Map pages sou

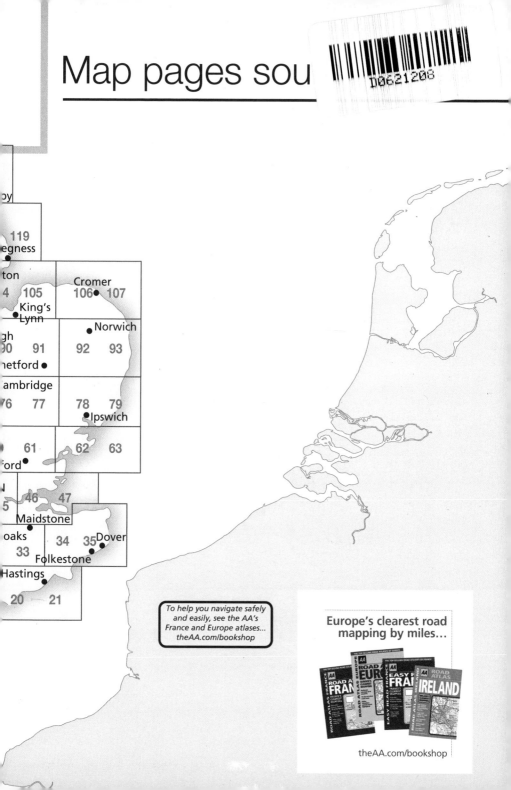

Atlas contents

Scale 1:250,000 or 3.95 miles to 1 inch

Map pages south	inside front cover

Route planner	II–VII

Mileage chart	VIII

Atlas Symbols	1

Road maps 1:250,000 scale	2–237
Western Isles 1:700,000 scale	232–233
Orkney Islands 1:636,000 scale	234
Shetland Islands 1:636,000 scale	235
Channel Islands 1:150,000 scale	236
Isle of Man 1:317,000 scale	237

Restricted junctions	238–239

Index to place names	240–320
County, administrative area map	240–241
Place name index	242–320

Ireland	321

Map pages north	inside back cover

8th edition June 2009

© AA Media Limited 2009

Cartography:

Now fully updated, the 1st edition of this atlas won the British Cartographic Society - Ordnance Survey Award for innovation in the design and presentation of spatial information. All cartography in this atlas edited, designed and produced by the Mapping Services Department of AA Publishing (A04060).

 This product includes mapping data licensed from Ordnance Survey® with the permission of the Controller of Her Majesty's Stationery Office. © Crown copyright 2009. All rights reserved. Licence number 100021153.

 This atlas includes Northern Ireland mapping. This material is based upon Crown Copyright and is reproduced with the permission of Land and Property Services under delegated authority from the Controller of Her Majesty's Stationery Office, © Crown copyright and database rights LA59. Permit No. 80247

© Ordnance Survey Ireland/ Government of Ireland Copyright Permit No. MP000109

Publisher's notes:

Published by AA Publishing (a trading name of AA Media Limited, whose registered office is Fanum House, Basing View, Basingstoke, Hampshire RG21 4EA, UK. Registered number 06112600).

All rights reserved. No part of this publication may be reproduced, stored in a retrieval system, or transmitted in any form or by any means – electronic, mechanical, photocopying, recording or otherwise – unless the permission of the publisher has been given beforehand.

ISBN: 978 0 7495 6256 4 (flexibound)

A CIP catalogue record for this book is available from The British Library.

The publishers would welcome information to correct any errors or omissions and to keep this atlas up to date. Please write to the Atlas Editor, AA Publishing, The Automobile Association, Fanum House, Basing View, Basingstoke, Hampshire RG21 4EA, UK. E-mail: roadatlasfeedback@theaa.com

Acknowledgements:

AA Publishing would like to thank the following for their assistance in producing this atlas:

RoadPilot® Information on fixed speed camera locations provided by RoadPilot © 2009 RoadPilot® Driving Technology. Information on truckstops and transport cafés kindly provided by John Eden (www.transportcafe.co.uk). Crematoria database provided by Cremation Society of Great Britain. Cadw, English Heritage, English Nature, Forestry Commission, Historic Scotland, Johnsons, National Trust and National Trust for Scotland, RSPB, Scottish Natural Heritage, The Countryside Agency, The Countryside Council for Wales.

Printer:

 Printed in Italy by Rotolito Lombarda, Milan.
Paper: 100gsm Matt Coated.

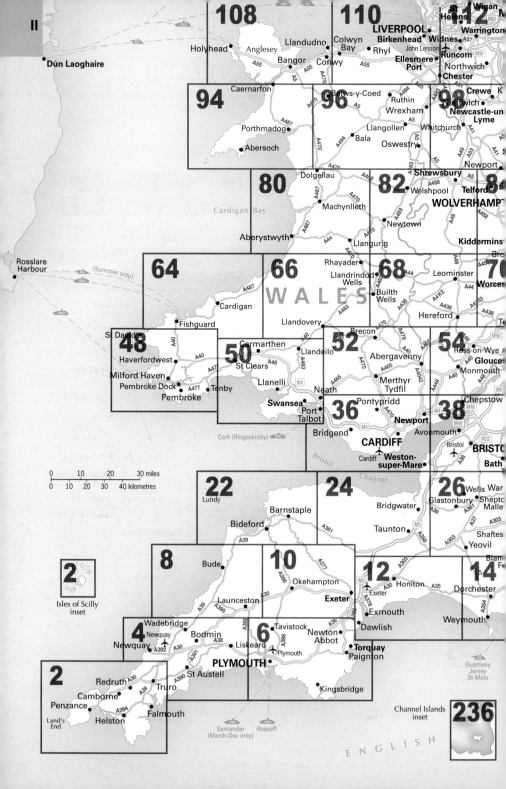

II

108
110
112
Wigan
Helens
LIVERPOOL
Birkenhead
Widnes
Warrington
M62
A57
Holyhead
Anglesey
Llandudno
Colwyn Bay
Rhyl
John Lennon
Runcorn
M56
Dún Laoghaire
Bangor
Conwy
A55
Ellesmere Port
Northwich
A55
A55
Chester
A5
A470

94
Caernarfon
96
Betws-y-Coed
Ruthin
Wrexham
98
Crewe
K
A494
A5
A5
A494
Nantwich
Newcastle-un-Lyme
A487
Porthmadog
Llangollen
Whitchurch
A5
A470
Bala
A41
Abersoch
Oswestry
A49
A53
Newport
A483

80
Dolgellau
82
Shrewsbury
A5
Welshpool
Telford
A487
A458
WOLVERHAMP
Cardigan Bay
Machynlleth
A483
A458
A470
Newtown
A49
A458
Aberystwyth
A44
Llangurig
A470
Kiddermins
A44
Bro

64
66
Rhayader
68
Leominster
Wores
A487
Llandrindod Wells
A44
A49
A44
A483
A412
Cardigan
W A L E S
Builth Wells
Hereford
A483
A438
A438
Fishguard
Llandovery
A483
A40
T

St David's
48
A40
Carmarthen
50
Brecon
52
Ross-on-Wye
54
M50
Haverfordwest
A40
Llandeilo
A479
A40
Glouce
Milford Haven
A477
St Clears
A48
A483
Abergavenny
A465
A40
Monmouth
A48
Pembroke Dock
Tenby
Llanelli
Neath
Merthyr Tydfil
A4042
M5
Pembroke
M4
A465
Chepstow
Swansea
Pontypridd
M48
Port Talbot
36
Newport
38
Avonmouth
M49
Bridgend
M4
CARDIFF
Avonmouth
Bristol
M32
Cork (Ringaskiddy)
Cardiff
Weston-super-Mare
BRISTC
Bristol Channel
Bath
A38

22
24
Wells
War
Lundy
Barnstaple
Glastonbury
Shepto
A361
Bridgwater
A39
Malle
Bideford
A361
A37
A303
A39
Taunton
M5
Shaftes
Bude
A386
A358
A303
Yeovil

8
10
Okehampton
12
Honiton
A35
14
Blan
A30
A377
M5
Dorchester
Fe
Launceston
A386
Exeter
Exeter
A35
A30
A354
A395
A386
Exmouth
Weymouth
Wadebridge
4
Newquay
A30
Tavistock
6
Dawlish
Guernsey
Newquay
A392
Bodmin
A38
Newton Abbot
Jersey
A30
A391
Liskeard
A386
Torquay
St-Malo
2
A390
PLYMOUTH
Plymouth
Paignton
Redruth
A30
St Austell
Camborne
A39
Truro
Kingsbridge
Channel Islands inset
Penzance
A394
Falmouth
236
Land's End
Helston
E N G L I S H

0   10   20   30 miles
0 10 20 30 40 kilometres

2
Isles of Scilly inset

Rosslare Harbour
(Summer only)

Santander (March-Dec only)
Roscoff

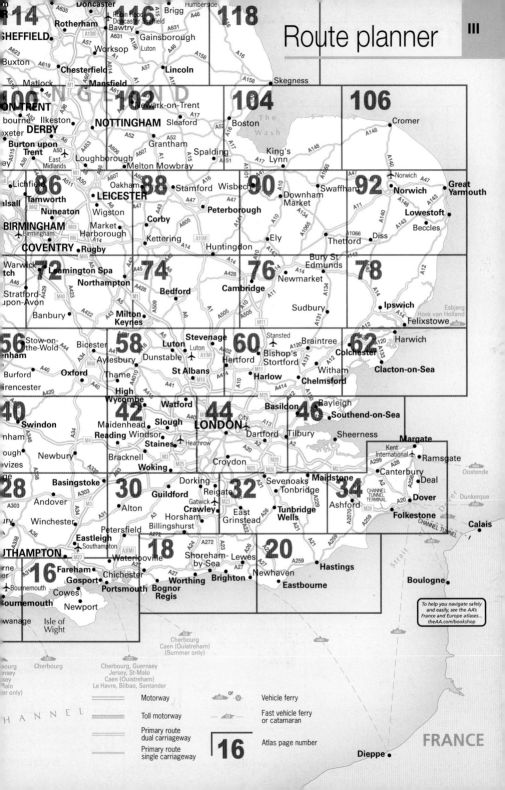

Route planner

114 Doncaster 116 Robin Hood Doncaster Sheffield, Brigg Humberside **118**
Rotherham Bawtry A46
A1(M) A57 A631 Gainsborough
SHEFFIELD Worksop A158 Luton A46 A16
Buxton A619 A1 A57 Lincoln A158
Matlock Chesterfield A57 A158 Skegness
M1 Mansfield
100 Newark-on-Trent **102** The **104** **106**
bourne Ilkeston NOTTINGHAM Sleaford Boston Wash Cromer
xeter DERBY A52 A148
Burton upon A50 A607 Grantham Spalding King's A148
Trent East A606 Melton Mowbray A151 A17 Lynn A1065 A140
Midlands Loughborough A16 Norwich A47 Great
Lichfield **86** Oakham A16 Wisbech A10 **92** Norwich A143 Yarmouth
Tamworth LEICESTER **88** Stamford A47 Downham Swaffham A146 A143
alsall M42 Nuneaton A47 A43 Peterborough Market A134 A11 Lowestoft
BIRMINGHAM M69 Wigston Corby A605 A10 A140 Diss A143 Beccles
Birmingham M6 Market Kettering A1(M) Ely Thetford A1066
COVENTRY Harborough A14 Huntingdon A10 Diss
Rugby A14 Bury St A12
Warwick M45 **72** Leamington Spa **74** A14 Edmonds **78**
tch A45 A428 **76** Newmarket A134 A14
Stratford A429 Northampton A428 Cambridge A11 Ipswich A14 Esbjerg
upon-Avon M40 M23 A5 Bedford A11 Hoek van Holland
Banbury A422 A43 Milton A509 A505 Sudbury A131 A14 Felixstowe
A420 Keynes A505 M11 A12
56 Stow-on- A5 Stevenage Stansted Harwich
the-Wold Bicester Luton Luton Braintree A120
enham A34 M40 Dunstable A1(M) Hertford Bishop's A120 Colchester **62**
Burford Aylesbury A41 Stortford A12 A133
Oxford Thame M1 St Albans Witham Clacton-on-Sea
irencester A40 A10 Harlow Chelmsford
A420 High A41 M10 A414
40 Wycombe Watford M25 Basildon Rayleigh
Swindon Maidenhead Slough A40 LONDON Dartford Tilbury Southend-on-Sea
nham A34 Reading Windsor City A13 Sheerness
ough Newbury Staines Heathrow A2 Margate
vizes Bracknell M3 M25 M20 Croydon M2 Kent A299 Ramsgate
ge A338 Woking M25 M26 M20 International Canterbury Deal
Basingstoke **30** Dorking Sevenoaks Maidstone A256 Dover
28 Andover A303 Guildford Reigate A21 Tonbridge A229 CHANNEL
A303 M3 Gatwick A23 TUNNEL Folkestone
ury Winchester A34 A31 Alton Crawley East Tunbridge Ashford A20 TERMINAL Calais
Eastleigh Petersfield Horsham Grinstead Wells A21 A2070 M20 CHANNEL TUNNEL
THAMPTON **16** Southampton A3(M) **18** Billingshurst A24 A272 A23 A259
rne Fareham M27 Waterlooville Shoreham- **20** Lewes Hastings
Gosport Chichester A27 by-Sea Brighton Newhaven Boulogne
ournemouth Cowes Portsmouth Bognor Worthing Eastbourne
Newport Regis

CHANNEL

Cherbourg
Caen (Ouistreham)
(Summer only)
Cherbourg, Guernsey
Jersey, St-Malo
Caen (Ouistreham)
Le Havre, Bilbao, Santander

FRANCE

Dieppe

	Motorway		Vehicle ferry
	Toll motorway		Fast vehicle ferry or catamaran
	Primary route dual carriageway		
	Primary route single carriageway	**16**	Atlas page number

To help you navigate safely and easily, see the AAs France and Europe atlases... theAA.com/bookshop

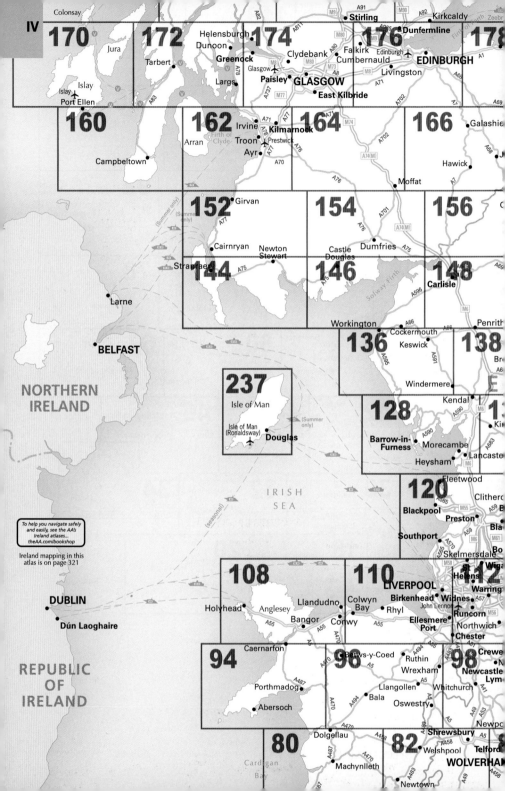

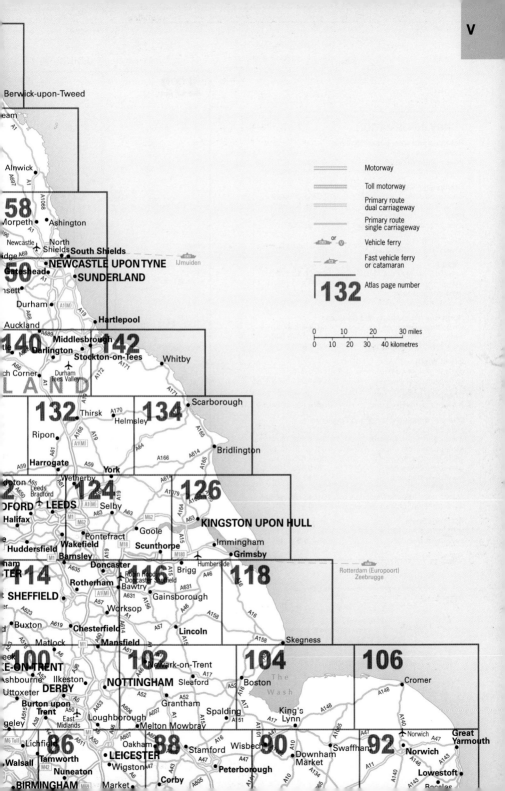

FERRY INFORMATION

Hebrides and west coast Scotland

www.calmac.co.uk	01475 650 100
www.skyeferry.co.uk	01599 522 273
www.western-ferries.co.uk	01368 704 452

Orkney and Shetland

www.northlinkferries.co.uk	0845 6000 449
www.pentlandferries.co.uk	01856 831 226
www.orkneyferries.co.uk	01856 872 044
www.shetland.gov.uk/ferries	01595 743 370

Isle of Man

www.steam-packet.com	0871 222 1333

Ireland

www.irishferries.com	08705 17 17 17
www.norfolkline.com	0870 870 1020
www.poirishsea.com	0870 2424 777
www.stenaline.co.uk	08705 70 70 70

North Sea (Scandinavia and Benelux)

www.dfdsseaways.co.uk	0871 522 9955
www.poferries.com	08716 645 645
www.stenaline.co.uk	08705 70 70 70

Isle of Wight

www.wightlink.co.uk	0871 376 1000
www.redfunnel.co.uk	0844 844 9988

Channel Islands

www.condorferries.com	0845 609 1024

Channel hopping (France and Belgium)

www.brittany-ferries.co.uk	0871 244 0744
www.condorferries.com	0845 609 1024
www.eurotunnel.com	08705 35 35 35
www.ldlines.com	0844 576 8836
www.norfolkline.com	0870 870 1020
www.poferries.com	08716 645 645
www.seafrance.com	0871 423 7119
www.transeuropaferries.co.uk	01843 595 522
www.transmancheferries.com	0800 917 1201

Northern Spain

www.brittany-ferries.co.uk	0871 244 0744
www.poferries.com	08716 645 645

Motorway	
Primary route dual carriageway	
Primary route single carriageway	
or Vehicle ferry	
Fast vehicle ferry or catamaran	

192 Atlas page number

0   10   20   30 miles
0 10 20 30 40 kilometres

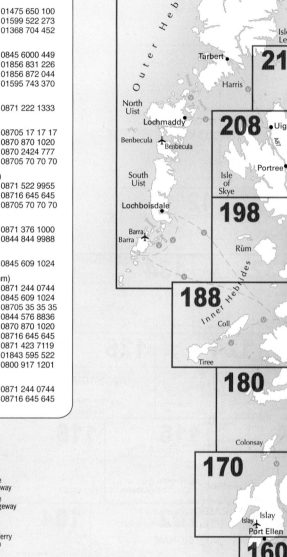

232
Western
Isles

Port of

Stornoway

Outer Hebrides

Isle of Lewis

Tarbert

218

Harris

Gai

North Uist

Lochmaddy

208 Uig

Benbecula

Portree

South Uist

Isle of Skye

Lochboisdale

198

Barra

Rùm

Mallaig

Eigg

Inner Hebrides

188

19

Coll

Tiree

Isle of Mu

180

Colonsay

170

Jura

Islay

Port Ellen

160

Campbeltow

Stornoway

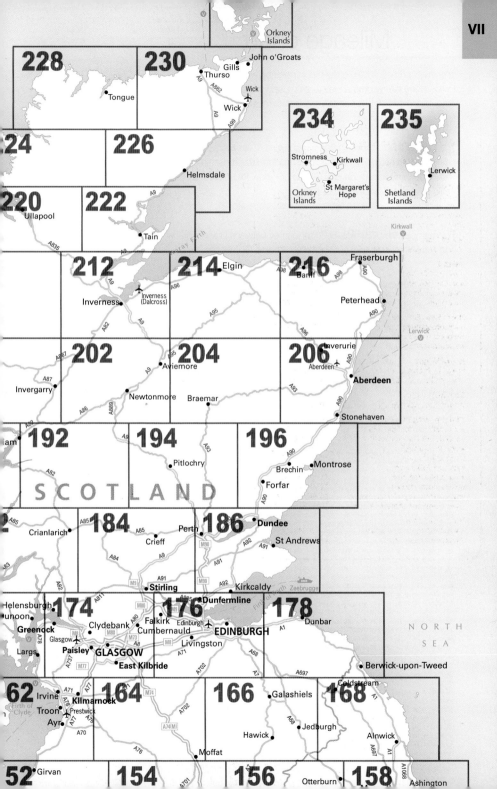

Mileage chart

The mileage chart shows distances in miles between two towns along AA-recommended routes. Using motorways and other main roads this is normally the fastest route, though not necessarily the shortest.

The journey times, shown in hours and minutes, are average off-peak driving times along AA-recommended routes. These times should be used as a guide only and do not allow for unforeseen traffic delays, rest breaks or fuel stops.

For example, the 378 miles (608 km) journey between Glasgow and Norwich should take approximately 7 hours 28 minutes.

journey time

City labels along the diagonal (top-left to bottom-right): Aberdeen, Aberystwyth, Barnstaple, Birmingham, Brighton, Bristol, Cambridge, Cardiff, Carlisle, Carmarthen, Dorchester, Dover, Edinburgh, Exeter, Fort William, Glasgow, Gloucester, Guildford, Hereford, Holyhead, Hull, Inverness, Kendal, Leeds, Lincoln, Liverpool, Maidstone, Manchester, Middlesbrough, Newcastle, Northampton, Norwich, Nottingham, Oxford, Penzance, Perth, Peterborough, Plymouth, Portsmouth, Preston, Salisbury, Sheffield, Shrewsbury, Southampton, Stoke-on-Trent, Stranraer, Taunton, Wick, York, LONDON

distances in miles (one mile equals 1.6093 km)

Atlas symbols

M4 — Motorway with number

Toll T4 — Toll motorway with toll station

3 — Restricted motorway junctions

S Fleet — Motorway service area

— Motorway and junction under construction

A3 — Primary route single/dual carriageway

1 — Primary route junction with and without number

3 — Restricted primary route junctions

S Grantham North — Primary route service area

— Transport café

BATH — Primary route destination

A1123 — Other A road single/dual carriageway

B2070 — B road single/dual carriageway

— Minor road, more than 4 metres wide, less than 4 metres wide

— Roundabout

— Interchange/junction

— Narrow primary/other A/B road with passing places (Scotland)

— Road under construction

— Road tunnel

Toll — Road toll, steep gradient (arrows point downhill)

5 — Distance in miles between symbols

— Railway station and level crossing

— Tourist railway

628 / 637 Lecht Summit — Height in metres, mountain pass

30 — Speed camera site (fixed location) with speed limit in mph

40 — Section of road with two or more fixed speed cameras, with speed limit in mph

50 50 — Average speed (SPECS™) camera system with speed limit in mph

V — Fixed speed camera site with variable speed limit

or V — Vehicle ferry

— Fast vehicle ferry or catamaran

⊕ Ⓗ Ⓕ — Airport, heliport, international freight terminal

Ⓗ — 24-hour Accident & Emergency hospital

Ⓒ — Crematorium

P·R — Park and Ride (at least 6 days per week)

— City, town, village or other built-up area

— National boundary, administrative boundary

— Scenic route

ℤℤ — Tourist Information Centre (all year/seasonal)

ℤ — Visitor or heritage centre

— Abbey, cathedral or priory

— Ruined abbey, cathedral or priory

✗ — Castle

— Historic house or building

— Museum or art gallery

— Industrial interest

ⅲ — Aqueduct or viaduct

✤ ♣ — Garden, arboretum

— Vineyard

♈ — Country park

♈ — Agricultural showground

☲ — Theme park

— Farm or animal centre

— Zoological or wildlife collection

— Bird collection, aquarium

RSPB — RSPB site

— National Nature Reserve (England, Scotland, Wales)

— Local nature reserve

···· — Forest drive

– – – — National trail

☀ ♣ — Viewpoint, picnic site

···· — Hill-fort

♣ ♣ — Prehistoric monument, Roman antiquity

✗ 1066 — Battle site with year

— Steam railway centre

☌ — Cave

✗ — Windmill

1 — Monument

ſ — Golf course

— County cricket ground

☌ — Rugby Union national stadium

✗ — International athletics stadium

— Horse racing, show jumping

— Air show venue, motor-racing circuit

— Ski slope (natural, artificial)

— National Trust property (England & Wales, Scotland)

✠ — English Heritage site

— Historic Scotland site

— Cadw (Welsh heritage) site

— Major shopping centre, other place of interest

— Attraction within urban area

◉ — World Heritage Site (UNESCO)

— National Park and National Scenic Areas

— Forest Park

— Heritage coast

Isles of Scilly

White Island

King Charles's Old Grimsby

ST MARTIN'S

St Martin's Head

BRYHER

Cromwell's

Old Blockhouse

Higher Town

Isles of Scilly Heritage Coast

New Grimsby

Lizard Point

Old Blockhouse

TRESCO

Tresco Abbey

Innisidgen Tomb

Great Ganilly

Crow Sound

Great Arthur

Samson

Bant's Carn Burial

A3110

ST MARY'S

Harry's Walls

Longstone

Deep Point

Hugh Town

Porth Hellick Downs Tombs

Garrison Walls

Old Town

Isles of Scilly (St Mary's)

Penrinis Head

Annet

St Mary's Sound

Gugh

Middle Town

ST AGNES

Horse Point

Western Rocks

Smith Sound

North West Channel

Broad Sound

0   1   2   3 miles

0 1 2 3 4 5 kilometres

Carn Naun Point

The Island or St Ives Head

St Ives

Zennor Head

Gurnards Head

St Ives Bay

South West Coast Path

Zennor

Halsetown

Towednack

Carbis Bay

Lelant

B3306

P·R

Pendeen Watch

Lighthouse

Penwith Heritage Coast

Morvah

Men-An-Tol

Carn Galver

Mulfra Quoit

Chysauster Ancient Village

Canonstown

St E

A30

Geevor Tin Mines

Pendeen

Lanyon Quoit

New Mill

Crowlas

Levant Mine and Beam Engine

Botallack

St Just Mining District

Trengwainton Garden

Gulval

Ludgvan

St Hila

Longrock

St Just

Madron

Heamoor

Penzance

Marazion

Cape Cornwall

A3071

Newbridge

Chyandour

Perranuthnoe

Gol

Ballowall Barrow

Kelynack

B3306

Carn Euny Ancient Village

Sancreed

Drift

A30

Penzance

Newlyn

St Michael's Mount

Whitesand Bay

Land's End

Crows-an-Wra

A30   10

Kerris

Paul

Mousehole

Sennen Cove

St Buryan

LAND'S END

Sennen

The Merry Maidens

Lamorna

MOUNT'S B

Trevescan

B3315

Trethewey

Treen

B3315

Merthen Point

Lamorna Cove

Porthcurno

Submarine Telegraphy

B3283

Porthgwarra

St Levan

Minack Open Air Theatre

Cribba Head

Gwennap Head

Higher

Lower

Dizzard Point

St
Gennys
Crackington Haven
Cambeak

Sweets

Witchcraft

Tresparrett

Mar

Pentire Point · Widemouth
Heritage Coast
Boscastle
Trevalga
Lesnewth

O

B3263

TINTAGEL HEAD
Castle
Tretheyey

Tintagel
Bossiney
Davidstow

Old Post Office
Penhallic Point
Treknow
Trewarmett

British Cycling
Tremai

South West Coast Path
Delabole
Pengelly
Camelford
Crow
Reser

Westdowns
Lanteglos
Trewalder
Helstone

Rumps
Point
Kelland
Head
Varley
Head
Port Isaac
Bay

Port Quin
Bay
Port
Quin
Port
Isaac
Port Gaverne

Pentire Point
Bee Centre
St Teath

Padstow Bay
Hayle Bay
Long
Cross
Treveighan

Stepper Point
Polzeath
Trelights
Pendoggett
Michaelstow

419
BROW
WILL

Trevose
Heritage Coast
Moth
Ivey
Bay
St Minver
St Endelli
relill
A39
Churchtown

TREVOSE HEAD
B3314
St Kew
St Breward

Dinas
Head
Trequite
St
Tudy
Jamai

Bay
Trevone
St Kew

4

0   1   2   3   4 miles

0 1 2 3 4   5 kilometres

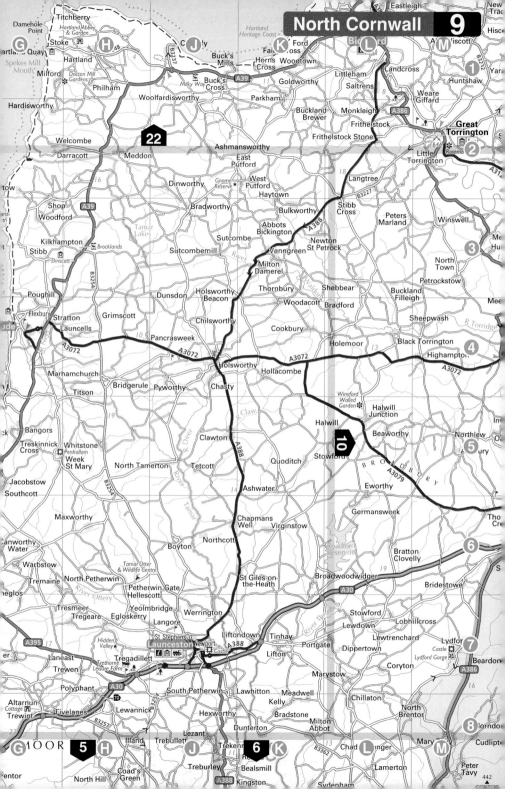

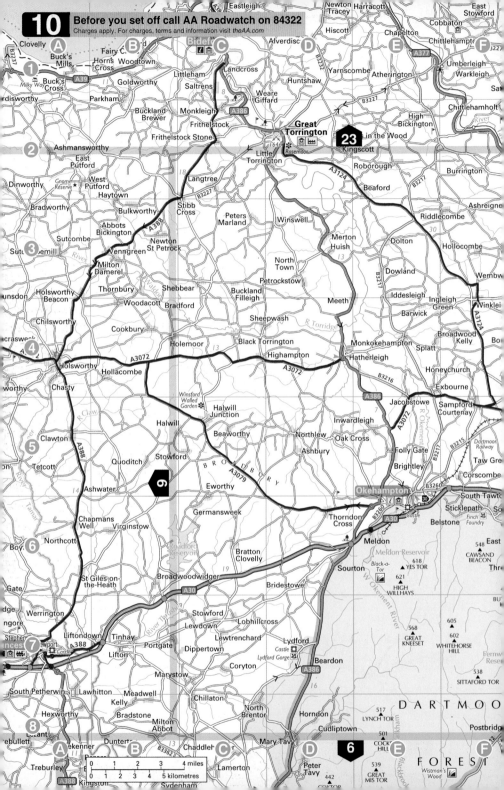

G H **29** J **30** K L M

Waltham Chase
Curdridge
Shedfield
Shirrell Heath
Soberton Heath
Newtown
Hambledon
Catherington
Chalton
Farm
Blendwo
imead
Anmore
Soake
Cowplain
chdean
Forestside
Singl
t Dea
Weald & Dow
ur Mus
Th
Tru

G Wickham
Curbridge
Burridge
Swanwick

H
Worlds End
North
Boarhunt
Boarhunt
Wallington

Stoughton
Bow Hill
Walderton
Woodend
West
Stoke

1

WATERLOOVILLE
Southwick
Purbrook
Stakes
Rowland's Castle
Staunton
Westbourne
Funtington
Woodmancote
West
Ashling
East Ashling
Mid
Lavant
Summersdale

M27
Titchfield
Abbey
Catisfield
10
Ports Down
Royal Armouries
Cosham
HAVANT
A259
Bedhampton
Drayton
Hambrook
Southbourne
Broadbridge
CH

FAREHAM
Titchfield
Portchester
Castle
12
Eartington
Langstone
Emsworth
Nutbourne
Chidham
Walton
Bosham
Fishbourne

2

ubbington
Hill Head
Bridgemary
Fort Brockhurst
Elson
Hardway
Portsmouth
Harbour
North
End
Brockhampton
Northney
North Hayling
Stoke
HAYLING
ISLAND
West
Thorney
West
Itchenor
Shipton
Green
Dell
Quay
Donnington
Apuldram
Hunstor

e-on-the-Solent
Rowner
GOSPORT
Alverstoke
Portsea
Fratton
Southsea
West Town
Fort
Cumberland
**South
Hayling**
THORNEY
ISLAND
Chichester
Harbour
West
Wittering
Birdham
Somerley
Stree
Sid
Highleig

3

Stokes Bay
Gilkicker Point
PORTSMOUTH
Eastney
Hayling Bay
Langstone
Harbour
Chichester
Harbour
East Wittering
Earnley
Bracklesham
30

18

Osborne
Osborne
House
Cowes
hippingham
Spithead
SPITHEAD
Spitbank
Fort
Bracklesham
Bay
Sels

4

Wootton
Bridge
Fishbourne
Ryde
Puckpool Point
Nettlestone Point
Seaview
Nettlestone
St Helens
(Summer only)
Cherbourg
Caen (Ouistreham)
SELS

Flamingo
Park
Binstead
Brickfields
Horse
Country
Havenstreet
Little
Whitefield
Isle of Wight
Steam Railway
Robin Hill
East
Ashey
Rosemary
Nunwell
The Duver
Bembridge
Bembridge
Windmill
Lifeboat Station
FORELAND
Cherbourg
Guernsey
Jersey
St-Malo
Caen (Ouistreham)
Bilbao
Le Havre
Santander

5

port
W · I · G · H · T
rreton
Newchurch
Haseley Manor
Brading
Alverstone
Bembridge
Down
Whitecliff Bay
Bembridge
Down

rstone
ley
Queen's
Bower
Winford
Dinosaur
Isle
Yaverland
Culver Cliff

Branstone
Sandown
Lake
Sandown Bay

A3020
Sandford
Apse
Heath
Whiteley
Bank
Shanklin

6

ll
Old Smithy
& Gardens
Appuldurcombe
House
Wroxall
Luccombe Village
Luccombe Chine
Shanklin Chine
Ventnor
Down
DUNNOSE

 well
Glass
55
St Lawrence
The Undercliffe
Ventnor
Botanic Garden

7

8

G H J K L M

Grid references: G, H, J, K, L, M (top and bottom); 1, 2, 3, 4, 5, 6, 7, 8 (right side)

St Leonards Forest, Horsham, Wakehurst Place, Hoathly, Highbrook, Sweethaws, Balcombe, Handcross, Nymans Garden, Staplefield, Borde Hill, Ardingly Reservoir, Ouse Valley, Bluebell Railway, Ardi, Horsted Keynes, Fairwarp, High Hurstwood, Pou Gre, Lower Beeding, Slaugham, Warninglid, Leonardslee, Crabtree, Cuckfield, Ansty, Haywards Heath, Scayne's Hill, Danehill, Nutley, Maresfield, Splayne's Green, Fletching, Piltdown, Five Ash Down, Buxted, `32`, Wivelsfield, North Chailey, Newick, Framfiel, Blac, Ridgewood, B210, Uckfield, New Town, `31`, Cowfold, Chalet Transport Café, Twineham, Hickstead, Sayers Common, Bolney, Bookers, Worlds End, Wivelsfield Green, Chailey, Town, Littleworth, East Sussex National, Lavender Line, Little Horsted, Halland, Shortgate, Whitese, Henfield, Blackstone, Albourne, Hurstpierpoint, Burgess Hill, Keymer, Ditchling, Plumpton Green, South Chailey, East Chiltington, Barcombe Cross, Upper Wellingham, Isfield, Bentley Wildfowl & Motor Museum, Woodmancote, Small Dole, Hassocks, Clayton, Pyecombe, B2116, Streat, Westmeston, Plumpton, Plumpton College, Barcombe, Hamsey, Ringmer, Laughton, Upper Beeding, Edburton, Fulking, Poynings, Pangdean, Saddlescombe, Devil's Dyke, Truleigh Hill, Ditchling Beacon 248, South Downs National Park (Proposed Area), Mount Harry 1264, Offham, Castle, South Malling, Glynde Place, Glynde, vingt, Bramber, Botolphs, ombes, Castle, Stanmer, Patcham, Coldean, Withdean, Hollingbury, Lewes, Wallands Park, Kingston near Lewes, Iford, Beddingham, Firle, Firle Place 219, Charleston Farmhouse, Firle Beacon, Lancing College Chapel, Mile Oak, Hangleton, West Blatchington, Portslade, Preston, Falmer, Moulsecoomb, South Downs Way, Rodmell, Monk's House, Tarring Neville, Berwick Dru, Old Shoreham, Shoreham-by-Sea, Southwick, Portslade-by-Sea, HOVE, BRIGHTON, Kemp Town, Newmarket Hill 197, Woodingdean, Breaky Bottom, Southease, South Heighton, Alfriston, Clergy House, Worthing, RTHING, lancing, Rottingdean, Ovingdean, Saltdean, Telscombe, Piddinghoe, Paradise Park, Denton, Newhaven, Norton, Bishopstone, East Blatchington, Sutton, Peacehaven, Fort, Seaford Bay, Seaford, Seaford Head, Sew, Dieppe (ferry), `20`

Road numbers: A23, A24, A272, A273, A275, A26, A27, A259, A270, A283, A281, A2037, A2300, A22, A2026, B2110, B2114, B2115, B2116, B2113, B2112, B2111, B2036, B2028, B2116, B2192, B2124, B2066

North West Point
Lundy Heritage Coast
LUNDY
▲142
Marisco
Surf Point
Shutter Point

BARNSTAPLE
OR
BIDEFORD BAY
Westw

Cro

HARTLAND POINT
Shipload Bay
Titchberry
Damehole Point
Hartland Abbey & Garden
Stoke
Abbo
Hartland Heritage Coast
Ford
Fairy Cross
Clovelly
Hartland Quay
Spekes Mill Mouth
B3248
Hartland
B3237
Buck's Mills
Horns Cross
Woodto
Milford
Docton Mill Gardens
4
Milky Way
Buck's Cross
A39
Goldwor
Philham
Woolfardisworthy
Parkham
Hardisworthy
Buc
B

Welcombe
Ashmansworthy
Darracott
Med
9
East Putford
Morwenstow
Dinworthy
Gnome Reserve ★
West Putford
Haytown
Higher Sharpnose Point
Shop
Woodford
A39
Bradworthy
Bulkwor
South West Coast Path
Lower Sharpnose Point
Tamar Lakes
Sutcombe
Abbots Bickington
Steeple Point
Kilkhampton
Brockl
Venn
Vence
bb
Dinscott
Sutcom
ill
Milton Damerel
B3254
Holsworthy
Thornbury

0 1 2 3 4 miles
0 1 2 3 4 5 kilometres

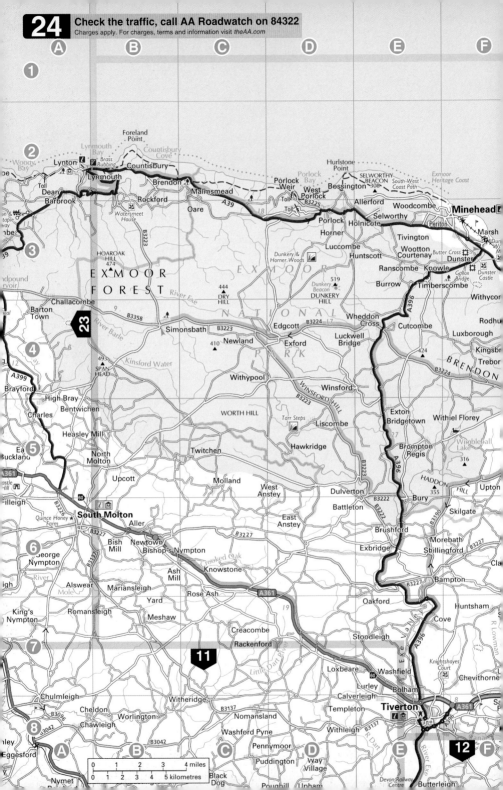

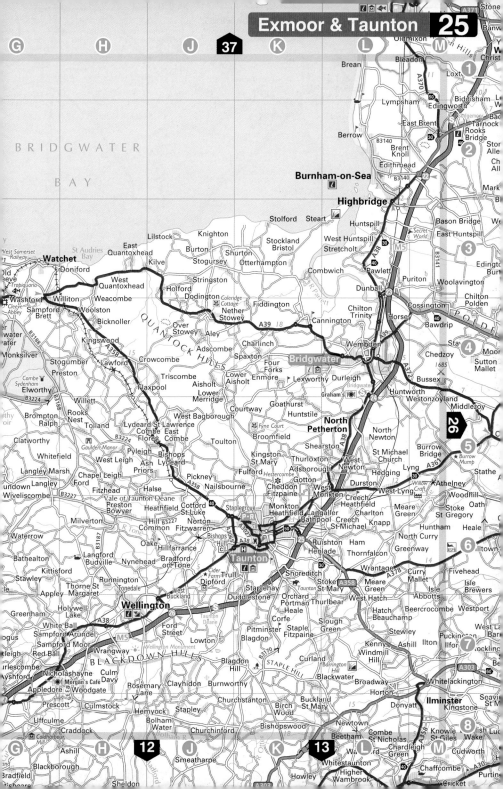

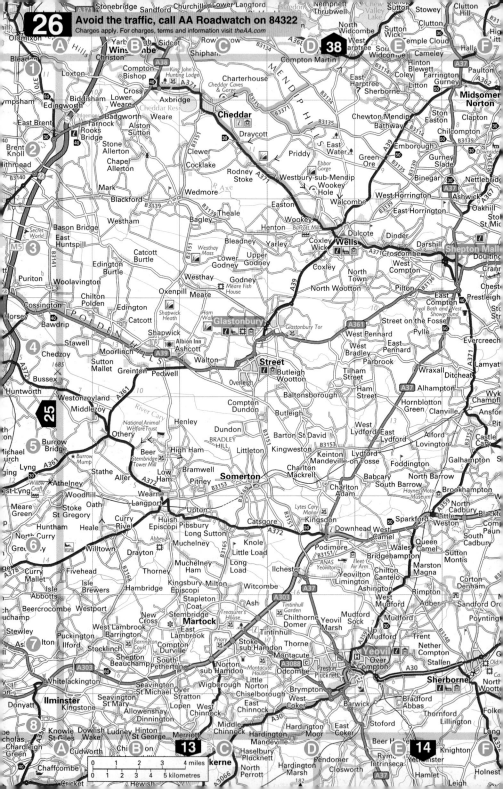

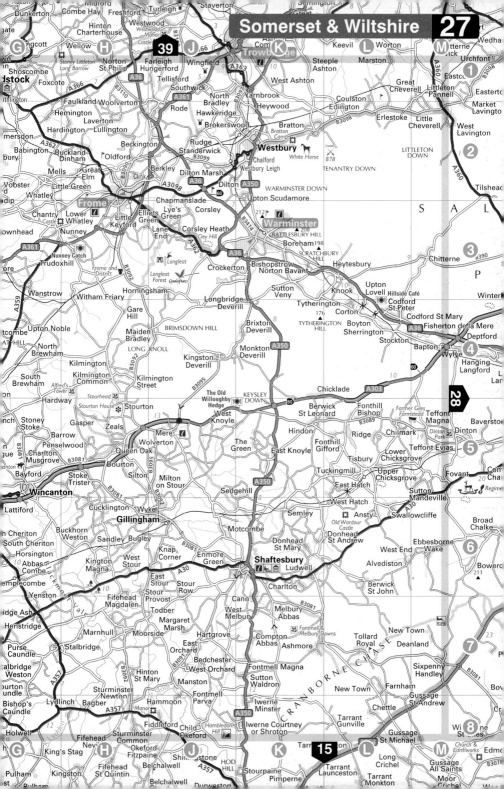

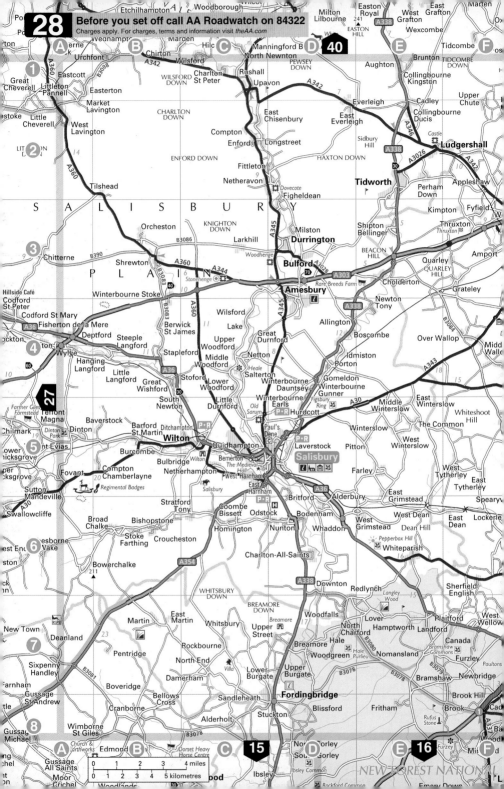

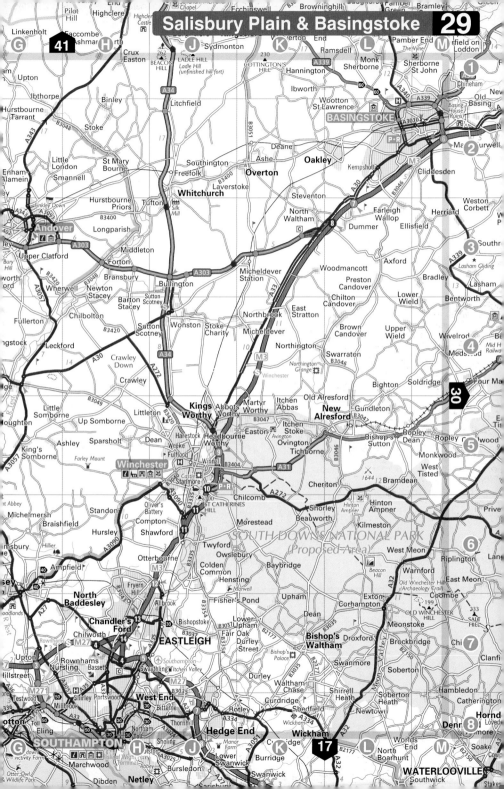

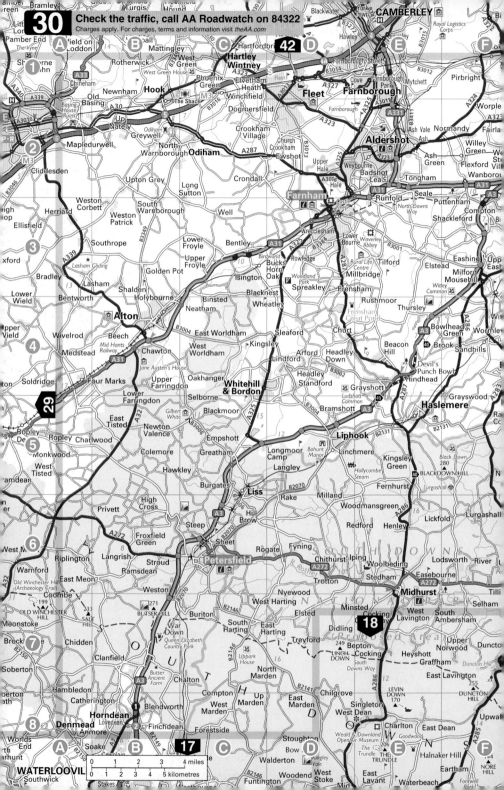

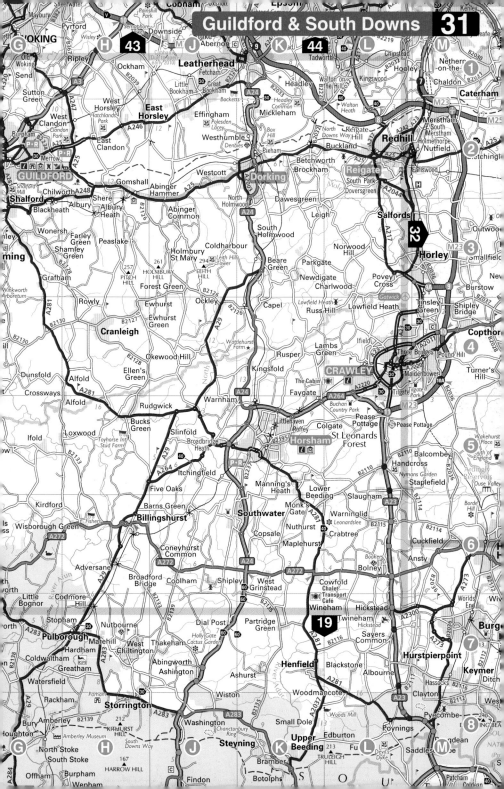

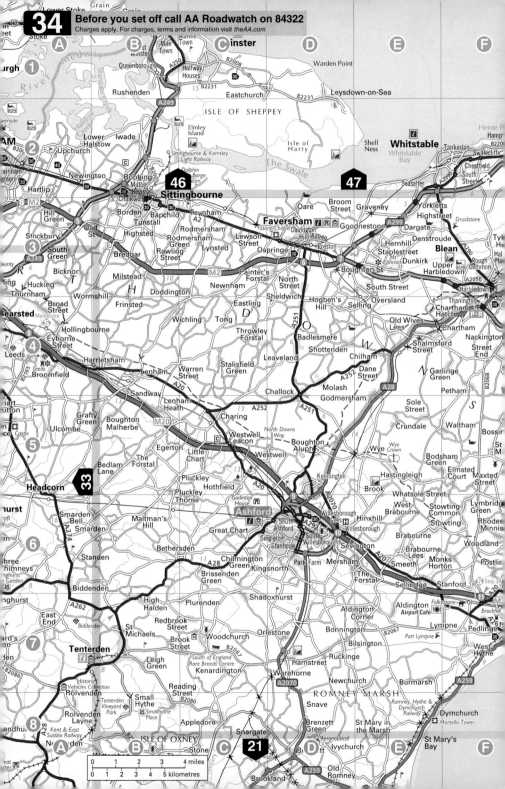

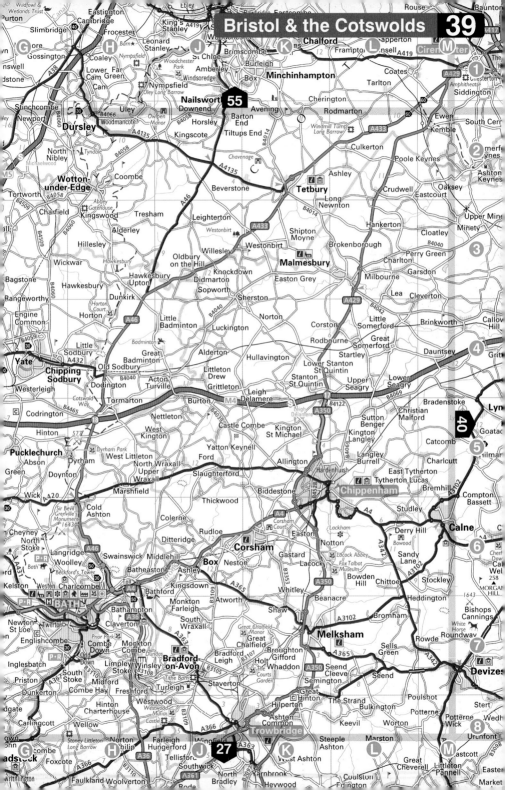

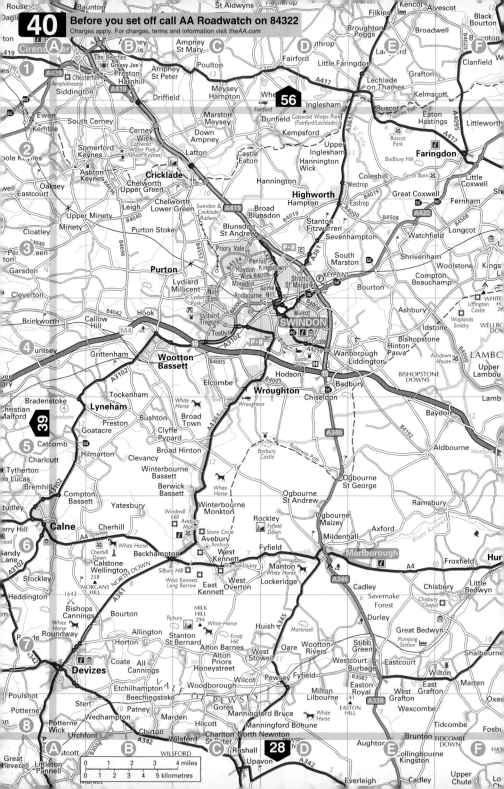

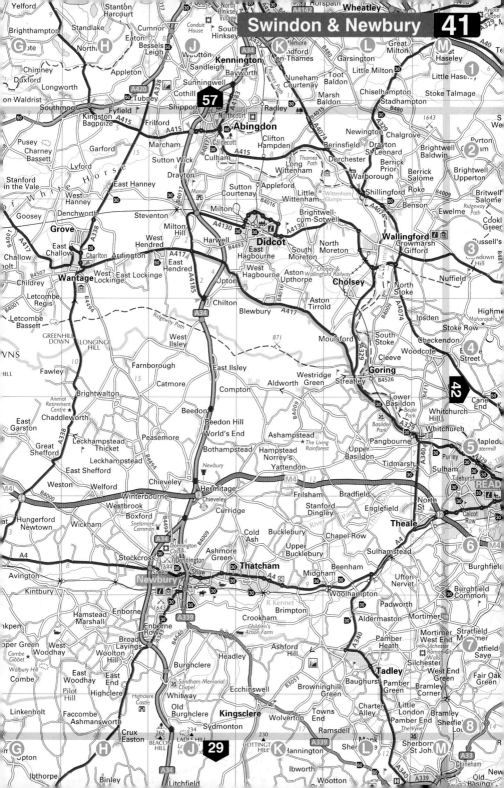

A B C D E F

1

Pen Brush

Pembrokeshire
Coast Path

Trefasser

Manorowen

300

St Nicholas

2

Ynys
Daullyn

Carreg Sampson

Granston

Abere

64

ngloffan

Jordar

Porthgain

Trefin

Mathry

16

A487

B4331

Abereiddy

Llanrhian

Berea

Croes-goch

Letters

Treleddyd-fawr

Treglemais

ST DAVID'S HEAD

Rhodiad-
y-brenin

Caer
Farchell

River Solva

B4330

Llandeloy

Whitesand
Bay

B3583

Bishop's
Palace

Whitchurch

Treffgarne
Owen

Hayscastle

Hayscas
Cross

3

St David's

RAMSEY
ISLAND

RSPB

Solva

A487

Pen-y-cwn

178
DUDWELL
MT

Lewesto

St David's Peninsula
Heritage Coast

Newgale

Roch

16

Wolfsdale

PEMBROKESHIRE
COAST
NATIONAL PARK

Simpson
Cross

Rickets Head

A487

Keeston

Ca

Pem

4

St Brides Bay

Nolton Haven

Nolton

St Brides Bay
Heritage Coast

Druidston

Haroldston
West

Portfield
Gate

B4341

Broad Haven

Broadway

B4327

Dree
Hill

Little Haven

Walton
West

4

Pembrokeshire
Coast Path

5

Talbenny

Tiers
Cross

Walwyn's
Castle

SKOMER
ISLAND

Wooltack Point

B4327

Marloes

St Ishmael's

Herbrandston

Steynto

6

Broad Sound

Marloes and Dale Heritage Coast

Dale

Hubberston

Hakin

Waterst

6

Llansta

SKOKHOLM
ISLAND

Westdale
Bay

Dale
Point

Great Castle
Head

Milford Haven
(Aberdaugleddau)

Per

St Anns Head

Angle

Angle
Bay

Rhoscrowthe

B4320

7

Rosslare Harbour

Freshwater
West

Castlemartin Brook

10

B4319

Castlemartin

Warren

Linney Head

PEMBROKESHIRE
NATIONAL F

Mer

8

Pembrokeshire
Coast Path

A B C D E F

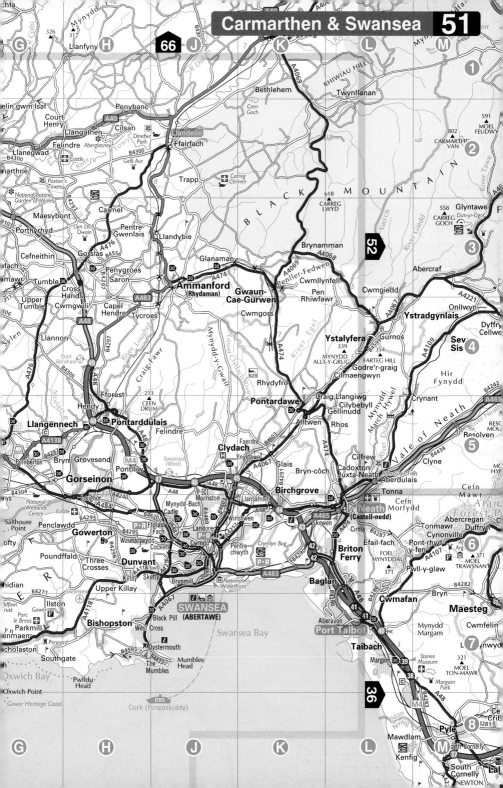

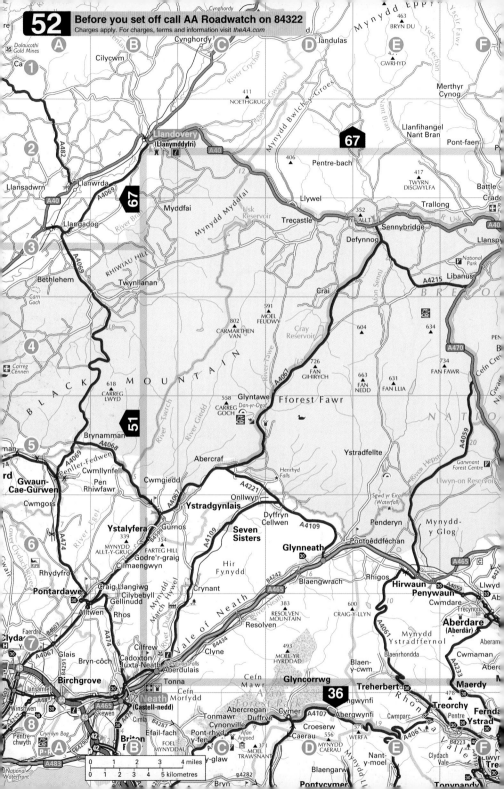

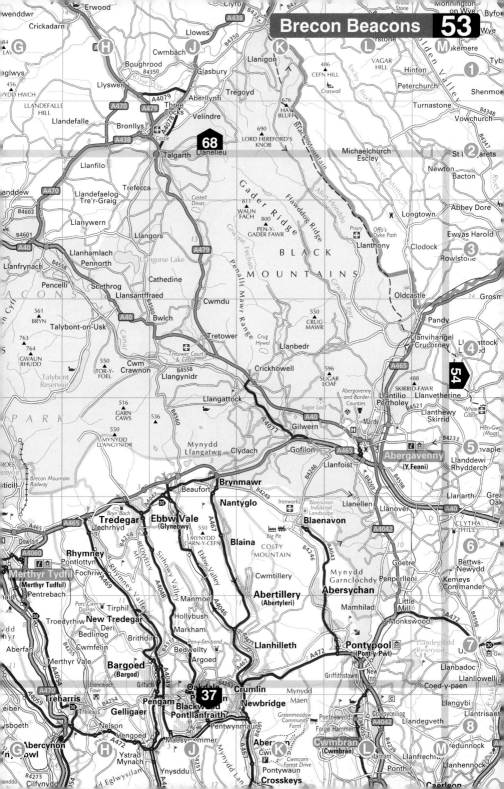

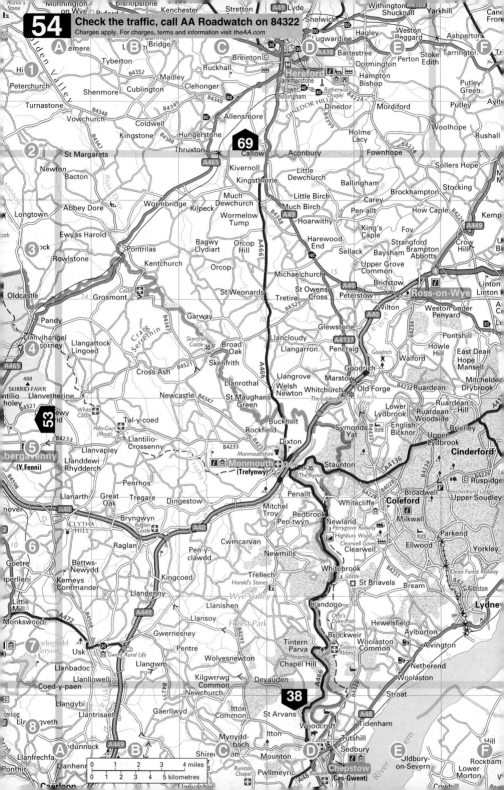

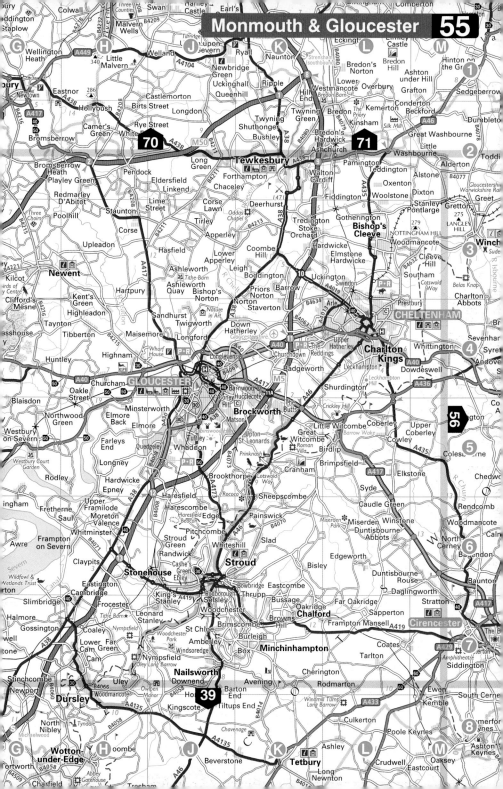

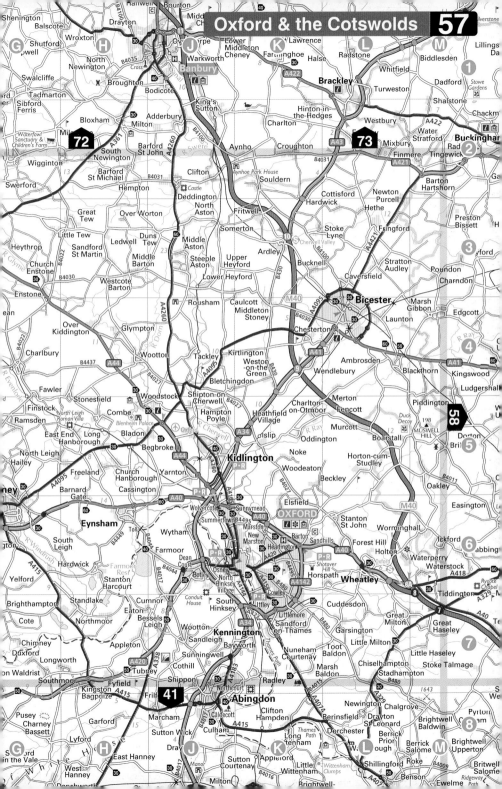

58

Before you set off call AA Roadwatch on 84322

Charges apply. For charges, terms and information visit *theAA.com*

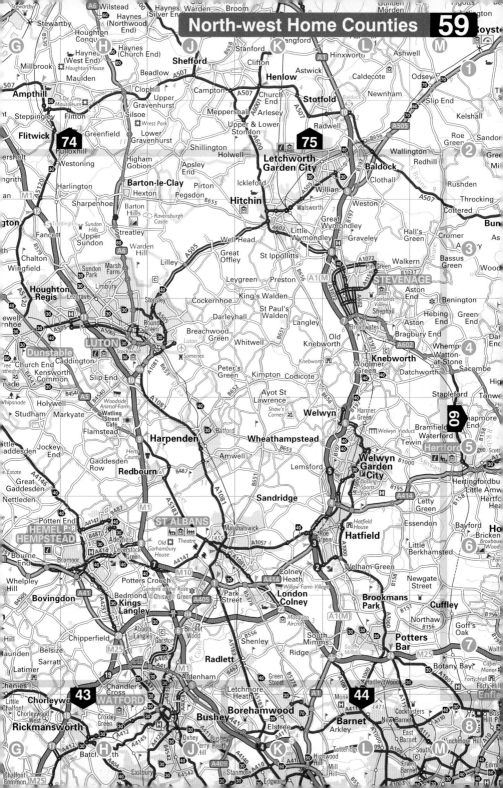

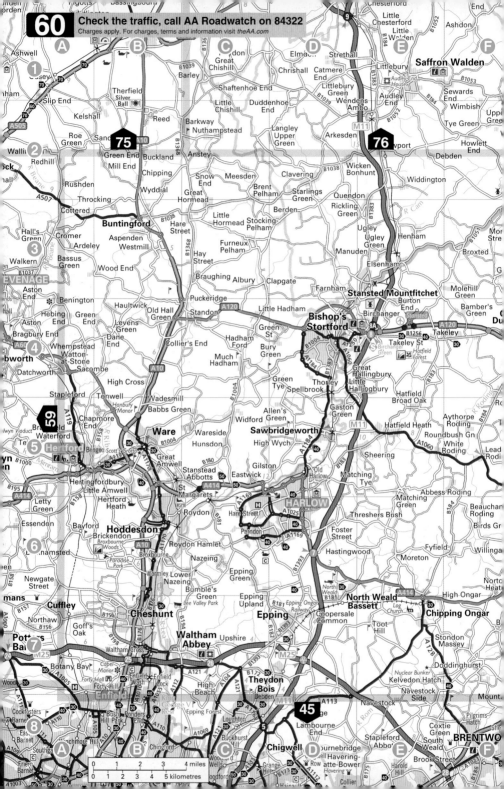

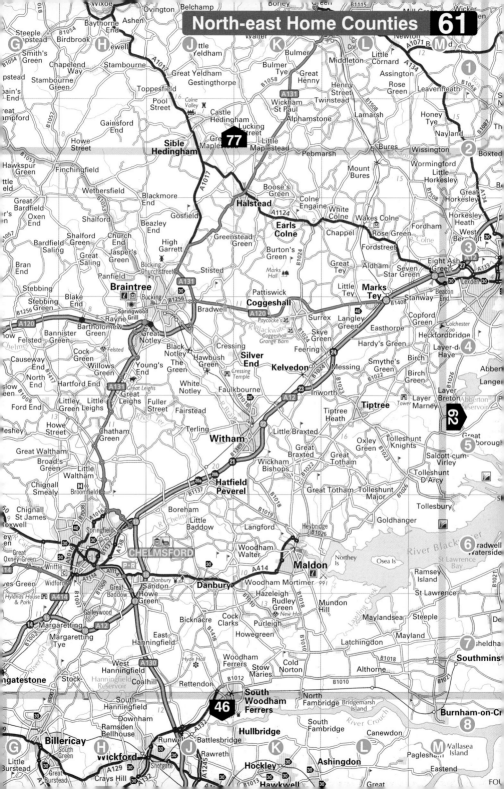

A   B   C   D   E   F

1

Mill
Wicker
Newton
A1071 Bo
Leavenheath
Honey Tye
Nayla
Rose Green
Wormingford
Little Horkesley
Great Horkesley
Horkesley Heath
West Bergholt
Eight Ash Green
Seven Star Green
Stanway
Beacon End
Copford Green
Heckfordbridge
Birch
Birch Green
Layer-de-la-Haye
Layer Breton
Layer Marney
Tollesh Knigl
Salcott-cum-Virley
Tolleshunt D'Arcy
Tollesbury

77

78

Layham
Raydon
Shelley
Lower Raydon
Polstead
Stoke-by-Nayland
Thorington Street
Higham
Stratford St Mary
Boxted
Boxted Cross
Langham
Dedham
Boxted

Great Wenham
Little Wenham
Capel St Mary
Holton St Mary
East Bergholt
Flatford Mills & Cottages
Manningtree
Lawford
Ardleigh Heath
Ardleigh
Ardleigh Truckstop

Wherstead
Freston
Tattingstone White Horse
Tattingstone
Holbrook
Stutton
Cattawade
Mistley Towers
New Mistley
Mistley
Bradfield
Bradfield Heath
Horsleycross Street
Wix

Nacton
Levington
Woolverstone
Shotley
Shotley Street
Wrabness
Ramsey
Upper Dovercourt
Little Oakley
Great Oakley

COLCHESTER
Lexden
Greenstead
Wivenhoe
Rowhedge
Fingringhoe
High Park Corner
Abberton
Langenhoe
Peldon
Abberton Reservoir

Elmstead Market
Frating Green
Frating
Alresford
Thorrington

Great Bentley
Little Bentley
Tendring Heath
Tendring Green
Goose Green
Tendring
Thorpe Green
Beaumont
Weeley
Weeley Heath
Aingers Green
Cook's Green
Little Clacton
Great Holland

Thorpe-le-Soken
Kirby le Soken
Kirby Cross
Horsey Island

Frin

Brightlingsea
Mersea Island
Great Wigborough
East Mersea
West Mersea

St Osyth
Jaywick
Rush Green
CLACTON-ON-SEA
Great Clacton
Holland-on-Sea

Colne Point

6

Shinglehead Point
Bradwell Waterside
St Lawrence Bay
Ramsey Island
St Lawrence
Sales Point
Bradwell-on-Sea
Tillingham

7

Steeple
May
Dengie
Asheldham
Southminster

8

Burnham-on-Crouch

47

Holliwell Point
Foulness Point

A   B   C   D   E   F

allasea Island
Paglesha
Eastend
Courtsend
FOULNESS

0 1 2 3 4 miles
0 1 2 3 4 5 kilometres

Hollesley
Bay

Alderton

Bawdsey

Falkenham

Old
Felixstowe

Felixstowe

79

ard Fort
guard

Hoek van Holland
Esbjerg

A B C D E F

1

2

3

4

5

Pembs
Coa

St Dogmaels Moylgrove
Heritage Coast

Moylegro

Trwyn-y-bwa

(Summer only)

Rosslare Harbour

Rosslare Harbour

Nevern

STRUMBLE HEAD

Carregwastad Head

Dinas Head
Heritage Coast

DINAS
HEAD

Newport
Bay

Newport

Fe
Far

6

Pen Brush

Llanwnda

Fishguard
Bay

Bryn-
Henllan

Dinas

Carreg
Coetan

Pentre
Ifan

Cros

Pwll Deri

Trefasser

Goodwick

Ocean Lab

Lower Town

Mynydd
Melyn

311

Pembrokeshire
Coast Path

Manorowen

Fishguard

(Abergwaun)

Llanychaer
Bridge

MYNYDD
CAREGOG

Penlan-Uchaf

St Nicholas

Scleddau

Pontfaen

PEMBROKESHIRE

Ynys
Daullyn

Carreg Sampson

Granston

Abercastle

A40

B4313

MYNYDD P

7

Porthgain

Trefin

Llangloffan

Mathry

Jordanston

Trecwn

NATIONAL

Foel
Eryr

536

FOEL
CWMCERWYN

Abereiddy
Berea

Llanrhian

Croes-goch

A487

16

48

B4331

Little
Newcastle

49

Puncheston

Rosebush

Preglemais

Caer
F...ell

Letterston

Castlebythe

Tufton

26

Maencloc

8

Whitchurch

River Solva

Llandeloy

B4330

Wolf's
Castle

Rinas

Henry's Moat
(Castell Hendre)

New
Moat

Lla...ln

B4313

Lla...

wr

Solva

A B C D E F

0 1 2 3   4 miles
0 1 2 3 4 5 kilometres

Hayscastle
Cross

Ambleston

Llys-y-frân
Res

New
Moat

Treffgarne

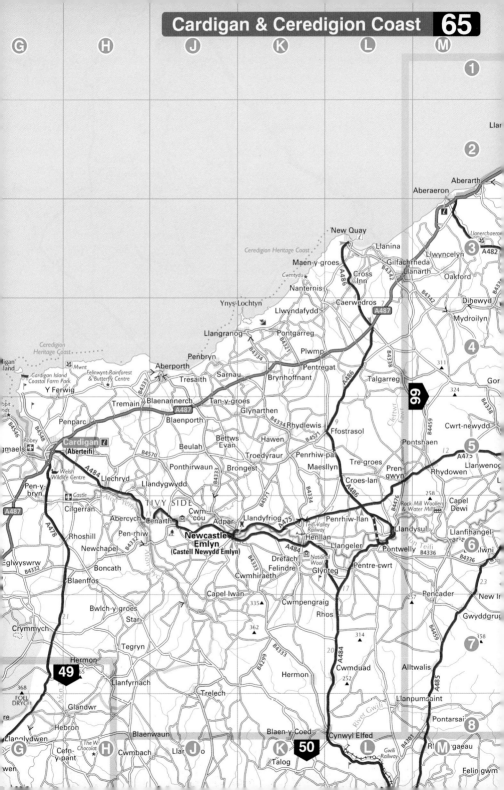

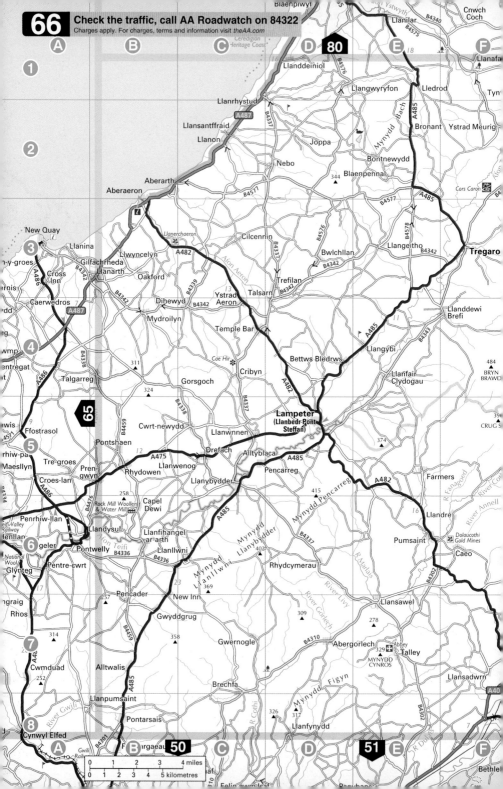

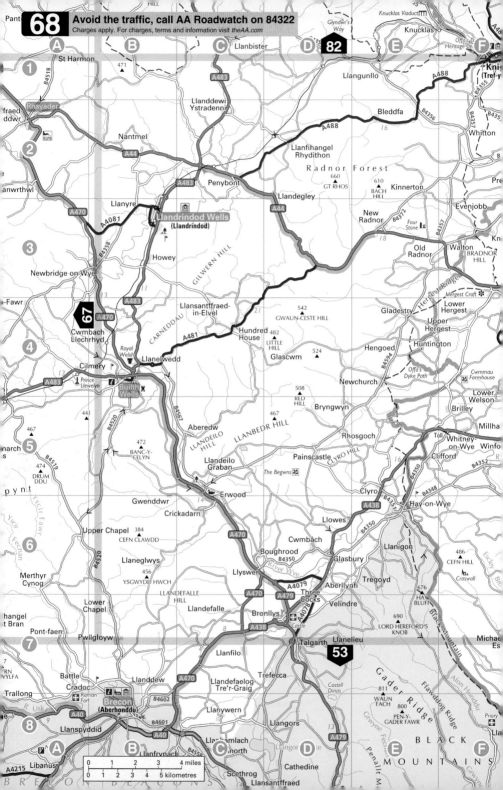

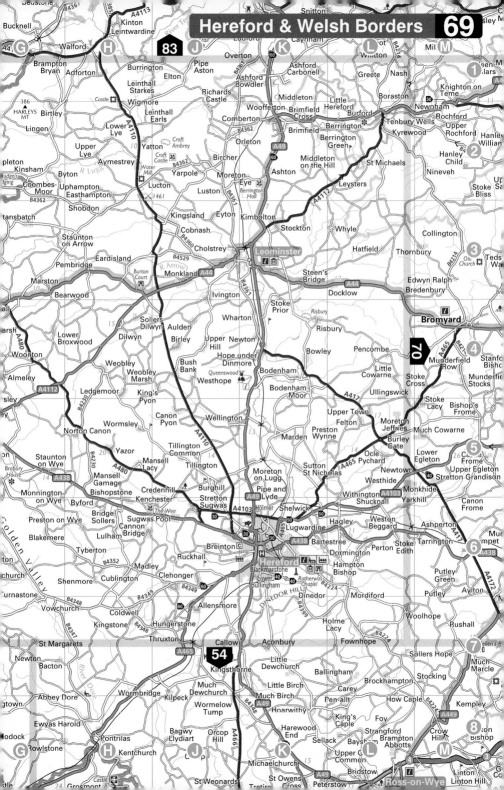

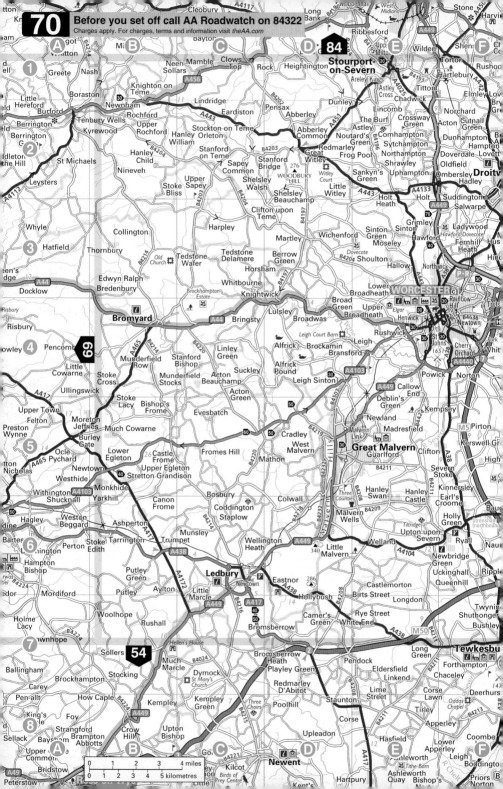

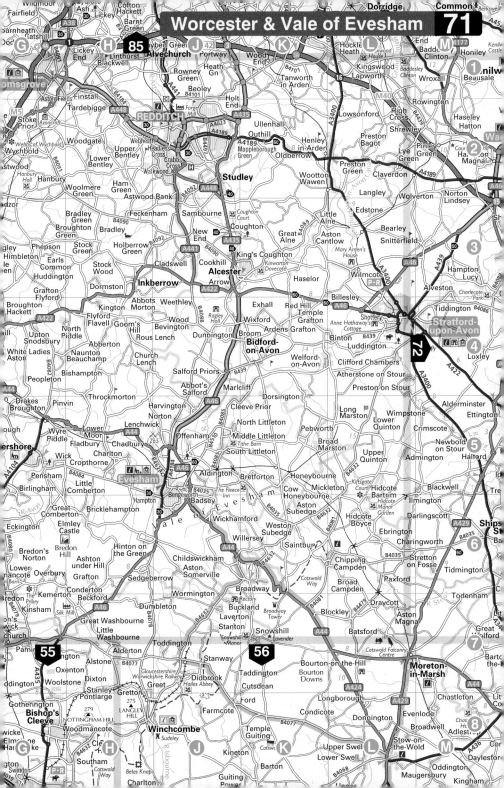

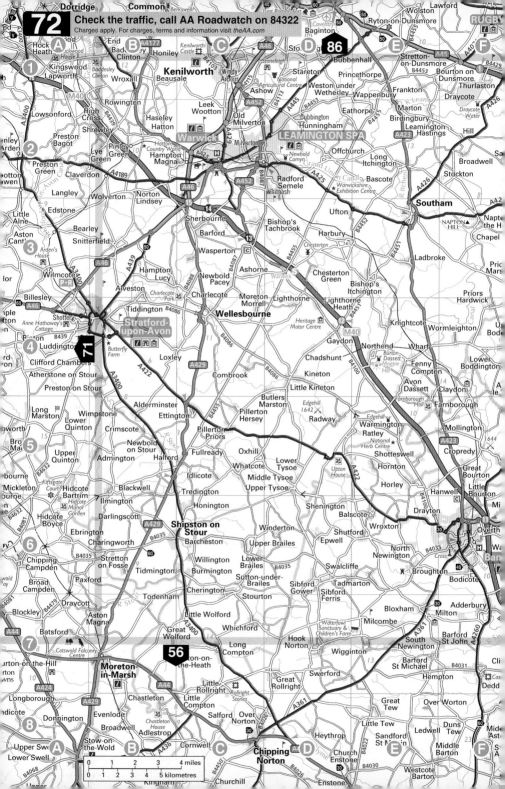

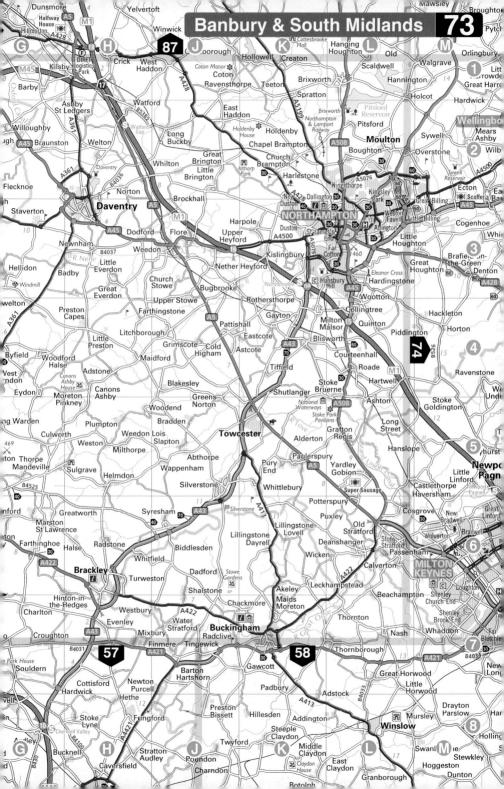

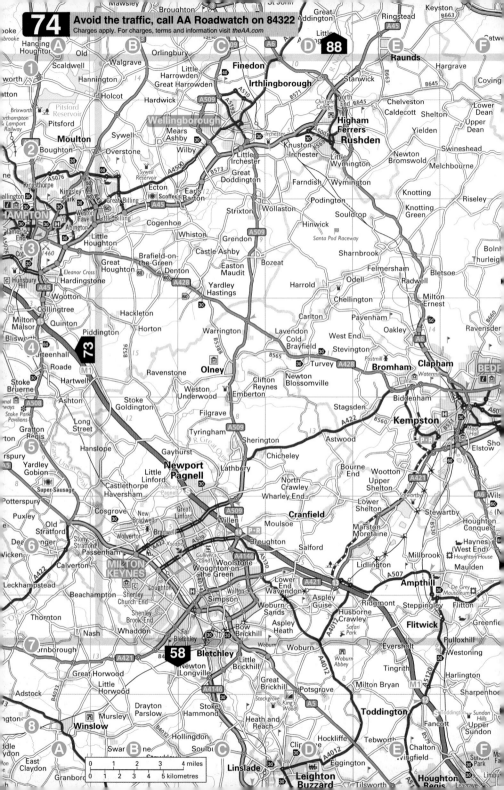

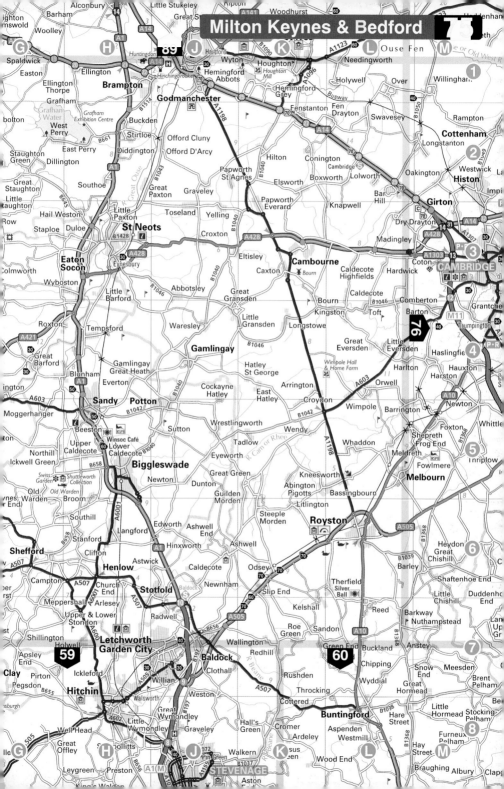

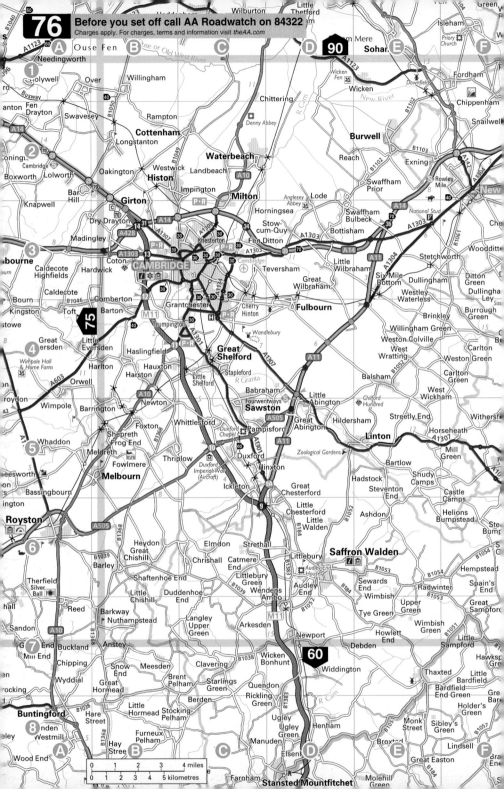

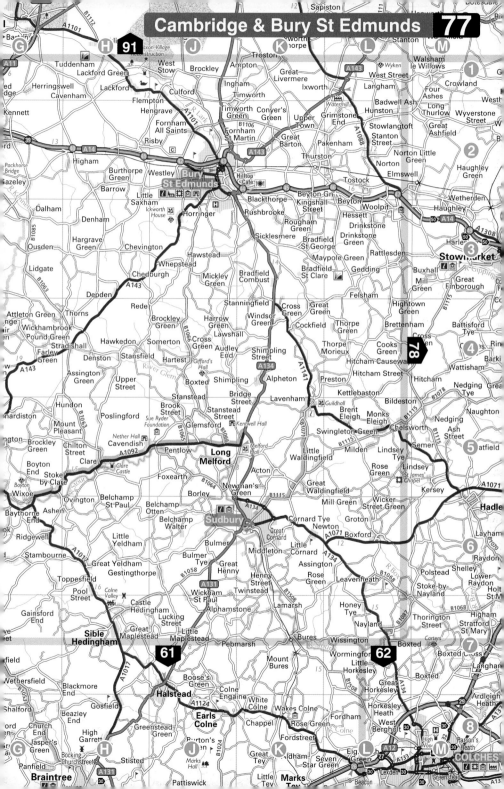

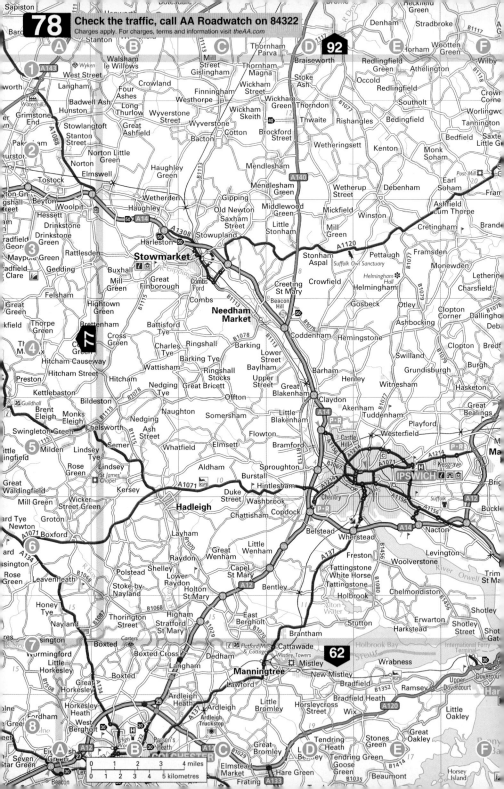

G H J 93 K L M

Cratfield
Cookley
Wenhaston
Blythburgh
Southwold
Huntingfield
Blackheath
Walpole
Bramfield
Thorington
Walberswick
Heveningham
B1117
Lakfield
A144
Suffolk
Coast
Ubbeston
Green
Darsham
Dunwich
Sibton
Peasenhall
Yoxford
Westleton
A1120
Badingham
Middleton
Minsmere
RSPB
Bruisyard
Middleton Moor
Eastbridge
Bruisyard
Street
Theberton
A12
Cransford
Rendham
Kelsale
Leiston
Abbey
Shawsgate
Carlton
Swefling
B1119
Saxmundham
th Green
Great
Glemham
Benhall
Street
Benhall
Green
Sternfield
Knodishall
Leiston
Aldringham
Thorpe
Ness
Stratford
St Andrew
B1119
Hacheston
Friday
Street
Farnham
Friston
Knodishall
Common
Thorpeness
Marlesford
Snape
B1121
A1094
B1122
RSPB
Little
Glemham
Snape
Street
The Maltings
Aldeburgh
Blaxhall
B1069
Iken
Campsea
Ash
High
Street
Aldeburgh
Bay
Tunstall
B1078
Rendlesham
Chillesford
Sudbourne
River Alde
Ufford
A1152
Eyke
Butley
B1084
Orford
Bromeswell
B1084
Castle
dge
Capel
St Andrew
Orford Ness
Sutton
Orfordness-
Havergate
RSPB
Boyton
ngfield
River Ore
Suffolk Heritage Coast
Shottisham
Hollesley
North Weir Point
Hollesley
Bay
B1083
ne
Alderton
nley
Bawdsey
ary
alkenham
ley
Old
Felixstowe
Felixstowe
River Deben
ard Fort
guard

Hoek van Holland
Esbjerg

G H J K L M

1 2 3 4 5 6 7 8

95

66

A B C D E F

Llane
Toll
Penmaenp
Barmouth
Barmouth Bridge ★
Barmouth
Bay
Fairbourne &
Barmouth
Steam Railway
Fairbourne
S N O W D O N I A
621
N A T I O N A L
P A R K
Tal-
20
Llwyngwril
Castell y Bere
Llangelynin
Abergyno
Rhoslefain
A493
Tal-y-Llyn Railway
Llanegryn
Dolgoch
633
Bryncrug B4405
Falls
TAREN
HENDRE
Aber
Dysynni
Pennal
Tywyn
Dove
C A R D I G A N
5
11
Aberdyfi A493
B A Y
Afon Dyfi River Dovey
A487
Dyfi
Furnace
18
B4353
Tre Taliesin
5
Borth
Tal-y-bont
B4353
Ceredigion
Heritage Coast
Llandre
Bont-g
Rhyd-y pennau
or Ele
Bow
Salem
B4572
Street
Clarach
Garth
Pen-bont
Bay
C
Penrhyncoch
Rhydybed
A4159
Capel-
Dewi
Capel
Aberystwyth
Bangor
Goginan
Waunfawr
Rheidol
P·R
Llanbadarn
Power Station
Fawr
Aberystwyth
Capel
12
A41
and District
Seion
Llanfarian
Llanfihangel-
y-Creuddyn
A485
Afon Ystwyth
Blaenplwyf
Cnwch
Coch
Llanilar
B4340
B4575
Ceredigion
Heritage Coast
18
Llanddeiniol
B4576
Llana
Llangwyryfon
Lledrod
Tyr
Llanrhystud

| 0 | 1 | 2 | 3 | 4 miles |
| 0 | 1 | 2 | 3 | 4 | 5 kilometres |

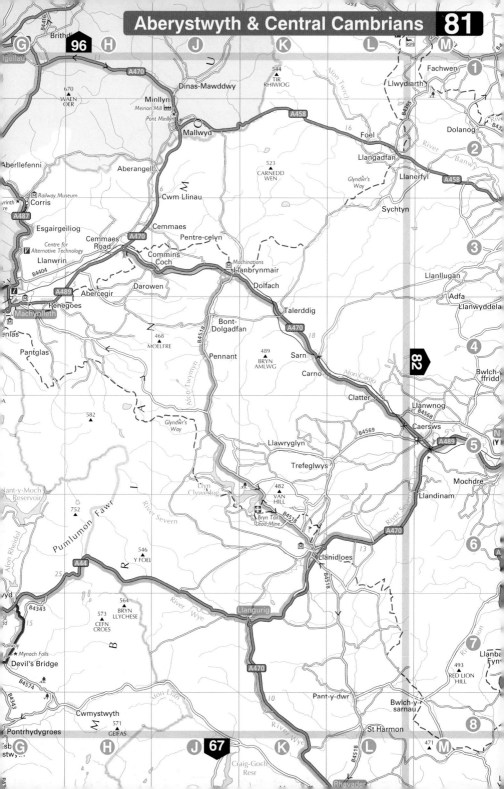

G | 96 | H | J | K | L | RSPB | M

B4404
Brithdir
Igellau
WAEN OER 670
A470
Dinas-Mawddwy
TIR RHIWIOG 544
Afon Twrch
Fachwen **1**
Llwydiarth
B4395
Minllyn
Meirion Mill
Pont Minllyn
Mallwyd
A458
16
Foel
River
Dolanog
B43
River

Aberllefenni
Aberangell
CARNEDD WEN 523
Glyndwr's Way
River Banwy
Llangadfan **2**
Llanerfyl
A458
Sychtyn

Railway Museum
Corris
A487
Esgairgeiliog
Cemmaes
Pentre-celyn
Cwm Llinau
6
Llanllugan **3**
Adfa
Llanwyddela

Centre for Alternative Technology
Cemmaes Road
A470
Commins Coch
Machinations
Llanbrynmair
Dolfach
Talerddig
A470
18
4
Bwlch-ffridd

Llanwrin
B4404
A489
Abercegir
Darowen
Sarn
Carno
Afon Carno
82
Llanwnog
B4568

Machynlleth
Penegoes
MOELFRE 468
Z
Bont-Dolgadfan
Pennant
BRYN AMLWG 489
Carno
Clatter
Caersws
A489
5
N

enlas
Pantglas
A
Afon Twymyn
Llawryglyn
Trefeglwys
B4569
Mochdre
River Severn
Llandinam

Pant-y-Moch Reservoir
582
Glyndwr's Way
Llyn Clywedog
VAN HILL 482
Bryn Tail Lead Mine
B4518
A470
6

Afon Rheidol
752
Pumlumon Fawr
R
River Severn
Llanidloes
13
B4518

yd
B4343
A44
Y FOEL 546
River Wye
Llangurig
7
Llanba Fyn

Railway
Mynach Falls
Devil's Bridge
25
B
BRYN LLYCHESE 564
CEFN CROES 573
River Wye
A470
RED LION HILL 493

B4574
esb y... stwy
B4343
Cwmystwyth
GEIFAS 571
Afon Elan
Pant-y-dwr
Bwlch-y-sarnau
8

Pontrhydygroes
River Wye
St Harmon
471
M

G | H | J | 67 | K | L | M

Craig-Goch Resr
Rhayader

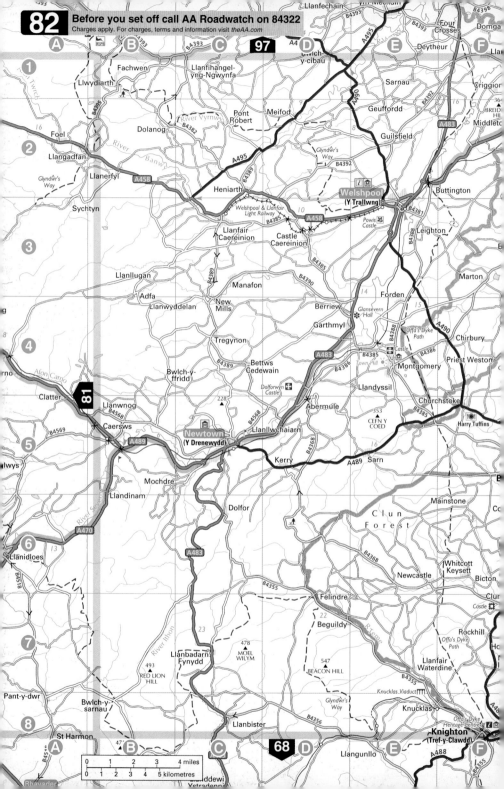

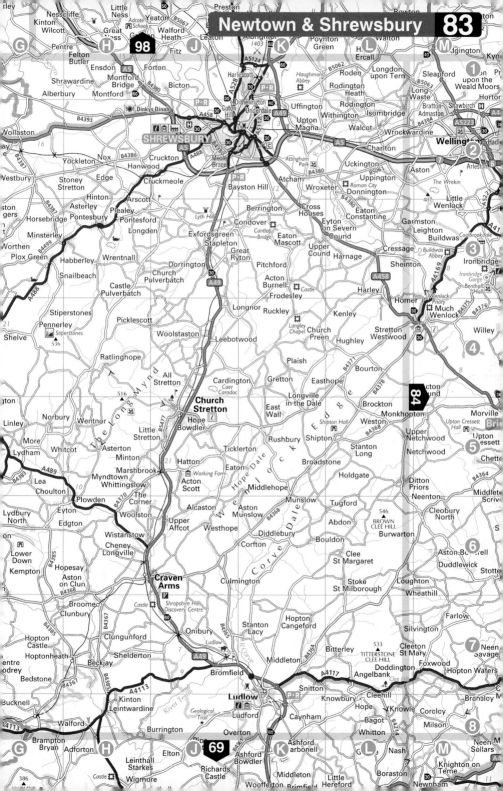

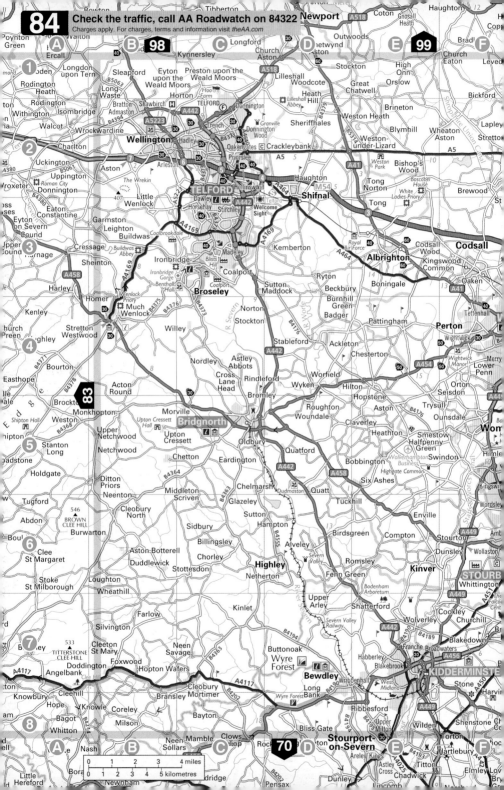

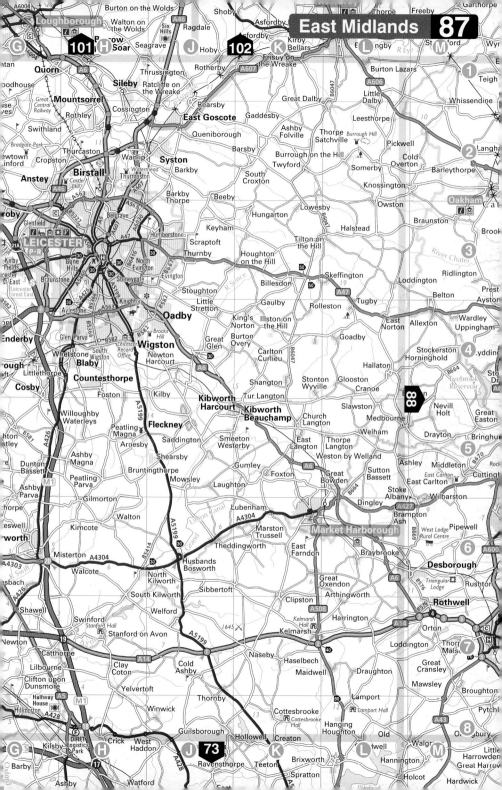

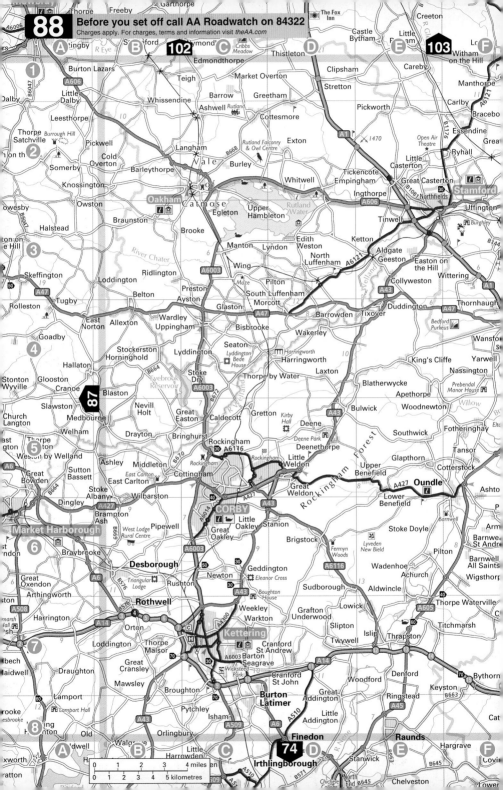

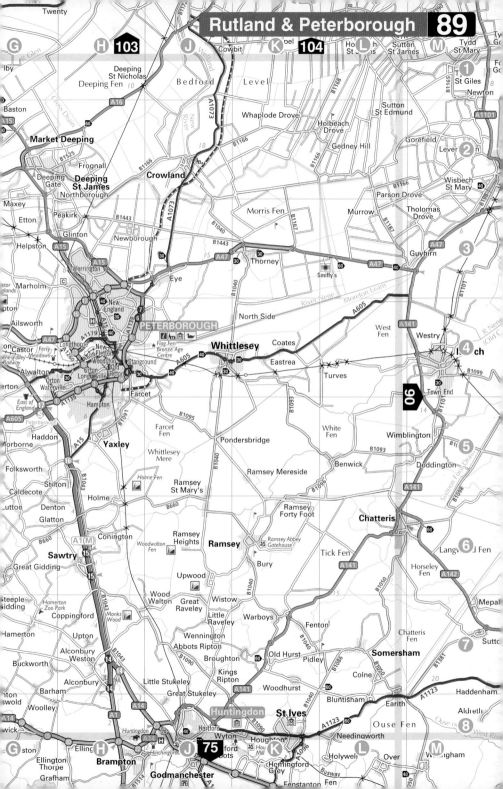

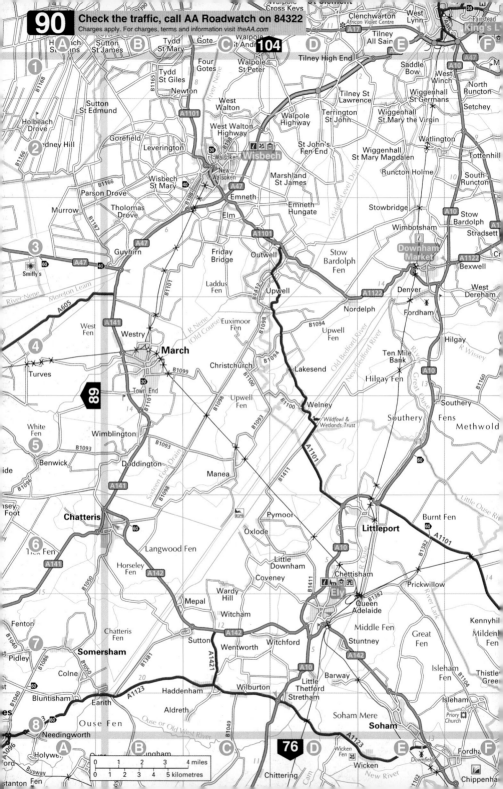

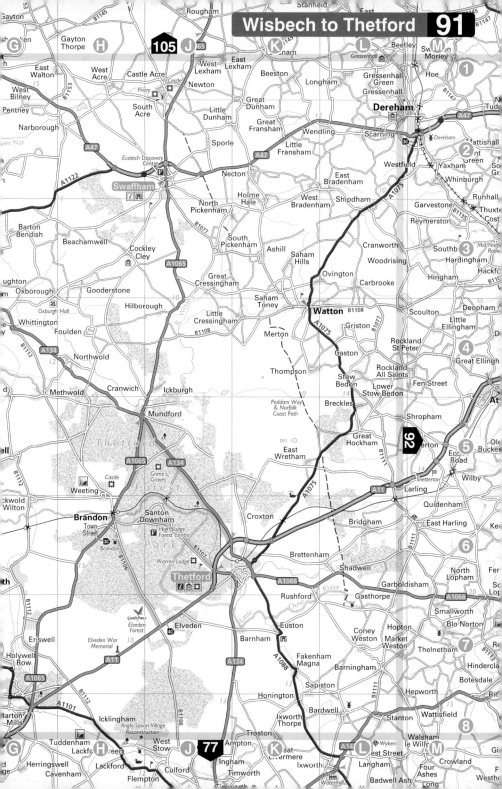

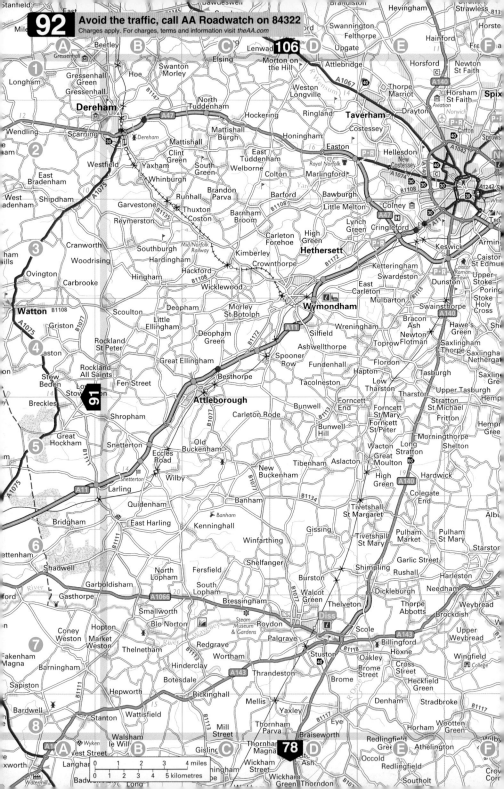

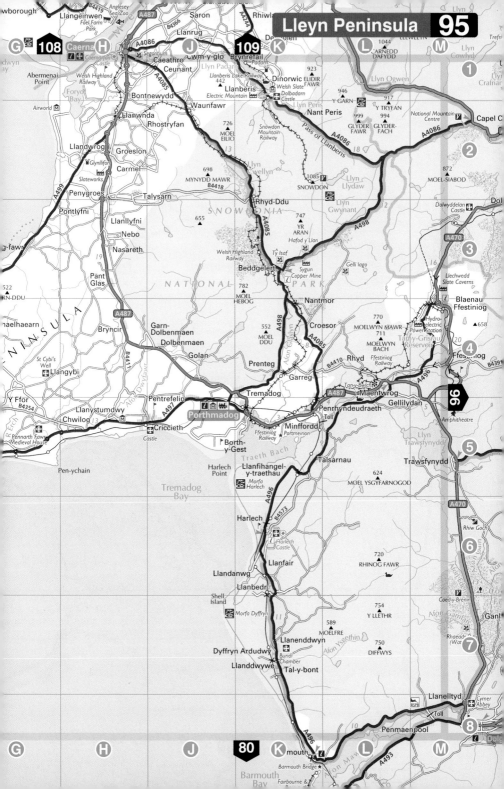

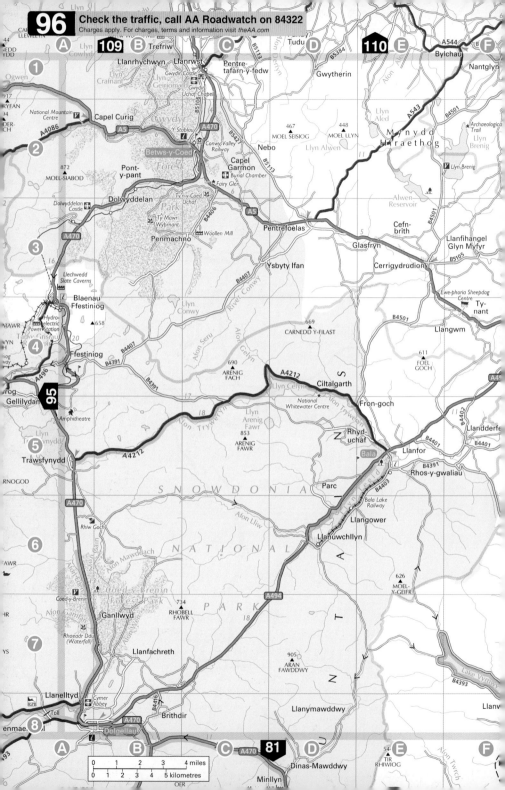

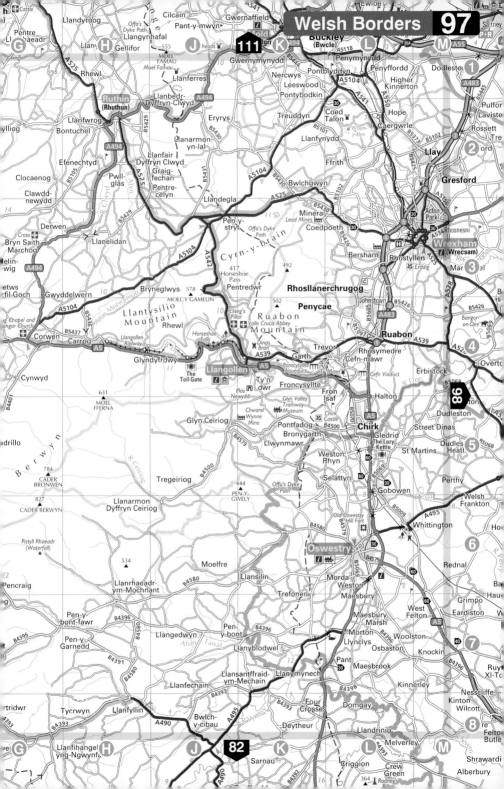

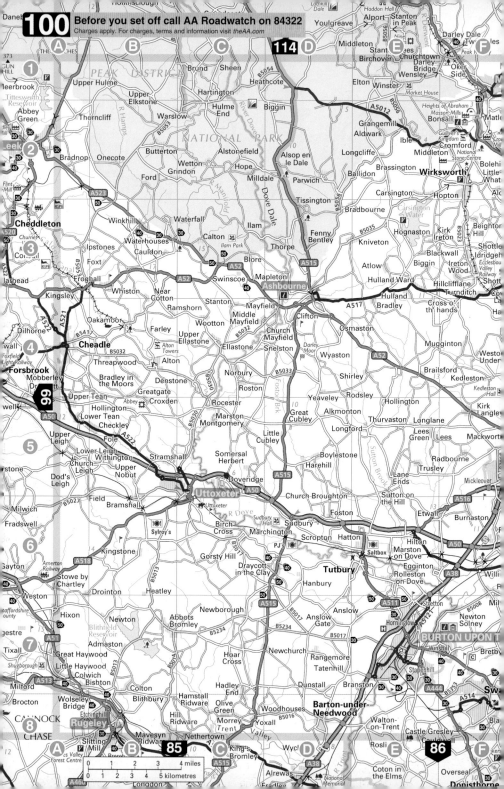

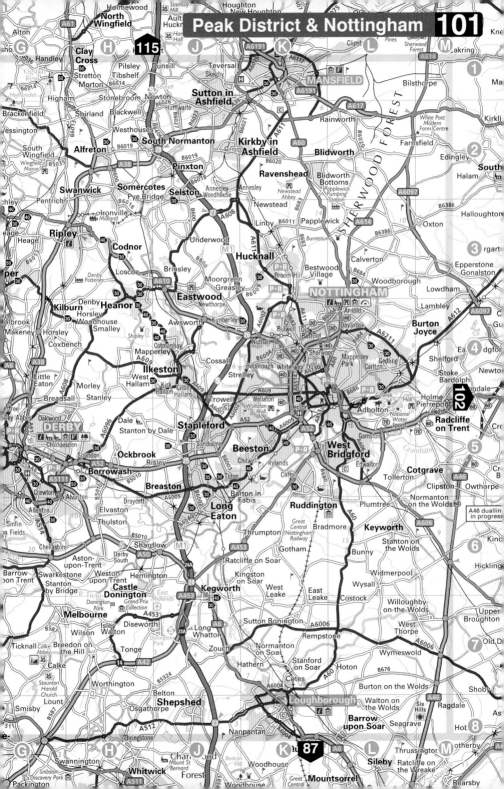

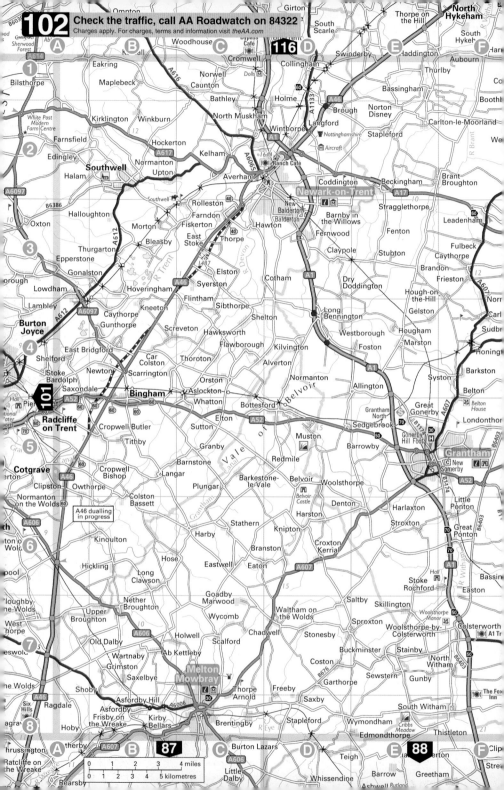

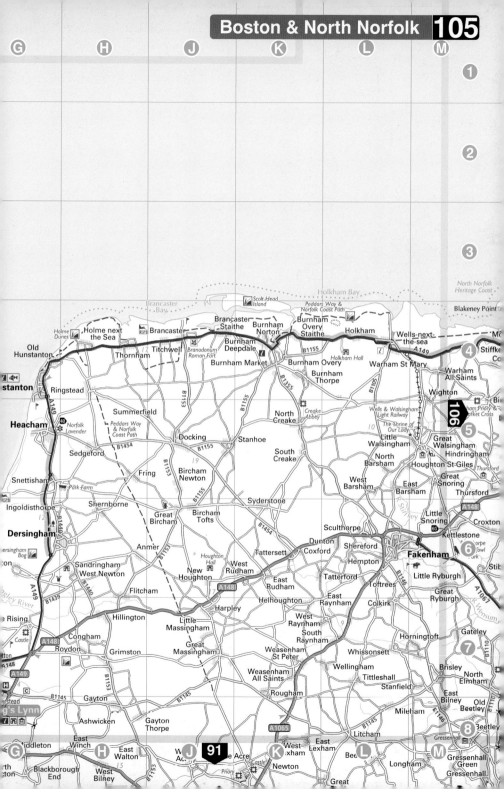

G **H** **J** **K** **L** **M**

1

2

3

North Norfolk
Heritage Coast

Blakeney Point

Holkham Bay

Brancaster
Bay

Scolt Head
Island

Peddars Way &
Norfolk Coast Path

Brancaster
Staithe

Burnham
Norton

Burnham
Overy
Staithe

Holkham

Wells-next-
the-sea

Holme next
the Sea

Holme
Dunes

Brancaster

Burnham
Deepdale

Burnham Overy

Wells Priory &
Market Cross

4

Stiffke
Co

Old
Hunstanton

Thornham

Titchwell

Branodunum
Roman Fort

Burnham Market

Burnham
Thorpe

Warham St Mary

Warham
All Saints

Wighton

106

Bi

stanton

Ringstead

B1153

B1155

B1355

North
Creake

Creake
Abbey

A149

Wells & Walsingham
Light Railway

The Shrine of
Our Lady

Great
Walsingham

5

Heacham

Norfolk
Lavender

Summerfield

Peddars Way
& Norfolk
Coast Path

Docking

Stanhoe

South
Creake

Little
Walsingham

North
Barsham

Houghton St Giles

Hindringham

Thursford

Great
Snoring

Thursford

Sedgeford

B1454

B1153

Fring

Bircham
Newton

B1155

19

Syderstone

West
Barsham

East
Barsham

Snettisham

Park Farm

Shernborne

Great
Bircham

Bircham
Tofts

B1454

Sculthorpe

Little
Snoring

60

Kettlestone

Croxton

Ingoldisthorpe

12

B1440

A148

Dunton

Shereford

Fakenham

6

orpe
owl

Stib

Dersingham

Anmer

B1153

Houghton
Hall

West
Rudham

Tattersett

Coxford

Hempton

Great
Ryburgh

Little Ryburgh

ersingham
Bog

ton

Sandringham
West Newton

A149

B1440

New
Houghton

East
Rudham

Tatterford

Toftrees

A1067

R. Wensum

Flitcham

A148

Helhoughton

East
Raynham

Colkirk

Great
Ryburgh

Gateley

7

Rising

Castle

A148

Hillington

Congham

Harpley

Little
Massingham

West
Raynham

South
Raynham

Horningtoft

Brisley

North
Elmham

Roydon

Grimston

Great
Massingham

Weasenham
St Peter

Whissonsett

Wellingham

Tittleshall

Stanfield

East
Bilney

Old
Beetley

A149

B1439

Weasenham
All Saints

Rougham

B1145

Gayton

B1145

Mileham

A1065

Beetle

8

g's Lynn

Ashwicken

Gayton
Thorpe

Litcham

Gressenhall

Gressenhall
Green
Gressenhall

iddleton

East
Winch

East
Walton

G   **H**   **J** ▼ **91**   **K**   **L**   **M**

Blackborough
End

West
Bilney

Newton

Beel

Longham

rth

West
xham

East
Lexham

G   H   J   K   L   M

1

2

3

4

gham

5

Mundesley
Stow Mill
Paston
B1159
apton
Edingthorpe   Bacton
Walcott
Edingthorpe
Green   Witton   Ridlington   Happisburgh
Meeting   Whimpwell Green
ouse Hill   Honing   Happisburgh
Common   Hempstead   6
Lessingham
Briggate   East   B1159   Ingham   Sea Palling
Worstead   Ruston   Ingham   Corner
Stalham   Waxham
Dilham   Calthorpe
Smallburgh   Street
2   A149   Hickling
Tunstead   Barton   Sutton   Hickling Green   Horsey
Turf   Wood   7
Neatishead   Catfield   Street   Hickling   Horsey Windpump
Barton   7   Broad
Irstead   Broad
Potter
Hoveton   Ludham   Heigham
Martham
Upper   Bastwick   Winterton-on-Sea
A1062   Hemsby   Hemsby
Street   Ormes   Hole   8
G   Horning   H   er Street   J   Broad   K   M
Woodbastwick   Bure   Repps   Orr   y
Marshes   esby   Orr St Margaret   Scratby
Broadland   Thurne   93
Conservation Centre   Clippesby   Burgh St   California
Salhouse   Pilson   Margaret Ormesby
Ranworth   St Michael

93

108
Check the traffic, call AA Roadwatch on 84322
Charges apply. For charges, terms and information visit *theAA.com*

North Anglesey Heritage Coast

The Skerries

Wylfa Head

Cemaes Bay

Porth Wen

Bull Bay

Amlw

CARMEL HEAD

Hen Borth

Cemlyn Bay

Cemaes

A5025

Burwen

Llan

Tregele

Rhosbeirio

Bodewryd

Penysarn

Llanfairynghornwy

Llanfechell

Carreglefn

Rhosybol

Holyhead Bay

Church Bay

Llanrhyddlad

Capel Parc

Dublin

Llanfaethlu

Llyn Alaw

B5111

Dún Laoghaire

Llanddeusant

Elim

Llanerchymedd

Porth Tywynmawr

Llanfwrog

Llyn Llywenan

B5112

Coedana

Capel Coch

North Stack

Breakwater Quarry

Holyhead Mountain Hut Group

Presaddfed

B5109

ANGLESEY

B5111

Gogarth Bay

South Stack

Holyhead (Caergybi)

Llanfachraeth

B5112

South Stack

Penrhos Feilw

Kingsland

Llanynghenedl

Valley A5025

Bodedern

Llynfaes

B5109

Holyhead Mountain Heritage Coast

Porth Dafarch

A55

Caergeiliog

Bryngwran

Bodffordd

Gwalchmai

Celni Reservoir

Oriel Ynys Mon

Penrhyn Mawr

B4545

Trefignath

Trearddur Bay

Four Mile Bridge

Llanfihangel yn Nhowyn

A4080

Anglesey

18

A5

A55

A5114

HOLY ISLAND

Llanfair-yn-Neubwll

Plas Cymyran

Ty Newydd

10

Cerrigceinwen

Llangristiol

Rhoscolyn

Rhoscolyn Head

Cymyran Bay

Pencarnisiog

Din-Dryfol

Pentre Be

Rhosneigr

A4080

Llanfaelog

Bethel

B4422

Capel Mawr

Hen Blas

Aberffraw

Barclodiad y Gawres

Ga

Llangadwaladr

Malltraeth

Llangaffo

A4080

Porth Trecastell

Aberffraw

Anglesey Circuit

Llanfair-y-Cwmwd

B4421

B4419

Dwyra

Llan

Aberffraw Bay

Newborough

Llangeinwe

Foel Far Park

Aberffraw Bay Heritage Coast

Malltraeth Bay

Caernar

Llanddwyn Island

Llanddwyn

95

Menai

Forya Bay

G H J K L M

① ② ③ ④ ⑤ ⑥ ⑦ ⑧

Dulas Bay

Seawatch Centre

Moelfre
Llanallgo

Benllech

Red Wharf Bay
rgoch
Red Wharf Bay

Pentraeth

Llanddona

Llandegfan

Llansadwrn

Beaumaris
Gaol & Courthouse
Beaumaris Castle

Penmon Priory,
Cross & Dovecote
Toll

Puffin Island

Black Point

Llangoed

GREAT ORMES HEAD

Great Orme
Heritage Coast

Little Ormes He

Conwy Bay

Llandudno

Deganwy

110

Penrhyn
ny

⑤

Llandrillo
yn-Rhos

Ri

Menai
Bridge
(Porthaethwy)

Anglesey Column

anfair P G

Bryn
Celli Ddu
Britannia Bridge
Plas Newydd

Bangor

Penrhyn
Llandygai

Tal-y-bont

Llandygai

Conwy
Conwy Castle

Llandudno
Junction

Llansanffraid
Glan C

Bry
y-M

⑥

Dwygyfylchi
Penmaenmawr

Llanfairfechan

14

Abergwyngregyn

Capelulo

Henryd

Rowen

S N O W D O N I A

610
TAL-Y-FAN

Tal-y-Cafn

Graig
Eglwysbach

Bodnant

Llanllechid

Moel Winion
580

Aber
Waterfall

N A T I O N A L

Llanbedr-y-Cennin

Ty'n-y-Groes

Tal-y-Bont

Dolgarrog

Vale of Conwy

⑦

Felinheli
Green Wood
Forest Park

Pentir
Rhyd-y groes

Glasinfryn

Tregarth

757
Y DROSGL

Rachub

Bethesda

942
FOEL-FRAS

Afon Dulyn

Bethel

Llanddeiniolen

Saron

Rhiwlas

Aron Caseg

Aron Ddu

Afon Anafon

Aron Dulyn

Llyn
Eigiau

P A R K

Llyn
Cowlyd

Trefriw Woollen Mill

Trefriw

Llanddoget

⑧

Llanrug

Deiniolen

1062
CARNEDD
LLEWELYN

1044
CARNEDD
DAFYDD

Llyn
Crafnant

Llanr

Llanrwst
Castle

Llanrwst

Pentre-
tafarn-y-fedw

ydd

aeathro
iant

Llyn Padarn

Brynrefail

Cwm-y-glo

G H 95 J K L 96 M

B4085

Waunfawr

Llanberis
Electric Mountain

Llanberis Lake Rly
442

923
C ELIDIR
FAWR

Welsh Slate
Dolbadarn Castle

946
Y GARN

580

917

Llyn Ogwen

Llyn Peris

Llyn
Crafnant

Geirionydd

Gwydir
Uchaf Chapel

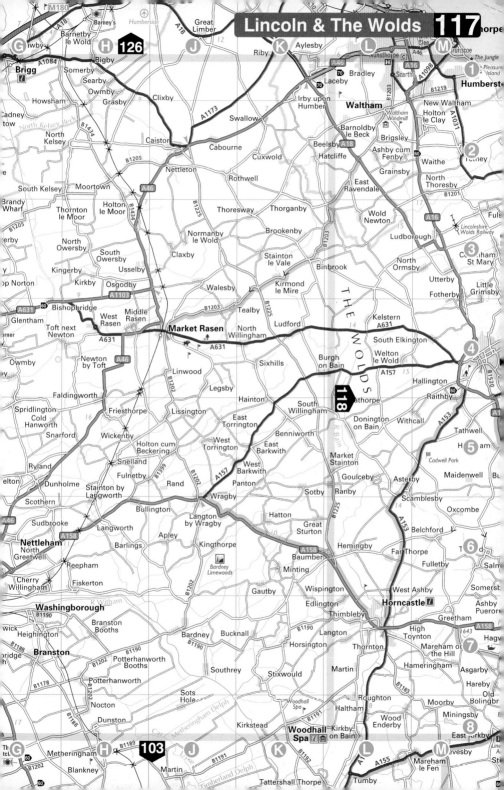

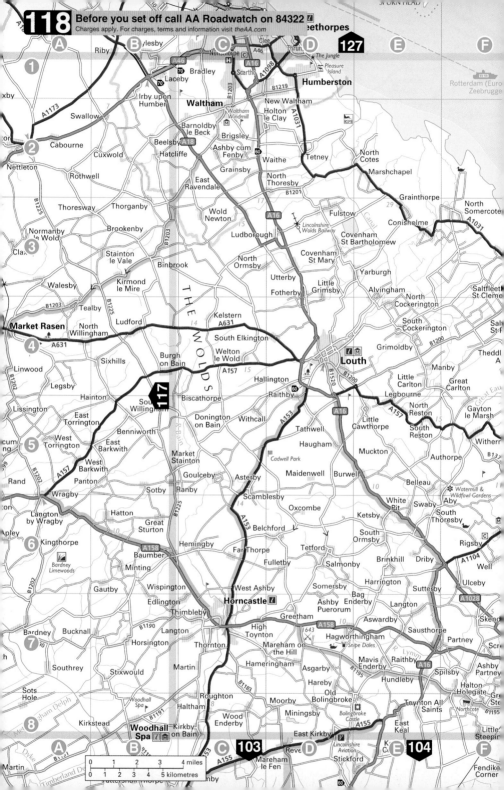

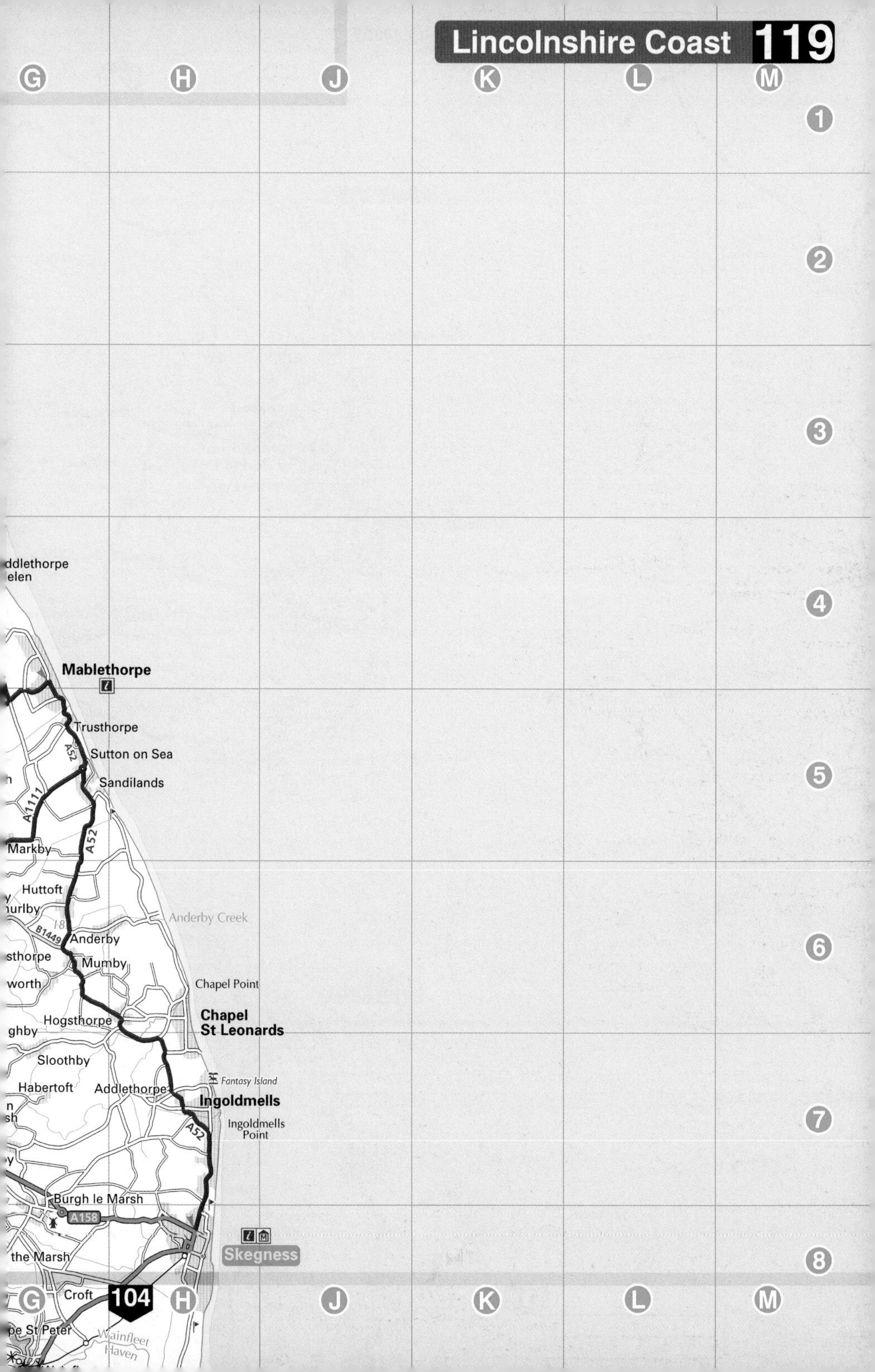
G
H
J
K
L
M
1
2
3
4
5
6
7
8
ddlethorpe
elen
Mablethorpe
Trusthorpe
A52
Sutton on Sea
Sandilands
A1111
Markby
Huttoft
urlby
Anderby Creek
B1449
Anderby
sthorpe
Mumby
worth
Chapel Point
Hogsthorpe
Chapel
St Leonards
ghby
Sloothby
Fantasy Island
Habertoft
Addlethorpe
Ingoldmells
Ingoldmells
Point
Burgh le Marsh
A158
Skegness
the Marsh
Croft
104
pe St Peter
Wainfleet
Haven

129

A   B   C   D   E   F

1

Glasson
Cockersand
Cockerl

Larne

🚢 Fleetwood
Rossall Point

Knott End-
on-Sea
Preesall
Piling
COCKERHA
Winmar

2
B5377
A588

River Wyre
Stalmine
Staynall
Eagland
Hill
Moss Edge

🚢 Cleveleys
B5268
A585

Thornton

Hambleton
Out
Rawcliffe
Great
Eccleston

3
A584
A586
Poulton-
le-Fylde
Little
Singleton
Copp
Singleton
Elswick
Thistleton
B5269

Warbreck
North
Shore
A585
B5266
Greenhalgh
Esprick
Wharles

BLACKPOOL
Staining
Weeton
M55

4
Model Village
Great
Marton
Great
Plumpton
Wesham
Treales
Kirkham
A583

South
Shore
A5230
Westby
Wrea
Green
Newton with
Scales
Freckleton
Warton

Blackpool
B5261
St Anne's
Royal Lytham & St Annes
Fairhaven
Ansdell
Kellamergh
A584
Lytham
River Ribble

5
Lytham
St Anne's
RSPB
Discovery
Centre

Hesketh
Bank
Wes

Hundred
End
Becconsall

6
Banks
Tarleton
A565
Mere Brow

SOUTHPORT
New Pleasureland
P·R
RSPB
Holmeswood
Ruffo
B5246

7
Birkdale
The Royal
Birkdale
P·R
Windmill
Animal Farm
Wildfowl &
Wetlands Trust
Scarisbrick
Bescar
Burscough
Bridge

Shirdley
Hill
A570
Heaton's
Bridge
Burscough
B5242

Ainsdale
A565
Halsall
B5240

8
Ainsdale
Sand-Dunes
Barton
Haskayne
Ormskirk
A577
B5

Cabin
Hill
Freshfield
Formby
Little
Altcar
Great
Altcar
B5195
Aughton Park
Skelmer

A   B   **111**   C   D   E   F

A506

Hightown
A565
Aughton
A5147

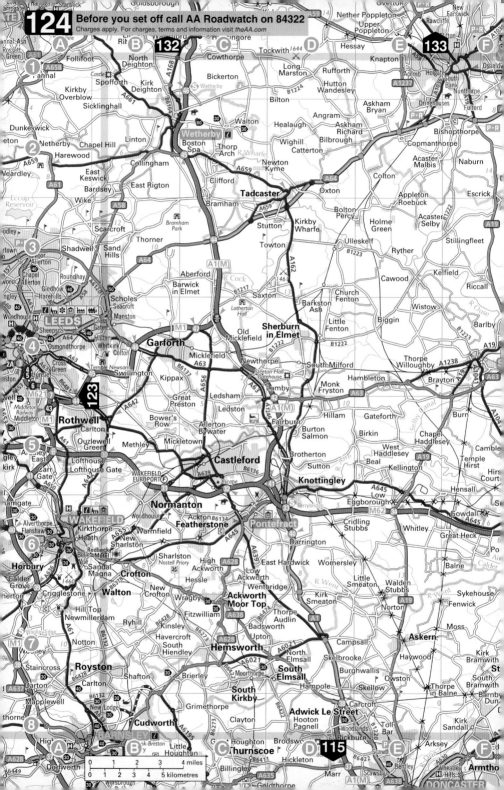

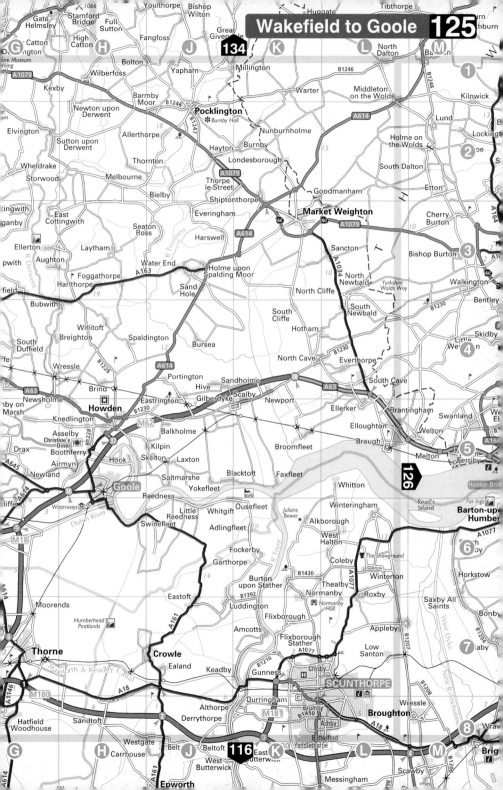

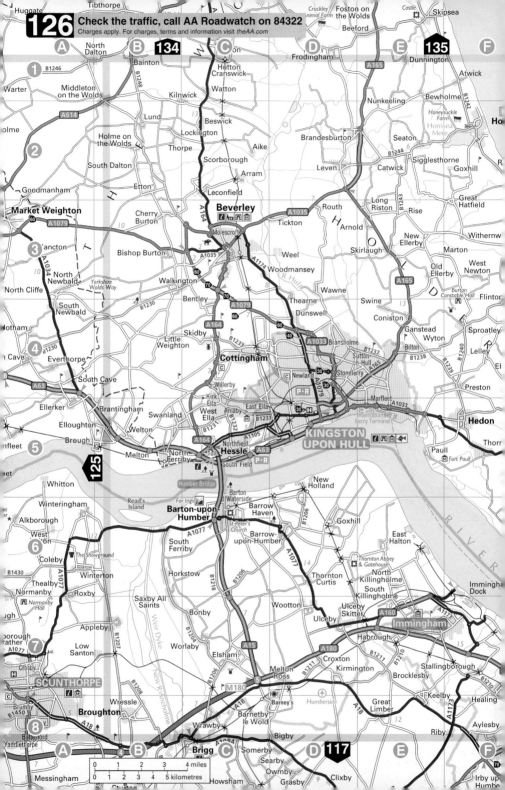

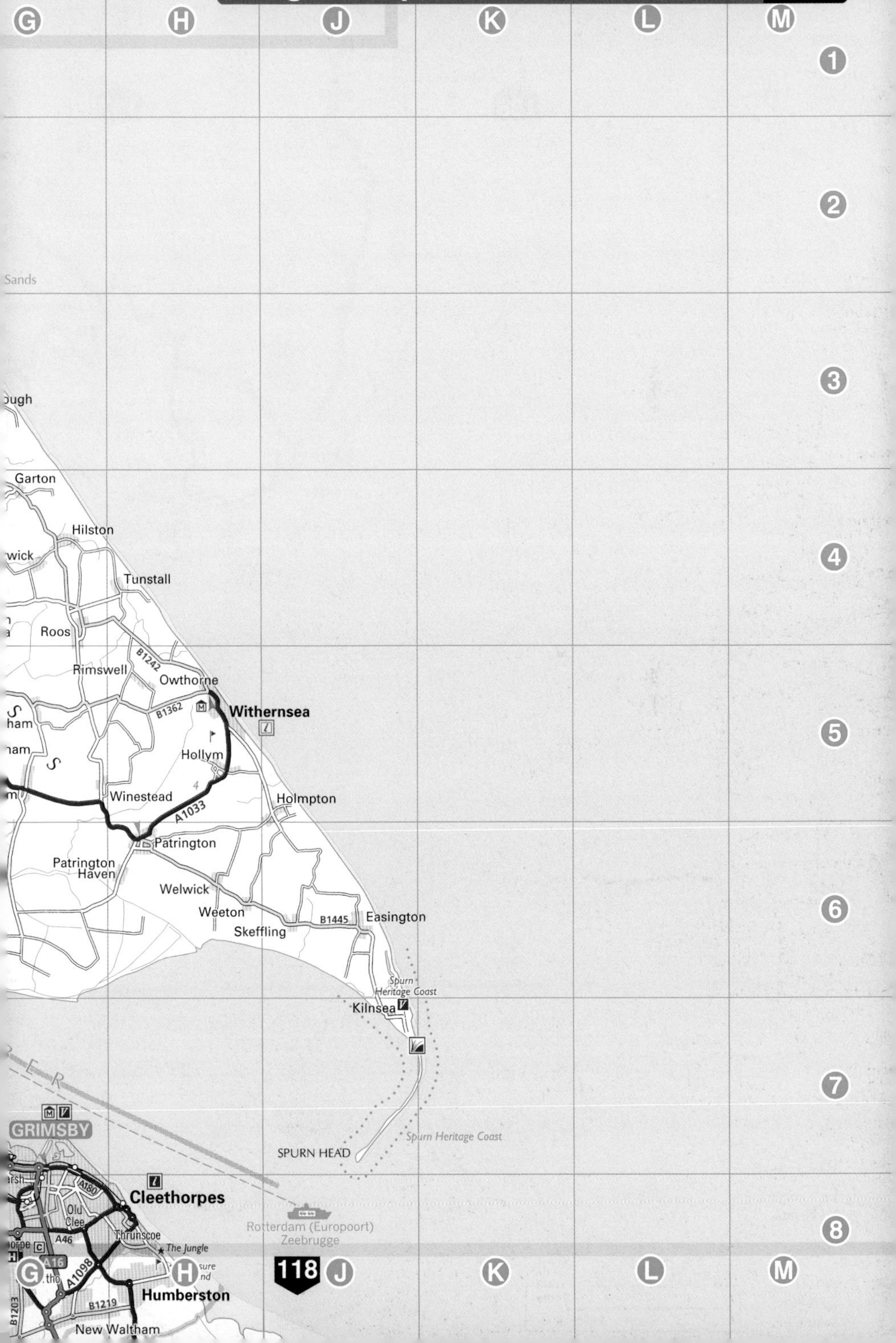

G   H   J   K   L   M

①
②
③

Sands

ough

Garton

Hilston

wick

Tunstall

Roos

B1242

Rimswell   Owthorne

B1362

Withernsea

Hollym

Winestead

A1033   Holmpton

Patrington

Patrington
Haven

Welwick

Weeton

Skeffling   B1445   Easington

Spurn
Heritage Coast

Kilnsea

Spurn Heritage Coast

SPURN HEAD

④
⑤
⑥
⑦

GRIMSBY

Cleethorpes

Thrunscoe

The Jungle

Rotterdam (Europoort)
Zeebrugge

⑧

118

G   H   J   K   L   M

Old
Clee   A46

sure
nd

Humberston

New Waltham

Seascale

Green

Eskdale

652
HARTER
FELL

136

Ravenglass
Roman Bath House

Muncaster

Ravenglass
and Eskdale
Railway

Devoke
Water

Hall
Dunnerdale

Seath

A595

137

LAKE   DISTR

Lane End
Waberthwaite

573
WHITFELL

Ulpha

N A T I O N A L

Broughton
Mills

A59

Hycemoor

Selker Bay

Bootle

Swinside Stone Circle

P A R K

Broughton-i

A595

Lady
Hall

Foxfield

600
BLACK
COMBE

Whitbeck

The Green

Gutterby Spa

Whicham

Silecroft

Kirksanton

A5093

The Hill

C Kirkby
Be

Soutergate

A595

12

Millom

RSPB

Haverigg

Haverigg
Point

Askam
in Furness

Ireleth

Lindal
in Furness
South Lakes
Animal Park

Sandscale Haws

North Walney

Dalton-
in-Furness

Newton

**BARROW-
IN-FURNESS**

Furness
Abbey

Bow
Bridge

Dendron

Vickerstown

Barrow
Island

30

A590

A5087

Ra

**ISLE OF
WALNEY**

Sheep
Island

Piel
Cast

Piel Is

Hilpsford Point

Piel

G · H · J · K · L · M · **1**

G · H **120** · J · K **121** · L · M

MORECAMBE

BAY

2

3

4

5

6

7

8

Kendal

137

138

130

Outgate
Troutbeck Bridge
Hawkshead Hill
Hawkshead
Bowness-on-Windermere
Garth Row
Grayrigg
Burneside
Far Sawrey
Near Sawrey
Hill Top
Crook
Underbarrow
Firbank
Grizedale
Winster
New Hutton
Blackwell
Killington
Satterthwaite
Furness Fells
Crosthwaite
Brigsteer
Oxenholme
Natland
Middleshaw
Thwaite Head
Graythwaite Hall
Row
Old Hutton
High Nibthwaite
Crosslands
Stott Park Bobbin Mill
Finsthwaite
Gummers How
Whitbarrow
Levens
Sedgwick
Stainton
Old Town
Oxen Park
Colton
Rusland
Fell Foot Park
Staveley
Newby Bridge
Lakeside and Haverthwaite Railway
Levens Hall
Hincaster
Westmorland
Endmoor
Preston Patrick
Lowick Green
Bouth
Spark Bridge
Haverthwaite
Witherslack
Ayside
Leasgill
Crooklands
Penny Bridge
Greenodd
High Newton
Low Newton
Heversham
Nook Lupton
Arrad Foot
Field Broughton
Lindale
Milnthorpe
Meathop
Whasset
Farleton
Kearstwick
Barrow Monument
Priory Gatehouse
Hampsfield Fell
Arnside
Beetham
Holme
Hutton Roof
High Biggins
Low Biggins
Kirkby
Lakeland Motor
Cartmel
Holker
Cark
Allithwaite
Grange-over-Sands
Arnside Knott
Hale
Lakeland Wildlife Oasis
Burton-in-Kendal
Holme Park Fell
Park Wood
Docker
Conishead Priory
Flookburgh
Silverdale
Leighton Hall
Yealand Redmayne
Priest Hutton
Whittington
Bardsea
Humphrey Head
Jack Scout
Heald Brow
Yealand Conyers
Truckhaven
Warton
Old Rectory
Borwick
Arkholme
Baycliff
Silverdale
Carnforth
Over Kellet
Gressingham
Wennington
Aldingham
Bolton le Sands
Nether Kellet
Hornby
Hest Bank
Aughton
Claughton
Caton Green
Brookhouse
Wray
Farleton
Morecambe
Bare
Slyne
Halton
Caton
Crossgill
Sandylands
Torrisholme
Skerton
River Lune Millennium Park
Lancaster
Heysham
Higher Heysham
Aldcliffe
Scotforth
WARD'S STONE
Overton
Ellel
Sunderland
Glasson
Galgate
Abbeystead
Cockersand
Dolphinholme
Knott End
Pilling
Cockerham
HAWTHORN FELL
Calder Fell

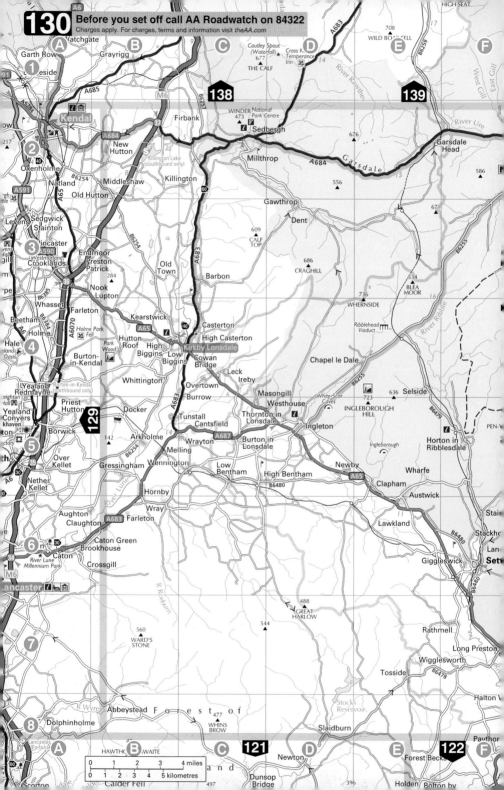

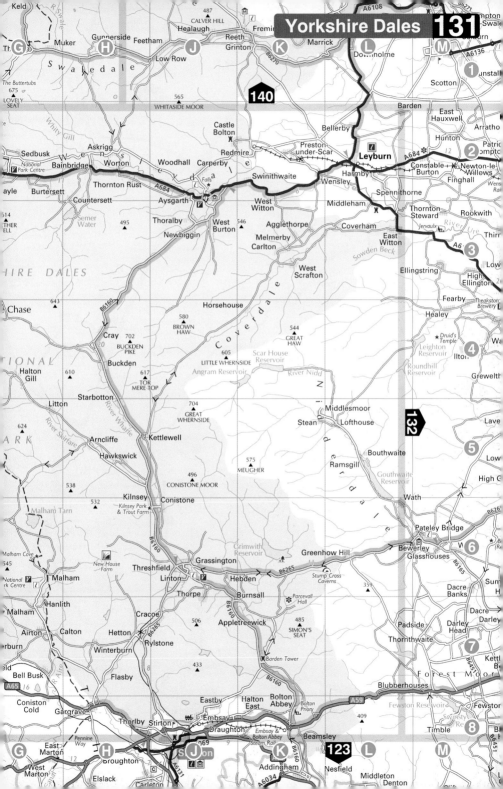

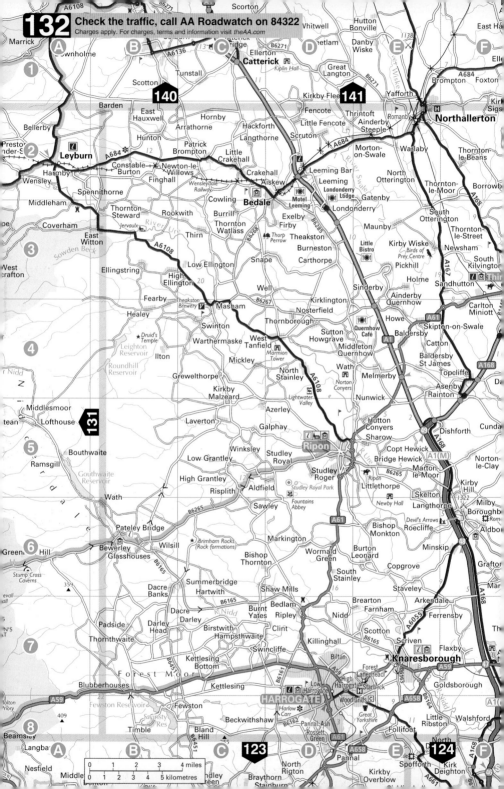

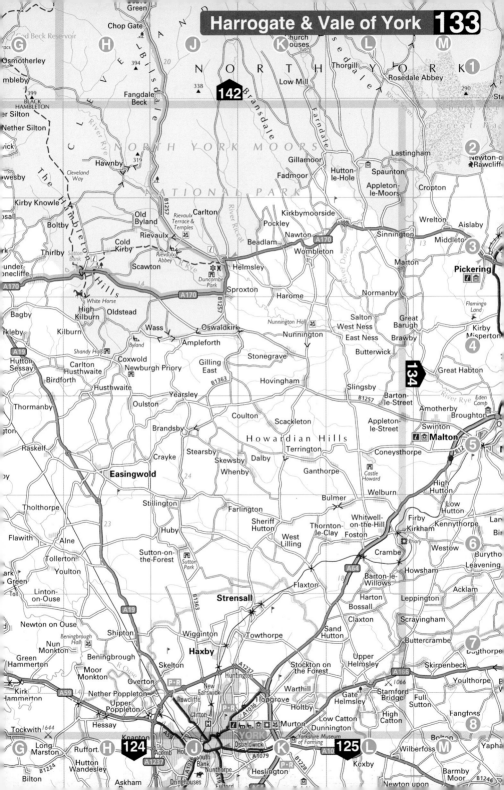

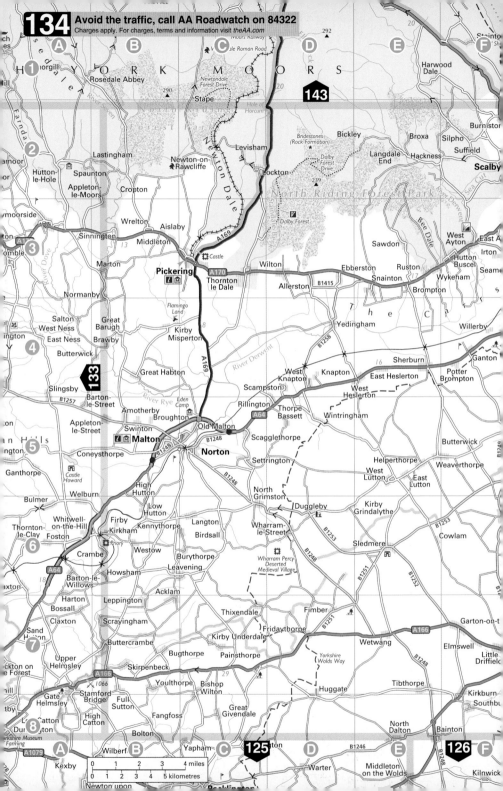

G　H　J　K　L　M

1
2
3
4
5
6
7
8

Scarborough
Hatherleigh
Deep Sea
Trawler
Oliver's Mount
A165
Osgodby
Cayton Bay
B1261
yton
The Wyke
Lebberston
A1039
Filey Brigg
Gristhorpe
R. Hertford
Muston
Filey
lkton
A1039
Filey Bay
Hunmanby
Fordon
Reighton
Flamborough Head
Heritage Coast
Wold Newton
Speeton
B1229
Thornwick Bay
Bempton Cliffs
RSPB
Burton Fleming
Buckton
Bempton
North Landing
A165
Grindale
B1229
Selwicks Bay
B1259
FLAMBOROUGH HEAD
Lighthouse
B1255
Flamborough
Sewerby
B1253
Bondville
Miniature Village
Rudston
Monolith
Boynton
Bridlington
BRIDLINGTON BAY
Bessingby
Hilderthorpe
Haisthorpe
Carnaby
Thornholme
Kilham
Burton Agnes
Norman Manor House
Parva
Harpham
A165
Lowthorpe
Fraisthorpe
A614
Nafferton
Gransmoor
Great Kelk
Lissett
Barmston
Wansford
B1242
Gembling
Ulrome
Cruckley
Animal Farm
Foston on the Wolds
Castle
Skipsea
B1249
Skerne
Beeford
Brigham
North Frodingham
A165
Dunnington
126
Atwick
Bewholme
B1242
Nunkeeling

G　H　J　K　L　M

136

Before you set off call AA Roadwatch on 84322
Charges apply. For charges, terms and information visit *theAA.com*

A B C D E F

1

147

Maryport

Crosscanonby
Crosby
Fort

Dearham

Flimby

Broughton
Moor
Standingstone Dovenby
Great
Broughton
Cameron Papcastle

2

Seaton

Workington

Moss
Bay

Great
Clifton 8

Stainburn Little
Clifton

Brigham

Greysouthen

Eaglesfield

A66

Mossbay
Westfield A596 A595
Salterbeck
Harrington

Deanscales

Dean
Pardshaw

Branthwaite

Ullock

Distington

Common End

Lowca
Parton

A595

Howgate
Low
Moresby

Gilgarran
Pica

Mockerkin

Lamplugh
572

Loweswater

3

Whitehaven

Saltom
Bay

Sandwith

Mirehouse

Hensingham

Frizington

Cleator
Moor

Arlecdon

Rowrah

Asby

Kirkland

High Leys

Ennerdale
Bridge

Enner
Wa

4

St Bees Head
St Bees Head
Heritage Coast

Rottington

Bigrigg

St Bees

Cleator

Egremont

River Ehen

River Calder

533
LANK
RIGG

5

Florence Mine

Haile

Worm Gill

River Bleng

Nethertown
Beckermet

Calder Bridge

Sellafield
Visitor
Centre

Cross

Wellington

Gosforth

Sar

6

B5343

Seascale

Hallsenna Moor

Drigg

Holmrook

Muncaster
Mill

7

Ravenglass

Roman
Bath
House

Muncaste

A595

128

Lan
Wabe

8

A B C D E F

Hycemoor

Selker Bay

Boo

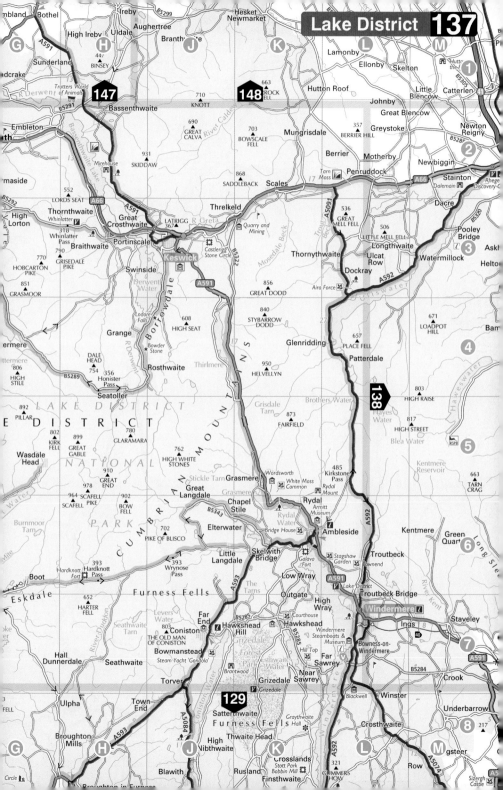

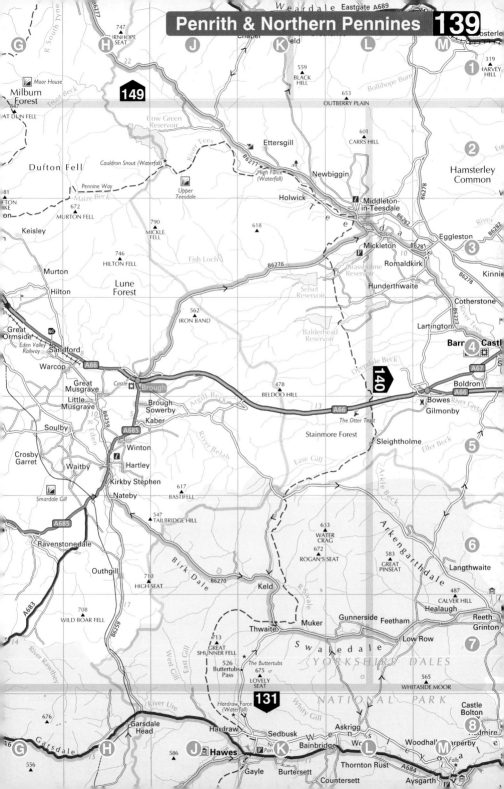

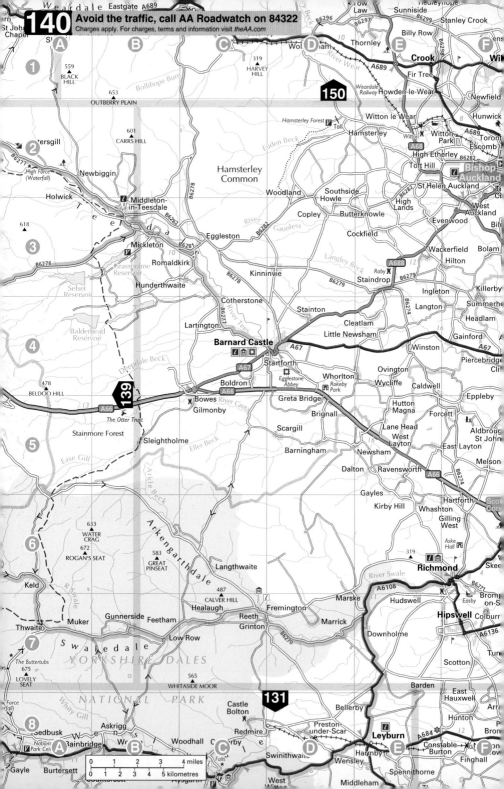

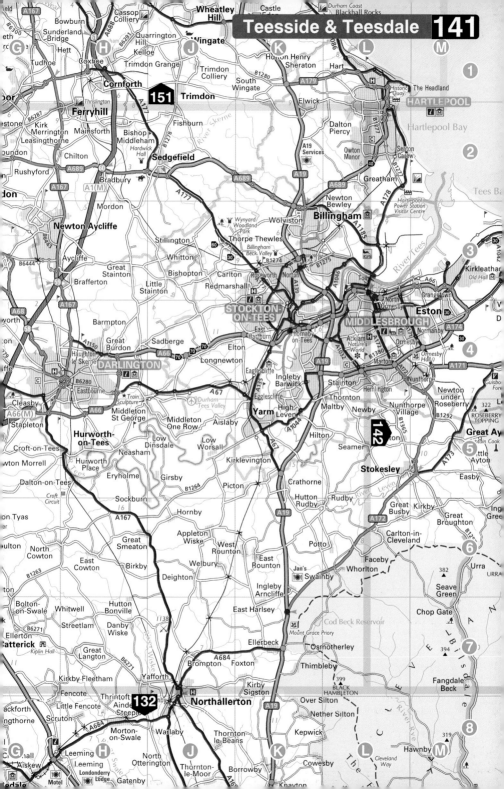

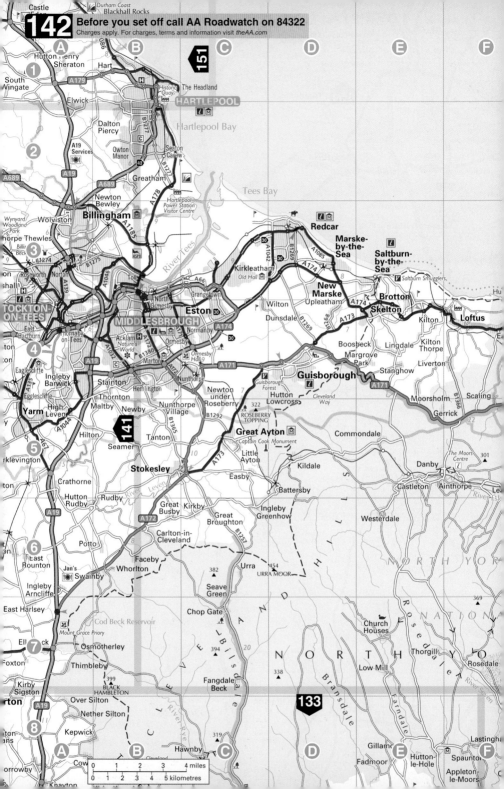

G H J K L M

1 2 3 4 5 6 7 8

aithes
Heritage Centre

Runswick Bay
North Yorkshire and
Cleveland Heritage Coast

Runswick
Ellerby
Goldsborough
Overdale
Wyke
kleby
A174
Lythe
Sandsend
Sandsend
Wyke
West Barnby
East Barnby
Whitby 🅸 🖼
Dunsley
Newholm
Abbey
Saltwick
Bay
Ugthorpe
A171
Ruswarp
Stainsacre
Aislaby
Briggswath
Sneaton
High Hawsker
Sleights
Uggglebarnby
B1447
Egton
Iburndale
Ness Point or
North Cheek
Grosmont
A169
Robin Hood's Bay
dge
B1416
Fylingthorpe
Robin
Hood's Bay
Old Peak or
South Cheek
Goathland
A171
Ravenscar
North Yorkshire
Moors Railway
292
Staintondale
Shire Horse Centre
Wheeldale Roman Road
Eller Beck
Hayburn
Wyke
M O O R S
20
Harwood
Dale
Newtondale
Forest Drive
Cloughton
Wyke
Stape
Hole of
Horcum
Cloughton
134
Cromer Point
Burniston
A165
Bridestones
(Rock Formation)
Bickley
Broxa
Silpho
Cleveland Way
Levisham
Dalby
Forest
Drive
Langdale
End
Hackness
Suffield
239
lock
Scalby
carborough
Falsgrave
Hatherleigh
Deep Sea
Trawler
North Riding Forest Park

G H J K L M

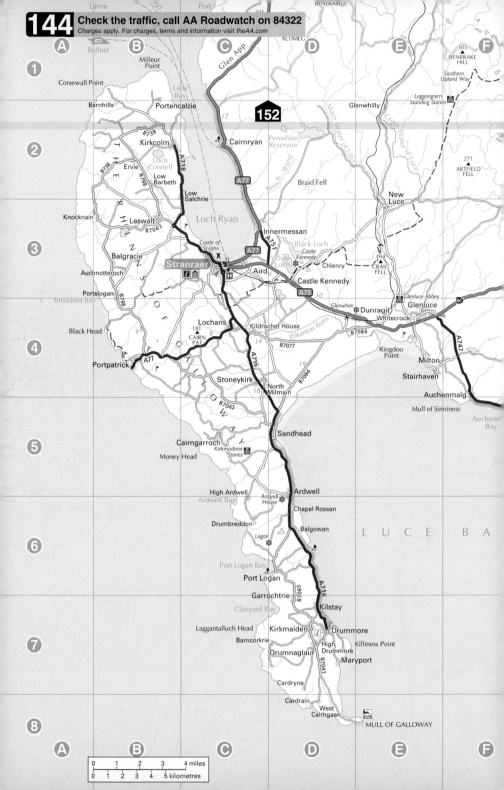

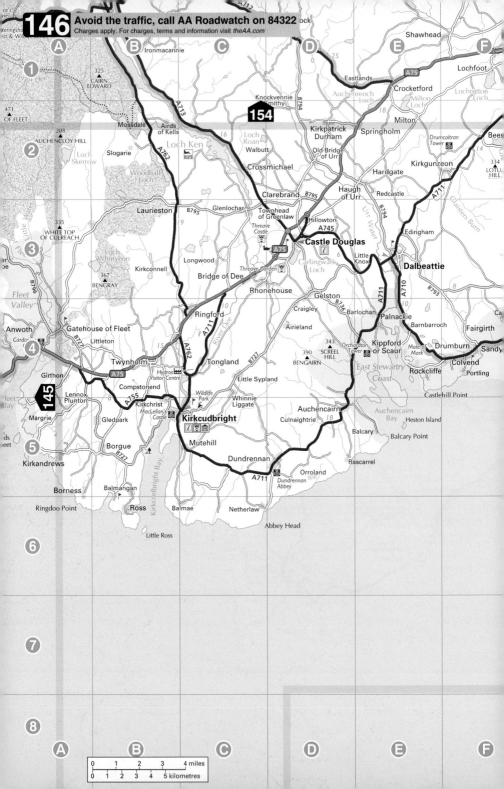

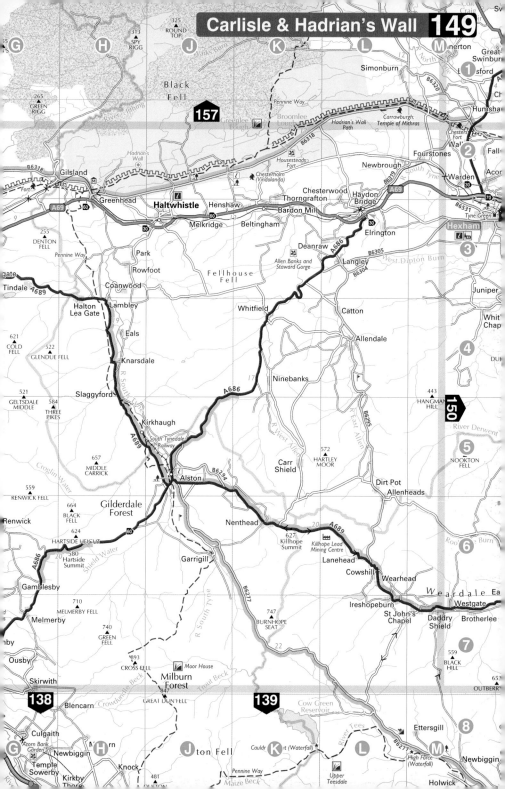

G H 325 J K L M
ROUND
TOP

313
SPY
RIGG

Works Burn

Pennine Way

Simonburn

Great
Swinbur
sford

B6320

 Merton

Black
Fell

157

Greenlee
Lough

Broomlee
Lough

Hadrian's Wall
Path

B6318

Carrawburgh:
Temple of Mithras

Humsha

Chesters
Fort

265
GREEN
RIGG

Hadrian's
Wall

Housesteads
Fort

Fourstones

Wal

Fall

Gilsland

Chesterholm
(Vindolanda)

Newbrough

Warden

Acor

B6318

Fort

A69

Greenhead

Haltwhistle

Henshaw

Melkridge

Beltingham

Chesterwood
Thorngrafton

Bardon Mill

Haydon
Bridge

A69

7

Tyne Green

B6531

30

70

255
DENTON
FELL

Park

Rowfoot

Deanraw

Elrington

Hexham

Pennine Way

Langley

B6305

West Dipton Burn

3

gate

Tindale

A689

Halton
Lea Gate

Lambley

Coanwood

Eals

Fellhouse
Fell

Allen Banks and
Staward Gorge

Whitfield

Catton

B6304

Juniper

Whit
Chap

621
COLD
FELL

522
GLENDUE FELL

Knarsdale

Allendale

4

DU

521
GELTSDALE
MIDDLE

584
THREE
PIKES

Slaggyford

A686

Ninebanks

443
HANGMAN
HILL

150

River Derwent

Kirkhaugh

South Tynedale
Railway

Carr
Shield

572
HARTLEY
MOOR

5
NOOKTON
FELL

559
RENWICK FELL

657
MIDDLE
CARRICK

Alston

B6294

Dirt Pot
Allenheads

B

Renwick

**Gilderdale
Forest**

664
BLACK
FELL

60

Nenthead

6

Burn

Gamblesby

624
HARTSIDE HEIGHT

580
Hartside
Summit

Garrigill

627
Killhope
Summit

A689

Killhope Lead
Mining Centre

Lanehead

Cowshill

Wearhead

Weardale

Ea

710
MELMERBY FELL

Ireshopeburn

Westgate

Melmerby

740
GREEN
FELL

B6277

747
BURNHOPE
SEAT

St John's
Chapel

Daddry
Shield

Brotherlee

7

559
BLACK
HILL

Ousby

Skirwith

893
CROSS FELL

Moor House

**Milburn
Forest**

22

653
OUTBERR

by

138

Blencarn

GREAT DUN FELL

842

139

Cow Green
Reservoir

Ettersgill

8

Culgaith

Acorn Bank
Garden

rn

Newbiggin

J ton Fell

Cauldr t (Waterfall)

L

B6277

High Force
(Waterfall)

Newbiggin

Temple
Sowerby

Knock

Pennine Way

Upper
Teesdale

Holwick

Kirkby
Thore

481

Maize Beck

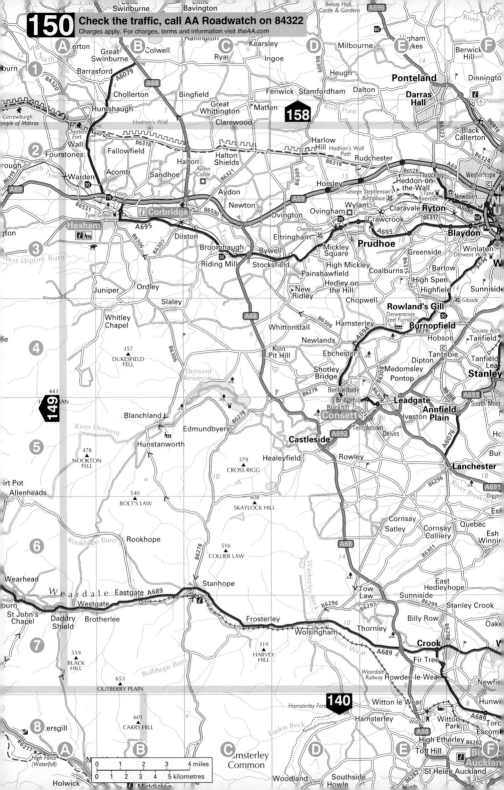

162

144

Culzean
Culzean & Country Park
Maidenhead Bay
Maidens
A719
Kir Sou Cott
Turnberry
Turnberry
Turnberry Bay
B60
A77
Dipple
Kilgran
B741
Water of
Old Daily
B60
Girvan
Dounepark
Penkill
B73
Woodland
C
60
Pinminnoch
8
60
297
GREY HILL
Pinmore
Balligmorrie
340 Ailsa Craig
RSPB
13
Lendalfoot
A714
A77
Bennane Head
Colmonell
9
B734
Pinwherry
B734
River Stinchar
Muck Water
B7044
Heronsford
Dusk River
Ballantrae
Water of Tig
Barrhi

Larne
(Summer only)
Larne
Currarie Port
437
BENERAIRD
Belfast
321
CARLOCK HILL
Belfast
387
ALTIMEG HILL
305
BENBRAKE HILL
Milleur Point
Glen App
Southern Upland Way
Corsewall Point
Lady Bay
Glenwhilly
Laggangairn Standing Stones
Barnhills
Portencalzie
17
Kirkcolm
Main Water of Luce
Cross Water of Luce
B738
271
ARTFIELD FELL
B738
Ervie
Loch Connell
Cairnryan
Braid Fell
Low Barbeth
B796
A718
New
Beoch Burn
Low Salchrie
h Ryan
Innermessan
Knockna
Castle of

0   1   2   3   4 miles
0 1 2 3 4 5 kilometres

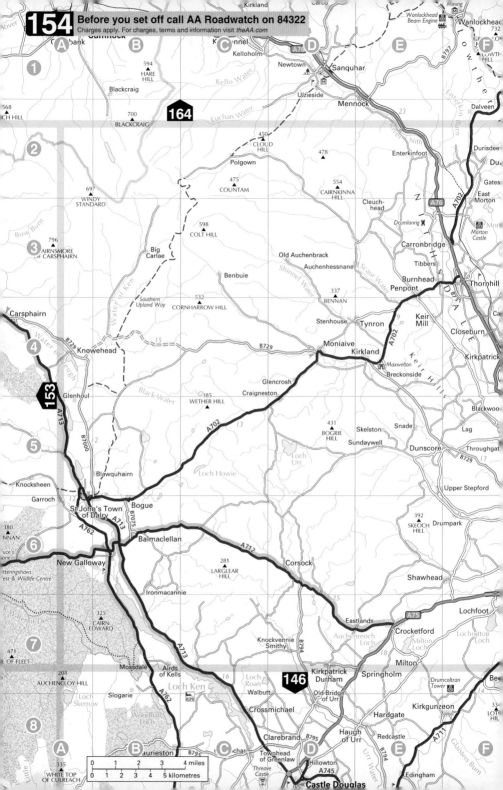

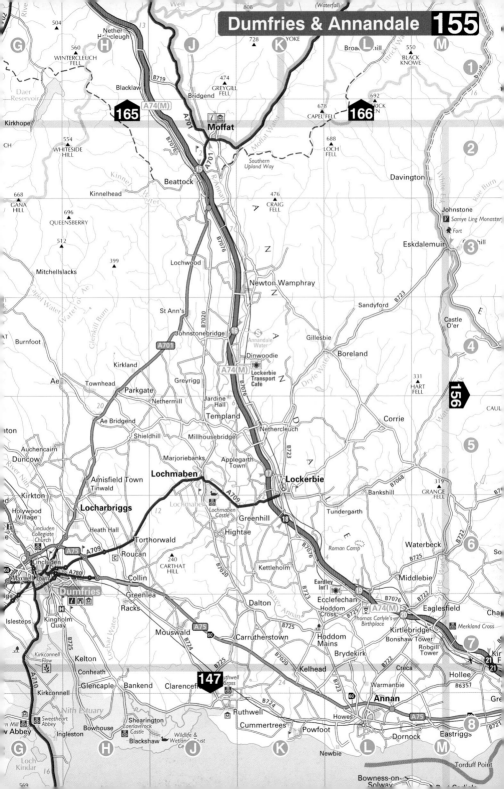

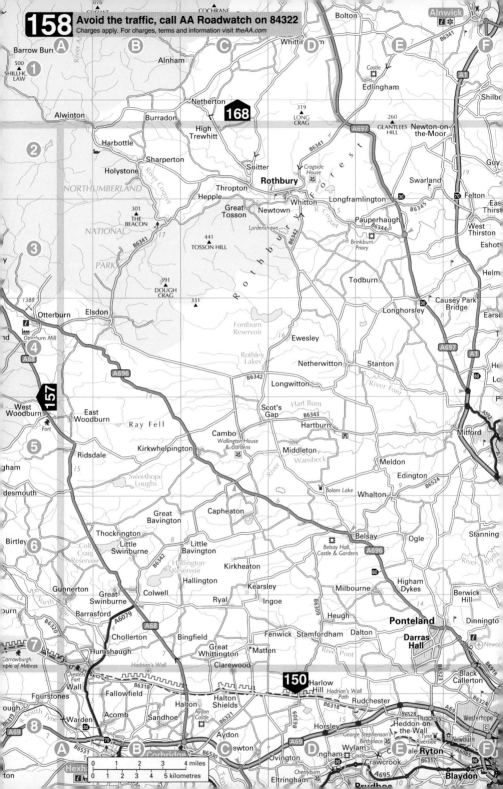

Check the traffic, call AA Roadwatch on 84322

Charges apply. For charges, terms and information visit *theAA.com*

Se

Portencross
Farland Head

B7

1

Pirnmill

Penrioch

hitefarland

715
BEINN
BHARRAIN

2 machar

Balliekine

North Arran

834
CAISTEAL ABHAIL

Loch
Tanna

Glen Iorsa

Glen Catacol

A841

adal

Sannox

Corrie

874
GOATFELL

792
BEINN
NUIS

Glen Rosa

Merkland Point

Brodick Castle, Garden
& Country Club

Brodick
Bay

FIRTH

OF

CLYD

V

Iorsa Water

 A R R A N

Auchagallon
Stone Circle

3 Machrie
Bay

Machrie

Tormore

Machrie Moor
Stone Circles

Moss Farm Road
Stone Circle

512
A'CHRUACH

Balmichael

503
BEINN BHREAC

Brodick

Strathwhillan

Corriegills

Clauchlands Point

Lamlash

Margnaheglish

Lamlash
Bay

Holy Island

Balmichael

Balmichael

Cordon

Torbeg

Shiskine

4 Drumadoon
Bay

Blackwaterfoot

Kilpatrick

Kilpatrick Dun

Brown Head

Glen Scorrodale

Carn Ban

Auchencairn

Whiting Bay

Glen Ashdale

Kingscross
Knockenkelly

Whiting
Bay

Largymore

Corriecravie

Torr a' Chaisteal Fort

Sliddery

Kilmory Water

161

5

Lagg

Kilmory

Torrylin
Cairn

Bennan

Largybeg

Dippen Dippen Head

Kildonan

Bennan Head

Pladda

6

7

152 Tu
Turnb
Ba

8

0 1 2 3 4 miles
0 1 2 3 4 5 kilometres

Ailsa Craig

RSPB

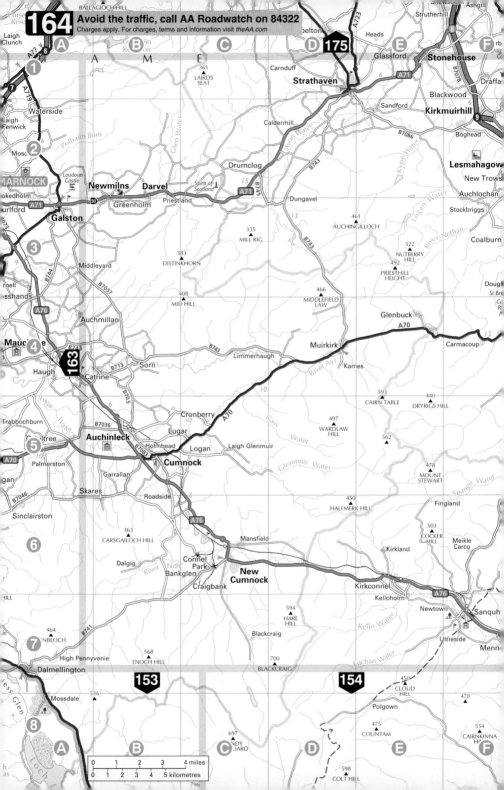

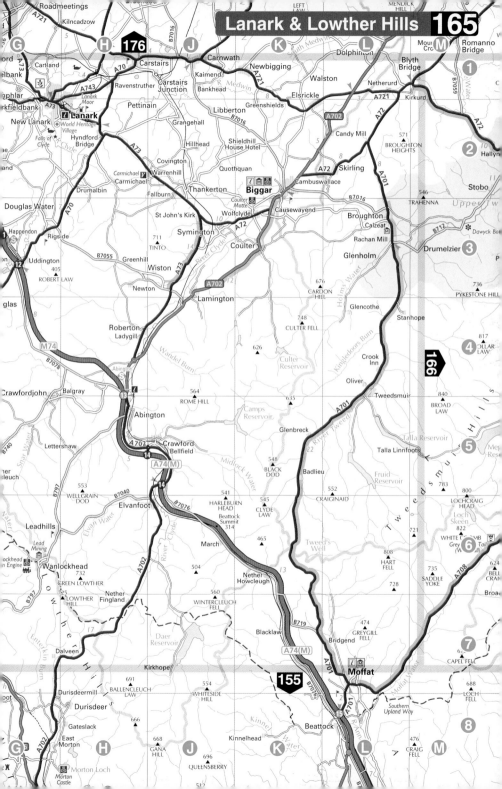

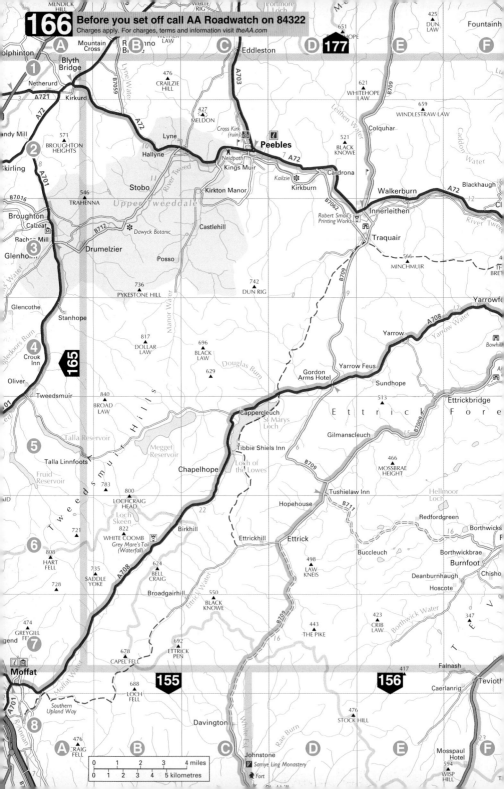

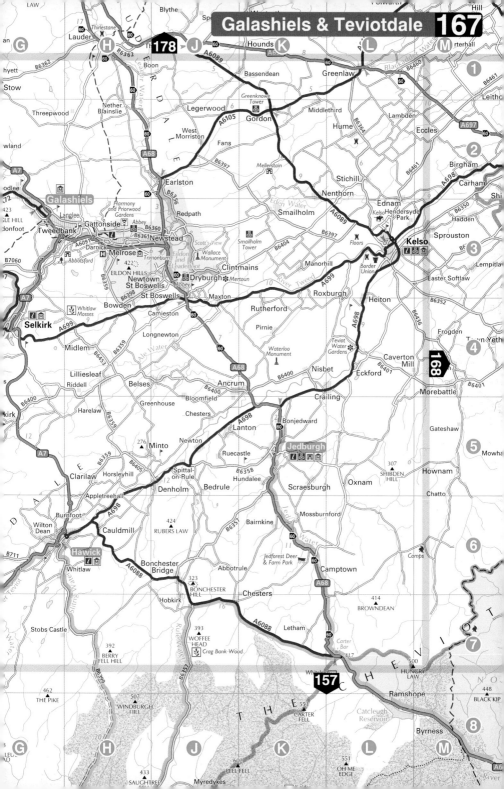

G H J K L M

① ② ③ ④ ⑤ ⑥ ⑦ ⑧

CAUSEWAY
FLOODED
AT HIGH TIDE

HOLY ISLAND

Holy
Island
Lindisfarne
Priory
Lindisfarne
Castle
Castle Point
Guile Point

Longstone
Lighthouse
FARNE
ISLANDS

Staple
Sound
Inner
Sound
North Northumberland
Heritage Coast

Budle
Bay
Bamburgh
B1342
Bamburgh
B1340

Belford
B6349

Seahouses
North Sunderland

B1341
Lucker
Beadnell

B6348
Warenford
Swinhoe
Beadnell
Bay

A1
Newstead
Chathill
Tughall
B1340
Newton-by-the-Sea
Embleton &
Newton Links

Ellingham
Preston
Brunton
Christon
Bank
Embleton
Embleton
Bay

267
CATERAN
HILL
Preston
Pele Tower

North
Charlton
Falloden
B1339
Dunstanburgh Castle

wick
Ditchburn
South
Charlton
B6347
Dunstan
Craster

346
Eglingham
Rock
Rennington
Stamford

eanley
B6341
B1340
Howick
Hall
Howick
Cullernose Point

Bolton
B6346
River Aln
Denwick
Longhoughton
Boulmer

Alnwick
Seaton Point

Lesbury

Castle
Edlingham
A1
Alnmouth

Shilbottle
A1068
Alnmouth
Bay

A697
GLANTLEES
HILL
Newton-on-
the-Moor
Warkworth Castle
& Hermitage
Warkworth

159

Amble
Coquet Island

Gloster Hill
Guyzance
Togston
High
Hauxley
Radcliffe

Swarland
Acklington
Broomhill

G ramlington
30
H
70
Felton
J
East
Thirston
K
South
Broomhill
L M

Pauperhaugh
B63
West
Thirston
60
Red Row
Druridge Bay

Brinkburn
B6344

Avoid the traffic, call AA Roadwatch on 84322

Charges apply. For charges, terms and information visit *theAA.com*

ISLA

Dub

Nave Island
Ardnave
Point
G

Ton Mhòr

Eilean Mòr

Kilnave

Sanaigmore

Rudha Lamanais

Loch
Gorr

Lecht Gruinart

RSPB

B8017

B8018

Saligo Bay

Loch
Gorm

Gruinart

Gleann Mòr

Coul Point

Sunderland

B8018

Machir
Bay

Kilchoman

A847

Loch
Indaal

Kilchiaran Bay

Bruichladdich

Bowmore

RHINNS OF ISLAY

231
BEINN TART A'MHILL

15
M

Port
Charlotte

i

Lossit Bay

Nereabolls

Duich R.

Riv

Rudha na
Faing

A847

Portnahaven

Port Wemyss

Laggan

Orsay

RHINNS
POINT

Bay

Rudha Mòr

Ki

165
MAOL BU

F

T H E

Lower
Killeyan

0   1   2   3   4 miles
0 1 2 3 4 5 kilometres

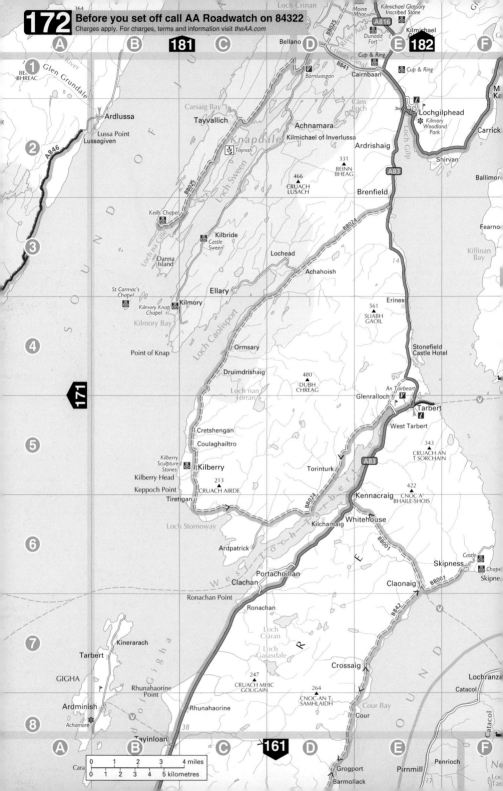

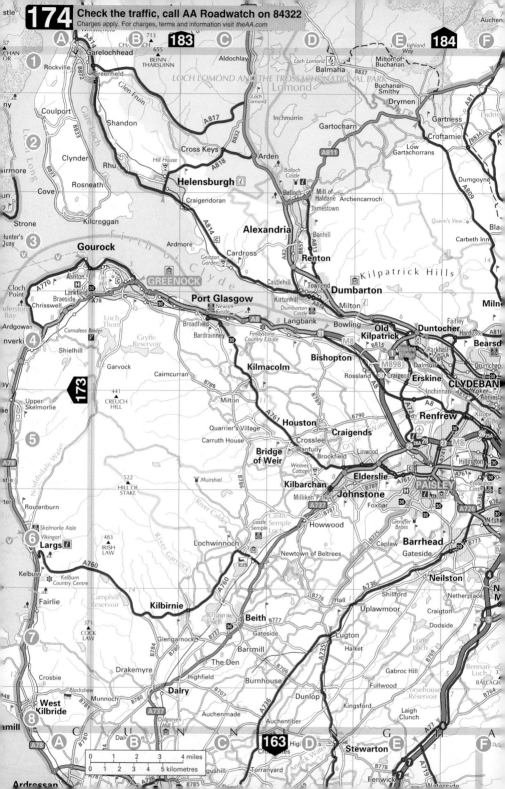

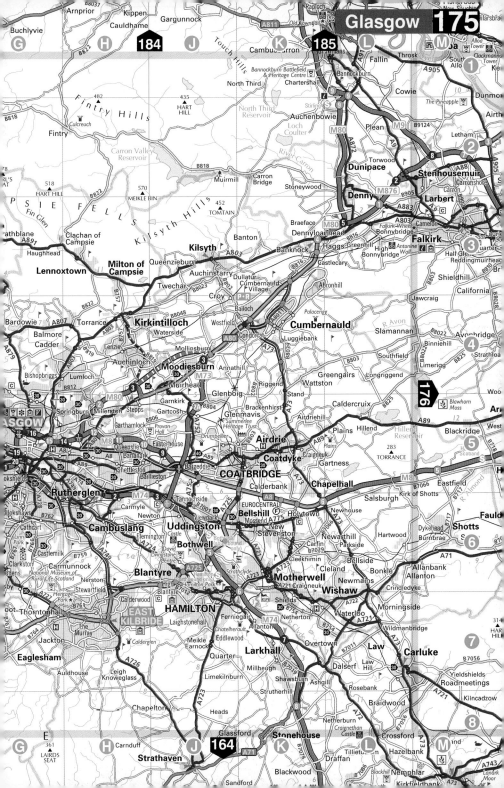

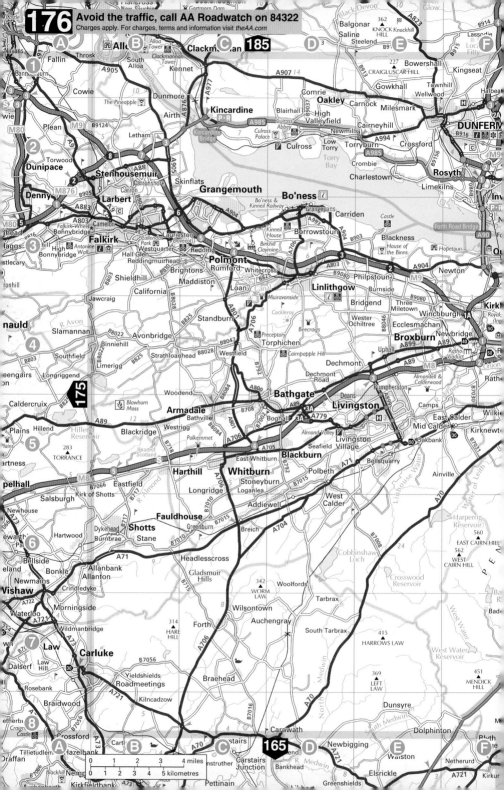

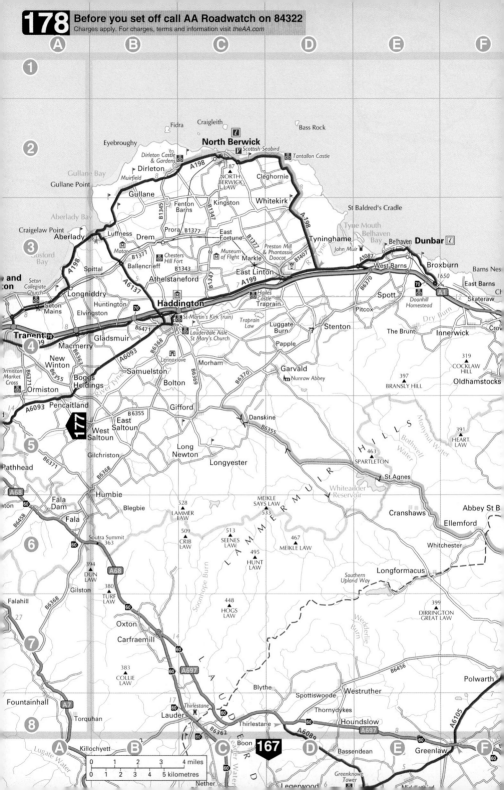

Map grid references (top): G   H   J   K   L   M
Row numbers (right): 1 2 3 4 5 6 7 8

ed Point
Cove
Pease Bay
Siccar Point
Fast Castle Head
ath
A1107
ST ABB'S HEAD
196 BROWN RIG
Coldingham Loch
St Abbs
Coldingham Bay
othern nd Way
terdean
Grantshouse
Coldingham
A1107
22
Houndwood
B6438
Eyemouth
od
262 HORSELEY HILL
Heugh Head
Cairncross
A1
B6355
14
Reston
Ayton
Burnmouth
A6112
Auchencrow
Marygold
Lintlaw
Lamberton
Marshall Meadows Bay
Preston
Cumledge
B6355
Chirnside
B6437
Foulden
North Northumberland Heritage Coast
Edrom Church
Edrom
Manderston
15
Chirnsidebridge
Foulden Tithe Barn
1333
Whiteadder Water
A6105
Berwick-upon-Tweed
Broadhaugh
Edington
Hutton
Castle
Allanton
Barracks
Blackadder
Paxton
Town Ramparts
ns
A6105
B6460
Hilton
B6461
Paxton
Tweedmouth
Whitsome
Spittal
isbet Hill
Sinclair's Hill
13
Horndean
Horncliffe
Huds Head
Blackadder
B6437
Murton
Scremerston
Ladykirk
Castle
Thornton
A1
Swinton
B6470
Norham
A698
Cheswick
Upsettlington
River Tweed
Simprim
Ancroft
Leitholm
A6112
B6461
Haggerston

Map grid references (bottom): G   H   J   K   L   M

CAUSEWAY FLOODED AT HIGH TIDE

A B C eag D **189** E F

1

Little Colonsay

 Staffa

Fingal's Cave

*Loch na Keal,
Isle of Mull*

Inch Kenneth
Inchkenneth Chapel
(ruin)

2

491
CREACH BHEINN

★ *Fossil Tree*

Burg

3

Rudha nan Cearc

Iona Abbey
& Nunnery

IONA

Baile Mòr

MacLean's Cross

Kintra

Fionnphort

Aridhglas

St Columba
Exhibition
Centre

Bunessan

Loch na
Lathaich

Loch

A849

Loch Assapol

Sound of Iona

ROSS OF MULL

Soa Island

Erraid

Uisken

Ardchiavaig

4

Rudha
Ardalanish

Torran Rocks

5

6

Eilean
Dubh

Balnahard Ru

Kiloran Bay

COLONSAY

Kiloran

7

Kilchattan

B8086

Scalasaig

B8085

Machrins

Garvard

8

A B C D **171** E F

Oronsay

Rudha
Bàn

Dubh Eilean

0 1 2 3 4 miles
0 1 2 3 4 5 kilometres

G H J K L M

190

1

ISLE OF MULL

Eorsa

Macquarie Mausoleum

BEINN NAN LUS

BEINN A' CHRAIG

BEINN MHEADHO

766 DUN DA GHAOITHE

Craignure

Mull & West Highland Narrow Gauge Railway

Torosay Castle

Duart Bay   Duart Point

Duart

Lochdonhead

Lochdon

Kilchera

2

966 BEN MORE

704 CRUACHAN DEARG

A849

Strathcoil

Loch Don

Gorten

Grass Point

KERRERA

Aird of Kinloch

Glen More

Loch Fuaran

717 BEN BUIE

698 BEN CREACH

247 CARN BAN

Pennycross   Pennyghael

A849

Loch Spelve

Croggan

Rudha Seanach

Ar

3

Leidle Water

503 BEINN NA CROISE

Lochbuie

Loch Uisg

337 MAOL BAN

376 BEINN CHREAGACH

Carsaig

Rudha Dubh

Loch Buie

377 DRUIM FADA

FIRTH

Insh Island

Clachan

Clachan-Seil

B844

Barrnacarry Bay

Malcolm's Point

Ellanbeich   Easdale

SEIL   Balvicar

4

Easdale

Cuan Ferry Village

B8003

OF

Colonsay, Oban

Garbh Eileach

Eilean Dubh Mòr

GARVELLACHS
Monastery & Beehive Cells

Eileach an Naoimh

LUNGA

Cullipool   Torsay House   Island   Island

LORNE

Seil Sound

LUING

Toberonochy

Degnish

182

Loch Melfor

Arduaine Garden   Arduaine

5

Scarba, Lunga and the Garvellachs

SCARBA

448 CRUACH SCARBA

Sound of Luing

SHUNA

Shuna Point

Shuna Sound

Craobh Haven

A

Craigdhu

Ardfe   Kint

6

Gulf of Corryvreckan

B8002

En Mhic

En Rig

Aird

Glengarrisdale Bay

295 CRUACH NA SEILCHEIG

Craignish Point

Island Macaskin

Clockavulli

Wood

rcles

7

Ri Cruin Ca

Poltalloc

Glendebadel Bay

364 BEN GARRISDALE

Lussa River

Leall Burn

JURA

Corpach Bay

466 BEINN BHREAC

Glen Grundale

Loch Crinan

Crinan

Kilmahumaig

Bellanoch

8

Barnluasgan

B8025

G H J K L M

Carsaig Bay

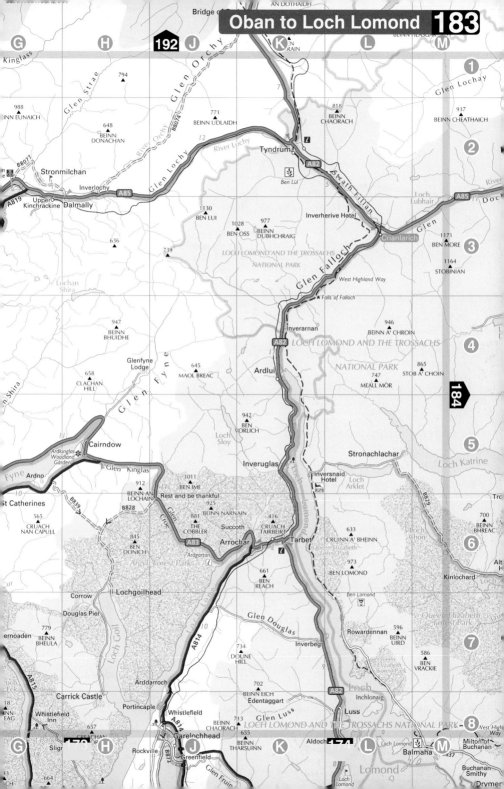

Grid references (top): G H 192 J K L M

Grid references (right): 1 2 3 4 184 5 6 7 8

Grid references (bottom): G H K L M

Kinglass

AN DOTHAIDH

Glen Lochay

988 INN EUNAICH

794

771 BEINN UDLAIDH

818 BEINN CHAORACH

937 BEINN CHEATHAICH

648 BEINN DONACHAN

Glen Strae

Glen Orchy

River Orchy

B8074

Glen Lochy

River Lochy

12

Tyndrum

A82

Strath Fillan

7

Loch Dochart

Stronmilchan

Inverlochy

A85

Ben Lùi

5

Loch Lubhair

A85

River Dochart

B8077

B8077

Upper Kinchrackine

Dalmally

A819

1130 BEN LUI

1028 BEN OSS

977 BEINN DUBHCHRAIG

Inverherive Hotel

Glen

Crianlarich

1171 BEN MORE

636

739

LOCH LOMOND AND THE TROSSACHS

NATIONAL PARK

Glen Falloch

West Highland Way

★ Falls of Falloch

1164 STOBINIAN

Lochan Shira

947 BEINN BHUIDHE

645 MAOL BREAC

Inverarnan

946 BEINN A' CHROIN

Glen Fyne

Glenfyne Lodge

658 CLACHAN HILL

A82

LOCH LOMOND AND THE TROSSACHS

NATIONAL PARK

865 STOB A' CHOIN

Ardlui

747 MEALL MÒR

n Shira

Glen Fyne

Ardkinglas Woodland Garden

Cairndow

942 BEN VORLICH

Stronachlachar

Loch Katrine

Fyne

Ardno

Glen Kinglas

10

Loch Sloy

Inveruglas

Inversnaid Hotel RSPB

Loch Arklet

B829

St Catherines

B839

912 BEINN AN LOCHAIN

1011 BEN IME

Rest and be thankful

B828

Glen Croe

925 BEINN NARNAIN

881 THE COBBLER

565 CRUACH NAN CAPULL

845 BEN DONICH

A83

Succoth

416 CRUACH TAIRBEIRT

Tarbet

633 CRUINN A' BHEINN

700 BEINN BHREAC

Argyll Forest Park

Ardgartan

Arrochar

Queen Elizabeth Forest Park

973 BEN LOMOND

Kinlochard

Loch Chon

661 BEN REACH

Ben Lomond

Queen Elizabeth Forest Park

Corrow

Lochgoilhead

Glen Douglas

Rowardennan

596 BEINN UIRD

Douglas Pier

Loch Goil

734 DOUNE HILL

Inverbeg

586 BEN VRACKIE

779 BEINN BHEULA

A814

Arddarroch

702 BEINN EICH

Edentaggart

Queen Elizabeth Forest Park

Glen Luss

Loch

A815

Carrick Castle

Portincaple

Whistlefield

A814

713 BEINN CHAORACH

655 BEINN THARSUINN

Inchlonaig

Luss

Lomond

Whistlefield Inn

INN EAG

657

Rockville

B872

Garelochhead

Greenfield

Aldoch

Loch Lomond

Balmaha

Milton of Buchanan

664

Sligr

Glen Fruin

Loch

Lomond

LOCH LOMOND AND THE TROSSACHS NATIONAL PARK

West High Way

B837

Buchanan Smithy

Drymen

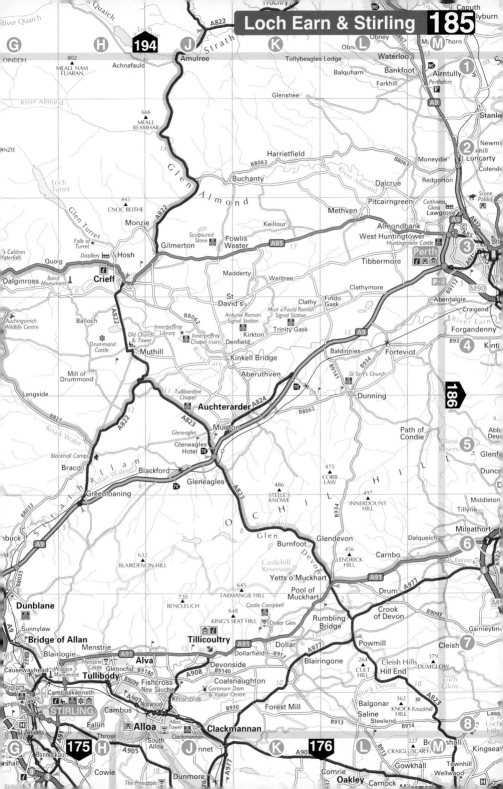

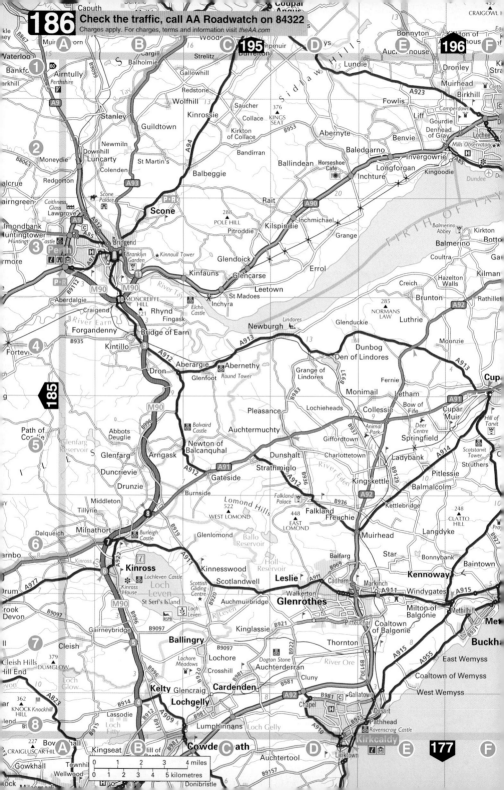

A B C D E F

1
2
3
4
5
6
7
8

Grishipol
Clabhach
Hogh Bay   Ballyhaug
Totronald
Acha
Feall Bay   Arileod
RSPB   Uig   Fri
Calgary Point   Crossapol Bay   Rudha Fàsachd
Gunna   Loch Breachacha

Rudha Port Bhiosd   Clachan Mor   Caoles   Rudha Dubh   V
Balephetrish Bay   B8069
Loch Bhasapoll   B8068   Ruaig
Haugh Bay   Ballevullin   Cornoigmore   Kenovay   Gott Bay
Kilkenneth   B8068   Tiree   Scarinish
Moss   Heylipoll   B8065
Middleton   Crossapoll   TIREE
Barrapoll   B8065
Loch a Phuill   B8067   Balemartine
Mannel
Rinn Thorbhais   Hynish
Balephuil Bay

0 1 2 3 4 miles
0 1 2 3 4 5 kilometres

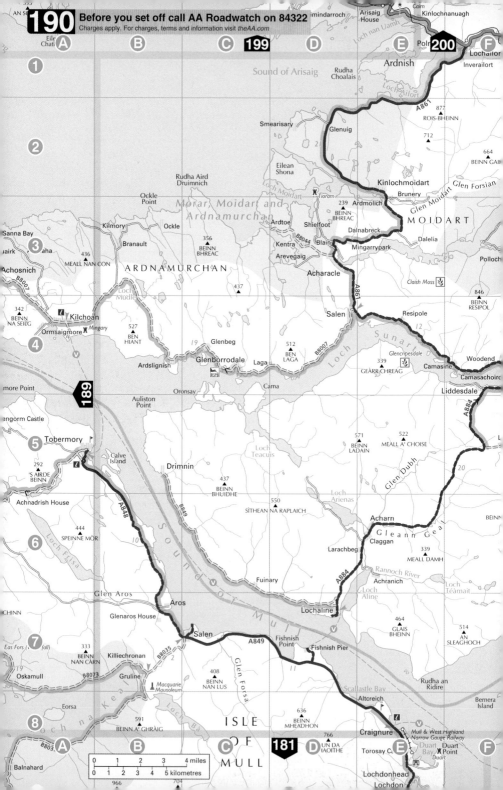

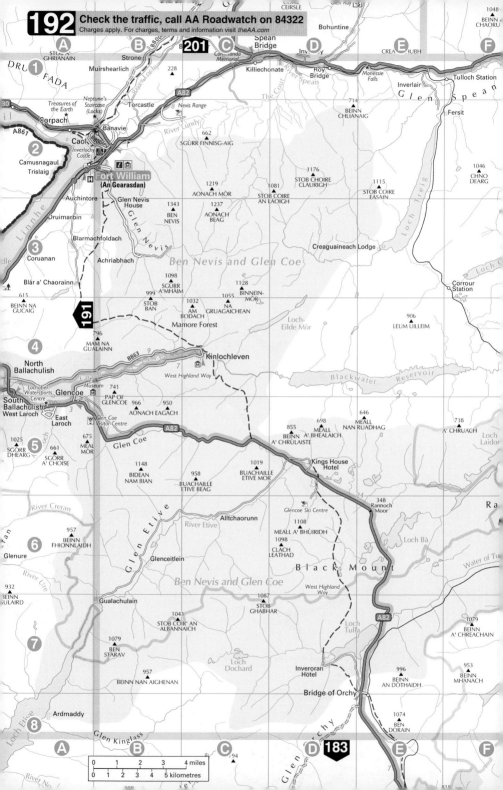

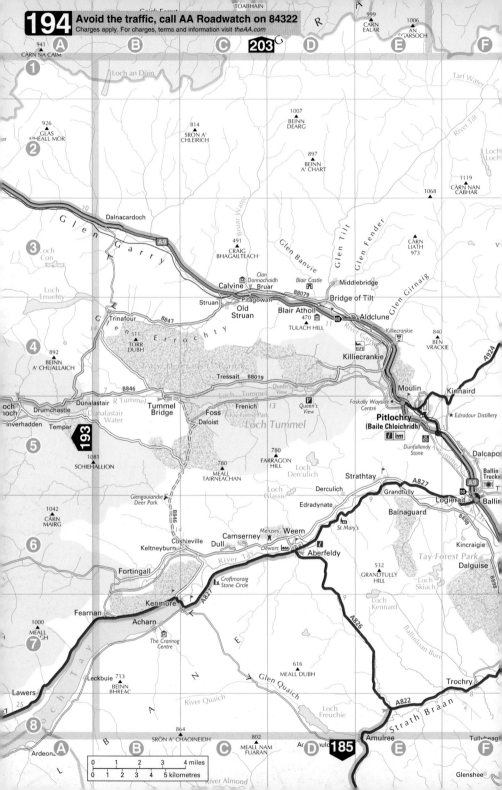

194
Avoid the traffic, call AA Roadwatch on 84322
Charges apply. For charges, terms and information visit *theAA.com*

TOABHAIN

203

999
CARN
EALAR

1006
AN
SGARSOCH

A
941
CARN NA CAIM

1

Loch an Duin

Tarf Water

River Tilt

2
926
GLAS
MHEALL MOR

814
SRON A'
CHLEIRICH

1007
BEINN
DEARG

897
BEINN
A' CHART

1119
CARN NAN
CABHAR
1068

Glen Garry

Dalnacardoch

A9

Bruar Water

Glen Banvie

Glen Tilt

Glen Fender

CARN
LIATH
973

Glen Girnaig

3
Loch
Con

Loch
Errochty

491
CRAIG
BHAGAILTEACH

Calvine

Clan
Donnachaidh
Bruar

Blair Castle

Middlebridge

Bridge of Tilt

840
BEN
VRACKIE

A924

Struan

Pitagowan

B8079

Blair Atholh

Aldclune

Killiecrankie

Trinafour

B847

Old
Struan

470
TULACH HILL

B0

Killiecrankie

4
892
BEINN
A' CHUALLAICH

511
TORR
DUBH

Glen Errochty

Tay Forest P

Tressait

B8019

River Garry

Moulin

Kinnaird

Loch Tummel

Queen's
View

Faskally Wayside
Centre

Edradour Distillery

5
Inverhadden

Drumchastle

Dunalastair

Tempar

193

1081
SCHIEHALLION

Dunalastair
Water

Tummel
Bridge

R Tummel

Foss

Daloist

Frenich

Queen's
View

Loch Tummel

Pitlochry
(Baile Chloichridh)

Dunfallandy
Stone

Dalcapo

Ballin
Trucks

6
1042
CARN
MAIRG

780
MEALL
TAIRNEACHAN

Glengoulandie
Deer Park

B846

780
FARRAGON
HILL

Loch
Derculich

Strathtay

Derculich

Grandtully

A827

Logierait

Balli

Loch
Glassie

Edradynate

Balnaguard

B898

Coshieville

Camserney

Menzies

Weem

St Mary's

532
GRANDTULLY
HILL

Kincraigie

Tay Forest Park

Dalguise

Keltneyburn

Dull

Dewars

Aberfeldy

River Tay

Croftmoraig
Stone Circle

Loch
Kennard

B598

Fortingall

7
1000
MEALL
GH

Fearnan

Kenmore

Acharn

The Crannog
Centre

616
MEALL DUBH

A826

Ballinloan Burn

Trochry

8
Leckbuie

713
BEINN
BHREAC

Loch Tay

Glen Quaich

Loch
Freuchie

A822

Strath Braan

Lawers

River Quaich

Amulree

Tullybeag

Ardeona

864
SRON A' CHAOINEIDH

802
MEALL NAM
FUARAN

185

Glenshee

River Almond

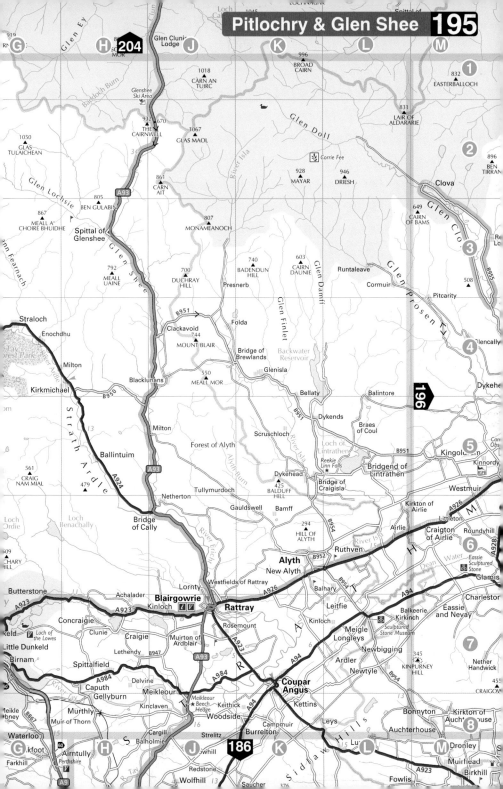

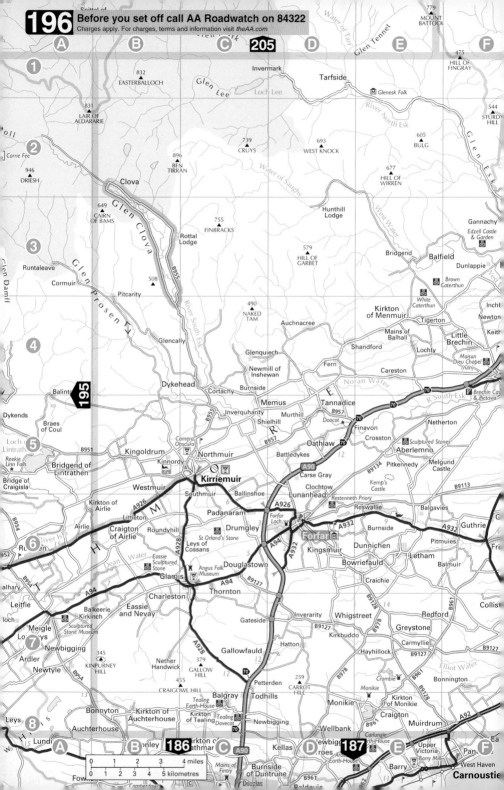

G · H · J · K · L · M

① ② ③ ④ ⑤ ⑥ ⑦ ⑧

206

LEACHIE HILL
Tannachie
Goosecruives
Drumlithie
Temple of Fiddes
v Mill
Glenbervie
Mondynes
465 GOYLE HILL
Bervie Water
Crawton
Fowlsheugh
Trelong Bay
454 Cairn o' Mount
414 FINELLA HILL
Auchenblae
Kinneff
Catterline
Todhead Point
B966
Fordoun
B967
Arbuthnott
A92
Pittarrow
Redmyre
Inverbervie
Bervie Bay
B9120
Mains of Haulkerton
Laurencekirk
Gourdon
B974
Sauchieburn
Redford
Benholm
B9120
·muir
·ermuir
Dykelands
A90
North Esk
Hospital
Logie Pert
Marykirk
Craigo
Logie
Lochside
Morphie
Bush
St Cyrus
Johnshaven
13
Milton Ness
A937
A935
Dun
House of Dun
Hillside
Montrose Air Station
Montrose
Montrose Basin
Scurdie Ness
Barnhead
Maryton
Ferryden
Craig
Usan
A934
Westerton
Boddin Point
Braehead
Lunan
Lunan Bay
Inverkeilor
Red Head
·pelton
·Cauldcots
13
A92
Marywell
Auchmithie
Carlingheugh Bay
The Deil's Head
Arbroath

198
Check the traffic, call AA Roadwatch on 84322
Charges apply. For charges, terms and information visit *theAA.com*

A B C D **208** E F

1

Bay Talisker

Glen Eynort

Gr

147
BEINN
BHREAC

Loch Eynort

2

434
AN CRÙACHIN
Glenbrittle House
Bualintur

Loch Brittle

Rudh' an Dùnain

3

Cu

4

CANNA

210
CARN A' GHAILL

Garrisdale Point

A'Chill

Canna
Harbour

Rudha
Shamhnan Insir

Sanday

Sound of Canna

302
MULLACH
MÒR

5

A Bhrideanach

570
ORVAL

Ki

Oigh-sgeir

RÙM

6

810
ASKIVAL

763
SGÙRR NAN
GILLEAN

The Small Isles

Rudha nam
Meirleach

7

Sou

Rudh

8

Eilean
nan Each

0   1   2   3   4 miles
0 1 2 3 4   5 kilometres

211

G **H** **J** **K** **L** **M**

Corrimony

1

578
SUIDHE
CHUIRMAIN

TOLL CREAGACH

Glen Affric

Tom

1182
CARN
EIGE

Loch Beinn
a Mheadhoin

1036
SGÙRR NA
LAPAICH

Affric
Lodge

Glen Affric

Loch
ma Stac

678
MEALL A'
CHRÀTHAICH

2

149
RR NAN
REAMHNAN

Loch a'
Chràthaich

River Affric

Glen Affric

Loch
Affric

Loch na
Beinne Bàine

677
CÀRN MHIC
AN TOISICH

884
AONACH
SHASUINN

705
CARN A'
CHAOCHAIN

981
CISTE
DHUBH

1102
MULLACH
FRAOCH-CHOIRE

Dundreggan

A887

705
CH

3

1120
A'CHRALAIG

River Doe

Dalchreichart

16

536

Inchnacardoch
Hotel

1108
SGURR NAN
CONBHAIREAN

Tomchrasky

Glen Moriston

Caledonian
Canal

Cluanie
Inn

Ceannacroc
Lodge

Fort Augustus

Cluanie
Lodge

Loch Cluanie

671
CEANN A'MHAIN

Auchteraw

4

CHRITH

947
CREAG
A'MHAIM

787
MEALL DUBH

Glen Tarff

PIDEAN
IALACH

996

Loch Loyne

A87

Glen Loyne

13

Loch
Lundie

Bridge
of Oich

Caledonian Canal

Newtown

Aberchalder
Lodge

202

5

Glenquoich Forest

Glen Garry

Glen Garry

Loch Garry

Invergarry

Inchlaggan

Tomdoun

Greenfield

Mandally

816
CÀRN DEARG

River Garry

A82

Laggan

ie
ange

556
GLAS BHEINN

901
BEN TEE

Kilfinnan

6

656
MEALL BLÀIR

821
MEALL COIRE
NAN SAOBHAIDH

Glengarry
Forest

935
SRON A'CHOIRE
GHAIRBH

Corriegour
Lodge Hotel

803
BEINNIARUINN

Brae Roy
Lodge

nich

Arkaig

Gleann Cia-aig

Loch Lochy

Glen Gloy

Glen Roy

834
CÀRN
DEARG

7

Ardechive

Clunes

Letterfinlay
Lodge Hotel

5

Glen Mallie

Achnacarry

Bunarkaig

Inverloy

Glenfintaig Lodge

654
COIRE
CEIRSLE

Glen Roy

1048
BEINN A'
CHAORUNN

796
BEINN BHAN

B8005

Great Glen Way

Bohuntine

Gairlochy

Glen Loy

Stronenaba

659
CREAG DHUBH

8

738
STOB A'
GHRIANAIN

B8004

Bracletter

Spean
Bridge

Commando
Memorial

192

Inverroy

Roy
Bridge

Inverlair

Strone

Muirs

ch

228

Falls

ulloch Station

FADA

A82

Nevis Range

The Co

Spean

714

Glen Spean

Neptune's
Staircase

Torcastle

Treasures of

202
Before you set off call AA Roadwatch on 84322
Charges apply. For charges, terms and information visit *theAA.com*

Tomich A B SUIDHE GHUIRMAIN C 212 D Lenie E Torness F

Aberarder

Loch ma Stac
Loch a' Chràthaich

678
MEALL A' CHRATHAICH

Loch nan Breac Deorga

696

Inverfarigaig
Aultnagoire

Farigaig

Errogie
Farraline

Dunmaglass Lodge

677
CÀRN MHIC AN TOISICH

Foyers

Gorthleck

Glebe

Loch Mhor

686
BEINN DUBHCHARAIOH

Achnaconeran

River Moriston

Invermoriston

Great Glen Way

Loch Knockie

Whitebridge

810
CÀRN NA SAOBHAIDHE

Dundreggan A88

16

605
BURACH

A82

Loch Killin

810
CÀRN NA LARAICHE MAOILE

hreichart

Glen Moriston

536

Inchnacardoch Hotel

Caledonian Canal

Fort Augustus

Glendoe Lodge

B862

Glen Doe

M o n a d h

MHAIN

Auchteraw

Glen Tarff

778
CÀRN EASGANN BÀNA

855
SGARAMAN NAM FIADH

4

Caledonian Canal

Newtown

816
CÀRN A' CHUILINN

201

Aberchalder Lodge

861
MEALL NA-H-AISRE

925
GEAL CHARN

CÀ LETH

Loch Lundie

Invergarry

891
CORRIEYAIRACK HILL

Glen Markie

Mandally

A82

881
CÀRN LEAC

Laggan

816
CÀRN DEARG

River Spey

Blargie Lagga

Crathie

gour Hotel

Loch Spey

Loch Crunachdan

Glenshero Lodge

563
BLACK CRAIG

A86

Catl

Strathmashie House

6

Brae Roy Lodge

803
BEINNIARUINN

1005
CÀRN LIATH

Kinlochlaggan

Gallovie

834
CÀRN DEARG

Creag Meagaidh

River Maghie

Co

Glen Roy

7

1128
CREAG MEAGAIDH

River Spean

29

River Pattack

Dalwhi

n Roy

1048
BEINN A' CHAORUNN

Dist

tine

A86

747
BINNEIN SHUAS

1049
GEAL CHARN

L CREAG MOR

659
CREAG DHUBH

Moy

8

Monessie Falls

714

Inverlai

G l

1088

0 1 2 3 4 miles
0 1 2 3 4 5 kilometres

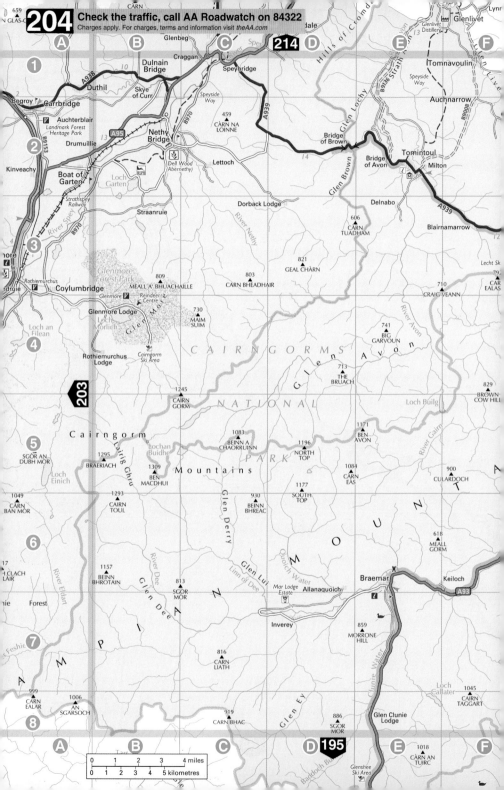

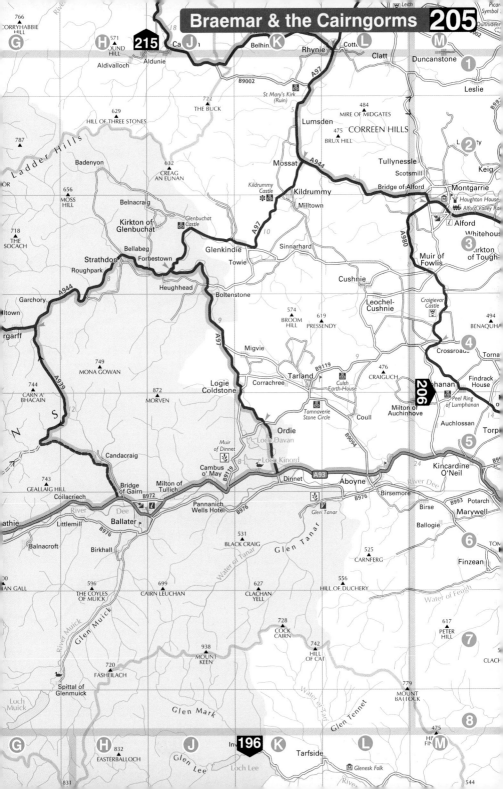

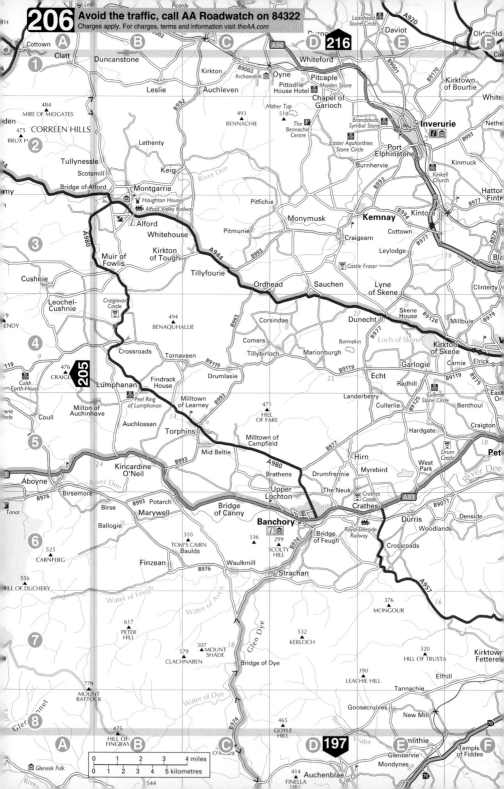

208

Before you set off call AA Roadwatch on 84322
Charges apply. For charges, terms and information visit *theAA.com*

A B C D E F

1

2

3

4

5

6

7

8

218

198

Duntul

Tairbeart
(Tarbert)

Lùb Score

Borneskitaig
Kilmuir
Kilvaxter

He

Balgown

Linicro
Totscore

Idrigill

Uig
(Uige

Earlish

Kingsb

Loch nam Madadh
(Lochmaddy)

Waternish Point

Ascrib
Islands

Loch Snizort

283
BEN
GEARY

Geary

Gillen

Trumpan

Hallin

Ardmore
Point

Stein

Lusta

214
BEN
DIUBAIG

Greshornish
House
Hotel

DUNVEGAN
HEAD

Isay

Mingay

Loch
Bay

Claigan

Bay

Treaslane

Flashader

Boreraig

Uig

327
BEINN
BHREAC

Upperglen

Edinbane

Bernisdale

Loch
Pooltiel

Feriniquarrie

Totaig

Dunvegan

Oisgill Bay

Milovaig

Glendale

Skeab

Waterstein

Lephin

Colbost

Colbost Croft

Toy

Skinidin

Dunvegan

Kilmuir

Giant Angus MacAskill

Lonmore

265
BEN
AKETIL

271
CRUACHAN BEINN
A' CHEARCAILL

Neist
Point

Roskhill

Moonen Bay

469
HEALAVAL
MORE

Roag

Orbost

Vatten

Ramasaig

Hoe Rape

488
HEALAVAL
BHEAG

Harlosh

Glen Ose

Ose

Hoe Point

368
BEINN NA
BOINEID

Harlosh
Island

Colbost
Point

Dun
Beag

Bracadale

Loch
Duag

Coillore

Tarner
Island

Struan

Loch Bracadale

Ullinish
Lodge Hotel

Wiay

Idrigill
Point

Oronsay

Portnalong

Fiskavaig

Rudha nan Clach

369
ARNAVAL

Carbost

Fernilea

Drynoch

Merkadale

Talisker
Bay

Talisker

Glen Eynort

447
BEINN
BHREAC

Grula

Loch Eynort

0 1 2 3 4 miles
0 1 2 3 4 5 kilometres

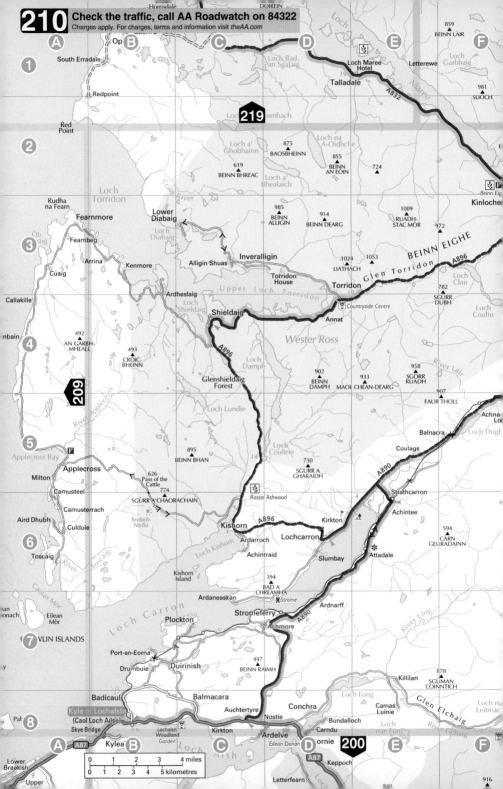

210

Check the traffic, call AA Roadwatch on 84322
Charges apply. For charges, terms and information visit *theAA.com*

A B C D E F

1 South Erradale
Horrisdale
DOIREIN
Loch
▲ 859
BEINN LÀIR
Op
Loch
Garbhaig

Redpoint
Loch Bad
nan Sgalaig
Loch Maree
Hotel
Letterewe
▲ 981
SLIOCH

219

Red
Point
Talladale
A832
Loch
Maree

2
Loch a'
Ghobhainn
Loch na
A-Oidhche
▲ 875
BAOSBHEINN
▲ 855
BEINN
AN EOIN
▲ 724
Beinn Eig

Rudha
na Fearn
Loch
Torridon
▲ 619
BEINN BHREAC
Loch a'
Bhealaich
Kinloche

3
Fearnmore
Ob
aig
Craig River
Lower
Diabaig
Loch
Diabaig
▲ 985
BEINN
ALLIGIN
▲ 914
BEINN DEARG
▲ 1009
RUADH-
STAC MÒR
▲ 972
BEINN EIGHE

Fearnbeg
Arrina
Kenmore
Allligin Shuas
Inveralligin
▲ 1024
LIATHACH
▲ 1053
Glen Torridon
A896
Loch
Clair
▲ 782
SGURR
DUBH

Cuaig
Ardheslaig
Torridon
House
Torridon
Countryside Centre
Loch
Coulin

Callakille
Loch
Shieldaig
Shieldaig
Upper Loch Torridon
Annat
Wester Ross

4
▲ 492
AN GARBH-
MHEALL
▲ 493
CRÒIC-
BHEINN
A896
Loch
Damph
▲ 902
BEINN
DAMPH
▲ 933
MAOL CHEAN-DEARG
▲ 958
SGORR
RUADH
River Lair

nbain
Glenshieldaig
Forest
Loch
Lundie
▲ 907
FAUR THOLL
Achna
Lo

209
River Applecross
Loch
Coultrie
▲ 730
SGURR A
GHARAIDH
A890
Balnacra
Coulags
Loch Dugh

5
Applecross Bay
▲ 895
BEINN BHAN
Strathcarron

Milton
Applecross
▲ 626
Pass of the
Cattle
▲ 774
SGÙRR A'CHAORACHAIN
Rassal Ashwood
Kirkton
Achintee

Camusteel
Bealach-
Na-Ba
Kishorn
A896
Slumbay
Attadale
▲ 594
CARN
GEURADAINN

Camusterrach
Ardarroch
Lochcarron

6
Aird Dhubh
Culduie
River
Toscaig
Kishorn
Island
Achintraid
▲ 394
BAD A
CHREAMHA
Ardnarff
River Ling

Toscaig
Loch Kishorn
Ardaneaskan
Strome
Glen Elchaig

7
Caolas Mòr
Eilean
Mòr
VLIN ISLANDS
Loch Carron
Plockton
Stromeferry
Achmore
A890
▲ 878
SGUMAN
COINNTICH
Killilan

Port-an-Eorna
Duirinish
▲ 447
BEINN RAIMH
Loch
Long
Loch na
Leitreac

Drumbuie
River

8
Pab
Badicaul
Balmacara
Auchtertyre
Conchra
Bundalloch
Camas
Luinie
Loch
nan Eun
River Elchaig

Lower
Breakish
Kyle of Lochalsh
(Caol Loch Ailse)
Skye Bridge
A87
Kylea
Lochalsh
Woodland
Garden
Kirkton
Nostie
Ardelve
Eilean Donan
Dornie
Carndu
Glen Elchaig

Upper
Letterfearn
Keppoch
A87

200

A B C D E F

0 — 1 — 2 — 3 — 4 miles
0 — 1 — 2 — 3 — 4 — 5 kilometres

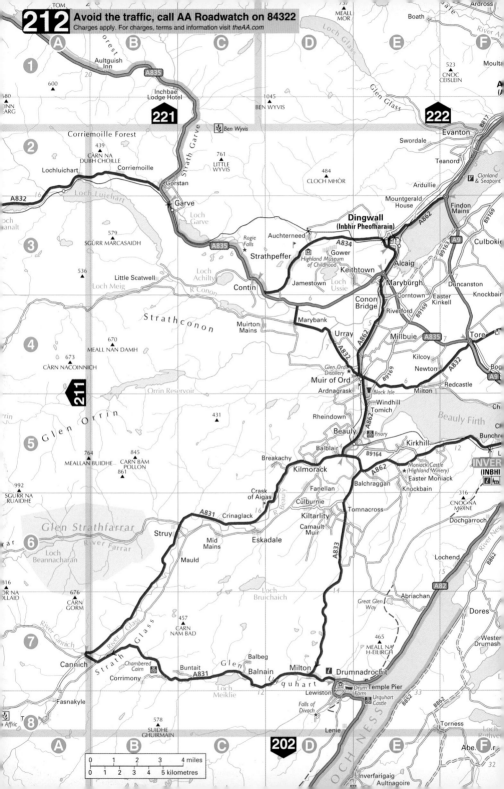

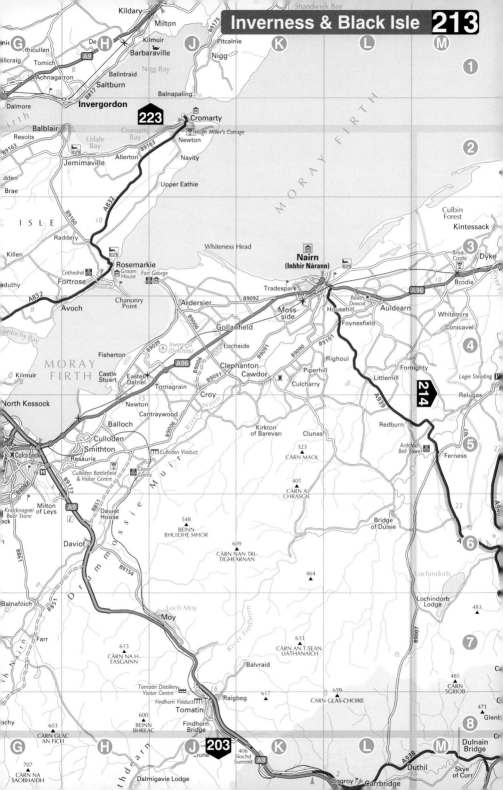

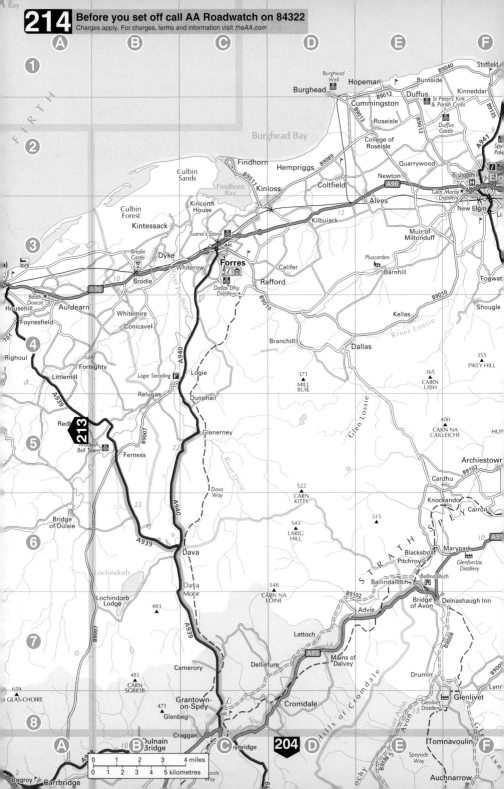

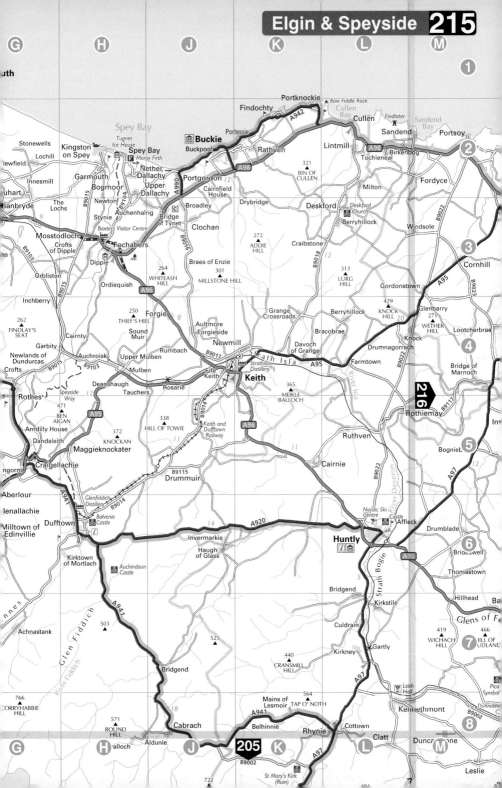

G H J K L M

1

Portknockie
Findochty ★ Bow Fiddle Rock
Cullen
Portessie A942 Bay Cullen Findlater Sandend
Rathven Sandend Bay Portsoy
Buckie Lintmill Tochieneal Birkenbog 2
Buckpool A98 321 Deskford
Stonewells Lochill Spey Bay BIN OF Fordyce
Kingston Tugnet CULLEN
on Spey Ice House Portgordon 12 Milton
iewfield Spey Bay Cairnfield Deskford
uth Garmouth Nether House Broadley Drybridge Deskford Church Windsole
Innesmill Bogmoor Dallachy Clochan Berryhillock B9022
Upper Berryhillock
uhart The Lochs Newton Dallachy 272 Craibstone Gordonstown Cornhill 3
anbryde Stynie Auchenhalrig ADDIE B9018 12
Mosstodloch Bridge HILL A95
Crofts of Tynet Braes of Enzie 313 B9023
of Dipple Fochabers 301 LURG Glenbarry
Dipple 264 MILLSTONE HILL HILL 429 271 4
Orbliston WHITEASH Grange KNOCK WETHER Lootcherbrae
Ordiequish HILL Crossroads Berryhillock HILL 20 HILL
Inchberry A96 Forgie Knock
250 Bracobrae Drumnagorrach Bridge of
262 THIEF'S HILL 8 Aultmore Davoch Marnoch
FINDLAY'S Cairnty Sound Forgieside of Grange Farmtown
SEAT Muir Newmill Strath Isla Bogniel 5
Garbity Auchroisk Rumbach B9017 Strathisla River Isla
Newlands of B9103 Upper Mulben Fife Distillery
Dundurcas B9015 Mulben Keith Keith A95
Crofts Deanshaugh Rosarie 365 216
Rothes Tauchers MEIKLE Rothiemay
471 Speyside BALLOCH
BEN Way A95 338 Ruthven
Arndilly House AIGAN HILL OF TOWIE Keith and Cairnie
Dandaleith 372 Dufftown B9115
Craigellachie KNOCKAN Railway 11
Maggieknockater Drummuir Strath Bogie
Aberlour Glenfiddich B9014 Nordic Ski Drumblade 6
lenallachie Distillery Centre Castle Briggswell
Milltown of Dufftown Balvenie A920 Affleck Thomastown
Edinvillie Castle Invermarkie Huntly Hillhead
Kirktown Haugh Glens of F
of Mortlach Auchindoun of Glass Kirkstile WICHACH 419 466 7
Castle Bridgend HILL HILL OF
503 Culdrain UDLAND
Achnastank Pica
525 Kirkney Gartly Leith Symbol
440 Hall
766 CRANSMILL Kennethmont
ORRYHABBIE 571 HILL 564 8
HILL ROUND Cabrach Mains of TAP O' NOTH Cottown
Aldunie HILL Belhinnie Rhynie Clatt
Halloch A941 A97
205 St Mary's Kirk
B9002 (Ruin)
G H J K L M

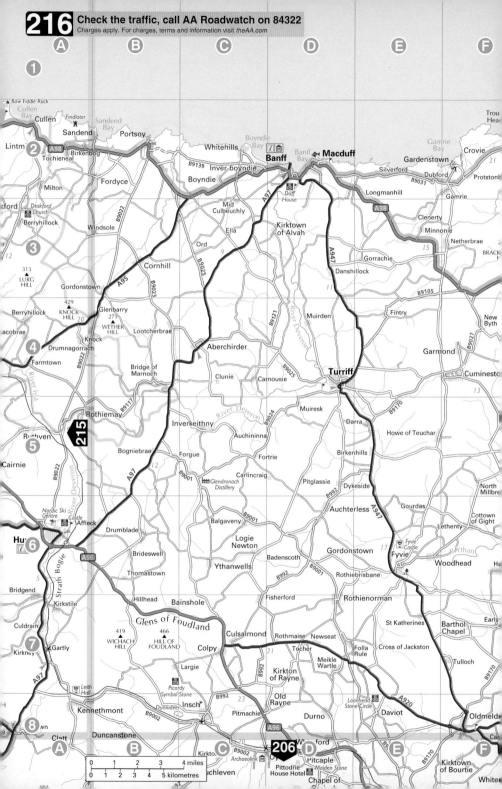

G   H   J   K   L   M

1

2

3

4

5

6

7

8

Rosehearty
Pittulie
Craigiefold
Peathill
Percyhorner
Coburby
Boyndlie
B9031
Mid Ardlaw
Aberdour Bay
A98
B9032
Memsie
Memsie Cairn
Newburgh
B9093
Strichen
New Leeds
B9093
234
WAUGHTON HILL
Denhead
Fetterangus
Maud
B9106
A950
A981
Deer Abbey
Dunshillock
Aden
Old Deer
Blackhill of Clackriach
Drymuir
Bulwark
B9029
B9029
Stuartfield
Millbreck
Nethermuir
Knaven
B9030
Kinnadie
Clola
Auchnagatt
Inkhorn
Coldwells
Kinknockie
A948
Arthrath
Muirtack
A952
Ythanbank
Auchedly
Birness
Artrochie
Kinharrachie
Ythsie
Ellon
P R
Esslemont
A920
Kirkton of Logie Buchan
Pitmedden
Logierieve
B90
Housieside
Udny Station
B9000
Pettymuk
Cultercullen
Foveran
A90

Castle Lighthouse & Museum
Sandhaven
Kinnaird Head
Kirktown
Fraserburgh
Fraserburgh Bay
Cairnbulg
Inverallochy
Maggie's Hoosie
Whitelinks Bay
A90
St Combs
B9033
Rathen
60
Crofts of Savoch
Lonmay
60
12
Loch of Strathbeg
Rattray Head
Crimond
Blackhill
60
18
Leys
Kirktown
St Fergus
Backfolds
A90
Rora
60
River Ugie
Longside
Inverugie
Mintlaw
Peterhead
Buchanhaven
Peterhead
A950
Inverquhomery
9
Peterhead Bay
Nether Kinmundy
Hillhead of Cocklaw
Burnhaven
Blackhill
Buchan Ness
Stirling
Boddam
Lendrum Terrace
Longhaven
A90
Bullers of Buchan
Auchiries
North Haven
Hatton
Slains
Cruden Bay
Bogbrae
Chapel Hill
Bay of Cruden
Whinnyfold
The Skares
A975
Colliston
Kirktown of Slains
32
Forvie

207
Newburgh

A B C D E F

1
2
3
4
5

Fladda-chùain

Eilean Trodday

Rudha Hunish

6

Tairbeart
(Tarbert)

Lùb Score

North
Duntulm

Duntulm   Kilmaluag

A855

Skye Museum
of Island Life   Flodigarry

Borneskitaig   Eilean Flodigarry

Kilmuir   Heribusta

Kilvaxter   542
MEAL NA   Staffin
Balgown   SUIREAMACH   Digg   Bay   Staffin Island

Brogaig

7

Linicro   Stenscholl   Staffin

Totscore   464
BIODA   Kilt Rock Waterfall
BUIDHE   *Trotternish*   Ellishader

208   **209**

Idrigill   Maligar   Valtos

Marishader   Rudha nam Brathairean

Loch nam Madadh   Uig Bay   611   Garros   Culnaknock
(Lochmaddy)   (Uige)   BEINN
8   Uig   EDRA

Earlish   Le   Tote

Loch S ort   A855

A   B   C   D   E   F

0   1   2   3   4 miles
0 1 2 3 4 5 kilometres

608

G H J K L M

1

Foibain

Badentarbat
Bay

Steornabhagh
(Stornoway)

Tanera
Beg

Tanera
Mòr

Horse
Island

Glas-leac Beag

Eilean Dubh

2

Priest
Island

Leac

Cailleach Head

Scoraig

Greenstone
Point

Rudha Beag

Stattic Point

GRUINARD
ISLAND

Badluachrach **3**

Little

Mellon
Udrigle

A832

Foura

Cove

Laide

Gruinard
Bay

Badcaul

Rudha Reidh

Mellon
Charles

Ormiscaig

Aultbea

Gruinard

296
AN
CUAIDH

B8057

ISLE
OF EWE

Little Gruinard River

Gruinard River

Gai

4

347
CREAG-
MHEAL BEAG

Melvaig

Aultgrishin

Loch Ewe

293
CNOC
BREAC

Inverasdale

Naast

Loch
Fada

681
BEINN A'
CHAISGEIN BEAG

220

Loc
Sea

5

North Erradale

B8021

Inverewe
Garden

13

Poolewe

Londubh

250
MEALL NA MEINE

Fionn

Wester Ross

BEIN

Big Sand

Strath

A832

Smithstown

Lonemore

Gairloch

Auchtercairn

Heritage
Museum

Charlestown

421
MEALL AN
DOIREIN

791
BEINN
AIRIDH CHARR

Loch

Dubh
Loch

6

Longa
Island

Loch
Gairloch

Port
Henderson

Eilean
Horrisdale

B8056

Badachro

Opinan

South Erradale

Redpoint

Red
Point

Loch Bad
an Sgalaig

Loch
Maree
Hotel

Talladale

19

Loch

Letterewe

Loch
Garbhaig

859
BEINN LÀIR

981
SLIOCH

A832

Maree

7

Loch Ghaineamhach

210

Loch
Ghoblachan

619
BEINN BHREAC

Loch a'
Bhealaich

875
BAOSBHEINN

Loch na
A'Oidhche

855
BEINN
AN EOIN

724

8

Beinn Eighe

Kinlochew

Rudha
na Fearn

Fearnn

Loch
Torridon

Lower
Diabaig

Loch
Diabaig

B
ALLIGIN

914
BEINN DEARG

1009
RUADH-
STAC MÒR

972

BEINN EIGHE

Òb
Chuaig

Fearnbeg

Craig River

G H J K L M

220

Before you set off call AA Roadwatch on 84322
Charges apply. For charges, terms and information visit *theAA.com*

A　B　C　D　E　F

1

STAC POLLAIDH
769 CUL BEAG
Polbain
Altibuie
Tanera Beg
Badentarbat Bay
Steornabhagh (Stornoway)
Tanera Mòr
glass
Loch Lurgainn

COIGACH

2

Eilean Dubh
Horse Island
Horse Sound
Achduart
652
BEN MORE COIGACH
224
Culn
Strathcanaird
Strath Canaird

Leac Dhonn
Isle Martin
Ardmair
A835

Greenstone Point
Rudha Beag
Cailleach Head
Scoraig
Annat Bay
Rhireavach
635 BEINN GHOBHLACH
Morefield
Ullapool (Ulapul)
M
A835

3

Mellon Udrigle
Stattic Point
Badluachrach
GRUINARD ISLAND
A832
Little Loch Broom
Badrallach
EILI

Laide
Gruinard Bay
Badcaul
Ardessie
Camusnagaul
Ardindrean
Letters

Mellon Charles
Ormiscaig
Gruinard
764 SAIL MHOR
Dundonnell
507 CARN BHIORAIN
Crofto

Aultbea
Little Gruinard River
Lochan Gaineamhaich
32

4

ISL OF EWE
Loch Fada
347 CREAG-MHEAL BEAG
Gruinard River
1062 AN TEALLACH
Strathnasheallag Forest

Loch Ewe
nverasdale
Inverewe Garden
13
681 BEINN A' CHAISGEIN BEAG
Loch na Sealga
601 MEALL AN T-SITHE

5

Poolewe
Londubh
250 MEALL NA MEINE
219
Fionn Loch
906 BEINN DEARG MHOR
Loch a' Bhraoin

32
airn
Wester Ross

lestown
421 MEALL AN DOIREIN
791 BEINN AIRIDH CHARR
Dubh Loch
974 SGÙRRBÀN
1019 MULLACH COIRE MHIC FHEARCHAIR
999 A' CHAILLEACH

6

Loch
859 BEINN LÀIR
Lochan Fada

Loch Bad an Sgalaig
Loch Maree Hotel
19
Letterewe
Loch Garbhaig

Talladale
A832
Maree
981 SLIOCH
711 BEINN NAN RAMH

7

Loch Gaineamhach
680 BEINN A' MHÙINIDH
Kinlochewe Forest

Loch a' Ghobhainn
875 BAOSBHEINN
Loch na A-Oidhche
210
933 FIONN BHEINN

619 BEINN BHREAC
Loch a' Bhealaich
855 BEINN AN EOIN
724
Beinn Eighe
Incheril

8

Kinlochewe
A832
Glen Docherty
10

A　B　C　D　E　F

L ALLIGIN
914
1009 RUADH
972
BEINN EIGHE

0　1　2　3　4 miles
0　1　2　3　4　5 kilometres

Colaboll

BEINN AN

A **B** **C** **D** **E** **F**

Ferrycroft
Countryside
Centre

1

Loch na
Claise Mòire

402
CNOC A' CHOIRE

323
BEN DOULA

Lairg

Tomich

Torrobull

225 A839

A839

226

Oykel Bridge
Hotel

2

A837 Rosehall

Achany

313
CREAGAN
GLAS

Doune

Altass

Linsidemore

B864

A836

A837

Falls of Shin

333
MEALL
EACHAINN

Loch Buidhe

Strath Oykel

493
BEINN
ULBHAIDH

463
BREAC BHEINN

Inveran

Invershin

Sleasdairidh

349
BEINN
DONUILL

River Evelis

412
CREAG
LOISGTE

3

506
MEALL
DHEIRGIDH

Brealangwell
Lodge

Culrain

A836

Kyle of
Sutherland

asha Burn

701
CARN A'
CHOIN DEIRG

Strathcarron

Croick

Lower
Gledfield

Dounie

Bonar
Bridge

Loch
Migdale

A949

Spinning

Dounie

Ardgay

4

Glencalvie Forest

River Carron

634
CÀRN BHREN

Kincardine

Upper Ardchronie

A836

Struie Hill

Dorn

Edderto

221

838
CARN
CHUINNEAG

477
BEINN CLACH
AN FHEADAIN

Edderto

Crom Loch

710
BEINN
THARSUINN

Aultnamain Inn

5

602
CÀRN CAS NAN GABHAR

EASTER ROSS

692
BEINN
THARSUINN

379
CNOC
T-SABH

771
MEALL A'
GHRIANAIN

Loch a
Chaorunn

Loch
Morie

Strath Rusdale

B9176

742
BEINN
NAN EUN

Ardross

6

737
MEALL
MÒR

Boath

River Alness

Achandunie

Rhicullen

Millcraig

Tomich

Achnag

A835

Inchbae
Lodge Hotel

ish

Loch Glass

523
CNOC
CEISLEIN

Moultavie

Alness
(Alanais)

7

479

1045
BEN WYVIS

Dalmore

Balblair

Forest

Ben Wyvis

Glen Glass

B817

Resolis

Corriemoille

761
LITTLE
WYVIS

212

Evanton

B9163

LE
Corriemoille

Strath Garve

Gorstan

484
CLOCH MHÒR

Teanord

Cullicudden

Brae

8

Garve

Mountgerald
House

Ardullie

Clanland
& Seaport

BLACK ISLE

A

Loch
Gar

B

Dingwall
(Inbhir Pheofharain)

C

Findon
Mains

D

E

Culbokie

F

255
MOUNT

CASAIDH

0 1 2 3 4 miles
0 1 2 3 4 5 kilometres

A834

A9

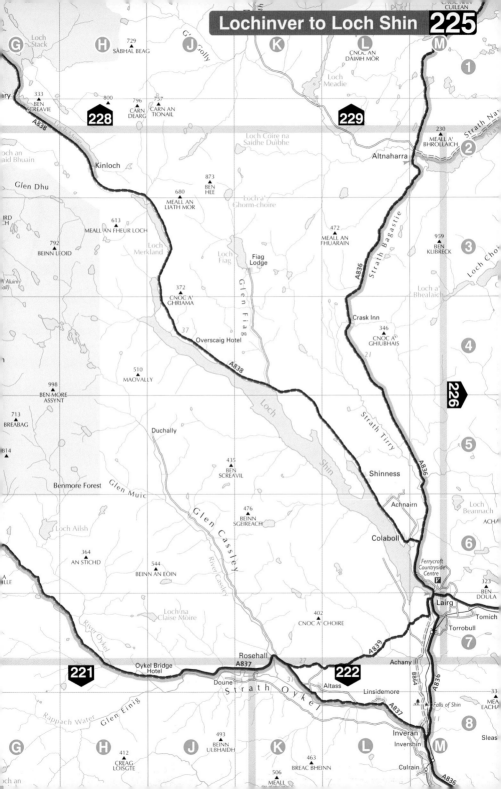

Altnabreac Station

G
CNOC
NAN GALL

H
Strathmore
Dalnawillan Lodge

J
Rumsdale Water
Loch
More
Loch an
Thulachan

K
Loch
Sand

Achavanich **L** Loch
Stemster
Loch
Rangag

M
Grey Cair
of Camst

1

226
COIRE
NA BEINN

248
STEMSTER HILL

230

348 ▲
BEN
ALISKY

287 ▲
BEN-A-
CHIELT

231

Roste
Hill

Upper
Lybster

Glutt Lodge

264 ▲
CNOCAN
CONACHREAG

Houstry

Swiney

Invershore

Landhallow

2

Lybster
Bay

Mid

Occu

NOCKFIN
EIGHTS

317 ▲
CNOC LOCH
MHADADH

Dunbeath Water

Smerral

Latheronwheel

Latheron

Forse

Janetstown

A9

37 ▲
COIRE
ARNA

Braemore

484 ▲
MAIDEN
PAP

Knockally

Laidhay Croft

Dunbeath

3

705 ▲
MORVEN

Ramscraigs

518 ▲
CNOC AN
EIREANNAICH

626 ▲
SCARABEN

Borgue

554 ▲
CREAG
SCALABSDALE

Langwell Forest

Newport

20

Langwell
House

Berriedale

4

416 ▲
EINN
BHAIN

401 ▲
CNOC NA
MAOILE

A897

A9

5

Torrish

River Helmsdale

404 ▲
CREAG
THORARAIDH

Ord of Caithness

Timespan

Navidale House Hotel

West
Helmsdale

East Helmsdale

Helmsdale

591 ▲
BEINN NA
MEILICH

Gartymore

Glen Loth

Portgower

6

Lothmore

thbeg

7

8

G **H** **J** **K** **L** **M**

228
Check the traffic, call AA Roadwatch on 84322
Charges apply. For charges, terms and information visit *theAA*.com

CAPE WRATH

Cléit Dhubh

Faraid Head

371 ▲ SCRIBHIS-BHEINN

297 ▲ CNOC A GHIUBHAIS

300 ▲ MAOVALLY

THE PARPH

457 ▲ FASHVEN

Balnakeil Bay

Balnakeil

Durness
Sangomore

Smoo

Keoldale

Sar

Loch Airigh na Beinne

Sandwood Bay

Sandwood Loch

485 ▲ CREAG RIABACH

331 ▲ GHLAS-BHEINN

Loch Meada

423 ▲ MEALL MEADHONA

Rudh' an Fhir Leithe

468 ▲ BEINN DEARG MHÒR

464 ▲ MEALL NA MÒINE

489 ▲ MEALL NA CRA

Laid

Strath Shinary

Strath Beag

AN LEA

Sheigra

355 ▲ AN SOCACH

521 ▲ FARVEALL

773 ▲ BEINN SPIONNAIDH

A838

Balchreick

Blairmore

Oldshoremore

801 ▲ CRANSTACKIE

Kinlochbervie

Badcall

Loch Clash

Strath Dionard

B801

Achriesgill

Loch Inchard

Rhiconich

Loch na Claise Càrnaich

River Dionard

Rudha Ruadh

Skerricha

908 ▲ FOINAVEN

Fanagmore

Loch Laxford

North-west Sutherland

Loch na Tuadh

Tarbet

Foindle

A838

HANDA ISLAND

Laxford Bridge

River Laxford

786 ▲ ARKLE

Glen

Scourie Bay

A894

Loch Stack

729 ▲ SÀBHAL BEAG

Scourie More

Scourie

Badcall

Loch a' Mhuilinn

386 ▲ BEN AUSKAIRD

721 ▲ BEN STACK

Strath Stack

Achfary

333 ▲ BEN SCREAVIE

800 ▲

796 ▲ CARN DEARG

757 ▲ CARN AN TIONAIL

Rudh' a' Mhucard

17

Badcall Bay

Loch More

A838

OLDANY ISLAND

Eddrachillis Bay

224

419 ▲ BEN STROME

Loch an Leathaid-Bhuain

Loch Glendhu

Glen Dhu

225

Kinloch

680 ▲ MEALL AN LIATH

Culkein Drumbeg

Drumbeg

Loch a' Chàirn Bhàin

Kylestrome

Kylesku

525 ▲ BEINN DA LO

613 ▲ MEALL AN FHEUR LOCH

Loch Merkland

Olda

Nedd

B869

Unapool

Loch Glencoul

792 ▲ BEINN LEOID

Loch Poll

0 1 2 3 4 miles
0 1 2 3 4 5 kilometres

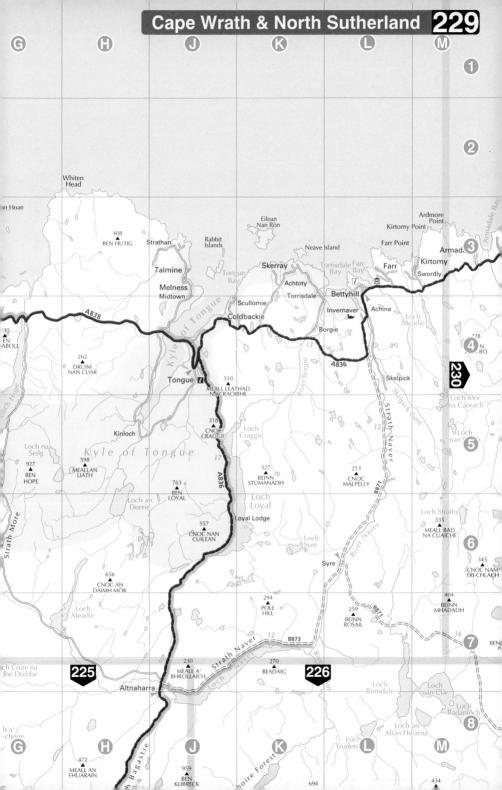

G H J K L M

1
2
3

Whiten Head

an Hoan

408
BEN HUTIG
Strathan

Talmine

Melness
Midtown

Rabbit
Islands

Eilean
Nan Ròn

Skerray

Neave Island

Achtoty

Scullomie

Torrisdale

Torrisdale Farr
Bay Bay

Kirtomy Point

Farr Point

Farr

Bettyhill

Invernaver

Borgie

Ardmore
Point

Armadale Bay

Armad.

Kirtomy
Swordly

Achina

Loch
Meadie

A838

Coldbackie

13

A836

Skelpick

230

N
BO

Kyle of Tongue

262
DRUIM
NAN CLIAR

Tongue

310
MEALL LEATHAD
NA CRAOIBHE

River Borgie

Strath Naver

Loch Mòr
na Caorach

Kinloch

318
CNOC
CRAGGIE

Loch
Craggie

Kyle of Tongue

17

Skelpick Burn

12

Loch
nan Ca

5

Loch na
Seilg

598
MEALLAN
LIATH

527
BEINN
STUMANADH

213
CNOC
MALPELLY

Loch Strathy

927
BEN
HOPE

763
BEN
LOYAL

A836

Loch an
Deerie

Loch
Loyal

B871

335
MEALL BAD
NA CUAICHE

557
CNOC NAN
CUILEAN

Loyal Lodge

Loch
Syre

6

Strath More

Syre

River Naver

345
CNOC NAM
TRI-CHLACH

656
CNOC AN
DÀIMH MÒR

294
POLE
HILL

259
BEINN
ROSAIL

404
BEINN
MHADADH

Loch
Meadie

B871

7

BEN

225

230
MEALL A'
BHROLLAICH

270
BEADAIG

226

12

B873

Strath Naver

16

Loch
Rimsdale

Loch
nan-Clàr

472
MEALL AN
FHUARAIN

Altnaharra

959
BEN
KLIBRECK

hoire Forest

Loch
Truders

Loch an
Altan Fhearna

8

Loch
Badanloch

G H J K L M

694

434

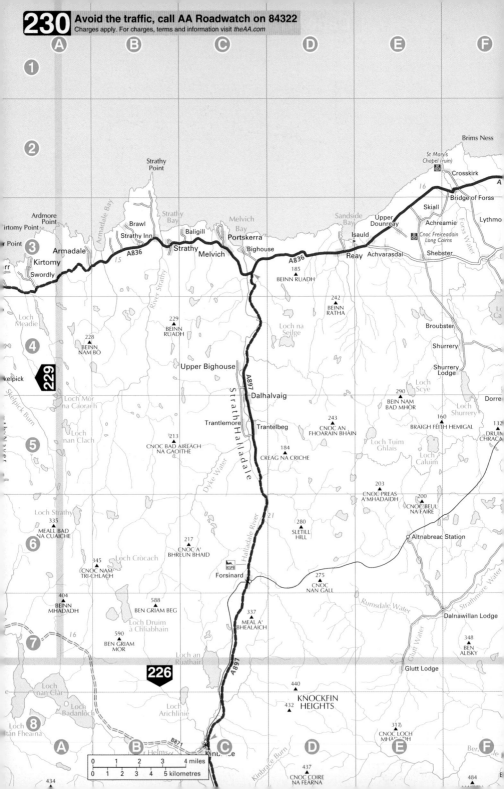

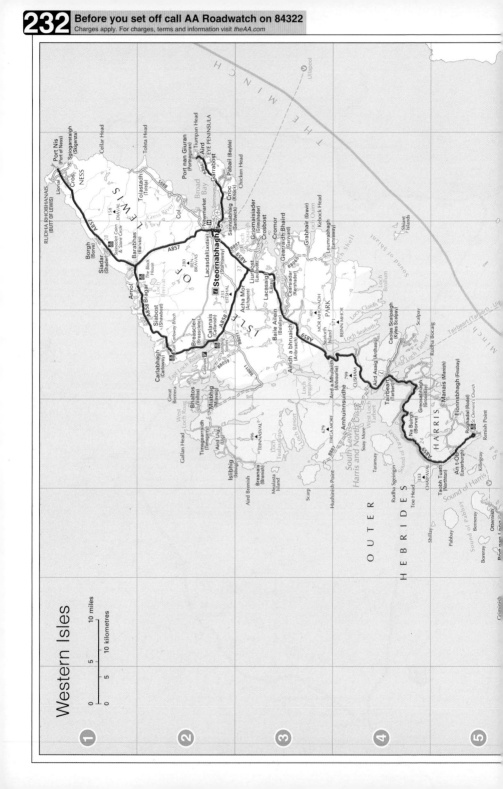

RONA

SCALPAY

RAASAY

ISLE OF SKYE

Uig
(Ùige)

Uig
(Ùige)

EIGG

MUCK

RÙM

CANNA

Loch nam Madadh
(Lochmaddy)

BEINN NA FAOGHLA
(BENBECULA)

Ronay

Wiay

UIBHIST A DEAS
(SOUTH UIST)

Rudha Hallagro

Rudha Bolum

Rudha Eyenort

Loch Baghasdail
(Lochboisdale)

Loch Euphoirt (Locheport)

Cairinis
(Carinish)

Griomasaigh

Gramsdail
(Gramsdale)

TÀBHAL

Clachan na Luib
(Clachan-a-Luib)

BEN TARBERT
165

BEINN MHÒR
620

HECLA
606

BEINN MHÒR
424

Druidbeg

Lionacleit

Creag Ghoraidh
(Creagorry)

Iochdar

Hornish Point

Our Lady of the Isles
27

Stadhlaigearraidh (Stilligarry)

Tobha Mòr
(Howmore)

Staoinebrig
(Stoneybridge)

Rudha Ardvule

Dalabrog
(Daliburgh)

South Uist

Machair

STÙLAVAL
374

Stuley

Ludag

Rubha Ban

KONE-VAL

ERISKAY

BEN
SCRIEN

Kilbay

Oilit

Hellisa

Bàgh a Tuath

Bruernish
Point

Fuiay

Sound of Barra

Scurrival
Point

Eolaigearraidh

Bàgh a Chàisteil
(Castlebay)

Muldoanich

Gighay

Sandray

Pabbay

BARRAIGH
(BARRA)

Borgh
(Borve)

Tangusdale

HEAVAL
383

A888

Flodday

Vatersay

Bhatarsaigh

Mingulay

Berneray

Heisker or
Monach Islands

Sound of Monach

Kirkibost Island

Scolpaig

Baile a Mhanaich
(Balivanich)

Grimsay

Oban

Oban

SEA OF THE HEBRIDES

SOUND OF BARRA (CONDUCTED)

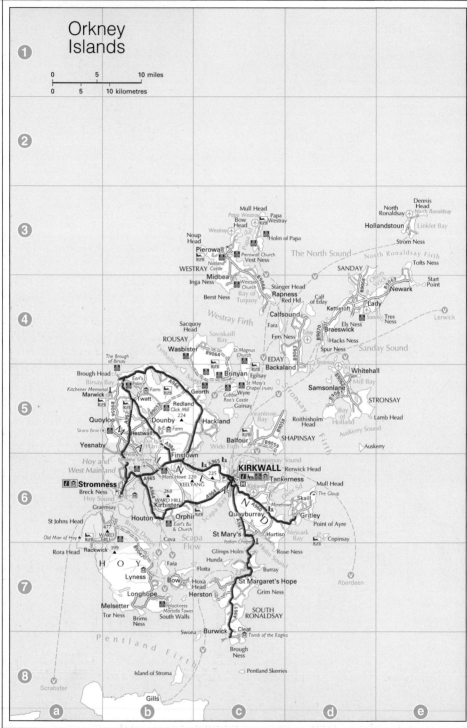

Orkney
Islands

0   5   10 miles
0 5   10 kilometres

Mull Head
Papa Westray
Bow Head
Papa Westray
Westray
Holm of Papa
Noup Head
Pierowall
Pierowall Church
Vest Ness
WESTRAY
Notland Castle
Midbea
Inga Ness
Westside Church
Stanger Head
Berst Ness
Rapness
Red Hd
Calf of Eday

Dennis Head
North Ronaldsay
North Ronaldsay
Hollandstoun
Linklet Bay
Strom Ness
Tofts Ness
SANDAY
B9069
Newark
Start Point
Kettletoft
Lady
Sandy
Tres Ness
Els Ness
Braeswick
Hacks Ness
Spur Ness
Sanday Sound
Lerwick

The North Sound
North Ronaldsay Firth

Sacquoy Head
ROUSAY
Wasbister
Saviskaill Bay
B9064
St Magnus Church
Brinyan
Egilsay
St Mary's Chapel (ruin)
Cubbie Roo's Castle
Wyre
Gairsay
EDAY
Backaland
Stronsay

Whitehall
Mill Bay
Samsonlane
STRONSAY

The Brough of Birsay
Brough Head
Birsay Bay
Kitchener Memorial
Marwick
Earl's Palace
Farm
Twatt
Redland
Click Mill
224
Georth
Dounby
Hackland
Balfour
SHAPINSAY
Wide Firth
B9059

Fers Ness
Eday
Fara
Veantrow Bay
Roithisholm Head
Bay of Holland
Lamb Ness
Auskerry Sound
Auskerry

Quoyloo
Hestwall
Yesnaby
Skara Brae
Ring of Brodgar
Ring of Neolithic Orkney
Finstown
Maes Howe 220
225
KEELYANG
KIRKWALL
Tankerness
Rerwick Head

Hoy and West Mainland
Stromness
Breck Ness
Hoy Sound
Graemsay
St Johns Head
Old Man of Hoy
Rora Head
Rackwick
HOY
Lyness
Longhope
Melsetter
Tor Ness
Brims Ness
Houton
Kirbister
Orphir
Earl's Bu & Church
St Mary's
Italian Chapel
Glimps Holm
Hunda
Flotta
Burray
Hoxa Head
Herston
St Margaret's Hope
Grim Ness
SOUTH RONALDSAY
Burwick
Cleat
Tomb of the Eagles
Brough Ness

WARD HILL
268
Kirbister
477
WARD HILL
Cava
Fara
Bow
Swona
South Walls
Hackness Martello Tower

Quoyburray
Hurtiso
Newark Bay
Gritley
Point of Ayre
Skaill
Minehowe
The Gloup
Mull Head
Copinsay

Shapinsay Sound
Deer Sd

Scapa Flow
Scapa Bay
Holm Sound
Rose Ness

Aberdeen

Pentland Firth
Island of Stroma
Pentland Skerries
Scrabster
Gills

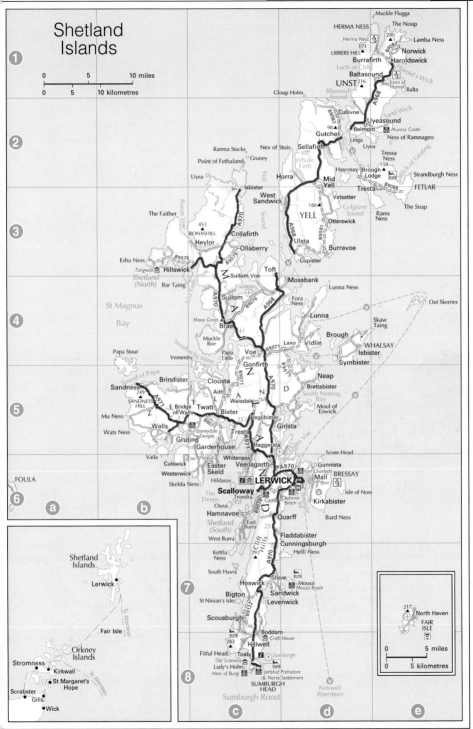

Shetland Islands

0   5   10 miles
0   5   10 kilometres

1

Muckle Flugga
HERMA NESS
The Noup
Herma Ness
171
Lamba Ness
LIBBERS HILL
280
Norwick
Burrafirth
Haroldswick
Harold's Wick
Baltasound
216
UNST
Keen of
Hamar
Balta

Gloup Holm
Bluemull
Sound
Sand Wick

2

Cullivoe
Uyeasound
98
Belmont
Muness Castle
Gutcher
Linga
Uyea
Ness of Ramnageo
Ramna Stacks
Nev of Stuis
Sellafirth
Point of Fethaland
Gruney
Whale
Firth
Hascosay
Tressa
Ness
159
Brough
Lodge
Uyea
Horra
Mid
Yell
Tresta
Strandburgh Ness
FETLAR
Isbister
West
Sandwick
Vatsetter
The Snap
453
RONASHILL
188
YELL
Colgrave
Sound
Rams
Ness
The Faither

3

Collafirth
Otterswick
Heylor
Ollaberry
Ulsta
Burravoe
Esha Ness
Copister
Tangwick
Hillswick
Shetland
(North)
Bar Taing
Sullom Voe
Toft
Mossbank
Lunna Ness
Out Skerries

4

St Magnus
Bay
Suillom
Fora
Ness
Lunna
Skaw
Taing
Mavis Grind
Brae
Laxo
Vidlin
Brough
WHALSAY
Papa Stour
Muckle
Roe
Papa
Little
Voe
Isbister
Vementry
Gonfirth
Neap
Symbister
Brindister
Clousta
Brettabister
Sandness
Aith
Moul of
Eswick
249
SANDNESS
HILL
Weisdale
South Nesting
Bay

5

Mu Ness
E Bridge
of Walls
Twatt
Bixter
Heglibister
Girlsta
Wats Ness
Walls
Tresta
Haggersta
Gruting
Garderhouse
Staneydale
Temple
Score Head
Vaila
Culswick
Whiteness
Veensgarth
Gunnista
Easter
Skeld
Fort Charlotte
BRESSAY
Westerwick
Hildasay
Skelda Ness
LERWICK
Mail
Isle of Noss

6

FOULA
Scalloway
Trondra
Clickimin
Broch
Kirkabister
The
Deeps
Castle
Bard Ness
Hamnavoe
Oxna
Quarff
Shetland
(South)
East
Burra
Fladdabister
Cunningsburgh
Helli Ness
West Burra
Kettla
Ness
Clift
Hills
293
Helli Ness

7

South Havra
Slove
Mousa
Mousa Broch
Hoswick
Sandwick
Bigton
Levenwick
St Ninian's Isle
Scousburgh

8

Boddam
Hillwell
Croft House
Fitful Head
Toab
Old Scatness
Sumburgh
Lady's Holm
Jarlshof Prehistoric
& Norse Settlement
Ness of Burgi
SUMBURGH
HEAD
Kirkwall
Aberdeen
Sumburgh Roost

a   b   c   d   e

Shetland Islands

Lerwick

To Aberdeen

Fair Isle

Orkney Islands

Stromness
Kirkwall
Scrabster
St Margaret's
Hope
Gills
Wick
To Aberdeen

217
North Haven
FAIR
ISLE

0   5 miles
0   5 kilometres

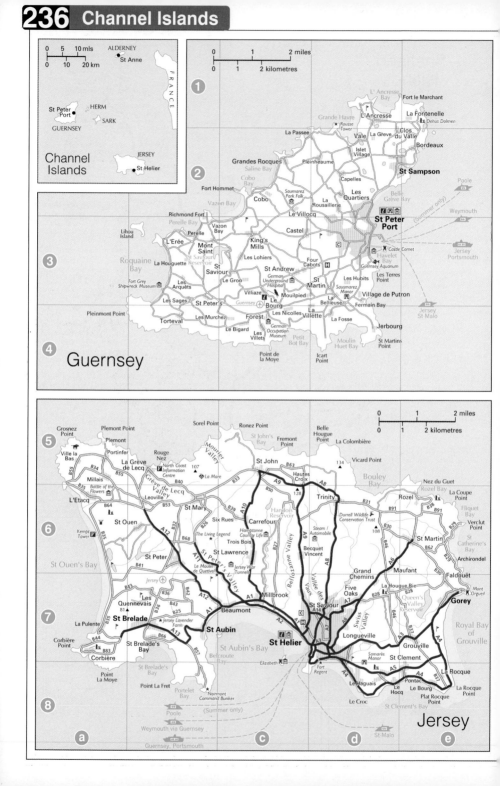

Channel Islands

ALDERNEY
St Anne

FRANCE

St Peter Port
HERM
SARK
GUERNSEY

JERSEY
St Helier

Guernsey

0 5 10 mls
0 10 20 km

0 1 2 miles
0 1 2 kilometres

L'Ancresse Bay
Fort le Marchant
L'Ancresse
La Grève
Clos du Valle
La Fontenelle
Dehus Dolmen
Grande Havre
Rousse Tower
Vale
Bordeaux
La Passee
Islet Village
Grandes Rocques
Pleinheaume
Capelles
St Sampson
Saline Bay
Les Quartiers
Cobo Bay
Fort Hommet
Samarez Park Folk
La Rousaillerie
Belle Grève Bay
Poole
Vazen Bay
Cobo
Le Villocq
St Peter Port
Weymouth
Richmond Fort
Perelle Bay
Vazon Bay
Castel
Guernsey (Summer only)
Lihou Island
Perelle
Castle Cornet
L'Erée
Mont Saint
King's Mills
Four Cabots
Havelet Bay
Jersey Portsmouth
Roquaine Bay
St Saviour Reservoir
Les Lohiers
St Andrew
Guernsey Aquarium
La Houguette
St Saviour
German Underground Hospital
Les Terres Point
Fort Grey Shipwreck Museum
Les Arquèts
Le Gron
St Martin
Les Hubits
Village de Putron
Les Sages
Villiaze
Moulipied
Sausmarez Manor
Fermain Bay
Les Murchez
St Peter's
Le Bourg
La Bellieuse
Pleinmont Point
Les Nicolles
La Villette
La Fosse
Jerbourg
Torteval
Forest
Le Bigard
German Occupation Museum
Les Villets
Moulin Huet Bay
St Martins Point
Point de la Moye
Icart Point
Petit Bot Bay

Jersey

0 1 2 miles
0 1 2 kilometres

Grosnez Point
Plemont Point
Sorel Point
Ronez Point
Belle Hougue Point
Vicard Point
Plemont
St John's Bay
Fremont Point
La Colombière
Ville la Bas
Portinfer
Rouge Nez
North Coast Information Centre
St John
B63
B31
134
Nez du Guet
La Coupe Point
Millais
Battle of the Flowers
La Mare
107
Hautes Croix
B50
A9
A8
Bouley Bay
Rozel Bay
La Grève de Lecq
Greve de Lecq Valley
B33
128
Trinity
Rozel
Fliquet Bay
L'Etacq
B64
B53
Leoville
St Mary
B39
Carrefour
Hamptonne Country Life
Steam / Automobile
Durrell Wildlife Conservation Trust
108
B30
B91
Verclut Point
Kempt Tower
St Ouen
Six Rues
The Living Legend
Trois Bois
B27
Bellozanne Valley
St Catherine's Bay
St Peter
B41
St Lawrence
Becquet Vincent
Grand Chemins
St Martin
B62
Archirondel
Jersey
Le Moulin de Quetivel
Maufant
B46
Faldouët
Les Quennevais
Quennevais
Le Hougue Bie
Mont Orgueil
La Pulente
St Brelade
Jersey Lavender Farm
Millbrook
Beaumont
St Saviour
A14
Five Oaks
Queen's Valley Reservoir
Gorey
Corbière Point
St Brelade's Bay
St Aubin
St Aubin's Bay
St Helier
Longueville
Royal Bay of Grouville
Corbière
Belcroute Bay
Elizabeth
Fort Regent
Grouville
A4
Point La Moye
Point La Fret
Portelet Bay
Normont Command Bunker
Samarès Manor
St Clement
La Rocque
Poole
Les Laveurs
Le Hocq
Le Bourg
Pontac
La Rocque Point
Weymouth via Guernsey
Le Croc
Plat Rocque Point
Guernsey, Portsmouth
(Summer only)
St Clement's Bay
St Malo

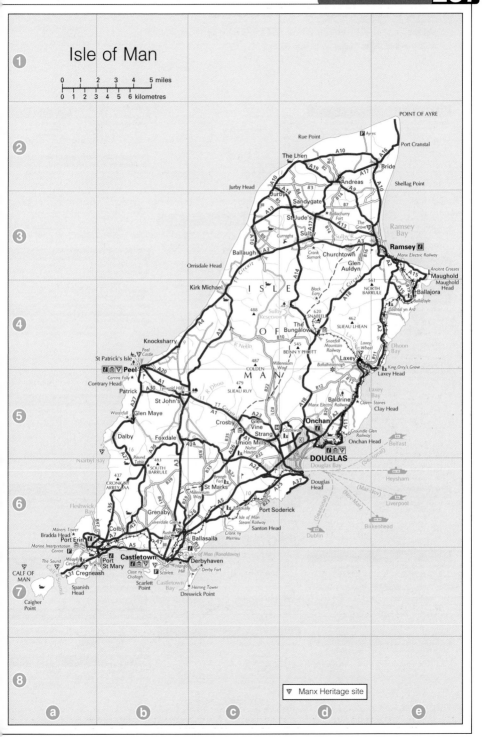

Isle of Man

```
0   1   2   3   4   5 miles
├───┼───┼───┼───┼───┤
0  1  2  3  4  5  6 kilometres
```

POINT OF AYRE

Rue Point

Port Cranstal

The Lhen

A10

Ayres

A16

Bride

Shellag Point

Jurby Head

A19

B6

A17

Andreas

A9

A10

Jurby

B3

B7

Sandygate

A14

St Jude's

A13

B16

The Grove

Ballachurry Fort

Ramsey Bay

Curraghs

Sulby

Sulby R.

A3

Ramsey

Manx Electric Railway

Ballaugh

A3

Cronk Sumark

Churchtown

Glen Auldyn

B16

A2

A15

Ancient Crosses

Maughold

Maughold Head

Orrisdale Head

Cashtal yn Ard

Ballajora

Ballafayle

Kirk Michael

I S L E

Sulby Reservoir

Block Eary

488

TT Circuit

A14

A18

561 NORTH BARRULE

A4

O F

620 SNAEFELL

The Bungalow

B10

462 SLIEAU LHEAN

Laxey Wheel

Dhoon Bay

Knocksharry

Peel Castle

545 BEINN Y PHOTT

Snaefell Mountain Railway

Laxey

King Orry's Grove

St Patrick's Isle

R. Neb

487 COLDEN

Millennium Way

Ballacheganagh

Laxey Head

Laxey Bay

Peel

A20

A3

M A N

479 SLIEAU RUY

A18

B12

Clay Head

Corrins Folly

Contrary Head

A30 Tynwald Hill

St John's

R. Dhoo

TT Circuit

A1

Manx Electric Railway

Baldrine

Cloven Stones

Patrick

A27

A23

B21

Onchan

A11

Waterfall

Glen Maye

Dalby

A36

Foxdale

A24

Crosby

Glen Vine

Strang

H

Castletown

C

Onchan Head

Groundle Glen Railway

Belfast

Round Table

483 SOUTH BARRULE

A3

Union Mills

Norse Houses

B32

DOUGLAS

Douglas Bay

Heysham

Niarbyl Bay

A25

A36

B39

St Marks

B41

Millennium Way

Brough Fort

A5

A24

A37

Douglas Head

Liverpool

Birkenhead

Fleshwick Bay

A36

Grenaby

Silverdale Glen

Ballakilley

Isle of Man Steam Railway

Port Soderick

Santon Head

Dublin

Miller's Tower

Bradda Head

Port Erin

Colby

A7

Ballabeg

Rushen Abbey

Ballasalla

Cronk ny Merriew

Marine Interpretation Centre

The Sound

Meayll Circle

Port St Mary

Castletown

St Mary

Close ny Chollagh

Hango Hill

Derbyhaven

Derby Fort

Isle of Man (Ronaldsway)

CALF OF MAN

Cregneash

A31

Scarlett

Scarlett Point

Castletown Bay

Herring Tower

Spanish Head

Dreswick Point

Caigher Point

☒ Manx Heritage site

Restricted Junctions

Motorway and Primary Route junctions which have access or exit restrictions are shown thus ■■3■■ , ■■56■■ on the map pages.

M1 London - Leeds

Junction	Northbound	Southbound
2	Access only from A1 (northbound)	Exit only to A1 (southbound)
4	Access only from A41 (northbound)	Exit only to A41 (southbound)
6A	Access only from M25 (no link from A405)	Exit only to M25 (no link from A405)
7	Access only from M10	Exit only to M10
17	Exit only to M45	Access only from M45
19	Exit only to northbound M6	Access only from M6
21A	Exit only to A46	Access only from A46
23A	Access only from A42	Exit only to A42
24A	Access only from A50	Exit only to A50
35A	Exit only to A616	Access only from A616
43	Exit only to M621	Access only from M621
48	Exit only to A1(M)	Access only from A1(M) (southbound)

M2 Rochester - Faversham

Junction	Westbound	Eastbound
1	Access only to A289 (eastbound)	Access only from A289 (westbound)

M3 Sunbury - Southampton

Junction	Southwestbound	Northeastbound
8	Exit only to A303	Access only from A303
10	Access only from Winchester & A31	Exit only to Winchester & A31
13	Exit only	No restriction
14	No access to M27 westbound	Access from M27 only No exit

M4 London - South Wales

Junction	Westbound	Eastbound
1	Access only from A4 (westbound)	Exit only to A4 (eastbound)
4A	No exit to A4 (westbound)	No restriction
21	Exit only to M48	Access only from M48
23	Access only from M48	Exit only to M48
25	Exit only	Access only from B4596
25A	Exit only	Access only from A4042
29	Exit only to A48(M)	Access only from A48(M)
38	Exit only	No restriction
39	Access only	No access/exit

M5 Birmingham - Exeter

Junction	Southwestbound	Northeastbound
10	Exit only	Access only
11A	Exit only to A417 (eastbound)	Access only from A417 (westbound)
18A	Access only from M49	Exit only to M49
29	Access only from A30 (westbound)	No restriction

M6 Toll Motorway

Junction	Northbound	Southbound
T1	Access only	No access or exit
T2	No access or exit	Exit only
T3	Staggered junction; follow signs - access only from A38	Staggered junction; follow signs - no restriction
T5	Access only from A5127 (southbound)	Exit only to A5148 (northbound)
T7	Exit only	Access only
T8	Exit only	Access only

M6 Rugby - Carlisle

Junction	Northbound	Southbound
3A	Exit only	Access only
4	No access from M42 (southbound). No exit to M42 (northbound)	No access from M42 (southbound). No exit to M42
4A	Access only from M42 (southbound)	Exit only to M42
5	Exit only to A452	Access only
10A	Exit only to M54	Access only from M54

11A	Access only	Exit only
20A (with M56)	No restriction	No access from M56 (westbound)
20	Access only from A50	No restriction
24	Access only from A58	Exit only to A58
25	Exit only	Access only
29	No direct access, use adjacent slip road to jct 29A	No direct exit, use adjacent slip road to jct 29A
29A	No direct exit, use adjacent slip road from jct 29	No direct access, use adjacent slip road to jct 29
30	Access only from M61	Exit only to M61
31A	Exit only	Access only
45	Exit only	Access only

M8 Edinburgh - Bishopton

Junction	Westbound	Eastbound
8	No access from M73 (southbound) or from A8 (eastbound) & A89	No exit to M73 (northbound) or to A8 (westbound) & A89
9	Access only	Exit only
13	Access only from M80 (southbound)	Exit only to M80 (northbound)
14	Access only	Exit only
16	Exit only to A804	Access only from A879
17	Access only from A82	No restriction
18	Access only from A82 (eastbound)	Exit only to A814
19	No access from A814 (westbound)	Exit only to A814 (westbound)
20	Exit only	Access only
21	Access only	Exit only to A8
22	Exit only to M77 (southbound)	Access only from M77 (northbound)
23	Exit only to B768	Access only from B768
25	No access or exit from or to A8	No access or exit from or to A8
25A	Access only	Exit only
28	Access only	Exit only
28A	Exit only to A737	Access only from A737

M9 Edinburgh - Dunblane

Junction	Northwestbound	Southeastbound
1A	Exit only to M9 spur	Access only from M9 spur
2	Access only	Exit only
3	Exit only	Access only
6	Access only from A904	Exit only to A905
8	Exit only to M876 (southwestbound)	Access only from M876 (northeastbound)

M10 St Albans - M1

Junction	Northwestbound	Southeastbound
with M1 (jct 7)	Exit only to M1 (northbound)	Access only from M1 (southbound)

M11 London - Cambridge

Junction	Northbound	Southbound
4	Access only from A406	Exit only to A406
5	Exit only to A1168	Access only from A1168
9	Exit only to A11	Access only from A11
13	Exit only to A1303	Access only from A1303
14	Exit only to A14 (eastbound)	Access only from A14

M20 Swanley - Folkestone

Junction	Southeastbound	Northwestbound
2	Staggered junction; follow signs - exit only to A227	Staggered junction; follow signs - access only from A227
3	Access only from M26 (eastbound)	Exit only to M26 (westbound)
5	For access follow signs - exit only to A20	Access only from A20
6	For exit follow signs	No restriction
11A	Exit only	Access only

M23 Hooley - Crawley

Junction	Southbound	Northbound
7	Access only from A23 (southbound)	Exit only to A23 (northbound)
10A	Exit only to B2036	Access only from B2036

M25 London Orbital Motorway

Junction	Clockwise	Anticlockwise
1B	No direct access, use slip road to jct 2. Exit only to A296	Access only from A296. No exit - use jct 2
5	No exit to M26	No access from M26
19	Exit only to A41	Access only from A41
21	Access only from M1 (southbound). Exit only to M1 (northbound)	Access only from M1 (southbound). Exit only to M1 (northbound)
31	No exit (use slip road via jct 30)	For access follow signs

M26 Sevenoaks - Wrotham

Junction	Westbound	Eastbound
with M25 (jct 5)	Access only from anticlockwise M25 (eastbound)	Exit only to clockwise M25 (westbound)
with M20 (jct 3)	Access only from M20 (southeastbound)	Access only from M20 (northwestbound)

M27 Cadnam - Portsmouth

Junction	Eastbound	Westbound
4	Staggered junction; follow signs - access only from M3 (southbound). Exit only to M3 (northbound)	Staggered junction; follow signs - access only from M3 (southbound). Exit only to M3 (northbound)
10	Access only	Exit only
12	Staggered junction; follow signs - access only from M275 (northbound)	Staggered junction; follow signs - exit only to M275 (southbound)

M40 London - Birmingham

Junction	Northwestbound	Southeastbound
3	Exit only to A40	Access only from A40
7	Exit only to A329	Access only from A329
8	Exit only to A40	Access only from A40
13	Exit only to A452	Access only from A452
14	Access only from A452	Exit only to A452
16	Access only from A3400	Exit only to A3400

M42 Bromsgrove - Measham

Junction	Northeastbound	Southwestbound
1	Access only from A38	Exit only to A38
7	Exit only to M6 (northwestbound)	Access only from M6 (northwestbound)
7A	Exit only to M6 (southeastbound)	No access or exit
8	Access only from M6 (southeastbound)	Exit only to M6 (northwestbound)

M45 Coventry - M1

Junction	Eastbound	Westbound
unnumbered (Dunchurch)	Exit only to A45 & B4429	Access only from A45 & B4429
with M1 (jct 17)	Exit only to M1 (southbound)	Access only from M1 (northbound)

M53 Mersey Tunnel - Chester

Junction	Southeastbound	Northwestbound
11	Access only from M56 (westbound). Exit only to M56 (eastbound)	Access only from M56 (westbound). Exit only to M56 (eastbound)

M54 Telford

Junction	Westbound	Eastbound
with M6 (jct 10A)	Access only from M6 (northbound)	Exit only to M6 (southbound)

M56 North Cheshire

Junction	Westbound	Eastbound
1	Access only from M60 (*westbound*)	Exit only to M60 (*eastbound*) & A34 (*northbound*)
2	Exit only to A560	Access only from A560
3	Access only from A5103	Exit only to A5103 & A560
4	Exit only	Access only
9	Exit to M6 (*southbound*) via A50 interchange	Access from M6 (*northbound*) via A50 interchange
15	Exit only to M53	Access only from M53

M57 Liverpool Outer Ring Road

Junction	Northwestbound	Southeastbound
3	Access only from A526	Exit only to A526
5	Access only from A580 (*westbound*)	Exit only to A580

M58 Liverpool - Wigan

Junction	Eastbound	Westbound
1	Access only	Exit Only

M60 Manchester Orbital

Junction	Clockwise	Anticlockwise
2	Access only from A560	Exit only to A560
3	No access from M56	Access only from A34 (*northbound*)
4	Access only from A34 (*northbound*). Exit only to M56	Access from M56 (*eastbound*). Exit only to A34 (*southbound*)
5	Access and exit only from and to A5103 (*southbound*)	Access and exit only from and to A5103 (*southbound*)
7	No direct access, use slip road to jct 8. Exit only to A56	Access only from A56. No exit - use jct 8
14	Access from A580 (*eastbound*)	Exit only to A580 (*westbound*)
16	Access only from A666	Exit only to A666
20	Exit only to A664	Access only from A664
22	No restriction	Exit only to A62
25	Exit only to A6017	No restriction
26	No restriction	No access or exit
27	Access only from A626	Exit only to A626

M61 Manchester - Preston

Junction	Northeastbound	Southeastbound
3	No access or exit	Exit only to A666
with M6 (jct 30)	Exit only to M6 (*northbound*)	Access only from M6 (*southbound*)

M62 Liverpool - Kingston upon Hull

Junction	Eastbound	Westbound
23	Exit only to A640	Access only from A640

M65 Preston - Colne

Junction	Northeastbound	Southwestbound
1	Access and exit to M6 only	Access and exit to M6 only
9	Exit only to A679	Access only from A679
11	Access only	Exit only

M66 Bury

Junction	Southbound	Northbound
with A56	Access only from A56 (*southbound*)	Exit only to A56 (*northbound*)
1	Exit only to A56	Access only from A56

M67 Hyde Bypass

Junction	Eastbound	Westbound
1	Exit only to A6017	Access only from A6017
2	Access only	Exit only to A57
3	No restriction	Exit only to A627

M69 Coventry - Leicester

Junction	Northbound	Southbound
2	Access only from B4669	Exit only to B4669

M73 East of Glasgow

Junction	Northbound	Southbound
2	No access from or exit to A89. No access from M8 (*eastbound*).	No access from or exit to A89. No exit to M8 (*westbound*)
3	Exit only to A80 (*northeastbound*)	Access only from A80 (*southwestbound*)

M74 and A74(M) Glasgow - Gretna

Junction	Southbound	Northbound
2	Access only from A763	Exit only to A763
3	Exit only	Access only
7	Exit only to A72	Access only from A72
9	Exit only to B7078	No access or exit
10	Access only from B7078	No restrictions
11	Exit only to B7078	Access only from B7078
12	Access only from A70	Exit only to A70
18	Access only from B723	Exit only to B723
21	Exit only to B6357	Access only from B6357
22	Exit only	Access only
23	Access only from A75	Exit only to A75

M77 South of Glasgow

Junction	Southbound	Northbound
with M8 (jct 22)	No access from M8 (*eastbound*)	No exit to M8 (*westbound*)
4	Exit only	Access only
6	Exit only	Access only
7	No restriction	Access only
8	No restriction	Access only from A77

M80 Stepps Bypass

Junction	Northeastbound	Southwestbound
1	Access only	No restriction
3	Exit only	Access only

M80 Bonnybridge - Stirling

Junction	Northbound	Southbound
5	Exit only to M876 (*northeastbound*)	Access only from M876 (*southwestbound*)

M90 Forth Road Bridge - Perth

Junction	Northbound	Southbound
2A	Exit only to A92 (*eastbound*)	Access only from A92 (*westbound*)
7	Access only from A91	Exit only to A91
8	Exit only to A91	Access only from A91
10	No access from A912. No exit to A912 (*southbound*).	No access from A912 (*northbound*). No exit to A912

M180 Doncaster - Grimsby

Junction	Eastbound	Westbound
1	Exit only A18	Access only from A18

M606 Bradford Spur

Junction	Northbound	Southbound
2	Exit only	No restriction

M621 Leeds - M1

Junction	Clockwise	Anticlockwise
2A	Access only	Exit only
4	Exit only	No restriction
5	Access only	Exit only
6	Exit only	Access only
with M1 (jct 43)	Access only from M1 (*southbound*)	Access only from M1 (*northbound*)

M876 Bonnybridge - Kincardine Bridge

Junction	Northeastbound	Southwestbound
with M80 (jct 5)	Access only from M80 (*northbound*)	Exit only to M80 (*southbound*)
2	Exit only to A9	Access only from A9
with M9 (jct 8)	Exit only to M9 (*eastbound*)	Access only from M9 (*westbound*)

A1(M) South Mimms - Baldock

Junction	Northbound	Southbound
2	Exit only to A1001	Access only from A1001
3	No restriction	Exit only
5	Access only	No access or exit

A1(M) East of Leeds

Junction	Northbound	Southbound
44	Access only from M1 (*northbound*)	Exit only to M1 (*southbound*)

A1(M) Scotch Corner - Newcastle upon Tyne

Junction	Northbound	Southbound
57	Exit only to A66(M) (*eastbound*)	Access only from Abb(M) (*westbound*)
65	No access Exit only to A194(M) & A1 (*northbound*)	No exit Access only from A194(M) and A1 (*southbound*)

A3(M) Horndean - Havant

Junction	Southbound	Northbound
1	Exit only to A3	Access only from A3
4	Access only	Exit only

A48(M) Cardiff Spur

Junction	Westbound	Eastbound
29	Access only from M4 (*westbound*)	Exit only to M4 (*eastbound*)
29A	Exit only to A48 (*westbound*)	Access only from A48 (*eastbound*)

A66(M) Darlington Spur

Junction	Eastbound	Westbound
with A1(M) (jct 57)	A1(M) (*northbound*)	Exit only to A1(M) (*southbound*)

A194(M) Newcastle upon Tyne

Junction	Northbound	Southbound
with A1(M) (jct 65)	Access only from A1(M) (*northbound*)	Exit only to A1(M) (*southbound*)

A12 M25 - Ipswich

Junction	Northeastbound	Southwestbound
13	Access only from B1002	No restriction
14	Exit only	Access only
20A	Exit only to B1137	Access only from B1137
20B	Access only B1137	Exit only to B1137
21	No restriction	Access only from B1389
23	Exit only to B1024	Access only from B1024
24	Access only from B1024	Exit only from B1024
27	Exit only to A113	Access only from A113
unnumbered (with A120)	Exit only A120	Access only from A120
29	Access only from A120 and A1232	Exit only to A120 and A1232
unnumbered	Exit only	Access only

A14 M1 - Felixstowe

Junction	Eastbound	Westbound
With M1/M6 (jct19)	Access only from M6 and M1 (*southbound*)	Exit only to M6 and M1 (*northbound*)
4	Access only from B669	Exit only to B669
31	Access only from A428 & M11. Exit only to A1307	Exit only to A428 & M11. Access only from A1307
34	Exit only to A1047	Access only from B1047
36	Access only from A11	Exit only to A11
38	Exit only to A11	Access only from A11
39	Access only from B1506	Exit only to B1506
49	Access only to A1308	Access only from A1308
61	Exit only to A154	Access only from A154

A55 Holyhead - Chester

Junction	Eastbound	Westbound
8A	Access only from A5	Exit only to A5
23A	Exit only	Access only
24A	No access or exit	Exit only
33A	No access from or exit to B5126	Exit only to B5126
33B	Access only from A494	Exit only to A494
35A (west)	Exit only A5104	Access only from A5104
35B (east)	Access only from A5104	Exit only to A5104

Index to place names

This index lists places appearing in the main-map section of the atlas in alphabetical order. The reference before each name gives the atlas page number and grid reference of the square in which the place appears. The map shows counties and administrative areas, together with a list of the abbreviated name forms used in the index. The top 100 places of tourist interest are indexed in **red**, motorway service areas in **blue** and airports in blue it*

England

BaNES	**Bath & N E Somerset (18)**
Barns	**Barnsley (19)**
Bed	**Bedford**
Birm	**Birmingham**
Bl w D	**Blackburn with Darwen (20)**
Bmouth	**Bournemouth**
Bolton	**Bolton (21)**
Bpool	**Blackpool**
Br & H	**Brighton & Hove (22)**
Br For	**Bracknell Forest (23)**
Bristl	**City of Bristol**
Bucks	**Buckinghamshire**
Bury	**Bury (24)**
C Beds	**Central Bedfordshire**
C Brad	**City of Bradford**
C Derb	**City of Derby**
C KuH	**City of Kingston upon Hull**
C Leic	**City of Leicester**
C Nott	**City of Nottingham**
C Pete	**City of Peterborough**
C Plym	**City of Plymouth**
C Port	**City of Portsmouth**
C Sotn	**City of Southampton**
C Stke	**City of Stoke-on-Trent**
C York	**City of York**
Calder	**Calderdale (25)**
Cambs	**Cambridgeshire**
Ches E	**Cheshire East**
Ches W	**Cheshire West and Chester**
Cnwll	**Cornwall**
Covtry	**Coventry**
Cumb	**Cumbria**
Darltn	**Darlington (26)**
Derbys	**Derbyshire**
Devon	**Devon**
Donc	**Doncaster (27)**
Dorset	**Dorset**
Dudley	**Dudley (28)**
Dur	**Durham**
E R Yk	**East Riding of Yorkshire**
E Susx	**East Sussex**
Essex	**Essex**
Gatesd	**Gateshead (29)**
Gloucs	**Gloucestershire**
Gt Lon	**Greater London**
Halton	**Halton (30)**
Hants	**Hampshire**
Hartpl	**Hartlepool (31)**
Herefs	**Herefordshire**
Herts	**Hertfordshire**
IoS	**Isles of Scilly**
IoW	**Isle of Wight**
Kent	**Kent**
Kirk	**Kirklees (32)**
Knows	**Knowsley (33)**
Lancs	**Lancashire**
Leeds	**Leeds**
Leics	**Leicestershire**
Lincs	**Lincolnshire**
Lpool	**Liverpool**

Luton	**Luton**
M Keyn	**Milton Keynes**
Manch	**Manchester**
Medway	**Medway**
Middsb	**Middlesbrough**
NE Lin	**North East Lincolnshire**
N Linc	**North Lincolnshire**
N Som	**North Somerset (34)**
N Tyne	**North Tyneside (35)**
N u Ty	**Newcastle upon Tyne**
N York	**North Yorkshire**
Nhants	**Northamptonshire**
Norfk	**Norfolk**
Notts	**Nottinghamshire**
Nthumb	**Northumberland**
Oldham	**Oldham (36)**
Oxon	**Oxfordshire**
Poole	**Poole**
R & Cl	**Redcar & Cleveland**
Readg	**Reading**
Rochdl	**Rochdale (37)**
Rothm	**Rotherham (38)**
Rutlnd	**Rutland**
S Glos	**South Gloucestershire (39)**
S on T	**Stockton-on-Tees (40)**
S Tyne	**South Tyneside (41)**
Salfd	**Salford (42)**
Sandw	**Sandwell (43)**
Sefton	**Sefton (44)**
Sheff	**Sheffield**
Shrops	**Shropshire**
Slough	**Slough (45)**
Solhll	**Solihull (46)**
Somset	**Somerset**
St Hel	**St Helens (47)**
Staffs	**Staffordshire**
Sthend	**Southend-on-Sea**
Stockp	**Stockport (48)**
Suffk	**Suffolk**
Sundld	**Sunderland**
Surrey	**Surrey**
Swindn	**Swindon**
Tamesd	**Tameside (49)**
Thurr	**Thurrock (50)**
Torbay	**Torbay**
Traffd	**Trafford (51)**
W & M	**Windsor and Maidenhead (52)**
W Berk	**West Berkshire**
W Susx	**West Sussex**
Wakefd	**Wakefield (53)**
Warrtn	**Warrington (54)**
Warwks	**Warwickshire**
Wigan	**Wigan (55)**
Wilts	**Wiltshire**
Wirral	**Wirral (56)**
Wokham	**Wokingham (57)**
Wolves	**Wolverhampton (58)**
Worcs	**Worcestershire**
Wrekin	**Telford & Wrekin (59)**
Wsall	**Walsall (60)**

Scotland

Abers	**Aberdeenshire**
Ag & B	**Argyll and Bute**
Angus	**Angus**
Border	**Scottish Borders**
C Aber	**City of Aberdeen**
C Dund	**City of Dundee**
C Edin	**City of Edinburgh**
C Glas	**City of Glasgow**
Clacks	**Clackmannanshire (1)**
D & G	**Dumfries & Galloway**
E Ayrs	**East Ayrshire**
E Duns	**East Dunbartonshire (2)**
E Loth	**East Lothian**
E Rens	**East Renfrewshire (3)**
Falk	**Falkirk**
Fife	**Fife**
Highld	**Highland**
Inver	**Inverclyde (4)**
Mdloth	**Midlothian (5)**
Moray	**Moray**
N Ayrs	**North Ayrshire**
N Lans	**North Lanarkshire (6)**
Ork	**Orkney Islands**
P & K	**Perth & Kinross**
Rens	**Renfrewshire (7)**
S Ayrs	**South Ayrshire**
Shet	**Shetland Islands**
S Lans	**South Lanarkshire**
Stirlg	**Stirling**
W Duns	**West Dunbartonshire (8)**
W Isls	**Western Isles (Na h-Eileanan an Iar)**
W Loth	**West Lothian**

Wales

Blae G	**Blaenau Gwent (9)**
Brdgnd	**Bridgend (10)**
Caerph	**Caerphilly (11)**
Cardif	**Cardiff**
Carmth	**Carmarthenshire**
Cerdgn	**Ceredigion**
Conwy	**Conwy**
Denbgs	**Denbighshire**
Flints	**Flintshire**
Gwynd	**Gwynedd**
IoA	**Isle of Anglesey**
Mons	**Monmouthshire**
Myr Td	**Merthyr Tydfil (12)**
Neath	**Neath Port Talbot (13)**
Newpt	**Newport (14)**
Pembks	**Pembrokeshire**
Powys	**Powys**
Rhondd	**Rhondda Cynon Taff (15)**
Swans	**Swansea**
Torfn	**Torfaen (16)**
V Glam	**Vale of Glamorgan (17)**
Wrexhm	**Wrexham**

Channel Islands & Isle of Man

Guern	**Guernsey**
Jersey	**Jersey**
IoM	**Isle of Man**

ORKNEY
ISLANDS

SHETLAND
ISLANDS

WESTERN ISLES (Na h-Eileanan an Iar)

HIGHLAND

MORAY

S C O T L A N D

ABERDEENSHIRE

Aberdeen

ANGUS

PERTH &
KINROSS

Dundee

ARGYLL
& BUTE

STIRLING

FIFE

FALK
1
W
LOTH

Edinburgh

E LOTH

8 2
Glasgow
7
4
3
6
5

NORTH
AYRSHIRE

S LANS

SCOTTISH
BORDERS

E AYRS

S AYRS

DUMFRIES &
GALLOWAY

NORTHUMBERLAND

Newcastle
upon Tyne
29 41
35

Sunderland

CUMBRIA

DURHAM

31
26 40 R & CL
Middlesbrough

IoM

NORTH YORKSHIRE

Blackpool

LANCASHIRE

Bradford

York

EAST RIDING
OF YORKSHIRE

Kingston
upon Hull

Leeds

20
55
21 24 37
44 47
33   36
30 54 51
56

25
32
42
39
48
Manchester
Sheffield

53
19
38
27

N LINCS

N E
LINCS

Liverpool

IoA

CONWY

FLINTS

CHES
W

CHES
E

DERBYS

NOTTS

LINCOLNSHIRE

DENBGS

Stoke-on-
Trent

GWYNEDD

WREXHAM

STAFFS

Derby

Nottingham

LEICS

RUTLAND

NORFOLK

SHROPSHIRE

59

58 60
28 43
46

Birmingham
Coventry

NHANTS

Leicester

Peterborough

CAMBS

SUFFOLK

POWYS

WORCS

WARWKS

Milton
Keynes

BED

CERDGN

HEREFS

W A L E S   E N G L A N D

BEDS

Luton

ESSEX

PEMBKS

CARMTH

MONS

GLOUCS

OXON

BUCKS

HERTS

Southend-
on-Sea

13
12
9
16
15 14
10 11
17
Cardiff
34 18
39
Bristol

Swansea

Swindon

WILTSHIRE

Reading
W BERKS

52 45
57 23

GREATER
LONDON

SURREY

50

MEDWAY

KENT

HAMPSHIRE

SOMERSET

DORSET

Southampton
Bournemouth
Poole
IoW

Portsmouth

W SUSX

E SUSX

22

DEVON

CORNWALL

Plymouth

Torbay

CHANNEL
ISLANDS

Guernsey

Jersey

IoS

A

27 G6 **Abbas Combe** Somset
70 D2 **Abberley** Worcs
70 D2 **Abberley Common** Worcs
62 B4 **Abberton** Essex
71 H4 **Abberton** Worcs
60 F5 **Abbess Roding** Essex
114 F5 **Abbeydale** Sheff
54 B3 **Abbey Dore** Herefs
99 L2 **Abbey Green** Staffs
178 F6 **Abbey St Bathans** Border
130 B8 **Abbeystead** Lancs
147 L5 **Abbey Town** Cumb
121 J6 **Abbey Village** Lancs
45 J4 **Abbey Wood** Gt Lon
167 J6 **Abbotrule** Border
9 K3 **Abbots Bickington** Devon
100 B7 **Abbots Bromley** Staffs
14 B5 **Abbotsbury** Dorset
186 B5 **Abbotts Deuglie** P & K
22 F6 **Abbotsham** Devon
7 K3 **Abbotskerswell** Devon
59 H7 **Abbots Langley** Herts
38 D5 **Abbots Leigh** N Som
75 J3 **Abbotsley** Cambs
71 H4 **Abbots Morton** Worcs
89 J7 **Abbots Ripton** Cambs
71 J4 **Abbot's Salford** Warwks
29 J5 **Abbots Worthy** Hants
29 G3 **Abbotts Ann** Hants
15 J3 **Abbott Street** Dorset
83 L6 **Abdon** Shrops
66 B3 **Aberaeron** Cerdgn
52 F7 **Aberaman** Rhondd
81 J2 **Aberangell** Gwynd
202 F1 **Aberarder** Highld
186 B4 **Aberargie** P & K
66 B2 **Aberarth** Cerdgn
51 L7 **Aberavon** Neath
53 G7 **Abercanaid** Myr Td
37 K2 **Abercarn** Caerph
64 B7 **Abercastle** Pembks
81 H3 **Abercegir** Powys
202 B5 **Aberchalder Lodge** Highld
216 C4 **Aberchirder** Abers
52 C5 **Abercraf** Powys
36 D2 **Abercregan** Neath
52 F7 **Abercwmboi** Rhondd
65 H6 **Abercych** Pembks
37 G2 **Abercynon** Rhondd
185 M4 **Aberdalgie** P & K
52 F7 **Aberdare** Rhondd
94 C7 **Aberdaron** Gwynd
207 H4 **Aberdeen** C Aber
207 G3 *Aberdeen Airport* C Aber
177 G2 **Aberdour** Fife
52 B7 **Aberdulais** Neath
80 E4 **Aberdyfi** Gwynd
68 C5 **Aberedw** Powys
48 D2 **Abereiddy** Pembks
95 G5 **Abererch** Gwynd
53 G7 **Aberfan** Myr Td
194 D6 **Aberfeldy** P & K
108 D7 **Aberffraw** IoA
124 C3 **Aberford** Leeds
184 C7 **Aberfoyle** Stirlg
53 L5 **Abergavenny** Mons
110 C6 **Abergele** Conwy
66 D7 **Abergorlech** Carmth
67 J4 **Abergwesyn** Powys
50 F2 **Abergwili** Carmth
36 D2 **Abergwynfi** Neath
109 J6 **Abergwyngregyn** Gwynd

80 F3 **Abergynolwyn** Gwynd
36 D4 **Aberkenfig** Brdgnd
178 B3 **Aberlady** E Loth
196 E5 **Aberlemno** Angus
81 G2 **Aberllefenni** Gwynd
68 D6 **Aberllynfi** Powys
215 G5 **Aberlour** Moray
82 D5 **Abermule** Powys
50 D2 **Abernant** Carmth
52 F7 **Aber-nant** Rhondd
186 C4 **Abernethy** P & K
186 D2 **Abernyte** P & K
65 J4 **Aberporth** Cerdgn
94 E6 **Abersoch** Gwynd
53 K7 **Abersychan** Torfn
36 F5 **Aberthin** V Glam
53 K7 **Abertillery** Blae G
37 H3 **Abertridwr** Caerph
97 G8 **Abertridwr** Powys
185 K4 **Aberuthven** P & K
80 D6 **Aberystwyth** Cerdgn
80 E6 **Aberystwyth Crematorium** Cerdgn
41 J2 **Abingdon** Oxon
31 J3 **Abinger Common** Surrey
31 H2 **Abinger Hammer** Surrey
73 L3 **Abington** Nhants
165 H6 **Abington** S Lans
75 K5 **Abington Pigotts** Cambs
165 H4 *Abington Services* S Lans
18 F3 **Abingworth** W Susx
102 B7 **Ab Kettleby** Leics
56 C6 **Ablington** Gloucs
114 D5 **Abney** Derbys
205 L5 **Aboyne** Abers
112 E2 **Abram** Wigan
212 E7 **Abriachan** Highld
45 J2 **Abridge** Essex
175 K3 **Abronhill** N Lans
39 G5 **Abson** S Glos
73 J5 **Abthorpe** Nhants
118 F5 **Aby** Lincs
124 E2 **Acaster Malbis** C York
124 E3 **Acaster Selby** N York
121 L5 **Accrington** Lancs
121 L5 **Accrington Crematorium** Lancs
188 F5 **Acha** Ag & B
172 D3 **Achahoish** Ag & B
195 H7 **Achalader** P & K
182 D1 **Achaleven** Ag & B
232 f3 **Acha Mor** W Isls
211 K3 **Achanalt** Highld
222 E6 **Achandunie** Highld
222 D2 **Achany** Highld
190 D3 **Acharacle** Highld
190 E6 **Acharn** Highld
194 B7 **Acharn** P & K
231 H6 **Achavanich** Highld
224 C7 **Achduart** Highld
228 D7 **Achfary** Highld
198 D4 **A'Chill** Highld
224 C6 **Achiltibuie** Highld
229 L4 **Achina** Highld
161 J6 **Achinhoan** Ag & B
210 E6 **Achintee** Highld
210 C6 **Achintraid** Highld
224 C4 **Achmelvich** Highld
210 D7 **Achmore** Highld
232 f3 **Achmore** W Isls
224 C3 **Achnacarnin** Highld
201 J7 **Achnacarry** Highld
199 J4 **Achnacloich** Highld
202 C2 **Achnaconeran** Highld
191 G7 **Achnacroish** Ag & B
189 L6 **Achnadrish House** Ag & B
185 J1 **Achnafauld** P & K
222 F7 **Achnagarron** Highld
189 L3 **Achnaha** Highld
224 B5 **Achnahaird** Highld

225 L6 **Achnairn** Highld
191 G4 **Achnalea** Highld
172 D2 **Achnamara** Ag & B
211 J3 **Achnasheen** Highld
210 F5 **Achnashellach Lodge** Highld
215 G7 **Achnastank** Moray
189 K3 **Achosnich** Highld
190 E6 **Achranich** Highld
230 E3 **Achreamie** Highld
192 B3 **Achriabhach** Highld
228 C5 **Achriesgill** Highld
229 K3 **Achtoty** Highld
88 E6 **Achurch** Nhants
222 F3 **Achvaich** Highld
230 E3 **Achvarasdal** Highld
231 L5 **Ackergill** Highld
141 L4 **Acklam** Middsb
134 B7 **Acklam** N York
84 D4 **Ackleton** Shrops
159 G2 **Acklington** Nthumb
124 C6 **Ackton** Wakefd
124 C7 **Ackworth Moor Top** Wakefd
93 J2 **Acle** Norfk
85 K6 **Acock's Green** Birm
35 J2 **Acol** Kent
124 E1 **Acomb** C York
150 B2 **Acomb** Nthumb
54 D2 **Aconbury** Herefs
98 F2 **Acton** Ches E
44 D4 **Acton** Gt Lon
99 J4 **Acton** Staffs
77 K5 **Acton** Suffk
70 E2 **Acton** Worcs
70 C4 **Acton Beauchamp** Herefs
112 E6 **Acton Bridge** Ches W
83 K3 **Acton Burnell** Shrops
70 C4 **Acton Green** Herefs
97 M3 **Acton Park** Wrexhm
84 B4 **Acton Round** Shrops
83 J5 **Acton Scott** Shrops
99 L8 **Acton Trussell** Staffs
39 J4 **Acton Turville** S Glos
99 H6 **Adbaston** Staffs
26 E7 **Adber** Dorset
101 L5 **Adbolton** Notts
72 F7 **Adderbury** Oxon
98 F4 **Adderley** Shrops
176 D5 **Addiewell** W Loth
123 J7 **Addingham** C Brad
58 C3 **Addington** Bucks
45 G7 **Addington** Gt Lon
33 H2 **Addington** Kent
45 G6 **Addiscombe** Gt Lon
43 H7 **Addlestone** Surrey
119 H7 **Addlethorpe** Lincs
59 H6 **Adeyfield** Herts
82 B4 **Adfa** Powys
69 H1 **Adforton** Herefs
35 G4 **Adisham** Kent
56 E3 **Adlestrop** Gloucs
125 K6 **Adlingfleet** E R Yk
121 J7 **Adlington** Lancs
100 B7 **Admaston** Staffs
84 B2 **Admaston** Wrekin
71 L5 **Admington** Warwks
65 J6 **Adpar** Cerdgn
25 L5 **Adsborough** Somset
25 J4 **Adscombe** Somset
58 C3 **Adstock** Bucks
73 H4 **Adstone** Nhants
31 H6 **Adversane** W Susx
214 D7 **Advie** Highld
124 E8 **Adwick Le Street** Donc
115 J2 **Adwick upon Dearne** Donc
155 H4 **Ae** D & G
155 H5 **Ae Bridgend** D & G
36 D2 **Afan Forest Park** Neath
216 B6 **Affleck** Abers
14 F4 **Affpuddle** Dorset
201 J2 **Affric Lodge** Highld

110 F6 **Afon-wen** Flints
16 D5 **Afton** IoW
113 J2 **Agecroft Crematorium** Salfd
131 K3 **Agglethorpe** N York
111 L4 **Aigburth** Lpool
126 C2 **Aike** E R Yk
148 E5 **Aiketgate** Cumb
148 B4 **Aikton** Cumb
89 G4 **Ailsworth** C Pete
132 E4 **Ainderby Quernhow** N York
132 E2 **Ainderby Steeple** N York
62 D4 **Aingers Green** Essex
120 D7 **Ainsdale** Sefton
148 F5 **Ainstable** Cumb
142 E5 **Ainthorpe** N York
176 F5 **Ainville** W Loth
181 M7 **Aird** Ag & B
144 D3 **Aird** D & G
232 g2 **Aird** W Isls
232 e3 **Aird a Mhulaidh** W Isls
232 e4 **Aird Asaig** W Isls
209 L6 **Aird Dhubh** Highld
182 E2 **Airdeny** Ag & B
181 H2 **Aird of Kinloch** Ag & B
199 J5 **Aird of Sleat** Highld
175 K5 **Airdrie** N Lans
175 K5 **Airdriehill** N Lans
182 E2 **Airds Bay** Ag & B
154 B7 **Airds of Kells** D & G
232 d2 **Aird Uig** W Isls
232 e3 **Airidh a bhruaich** W Isls
146 D4 **Airieland** D & G
195 L6 **Airlie** Angus
125 H5 **Airmyn** E R Yk
186 A1 **Airntully** P & K
199 L4 **Airor** Highld
176 B2 **Airth** Falk
131 G7 **Airton** N York
103 G5 **Aisby** Lincs
116 E3 **Aisby** Lincs
7 G4 **Aish** Devon
7 J4 **Aish** Devon
25 J4 **Aisholt** Somset
132 D2 **Aiskew** N York
134 B3 **Aislaby** N York
143 H5 **Aislaby** N York
141 J5 **Aislaby** S on T
116 F5 **Aisthorpe** Lincs
235 c5 **Aith** Shet
168 E4 **Akeld** Nthumb
73 K6 **Akeley** Bucks
78 D6 **Akenham** Suffk
6 B2 **Albaston** Cnwll
83 G1 **Alberbury** Shrops
19 H3 **Albourne** W Susx
84 E3 **Albrighton** Shrops
98 C8 **Albrighton** Shrops
92 F6 **Alburgh** Norfk
60 C3 **Albury** Herts
31 H2 **Albury** Surrey
31 H3 **Albury Heath** Surrey
212 E3 **Alcaig** Highld
83 J6 **Alcaston** Shrops
71 K3 **Alcester** Warwks
20 B5 **Alciston** E Susx
89 H7 **Alconbury** Cambs
89 H7 **Alconbury Weston** Cambs
132 F6 **Aldborough** N York
106 E5 **Aldborough** Norfk
40 E5 **Aldbourne** Wilts
127 G3 **Aldbrough** E R Yk
140 F5 **Aldbrough St John** N York
58 F5 **Aldbury** Herts
129 K7 **Aldcliffe** Lancs
194 E4 **Aldclune** P & K
79 K3 **Aldeburgh** Suffk
93 J5 **Aldeby** Norfk
43 J2 **Aldenham** Herts
28 D6 **Alderbury** Wilts

106 D8	**Alderford** Norfk	
28 C8	**Alderholt** Dorset	
39 H3	**Alderley** Gloucs	
113 J5	**Alderley Edge** Ches E	
86 D6	**Aldermans Green** Covtry	
41 L7	**Aldermaston** W Berk	
72 B5	**Alderminster** Warwks	
30 E2	**Aldershot** Hants	
55 M2	**Alderton** Gloucs	
73 K5	**Alderton** Nhants	
79 H6	**Alderton** Suffk	
39 J4	**Alderton** Wilts	
100 F2	**Alderwasley** Derbys	
132 D5	**Aldfield** N York	
98 B2	**Aldford** Ches W	
88 E3	**Aldgate** Rutlnd	
61 L3	**Aldham** Essex	
78 C5	**Aldham** Suffk	
18 C5	**Aldingbourne** W Susx	
129 G5	**Aldingham** Cumb	
34 E7	**Aldington** Kent	
71 J5	**Aldington** Worcs	
34 E7	**Aldington Corner** Kent	
205 H1	**Aldivalloch** Moray	
174 C1	**Aldochlay** Ag & B	
90 C8	**Aldreth** Cambs	
85 J4	**Aldridge** Wsall	
79 J3	**Aldringham** Suffk	
56 D6	**Aldsworth** Gloucs	
215 H8	**Aldunie** Moray	
100 E2	**Aldwark** Derbys	
133 G6	**Aldwark** N York	
18 C6	**Aldwick** W Susx	
88 E6	**Aldwincle** Nhants	
41 K4	**Aldworth** W Berk	
174 D3	**Alexandria** W Duns	
25 J4	**Aley** Somset	
12 E3	**Alfington** Devon	
31 H5	**Alfold** Surrey	
31 H4	**Alfold Crossways** Surrey	
206 B3	**Alford** Abers	
118 F6	**Alford** Lincs	
26 E5	**Alford** Somset	
118 F6	**Alford Crematorium** Lincs	
101 H2	**Alfreton** Derbys	
70 D4	**Alfrick** Worcs	
70 D4	**Alfrick Pound** Worcs	
20 B5	**Alfriston** E Susx	
103 M5	**Algarkirk** Lincs	
26 F4	**Alhampton** Somset	
125 K6	**Alkborough** N Linc	
35 H6	**Alkham** Kent	
100 D5	**Alkmonton** Derbys	
7 J5	**Allaleigh** Devon	
204 D6	**Allanaquoich** Abers	
175 L6	**Allanbank** N Lans	
179 H7	**Allanton** Border	
175 L6	**Allanton** N Lans	
175 K7	**Allanton** S Lans	
54 F6	**Allaston** Gloucs	
29 J7	**Allbrook** Hants	
40 B7	**All Cannings** Wilts	
149 L4	**Allendale** Nthumb	
85 L4	**Allen End** Warwks	
149 L6	**Allenheads** Nthumb	
60 D5	**Allen's Green** Herts	
69 J7	**Allensmore** Herefs	
101 G6	**Allenton** C Derb	
24 B6	**Aller** Devon	
26 B5	**Aller** Somset	
147 J6	**Allerby** Cumb	
12 D4	**Allercombe** Devon	
24 D3	**Allerford** Somset	
134 D3	**Allerston** N York	
125 J2	**Allerthorpe** E R Yk	
123 G4	**Allerton** C Brad	
213 H2	**Allerton** Highld	
111 L4	**Allerton** Lpool	
124 C5	**Allerton Bywater** Leeds	
132 F7	**Allerton Mauleverer** N York	
86 C7	**Allesley** Covtry	
101 G5	**Allestree** C Derb	
88 B4	**Allexton** Leics	
113 L7	**Allgreave** Ches E	
46 D4	**Allhallows** Medway	
210 C3	**Alligin Shuas** Highld	
13 L4	**Allington** Dorset	
102 E4	**Allington** Lincs	
28 D4	**Allington** Wilts	
39 K5	**Allington** Wilts	
40 B7	**Allington** Wilts	
129 J4	**Allithwaite** Cumb	
147 J6	**Allonby** Cumb	
163 J5	**Alloway** S Ayrs	
26 B8	**Allowenshay** Somset	
83 J4	**All Stretton** Shrops	
192 C6	**Alltchaorunn** Highld	
66 B7	**Alltwalis** Carmth	
51 K5	**Alltwen** Neath	
66 C5	**Alltyblaca** Cerdgn	
26 F8	**Allweston** Dorset	
69 G4	**Almeley** Herefs	
99 G5	**Almington** Staffs	
185 M3	**Almondbank** P & K	
123 H7	**Almondbury** Kirk	
38 E4	**Almondsbury** S Glos	
133 G6	**Alne** N York	
222 E7	**Alness** Highld	
168 E7	**Alnham** Nthumb	
169 J7	**Alnmouth** Nthumb	
169 J6	**Alnwick** Nthumb	
44 D4	**Alperton** Gt Lon	
77 K4	**Alphamstone** Essex	
77 K4	**Alpheton** Suffk	
11 L6	**Alphington** Devon	
114 E8	**Alport** Derbys	
98 E1	**Alpraham** Ches E	
62 C4	**Alresford** Essex	
85 L1	**Alrewas** Staffs	
99 H2	**Alsager** Ches E	
100 D3	**Alsop en le Dale** Derbys	
149 J5	**Alston** Cumb	
13 H2	**Alston** Devon	
55 M2	**Alstone** Gloucs	
100 C2	**Alstonefield** Staffs	
26 B2	**Alston Sutton** Somset	
23 L8	**Alswear** Devon	
224 B6	**Altandhu** Highld	
9 G8	**Altarnun** Cnwll	
222 C2	**Altass** Highld	
190 D8	**Altcreich** Ag & B	
173 H4	**Altgaltraig** Ag & B	
61 L7	**Althorne** Essex	
125 K8	**Althorpe** N Linc	
230 E6	**Altnabreac Station** Highld	
182 B2	**Altnacraig** Ag & B	
225 M2	**Altnaharra** Highld	
115 G8	**Alton** Derbys	
30 B4	**Alton** Hants	
100 B4	**Alton** Staffs	
40 C7	**Alton Barnes** Wilts	
14 D3	**Alton Pancras** Dorset	
40 C7	**Alton Priors** Wilts	
100 B4	**Alton Towers** Staffs	
113 H4	**Altrincham** Traffd	
113 G4	**Altrincham Crematorium** Traffd	
184 B6	**Altskeith Hotel** Stirlg	
185 J7	**Alva** Clacks	
112 C6	**Alvanley** Ches W	
101 H5	**Alvaston** C Derb	
85 J8	**Alvechurch** Worcs	
86 B3	**Alvecote** Warwks	
27 L6	**Alvediston** Wilts	
84 D6	**Alveley** Shrops	
23 H6	**Alverdiscott** Devon	
17 H3	**Alverstoke** Hants	
17 H5	**Alverstone** IoW	
123 L6	**Alverthorpe** Wakefd	
102 C4	**Alverton** Notts	
214 E6	**Alves** Moray	
56 F6	**Alvescot** Oxon	
38 F3	**Alveston** S Glos	
72 B3	**Alveston** Warwks	
118 E4	**Alvingham** Lincs	
54 E7	**Alvington** Gloucs	
89 G4	**Alwalton** C Pete	
168 D7	**Alwinton** Nthumb	
123 K3	**Alwoodley** Leeds	
195 K6	**Alyth** P & K	
101 G3	**Ambergate** Derbys	
55 J7	**Amberley** Gloucs	
18 D3	**Amberley** W Susx	
159 G2	**Amble** Nthumb	
84 F6	**Amblecote** Dudley	
123 G5	**Ambler Thorn** C Brad	
137 K6	**Ambleside** Cumb	
49 G3	**Ambleston** Pembks	
57 L4	**Ambrosden** Oxon	
125 K7	**Amcotts** N Linc	
42 F2	**Amersham** Bucks	
42 F2	**Amersham Common** Bucks	
42 F2	**Amersham Old Town** Bucks	
58 F7	**Amersham on the Hill** Bucks	
28 D3	**Amesbury** Wilts	
232 d4	**Amhuinnsuidhe** W Isls	
86 B3	**Amington** Staffs	
155 H5	**Amisfield Town** D & G	
108 F3	**Amlwch** IoA	
51 J3	**Ammanford** Carmth	
134 B5	**Amotherby** N York	
29 H6	**Ampfield** Hants	
133 J4	**Ampleforth** N York	
56 B7	**Ampney Crucis** Gloucs	
56 C7	**Ampney St Mary** Gloucs	
56 B7	**Ampney St Peter** Gloucs	
28 F3	**Amport** Hants	
74 F6	**Ampthill** C Beds	
77 J1	**Ampton** Suffk	
49 K6	**Amroth** Pembks	
185 J1	**Amulree** P & K	
59 K5	**Amwell** Herts	
191 G4	**Anaheilt** Highld	
103 G4	**Ancaster** Lincs	
168 E1	**Ancroft** Nthumb	
167 K4	**Ancrum** Border	
119 G6	**Anderby** Lincs	
29 G3	**Andover** Hants	
56 A4	**Andoversford** Gloucs	
237 d2	**Andreas** IoM	
45 G6	**Anerley** Gt Lon	
111 K3	**Anfield** Lpool	
111 K3	**Anfield Crematorium** Lpool	
3 G4	**Angarrack** Cnwll	
83 L7	**Angelbank** Shrops	
48 E6	**Angle** Pembks	
108 E5	**Anglesey** IoA	
18 E5	**Angmering** W Susx	
124 D2	**Angram** N York	
223 H6	**Ankerville** Highld	
126 C5	**Anlaby** E R Yk	
105 H6	**Anmer** Norfk	
17 J1	**Anmore** Hants	
147 L2	**Annan** D & G	
155 J4	**Annandale Water Services** D & G	
210 D4	**Annat** Highld	
175 J4	**Annathill** N Lans	
29 G3	**Anna Valley** Hants	
163 K5	**Annbank** S Ayrs	
71 L4	**Anne Hathaway's Cottage** Warwks	
101 J2	**Annesley** Notts	
101 J2	**Annesley Woodhouse** Notts	
150 F5	**Annfield Plain** Dur	
174 F5	**Anniesland** C Glas	
120 D5	**Ansdell** Lancs	
26 F5	**Ansford** Somset	
86 C5	**Ansley** Warwks	
100 E7	**Anslow** Staffs	
100 D7	**Anslow Gate** Staffs	
60 C2	**Anstey** Herts	
87 G2	**Anstey** Leics	
187 J6	**Anstruther** Fife	
19 J2	**Ansty** W Susx	
86 E6	**Ansty** Warwks	
27 L6	**Ansty** Wilts	
147 L4	**Anthorn** Cumb	
106 F5	**Antingham** Norfk	
232 d5	**An t-Ob** W Isls	
103 M3	**Anton's Gowt** Lincs	
6 B5	**Antony** Cnwll	
112 F5	**Antrobus** Ches W	
103 J3	**Anwick** Lincs	
145 M4	**Anwoth** D & G	
32 D2	**Aperfield** Gt Lon	
88 E4	**Apethorpe** Nhants	
117 J6	**Apley** Lincs	
115 G5	**Apperknowle** Derbys	
55 K3	**Apperley** Gloucs	
191 J6	**Appin** Ag & B	
126 B7	**Appleby** N Linc	
139 G3	**Appleby-in-Westmorland** Cumb	
86 C2	**Appleby Magna** Leics	
86 C2	**Appleby Parva** Leics	
209 L5	**Applecross** Highld	
23 G5	**Appledore** Devon	
25 G8	**Appledore** Devon	
34 C8	**Appledore** Kent	
41 K2	**Appleford** Oxon	
155 J5	**Applegarth Town** D & G	
28 F2	**Appleshaw** Hants	
112 D4	**Appleton** Halton	
57 H7	**Appleton** Oxon	
112 F5	**Appleton** Warrtn	
133 L3	**Appleton-le-Moors** N York	
134 B5	**Appleton-le-Street** N York	
124 E3	**Appleton Roebuck** N York	
112 F5	**Appleton Thorn** Warrtn	
141 J6	**Appleton Wiske** N York	
167 H6	**Appletreehall** Border	
131 K7	**Appletreewick** N York	
25 G6	**Appley** Somset	
121 G8	**Appley Bridge** Lancs	
17 G5	**Apse Heath** IoW	
59 J2	**Apsley End** C Beds	
18 A5	**Apuldram** W Susx	
223 H6	**Arabella** Highld	
196 F7	**Arbirlot** Angus	
223 J5	**Arboll** Highld	
42 C6	**Arborfield** Wokham	
42 C6	**Arborfield Cross** Wokham	
197 G7	**Arbroath** Angus	
197 K2	**Arbuthnott** Abers	
50 F5	**Archddu** Carmth	
141 G4	**Archdeacon Newton** Darltn	
174 D3	**Archencarroch** W Duns	
214 F5	**Archiestown** Moray	
99 H1	**Arclid Green** Ches E	
217 J6	**Ardallie** Abers	
182 F3	**Ardanaiseig Hotel** Ag & B	
210 C7	**Ardaneaskan** Highld	
210 C6	**Ardarroch** Highld	
160 D1	**Ardbeg** Ag & B	
173 J5	**Ardbeg** Ag & B	
173 K2	**Ardbeg** Ag & B	
220 F4	**Ardcharnich** Highld	
180 E4	**Ardchiavaig** Ag & B	
182 D5	**Ardchonnel** Ag & B	
184 D5	**Ardchullarie More** Stirlg	
183 J7	**Arddarroch** Ag & B	
201 H7	**Ardechive** Highld	
163 H2	**Ardeer** N Ayrs	
60 A3	**Ardeley** Herts	

210 D8 **Ardelve** Highld
174 C2 **Arden** Ag & B
71 K4 **Ardens Grafton**
Warwks
182 B3 **Ardentallen** Ag & B
173 L2 **Ardentinny** Ag & B
173 H4 **Ardentraive** Ag & B
184 E1 **Ardeonaig** Stirlg
213 J4 **Ardersier** Highld
220 D8 **Ardessie** Highld
182 A6 **Ardfern** Ag & B
171 K4 **Ardfernal** Ag & B
222 D4 **Ardgay** Highld
191 K4 **Ardgour** Highld
173 L4 **Ardgowan** Inver
173 K4 **Ardhallow** Ag & B
232 e4 **Ardhasig** W Isls
210 B3 **Ardheslaig** Highld
220 F4 **Ardindrean** Highld
32 C7 **Ardingly** W Susx
41 H3 **Ardington** Oxon
173 G5 **Ardlamont** Ag & B
62 C3 **Ardleigh** Essex
62 C2 **Ardleigh Heath** Essex
195 L7 **Ardler** P & K
57 K3 **Ardley** Oxon
183 K4 **Ardlui** Ag & B
172 B2 **Ardlussa** Ag & B
191 L8 **Ardmaddy** Ag & B
220 E2 **Ardmair** Highld
173 J5 **Ardmaleish** Ag & B
172 B8 **Ardminish** Ag & B
190 E3 **Ardmolich** Highld
174 C3 **Ardmore** Ag & B
222 F4 **Ardmore** Highld
173 K3 **Ardnadam** Ag & B
212 E4 **Ardnagrask** Highld
210 D7 **Ardnarff** Highld
190 F4 **Ardnastang** Highld
183 G5 **Ardno** Ag & B
172 C6 **Ardpatrick** Ag & B
172 E2 **Ardrishaig** Ag & B
222 E6 **Ardross** Highld
163 G2 **Ardrossan** N Ayrs
123 K5 **Ardsley East** Leeds
190 B4 **Ardslignish** Highld
171 J7 **Ardtalla** Ag & B
190 C3 **Ardtoe** Highld
182 A5 **Arduaine** Ag & B
212 E2 **Ardullie** Highld
199 K5 **Ardvasar** Highld
184 D3 **Ardvorlich** P & K
232 e3 **Ardvourlie** W Isls
144 D5 **Ardwell** D & G
113 J3 **Ardwick** Manch
70 E1 **Areley Kings** Worcs
190 D3 **Arevegaig** Highld
30 D4 **Arford** Hants
53 J7 **Argoed** Caerph
183 J6 **Argyll Forest Park**
Ag & B
232 e3 **Aribruach** W Isls
180 D3 **Aridhglas** Ag & B
188 F5 **Arileod** Ag & B
189 G5 **Arinagour** Ag & B
182 C3 **Ariogan** Ag & B
199 K7 **Arisaig** Highld
199 L7 **Arisaig House** Highld
132 F7 **Arkendale** N York
76 C7 **Arkesden** Essex
130 B5 **Arkholme** Lancs
156 C4 **Arkleton** D & G
44 E2 **Arkley** Gt Lon
115 L1 **Arksey** Donc
115 H7 **Arkwright Town**
Derbys
55 L4 **Arle** Gloucs
136 E4 **Arlecdon** Cumb
75 H7 **Arlesey** C Beds
84 B2 **Arleston** Wrekin
112 F5 **Arley** Ches E
86 C5 **Arley** Warwks
55 G6 **Arlingham** Gloucs
23 K4 **Arlington** Devon
20 B4 **Arlington** E Susx
199 K5 **Armadale** Highld

230 A3 **Armadale** Highld
176 C5 **Armadale** W Loth
137 G2 **Armaside** Cumb
148 E5 **Armathwaite** Cumb
92 F3 **Arminghall** Norfk
85 J1 **Armitage** Staffs
123 K4 **Armley** Leeds
88 F6 **Armston** Nhants
115 L1 **Armthorpe** Donc
188 F4 **Arnabost** Ag & B
131 H5 **Arncliffe** N York
187 H6 **Arncroach** Fife
215 G5 **Arndilly House** Moray
15 H5 **Arne** Dorset
87 H5 **Arnesby** Leics
186 B5 **Arngask** P & K
200 C3 **Arnisdale** Highld
209 J5 **Arnish** Highld
177 K6 **Arniston** Mdloth
232 f1 **Arnol** W Isls
126 E3 **Arnold** E R Yk
101 L4 **Arnold** Notts
184 D7 **Arnprior** Stirlg
129 K4 **Arnside** Cumb
190 B7 **Aros** Ag & B
129 G4 **Arrad Foot** Cumb
126 C2 **Arram** E R Yk
162 B3 **Arran** N Ayrs
132 C2 **Arrathorne** N York
17 G5 **Arreton** IoW
210 B3 **Arrina** Highld
75 K4 **Arrington** Cambs
183 K6 **Arrochar** Ag & B
71 J3 **Arrow** Warwks
83 J2 **Arscott** Shrops
212 F4 **Artafallie** Highld
123 K2 **Arthington** Leeds
87 L7 **Arthingworth** Nhants
217 H6 **Arthrath** Abers
217 J7 **Artrochie** Abers
18 D4 **Arundel** W Susx
136 E3 **Asby** Cumb
173 J5 **Ascog** Ag & B
42 F6 **Ascot** W & M
56 F4 **Ascott-under-**
Wychwood Oxon
132 F4 **Asenby** N York
102 B8 **Asfordby** Leics
102 B8 **Asfordby Hill** Leics
103 J4 **Asgarby** Lincs
118 D7 **Asgarby** Lincs
35 H3 **Ash** Kent
45 L6 **Ash** Kent
26 C7 **Ash** Somset
30 E2 **Ash** Surrey
41 K5 **Ashampstead** W Berk
78 E4 **Ashbocking** Suffk
100 D3 **Ashbourne** Derbys
25 G6 **Ashbrittle** Somset
7 H2 **Ashburton** Devon
10 D5 **Ashbury** Devon
40 E4 **Ashbury** Oxon
125 L8 **Ashby** N Linc
118 F7 **Ashby by Partney**
Lincs
118 C2 **Ashby cum Fenby**
NE Lin
103 H2 **Ashby de la Launde**
Lincs
86 D1 **Ashby-de-la-Zouch**
Leics
87 K2 **Ashby Folville** Leics
87 H5 **Ashby Magna** Leics
87 G5 **Ashby Parva** Leics
118 D7 **Ashby Puerorum**
Lincs
73 H2 **Ashby St Ledgers**
Nhants
93 G3 **Ashby St Mary** Norfk
55 L2 **Ashchurch** Gloucs
11 L8 **Ashcombe** Devon
37 M7 **Ashcombe** N Som
26 C4 **Ashcott** Somset
76 E6 **Ashdon** Essex
29 K2 **Ashe** Hants
62 A7 **Asheldham** Essex

77 H6 **Ashen** Essex
58 B5 **Ashendon** Bucks
58 C7 **Asheridge** Bucks
185 G6 **Ashfield** Stirlg
78 E3 **Ashfield cum Thorpe**
Suffk
92 F8 **Ashfield Green** Suffk
7 G6 **Ashford** Devon
23 H4 **Ashford** Devon
34 D6 **Ashford** Kent
43 H6 **Ashford** Surrey
69 K1 **Ashford Bowdler**
Shrops
69 K1 **Ashford Carbonell**
Shrops
41 K7 **Ashford Hill** Hants
114 D7 **Ashford in the Water**
Derbys
175 K7 **Ashgill** S Lans
30 E2 **Ash Green** Surrey
86 D6 **Ash Green** Warwks
12 E1 **Ashill** Devon
91 K3 **Ashill** Norfk
25 L7 **Ashill** Somset
46 E2 **Ashingdon** Essex
159 G5 **Ashington** Nthumb
26 E6 **Ashington** Somset
18 F3 **Ashington** W Susx
167 G5 **Ashkirk** Border
55 J3 **Ashleworth** Gloucs
55 J3 **Ashleworth Quay**
Gloucs
77 G3 **Ashley** Cambs
113 H5 **Ashley** Ches E
10 F5 **Ashley** Devon
39 L2 **Ashley** Gloucs
16 B4 **Ashley** Hants
29 G5 **Ashley** Hants
35 J5 **Ashley** Kent
87 L5 **Ashley** Nhants
99 H5 **Ashley** Staffs
39 J6 **Ashley** Wilts
58 F6 **Ashley Green** Bucks
98 E4 **Ash Magna** Shrops
41 H8 **Ashmansworth** Hants
22 E7 **Ashmansworthy**
Devon
24 C6 **Ash Mill** Devon
27 K7 **Ashmore** Dorset
41 J6 **Ashmore Green**
W Berk
72 C3 **Ashorne** Warwks
115 G8 **Ashover** Derbys
72 C1 **Ashow** Warwks
70 B6 **Ashperton** Herefs
7 J4 **Ashprington** Devon
25 J5 **Ash Priors** Somset
10 F3 **Ashreigney** Devon
78 B5 **Ash Street** Suffk
44 D8 **Ashtead** Surrey
12 C1 **Ash Thomas** Devon
112 D7 **Ashton** Ches W
3 G5 **Ashton** Cnwll
11 K7 **Ashton** Devon
69 K2 **Ashton** Herefs
173 L3 **Ashton** Inver
73 L5 **Ashton** Nhants
88 F5 **Ashton** Nhants
39 K8 **Ashton Common**
Wilts
112 E2 **Ashton-in-**
Makerfield Wigan
40 B2 **Ashton Keynes** Wilts
71 H6 **Ashton under Hill**
Worcs
113 L2 **Ashton-under-Lyne**
Tamesd
16 D1 **Ashurst** Hants
32 F5 **Ashurst** Kent
19 G3 **Ashurst** W Susx
32 D5 **Ashurstwood** W Susx
30 E2 **Ash Vale** Surrey
9 K5 **Ashwater** Devon
75 J6 **Ashwell** Herts
88 C2 **Ashwell** Rutlnd
75 J6 **Ashwell End** Herts

92 D4 **Ashwellthorpe** Norfk
26 F2 **Ashwick** Somset
105 H8 **Ashwicken** Norfk
128 F4 **Askam in Furness**
Cumb
124 E7 **Askern** Donc
14 A4 **Askerswell** Dorset
58 D6 **Askett** Bucks
138 D3 **Askham** Cumb
116 C6 **Askham** Notts
124 E3 **Askham Bryan** C York
124 E2 **Askham Richard**
C York
172 F1 **Asknish** Ag & B
131 H2 **Askrigg** N York
123 H2 **Askwith** N York
103 H6 **Aslackby** Lincs
92 D5 **Aslacton** Norfk
102 C4 **Aslockton** Notts
147 K6 **Aspatria** Cumb
60 B3 **Aspenden** Herts
74 D7 **Aspley Guise** C Beds
74 D7 **Aspley Heath** C Beds
121 J8 **Aspull** Wigan
125 H5 **Asselby** E R Yk
77 L6 **Assington** Suffk
77 H4 **Assington Green**
Suffk
99 J1 **Astbury** Ches E
73 J4 **Astcote** Nhants
118 C5 **Asterby** Lincs
83 H3 **Asterley** Shrops
83 H5 **Asterton** Shrops
56 F5 **Asthall** Oxon
56 F5 **Asthall Leigh** Oxon
223 G3 **Astle** Highld
98 D8 **Astley** Shrops
86 C5 **Astley** Warwks
113 G2 **Astley** Wigan
70 D2 **Astley** Worcs
84 C4 **Astley Abbots** Shrops
121 K7 **Astley Bridge** Bolton
70 E1 **Astley Cross** Worcs
98 E3 **Aston** Ches E
112 E5 **Aston** Ches E
114 D5 **Aston** Derbys
111 J7 **Aston** Flints
59 L4 **Aston** Herts
57 G7 **Aston** Oxon
115 J4 **Aston** Rothm
84 E5 **Aston** Shrops
98 D6 **Aston** Shrops
99 H4 **Aston** Staffs
99 K6 **Aston** Staffs
99 K7 **Aston** Staffs
42 C4 **Aston** Wokham
84 B2 **Aston** Wrekin
58 D4 **Aston Abbotts** Bucks
84 B6 **Aston Botterell**
Shrops
71 K3 **Aston Cantlow**
Warwks
58 E5 **Aston Clinton** Bucks
54 F4 **Aston Crews** Herefs
59 L3 **Aston End** Herts
71 G1 **Aston Fields** Worcs
86 F5 **Aston Flamville** Leics
55 G4 **Aston Ingham** Herefs
72 F4 **Aston le Walls** Nhants
71 L7 **Aston Magna** Gloucs
83 K6 **Aston Munslow**
Shrops
83 H6 **Aston on Clun** Shrops
83 G3 **Aston Pigott** Shrops
83 G3 **Aston Rogers** Shrops
58 B7 **Aston Rowant** Oxon
71 J6 **Aston Somerville**
Worcs
71 K6 **Aston Subedge**
Gloucs
41 K3 **Aston Tirrold** Oxon
101 H6 **Aston-upon-Trent**
Derbys
41 K3 **Aston Upthorpe**
Oxon
75 J6 **Astwick** C Beds

74 D5 **Astwood** M Keyn	77 J4 **Audley End** Suffk	116 B5 **Babworth** Notts	187 K5 **Balcomie Links** Fife
71 G2 **Astwood** Worcs	76 D6 **Audley End House** Essex	234 d4 **Backaland** Ork	132 E4 **Baldersby** N York
71 J3 **Astwood Bank** Worcs	148 A7 **Aughertree** Cumb	217 J4 **Backfolds** Abers	132 E4 **Baldersby St James** N York
70 F3 **Astwood Crematorium** Worcs	125 G3 **Aughton** E R Yk	111 L6 **Backford** Ches W	121 J4 **Balderstone** Lancs
103 H4 **Aswarby** Lincs	111 L1 **Aughton** Lancs	223 H2 **Backies** Highld	102 D3 **Balderton** Notts
118 E7 **Aswardby** Lincs	129 L6 **Aughton** Lancs	199 K7 **Back of Keppoch** Highld	187 G5 **Baldinnie** Fife
83 K2 **Atcham** Shrops	115 J4 **Aughton** Rothm	38 C6 **Backwell** N Som	185 L4 **Baldinnies** P & K
14 E4 **Athelhampton** Dorset	28 E1 **Aughton** Wilts	106 D5 **Baconsthorpe** Norfk	75 J7 **Baldock** Herts
78 E1 **Athelington** Suffk	112 B1 **Aughton Park** Lancs	54 A2 **Bacton** Herefs	75 J6 **Baldock Services** Herts
25 M5 **Athelney** Somset	213 L4 **Auldearn** Highld	107 H5 **Bacton** Norfk	187 G2 **Baldovie** C Dund
178 C3 **Athelstaneford** E Loth	69 J4 **Aulden** Herefs	78 C2 **Bacton** Suffk	237 d5 **Baldrine** IoM
23 J6 **Atherington** Devon	154 F5 **Auldgirth** D & G	122 C6 **Bacup** Lancs	20 F3 **Baldslow** E Susx
86 C4 **Atherstone** Warwks	175 H7 **Auldhouse** S Lans	219 J6 **Badachro** Highld	106 B5 **Bale** Norfk
72 B4 **Atherstone on Stour** Warwks	200 E2 **Ault a' chruinn** Highld	40 D4 **Badbury** Swindn	186 D2 **Baledgarno** P & K
113 G2 **Atherton** Wigan	219 K4 **Aultbea** Highld	73 H3 **Badby** Nhants	188 C7 **Balemartine** Ag & B
100 E3 **Atlow** Derbys	219 H4 **Aultgrishin** Highld	228 B7 **Badcall** Highld	177 G5 **Balerno** C Edin
210 E6 **Attadale** Highld	221 J7 **Aultguish Inn** Highld	228 C4 **Badcall** Highld	186 D6 **Balfarg** Fife
117 G3 **Atterby** Lincs	115 J7 **Ault Hucknall** Derbys	220 D3 **Badcaul** Highld	196 E3 **Balfield** Angus
115 G4 **Attercliffe** Sheff	215 J4 **Aultmore** Moray	86 B8 **Baddesley Clinton** Warwks	234 c5 **Balfour** Ork
86 D4 **Atterton** Leics	202 E2 **Aultnagoire** Highld	86 C4 **Baddesley Ensor** Warwks	174 F1 **Balfron** Stirlg
92 C4 **Attleborough** Norfk	222 F5 **Aultnamain Inn** Highld	224 D4 **Baddidarrach** Highld	216 C6 **Balgaveny** Abers
86 D5 **Attleborough** Warwks	103 H5 **Aunsby** Lincs	176 F7 **Baddinsgill** Border	196 E6 **Balgavies** Angus
92 D1 **Attlebridge** Norfk	38 E3 **Aust** S Glos	216 D6 **Badenscoth** Abers	185 L8 **Balgonar** Fife
77 G4 **Attleton Green** Suffk	116 A3 **Austerfield** Donc	205 H2 **Badenyon** Abers	144 D6 **Balgowan** D & G
126 F1 **Atwick** E R Yk	86 C3 **Austrey** Warwks	84 D4 **Badger** Shrops	202 F6 **Balgowan** Highld
39 J7 **Atworth** Wilts	130 E5 **Austwick** N York	55 K4 **Badgeworth** Gloucs	218 B7 **Balgown** Highld
116 F8 **Aubourn** Lincs	118 E5 **Authorpe** Lincs	26 B2 **Badgworth** Somset	144 B3 **Balgracie** D & G
217 G7 **Auchedly** Abers	40 C6 **Avebury** Wilts	210 B8 **Badicaul** Highld	196 C8 **Balgray** Angus
197 H1 **Auchenblae** Abers	45 L4 **Aveley** Thurr	79 G2 **Badingham** Suffk	165 H5 **Balgray** S Lans
175 L2 **Auchenbowie** Stirlg	39 K2 **Avening** Gloucs	34 D4 **Badlesmere** Kent	44 F5 **Balham** Gt Lon
146 D5 **Auchencairn** D & G	102 C2 **Averham** Notts	165 K5 **Badlieu** Border	195 L6 **Balhary** P & K
155 G5 **Auchencairn** D & G	7 G6 **Aveton Gifford** Devon	231 J5 **Badlipster** Highld	186 B1 **Balholmie** P & K
162 D4 **Auchencairn** N Ayrs	203 L3 **Aviemore** Highld	220 C3 **Badluachrach** Highld	230 C3 **Baligill** Highld
179 H6 **Auchencrow** Border	41 G6 **Avington** W Berk	223 G3 **Badninish** Highld	195 L5 **Balintore** Angus
177 H6 **Auchendinny** Mdloth	213 G4 **Avoch** Highld	220 D3 **Badrallach** Highld	223 J6 **Balintore** Highld
176 D7 **Auchengray** S Lans	15 L3 **Avon** Hants	71 J5 **Badsey** Worcs	223 G7 **Balintraid** Highld
215 J3 **Auchenhalrig** Moray	176 B4 **Avonbridge** Falk	30 E2 **Badshot Lea** Surrey	233 b6 **Balivanich** W Isls
164 F2 **Auchenheath** S Lans	72 E4 **Avon Dassett** Warwks	124 C7 **Badsworth** Wakefd	196 B7 **Balkeerie** Angus
154 E3 **Auchenhessnane** D & G	38 D5 **Avonmouth** Bristl	78 B2 **Badwell Ash** Suffk	125 J3 **Balkholme** E R Yk
173 G4 **Auchenlochan** Ag & B	7 G4 **Avonwick** Devon	27 H8 **Bagber** Dorset	237 e4 **Ballajora** IoM
174 C8 **Auchenmade** N Ayrs	28 F6 **Awbridge** Hants	133 G4 **Bagby** N York	173 H6 **Ballanlay** Ag & B
144 F4 **Auchenmalg** D & G	12 E3 **Awliscombe** Devon	118 E6 **Bag Enderby** Lincs	152 C5 **Ballantrae** S Ayrs
174 C8 **Auchentiber** N Ayrs	55 G6 **Awre** Gloucs	56 A6 **Bagendon** Gloucs	237 b6 **Ballasalla** IoM
184 C8 **Auchentroig** Stirlg	101 J4 **Awsworth** Notts	233 b9 **Bagh a Chaisteil** W Isls	205 J6 **Ballater** Abers
221 G5 **Auchindrean** Highld	26 B1 **Axbridge** Somset	233 b9 **Bagh a Tuath** W Isls	237 c3 **Ballaugh** IoM
216 C5 **Auchininna** Abers	29 L3 **Axford** Hants	111 H6 **Bagillt** Flints	223 G6 **Ballchraggan** Highld
164 B5 **Auchinleck** E Ayrs	40 E6 **Axford** Wilts	86 D8 **Baginton** Warwks	178 B3 **Ballencrieff** E Loth
175 J3 **Auchinstarry** N Lans	13 H3 **Axminster** Devon	51 L6 **Baglan** Neath	188 B6 **Ballevullin** Ag & B
191 L2 **Auchintore** Highld	13 G4 **Axmouth** Devon	98 B6 **Bagley** Shrops	100 D2 **Ballidon** Derbys
217 K6 **Auchiries** Abers	141 G3 **Aycliffe** Dur	26 C3 **Bagley** Somset	161 L2 **Balliekine** N Ayrs
207 G6 **Auchlee** Abers	150 C2 **Aydon** Nthumb	99 L3 **Bagnall** Staffs	182 F7 **Balliemore** Ag & B
206 C1 **Auchleven** Abers	54 E7 **Aylburton** Gloucs	83 L8 **Bagot** Shrops	152 F4 **Balligmorrie** S Ayrs
164 F3 **Auchlochan** S Lans	12 D4 **Aylesbeare** Devon	42 E7 **Bagshot** Surrey	172 F2 **Ballimore** Ag & B
206 B5 **Auchlossan** Abers	58 D5 **Aylesbury** Bucks	39 G3 **Bagstone** S Glos	184 C4 **Ballimore** Stirlg
184 B2 **Auchlyne** Stirlg	126 F8 **Aylesby** NE Lin	86 F2 **Bagworth** Leics	214 E6 **Ballindalloch** Moray
164 A4 **Auchmillan** E Ayrs	33 J2 **Aylesford** Kent	54 C3 **Bagwy Llydiart** Herefs	186 D2 **Ballindean** P & K
197 G7 **Auchmithie** Angus	35 H4 **Aylesham** Kent	123 H3 **Baildon** C Brad	58 E7 **Ballinger Common** Bucks
186 C6 **Auchmuirbridge** Fife	87 H4 **Aylestone** C Leic	123 H3 **Baildon Green** C Brad	54 E2 **Ballingham** Herefs
196 D4 **Auchnacree** Angus	106 E5 **Aylmerton** Norfk	232 f3 **Baile Ailein** W Isls	186 C7 **Ballingry** Fife
217 H6 **Auchnagatt** Abers	106 E6 **Aylsham** Norfk	233 b6 **Baile a Mhanaich** W Isls	194 F6 **Ballinluig** P & K
204 F2 **Auchnarrow** Moray	70 B6 **Aylton** Herefs	180 D3 **Baile Mor** Ag & B	196 C5 **Ballinshoe** Angus
144 B3 **Auchnotteroch** D & G	56 C4 **Aylworth** Gloucs	175 J5 **Baillieston** C Glas	195 H5 **Ballintuim** P & K
215 H4 **Auchroisk** Moray	69 H2 **Aymestrey** Herefs	131 H2 **Bainbridge** N York	213 H5 **Balloch** Highld
185 K5 **Auchterarder** P & K	57 K2 **Aynho** Nhants	216 B7 **Bainshole** Abers	175 K4 **Balloch** N Lans
202 B4 **Auchteraw** Highld	59 K5 **Ayot St Lawrence** Herts	89 G3 **Bainton** C Pete	185 H4 **Balloch** P & K
203 L2 **Auchterblair** Highld	163 J5 **Ayr** S Ayrs	126 B1 **Bainton** E R Yk	153 G3 **Balloch** S Ayrs
219 J6 **Auchtercairn** Highld	131 J2 **Aysgarth** N York	186 F6 **Baintown** Fife	174 D3 **Balloch** W Duns
186 C7 **Auchterderran** Fife	25 G7 **Ayshford** Devon	167 K6 **Bairnkine** Border	206 B6 **Ballogie** Abers
196 B8 **Auchterhouse** Angus	129 J3 **Ayside** Cumb	114 E7 **Bakewell** Derbys	31 G6 **Balls Cross** W Susx
216 D6 **Auchterless** Abers	88 C4 **Ayston** Rutlnd	96 E5 **Bala** Gwynd	32 E6 **Balls Green** E Susx
186 D5 **Auchtermuchty** Fife	60 F5 **Aythorpe Roding** Essex	232 f3 **Balallan** W Isls	189 K7 **Ballygown** Ag & B
212 D3 **Auchterneed** Highld	179 J6 **Ayton** Border	212 C7 **Balbeg** Highld	171 G5 **Ballygrant** Ag & B
177 H1 **Auchtertool** Fife	132 C5 **Azerley** N York	186 C2 **Balbeggie** P & K	188 F5 **Ballyhaugh** Ag & B
210 C8 **Auchtertyre** Highld		212 D5 **Balblair** Highld	154 B6 **Balmaclellan** D & G
184 C4 **Auchtubh** Stirlg	**B**	213 G2 **Balblair** Highld	146 C6 **Balmae** D & G
231 L3 **Auckengill** Highld		115 K2 **Balby** Donc	174 D1 **Balmaha** Stirlg
115 M2 **Auckley** Donc	7 L3 **Babbacombe** Torbay	146 E5 **Balcary** D & G	186 E5 **Balmalcolm** Fife
113 K3 **Audenshaw** Tamesd	60 C5 **Babbs Green** Herts	212 E5 **Balchraggan** Highld	146 B5 **Balmangan** D & G
98 F4 **Audlem** Ches E	26 E5 **Babcary** Somset	228 B4 **Balchreick** Highld	207 H2 **Balmedie** Abers
99 J3 **Audley** Staffs	27 G2 **Babington** Somset	32 B6 **Balcombe** W Susx	186 F3 **Balmerino** Fife
76 D6 **Audley End** Essex	76 D4 **Babraham** Cambs		162 B3 **Balmichael** N Ayrs
			205 G6 **Balmoral Castle Grounds** Abers

175 G4 **Balmore** E Duns
223 J5 **Balmuchy** Highld
196 F6 **Balmuir** Angus
177 G2 **Balmule** Fife
187 G4 **Balmullo** Fife
226 E6 **Balnacoil Lodge** Highld
210 F5 **Balnacra** Highld
205 G6 **Balnacroft** Abers
213 G7 **Balnafoich** Highld
194 E6 **Balnaguard** P & K
180 F1 **Balnahard** Ag & B
180 F7 **Balnahard** Ag & B
212 C7 **Balnain** Highld
228 F2 **Balnakeil** Highld
223 H7 **Balnapaling** Highld
124 F6 **Balne** N York
185 L1 **Balquharn** P & K
184 C3 **Balquhidder** Stirlg
86 B7 **Balsall Common** Solhll
85 J6 **Balsall Heath** Birm
72 E6 **Balscote** Oxon
76 E4 **Balsham** Cambs
235 e1 **Baltasound** Shet
145 J3 **Baltersan** D & G
26 D4 **Baltonsborough** Somset
181 M4 **Balvicar** Ag & B
200 C3 **Balvraid** Highld
213 K7 **Balvraid** Highld
121 H5 **Bamber Bridge** Lancs
60 F4 **Bamber's Green** Essex
169 H3 **Bamburgh** Nthumb
169 H3 **Bamburgh Castle** Nthumb
195 K6 **Bamff** P & K
114 E5 **Bamford** Derbys
138 D4 **Bampton** Cumb
24 E6 **Bampton** Devon
56 F7 **Bampton** Oxon
138 D4 **Bampton Grange** Cumb
191 L2 **Banavie** Highld
72 F6 **Banbury** Oxon
72 F6 **Banbury Crematorium** Oxon
50 F3 **Bancffosfelen** Carmth
206 D6 **Banchory** Abers
207 G5 **Banchory-Devenick** Abers
50 E3 **Bancycapel** Carmth
50 D2 **Bancyfelin** Carmth
186 C2 **Bandirran** P & K
216 D2 **Banff** Abers
109 H6 **Bangor** Gwynd
109 H6 **Bangor Crematorium** Gwynd
98 B4 **Bangor-is-y-coed** Wrexhm
9 G5 **Bangors** Cnwll
92 C6 **Banham** Norfk
16 C2 **Bank** Hants
147 H2 **Bankend** D & G
185 M1 **Bankfoot** P & K
164 C6 **Bankglen** E Ayrs
207 G4 **Bankhead** C Aber
165 J1 **Bankhead** S Lans
175 K3 **Banknock** Falk
120 E6 **Banks** Lancs
155 L5 **Bankshill** D & G
106 F6 **Banningham** Norfk
61 H4 **Bannister Green** Essex
175 L1 **Bannockburn** Stirlg
44 E7 **Banstead** Surrey
6 F3 **Bantham** Devon
175 K3 **Banton** N Lans
38 B8 **Banwell** N Som
34 C3 **Bapchild** Kent
27 M4 **Bapton** Wilts
232 f1 **Barabhas** W Isls
163 J3 **Barassie** S Ayrs
223 G6 **Barbaraville** Highld

163 K5 **Barbieston** S Ayrs
130 C3 **Barbon** Cumb
23 L2 **Barbrook** Devon
73 G1 **Barby** Nhants
191 J7 **Barcaldine** Ag & B
72 C6 **Barcheston** Warwks
19 L3 **Barcombe** E Susx
19 L3 **Barcombe Cross** E Susx
131 L2 **Barden** N York
33 G4 **Barden Park** Kent
61 G2 **Bardfield End Green** Essex
61 G3 **Bardfield Saling** Essex
117 J7 **Bardney** Lincs
86 F2 **Bardon** Leics
149 K3 **Bardon Mill** Nthumb
175 G4 **Bardowie** E Duns
174 C4 **Bardrainney** Inver
129 G5 **Bardsea** Cumb
124 B2 **Bardsey** Leeds
94 B7 **Bardsey Island** Gwynd
91 L8 **Bardwell** Suffk
129 K6 **Bare** Lancs
145 G2 **Barfad** D & G
92 D3 **Barford** Norfk
72 C3 **Barford** Warwks
57 H2 **Barford St John** Oxon
28 B5 **Barford St Martin** Wilts
57 H2 **Barford St Michael** Oxon
35 H5 **Barfrestone** Kent
175 J5 **Bargeddie** N Lans
53 J7 **Bargoed** Caerph
153 H6 **Bargrennan** D & G
89 G7 **Barham** Cambs
35 G5 **Barham** Kent
78 D4 **Barham** Suffk
35 G5 **Barham Crematorium** Kent
75 L2 **Bar Hill** Cambs
88 F2 **Barholm** Lincs
87 J2 **Barkby** Leics
87 J2 **Barkby Thorpe** Leics
102 C5 **Barkestone-le-Vale** Leics
42 C6 **Barkham** Wokham
45 H3 **Barking** Gt Lon
78 C4 **Barking** Suffk
45 H3 **Barkingside** Gt Lon
78 C4 **Barking Tye** Suffk
122 F6 **Barkisland** Calder
3 J2 **Barkla Shop** Cnwll
102 F4 **Barkston** Lincs
124 D4 **Barkston Ash** N York
75 L7 **Barkway** Herts
175 H5 **Barlanark** C Glas
99 K5 **Barlaston** Staffs
18 C3 **Barlavington** W Susx
115 J6 **Barlborough** Derbys
124 F4 **Barlby** N York
86 E3 **Barlestone** Leics
76 B6 **Barley** Herts
122 B3 **Barley** Lancs
88 B2 **Barleythorpe** Rutlnd
46 F3 **Barling** Essex
117 H6 **Barlings** Lincs
146 E4 **Barlochan** D & G
115 G6 **Barlow** Derbys
150 E3 **Barlow** Gatesd
124 F5 **Barlow** N York
125 J2 **Barmby Moor** E R Yk
125 G5 **Barmby on the Marsh** E R Yk
161 K1 **Barmollack** Ag & B
80 E1 **Barmouth** Gwynd
141 H4 **Barmpton** Darltn
135 J7 **Barmston** E R Yk
182 E8 **Barnacarry** Ag & B
88 F3 **Barnack** C Pete
140 D4 **Barnard Castle** Dur
57 H6 **Barnard Gate** Oxon
77 G5 **Barnardiston** Suffk

146 E4 **Barnbarroch** D & G
115 J2 **Barnburgh** Donc
93 K5 **Barnby** Suffk
124 F8 **Barnby Dun** Donc
102 E3 **Barnby in the Willows** Notts
116 A5 **Barnby Moor** Notts
144 D5 **Barncorkrie** D & G
44 E5 **Barnes** Gt Lon
33 H4 **Barnes Street** Kent
44 E2 **Barnet** Gt Lon
126 C8 **Barnetby le Wold** N Linc
106 B6 **Barney** Norfk
91 K7 **Barnham** Suffk
18 C5 **Barnham** W Susx
92 C3 **Barnham Broom** Norfk
197 G5 **Barnhead** Angus
187 H2 **Barnhill** C Dund
214 E3 **Barnhill** Moray
152 B7 **Barnhills** D & G
140 D5 **Barningham** Dur
91 L7 **Barningham** Suffk
118 C2 **Barnoldby le Beck** NE Lin
122 C2 **Barnoldswick** Lancs
31 J6 **Barns Green** W Susx
115 G1 **Barnsley** Barns
56 B6 **Barnsley** Gloucs
115 G1 **Barnsley Crematorium** Barns
23 J5 **Barnstaple** Devon
61 G4 **Barnston** Essex
111 J5 **Barnston** Wirral
102 B5 **Barnstone** Notts
85 H8 **Barnt Green** Worcs
177 G4 **Barnton** C Edin
112 F6 **Barnton** Ches W
88 F6 **Barnwell All Saints** Nhants
88 F6 **Barnwell St Andrew** Nhants
55 K4 **Barnwood** Gloucs
153 G4 **Barr** S Ayrs
233 b9 **Barra** W Isls
145 H5 **Barrachan** D & G
233 b9 **Barraigh** W Isls
188 B7 **Barrapoll** Ag & B
158 A7 **Barrasford** Nthumb
174 F2 **Barrhead** E Rens
152 F5 **Barrhill** S Ayrs
76 B5 **Barrington** Cambs
26 B7 **Barrington** Somset
3 H4 **Barripper** Cnwll
174 C7 **Barrmill** N Ayrs
182 B3 **Barrnacarry Bay** Ag & B
231 J2 **Barrock** Highld
55 K3 **Barrow** Gloucs
121 L7 **Barrow** Lancs
88 C1 **Barrow** Rutlnd
27 G5 **Barrow** Somset
77 H2 **Barrow** Suffk
168 C7 **Barrow Burn** Nthumb
102 E5 **Barrowby** Lincs
88 D4 **Barrowden** Rutlnd
122 C3 **Barrowford** Lancs
38 D6 **Barrow Gurney** N Som
126 D6 **Barrow Haven** N Linc
128 E5 **Barrow-in-Furness** Cumb
128 E5 **Barrow Island** Cumb
126 D6 **Barrow-upon-Humber** N Linc
101 L8 **Barrow upon Soar** Leics
101 G6 **Barrow upon Trent** Derbys
187 J1 **Barry** Angus
37 H6 **Barry** V Glam
37 H6 **Barry Island** V Glam
87 K2 **Barsby** Leics
93 H5 **Barsham** Suffk

86 B7 **Barston** Solhll
69 L6 **Bartestree** Herefs
216 F7 **Barthol Chapel** Abers
61 H4 **Bartholomew Green** Essex
99 H3 **Barthomley** Ches E
28 F8 **Bartley** Hants
85 H6 **Bartley Green** Birm
76 E5 **Bartlow** Cambs
76 B4 **Barton** Cambs
98 C2 **Barton** Ches W
56 C3 **Barton** Gloucs
120 E8 **Barton** Lancs
121 G3 **Barton** Lancs
141 G5 **Barton** N York
57 K6 **Barton** Oxon
7 K3 **Barton** Torbay
91 G3 **Barton Bendish** Norfk
39 J2 **Barton End** Gloucs
57 M2 **Barton Hartshorn** Bucks
101 K6 **Barton in Fabis** Notts
86 E3 **Barton in the Beans** Leics
59 H2 **Barton-le-Clay** C Beds
133 L5 **Barton-le-Street** N York
133 L6 **Barton-le-Willows** N York
91 G8 **Barton Mills** Suffk
16 B4 **Barton-on-Sea** Hants
56 E2 **Barton-on-the-Heath** Warwks
26 D5 **Barton St David** Somset
88 C7 **Barton Seagrave** Nhants
29 H3 **Barton Stacey** Hants
23 L4 **Barton Town** Devon
107 H7 **Barton Turf** Norfk
100 D8 **Barton-under-Needwood** Staffs
126 C6 **Barton-upon-Humber** N Linc
126 C6 **Barton Waterside** N Linc
232 f1 **Barvas** W Isls
90 D7 **Barway** Cambs
86 F4 **Barwell** Leics
10 E4 **Barwick** Devon
26 E8 **Barwick** Somset
124 B3 **Barwick in Elmet** Leeds
98 B7 **Baschurch** Shrops
72 E2 **Bascote** Warwks
121 K2 **Bashall Eaves** Lancs
46 B3 **Basildon** Essex
46 C3 **Basildon & District Crematorium** Essex
29 M2 **Basingstoke** Hants
29 K3 **Basingstoke Crematorium** Hants
114 E6 **Baslow** Derbys
25 M3 **Bason Bridge** Somset
37 L3 **Bassaleg** Newpt
167 K1 **Bassendean** Border
137 H2 **Bassenthwaite** Cumb
29 H7 **Bassett** C Sotn
75 K5 **Bassingbourn** Cambs
102 E1 **Bassingham** Lincs
102 E5 **Bassingthorpe** Lincs
60 A3 **Bassus Green** Herts
89 G2 **Baston** Lincs
107 J8 **Bastwick** Norfk
43 H2 **Batchworth** Herts
14 C2 **Batcombe** Dorset
27 G4 **Batcombe** Somset
59 J5 **Batford** Herts
39 H7 **Bath** BaNES
39 H7 **Bathampton** BaNES
25 G6 **Bathealton** Somset
39 H6 **Batheaston** BaNES
39 H6 **Bathford** BaNES
176 D5 **Bathgate** W Loth
102 C2 **Bathley** Notts
5 L2 **Bathpool** Cnwll

25 K6 **Bathpool** Somset
62 F2 **Bath Side** Essex
176 C5 **Bathville** W Loth
26 E2 **Bathway** Somset
123 J5 **Batley** Kirk
71 L7 **Batsford** Gloucs
142 D5 **Battersby** N York
44 F5 **Battersea** Gt Lon
78 B4 **Battisford Tye** Suffk
20 F3 **Battle** E Susx
52 F2 **Battle** Powys
196 D5 **Battledykes** Angus
103 L2 **Battle of Britain Memorial Flight** Lincs
46 C2 **Battlesbridge** Essex
24 E6 **Battleton** Somset
70 F6 **Baughton** Worcs
41 L7 **Baughurst** Hants
206 B6 **Baulds** Abers
40 F3 **Baulking** Oxon
117 L6 **Baumber** Lincs
56 A6 **Baunton** Gloucs
28 B5 **Baverstock** Wilts
92 D2 **Bawburgh** Norfk
106 C7 **Bawdeswell** Norfk
25 M4 **Bawdrip** Somset
79 H6 **Bawdsey** Suffk
115 M3 **Bawtry** Donc
122 B5 **Baxenden** Lancs
86 C4 **Baxterley** Warwks
208 D4 **Bay** Highld
232 g2 **Bayble** W Isls
29 K6 **Baybridge** Hants
129 G5 **Baycliff** Cumb
40 F5 **Baydon** Wilts
60 A6 **Bayford** Herts
27 G5 **Bayford** Somset
233 b6 **Bayhead** W Isls
84 E3 **Baylham** Suffk
54 E3 **Baysham** Herefs
83 J2 **Bayston Hill** Shrops
77 G6 **Baythorne End** Essex
84 C8 **Bayton** Worcs
57 J7 **Bayworth** Oxon
73 L6 **Beachampton** Bucks
91 H3 **Beachamwell** Norfk
20 C6 **Beachy Head** E Susx
12 F2 **Beacon** Devon
62 A3 **Beacon End** Essex
30 E4 **Beacon Hill** Surrey
78 D4 **Beacon Hill Services** Suffk
42 C2 **Beacon's Bottom** Bucks
42 F3 **Beaconsfield** Bucks
42 F3 **Beaconsfield Services** Bucks
133 K3 **Beadlam** N York
75 G6 **Beadlow** C Beds
169 J4 **Beadnell** Nthumb
10 E2 **Beaford** Devon
124 E5 **Beal** N York
169 G2 **Beal** Nthumb
6 A1 **Bealsmill** Cnwll
13 L3 **Beaminster** Dorset
150 F4 **Beamish** Dur
131 K8 **Beamsley** N York
39 K7 **Beanacre** Wilts
169 G5 **Beanley** Nthumb
10 D7 **Beardon** Devon
12 C3 **Beare** Devon
31 K3 **Beare Green** Surrey
71 L3 **Bearley** Warwks
151 G6 **Bearpark** Dur
174 F4 **Bearsden** E Duns
33 K3 **Bearsted** Kent
99 G5 **Bearstone** Shrops
85 H6 **Bearwood** Birm
69 H4 **Bearwood** Herefs
15 K3 **Bearwood** Poole
155 J2 **Beattock** D & G
60 F6 **Beauchamp Roding** Essex
53 J5 **Beaufort** Blae G
16 E3 **Beaulieu** Hants
16 E2 **Beaulieu House** Hants

212 E5 **Beauly** Highld
109 H6 **Beaumaris** IoA
148 C3 **Beaumont** Cumb
62 E3 **Beaumont** Essex
236 c7 **Beaumont** Jersey
72 B1 **Beausale** Warwks
29 L6 **Beauworth** Hants
10 C5 **Beaworthy** Devon
61 H3 **Beazley End** Essex
111 K5 **Bebington** Wirral
93 J5 **Beccles** Suffk
120 F6 **Becconsall** Lancs
84 D3 **Beckbury** Shrops
45 G6 **Beckenham** Gt Lon
45 G6 **Beckenham Crematorium** Gt Lon
136 E6 **Beckermet** Cumb
147 J5 **Beckfoot** Cumb
71 H7 **Beckford** Worcs
40 C6 **Beckhampton** Wilts
102 E2 **Beckingham** Lincs
116 C4 **Beckingham** Notts
27 J2 **Beckington** Somset
83 H7 **Beckjay** Shrops
21 G2 **Beckley** E Susx
57 K5 **Beckley** Oxon
91 G7 **Beck Row** Suffk
128 F3 **Beck Side** Cumb
45 H4 **Beckton** Gt Lon
132 D8 **Beckwithshaw** N York
45 J3 **Becontree** Gt Lon
132 D2 **Bedale** N York
27 J7 **Bedchester** Dorset
37 G4 **Beddau** Rhondd
95 K3 **Beddgelert** Gwynd
19 L4 **Beddingham** E Susx
44 F6 **Beddington** Gt Lon
44 F6 **Beddington Corner** Gt Lon
78 F2 **Bedfield** Suffk
74 F5 **Bedford** Bed
75 G4 **Bedford Crematorium** Bed
17 K2 **Bedhampton** Hants
78 E2 **Bedingfield** Suffk
132 D2 **Bedlam** N York
34 B5 **Bedlam Lane** Kent
159 G5 **Bedlington** Nthumb
53 H7 **Bedlinog** Myr Td
38 E6 **Bedminster** Bristl
38 E6 **Bedminster Down** Bristl
59 J7 **Bedmond** Herts
99 L8 **Bednall** Staffs
167 J5 **Bedrule** Border
83 G7 **Bedstone** Shrops
37 J3 **Bedwas** Caerph
53 J7 **Bedwellty** Caerph
86 D6 **Bedworth** Warwks
87 J2 **Beeby** Leics
30 B4 **Beech** Hants
99 J5 **Beech** Staffs
42 B7 **Beech Hill** W Berk
40 C8 **Beechingstoke** Wilts
41 J5 **Beedon** W Berk
41 J5 **Beedon Hill** W Berk
135 H8 **Beeford** E R Yk
114 E7 **Beeley** Derbys
117 K2 **Beelsby** NE Lin
41 L6 **Beenham** W Berk
13 L6 **Beer** Devon
26 B5 **Beer** Somset
25 L7 **Beercrocombe** Somset
14 B1 **Beer Hackett** Dorset
7 J7 **Beesands** Devon
118 F5 **Beesby** Lincs
7 J7 **Beeson** Devon
75 H5 **Beeston** C Beds
98 D2 **Beeston** Ches W
123 K4 **Beeston** Leeds
91 K1 **Beeston** Norfk
101 K5 **Beeston** Notts
106 E4 **Beeston Regis** Norfk
146 F2 **Beeswing** D & G

129 K4 **Beetham** Cumb
25 L8 **Beetham** Somset
106 A8 **Beetley** Norfk
57 J5 **Begbroke** Oxon
49 J6 **Begelly** Pembks
82 D7 **Beguildy** Powys
93 H2 **Beighton** Norfk
115 H5 **Beighton** Sheff
100 F3 **Beighton Hill** Derbys
233 c7 **Beinn Na Faoghla** W Isls
174 C7 **Beith** N Ayrs
35 G4 **Bekesbourne** Kent
107 G8 **Belaugh** Norfk
85 G7 **Belbroughton** Worcs
14 E1 **Belchalwell** Dorset
14 F1 **Belchalwell Street** Dorset
77 J6 **Belchamp Otten** Essex
77 H6 **Belchamp St Paul** Essex
77 J6 **Belchamp Walter** Essex
118 D6 **Belchford** Lincs
169 G3 **Belford** Nthumb
87 H3 **Belgrave** C Leic
178 E3 **Belhaven** E Loth
207 H2 **Belhelvie** Abers
215 K8 **Belhinnie** Abers
205 H3 **Bellabeg** Abers
182 A8 **Bellanoch** Ag & B
195 K4 **Bellaty** Angus
131 G7 **Bell Busk** N York
118 E5 **Belleau** Lincs
85 G7 **Bell End** Worcs
131 L2 **Bellerby** N York
148 C4 **Belle Vue** Cumb
123 L6 **Belle Vue** Wakefd
164 F3 **Bellfield** S Lans
165 J5 **Bellfield** S Lans
58 F6 **Bellingdon** Bucks
157 L5 **Bellingham** Nthumb
161 H2 **Belloch** Ag & B
161 H3 **Bellochantuy** Ag & B
98 D4 **Bell o' th' Hill** Ches W
175 J6 **Bellshill** N Lans
175 L6 **Bellside** N Lans
176 E5 **Bellsquarry** W Loth
33 G6 **Bells Yew Green** E Susx
38 E7 **Belluton** BaNES
213 G3 **Belmaduthy** Highld
121 K7 **Belmont** Bl w D
44 E7 **Belmont** Gt Lon
163 J5 **Belmont** S Ayrs
235 d2 **Belmont** Shet
205 J3 **Belnacraig** Abers
101 G3 **Belper** Derbys
101 G3 **Belper Lane End** Derbys
158 D6 **Belsay** Nthumb
167 J4 **Belses** Border
7 H4 **Belsford** Devon
59 G7 **Belsize** Herts
78 D6 **Belstead** Suffk
10 F6 **Belstone** Devon
121 L5 **Belthorn** Lancs
47 K6 **Beltinge** Kent
149 K3 **Beltingham** Nthumb
116 D1 **Beltoft** N Linc
101 H7 **Belton** Leics
102 F4 **Belton** Lincs
116 C1 **Belton** N Linc
93 K3 **Belton** Norfk
88 B3 **Belton** Rutlnd
45 J4 **Belvedere** Gt Lon
102 D5 **Belvoir** Leics
102 D5 **Belvoir Castle** Leics
17 J5 **Bembridge** IoW
28 C5 **Bemerton** Wilts
135 J5 **Bempton** E R Yk
93 K6 **Benacre** Suffk
233 c7 **Benbecula** W Isls
233 c6 *Benbecula Airport* W Isls

154 C3 **Benbuie** D & G
191 H8 **Benderloch** Ag & B
33 K6 **Benenden** Kent
150 D4 **Benfieldside** Dur
60 A5 **Bengeo** Herts
71 J5 **Bengeworth** Worcs
79 H3 **Benhall Green** Suffk
79 H3 **Benhall Street** Suffk
197 K3 **Benholm** Abers
133 H7 **Beningbrough** N York
59 M4 **Benington** Herts
104 C3 **Benington** Lincs
109 G5 **Benllech** IoA
173 K2 **Benmore** Ag & B
162 C5 **Bennan** N Ayrs
192 B3 **Ben Nevis** Highld
117 K5 **Benniworth** Lincs
33 J4 **Benover** Kent
123 H2 **Ben Rhydding** C Brad
163 J2 **Benslie** N Ayrs
41 L3 **Benson** Oxon
206 F5 **Benthoul** C Aber
115 K1 **Bentley** Donc
126 C4 **Bentley** E R Yk
30 C3 **Bentley** Hants
78 D6 **Bentley** Suffk
86 C4 **Bentley** Warwks
156 B4 **Bentpath** D & G
24 B5 **Bentwichen** Devon
30 A4 **Bentworth** Hants
186 E2 **Benvie** Angus
14 A2 **Benville** Dorset
89 L5 **Benwick** Cambs
71 J1 **Beoley** Worcs
199 L6 **Beoraidbeg** Highld
18 B3 **Bepton** W Susx
60 D3 **Berden** Essex
48 D2 **Berea** Pembks
6 C3 **Bere Alston** Devon
6 C3 **Bere Ferrers** Devon
14 F4 **Bere Regis** Dorset
93 G4 **Bergh Apton** Norfk
41 L2 **Berinsfield** Oxon
55 G7 **Berkeley** Gloucs
59 G6 **Berkhamsted** Herts
27 J2 **Berkley** Somset
86 B7 **Berkswell** Solhll
45 G4 **Bermondsey** Gt Lon
200 C2 **Bernera** Highld
208 F4 **Bernisdale** Highld
41 L2 **Berrick Prior** Oxon
41 L2 **Berrick Salome** Oxon
227 K4 **Berriedale** Highld
137 L2 **Berrier** Cumb
82 D4 **Berriew** Powys
83 K3 **Berrington** Shrops
69 L2 **Berrington** Worcs
69 L2 **Berrington Green** Worcs
25 L2 **Berrow** Somset
70 D3 **Berrow Green** Worcs
215 L3 **Berryhillock** Moray
215 L4 **Berryhillock** Moray
23 J3 **Berrynarbor** Devon
7 J4 **Berry Pomeroy** Devon
97 L3 **Bersham** Wrexhm
20 B5 **Berwick** E Susx
40 C5 **Berwick Bassett** Wilts
158 F6 **Berwick Hill** Nthumb
28 B4 **Berwick St James** Wilts
27 L6 **Berwick St John** Wilts
27 L5 **Berwick St Leonard** Wilts
179 K7 **Berwick-upon-Tweed** Nthumb
120 E7 **Bescar** Lancs
71 G5 **Besford** Worcs
115 L2 **Bessacarr** Donc
57 J7 **Bessels Leigh** Oxon
135 J6 **Bessingby** E R Yk
106 E5 **Bessingham** Norfk
92 C4 **Besthorpe** Norfk
116 D8 **Besthorpe** Notts

101 K3 **Bestwood Village** Notts
126 C2 **Beswick** E R Yk
31 K2 **Betchworth** Surrey
62 C1 **Beth Chatto Garden** Essex
109 G7 **Bethel** Gwynd
108 E7 **Bethel** IoA
34 C6 **Bethersden** Kent
109 J7 **Bethesda** Gwynd
49 J4 **Bethesda** Pembks
51 K1 **Bethlehem** Carmth
45 G4 **Bethnal Green** Gt Lon
99 H3 **Betley** Staffs
45 L5 **Betsham** Kent
35 J4 **Betteshanger** Kent
13 K3 **Bettiscombe** Dorset
98 C5 **Bettisfield** Wrexhm
37 L3 **Bettws** Newpt
66 D4 **Bettws Bledrws** Cerdgn
82 C4 **Bettws Cedewain** Powys
65 J5 **Bettws Evan** Cerdgn
54 A6 **Bettws-Newydd** Mons
229 L3 **Bettyhill** Highld
36 D3 **Betws** Brdgnd
97 G3 **Betws Gwerfil Goch** Denbgs
96 C2 **Betws-y-Coed** Conwy
110 C6 **Betws-yn-Rhos** Conwy
65 J5 **Beulah** Cerdgn
67 K4 **Beulah** Powys
116 B6 **Bevercotes** Notts
126 C3 **Beverley** E R Yk
39 K2 **Beverstone** Gloucs
156 F7 **Bewcastle** Cumb
84 D7 **Bewdley** Worcs
132 B6 **Bewerley** N York
126 E1 **Bewholme** E R Yk
20 E4 **Bexhill** E Susx
45 J5 **Bexley** Gt Lon
45 J5 **Bexleyheath** Gt Lon
90 F3 **Bexwell** Norfk
77 L2 **Beyton** Suffk
77 L2 **Beyton Green** Suffk
232 d2 **Bhaltos** W Isls
233 b10 **Bhatarsaigh** W Isls
56 C6 **Bibury** Gloucs
57 L4 **Bicester** Oxon
85 L6 **Bickenhill** Solhll
103 L5 **Bicker** Lincs
112 C2 **Bickerstaffe** Lancs
124 C1 **Bickerton** N York
84 F2 **Bickford** Staffs
7 J2 **Bickington** Devon
23 H5 **Bickington** Devon
6 D4 **Bickleigh** Devon
12 B2 **Bickleigh** Devon
98 D3 **Bickley** Ches W
45 H6 **Bickley** Gt Lon
134 E2 **Bickley** N York
61 J7 **Bicknacre** Essex
25 H4 **Bicknoller** Somset
33 L2 **Bicknor** Kent
82 F6 **Bicton** Shrops
83 J1 **Bicton** Shrops
32 F5 **Bidborough** Kent
33 L5 **Biddenden** Kent
74 E4 **Biddenham** Bed
39 K5 **Biddestone** Wilts
26 B2 **Biddisham** Somset
73 J6 **Biddlesden** Bucks
99 K2 **Biddulph** Staffs
99 K2 **Biddulph Moor** Staffs
23 G6 **Bideford** Devon
71 K4 **Bidford-on-Avon** Warwks
125 J2 **Bielby** E R Yk
207 G5 **Bieldside** C Aber
17 G6 **Bierley** IoW
58 D5 **Bierton** Bucks
145 H6 **Big Balcraig** D & G
6 F6 **Bigbury** Devon

6 F6 **Bigbury-on-Sea** Devon
117 H1 **Bigby** Lincs
154 B3 **Big Carlae** D & G
165 K2 **Biggar** S Lans
100 D2 **Biggin** Derbys
100 E3 **Biggin** Derbys
124 E4 **Biggin** N York
32 D2 **Biggin Hill** Gt Lon
45 H7 **Biggin Hill Airport** Gt Lon
75 H5 **Biggleswade** C Beds
156 B6 **Bigholms** D & G
230 C3 **Bighouse** Highld
29 L4 **Bighton** Hants
148 A4 **Biglands** Cumb
18 D3 **Bignor** W Susx
53 K6 **Big Pit Blaenavon** Torfn
136 D5 **Bigrigg** Cumb
219 H5 **Big Sand** Highld
235 C7 **Bigton** Shet
101 K4 **Bilborough** C Nott
25 G3 **Bilbrook** Somset
124 E2 **Bilbrough** N York
231 K5 **Bilbster** Highld
140 F3 **Bildershaw** Dur
78 B5 **Bildeston** Suffk
46 B2 **Billericay** Essex
87 K3 **Billesdon** Leics
71 K3 **Billesley** Warwks
103 J5 **Billingborough** Lincs
112 D2 **Billinge** St Hel
92 E7 **Billingford** Norfk
106 B7 **Billingford** Norfk
141 K3 **Billingham** S on T
103 J2 **Billinghay** Lincs
115 H1 **Billingley** Barns
31 H6 **Billingshurst** W Susx
84 C6 **Billingsley** Shrops
58 F4 **Billington** C Beds
121 L4 **Billington** Lancs
93 J2 **Billockby** Norfk
150 E7 **Billy Row** Dur
121 G3 **Bilsborrow** Lancs
119 G6 **Bilsby** Lincs
18 D5 **Bilsham** W Susx
34 D7 **Bilsington** Kent
101 M1 **Bilsthorpe** Notts
177 H5 **Bilston** Mdloth
85 G4 **Bilston** Wolves
86 D3 **Bilstone** Leics
126 E4 **Bilton** E R Yk
124 D1 **Bilton** N York
132 D7 **Bilton** N York
86 F8 **Bilton** Warwks
117 K3 **Binbrook** Lincs
14 D5 **Bincombe** Dorset
26 E2 **Binegar** Somset
42 D6 **Binfield** Br For
42 C5 **Binfield Heath** Oxon
158 B7 **Bingfield** Nthumb
102 B4 **Bingham** Notts
123 G3 **Bingley** C Brad
106 B5 **Binham** Norfk
86 E7 **Binley** Covtry
29 H2 **Binley** Hants
86 E7 **Binley Woods** Warwks
15 G5 **Binnegar** Dorset
176 B4 **Binniehill** Falk
30 F3 **Binscombe** Surrey
17 H4 **Binstead** IoW
30 C3 **Binsted** Hants
18 D4 **Binsted** W Susx
71 K4 **Binton** Warwks
106 B7 **Bintree** Norfk
61 M4 **Birch** Essex
105 J5 **Bircham Newton** Norfk
105 J6 **Bircham Tofts** Norfk
60 E4 **Birchanger** Essex
60 E4 **Birchanger Green Services** Essex
100 C6 **Birch Cross** Staffs
69 J2 **Bircher** Herefs
61 M4 **Birch Green** Essex

37 J4 **Birchgrove** Cardif
51 K5 **Birchgrove** Swans
32 D7 **Birchgrove** W Susx
35 J2 **Birchington** Kent
86 C5 **Birchley Heath** Warwks
100 E1 **Birchover** Derbys
122 C8 **Birch Services** Rochdl
114 A4 **Birch Vale** Derbys
25 K8 **Birch Wood** Somset
112 F4 **Birchwood** Warrtn
115 M3 **Bircotes** Notts
77 G6 **Birdbrook** Essex
133 G4 **Birdforth** N York
17 M3 **Birdham** W Susx
72 E2 **Birdingbury** Warwks
55 L5 **Birdlip** Gloucs
134 C6 **Birdsall** N York
123 J8 **Birds Edge** Kirk
60 F6 **Birds Green** Essex
84 D6 **Birdsgreen** Shrops
13 K3 **Birdsmoorgate** Dorset
115 G2 **Birdwell** Barns
168 B2 **Birgham** Border
223 G3 **Birichin** Highld
141 H6 **Birkby** N York
120 D7 **Birkdale** Sefton
215 L2 **Birkenbog** Abers
111 K4 **Birkenhead** Wirral
216 E5 **Birkenhills** Abers
123 J5 **Birkenshaw** Kirk
205 H6 **Birkhall** Abers
186 F1 **Birkhill** Angus
166 B6 **Birkhill** D & G
124 E5 **Birkin** N York
69 J4 **Birley** Herefs
115 G3 **Birley Carr** Sheff
46 B7 **Birling** Kent
71 G5 **Birlingham** Worcs
85 L6 **Birmingham** Birm
85 L6 **Birmingham Airport** Solhll
195 G7 **Birnam** P & K
217 J2 **Birness** Abers
206 B6 **Birse** Abers
205 L5 **Birsemore** Abers
123 J5 **Birstall** Kirk
87 H2 **Birstall** Leics
132 C7 **Birstwith** N York
151 G4 **Birtley** Gatesd
69 G2 **Birtley** Herefs
157 L6 **Birtley** Nthumb
151 G4 **Birtley Crematorium** Gatesd
70 D7 **Birts Street** Worcs
88 C4 **Bisbrooke** Rutlnd
118 C5 **Biscathorpe** Lincs
42 D4 **Bisham** W & M
71 H4 **Bishampton** Worcs
24 B6 **Bish Mill** Devon
140 F2 **Bishop Auckland** Dur
117 G4 **Bishopbridge** Lincs
175 G4 **Bishopbriggs** E Duns
126 B3 **Bishop Burton** E R Yk
141 H2 **Bishop Middleham** Dur
214 F2 **Bishopmill** Moray
132 E6 **Bishop Monkton** N York
117 G3 **Bishop Norton** Lincs
35 G4 **Bishopsbourne** Kent
40 B7 **Bishops Cannings** Wilts
83 G5 **Bishop's Castle** Shrops
27 G8 **Bishop's Caundle** Dorset
55 L3 **Bishop's Cleeve** Gloucs
70 B5 **Bishop's Frome** Herefs
61 G4 **Bishop's Green** Essex
25 J6 **Bishops Hull** Somset
72 E3 **Bishop's Itchington** Warwks

25 J5 **Bishops Lydeard** Somset
55 J3 **Bishop's Norton** Gloucs
24 B6 **Bishop's Nympton** Devon
99 H6 **Bishop's Offley** Staffs
60 D4 **Bishop's Stortford** Herts
29 L5 **Bishop's Sutton** Hants
72 C3 **Bishop's Tachbrook** Warwks
23 J5 **Bishop's Tawton** Devon
7 K2 **Bishopsteignton** Devon
29 J7 **Bishopstoke** Hants
51 H7 **Bishopston** Swans
58 D6 **Bishopstone** Bucks
19 M5 **Bishopstone** E Susx
69 H5 **Bishopstone** Herefs
47 K6 **Bishopstone** Kent
40 E4 **Bishopstone** Swindn
28 B6 **Bishopstone** Wilts
27 K3 **Bishopstrow** Wilts
38 E7 **Bishop Sutton** BaNES
29 K7 **Bishop's Waltham** Hants
25 K8 **Bishopswood** Somset
84 E2 **Bishop's Wood** Staffs
38 E6 **Bishopsworth** Bristl
132 D6 **Bishop Thornton** N York
124 F2 **Bishopthorpe** C York
141 J3 **Bishopton** Darltn
174 E4 **Bishopton** Rens
134 C7 **Bishop Wilton** E R Yk
38 B3 **Bishton** Newpt
100 A7 **Bishton** Staffs
55 K6 **Bisley** Gloucs
42 F8 **Bisley** Surrey
3 K3 **Bissoe** Cnwll
15 L3 **Bisterne** Hants
103 G6 **Bitchfield** Lincs
23 J3 **Bittadon** Devon
6 F4 **Bittaford** Devon
83 L7 **Bitterley** Shrops
29 J8 **Bitterne** C Sotn
87 G6 **Bitteswell** Leics
39 G6 **Bitton** S Glos
42 B4 **Bix** Oxon
235 C5 **Bixter** Shet
87 H4 **Blaby** Leics
179 H7 **Blackadder** Border
7 J5 **Blackawton** Devon
12 E1 **Blackborough** Devon
90 F1 **Blackborough End** Norfk
56 F6 **Black Bourton** Oxon
20 B2 **Blackboys** E Susx
101 G3 **Blackbrook** Derbys
112 D3 **Blackbrook** St Hel
99 H5 **Blackbrook** Staffs
206 F3 **Blackburn** Abers
121 K5 **Blackburn** Bl w D
176 D5 **Blackburn** W Loth
121 K5 **Blackburn with Darwen Services** Bl w D
150 F2 **Black Callerton** N u Ty
164 C3 **Blackcraig** E Ayrs
182 D1 **Black Crofts** Ag & B
207 H3 **Blackdog** Abers
11 J3 **Black Dog** Devon
13 K2 **Blackdown** Dorset
115 G2 **Blacker Hill** Barns
45 J5 **Blackfen** Gt Lon
16 E3 **Blackfield** Hants
185 J5 **Blackford** P & K
26 B2 **Blackford** Somset
26 F6 **Blackford** Somset
101 G8 **Blackfordby** Leics
177 G4 **Blackhall** C Edin
151 K6 **Blackhall Colliery** Dur
166 F2 **Blackhaugh** Border

45 G5 **Blackheath** Gt Lon
85 H6 **Blackheath** Sandw
93 J8 **Blackheath** Suffk
31 G3 **Blackheath** Surrey
217 K3 **Blackhill** Abers
217 K5 **Blackhill** Abers
150 D5 **Blackhill** Dur
217 H5 **Blackhill of Clackirn** Abers
12 C4 **Blackhorse** Devon
165 K7 **Blacklaw** D & G
113 J2 **Blackley** Manch
113 J2 **Blackley Crematorium** Manch
195 J4 **Blacklunans** P & K
69 K6 **Blackmarstone** Herefs
36 E3 **Blackmill** Brdgnd
30 C5 **Blackmoor** Hants
38 C7 **Blackmoor** N Som
123 G7 **Blackmoorfoot** Kirk
60 F7 **Blackmore** Essex
61 H2 **Blackmore End** Essex
176 E3 **Blackness** Falk
30 D3 **Blacknest** Hants
61 J4 **Black Notley** Essex
122 C3 **Blacko** Lancs
51 J7 **Black Pill** Swans
120 D4 **Blackpool** Bpool
7 K6 **Blackpool** Devon
120 D4 *Blackpool Airport Lancs*
176 B5 **Blackridge** W Loth
121 J7 **Blackrod** Bolton
214 E6 **Blacksboat** Moray
147 J2 **Blackshaw** D & G
122 E5 **Blackshaw Head** Calder
121 K6 **Blacksnape** Bl w D
19 H3 **Blackstone** W Susx
6 K6 **Black Street** Suffk
57 L4 **Blackthorn** Oxon
77 K2 **Blackthorpe** Suffk
125 J5 **Blacktoft** E R Yk
207 G4 **Blacktop** C Aber
10 C4 **Black Torrington** Devon
100 E3 **Blackwall** Derbys
3 J3 **Blackwater** Cnwll
42 D7 **Blackwater** Hants
25 K7 **Blackwater** IoW
25 K7 **Blackwater** Somset
162 A4 **Blackwaterfoot** N Ayrs
148 D4 **Blackwell** Cumb
101 H2 **Blackwell** Derbys
114 C6 **Blackwell** Derbys
72 B5 **Blackwell** Warwks
71 H1 **Blackwell** Worcs
37 J2 **Blackwood** Caerph
154 F5 **Blackwood** D & G
164 F1 **Blackwood** S Lans
111 L7 **Blacon** Ches W
145 J4 **Bladnoch** D & G
57 J5 **Bladon** Oxon
65 H5 **Blaenannerch** Cerdgn
96 A4 **Blaenau Ffestiniog** Gwynd
53 K6 **Blaenavon** Torfn
65 H6 **Blaenffos** Pembks
36 D2 **Blaengarw** Brdgnd
52 D6 **Blaengwrach** Neath
36 D2 **Blaengwynfi** Neath
66 E2 **Blaenpennal** Cerdgn
80 D7 **Blaenplwyf** Cerdgn
65 J5 **Blaenporth** Cerdgn
52 E7 **Blaenrhondda** Rhondd
50 B1 **Blaenwaun** Carmth
50 D1 **Blaen-y-Coed** Carmth
52 E7 **Blaen-y-cwm** Rhondd
38 D8 **Blagdon** N Som
25 K7 **Blagdon** Somset
7 K4 **Blagdon** Torbay
25 K7 **Blagdon Hill** Somset
191 K2 **Blaich** Highld

190 D3 **Blain** Highld
53 J6 **Blaina** Blae G
194 D4 **Blair Atholl** P & K
184 F7 **Blair Drummond** Stirlg
195 J7 **Blairgowrie** P & K
176 D2 **Blairhall** Fife
185 K7 **Blairingone** P & K
185 H7 **Blairlogie** Stirlg
173 L2 **Blairmore** Ag & B
228 C4 **Blairmore** Highld
204 F3 **Blairnamarrow** Moray
173 G4 **Blair's Ferry** Ag & B
55 G5 **Blaisdon** Gloucs
84 E7 **Blakebrook** Worcs
84 F7 **Blakedown** Worcs
61 H4 **Blake End** Essex
112 D7 **Blakemere** Ches W
69 G6 **Blakemere** Herefs
85 H3 **Blakenall Heath** Wsall
54 F6 **Blakeney** Gloucs
106 B4 **Blakeney** Norfk
99 G3 **Blakenhall** Ches E
85 G4 **Blakenhall** Wolves
150 B5 **Blakesley** Nhants
15 G2 **Blanchland** Nthumb
15 G2 **Blandford Forum** Dorset
15 G2 **Blandford St Mary** Dorset
132 C8 **Bland Hill** N York
174 F3 **Blanefield** Stirlg
103 H1 **Blankney** Lincs
175 J6 **Blantyre** S Lans
191 L3 **Blar a' Chaorainn** Highld
202 F6 **Blargie** Highld
191 L3 **Blarmachfoldach** Highld
88 B4 **Blaston** Leics
88 D4 **Blatherwycke** Nhants
129 G2 **Blawith** Cumb
154 B5 **Blawquhairn** D & G
79 H3 **Blaxhall** Suffk
116 A2 **Blaxton** Donc
150 F3 **Blaydon** Gatesd
26 C3 **Bleadney** Somset
25 M1 **Bleadon** N Som
34 F3 **Blean** Kent
102 B3 **Bleasby** Notts
121 H2 **Bleasdale** Lancs
187 G4 **Blebocraigs** Fife
68 E2 **Bleddfa** Powys
56 E4 **Bledington** Gloucs
58 C7 **Bledlow** Bucks
42 D2 **Bledlow Ridge** Bucks
178 B6 **Blegbie** E Loth
138 F2 **Blencarn** Cumb
147 L5 **Blencogo** Cumb
30 B8 **Blendworth** Hants
147 L6 **Blennerhasset** Cumb
57 J4 **Bletchingdon** Oxon
32 B3 **Bletchingley** Surrey
58 E2 **Bletchley** M Keyn
98 F5 **Bletchley** Shrops
49 H4 **Bletherston** Pembks
74 E3 **Bletsoe** Bed
41 K4 **Blewbury** Oxon
106 E6 **Blickling** Norfk
101 L2 **Blidworth** Notts
101 L2 **Blidworth Bottoms** Notts
147 K7 **Blindcrake** Cumb
32 C4 **Blindley Heath** Surrey
5 H2 **Blisland** Cnwll
28 D8 **Blissford** Hants
84 D8 **Bliss Gate** Worcs
73 K4 **Blisworth** Nhants
100 B8 **Blithbury** Staffs
71 L7 **Blockley** Gloucs
93 G2 **Blofield** Norfk
93 G2 **Blofield Heath** Norfk
92 B7 **Blo Norton** Norfk
167 J4 **Bloomfield** Border
99 G5 **Blore** Staffs

100 C3 **Blore** Staffs
72 E7 **Bloxham** Oxon
103 H2 **Bloxholm** Lincs
85 H3 **Bloxwich** Wsall
15 G4 **Bloxworth** Dorset
132 B7 **Blubberhouses** N York
24 F3 **Blue Anchor** Somset
46 C7 **Blue Bell Hill** Kent
114 C5 **Blue John Cavern** Derbys
111 J2 **Blundellsands** Sefton
93 L4 **Blundeston** Suffk
75 H4 **Blunham** C Beds
40 C3 **Blunsdon St Andrew** Swindn
84 F8 **Bluntington** Worcs
89 L8 **Bluntisham** Cambs
116 F3 **Blyborough** Lincs
93 J7 **Blyford** Suffk
84 E2 **Blymhill** Staffs
115 L4 **Blyth** Notts
159 H5 **Blyth** Nthumb
165 M1 **Blyth Bridge** Border
93 J7 **Blythburgh** Suffk
159 H5 **Blyth Crematorium** Nthumb
178 D7 **Blythe** Border
115 L4 **Blyth Services** Notts
116 D3 **Blyton** Lincs
187 J5 **Boarhills** Fife
17 H2 **Boarhunt** Hants
57 L5 **Boarstall** Bucks
222 D6 **Boath** Highld
203 L2 **Boat of Garten** Highld
46 E6 **Bobbing** Kent
84 E5 **Bobbington** Staffs
61 J4 **Bocking** Essex
61 J3 **Bocking Churchstreet** Essex
217 L6 **Boddam** Abers
235 C4 **Boddam** Shet
55 K3 **Boddington** Gloucs
108 D5 **Bodedern** IoA
110 D6 **Bodelwyddan** Denbgs
69 K4 **Bodenham** Herefs
28 D6 **Bodenham** Wilts
69 K4 **Bodenham Moor** Herefs
108 E4 **Bodewryd** IoA
110 F7 **Bodfari** Denbgs
108 F6 **Bodffordd** IoA
94 F5 **Bodfuan** Gwynd
106 D4 **Bodham** Norfk
33 K7 **Bodiam** E Susx
33 K7 **Bodiam Castle** E Susx
72 F6 **Bodicote** Oxon
5 H5 **Bodinnick** Cnwll
20 D3 **Bodle Street Green** E Susx
5 G3 **Bodmin** Cnwll
5 J1 **Bodmin Moor** Cnwll
109 M6 **Bodnant Garden** Conwy
34 E5 **Bodsham Green** Kent
5 G4 **Bodwen** Cnwll
212 F4 **Bogallan** Highld
217 J7 **Bogbrae** Abers
163 K3 **Bogend** S Ayrs
177 L4 **Boggs Holdings** E Loth
177 H5 **Boghall** Mdloth
176 D3 **Boghall** W Loth
164 F2 **Boghead** S Lans
215 H2 **Bogmoor** Moray
197 G3 **Bogmuir** Abers
216 B5 **Bogniebrae** Abers
18 C6 **Bognor Regis** W Susx
203 L2 **Bogroy** Highld
154 B6 **Bogue** D & G
3 L5 **Bohortha** Cnwll
201 L8 **Bohuntine** Highld
140 F3 **Bolam** Dur
7 G7 **Bolberry** Devon
85 K5 **Boldmere** Birm

16 C3 **Boldre** Hants
140 C4 **Boldron** Dur
116 C4 **Bole** Notts
100 F2 **Bolehill** Derbys
24 E7 **Bolham** Devon
25 J8 **Bolham Water** Devon
3 K1 **Bolingey** Cnwll
113 L6 **Bollington** Ches E
31 L6 **Bolney** W Susx
74 F3 **Bolnhurst** Bed
197 G6 **Bolshan** Angus
115 J7 **Bolsover** Derbys
114 F3 **Bolsterstone** Sheff
133 G3 **Boltby** N York
205 J3 **Boltenstone** Abers
121 L8 **Bolton** Bolton
138 F3 **Bolton** Cumb
178 B4 **Bolton** E Loth
125 J1 **Bolton** E R Yk
169 G6 **Bolton** Nthumb
131 K8 **Bolton Abbey** N York
122 B1 **Bolton by Bowland** Lancs
148 E2 **Boltonfellend** Cumb
147 M6 **Boltongate** Cumb
129 K6 **Bolton le Sands** Lancs
147 M6 **Bolton Low Houses** Cumb
141 G7 **Bolton-on-Swale** N York
124 E3 **Bolton Percy** N York
115 J2 **Bolton Upon Dearne** Barns
121 J7 *Bolton West Services Lancs*
5 J1 **Bolventor** Cnwll
98 C8 **Bomere Heath** Shrops
222 E3 **Bonar Bridge** Highld
182 E2 **Bonawe** Ag & B
126 C7 **Bonby** N Linc
65 H6 **Boncath** Pembks
167 J6 **Bonchester Bridge** Border
10 F4 **Bondleigh** Devon
121 G2 **Bonds** Lancs
176 D3 **Bo'ness** Falk
85 J2 **Boney Hay** Staffs
174 D3 **Bonhill** W Duns
84 E3 **Boningale** Shrops
167 K5 **Bonjedward** Border
175 L6 **Bonkle** N Lans
196 F7 **Bonnington** Angus
34 E7 **Bonnington** Kent
186 F6 **Bonnybank** Fife
175 L3 **Bonnybridge** Falk
217 G4 **Bonnykelly** Abers
177 J5 **Bonnyrigg** Mdloth
196 B8 **Bonnyton** Angus
100 F2 **Bonsall** Derbys
155 M7 **Bonshaw Tower** D & G
81 J4 **Bont-Dolgadfan** Powys
80 F6 **Bont-goch or Elerch** Cerdgn
66 E2 **Bontnewydd** Cerdgn
95 H1 **Bontnewydd** Gwynd
97 G2 **Bontuchel** Denbgs
37 G5 **Bonvilston** V Glam
23 H4 **Boode** Devon
42 D3 **Booker** Bucks
167 J1 **Boon** Border
142 E4 **Boosbeck** R & Cl
61 K2 **Boose's Green** Essex
137 G6 **Boot** Cumb
122 F5 **Booth** Calder
103 G2 **Boothby Graffoe** Lincs
102 F6 **Boothby Pagnell** Lincs
125 H5 **Boothferry** E R Yk
113 G2 **Boothstown** Salfd
128 D2 **Bootle** Cumb
111 K3 **Bootle** Sefton
70 B1 **Boraston** Shrops

236 e2 **Bordeaux** Guern
34 B3 **Borden** Kent
157 G5 **Border Forest Park**
61 J6 **Boreham** Essex
27 K3 **Boreham** Wilts
20 D4 **Boreham Street** E Susx
44 D2 **Borehamwood** Herts
155 L4 **Boreland** D & G
208 C4 **Boreraig** Highld
232 f1 **Borgh** W Isls
233 b9 **Borgh** W Isls
229 K4 **Borgie** Highld
146 B5 **Borgue** D & G
227 K4 **Borgue** Highld
77 J6 **Borley** Essex
218 B7 **Borneskitaig** Highld
146 A5 **Borness** D & G
132 F6 **Boroughbridge** N York
33 G2 **Borough Green** Kent
101 H5 **Borrowash** Derbys
132 F2 **Borrowby** N York
176 D3 **Borrowstoun** Falk
46 B6 **Borstal** Medway
80 E5 **Borth** Cerdgn
166 F6 **Borthwickbrae** Border
166 F6 **Borthwickshiels** Border
95 K5 **Borth-y-Gest** Gwynd
209 G5 **Borve** Highld
232 d4 **Borve** W Isls
232 f1 **Borve** W Isls
233 b9 **Borve** W Isls
129 L5 **Borwick** Lancs
70 C5 **Bosbury** Herefs
8 E6 **Boscastle** Cnwll
15 L4 **Boscombe** Bmouth
28 D4 **Boscombe** Wilts
17 L2 **Bosham** W Susx
49 G8 **Bosherston** Pembks
113 K7 **Bosley** Ches E
133 L7 **Bossall** N York
8 E6 **Bossiney** Cnwll
34 F5 **Bossingham** Kent
24 D2 **Bossington** Somset
112 F7 **Bostock Green** Ches W
104 B4 **Boston** Lincs
104 A4 **Boston Crematorium** Lincs
124 C2 **Boston Spa** Leeds
4 F7 **Boswinger** Cnwll
2 C5 **Botallack** Cnwll
59 M7 **Botany Bay** Gt Lon
92 C7 **Botesdale** Suffk
159 G5 **Bothal** Nthumb
41 J5 **Bothampstead** W Berk
116 A6 **Bothamsall** Notts
147 L6 **Bothel** Cumb
13 L4 **Bothenhampton** Dorset
175 J6 **Bothwell** S Lans
175 J6 **Bothwell Services** S Lans
59 G7 **Botley** Bucks
29 K8 **Botley** Hants
57 J6 **Botley** Oxon
58 B3 **Botolph Claydon** Bucks
19 G4 **Botolphs** W Susx
102 D5 **Bottesford** Leics
116 E1 **Bottesford** N Linc
76 D3 **Bottisham** Cambs
186 F3 **Bottomcraig** Fife
122 D6 **Bottoms** Calder
6 B4 **Botusfleming** Cnwll
94 E6 **Botwnnog** Gwynd
32 M4 **Bough Beech** Kent
68 C6 **Boughrood** Powys
73 L2 **Boughton** Nhants
91 G3 **Boughton** Norfk
116 B7 **Boughton** Notts
34 D5 **Boughton Aluph** Kent

33 K3 **Boughton Green** Kent
34 B5 **Boughton Malherbe** Kent
33 K3 **Boughton Monchelsea** Kent
34 E3 **Boughton Street** Kent
83 K6 **Bouldon** Shrops
169 K6 **Boulmer** Nthumb
116 F7 **Boultham** Lincs
75 K3 **Bourn** Cambs
103 H7 **Bourne** Lincs
45 J2 **Bournebridge** Essex
85 J6 **Bournebrook** Birm
42 E3 **Bourne End** Bucks
74 D5 **Bourne End** C Beds
59 G6 **Bourne End** Herts
15 K4 **Bournemouth** Bmouth
15 L3 *Bournemouth Airport Dorset*
15 L4 **Bournemouth Crematorium** Bmouth
46 E3 **Bournes Green** Sthend
85 G8 **Bournheath** Worcs
85 J7 **Bournville** Birm
27 H5 **Bourton** Dorset
40 E3 **Bourton** Oxon
83 L4 **Bourton** Shrops
40 B7 **Bourton** Wilts
72 E1 **Bourton on Dunsmore** Warwks
56 D2 **Bourton-on-the-Hill** Gloucs
56 D4 **Bourton-on-the-Water** Gloucs
189 G4 **Bousd** Ag & B
129 H3 **Bouth** Cumb
131 L2 **Bouthwaite** N York
28 B7 **Boveridge** Dorset
7 J1 **Bovey Tracey** Devon
59 G7 **Bovingdon** Herts
14 F5 **Bovington Tank Museum** Dorset
11 G4 **Bow** Devon
45 G4 **Bow** Gt Lon
234 b7 **Bow** Ork
74 C7 **Bow Brickhill** M Keyn
55 J6 **Bowbridge** Gloucs
151 H7 **Bowburn** Dur
16 F5 **Bowcombe** IoW
12 E4 **Bowd** Devon
167 H4 **Bowden** Border
39 J4 **Bowden Hill** Wilts
113 H4 **Bowdon** Traffd
231 J3 **Bower** Highld
28 A6 **Bowerchalke** Wilts
231 J3 **Bowermadden** Highld
99 J5 **Bowers** Staffs
46 C3 **Bowers Gifford** Essex
176 F1 **Bowershall** Fife
124 B5 **Bower's Row** Leeds
140 C4 **Bowes** Dur
121 G2 **Bowgreave** Lancs
147 H2 **Bowhouse** D & G
167 G2 **Bowland** Border
69 K4 **Bowley** Herefs
30 K4 **Bowlhead Green** Surrey
123 H4 **Bowling** C Brad
174 E4 **Bowling** W Duns
137 J7 **Bowmanstead** Cumb
170 F6 **Bowmore** Ag & B
147 L3 **Bowness-on-Solway** Cumb
137 L7 **Bowness-on-Windermere** Cumb
186 E5 **Bow of Fife** Fife
196 E6 **Bowriefauld** Angus
168 E2 **Bowsden** Nthumb
80 E6 **Bow Street** Cerdgn
55 K7 **Box** Gloucs

39 J6 **Box** Wilts
77 L6 **Boxford** Suffk
41 H6 **Boxford** W Berk
18 B4 **Boxgrove** W Susx
33 K2 **Boxley** Kent
59 H6 **Boxmoor** Herts
62 B2 **Boxted** Essex
62 B2 **Boxted** Essex
77 J4 **Boxted** Suffk
62 B2 **Boxted Cross** Essex
75 L2 **Boxworth** Cambs
47 L6 **Boyden Gate** Kent
100 D5 **Boylestone** Derbys
216 C2 **Boyndie** Abers
217 G2 **Boyndlie** Abers
135 H6 **Boynton** E R Yk
197 G6 **Boysack** Angus
9 J6 **Boyton** Cnwll
79 H5 **Boyton** Suffk
27 L4 **Boyton** Wilts
61 G6 **Boyton Cross** Essex
77 G5 **Boyton End** Suffk
74 C3 **Bozeat** Nhants
34 E6 **Brabourne** Kent
34 E6 **Brabourne Lees** Kent
231 K2 **Brabstermire** Highld
208 E6 **Bracadale** Highld
88 F2 **Braceborough** Lincs
117 G7 **Bracebridge Heath** Lincs
116 F7 **Bracebridge Low Fields** Lincs
103 G5 **Braceby** Lincs
122 C2 **Bracewell** Lancs
101 G2 **Brackenfield** Derbys
175 K5 **Brackenhirst** N Lans
17 L3 **Bracklesham** W Susx
201 J8 **Brackletter** Highld
73 H6 **Brackley** Nhants
42 E6 **Bracknell** Br For
185 H5 **Braco** P & K
215 L4 **Bracobrae** Moray
92 E4 **Bracon Ash** Norfk
199 L6 **Bracora** Highld
199 L6 **Bracorina** Highld
100 D3 **Bradbourne** Derbys
141 H2 **Bradbury** Dur
73 J5 **Bradden** Nhants
42 D2 **Bradenham** Bucks
39 M4 **Bradenstoke** Wilts
12 D1 **Bradfield** Devon
62 D2 **Bradfield** Essex
106 F5 **Bradfield** Norfk
114 F3 **Bradfield** Sheff
41 L6 **Bradfield** W Berk
77 K3 **Bradfield Combust** Suffk
99 G2 **Bradfield Green** Ches E
62 D3 **Bradfield Heath** Essex
77 K3 **Bradfield St Clare** Suffk
77 K3 **Bradfield St George** Suffk
123 H4 **Bradford** C Brad
9 L4 **Bradford** Devon
26 E8 **Bradford Abbas** Dorset
39 J7 **Bradford Leigh** Wilts
39 J7 **Bradford-on-Avon** Wilts
25 J6 **Bradford-on-Tone** Somset
14 C4 **Bradford Peverell** Dorset
23 J5 **Bradiford** Devon
17 H5 **Brading** IoW
100 E4 **Bradley** Derbys
29 M3 **Bradley** Hants
118 C1 **Bradley** NE Lin
99 K8 **Bradley** Staffs
85 G4 **Bradley** Wolves
71 H3 **Bradley** Worcs
71 H3 **Bradley Green** Worcs

100 B4 **Bradley in the Moors** Staffs
38 E4 **Bradley Stoke** S Glos
101 L6 **Bradmore** Notts
12 C2 **Bradninch** Devon
100 A2 **Bradnop** Staffs
13 L4 **Bradpole** Dorset
123 G4 **Bradshaw** Calder
9 K8 **Bradstone** Devon
113 H8 **Bradwall Green** Ches E
114 D5 **Bradwell** Derbys
61 J4 **Bradwell** Essex
74 B6 **Bradwell** M Keyn
93 K3 **Bradwell** Norfk
99 J3 **Bradwell Crematorium** Staffs
62 B6 **Bradwell-on-Sea** Essex
62 B6 **Bradwell Waterside** Essex
9 J3 **Bradworthy** Devon
213 G2 **Brae** Highld
235 c4 **Brae** Shet
175 K3 **Braeface** Falk
197 H5 **Braehead** Angus
145 J4 **Braehead** D & G
176 C7 **Braehead** S Lans
204 E6 **Braemar** Abers
221 G5 **Braemore** Highld
227 J3 **Braemore** Highld
201 L6 **Brae Roy Lodge** Highld
173 L4 **Braeside** Inver
195 L5 **Braes of Coul** Angus
215 J3 **Braes of Enzie** Moray
234 d4 **Braeswick** Ork
182 D6 **Braevallich** Ag & B
141 H3 **Brafferton** Darltn
132 F5 **Brafferton** N York
74 B3 **Brafield-on-the-Green** Nhants
232 f2 **Bragar** W Isls
59 L4 **Bragbury End** Herts
175 L8 **Braidwood** S Lans
100 E4 **Brailsford** Derbys
61 J4 **Braintree** Essex
78 D1 **Braiseworth** Suffk
29 G6 **Braishfield** Hants
137 H3 **Braithwaite** Cumb
115 K3 **Braithwell** Donc
19 G4 **Bramber** W Susx
86 E5 **Bramcote** Warwks
101 J5 **Bramcote Crematorium** Notts
29 L5 **Bramdean** Hants
93 G3 **Bramerton** Norfk
59 M5 **Bramfield** Herts
93 H8 **Bramfield** Suffk
78 D5 **Bramford** Suffk
113 K5 **Bramhall** Stockp
124 C2 **Bramham** Leeds
123 K2 **Bramhope** Leeds
41 M8 **Bramley** Hants
124 K4 **Bramley** Leeds
115 J3 **Bramley** Rothm
31 G3 **Bramley** Surrey
41 M8 **Bramley Corner** Hants
35 G4 **Bramling** Kent
11 L5 **Brampford Speke** Devon
75 J1 **Brampton** Cambs
138 F3 **Brampton** Cumb
148 F3 **Brampton** Cumb
116 D5 **Brampton** Lincs
106 F7 **Brampton** Norfk
115 H2 **Brampton** Rothm
93 J6 **Brampton** Suffk
54 E3 **Brampton Abbotts** Herefs
87 L6 **Brampton Ash** Nhants
83 G8 **Brampton Bryan** Herefs

115 J4	Brampton-en-le-Morthen Rothm
100 B6	Bramshall Staffs
28 F7	Bramshaw Hants
30 D5	Bramshott Hants
26 B5	Bramwell Somset
190 B3	Branault Highld
105 J4	Brancaster Norfk
105 J4	Brancaster Staithe Norfk
150 F7	Brancepeth Dur
214 D4	Branchill Moray
214 F1	Branderburgh Moray
126 E2	Brandesburton E R Yk
78 F3	Brandeston Suffk
106 D7	Brandiston Norfk
151 G6	Brandon Dur
102 E3	Brandon Lincs
91 H6	Brandon Suffk
86 E7	Brandon Warwks
92 C2	Brandon Parva Norfk
133 J5	Brandsby N York
117 G3	Brandy Wharf Lincs
61 G3	Bran End Essex
15 K4	Branksome Poole
15 K4	Branksome Park Poole
29 H3	Bransbury Hants
116 E5	Bransby Lincs
12 F5	Branscombe Devon
70 E4	Bransford Worcs
16 A3	Bransgore Hants
126 D4	Bransholme C KuH
84 B7	Bransley Shrops
102 D6	Branston Leics
117 G7	Branston Lincs
100 E7	Branston Staffs
117 H7	Branston Booths Lincs
17 G2	Branstone IoW
102 E2	Brant Broughton Lincs
78 D7	Brantham Suffk
136 E3	Branthwaite Cumb
148 B7	Branthwaite Cumb
125 L5	Brantingham E R Yk
115 M2	Branton Donc
168 F6	Branton Nthumb
132 F6	Branton Green N York
168 D2	Branxton Nthumb
100 E2	Brassington Derbys
32 E3	Brasted Kent
32 E3	Brasted Chart Kent
206 D5	Brathens Abers
119 G8	Bratoft Lincs
117 J5	Brattleby Lincs
27 K2	Bratton Wilts
84 B2	Bratton Wrekin
10 C6	Bratton Clovelly Devon
23 K4	Bratton Fleming Devon
26 F5	Bratton Seymour Somset
60 C3	Braughing Herts
73 G2	Braunston Nhants
88 B3	Braunston Rutlnd
87 G3	Braunstone Leics
23 H4	Braunton Devon
134 B4	Brawby N York
230 B3	Brawl Highld
42 E4	Bray W & M
87 L6	Braybrooke Nhants
23 L4	Brayford Devon
5 M2	Bray Shop Cnwll
123 K2	Braythorn N York
124 F4	Brayton N York
42 E4	Braywick W & M
59 J4	Breachwood Green Herts
101 G5	Breadsall Derbys
55 G7	Breadstone Gloucs
3 G5	Breage Cnwll
212 D5	Breakachy Highld

43 H3	Breakspear Crematorium Gt Lon
222 C3	Brealangwell Lodge Highld
54 E6	Bream Gloucs
28 D7	Breamore Hants
25 L1	Brean Somset
232 d3	Breanais W Isls
132 E7	Brearton N York
232 e2	Breascleit W Isls
232 e2	Breasclete W Isls
101 J5	Breaston Derbys
66 C7	Brechfa Carmth
196 F4	Brechin Angus
91 L5	Breckles Norfk
154 E4	Breckonside D & G
53 G3	Brecon Powys
52 F3	Brecon Beacons National Park
113 L3	Bredbury Stockp
21 G3	Brede E Susx
69 L3	Bredenbury Herefs
78 F4	Bredfield Suffk
34 B3	Bredgar Kent
46 D7	Bredhurst Kent
71 G6	Bredon Worcs
71 G7	Bredon's Hardwick Worcs
71 G6	Bredon's Norton Worcs
69 G5	Bredwardine Herefs
101 H7	Breedon on the Hill Leics
176 C6	Breich W Loth
121 L8	Breightmet Bolton
125 G4	Breighton E R Yk
69 J6	Breinton Herefs
39 L5	Bremhill Wilts
33 H5	Brenchley Kent
24 B2	Brendon Devon
172 E2	Brenfield Ag & B
232 d3	Brenish W Isls
77 L5	Brent Eleigh Suffk
44 D5	Brentford Gt Lon
102 C8	Brentingby Leics
25 M2	Brent Knoll Somset
7 G4	Brent Mill Devon
60 C2	Brent Pelham Herts
45 L2	Brentwood Essex
21 K1	Brenzett Kent
34 D8	Brenzett Green Kent
85 J1	Brereton Staffs
113 H8	Brereton Green Ches E
235 d6	Bressay Shet
92 C7	Bressingham Norfk
100 F7	Bretby Derbys
100 F7	Bretby Crematorium Derbys
86 E7	Bretford Warwks
71 K5	Bretforton Worcs
121 G6	Bretherton Lancs
235 d5	Brettabister Shet
91 L6	Brettenham Norfk
77 L4	Brettenham Suffk
111 K8	Bretton Flints
84 F2	Brewood Staffs
14 F4	Briantspuddle Dorset
60 A6	Brickendon Herts
59 J7	Bricket Wood Herts
114 F5	Brick Houses Sheff
71 H6	Bricklehampton Worcs
237 e2	Bride IoM
147 K7	Bridekirk Cumb
10 D6	Bridestowe Devon
216 B6	Brideswell Abers
11 J7	Bridford Devon
35 G4	Bridge Kent
26 E6	Bridgehampton Somset
132 E5	Bridge Hewick N York
150 D5	Bridgehill Dur
17 H2	Bridgemary Hants
215 L7	Bridgend Abers
171 G6	Bridgend Ag & B

196 E3	Bridgend Angus
36 E4	Bridgend Brdgnd
165 L7	Bridgend D & G
6 E6	Bridgend Devon
186 F5	Bridgend Fife
215 J7	Bridgend Moray
186 B3	Bridgend P & K
176 E3	Bridgend W Loth
195 L5	Bridgend of Lintrathen Angus
206 B2	Bridge of Alford Abers
185 G7	Bridge of Allan Stirlg
204 E2	Bridge of Avon Moray
214 E7	Bridge of Avon Moray
193 J6	Bridge of Balgie P & K
195 J4	Bridge of Brewlands Angus
204 D2	Bridge of Brown Highld
195 J6	Bridge of Cally P & K
206 C6	Bridge of Canny Abers
146 C3	Bridge of Dee D & G
207 H4	Bridge of Don C Aber
213 L6	Bridge of Dulsie Highld
206 C7	Bridge of Dye Abers
186 B4	Bridge of Earn P & K
193 H5	Bridge of Ericht P & K
206 D6	Bridge of Feugh Abers
230 F2	Bridge of Forss Highld
205 H6	Bridge of Gairn Abers
193 H5	Bridge of Gaur P & K
216 B4	Bridge of Marnoch Abers
192 E7	Bridge of Orchy Ag & B
194 D4	Bridge of Tilt P & K
215 J3	Bridge of Tynet Moray
235 b5	Bridge of Walls Shet
174 D5	Bridge of Weir Rens
9 H4	Bridgerule Devon
69 H6	Bridge Sollers Herefs
77 K5	Bridge Street Suffk
24 E5	Bridgetown Somset
112 C7	Bridge Trafford Ches W
91 L6	Bridgham Norfk
84 C5	Bridgnorth Shrops
25 L4	Bridgwater Somset
25 L4	Bridgwater Services Somset
135 J6	Bridlington E R Yk
13 L4	Bridport Dorset
54 E3	Bridstow Herefs
122 C3	Brierfield Lancs
124 C7	Brierley Barns
54 F5	Brierley Gloucs
85 G6	Brierley Hill Dudley
117 G1	Brigg N Linc
107 G6	Briggate Norfk
143 H5	Briggswath N York
136 F2	Brigham Cumb
135 G8	Brigham E R Yk
123 H6	Brighouse Calder
16 E5	Brighstone IoW
57 G7	Brighthampton Oxon
10 E5	Brightley Devon
20 D2	Brightling E Susx
62 C5	Brightlingsea Essex
19 J5	Brighton Br & H
111 J2	Brighton le Sands Sefton
176 C3	Brightons Falk
41 H5	Brightwalton W Berk
78 F5	Brightwell Suffk
41 M2	Brightwell Baldwin Oxon

41 L3	Brightwell-cum-Sotwell Oxon
42 A2	Brightwell Upperton Oxon
140 D5	Brignall Dur
184 C6	Brig o'Turk Stirlg
118 C2	Brigsley NE Lin
129 K2	Brigsteer Cumb
88 D6	Brigstock Nhants
58 A5	Brill Bucks
3 J5	Brill Cnwll
68 F5	Brilley Herefs
69 K2	Brimfield Herefs
69 K2	Brimfield Cross Herefs
115 H6	Brimington Derbys
7 J1	Brimley Devon
55 L5	Brimpsfield Gloucs
41 K7	Brimpton W Berk
55 K7	Brimscombe Gloucs
111 J5	Brimstage Wirral
115 F4	Brincliffe Sheff
125 H4	Brind E R Yk
235 c5	Brindister Shet
121 J5	Brindle Lancs
84 E2	Brineton Staffs
88 B5	Bringhurst Leics
70 C4	Bringsty Herefs
88 F7	Brington Cambs
106 C5	Briningham Norfk
118 E6	Brinkhill Lincs
76 F4	Brinkley Cambs
86 E7	Brinklow Warwks
40 A4	Brinkworth Wilts
121 J6	Brinscall Lancs
101 J3	Brinsley Notts
115 H4	Brinsworth Rothm
106 C5	Brinton Norfk
234 c5	Brinyan Ork
105 M7	Brisley Norfk
38 F6	Brislington Bristl
34 C6	Brissenden Green Kent
38 E5	Bristol Bristl
38 D7	Bristol Airport N Som
38 E5	Bristol Zoo Bristl
106 C6	Briston Norfk
28 D5	Britford Wilts
53 J7	Brithdir Caerph
96 B8	Brithdir Gwynd
33 J2	British Legion Village Kent
51 L6	Briton Ferry Neath
42 A2	Britwell Salome Oxon
7 L5	Brixham Torbay
6 E5	Brixton Devon
44 F5	Brixton Gt Lon
27 K4	Brixton Deverill Wilts
73 L1	Brixworth Nhants
56 F6	Brize Norton Oxon
56 F6	Brize Norton Airport Oxon
70 F2	Broad Alley Worcs
40 D3	Broad Blunsdon Swindn
113 M3	Broadbottom Tamesd
17 M2	Broadbridge W Susx
31 J5	Broadbridge Heath W Susx
71 L6	Broad Campden Gloucs
123 G6	Broad Carr Calder
28 B6	Broad Chalke Wilts
12 C3	Broadclyst Devon
174 C4	Broadfield Inver
199 K2	Broadford Highld
31 H6	Broadford Bridge W Susx
166 C7	Broadgairhill Border
70 D4	Broad Green Worcs
179 H7	Broadhaugh Border
48 E5	Broad Haven Pembks
113 H4	Broadheath Traffd
12 E2	Broadhembury Devon

7 J3 **Broadhempston** Devon
40 C5 **Broad Hinton** Wilts
21 G2 **Broadland Row** E Susx
41 H7 **Broad Layings** Hants
215 J3 **Broadley** Moray
71 K5 **Broad Marston** Worcs
14 D5 **Broadmayne** Dorset
49 K6 **Broadmoor** Pembks
13 K3 **Broadoak** Dorset
20 C2 **Broad Oak** E Susx
21 G2 **Broad Oak** E Susx
54 C4 **Broad Oak** Herefs
35 C4 **Broad Oak** Kent
112 D3 **Broad Oak** St Hel
61 H5 **Broad's Green** Essex
35 K2 **Broadstairs** Kent
15 J4 **Broadstone** Poole
83 K5 **Broadstone** Shrops
21 H3 **Broad Street** E Susx
33 L2 **Broad Street** Kent
40 C5 **Broad Town** Wilts
70 D4 **Broadwas** Worcs
59 L4 **Broadwater** Herts
18 F5 **Broadwater** W Susx
84 C4 **Broadwaters** Worcs
48 E5 **Broadway** Pembks
25 L7 **Broadway** Somset
71 K6 **Broadway** Worcs
54 E5 **Broadwell** Gloucs
56 D3 **Broadwell** Gloucs
56 E6 **Broadwell** Oxon
72 F2 **Broadwell** Warwks
13 K2 **Broadwindsor** Dorset
10 F4 **Broadwood Kelly** Devon
9 K6 **Broadwoodwidger** Devon
209 J5 **Brochel** Highld
70 D4 **Brockamin** Worcs
29 L7 **Brockbridge** Hants
92 E7 **Brockdish** Norfk
16 C3 **Brockenhurst** Hants
164 F2 **Brocketsbrae** S Lans
78 D2 **Brockford Street** Suffk
73 J2 **Brockhall** Nhants
31 K1 **Brockham** Surrey
56 B4 **Brockhampton** Gloucs
17 K2 **Brockhampton** Hants
54 E2 **Brockhampton** Herefs
70 C4 **Brockhampton Estate** Herefs
123 H7 **Brockholes** Kirk
126 E7 **Brocklesby** Lincs
38 C6 **Brockley** N Som
77 J1 **Brockley** Suffk
77 G5 **Brockley Green** Suffk
77 J4 **Brockley Green** Suffk
83 G3 **Brockton** Shrops
83 G6 **Brockton** Shrops
83 L5 **Brockton** Shrops
99 J6 **Brockton** Staffs
54 D7 **Brockweir** Gloucs
55 K5 **Brockworth** Gloucs
99 L8 **Brocton** Staffs
162 C3 **Brodick** N Ayrs
214 B3 **Brodie** Moray
115 J1 **Brodsworth** Donc
218 C7 **Brogaig** Highld
39 K3 **Brokenborough** Wilts
113 K6 **Broken Cross** Ches E
27 J2 **Brokerswood** Wilts
111 K5 **Bromborough** Wirral
92 D7 **Brome** Suffk
92 D7 **Brome Street** Suffk
79 G4 **Bromeswell** Suffk
147 L5 **Bromfield** Cumb
83 J7 **Bromfield** Shrops
74 E4 **Bromham** Bed
39 L7 **Bromham** Wilts
45 H6 **Bromley** Gt Lon
84 D4 **Bromley** Shrops

46 C6 **Brompton** Medway
134 E3 **Brompton** N York
141 J7 **Brompton** N York
140 F7 **Brompton-on-Swale** N York
25 G5 **Brompton Ralph** Somset
24 E5 **Brompton Regis** Somset
70 D7 **Bromsberrow** Gloucs
55 G2 **Bromsberrow Heath** Gloucs
71 G1 **Bromsgrove** Worcs
70 B4 **Bromyard** Herefs
66 E2 **Bronant** Cerdgn
65 K5 **Brongest** Cerdgn
98 C4 **Bronington** Wrexhm
68 D7 **Bronllys** Powys
50 E2 **Bronwydd** Carmth
97 K5 **Bronygarth** Shrops
110 A5 **Bron-y-Nant Crematorium** Conwy
28 F8 **Brook** Hants
16 E5 **Brook** IoW
34 E6 **Brook** Kent
30 F4 **Brook** Surrey
93 G4 **Brooke** Norfk
88 B3 **Brooke** Rutlnd
117 K3 **Brookenby** Lincs
174 D5 **Brookfield** Rens
26 F5 **Brookhampton** Somset
28 F8 **Brook Hill** Hants
129 L6 **Brookhouse** Lancs
115 K4 **Brookhouse** Rothm
99 J1 **Brookhouse Green** Ches E
114 B4 **Brookhouses** Derbys
21 K1 **Brookland** Kent
113 H4 **Brooklands** Traffd
59 L7 **Brookmans Park** Herts
45 L2 **Brook Street** Essex
34 C7 **Brook Street** Kent
77 J5 **Brook Street** Suffk
55 J5 **Brookthorpe** Gloucs
42 F8 **Brookwood** Surrey
75 H6 **Broom** C Beds
151 G6 **Broom** Dur
115 H3 **Broom** Rothm
71 K4 **Broom** Warwks
93 H5 **Broome** Norfk
83 H7 **Broome** Shrops
84 F7 **Broome** Worcs
113 G4 **Broomedge** Warrtn
61 H5 **Broomfield** Essex
33 L3 **Broomfield** Kent
47 K6 **Broomfield** Kent
25 K5 **Broomfield** Somset
125 K5 **Broomfleet** E R Yk
150 E3 **Broomhaugh** Nthumb
115 H2 **Broom Hill** Barns
101 H3 **Broom Hill** Notts
159 G2 **Broomhill** Nthumb
34 D3 **Broom Street** Kent
226 F7 **Brora** Highld
84 C3 **Broseley** Shrops
150 A7 **Brotherlee** Dur
124 D5 **Brotherton** N York
142 E4 **Brotton** R & Cl
230 F4 **Broubster** Highld
139 H4 **Brough** Cumb
125 L5 **Brough** E R Yk
231 J2 **Brough** Highld
102 D2 **Brough** Notts
235 d4 **Brough** Shet
98 E4 **Broughall** Shrops
235 d2 **Brough Lodge** Shet
139 H5 **Brough Sowerby** Cumb
165 L3 **Broughton** Border
89 K7 **Broughton** Cambs
111 K8 **Broughton** Flints
28 F5 **Broughton** Hants
121 G4 **Broughton** Lancs

74 C6 **Broughton** M Keyn
126 B8 **Broughton** N Linc
122 D1 **Broughton** N York
134 B5 **Broughton** N York
88 B7 **Broughton** Nhants
72 E6 **Broughton** Oxon
113 J2 **Broughton** Salfd
99 H5 **Broughton** Staffs
36 E6 **Broughton** V Glam
87 G5 **Broughton Astley** Leics
39 K7 **Broughton Gifford** Wilts
71 G3 **Broughton Green** Worcs
71 G4 **Broughton Hackett** Worcs
128 F3 **Broughton-in-Furness** Cumb
145 J6 **Broughton Mains** D & G
128 F2 **Broughton Mills** Cumb
147 J7 **Broughton Moor** Cumb
56 E7 **Broughton Poggs** Oxon
187 H2 **Broughty Ferry** C Dund
29 L4 **Brown Candover** Hants
99 K2 **Brown Edge** Staffs
217 G6 **Brownhill** Abers
187 H4 **Brownhills** Fife
85 J3 **Brownhills** Wsall
41 L7 **Browninghill Green** Hants
99 K2 **Brown Lees** Staffs
15 J5 **Brownsea Island** Dorset
55 K7 **Browns Hill** Gloucs
7 G5 **Brownston** Devon
134 E2 **Broxa** N York
60 B6 **Broxbourne** Herts
178 E3 **Broxburn** E Loth
176 E4 **Broxburn** W Loth
60 F3 **Broxted** Essex
231 K7 **Bruan** Highld
194 C3 **Bruar** P & K
223 K4 **Brucefield** Highld
173 J6 **Bruchag** Ag & B
170 E6 **Bruichladdich** Ag & B
79 G2 **Bruisyard** Suffk
79 G2 **Bruisyard Street** Suffk
125 K8 **Brumby** N Linc
100 C1 **Brund** Staffs
93 G2 **Brundall** Norfk
78 F1 **Brundish** Suffk
78 F1 **Brundish Street** Suffk
190 E3 **Brunery** Highld
159 G7 **Brunswick Village** N u Ty
122 F2 **Brunthwaite** C Brad
87 H5 **Bruntingthorpe** Leics
186 E3 **Brunton** Fife
169 J4 **Brunton** Nthumb
28 E1 **Brunton** Wilts
24 E6 **Brushford** Somset
11 G4 **Brushford Barton** Devon
27 G4 **Bruton** Somset
70 F2 **Bryan's Green** Worcs
15 G2 **Bryanston** Dorset
155 L7 **Brydekirk** D & G
2 a1 **Bryher** IoS
26 D7 **Brympton** Somset
51 G5 **Bryn** Carmth
36 C3 **Bryn** Neath
51 K3 **Brynamman** Carmth
64 F7 **Brynberian** Pembks
95 H4 **Bryncir** Gwynd
51 L5 **Bryn-coch** Neath
94 D6 **Bryncroes** Gwynd
80 E3 **Bryncrug** Gwynd
97 H3 **Bryneglwys** Denbgs

111 G6 **Brynford** Flints
112 E2 **Bryn Gates** Wigan
108 D6 **Bryngwran** IoA
54 B6 **Bryngwyn** Mons
68 D5 **Bryngwyn** Powys
64 E6 **Bryn-Henllan** Pembks
65 K4 **Brynhoffnant** Cerdgn
53 J5 **Brynmawr** Blae G
94 D5 **Bryn-mawr** Gwynd
36 D4 **Brynmenyn** Brdgnd
51 J6 **Brynmill** Swans
36 F4 **Brynna** Rhondd
109 H8 **Brynrefail** Gwynd
37 G4 **Brynsadler** Rhondd
97 G3 **Bryn Saith Marchog** Denbgs
108 F7 **Brynsiencyn** IoA
110 B6 **Bryn-y-Maen** Conwy
198 F2 **Bualintur** Highld
86 D8 **Bubbenhall** Warwks
125 H4 **Bubwith** E R Yk
166 E6 **Buccleuch** Border
174 E1 **Buchanan Smithy** Stirlg
217 L5 **Buchanhaven** Abers
185 J2 **Buchanty** P & K
184 F6 **Buchany** Stirlg
184 C8 **Buchlyvie** Stirlg
148 C5 **Buckabank** Cumb
75 H2 **Buckden** Cambs
131 H4 **Buckden** N York
93 H3 **Buckenham** Norfk
12 E3 **Buckerell** Devon
7 H3 **Buckfast** Devon
7 H3 **Buckfastleigh** Devon
186 F7 **Buckhaven** Fife
54 D5 **Buckholt** Mons
27 H6 **Buckhorn Weston** Dorset
45 H2 **Buckhurst Hill** Essex
215 J2 **Buckie** Moray
73 K7 **Buckingham** Bucks
58 E5 **Buckland** Bucks
7 G6 **Buckland** Devon
71 J7 **Buckland** Gloucs
75 L7 **Buckland** Herts
35 J6 **Buckland** Kent
41 G2 **Buckland** Oxon
31 K2 **Buckland** Surrey
22 F7 **Buckland Brewer** Devon
58 F6 **Buckland Common** Bucks
27 H2 **Buckland Dinham** Somset
10 C3 **Buckland Filleigh** Devon
7 G2 **Buckland in the Moor** Devon
6 D3 **Buckland Monachorum** Devon
14 D2 **Buckland Newton** Dorset
14 C6 **Buckland Ripers** Dorset
25 L8 **Buckland St Mary** Somset
7 H6 **Buckland-Tout-Saints** Devon
41 K6 **Bucklebury** W Berk
16 E3 **Bucklers Hard** Hants
78 F6 **Bucklesham** Suffk
111 J8 **Buckley** Flints
113 G5 **Bucklow Hill** Ches E
102 E7 **Buckminster** Leics
99 K3 **Bucknall** C Stke
117 K7 **Bucknall** Lincs
57 K3 **Bucknell** Oxon
83 G8 **Bucknell** Shrops
215 J2 **Buckpool** Moray
207 G4 **Bucksburn** C Aber
22 E6 **Buck's Cross** Devon
31 H5 **Bucks Green** W Susx
121 H6 **Buckshaw Village** Lancs

30 D3 **Bucks Horn Oak**
Hants
22 E6 **Buck's Mills** Devon
135 J5 **Buckton** E R Yk
169 G2 **Buckton** Nthumb
89 G7 **Buckworth** Cambs
115 L7 **Budby** Notts
187 H2 **Buddon** Angus
9 G4 **Bude** Cnwll
5 M4 **Budge's Shop** Cnwll
12 D6 **Budleigh Salterton**
Devon
3 K5 **Budock Water** Cnwll
99 G4 **Buerton** Ches E
73 J3 **Bugbrooke** Nhants
4 F4 **Bugle** Cnwll
27 H6 **Bugley** Dorset
134 B7 **Bugthorpe** E R Yk
84 B3 **Buildwas** Shrops
68 B4 **Builth Wells** Powys
28 C5 **Bulbridge** Wilts
28 D3 **Bulford** Wilts
98 D2 **Bulkeley** Ches E
86 E6 **Bulkington** Warwks
39 L8 **Bulkington** Wilts
9 K3 **Bulkworthy** Devon
42 E6 **Bullbrook** Br For
29 J3 **Bullington** Hants
117 H6 **Bullington** Lincs
77 J6 **Bulmer** Essex
133 L6 **Bulmer** N York
77 J6 **Bulmer Tye** Essex
45 M3 **Bulphan** Thurr
217 H5 **Bulwark** Abers
101 K4 **Bulwell** C Nott
88 D5 **Bulwick** Nhants
60 C6 **Bumble's Green** Essex
199 K7 **Bunacaimb** Highld
201 J7 **Bunarkaig** Highld
98 E2 **Bunbury** Ches E
212 F5 **Bunchrew** Highld
210 D8 **Bundalloch** Highld
180 E3 **Bunessan** Ag & B
93 G5 **Bungay** Suffk
171 H4 **Bunnahabhain**
Ag & B
101 L6 **Bunny** Notts
212 C7 **Buntait** Highld
60 B3 **Buntingford** Herts
92 D5 **Bunwell** Norfk
92 D5 **Bunwell Hill** Norfk
86 F5 **Burbage** Leics
40 E7 **Burbage** Wilts
42 D4 **Burchett's Green**
W & M
28 B5 **Burcombe** Wilts
58 E4 **Burcott** Bucks
77 K7 **Bures** Essex
56 E5 **Burford** Oxon
69 L2 **Burford** Shrops
189 J7 **Burg** Ag & B
30 C5 **Burgates** Hants
19 J2 **Burgess Hill** W Susx
78 F4 **Burgh** Suffk
148 B3 **Burgh by Sands**
Cumb
93 K3 **Burgh Castle** Norfk
41 J7 **Burghclere** Hants
214 D1 **Burghead** Moray
42 A6 **Burghfield** W Berk
42 A6 **Burghfield Common**
W Berk
44 E7 **Burgh Heath** Surrey
69 J5 **Burghill** Herefs
6 F6 **Burgh Island** Devon
119 G7 **Burgh le Marsh** Lincs
106 F7 **Burgh next Aylsham**
Norfk
117 I4 **Burgh on Bain** Lincs
93 J2 **Burgh St Margaret**
Norfk
93 K5 **Burgh St Peter** Norfk
124 E7 **Burghwallis** Donc
46 B7 **Burham** Kent
30 C7 **Buriton** Hants
98 E2 **Burland** Ches E

4 F2 **Burlawn** Cnwll
55 K7 **Burleigh** Gloucs
25 G7 **Burlescombe** Devon
14 E4 **Burleston** Dorset
16 B2 **Burley** Hants
88 C2 **Burley** Rutlnd
98 E4 **Burleydam** Ches E
69 L5 **Burley Gate** Herefs
123 H2 **Burley in Wharfedale**
C Brad
16 B2 **Burley Street** Hants
123 H2 **Burley Wood Head**
C Brad
98 C7 **Burlton** Shrops
34 E7 **Burmarsh** Kent
72 C6 **Burmington** Warwks
124 F5 **Burn** N York
113 K3 **Burnage** Manch
100 F6 **Burnaston** Derbys
176 B6 **Burnbrae** N Lans
125 K2 **Burnby** E R Yk
138 D7 **Burneside** Cumb
132 D3 **Burneston** N York
38 F7 **Burnett** BaNES
166 F6 **Burnfoot** Border
167 H6 **Burnfoot** Border
155 G4 **Burnfoot** D & G
156 C3 **Burnfoot** D & G
156 C4 **Burnfoot** D & G
185 K6 **Burnfoot** P & K
42 F4 **Burnham** Bucks
105 J4 **Burnham Deepdale**
Norfk
105 K4 **Burnham Market**
Norfk
105 K4 **Burnham Norton**
Norfk
46 F2 **Burnham-on-Crouch**
Essex
25 L2 **Burnham-on-Sea**
Somset
105 K4 **Burnham Overy**
Norfk
105 K4 **Burnham Overy**
Staithe Norfk
105 K4 **Burnham Thorpe**
Norfk
217 L5 **Burnhaven** Abers
154 E3 **Burnhead** D & G
206 D2 **Burnhervie** Abers
84 E4 **Burnhill Green** Staffs
150 F5 **Burnhope** Dur
174 D7 **Burnhouse** N Ayrs
134 F2 **Burniston** N York
122 C4 **Burnley** Lancs
122 B4 **Burnley**
Crematorium Lancs
151 H5 **Burnmoor** Dur
179 K6 **Burnmouth** Border
184 F6 **Burn of Cambus**
Stirlg
150 F4 **Burnopfield** Dur
131 J7 **Burnsall** N York
196 C4 **Burnside** Angus
196 E6 **Burnside** Angus
186 B5 **Burnside** Fife
214 E1 **Burnside** Moray
176 E3 **Burnside** W Loth
187 G1 **Burnside of**
Duntrune Angus
177 H2 **Burntisland** Fife
85 J2 **Burntwood** Staffs
85 J2 **Burntwood Green**
Staffs
132 C7 **Burnt Yates** N York
25 J7 **Burnworthy** Somset
31 G2 **Burpham** Surrey
18 E4 **Burpham** W Susx
168 E7 **Burradon** Nthumb
235 e1 **Burrafirth** Shet
235 d3 **Burravoe** Shet
138 F4 **Burrells** Cumb
195 K8 **Burrelton** P & K
13 H2 **Burridge** Devon
17 G1 **Burridge** Hants
132 C3 **Burrill** N York

125 K8 **Burringham** N Linc
10 F2 **Burrington** Devon
69 J1 **Burrington** Herefs
38 C8 **Burrington** N Som
76 F4 **Burrough Green**
Cambs
87 L2 **Burrough on the Hill**
Leics
130 C4 **Burrow** Lancs
24 E3 **Burrow** Somset
26 A5 **Burrow Bridge**
Somset
42 F7 **Burrowhill** Surrey
50 F7 **Burry Green** Swans
50 F5 **Burry Port** Carmth
120 F5 **Burscough** Lancs
120 F7 **Burscough Bridge**
Lancs
125 J4 **Bursea** E R Yk
16 F1 **Bursledon** Hants
99 K3 **Burslem** C Stke
78 D5 **Burstall** Suffk
13 K2 **Burstock** Dorset
92 D6 **Burston** Norfk
32 B5 **Burstow** Surrey
126 F5 **Burstwick** E R Yk
131 G2 **Burtersett** N York
148 F3 **Burtholme** Cumb
77 H2 **Burthorpe Green**
Suffk
103 L5 **Burtoft** Lincs
111 K6 **Burton** Ches W
112 D8 **Burton** Ches W
15 M4 **Burton** Dorset
116 F6 **Burton** Lincs
49 G6 **Burton** Pembks
25 J3 **Burton** Somset
39 J4 **Burton** Wilts
135 H6 **Burton Agnes** E R Yk
13 L4 **Burton Bradstock**
Dorset
103 G7 **Burton Coggles** Lincs
126 F4 **Burton Constable**
Hall E R Yk
60 E4 **Burton End** Essex
135 G5 **Burton Fleming**
E R Yk
86 E5 **Burton Hastings**
Warwks
129 L4 **Burton-in-Kendal**
Cumb
129 L4 **Burton-in-Kendal**
Services Cumb
130 C5 **Burton in Lonsdale**
N York
101 M4 **Burton Joyce** Notts
88 C8 **Burton Latimer**
Nhants
87 L1 **Burton Lazars** Leics
132 E6 **Burton Leonard**
N York
101 L7 **Burton on the Wolds**
Leics
87 J4 **Burton Overy** Leics
103 J4 **Burton Pedwardine**
Lincs
127 G4 **Burton Pidsea** E R Yk
124 D5 **Burton Salmon**
N York
61 K3 **Burton's Green** Essex
125 K6 **Burton upon Stather**
N Linc
100 E7 **Burton upon Trent**
Staffs
116 F6 **Burton Waters** Lincs
112 E3 **Burtonwood** Warrtn
112 E4 **Burtonwood**
Services Warrtn
98 D2 **Burwardsley** Ches W
84 B6 **Burwarton** Shrops
33 H7 **Burwash** E Susx
20 D2 **Burwash Common**
E Susx
20 D2 **Burwash Weald**
E Susx
76 E2 **Burwell** Cambs

118 E5 **Burwell** Lincs
108 E3 **Burwen** IoA
234 C8 **Burwick** Ork
122 B7 **Bury** Bury
89 K6 **Bury** Cambs
24 E6 **Bury** Somset
18 D3 **Bury** W Susx
60 D4 **Bury Green** Herts
77 J2 **Bury St Edmunds**
Suffk
134 C6 **Burythorpe** N York
175 G6 **Busby** E Rens
40 E2 **Buscot** Oxon
197 J4 **Bush** Abers
69 J4 **Bush Bank** Herefs
85 G3 **Bushbury** Wolves
85 G3 **Bushbury**
Crematorium Wolves
43 J2 **Bushey** Herts
43 J2 **Bushey Heath** Herts
45 G2 **Bush Hill Park** Gt Lon
70 F7 **Bushley** Worcs
40 B5 **Bushton** Wilts
55 K7 **Bussage** Gloucs
26 A4 **Bussex** Somset
38 D7 **Butcombe** N Som
173 H4 **Bute** Ag & B
26 D5 **Butleigh** Somset
26 D4 **Butleigh Wootton**
Somset
72 D4 **Butlers Marston**
Warwks
79 H4 **Butley** Suffk
133 L7 **Buttercrambe** N York
179 G5 **Butterdean** Border
140 E3 **Butterknowle** Dur
12 C2 **Butterleigh** Devon
137 G4 **Buttermere** Cumb
123 H5 **Buttershaw** C Brad
195 G7 **Butterstone** P & K
99 J4 **Butterton** Staffs
100 B2 **Butterton** Staffs
104 C4 **Butterwick** Lincs
133 L4 **Butterwick** N York
134 F5 **Butterwick** N York
82 E2 **Buttington** Powys
84 D7 **Buttonoak** Shrops
78 B3 **Buxhall** Suffk
20 A2 **Buxted** E Susx
114 B6 **Buxton** Derbys
106 F7 **Buxton** Norfk
106 E7 **Buxton Heath** Norfk
53 J4 **Bwlch** Powys
97 K2 **Bwlchgwyn** Wrexhm
66 D3 **Bwlchllan** Cerdgn
94 E7 **Bwlchtocyn** Gwynd
97 J8 **Bwlch-y-cibau** Powys
82 B4 **Bwlch-y-ffridd** Powys
65 H7 **Bwlch-y-groes**
Pembks
82 B8 **Bwlch-y-sarnau**
Powys
150 F7 **Byers Green** Dur
73 G4 **Byfield** Nhants
43 H7 **Byfleet** Surrey
69 H6 **Byford** Herefs
151 G3 **Byker** N u Ty
110 D8 **Bylchau** Conwy
113 G7 **Byley** Ches W
157 K2 **Byrness** Nthumb
12 D5 **Bystock** Devon
88 F7 **Bythorn** Cambs
69 G2 **Byton** Herefs
150 D3 **Bywell** Nthumb
31 G7 **Byworth** W Susx

C

117 J2 **Cabourne** Lincs
171 J5 **Cabrach** Ag & B
215 J8 **Cabrach** Moray
121 G2 **Cabus** Lancs
11 L4 **Cadbury** Devon
175 G4 **Cadder** E Duns
59 H4 **Caddington** C Beds

167 G3 **Caddonfoot** Border
115 K2 **Cadeby** Donc
86 E3 **Cadeby** Leics
11 L4 **Cadeleigh** Devon
20 C2 **Cade Street** E Susx
3 J7 **Cadgwith** Cnwll
186 D6 **Cadham** Fife
113 G3 **Cadishead** Salfd
51 J6 **Cadle** Swans
121 G4 **Cadley** Lancs
28 E2 **Cadley** Wilts
40 E6 **Cadley** Wilts
42 C3 **Cadmore End** Bucks
28 F8 **Cadnam** Hants
117 G2 **Cadney** N Linc
37 H6 **Cadoxton** V Glam
51 L5 **Cadoxton Juxta-Neath** Neath
95 J1 **Caeathro** Gwynd
117 G4 **Caenby** Lincs
66 F6 **Caeo** Carmth
36 D2 **Caerau** Brdgnd
37 H5 **Caerau** Cardif
48 D3 **Caer Farchell** Pembks
108 D5 **Caergeiliog** IoA
97 L2 **Caergwrle** Flints
156 D2 **Caerlanrig** Border
37 M3 **Caerleon** Newpt
37 M3 **Caerleon Roman Amphitheatre** Newpt
108 F8 **Caernarfon** Gwynd
108 F8 **Caernarfon Castle** Gwynd
37 J3 **Caerphilly** Caerph
82 B5 **Caersws** Powys
65 L4 **Caerwedros** Cerdgn
38 C3 **Caerwent** Mons
110 F6 **Caerwys** Flints
233 c6 **Cairinis** W Isls
172 E1 **Cairnbaan** Ag & B
217 J2 **Cairnbulg** Abers
179 J5 **Cairncross** Border
174 C4 **Cairncurran** Inver
183 H5 **Cairndow** Ag & B
176 E2 **Cairneyhill** Fife
215 J3 **Cairnfield House** Moray
144 C5 **Cairngarroch** D & G
204 B5 **Cairngorm Mountains**
215 K5 **Cairnie** Abers
217 G6 **Cairnorrie** Abers
144 C2 **Cairnryan** D & G
215 H4 **Cairnty** Moray
93 L2 **Caister-on-Sea** Norfk
117 J2 **Caistor** Lincs
92 F3 **Caistor St Edmund** Norfk
232 e2 **Calanais** W Isls
16 E5 **Calbourne** IoW
111 G6 **Calcot** Flints
56 C6 **Calcot** Gloucs
42 A6 **Calcot Row** W Berk
215 G2 **Calcots** Moray
148 B6 **Caldbeck** Cumb
75 L3 **Caldecote** Cambs
89 G5 **Caldecote** Cambs
75 J6 **Caldecote** Herts
75 L3 **Caldecote Highfields** Cambs
74 E2 **Caldecott** Nhants
41 J2 **Caldecott** Oxon
88 C5 **Caldecott** Rutlnd
175 K5 **Calderbank** N Lans
136 E6 **Calder Bridge** Cumb
175 L5 **Caldercruix** N Lans
123 L6 **Calder Grove** Wakefd
164 D2 **Caldermill** S Lans
121 G2 **Calder Vale** Lancs
175 H7 **Calderwood** S Lans
49 K7 **Caldey Island** Pembks
38 C3 **Caldicot** Mons
85 H4 **Caldmore** Wsall
140 E5 **Caldwell** N York
237 a7 **Calf of Man** IoM
234 d4 **Calfsound** Ork

189 J6 **Calgary** Ag & B
214 D3 **Califer** Moray
176 B3 **California** Falk
93 K1 **California** Norfk
101 G7 **Calke** Derbys
209 L4 **Callakille** Highld
184 D5 **Callander** Stirlg
232 e2 **Callanish** W Isls
3 K2 **Callestick** Cnwll
199 K5 **Calligarry** Highld
6 A3 **Callington** Cnwll
69 J7 **Callow** Herefs
70 E4 **Callow End** Worcs
40 B4 **Callow Hill** Wilts
29 G7 **Calmore** Hants
56 B6 **Calmsden** Gloucs
39 M6 **Calne** Wilts
16 F3 **Calshot** Hants
6 C3 **Calstock** Cnwll
40 B6 **Calstone Wellington** Wilts
106 E6 **Calthorpe** Norfk
107 J7 **Calthorpe Street** Norfk
148 E6 **Calthwaite** Cumb
131 G7 **Calton** N York
100 C3 **Calton** Staffs
98 E2 **Calveley** Ches E
114 E6 **Calver** Derbys
98 E5 **Calverhall** Shrops
11 L3 **Calverleigh** Devon
73 L6 **Calverton** M Keyn
101 L3 **Calverton** Notts
194 C3 **Calvine** P & K
147 K4 **Calvo** Cumb
165 L3 **Calzeat** Border
55 H7 **Cam** Gloucs
190 F4 **Camasachoirce** Highld
190 F4 **Camasine** Highld
210 E8 **Camas Luinie** Highld
209 H6 **Camastianavaig** Highld
212 D6 **Camault Muir** Highld
21 J2 **Camber** E Susx
42 E7 **Camberley** Surrey
44 F5 **Camberwell** Gt Lon
124 F5 **Camblesforth** N York
158 C5 **Cambo** Nthumb
3 H4 **Camborne** Cnwll
75 K3 **Cambourne** Cambs
76 C3 **Cambridge** Cambs
55 H7 **Cambridge** Gloucs
76 C3 *Cambridge Airport* Cambs
76 B3 **Cambridge City Crematorium** Cambs
75 L2 **Cambridge Services** Cambs
3 H3 **Cambrose** Cnwll
185 H8 **Cambus** Clacks
223 G8 **Cambusavie Platform** Highld
185 G8 **Cambusbarron** Stirlg
185 G8 **Cambuskenneth** Stirlg
175 H6 **Cambuslang** S Lans
205 J5 **Cambus o' May** Abers
165 K2 **Cambuswallace** S Lans
44 F4 **Camden Town** Gt Lon
38 E8 **Cameley** BaNES
8 E7 **Camelford** Cnwll
176 B3 **Camelon** Falk
214 C7 **Camerory** Highld
70 D7 **Camer's Green** Worcs
39 G8 **Camerton** BaNES
136 E2 **Camerton** Cumb
193 J5 **Camghouran** P & K
167 J4 **Camieston** Border
207 G6 **Cammachmore** Abers
116 F5 **Cammeringham** Lincs
223 G4 **Camore** Highld
161 J5 **Campbeltown** Ag & B
161 H5 *Campbeltown Airport* Ag & B

154 F4 **Cample** D & G
195 K8 **Campmuir** P & K
176 E5 **Camps** W Loth
124 E7 **Campsall** Donc
79 G4 **Campsea Ash** Suffk
75 G6 **Campton** C Beds
167 K6 **Camptown** Border
48 F4 **Camrose** Pembks
194 C6 **Camserney** P & K
191 L2 **Camusnagaul** Highld
220 D4 **Camusnagaul** Highld
209 L6 **Camusteel** Highld
209 L6 **Camusterrach** Highld
28 F7 **Canada** Hants
205 H5 **Candacraig** Abers
118 F7 **Candlesby** Lincs
165 L2 **Candy Mill** Border
42 B4 **Cane End** Oxon
46 E2 **Canewdon** Essex
15 K5 **Canford Cliffs** Poole
38 E5 **Canford Crematorium** Bristl
15 J4 **Canford Heath** Poole
231 L2 **Canisbay** Highld
86 C7 **Canley** Covtry
86 C7 **Canley Crematorium** Covtry
27 K7 **Cann** Dorset
198 C4 **Canna** Highld
211 L7 **Cannich** Highld
25 K4 **Cannington** Somset
45 H4 **Canning Town** Gt Lon
85 H2 **Cannock** Staffs
99 M8 **Cannock Chase** Staffs
69 H6 **Cannon Bridge** Herefs
156 C6 **Canonbie** D & G
70 B5 **Canon Frome** Herefs
69 J5 **Canon Pyon** Herefs
73 H4 **Canons Ashby** Nhants
2 F4 **Canonstown** Cnwll
34 F3 **Canterbury** Kent
34 F3 **Canterbury Cathedral** Kent
93 H3 **Cantley** Norfk
37 J5 **Canton** Cardif
213 J5 **Cantraywood** Highld
130 C5 **Cantsfield** Lancs
46 D4 **Canvey Island** Essex
117 G7 **Canwick** Lincs
9 G6 **Canworthy Water** Cnwll
191 L2 **Caol** Highld
232 e4 **Caolas Scalpaigh** W Isls
188 D6 **Caoles** Ag & B
201 G6 **Caonich** Highld
33 H4 **Capel** Kent
31 K4 **Capel** Surrey
80 E7 **Capel Bangor** Cerdgn
108 F5 **Capel Coch** IoA
96 A2 **Capel Curig** Conwy
50 F2 **Capel Dewi** Carmth
66 B6 **Capel Dewi** Cerdgn
80 E6 **Capel-Dewi** Cerdgn
96 C2 **Capel Garmon** Conwy
51 H4 **Capel Hendre** Carmth
65 J7 **Capel Iwan** Carmth
35 H6 **Capel le Ferne** Kent
108 E6 **Capel Mawr** IoA
108 F4 **Capel Parc** IoA
79 H5 **Capel St Andrew** Suffk
78 C6 **Capel St Mary** Suffk
80 E7 **Capel Seion** Cerdgn
109 L6 **Capelulo** Conwy
111 K6 **Capenhurst** Ches W
158 C6 **Capheaton** Nthumb
174 E6 **Caplaw** E Rens
166 C5 **Cappercleuch** Border
7 J5 **Capton** Devon
195 H7 **Caputh** P & K
174 F3 **Carbeth Inn** Stirlg
2 F4 **Carbis Bay** Cnwll
208 F5 **Carbost** Highld
208 F7 **Carbost** Highld

115 G4 **Carbrook** Sheff
91 L3 **Carbrooke** Norfk
102 B4 **Car Colston** Notts
124 E8 **Carcroft** Donc
186 C7 **Cardenden** Fife
214 F5 **Cardhu** Moray
37 J5 **Cardiff** Cardif
37 G6 *Cardiff Airport* V Glam
37 K4 **Cardiff Gate Services** Cardif
37 H4 **Cardiff West Services** Cardif
65 G5 **Cardigan** Cerdgn
74 F5 **Cardington** Bed
83 K4 **Cardington** Shrops
5 H3 **Cardinham** Cnwll
144 D8 **Cardrain** D & G
166 D2 **Cardrona** Border
174 C3 **Cardross** Ag & B
144 D7 **Cardryne** D & G
147 L3 **Cardurnock** Cumb
88 E1 **Careby** Lincs
196 E4 **Careston** Angus
49 H6 **Carew** Pembks
49 H6 **Carew Cheriton** Pembks
49 H6 **Carew Newton** Pembks
54 E2 **Carey** Herefs
175 K6 **Carfin** N Lans
178 B7 **Carfraemill** Border
93 H2 **Cargate Green** Norfk
155 G6 **Cargenbridge** D & G
195 J8 **Cargill** P & K
148 C3 **Cargo** Cumb
6 C4 **Cargreen** Cnwll
168 B2 **Carham** Nthumb
24 F3 **Carhampton** Somset
3 J3 **Carharrack** Cnwll
193 K5 **Carie** P & K
233 c6 **Carinish** W Isls
16 F5 **Carisbrooke** IoW
129 H4 **Cark** Cumb
6 B4 **Carkeel** Cnwll
232 e2 **Carlabhagh** W Isls
140 F4 **Carlbury** Darltn
88 F2 **Carlby** Lincs
168 C6 **Carlcroft** Nthumb
3 G5 **Carleen** Cnwll
122 E1 **Carleton** N York
120 D3 **Carleton Crematorium** Bpool
92 C3 **Carleton Forehoe** Norfk
92 D5 **Carleton Rode** Norfk
93 H3 **Carleton St Peter** Norfk
216 D5 **Carlincraig** Abers
39 G8 **Carlingcott** BaNES
148 D4 **Carlisle** Cumb
148 E3 *Carlisle Airport* Cumb
148 C4 **Carlisle Crematorium** Cumb
177 G6 **Carlops** Border
232 e2 **Carloway** W Isls
124 B7 **Carlton** Barns
74 D4 **Carlton** Bed
76 F4 **Carlton** Cambs
123 L5 **Carlton** Leeds
86 E3 **Carlton** Leics
124 F5 **Carlton** N York
131 K3 **Carlton** N York
133 J3 **Carlton** N York
101 L4 **Carlton** Notts
141 J3 **Carlton** S on T
79 H2 **Carlton** Suffk
93 K5 **Carlton Colville** Suffk
87 K4 **Carlton Curlieu** Leics
76 F4 **Carlton Green** Cambs
133 G4 **Carlton Husthwaite** N York
142 B6 **Carlton-in-Cleveland** N York
115 L5 **Carlton in Lindrick** Notts

102 E2 **Carlton-le-Moorland** Lincs
132 F4 **Carlton Miniott** N York
116 D8 **Carlton-on-Trent** Notts
102 F4 **Carlton Scroop** Lincs
175 L7 **Carluke** S Lans
164 F4 **Carmacoup** S Lans
50 E2 **Carmarthen** Carmth
51 H3 **Carmel** Carmth
111 G6 **Carmel** Flints
95 H2 **Carmel** Gwynd
165 H2 **Carmichael** S Lans
99 K3 **Carmountside Crematorium** C Stke
175 G6 **Carmunnock** C Glas
175 H6 **Carmyle** C Glas
196 E7 **Carmyllie** Angus
135 H6 **Carnaby** E R Yk
187 J6 **Carnbee** Fife
185 L6 **Carnbo** P & K
3 H3 **Carn Brea** Cnwll
216 F8 **Carnbrogie** Abers
210 D8 **Carndu** Highld
164 D1 **Carnduff** S Lans
163 L3 **Carnell** E Ayrs
129 K5 **Carnforth** Lancs
200 E2 **Carn-gorm** Highld
3 G4 **Carnhell Green** Cnwll
206 F4 **Carnie** Abers
3 H4 **Carnkie** Cnwll
3 J4 **Carnkie** Cnwll
81 K4 **Carno** Powys
200 D6 **Carnoch** Highld
176 E1 **Carnock** Fife
4 C7 **Carnon Downs** Cnwll
216 C4 **Carnousie** Abers
187 J1 **Carnoustie** Angus
165 J1 **Carnwath** S Lans
131 J2 **Carol Green** Solhll
161 K2 **Carperby** N York
203 L2 **Carradale** Ag & B
236 C6 **Carrbridge** Highld
236 C6 **Carrefour** Jersey
108 E4 **Carreglefn** IoA
123 L5 **Carr Gate** Wakefd
116 C1 **Carrhouse** N Linc
172 F2 **Carrick** Ag & B
183 H8 **Carrick Castle** Ag & B
176 D3 **Carriden** Falk
177 J6 **Carrington** Mdloth
113 H3 **Carrington** Traffd
97 H4 **Carrog** Denbgs
176 B2 **Carron** Falk
214 F6 **Carron** Moray
154 F3 **Carronbridge** D & G
175 K2 **Carron Bridge** Stirlg
176 B2 **Carronshore** Falk
149 K5 **Carr Shield** Nthumb
155 J7 **Carrutherstown** D & G
174 C5 **Carruth House** Inver
151 H6 **Carrville** Dur
181 H3 **Carsaig** Ag & B
190 D5 **Carse Gray** Angus
145 G2 **Carseriggan** D & G
147 H3 **Carsethorn** D & G
44 F6 **Carshalton** Gt Lon
100 E2 **Carsington** Derbys
161 H7 **Carskey** Ag & B
145 K4 **Carsluith** D & G
153 L4 **Carsphairn** D & G
165 H1 **Carstairs** S Lans
165 J1 **Carstairs Junction** S Lans
56 F6 **Carterton** Oxon
4 F5 **Carthew** Cnwll
132 D3 **Carthorpe** N York
165 G1 **Cartland** S Lans
129 H4 **Cartmel** Cumb
50 F4 **Carway** Carmth
55 J6 **Cashe's Green** Gloucs
57 J5 **Cassington** Oxon
151 J7 **Cassop Colliery** Dur
236 C3 **Castel** Guern

130 C4 **Casterton** Cumb
91 J1 **Castle Acre** Norfk
74 C3 **Castle Ashby** Nhants
233 b9 **Castlebay** W Isls
131 J2 **Castle Bolton** N York
85 K5 **Castle Bromwich** Solhll
103 G8 **Castle Bytham** Lincs
49 H2 **Castlebythe** Pembks
82 D3 **Castle Caereinion** Powys
76 F6 **Castle Camps** Cambs
148 F4 **Castle Carrock** Cumb
175 K3 **Castlecary** Falk
26 F5 **Castle Cary** Somset
39 J5 **Castle Combe** Wilts
101 H6 **Castle Donington** Leics
146 D3 **Castle Douglas** D & G
40 C2 **Castle Eaton** Swindn
151 K7 **Castle Eden** Dur
124 C5 **Castleford** Wakefd
70 C5 **Castle Frome** Herefs
100 F8 **Castle Gresley** Derbys
77 H7 **Castle Hedingham** Essex
166 C3 **Castlehill** Border
231 H2 **Castlehill** Highld
78 D5 **Castle Hill** Suffk
174 D3 **Castlehill** W Duns
144 D3 **Castle Kennedy** D & G
182 E7 **Castle Lachlan** Ag & B
48 F7 **Castlemartin** Pembks
175 G6 **Castlemilk** C Glas
70 E6 **Castlemorton** Worcs
156 A4 **Castle O'er** D & G
83 H3 **Castle Pulverbatch** Shrops
137 J3 **Castlerigg Stone Circle** Cumb
105 G7 **Castle Rising** Norfk
150 D5 **Castleside** Dur
213 H4 **Castle Stuart** Highld
74 B5 **Castlethorpe** M Keyn
156 E4 **Castleton** Border
114 D5 **Castleton** Derbys
142 E5 **Castleton** N York
37 K4 **Castleton** Newpt
122 D7 **Castleton** Rochdl
231 H3 **Castletown** Highld
237 b7 **Castletown** IoM
151 J4 **Castletown** Sundld
123 K2 **Castley** N York
91 L4 **Caston** Norfk
89 G4 **Castor** C Pete
172 F7 **Catacol** N Ayrs
115 H4 **Catcliffe** Rothm
40 A5 **Catcomb** Wilts
26 B4 **Catcott** Somset
26 B3 **Catcott Burtle** Somset
32 C3 **Caterham** Surrey
107 H7 **Catfield** Norfk
45 G5 **Catford** Gt Lon
121 G4 **Catforth** Lancs
175 G6 **Cathcart** C Glas
53 H3 **Cathedine** Powys
30 B8 **Catherington** Hants
13 J4 **Catherston Leweston** Dorset
17 G2 **Catisfield** Hants
202 F6 **Catlodge** Highld
76 C6 **Catmere End** Essex
41 J4 **Catmore** W Berk
129 L6 **Caton** Lancs
129 L6 **Caton Green** Lancs
164 B4 **Catrine** E Ayrs
20 F3 **Catsfield** E Susx
26 D6 **Catsgore** Somset
85 G8 **Catshill** Worcs
161 H7 **Cattadale** Ag & B
133 G8 **Cattal** N York
62 D2 **Cattawade** Suffk
121 G3 **Catterall** Lancs
141 G7 **Catterick** N York

141 G7 **Catterick Bridge** N York
148 E7 **Catterlen** Cumb
197 L2 **Catterline** Abers
124 D2 **Catterton** N York
31 G3 **Catteshall** Surrey
87 G7 **Catthorpe** Leics
14 B3 **Cattistock** Dorset
132 E4 **Catton** N York
92 F2 **Catton** Norfk
149 L4 **Catton** Nthumb
126 E2 **Catwick** E R Yk
88 F8 **Catworth** Cambs
55 L6 **Caudle Green** Gloucs
57 K3 **Caulcott** Oxon
197 G6 **Cauldcots** Angus
184 E8 **Cauldhame** Stirlg
167 H6 **Cauldmill** Border
100 B3 **Cauldon** Staffs
86 B1 **Cauldwell** Derbys
147 G4 **Caulkerbush** D & G
156 D6 **Caulside** D & G
27 G8 **Caundle Marsh** Dorset
102 C1 **Caunton** Notts
145 J3 **Causeway End** D & G
61 G4 **Causeway End** Essex
165 K3 **Causewayend** S Lans
185 G7 **Causewayhead** Stirlg
207 H2 **Causeyend** Abers
158 F3 **Causey Park Bridge** Nthumb
77 J5 **Cavendish** Suffk
77 H1 **Cavenham** Suffk
57 L3 **Caversfield** Oxon
42 B5 **Caversham** Readg
99 L4 **Caverswall** Staffs
167 L4 **Caverton Mill** Border
213 K4 **Cawdor** Highld
124 E3 **Cawood** N York
6 C5 **Cawsand** Cnwll
106 D7 **Cawston** Norfk
123 K8 **Cawthorne** Barns
75 K3 **Caxton** Cambs
83 K8 **Caynham** Shrops
102 F3 **Caythorpe** Lincs
102 B4 **Caythorpe** Notts
135 G3 **Cayton** N York
233 b6 **Ceann a Bhaigh** W Isls
201 K3 **Ceannacroc Lodge** Highld
232 f3 **Cearsiadar** W Isls
37 L3 **Cefn** Newpt
96 E3 **Cefn-brith** Conwy
36 D4 **Cefn Cribwr** Brdgnd
51 G3 **Cefneithin** Carmth
67 J5 **Cefngorwydd** Powys
97 L4 **Cefn-mawr** Wrexhm
49 K3 **Cefn-y-pant** Carmth
187 J6 **Cellardyke** Fife
99 L3 **Cellarhead** Staffs
108 E3 **Cemaes** IoA
81 H3 **Cemmaes** Powys
81 H3 **Cemmaes Road** Powys
65 J6 **Cenarth** Cerdgn
186 F5 **Ceres** Fife
14 C3 **Cerne Abbas** Dorset
40 B2 **Cerney Wick** Gloucs
108 E6 **Cerrigceinwen** IoA
96 E3 **Cerrigydrudion** Conwy
95 J1 **Ceunant** Gwynd
55 J2 **Chaceley** Gloucs
3 K3 **Chacewater** Cnwll
73 K7 **Chackmore** Bucks
72 F5 **Chacombe** Nhants
71 H5 **Chadbury** Worcs
113 K1 **Chadderton** Oldham
101 G5 **Chaddesden** C Derb
84 F8 **Chaddesley Corbett** Worcs
6 C1 **Chaddlehanger** Devon
41 H5 **Chaddleworth** W Berk

57 G4 **Chadlington** Oxon
72 D4 **Chadshunt** Warwks
102 C7 **Chadwell** Leics
45 J3 **Chadwell Heath** Gt Lon
45 M4 **Chadwell St Mary** Thurr
70 E2 **Chadwick** Worcs
86 B8 **Chadwick End** Solhll
13 J1 **Chaffcombe** Somset
11 G7 **Chagford** Devon
19 K2 **Chailey** E Susx
33 J4 **Chainhurst** Kent
32 B3 **Chaldon** Surrey
16 F6 **Chale** IoW
16 F6 **Chale Green** IoW
43 G3 **Chalfont Common** Bucks
43 G2 **Chalfont St Giles** Bucks
43 G3 **Chalfont St Peter** Bucks
55 K7 **Chalford** Gloucs
27 K2 **Chalford** Wilts
41 M2 **Chalgrove** Oxon
46 A5 **Chalk** Kent
34 B2 **Chalkwell** Kent
23 L3 **Challacombe** Devon
145 H2 **Challoch** D & G
34 D5 **Challock** Kent
59 G3 **Chalton** C Beds
30 B7 **Chalton** Hants
42 F4 **Chalvey** Slough
20 B4 **Chalvington** E Susx
43 H2 **Chandler's Cross** Herts
29 H7 **Chandler's Ford** Hants
126 D4 **Chanterlands Crematorium** C KuH
27 G3 **Chantry** Somset
78 D5 **Chantry** Suffk
186 D8 **Chapel** Fife
123 L3 **Chapel Allerton** Leeds
26 B2 **Chapel Allerton** Somset
4 F2 **Chapel Amble** Cnwll
73 K2 **Chapel Brampton** Nhants
99 J5 **Chapel Chorlton** Staffs
77 K6 **Chapelend Way** Essex
114 B5 **Chapel-en-le-Frith** Derbys
72 F3 **Chapel Green** Warwks
124 E5 **Chapel Haddlesey** N York
175 K5 **Chapelhall** N Lans
217 K2 **Chapel Hill** Abers
103 K2 **Chapel Hill** Lincs
54 D7 **Chapel Hill** Mons
123 L2 **Chapel Hill** N York
166 C5 **Chapelhope** Border
156 B7 **Chapelknowe** D & G
82 F7 **Chapel Lawn** Shrops
130 E4 **Chapel le Dale** N York
25 H5 **Chapel Leigh** Somset
206 D1 **Chapel of Garioch** Abers
144 D6 **Chapel Rossan** D & G
41 L6 **Chapel Row** W Berk
119 L6 **Chapel St Leonards** Lincs
137 K6 **Chapel Stile** Cumb
197 G6 **Chapelton** Angus
23 J6 **Chapelton** Devon
175 J8 **Chapelton** S Lans
121 L7 **Chapeltown** Bl w D
204 F2 **Chapeltown** Moray
115 G3 **Chapeltown** Sheff
27 J2 **Chapmanslade** Wilts
9 J6 **Chapmans Well** Devon
60 B8 **Chapmore End** Herts
61 L3 **Chappel** Essex
13 H2 **Chard** Somset

13 J2	**Chard Junction** Somset
13 H1	**Chardleigh Green** Somset
13 H2	**Chardstock** Devon
39 G3	**Charfield** S Glos
34 C5	**Charing** Kent
34 C5	**Charing Crematorium** Kent
71 L6	**Charingworth** Gloucs
57 G4	**Charlbury** Oxon
39 H6	**Charlcombe** BaNES
39 M5	**Charlcutt** Wilts
72 C3	**Charlecote** Warwks
85 H5	**Charlemont** Sandw
23 L5	**Charles** Devon
196 C7	**Charleston** Angus
207 H5	**Charlestown** C Aber
123 H3	**Charlestown** C Brad
122 E5	**Charlestown** Calder
5 G5	**Charlestown** Cnwll
176 E2	**Charlestown** Fife
213 G5	**Charlestown** Highld
219 J6	**Charlestown** Highld
113 J2	**Charlestown** Salfd
78 B4	**Charles Tye** Suffk
114 A3	**Charlesworth** Derbys
25 K4	**Charlinch** Somset
186 E5	**Charlottetown** Fife
45 H4	**Charlton** Gt Lon
73 G7	**Charlton** Nhants
157 K3	**Charlton** Nthumb
41 H3	**Charlton** Oxon
25 L6	**Charlton** Somset
27 G2	**Charlton** Somset
18 B3	**Charlton** W Susx
27 K6	**Charlton** Wilts
39 L3	**Charlton** Wilts
71 H5	**Charlton** Worcs
83 L2	**Charlton** Wrekin
56 B3	**Charlton Abbots** Gloucs
26 D5	**Charlton Adam** Somset
28 D6	**Charlton-All-Saints** Wilts
14 D4	**Charlton Down** Dorset
26 F6	**Charlton Horethorne** Somset
55 L4	**Charlton Kings** Gloucs
26 D5	**Charlton Mackrell** Somset
15 G2	**Charlton Marshall** Dorset
27 G5	**Charlton Musgrove** Somset
57 K5	**Charlton-on-Otmoor** Oxon
15 G2	**Charlton on the Hill** Dorset
28 C1	**Charlton St Peter** Wilts
30 A5	**Charlwood** Hants
31 L3	**Charlwood** Surrey
14 D4	**Charminster** Dorset
13 J4	**Charmouth** Dorset
58 A3	**Charndon** Bucks
41 G2	**Charney Bassett** Oxon
121 H7	**Charnock Richard** Lancs
121 H6	**Charnock Richard Crematorium** Lancs
121 H7	**Charnock Richard Services** Lancs
78 F3	**Charsfield** Suffk
41 L8	**Charter Alley** Hants
179 G8	**Charterhall** Border
26 D1	**Charterhouse** Somset
175 K1	**Chartershall** Stirlg
34 E4	**Chartham** Kent
34 E4	**Chartham Hatch** Kent
58 F7	**Chartridge** Bucks
33 K4	**Chart Sutton** Kent
42 C5	**Charvil** Wokham
73 G4	**Charwelton** Nhants
85 J2	**Chase Terrace** Staffs
85 J2	**Chasetown** Staffs
56 E3	**Chastleton** Oxon
9 J4	**Chasty** Devon
122 B2	**Chatburn** Lancs
99 H5	**Chatcull** Staffs
46 C6	**Chatham** Medway
61 H5	**Chatham Green** Essex
169 J4	**Chathill** Nthumb
114 E7	**Chatsworth House** Derbys
46 C5	**Chattenden** Medway
90 B6	**Chatteris** Cambs
122 B6	**Chatterton** Lancs
78 C6	**Chattisham** Suffk
168 B5	**Chatto** Border
168 F4	**Chatton** Nthumb
11 G3	**Chawleigh** Devon
30 B4	**Chawton** Hants
100 A4	**Cheadle** Staffs
113 K4	**Cheadle** Stockp
113 K4	**Cheadle Hulme** Stockp
44 E7	**Cheam** Gt Lon
58 B6	**Chearsley** Bucks
99 J6	**Chebsey** Staffs
42 A4	**Checkendon** Oxon
99 G4	**Checkley** Ches E
100 B5	**Checkley** Staffs
77 H3	**Chedburgh** Suffk
26 C2	**Cheddar** Somset
58 F4	**Cheddington** Bucks
99 L3	**Cheddleton** Staffs
25 K6	**Cheddon Fitzpaine** Somset
93 H4	**Chedgrave** Norfk
13 L2	**Chedington** Dorset
93 H7	**Chediston** Suffk
56 B5	**Chedworth** Gloucs
25 M4	**Chedzoy** Somset
113 J2	**Cheetham Hill** Manch
11 H3	**Cheldon** Devon
113 J6	**Chelford** Ches E
101 G6	**Chellaston** C Derb
74 D4	**Chellington** Bed
84 C5	**Chelmarsh** Shrops
78 E6	**Chelmondiston** Suffk
114 C7	**Chelmorton** Derbys
61 H6	**Chelmsford** Essex
61 H6	**Chelmsford Crematorium** Essex
85 L6	**Chelmsley Wood** Solhll
44 F4	**Chelsea** Gt Lon
45 J7	**Chelsfield** Gt Lon
77 L5	**Chelsworth** Suffk
55 L4	**Cheltenham** Gloucs
55 L4	**Cheltenham Crematorium** Gloucs
74 E1	**Chelveston** Nhants
38 C6	**Chelvey** N Som
38 F7	**Chelwood** BaNES
32 D6	**Chelwood Gate** E Susx
40 C2	**Chelworth Lower Green** Wilts
40 B2	**Chelworth Upper Green** Wilts
83 H6	**Cheney Longville** Shrops
43 G2	**Chenies** Bucks
38 D2	**Chepstow** Mons
40 B6	**Cherhill** Wilts
55 K7	**Cherington** Gloucs
72 C6	**Cherington** Warwks
29 L5	**Cheriton** Hants
35 G7	**Cheriton** Kent
50 F6	**Cheriton** Swans
11 H6	**Cheriton Bishop** Devon
11 K4	**Cheriton Fitzpaine** Devon
49 G7	**Cheriton or Stackpole Elidor** Pembks
98 F8	**Cherrington** Wrekin
126 B3	**Cherry Burton** E R Yk
76 C3	**Cherry Hinton** Cambs
70 F4	**Cherry Orchard** Worcs
117 G6	**Cherry Willingham** Lincs
43 H6	**Chertsey** Surrey
57 K3	**Cherwell Valley Services** Oxon
14 E3	**Cheselbourne** Dorset
58 F7	**Chesham** Bucks
122 B7	**Chesham** Bury
58 F7	**Chesham Bois** Bucks
60 B7	**Cheshunt** Herts
14 B6	**Chesil Beach** Dorset
85 H3	**Cheslyn Hay** Staffs
85 L8	**Chessetts Wood** Warwks
44 D7	**Chessington** Gt Lon
44 D7	**Chessington World of Adventures** Gt Lon
112 B7	**Chester** Ches W
26 F3	**Chesterblade** Somset
112 B7	**Chester Cathedral** Ches W
111 L7	**Chester Crematorium** Ches W
115 G7	**Chesterfield** Derbys
115 H6	**Chesterfield Crematorium** Derbys
101 H1	**Chesterfield Services** Derbys
177 K5	**Chesterhill** Mdloth
151 G5	**Chester-le-Street** Dur
151 G5	**Chester Moor** Dur
167 J5	**Chesters** Border
167 K7	**Chesters** Border
112 C6	**Chester Services** Ches W
76 C3	**Chesterton** Cambs
89 G4	**Chesterton** Cambs
56 A7	**Chesterton** Gloucs
57 K4	**Chesterton** Oxon
84 D4	**Chesterton** Shrops
72 D3	**Chesterton Green** Warwks
149 L2	**Chesterwood** Nthumb
112 B7	**Chester Zoo** Ches W
47 J6	**Chestfield** Kent
7 G4	**Cheston** Devon
99 G6	**Cheswardine** Shrops
168 F1	**Cheswick** Nthumb
14 B2	**Chetnole** Dorset
90 D6	**Chettisham** Cambs
27 L8	**Chettle** Dorset
84 B5	**Chetton** Shrops
99 G7	**Chetwynd** Wrekin
99 H8	**Chetwynd Aston** Wrekin
76 F3	**Cheveley** Cambs
32 E2	**Chevening** Kent
77 H3	**Chevington** Suffk
168 A7	**Cheviot Hills**
24 F7	**Chevithorne** Devon
38 E7	**Chew Magna** BaNES
38 E7	**Chew Stoke** BaNES
38 F6	**Chewton Keynsham** BaNES
26 E2	**Chewton Mendip** Somset
74 C5	**Chicheley** M Keyn
18 B5	**Chichester** W Susx
18 B4	**Chichester Crematorium** W Susx
14 C6	**Chickerell** Dorset
27 K4	**Chicklade** Wilts
30 A7	**Chidden** Hants
30 F4	**Chiddingfold** Surrey
20 B3	**Chiddingly** E Susx
32 E4	**Chiddingstone** Kent
32 F4	**Chiddingstone Causeway** Kent
13 K4	**Chideock** Dorset
17 L2	**Chidham** W Susx
123 K6	**Chidswell** Kirk
41 J5	**Chieveley** W Berk
41 J6	**Chieveley Services** W Berk
61 G6	**Chignall St James** Essex
61 G5	**Chignall Smealy** Essex
45 H2	**Chigwell** Essex
45 J2	**Chigwell Row** Essex
29 H4	**Chilbolton** Hants
29 J5	**Chilcomb** Hants
13 M4	**Chilcombe** Dorset
26 F2	**Chilcompton** Somset
86 C2	**Chilcote** Leics
111 K6	**Childer Thornton** Ches W
27 J8	**Child Okeford** Dorset
41 G3	**Childrey** Oxon
98 F7	**Child's Ercall** Shrops
71 J6	**Childswickham** Worcs
112 B4	**Childwall** Lpool
14 B3	**Chilfrome** Dorset
18 A3	**Chilgrove** W Susx
34 E4	**Chilham** Kent
10 C3	**Chillaton** Devon
35 H4	**Chillenden** Kent
16 F5	**Chillerton** IoW
79 H4	**Chillesford** Suffk
168 F4	**Chillingham** Nthumb
7 J7	**Chillington** Devon
13 K1	**Chillington** Somset
27 L5	**Chilmark** Wilts
34 C6	**Chilmington Green** Kent
56 F4	**Chilson** Oxon
6 B2	**Chilsworthy** Cnwll
9 J4	**Chilsworthy** Devon
42 C2	**Chiltern Hills**
42 F2	**Chilterns Crematorium** Bucks
26 D7	**Chilthorne Domer** Somset
58 B5	**Chilton** Bucks
141 H2	**Chilton** Dur
41 J4	**Chilton** Oxon
29 L4	**Chilton Candover** Hants
26 E6	**Chilton Cantelo** Somset
40 F6	**Chilton Foliat** Wilts
26 B4	**Chilton Polden** Somset
77 H5	**Chilton Street** Suffk
25 L4	**Chilton Trinity** Somset
101 K5	**Chilwell** Notts
29 H7	**Chilworth** Hants
31 G3	**Chilworth** Surrey
57 G7	**Chimney** Oxon
30 A1	**Chineham** Hants
45 G2	**Chingford** Gt Lon
114 B5	**Chinley** Derbys
58 C7	**Chinnor** Oxon
99 G6	**Chipnall** Shrops
76 F1	**Chippenham** Cambs
39 L5	**Chippenham** Wilts
59 H7	**Chipperfield** Herts
60 B2	**Chipping** Herts
121 J2	**Chipping** Lancs
71 L6	**Chipping Campden** Gloucs
56 F3	**Chipping Norton** Oxon
60 E7	**Chipping Ongar** Essex
39 G4	**Chipping Sodbury** S Glos
72 F5	**Chipping Warden** Nhants
25 G6	**Chipstable** Somset
32 E3	**Chipstead** Kent
32 B2	**Chipstead** Surrey
82 F4	**Chirbury** Shrops
97 L5	**Chirk** Wrexhm
179 H6	**Chirnside** Border

Ref	Place
179 H7	Chirnsidebridge Border
40 B8	Chirton Wilts
40 F6	Chisbury Wilts
26 C8	Chiselborough Somset
40 D4	Chiseldon Swindn
57 L7	Chiselhampton Oxon
166 F6	Chisholme Border
45 H6	Chislehurst Gt Lon
47 L6	Chislet Kent
122 F5	Chisley Calder
59 J6	Chiswell Green Herts
44 E4	Chiswick Gt Lon
113 M3	Chisworth Derbys
30 D6	Chithurst W Susx
76 C1	Chittering Cambs
27 M3	Chitterne Wilts
23 K7	Chittlehamholt Devon
23 K6	Chittlehampton Devon
39 L6	Chittoe Wilts
7 H7	Chivelstone Devon
23 H4	Chivenor Devon
144 D3	Chlenry D & G
42 F7	Chobham Surrey
28 E3	Cholderton Wilts
58 F6	Cholesbury Bucks
158 B7	Chollerton Nthumb
41 L3	Cholsey Oxon
69 J3	Cholstrey Herefs
142 C7	Chop Gate N York
159 G5	Choppington Nthumb
150 E4	Chopwell Gatesd
98 E3	Chorley Ches E
121 H6	Chorley Lancs
84 C6	Chorley Shrops
43 H2	Chorleywood Herts
43 G2	Chorleywood West Herts
99 G3	Chorlton Ches E
113 J3	Chorlton-cum-Hardy Manch
98 C3	Chorlton Lane Ches W
83 H5	Choulton Shrops
76 C6	Chrishall Essex
173 L4	Chrisswell Inver
90 C4	Christchurch Cambs
15 M4	Christchurch Dorset
37 M3	Christchurch Newpt
39 L5	Christian Malford Wilts
112 C7	Christleton Ches W
38 B8	Christon N Som
169 J5	Christon Bank Nthumb
11 J7	Christow Devon
11 K8	Chudleigh Devon
7 J1	Chudleigh Knighton Devon
11 G3	Chulmleigh Devon
121 L5	Church Lancs
55 H4	Churcham Gloucs
99 H8	Church Aston Wrekin
73 K2	Church Brampton Nhants
100 D5	Church Broughton Derbys
3 J8	Church Cove Cnwll
30 D2	Church Crookham Hants
55 K4	Churchdown Gloucs
99 J8	Church Eaton Staffs
59 G4	Church End C Beds
75 H6	Church End C Beds
47 G2	Churchend Essex
61 H3	Church End Essex
44 E3	Church End Gt Lon
57 G3	Church Enstone Oxon
124 D3	Church Fenton N York
85 H5	Churchfield Sandw
12 F3	Church Green Devon
57 H5	Church Hanborough Oxon
142 E7	Church Houses N York
13 H3	Churchill Devon
38 C7	Churchill N Som
56 F3	Churchill Oxon
71 G4	Churchill Worcs
84 F7	Churchill Worcs
25 K8	Churchinford Somset
15 H6	Church Knowle Dorset
87 K5	Church Langton Leics
86 F7	Church Lawford Warwks
100 A5	Church Leigh Staffs
71 H4	Church Lench Worcs
100 D4	Church Mayfield Staffs
98 H1	Church Minshull Ches E
18 B6	Church Norton W Susx
87 G7	Churchover Warwks
83 K4	Church Preen Shrops
83 H3	Church Pulverbatch Shrops
25 J8	Churchstanton Somset
82 F5	Churchstoke Powys
7 G6	Churchstow Devon
73 J3	Church Stowe Nhants
46 B5	Church Street Kent
83 J5	Church Stretton Shrops
5 H1	Churchtown Cnwll
114 E8	Churchtown Derbys
237 d3	Churchtown IoM
121 G2	Churchtown Lancs
37 G3	Church Village Rhondd
115 K7	Church Warsop Notts
7 K5	Churston Ferrers Torbay
30 D4	Churt Surrey
98 B2	Churton Ches W
123 K8	Churwell Leeds
95 G5	Chwilog Gwynd
2 E5	Chyandour Cnwll
2 E4	Chysauster Cnwll
111 G7	Cilcain Flints
66 C3	Cilcennin Cerdgn
52 B7	Cilfrew Neath
37 G3	Cilfynydd Rhondd
65 H6	Cilgerran Pembks
51 L4	Cilmaengwyn Neath
67 L4	Cilmery Powys
51 H2	Cilsan Carmth
96 D4	Ciltalgarth Gwynd
67 G6	Cilycwm Carmth
36 B2	Cimla Neath
54 F5	Cinderford Gloucs
42 F4	Cippenham Slough
56 A7	Cirencester Gloucs
45 G4	City Gt Lon
45 G4	City Airport Gt Lon
45 H3	City of London Gt Lon
45 H3	City of London Crematorium Gt Lon
188 F5	Clabhach Ag & B
173 J3	Clachaig Ag & B
172 C6	Clachan Ag & B
182 A4	Clachan Ag & B
191 G7	Clachan Ag & B
209 H6	Clachan Highld
233 c6	Clachan-a-Luib W Isls
188 C6	Clachan Mor Ag & B
233 c6	Clachan na Luib W Isls
175 G3	Clachan of Campsie E Duns
181 M4	Clachan-Seil Ag & B
213 G5	Clachnaharry Highld
224 C3	Clachtoll Highld
195 J4	Clackavoid P & K
32 D3	Clacket Lane Services Surrey
185 J8	Clackmannan Clacks
214 F3	Clackmarras Moray
62 E5	Clacton-on-Sea Essex
182 F3	Cladich Ag & B
71 J3	Cladswell Worcs
190 E6	Claggan Highld
208 C4	Claigan Highld
30 B7	Clanfield Hants
56 F7	Clanfield Oxon
28 F2	Clanville Hants
26 F5	Clanville Somset
172 E6	Claonaig Ag & B
60 C3	Clapgate Herts
74 F4	Clapham Bed
44 F5	Clapham Gt Lon
130 E5	Clapham N York
18 F4	Clapham W Susx
13 K2	Clapton Somset
26 F2	Clapton Somset
38 C5	Clapton-in-Gordano N Som
56 D4	Clapton-on-the-Hill Gloucs
150 E3	Claravale Gatesd
49 H3	Clarbeston Pembks
49 H4	Clarbeston Road Pembks
116 B5	Clarborough Notts
77 H5	Clare Suffk
146 D2	Clarebrand D & G
147 J2	Clarencefield D & G
150 C2	Clarewood Nthumb
167 H5	Clarilaw Border
175 G6	Clarkston E Rens
223 G4	Clashmore Highld
224 C3	Clashmore Highld
224 C3	Clashnessie Highld
204 F2	Clashnoir Moray
185 K4	Clathy P & K
185 L3	Clathymore P & K
205 L1	Clatt Abers
81 L5	Clatter Powys
25 G5	Clatworthy Somset
121 G3	Claughton Lancs
130 B6	Claughton Lancs
111 J4	Claughton Wirral
71 L2	Claverdon Warwks
38 C6	Claverham N Som
60 D2	Clavering Essex
84 E5	Claverley Shrops
39 H7	Claverton BaNES
37 G5	Clawdd-coch V Glam
97 G3	Clawdd-newydd Denbgs
9 J5	Clawton Devon
117 J3	Claxby Lincs
133 L7	Claxton N York
93 H3	Claxton Norfk
86 F5	Claybrooke Magna Leics
87 H7	Clay Coton Nhants
115 H8	Clay Cross Derbys
72 F4	Claydon Oxon
78 D5	Claydon Suffk
156 D6	Claygate D & G
33 J4	Claygate Kent
44 D7	Claygate Surrey
45 H3	Clayhall Gt Lon
24 F6	Clayhanger Devon
25 J7	Clayhidon Devon
21 G2	Clayhill E Susx
231 H4	Clayock Highld
55 H6	Claypits Gloucs
102 D3	Claypole Lincs
123 G4	Clayton C Brad
124 C8	Clayton Donc
19 J3	Clayton W Susx
121 L4	Clayton-le-Moors Lancs
121 H6	Clayton-le-Woods Lancs
123 K7	Clayton West Kirk
116 B4	Clayworth Notts
199 G7	Cleadale Highld
151 J3	Cleadon S Tyne
6 D3	Clearbrook Devon
54 E6	Clearwell Gloucs
141 G5	Cleasby N York
234 c8	Cleat Ork
140 E4	Cleatlam Dur
136 D4	Cleator Cumb
136 E4	Cleator Moor Cumb
123 J5	Cleckheaton Kirk
83 L7	Cleehill Shrops
175 K6	Cleekhimin N Lans
83 L6	Clee St Margaret Shrops
127 H8	Cleethorpes NE Lin
84 B7	Cleeton St Mary Shrops
38 C7	Cleeve N Som
41 L4	Cleeve Oxon
55 M3	Cleeve Hill Gloucs
71 J5	Cleeve Prior Worcs
178 D2	Cleghornie E Loth
69 J6	Clehonger Herefs
186 A7	Cleish P & K
175 L6	Cleland N Lans
182 C2	Clenamacrie Ag & B
104 F7	Clenchwarton Norfk
216 E3	Clenerty Abers
85 G7	Clent Worcs
84 C7	Cleobury Mortimer Shrops
84 B6	Cleobury North Shrops
161 H3	Cleongart Ag & B
213 J4	Clephanton Highld
156 A3	Clerkhill D & G
154 E3	Cleuch-head D & G
40 B5	Clevancy Wilts
38 B6	Clevedon N Som
120 D2	Cleveleys Lancs
39 L4	Cleverton Wilts
26 C2	Clewer Somset
106 C4	Cley next the Sea Norfk
138 E3	Cliburn Cumb
29 M2	Cliddesden Hants
46 C5	Cliffe Medway
125 G4	Cliffe N York
140 F4	Cliffe N York
21 H3	Cliff End E Susx
46 C5	Cliffe Woods Medway
68 E5	Clifford Herefs
124 C2	Clifford Leeds
71 L4	Clifford Chambers Warwks
55 G4	Clifford's Mesne Gloucs
38 E5	Clifton Bristl
75 H6	Clifton C Beds
101 K5	Clifton C Nott
133 J8	Clifton C York
123 H6	Clifton Calder
138 D2	Clifton Cumb
100 D4	Clifton Derbys
23 J3	Clifton Devon
115 K3	Clifton Donc
120 F4	Clifton Lancs
123 J2	Clifton N York
57 J2	Clifton Oxon
70 F5	Clifton Worcs
86 B2	Clifton Campville Staffs
41 K2	Clifton Hampden Oxon
74 C4	Clifton Reynes M Keyn
87 G7	Clifton upon Dunsmore Warwks
70 C3	Clifton upon Teme Worcs
35 K1	Cliftonville Kent
18 D5	Climping W Susx
27 H2	Clink Somset
132 D7	Clint N York
206 F3	Clinterty C Aber
92 B2	Clint Green Norfk
167 J3	Clintmains Border
93 J2	Clippesby Norfk
88 D1	Clipsham Rutlnd
87 K7	Clipston Nhants

101 M5	**Clipston** Notts
58 F3	**Clipstone** C Beds
115 L8	**Clipstone** Notts
121 L3	**Clitheroe** Lancs
98 D7	**Clive** Shrops
117 J2	**Clixby** Lincs
39 M3	**Cloatley** Wilts
97 G2	**Clocaenog** Denbgs
215 J3	**Clochan** Moray
196 D5	**Clochtow** Angus
53 L3	**Clodock** Herefs
217 J5	**Ciola** Abers
74 F6	**Clophill** C Beds
88 F7	**Clopton** Nhants
78 F4	**Clopton** Suffk
78 F4	**Clopton Corner** Suffk
236 d2	**Clos du Valle** Guern
154 F4	**Closeburn** D & G
154 F3	**Closeburnmill** D & G
14 B1	**Closworth** Somset
59 L2	**Clothall** Herts
112 D8	**Clotton** Ches W
122 D5	**Clough Foot** Calder
123 G6	**Clough Head** Calder
143 K7	**Cloughton** N York
235 C5	**Clousta** Shet
196 B2	**Clova** Angus
22 E6	**Clovelly** Devon
167 G3	**Clovenfords** Border
191 K4	**Clovulin** Highld
122 C5	**Clow Bridge** Lancs
115 J6	**Clowne** Derbys
70 C1	**Clows Top** Worcs
201 G3	**Cluanie Inn** Highld
201 G3	**Cluanie Lodge** Highld
145 H4	**Clugston** D & G
82 F7	**Clun** Shrops
213 K5	**Clunas** Highld
83 G7	**Clunbury** Shrops
49 J4	**Clunderwen** Carmth
203 J1	**Clune** Highld
201 J7	**Clunes** Highld
83 H7	**Clungunford** Shrops
216 C4	**Clunie** Abers
195 H7	**Clunie** P & K
83 G7	**Clunton** Shrops
186 D7	**Cluny** Fife
38 F8	**Clutton** BaNES
98 C2	**Clutton** Ches W
38 F8	**Clutton Hill** BaNES
53 K5	**Clydach** Mons
51 K5	**Clydach** Swans
36 F2	**Clydach Vale** Rhondd
174 F4	**Clydebank** W Duns
40 B5	**Clyffe Pypard** Wilts
174 A2	**Clynder** Ag & B
52 C7	**Clyne** Neath
95 G3	**Clynnog-fawr** Gwynd
68 E5	**Clyro** Powys
12 C4	**Clyst Honiton** Devon
12 D3	**Clyst Hydon** Devon
12 C5	**Clyst St George** Devon
12 D3	**Clyst St Lawrence** Devon
12 C4	**Clyst St Mary** Devon
232 g2	**Cnoc** W Isls
80 F8	**Cnwch Coch** Cerdgn
5 L1	**Coad's Green** Cnwll
164 F3	**Coalburn** S Lans
150 E3	**Coalburns** Gatesd
55 H7	**Coaley** Gloucs
61 J7	**Coalhill** Essex
38 F4	**Coalpit Heath** S Glos
84 C3	**Coalport** Wrekin
185 J7	**Coalsnaughton** Clacks
186 E7	**Coaltown of Balgonie** Fife
186 E7	**Coaltown of Wemyss** Fife
86 E2	**Coalville** Leics
149 H3	**Coanwood** Nthumb
26 C7	**Coat** Somset
175 J5	**Coatbridge** N Lans
175 K5	**Coatdyke** N Lans
40 D4	**Coate** Swindn
40 B7	**Coate** Wilts
89 K4	**Coates** Cambs
55 L7	**Coates** Gloucs
116 E5	**Coates** Lincs
18 D3	**Coates** W Susx
23 K6	**Cobbaton** Devon
55 L5	**Coberley** Gloucs
46 A6	**Cobham** Kent
43 J7	**Cobham** Surrey
43 J8	Cobham Services Surrey
69 J3	**Cobnash** Herefs
236 C2	**Cobo** Guern
217 H2	**Coburby** Abers
75 J5	**Cockayne Hatley** C Beds
205 G4	**Cock Bridge** Abers
179 G4	**Cockburnspath** Border
61 K7	**Cock Clarks** Essex
177 L4	**Cockenzie and Port Seton** E Loth
120 F1	**Cockerham** Lancs
136 F2	**Cockermouth** Cumb
59 J4	**Cockernhoe** Herts
51 J6	**Cockett** Swans
140 E3	**Cockfield** Dur
77 K4	**Cockfield** Suffk
44 F2	**Cockfosters** Gt Lon
61 H4	**Cock Green** Essex
18 B3	**Cocking** W Susx
18 B2	**Cocking Causeway** W Susx
7 K3	**Cockington** Torbay
26 C2	**Cocklake** Somset
91 H3	**Cockley Cley** Norfk
21 H2	**Cock Marling** E Susx
42 D4	**Cockpole Green** Wokham
98 B6	**Cockshutt** Shrops
106 B4	**Cockthorpe** Norfk
12 C6	**Cockwood** Devon
114 B5	**Cockyard** Derbys
78 D4	**Coddenham** Suffk
70 C6	**Coddington** Herefs
102 D2	**Coddington** Notts
27 L4	**Codford St Mary** Wilts
27 L4	**Codford St Peter** Wilts
59 K4	**Codicote** Herts
31 H7	**Codmore Hill** W Susx
101 H3	**Codnor** Derbys
39 G5	**Codrington** S Glos
84 F3	**Codsall** Staffs
84 F3	**Codsall Wood** Staffs
108 F5	**Coedana** IoA
97 L3	**Coedpoeth** Wrexhm
97 L2	**Coed Talon** Flints
53 M7	**Coed-y-paen** Mons
7 K3	**Coffinswell** Devon
12 C6	**Cofton** Devon
85 H7	**Cofton Hackett** Worcs
37 J6	**Cogan** V Glam
74 B3	**Cogenhoe** Nhants
61 K4	**Coggeshall** Essex
203 H2	**Coignafearn** Highld
205 H6	**Coilacriech** Abers
184 D6	**Coilantogle** Stirlg
208 E6	**Coillore** Highld
36 H4	**Coity** Brdgnd
232 g2	**Col** W Isls
225 L6	**Colaboll** Highld
4 D4	**Colan** Cnwll
12 D5	**Colaton Raleigh** Devon
208 C5	**Colbost** Highld
140 F7	**Colburn** N York
138 F3	**Colby** Cumb
237 b6	**Colby** IoM
62 B3	**Colchester** Essex
62 B4	**Colchester Crematorium** Essex
41 K6	**Cold Ash** W Berk
87 J7	**Cold Ashby** Nhants
39 H6	**Cold Ashton** S Glos
56 C4	**Cold Aston** Gloucs
229 J1	**Coldbackie** Highld
74 D4	**Cold Brayfield** M Keyn
19 J4	**Coldean** Br & H
7 J2	**Coldeast** Devon
122 E5	**Colden** Calder
29 J6	**Colden Common** Hants
117 G5	**Cold Hanworth** Lincs
31 J3	**Coldharbour** Surrey
73 J4	**Cold Higham** Nhants
179 J5	**Coldingham** Border
133 H3	**Cold Kirby** N York
99 J6	**Coldmeece** Staffs
61 K7	**Cold Norton** Essex
88 B2	**Cold Overton** Leics
35 H5	**Coldred** Kent
11 G4	**Coldridge** Devon
168 C2	**Coldstream** Border
18 D3	**Coldwaltham** W Susx
69 H7	**Coldwell** Herefs
217 H6	**Coldwells** Abers
26 F5	**Cole** Somset
83 G6	**Colebatch** Shrops
12 C2	**Colebrook** Devon
11 H5	**Colebrooke** Devon
102 F1	**Coleby** Lincs
125 L6	**Coleby** N Linc
11 H5	**Coleford** Devon
54 E6	**Coleford** Gloucs
27 G2	**Coleford** Somset
92 E6	**Colegate End** Norfk
15 J3	**Colehill** Dorset
32 D6	**Coleman's Hatch** E Susx
98 B5	**Colemere** Shrops
30 B5	**Colemore** Hants
186 B2	**Colenden** P & K
39 M3	**Colerne** Wilts
56 A5	**Colesbourne** Gloucs
42 F2	**Coleshill** Bucks
40 E2	**Coleshill** Oxon
85 L5	**Coleshill** Warwks
26 E1	**Coley** BaNES
31 L5	**Colgate** W Susx
187 H6	**Colinsburgh** Fife
177 H5	**Colinton** C Edin
173 H4	**Colintraive** Ag & B
105 L7	**Colkirk** Norfk
189 G5	**Coll** Ag & B
186 C2	**Collace** P & K
235 c3	**Collafirth** Shet
7 G7	**Collaton** Devon
7 K4	**Collaton St Mary** Torbay
214 E2	**College of Roseisle** Moray
42 D7	**College Town** Br For
186 E5	**Collessie** Fife
45 J2	**Collier Row** Gt Lon
60 B4	**Collier's End** Herts
33 J4	**Collier Street** Kent
217 K8	**Collieston** Abers
155 H6	**Collin** D & G
28 E2	**Collingbourne Ducis** Wilts
28 E1	**Collingbourne Kingston** Wilts
124 B2	**Collingham** Leeds
102 D1	**Collingham** Notts
70 B3	**Collington** Herefs
73 L4	**Collingtree** Nhants
112 E3	**Collins Green** Warrtn
196 F7	**Colliston** Angus
12 E2	**Colliton** Devon
88 E3	**Collyweston** Nhants
152 D5	**Colmonell** S Ayrs
75 G3	**Colmworth** Bed
43 G5	**Colnbrook** Slough
89 L7	**Colne** Cambs
122 B3	**Colne** Lancs
61 K3	**Colne Engaine** Essex
92 E3	**Colney** Norfk
59 K6	**Colney Heath** Herts
56 B6	**Coln Rogers** Gloucs
56 C6	**Coln St Aldwyns** Gloucs
56 B5	**Coln St Dennis** Gloucs
180 E7	**Colonsay** Ag & B
216 C7	**Colpy** Abers
166 E2	**Colquhar** Border
102 F7	**Colsterworth** Lincs
102 B5	**Colston Bassett** Notts
214 D2	**Coltfield** Moray
106 F8	**Coltishall** Norfk
129 G3	**Colton** Cumb
124 B4	**Colton** Leeds
124 E2	**Colton** N York
92 D2	**Colton** Norfk
100 B7	**Colton** Staffs
33 H4	**Colt's Hill** Kent
146 F4	**Colvend** D & G
70 D6	**Colwall** Herefs
158 B6	**Colwell** Nthumb
100 A7	**Colwich** Staffs
36 E5	**Colwinston** V Glam
18 C5	**Colworth** W Susx
110 B5	**Colwyn Bay** Conwy
13 G4	**Colyford** Devon
13 G4	**Colyton** Devon
57 H5	**Combe** Oxon
41 G7	**Combe** W Berk
39 H7	**Combe Down** BaNES
7 J3	**Combe Fishacre** Devon
25 J5	**Combe Florey** Somset
39 G7	**Combe Hay** BaNES
7 K2	**Combeinteignhead** Devon
23 J3	**Combe Martin** Devon
12 F3	**Combe Raleigh** Devon
112 F6	**Comberbach** Ches W
85 L3	**Comberford** Staffs
75 L4	**Comberton** Cambs
69 K2	**Comberton** Herefs
13 H1	**Combe St Nicholas** Somset
72 C4	**Combrook** Warwks
114 B6	**Combs** Derbys
78 C3	**Combs** Suffk
78 C3	**Combs Ford** Suffk
25 K3	**Combwich** Somset
206 D4	**Comers** Abers
70 E2	**Comhampton** Worcs
49 K4	**Commercial** Pembks
81 J3	**Commins Coch** Powys
142 E5	**Commondale** N York
136 D3	**Common End** Cumb
5 K2	**Common Moor** Cnwll
113 L4	**Compstall** Stockp
146 B4	**Compstonend** D & G
7 K3	**Compton** Devon
29 J6	**Compton** Hants
84 E6	**Compton** Staffs
30 F3	**Compton** Surrey
41 K4	**Compton** W Berk
30 C7	**Compton** W Susx
28 C2	**Compton** Wilts
27 K7	**Compton Abbas** Dorset
56 B5	**Compton Abdale** Gloucs
40 B6	**Compton Bassett** Wilts
40 F3	**Compton Beauchamp** Oxon
26 B1	**Compton Bishop** Somset
28 B5	**Compton Chamberlayne** Wilts
38 F7	**Compton Dando** BaNES
26 C5	**Compton Dundon** Somset
26 B7	**Compton Durville** Somset
38 E4	**Compton Greenfield** S Glos

38 D8 **Compton Martin** BaNES
26 F6 **Compton Pauncefoot** Somset
14 B4 **Compton Valence** Dorset
176 D1 **Comrie** Fife
185 G3 **Comrie** P & K
191 K3 **Conaglen House** Highld
210 D8 **Conchra** Highld
195 H7 **Concraigie** P & K
71 G6 **Conderton** Worcs
56 D3 **Condicote** Gloucs
175 K4 **Condorrat** N Lans
83 J3 **Condover** Shrops
55 J4 **Coney Hill** Gloucs
31 J6 **Coneyhurst Common** W Susx
133 L5 **Coneythorpe** N York
91 L7 **Coney Weston** Suffk
86 D3 **Congerstone** Leics
105 H7 **Congham** Norfk
113 J8 **Congleton** Ches E
38 C7 **Congresbury** N Som
147 H2 **Conheath** D & G
214 B4 **Conicavel** Moray
103 L2 **Coningsby** Lincs
75 K2 **Conington** Cambs
89 H6 **Conington** Cambs
115 K2 **Conisbrough** Donc
118 E3 **Conisholme** Lincs
137 J7 **Coniston** Cumb
126 E4 **Coniston** E R Yk
131 G8 **Coniston Cold** N York
131 J6 **Conistone** N York
111 J7 **Connah's Quay** Flints
182 C1 **Connel** Ag & B
164 C6 **Connel Park** E Ayrs
3 G4 **Connor Downs** Cnwll
212 E4 **Conon Bridge** Highld
122 E2 **Cononley** N York
99 M3 **Consall** Staffs
150 E5 **Consett** Dur
132 B2 **Constable Burton** N York
3 J5 **Constantine** Cnwll
4 D2 **Constantine Bay** Cnwll
212 C3 **Contin** Highld
109 L6 **Conwy** Conwy
77 K2 **Conyer's Green** Suffk
20 E4 **Cooden** E Susx
9 K4 **Cookbury** Devon
42 E4 **Cookham** W & M
42 E4 **Cookham Dean** W & M
42 E4 **Cookham Rise** W & M
71 J3 **Cookhill** Worcs
93 H7 **Cookley** Suffk
84 E7 **Cookley** Worcs
42 B3 **Cookley Green** Oxon
207 G6 **Cookney** Abers
62 E4 **Cook's Green** Essex
77 L4 **Cooks Green** Suffk
61 G6 **Cooksmill Green** Essex
31 J6 **Coolham** W Susx
46 C5 **Cooling** Medway
4 E5 **Coombe** Cnwll
7 L2 **Coombe** Devon
12 E4 **Coombe** Devon
39 H2 **Coombe** Gloucs
30 A7 **Coombe** Hants
28 C6 **Coombe Bissett** Wilts
7 K2 **Coombe Cellars** Devon
55 K3 **Coombe Hill** Gloucs
14 F5 **Coombe Keynes** Dorset
7 L3 **Coombe Pafford** Torbay
19 G4 **Coombes** W Susx
69 G2 **Coombes-Moor** Herefs

60 D7 **Coopersale Common** Essex
78 D6 **Copdock** Suffk
61 L4 **Copford Green** Essex
132 E6 **Copgrove** N York
235 d3 **Copister** Shet
75 G5 **Cople** Bed
140 D3 **Copley** Dur
124 E2 **Copmanthorpe** C York
99 J6 **Copmere End** Staffs
120 F3 **Copp** Lancs
99 K8 **Coppenhall** Staffs
2 F4 **Copperhouse** Cnwll
89 H7 **Coppingford** Cambs
11 H4 **Copplestone** Devon
121 H7 **Coppull** Lancs
31 K6 **Copsale** W Susx
121 K4 **Copster Green** Lancs
86 F5 **Copston Magna** Warwks
35 J3 **Cop Street** Kent
132 E5 **Copt Hewick** N York
32 B5 **Copthorne** W Susx
86 F2 **Copt Oak** Leics
28 F8 **Copythorne** Hants
45 K3 **Corbets Tey** Gt Lon
236 a7 **Corbiere** Jersey
150 C3 **Corbridge** Nthumb
88 C5 **Corby** Nhants
103 G7 **Corby Glen** Lincs
162 D4 **Cordon** N Ayrs
84 B8 **Coreley** Shrops
25 K7 **Corfe** Somset
15 H6 **Corfe Castle** Dorset
15 J3 **Corfe Mullen** Dorset
83 J6 **Corfton** Shrops
205 G4 **Corgarff** Abers
29 L7 **Corhampton** Hants
86 C6 **Corley** Warwks
86 C6 **Corley Services** Warwks
195 L3 **Cormuir** Angus
77 K6 **Cornard Tye** Suffk
151 H7 **Cornforth** Dur
216 B3 **Cornhill** Abers
168 C2 **Cornhill-on-Tweed** Nthumb
122 D5 **Cornholme** Calder
188 C6 **Cornoigmore** Ag & B
150 E6 **Cornsay** Dur
150 E6 **Cornsay Colliery** Dur
212 E3 **Corntown** Highld
36 E5 **Corntown** V Glam
56 F3 **Cornwell** Oxon
6 E4 **Cornwood** Devon
7 J5 **Cornworthy** Devon
191 L2 **Corpach** Highld
106 D6 **Corpusty** Norfk
205 K4 **Corrachree** Abers
191 K4 **Corran** Highld
200 C4 **Corran** Highld
155 L5 **Corrie** D & G
162 C2 **Corrie** N Ayrs
162 B5 **Corriecravie** N Ayrs
162 D3 **Corriegills** N Ayrs
201 K6 **Corriegour Lodge Hotel** Highld
212 B2 **Corriemoille** Highld
212 B7 **Corrimony** Highld
116 E4 **Corringham** Lincs
46 B4 **Corringham** Thurr
81 G2 **Corris** Gwynd
81 G2 **Corris Uchaf** Gwynd
183 H7 **Corrow** Ag & B
199 K1 **Corry** Highld
10 F5 **Corscombe** Devon
13 M2 **Corscombe** Dorset
55 H3 **Corse** Gloucs
55 J2 **Corse Lawn** Gloucs
39 K6 **Corsham** Wilts
206 D4 **Corsindae** Abers
27 J3 **Corsley** Wilts
27 J3 **Corsley Heath** Wilts
154 D6 **Corsock** D & G
39 G7 **Corston** BaNES

39 L4 **Corston** Wilts
177 G4 **Corstorphine** C Edin
196 C4 **Cortachy** Angus
93 L4 **Corton** Suffk
27 L4 **Corton** Wilts
26 F6 **Corton Denham** Somset
191 L3 **Coruanan** Highld
97 G4 **Corwen** Denbgs
10 C7 **Coryton** Devon
46 C4 **Coryton** Thurr
87 G4 **Cosby** Leics
85 G5 **Coseley** Dudley
73 L6 **Cosgrove** Nhants
17 J2 **Cosham** C Port
49 G6 **Cosheston** Pembks
194 C6 **Coshieville** P & K
101 J4 **Cossall** Notts
87 H2 **Cossington** Leics
26 A4 **Cossington** Somset
92 E2 **Costessey** Norfk
101 L7 **Costock** Notts
102 D7 **Coston** Leics
92 C3 **Coston** Norfk
57 G7 **Cote** Oxon
112 E7 **Cotebrook** Ches W
148 E5 **Cotehill** Cumb
101 K7 **Cotes** Leics
87 G6 **Cotesbach** Leics
25 J6 **Cotford St Luke** Somset
101 M5 **Cotgrave** Notts
207 G3 **Cothal** Abers
102 C3 **Cotham** Notts
140 C4 **Cotherstone** Dur
57 J7 **Cothill** Oxon
13 G3 **Cotleigh** Devon
101 J4 **Cotmanhay** Derbys
76 B3 **Coton** Cambs
73 J1 **Coton** Nhants
99 J7 **Coton** Staffs
99 K7 **Coton Clanford** Staffs
83 J2 **Coton Hill** Shrops
86 B1 **Coton in the Elms** Derbys
55 M6 **Cotswolds**
7 H4 **Cott** Devon
121 G4 **Cottam** Lancs
116 D5 **Cottam** Notts
76 C2 **Cottenham** Cambs
60 A3 **Cottered** Herts
88 F5 **Cotterstock** Nhants
87 K8 **Cottesbrooke** Nhants
88 C2 **Cottesmore** Rutlnd
126 C4 **Cottingham** E R Yk
88 B5 **Cottingham** Nhants
123 G3 **Cottingley** C Brad
123 K4 **Cottingley Hall Crematorium** Leeds
57 L2 **Cottisford** Oxon
78 C2 **Cotton** Suffk
206 E3 **Cottown** Abers
215 L8 **Cottown** Abers
216 F6 **Cottown of Gight** Abers
6 C3 **Cotts** Devon
71 J3 **Coughton** Warwks
172 C5 **Coulaghailtro** Ag & B
210 E5 **Coulags** Highld
205 L5 **Coull** Abers
173 L2 **Coulport** Ag & B
32 B2 **Coulsdon** Gt Lon
27 L2 **Coulston** Wilts
165 K3 **Coulter** S Lans
133 K5 **Coulton** N York
186 F3 **Coultra** Fife
83 L3 **Cound** Shrops
141 G2 **Coundon** Dur
131 H2 **Countersett** N York
12 B4 **Countess Wear** Devon
87 H4 **Countesthorpe** Leics
24 B2 **Countisbury** Devon
195 K7 **Coupar Angus** P & K
168 D3 **Coupland** Nthumb
172 D8 **Cour** Ag & B

199 L6 **Courteachan** Highld
73 L4 **Courteenhall** Nhants
51 H2 **Court Henry** Carmth
47 G2 **Courtsend** Essex
25 J5 **Courtway** Somset
177 K5 **Cousland** Mdloth
33 H6 **Cousley Wood** E Susx
173 L2 **Cove** Ag & B
179 G4 **Cove** Border
24 E7 **Cove** Devon
30 E1 **Cove** Hants
219 J3 **Cove** Highld
207 H5 **Cove Bay** C Aber
93 L6 **Covehithe** Suffk
85 G3 **Coven** Staffs
90 C6 **Coveney** Cambs
118 D3 **Covenham St Bartholomew** Lincs
118 D3 **Covenham St Mary** Lincs
86 D7 **Coventry** Covtry
86 D8 **Coventry Airport** Warwks
3 K7 **Coverack** Cnwll
3 H5 **Coverack Bridges** Cnwll
131 L3 **Coverham** N York
74 F1 **Covington** Cambs
165 J2 **Covington** S Lans
130 C4 **Cowan Bridge** Lancs
20 C3 **Cowbeech** E Susx
103 L8 **Cowbit** Lincs
36 F5 **Cowbridge** V Glam
32 E5 **Cowden** Kent
177 G1 **Cowdenbeath** Fife
100 F3 **Cowers Lane** Derbys
16 F3 **Cowes** IoW
133 G2 **Cowesby** N York
31 K6 **Cowfold** W Susx
38 E3 **Cowhill** S Glos
71 K5 **Cow Honeybourne** Worcs
175 L1 **Cowie** Stirlg
134 E6 **Cowlam** E R Yk
11 K5 **Cowley** Devon
55 L5 **Cowley** Gloucs
43 H4 **Cowley** Gt Lon
57 K7 **Cowley** Oxon
121 H6 **Cowling** Lancs
122 E2 **Cowling** N York
132 C3 **Cowling** N York
77 G4 **Cowlinge** Suffk
159 H5 **Cowpen** Nthumb
17 K1 **Cowplain** Hants
149 L6 **Cowshill** Dur
38 C7 **Cowslip Green** N Som
132 F8 **Cowthorpe** N York
98 F4 **Coxbank** Ches E
101 G4 **Coxbench** Derbys
8 F5 **Coxford** Cnwll
105 K6 **Coxford** Norfk
33 J3 **Coxheath** Kent
151 H7 **Coxhoe** Dur
26 D3 **Coxley** Somset
26 D3 **Coxley Wick** Somset
45 K2 **Coxtie Green** Essex
133 H4 **Coxwold** N York
36 E4 **Coychurch** Brdgnd
36 E4 **Coychurch Crematorium** Brdgnd
163 K5 **Coylton** S Ayrs
203 L3 **Coylumbridge** Highld
36 D4 **Coytrahen** Brdgnd
71 J2 **Crabbs Cross** Worcs
31 K6 **Crabtree** W Susx
138 F3 **Crackenthorpe** Cumb
8 F5 **Crackington Haven** Cnwll
84 D2 **Crackleybank** Shrops
131 J7 **Cracoe** N York
25 G8 **Craddock** Devon
85 G6 **Cradley** Dudley
70 D5 **Cradley** Herefs
85 G6 **Cradley Heath** Sandw
52 F2 **Cradoc** Powys
6 B5 **Crafthole** Cnwll

204 C1 **Craggan** Highld
150 F5 **Craghead** Dur
52 D3 **Crai** Powys
215 L3 **Craibstone** Moray
196 E6 **Craichie** Angus
197 H5 **Craig** Angus
211 G4 **Craig** Highld
164 C6 **Craigbank** E Ayrs
177 H7 **Craigburn** Border
156 C5 **Craigcleuch** D & G
216 F7 **Craigdam** Abers
182 B6 **Craigdhu** Ag & B
206 D3 **Craigearn** Abers
215 G5 **Craigellachie** Moray
186 B4 **Craigend** P & K
174 E4 **Craigend** Rens
174 C3 **Craigendoran** Ag & B
174 D5 **Craigends** Rens
145 G3 **Craighlaw** D & G
171 K5 **Craighouse** Ag & B
195 H7 **Craigie** P & K
163 K3 **Craigie** S Ayrs
217 H2 **Craigiefold** Abers
146 D4 **Craigley** D & G
51 K4 **Craig Llangiwg** Neath
177 H4 **Craiglockhart** C Edin
177 J4 **Craigmillar** C Edin
154 D5 **Craigneston** D & G
175 K5 **Craigneuk** N Lans
175 K6 **Craigneuk** N Lans
190 E8 **Craignure** Ag & B
197 H4 **Craigo** Angus
186 F5 **Craigrothie** Fife
184 B4 **Craigruie** Stirlg
196 E8 **Craigton** Angus
206 F5 **Craigton** C Aber
174 F7 **Craigton** E Rens
196 B6 **Craigton of Airlie** Angus
187 K7 **Crail** Fife
167 L4 **Crailing** Border
116 C2 **Craiselound** N Linc
132 C2 **Crakehall** N York
133 L6 **Crambe** N York
159 G6 **Cramlington** Nthumb
177 G3 **Cramond** C Edin
177 G4 **Cramond Bridge** C Edin
113 H7 **Cranage** Ches E
99 J5 **Cranberry** Staffs
28 B8 **Cranborne** Dorset
42 F5 **Cranbourne** Br For
33 K6 **Cranbrook** Kent
74 D6 **Cranfield** C Beds
43 J5 **Cranford** Gt Lon
88 D7 **Cranford St Andrew** Nhants
88 D7 **Cranford St John** Nhants
55 K5 **Cranham** Gloucs
112 D2 **Crank** St Hel
31 H4 **Cranleigh** Surrey
26 F3 **Cranmore** Somset
87 L4 **Cranoe** Leics
79 G2 **Cransford** Suffk
178 E6 **Cranshaws** Border
4 C4 **Crantock** Cnwll
103 G3 **Cranwell** Lincs
91 H4 **Cranwich** Norfk
92 B3 **Cranworth** Norfk
182 A6 **Craobh Haven** Ag & B
182 E7 **Crarae** Ag & B
225 L4 **Crask Inn** Highld
212 D6 **Crask of Aigas** Highld
169 K5 **Craster** Nthumb
93 G7 **Cratfield** Suffk
206 E6 **Crathes** Abers
206 D6 **Crathes Castle** Abers
205 G6 **Crathie** Abers
202 E6 **Crathie** Highld
141 K5 **Crathorne** N York
83 H6 **Craven Arms** Shrops
150 E3 **Crawcrook** Gatesd
165 J5 **Crawford** S Lans
165 G5 **Crawfordjohn** S Lans
29 H4 **Crawley** Hants

57 G5 **Crawley** Oxon
31 L4 **Crawley** W Susx
32 C5 **Crawley Down** W Susx
122 B5 **Crawshawbooth** Lancs
197 L1 **Crawton** Abers
131 H4 **Cray** N York
45 K5 **Crayford** Gt Lon
133 H5 **Crayke** N York
46 B2 **Crays Hill** Essex
24 C7 **Creacombe** Devon
191 J7 **Creagan Inn** Ag & B
233 C7 **Creag Ghoraidh** W Isls
233 c7 **Creagorry** W Isls
192 E3 **Creaguaineach Lodge** Highld
73 K1 **Creaton** Nhants
155 M7 **Creca** D & G
69 J5 **Credenhill** Herefs
11 J5 **Crediton** Devon
153 H6 **Creebank** D & G
145 J2 **Creebridge** D & G
25 L6 **Creech Heathfield** Somset
25 L6 **Creech St Michael** Somset
4 E6 **Creed** Cnwll
45 J4 **Creekmouth** Gt Lon
78 D3 **Creeting St Mary** Suffk
103 G8 **Creeton** Lincs
145 K3 **Creetown** D & G
237 a7 **Cregneash** IoM
186 E3 **Creich** Fife
37 G4 **Creigiau** Cardif
6 C5 **Cremyll** Cnwll
83 L3 **Cressage** Shrops
114 D6 **Cressbrook** Derbys
49 H6 **Cresselly** Pembks
42 D3 **Cressex** Bucks
61 J4 **Cressing** Essex
159 H4 **Cresswell** Nthumb
49 H6 **Cresswell** Pembks
99 L5 **Cresswell** Staffs
115 K6 **Creswell** Derbys
78 F3 **Cretingham** Suffk
172 C5 **Cretshengan** Ag & B
99 G2 **Crewe** Ches E
98 B2 **Crewe** Ches W
99 G2 **Crewe Crematorium** Ches E
99 G2 **Crewe Green** Ches E
83 G1 **Crew Green** Powys
13 K1 **Crewkerne** Somset
101 G5 **Crewton** C Derb
183 L3 **Crianlarich** Stirlg
66 C4 **Cribyn** Cerdgn
95 J5 **Criccieth** Gwynd
101 G2 **Crich** Derbys
177 K6 **Crichton** Mdloth
87 H8 **Crick** Nhants
68 C6 **Crickadarn** Powys
13 J2 **Cricket St Thomas** Somset
53 K4 **Crickhowell** Powys
40 C2 **Cricklade** Wilts
44 E3 **Cricklewood** Gt Lon
124 D6 **Cridling Stubbs** N York
185 H3 **Crieff** P & K
82 F1 **Criggion** Powys
123 L7 **Crigglestone** Wakefd
217 K3 **Crimond** Abers
90 F3 **Crimplesham** Norfk
72 B5 **Crimscote** Warwks
212 C6 **Crinaglack** Highld
182 A8 **Crinan** Ag & B
175 L6 **Crindledyke** N Lans
92 E3 **Cringleford** Norfk
49 J5 **Crinow** Pembks
213 G8 **Croachy** Highld
45 J6 **Crockenhill** Kent
42 B3 **Crocker End** Oxon
11 H6 **Crockernwell** Devon
27 K3 **Crockerton** Wilts

154 E7 **Crocketford** D & G
32 D3 **Crockham Hill** Kent
36 D2 **Croeserw** Neath
48 D2 **Croes-goch** Pembks
65 L5 **Croes-lan** Cerdgn
95 L4 **Croesor** Gwynd
50 E3 **Croesyceiliog** Carmth
37 L2 **Croesyceiliog** Torfn
87 G4 **Croft** Leics
104 E1 **Croft** Lincs
112 F3 **Croft** Warrtn
174 E2 **Croftamie** Stirlg
124 B6 **Crofton** Wakefd
141 H5 **Croft-on-Tees** N York
220 F5 **Croftown** Highld
215 G4 **Crofts** Moray
215 H3 **Crofts of Dipple** Moray
217 K3 **Crofts of Savoch** Abers
51 G6 **Crofty** Swans
181 L3 **Croggan** Ag & B
148 F5 **Croglin** Cumb
222 B3 **Croick** Highld
223 H7 **Cromarty** Highld
176 E2 **Crombie** Fife
214 D8 **Cromdale** Highld
59 M3 **Cromer** Herts
106 F4 **Cromer** Norfk
100 F2 **Cromford** Derbys
39 G3 **Cromhall** S Glos
232 f3 **Cromor** W Isls
102 D1 **Cromwell** Notts
164 C5 **Cronberry** E Ayrs
30 C2 **Crondall** Hants
112 C4 **Cronton** Knows
138 C7 **Crook** Cumb
150 E7 **Crook** Dur
163 L3 **Crookedholm** E Ayrs
168 D2 **Crookham** Nthumb
41 K7 **Crookham** W Berk
30 C2 **Crookham Village** Hants
165 L4 **Crook Inn** Border
129 L3 **Crooklands** Cumb
185 L7 **Crook of Devon** P & K
72 F5 **Cropredy** Oxon
87 G2 **Cropston** Leics
71 H5 **Cropthorne** Worcs
134 B2 **Cropton** N York
102 B5 **Cropwell Bishop** Notts
102 B5 **Cropwell Butler** Notts
232 g1 **Cros** W Isls
173 L7 **Crosbie** N Ayrs
232 f3 **Crosbost** W Isls
147 J7 **Crosby** Cumb
237 C5 **Crosby** IoM
125 K7 **Crosby** N Linc
111 J2 **Crosby** Sefton
139 G5 **Crosby Garret** Cumb
138 F4 **Crosby Ravensworth** Cumb
26 E3 **Croscombe** Somset
26 B1 **Cross** Somset
172 E7 **Crossaig** Ag & B
188 C7 **Crossapol** Ag & B
54 B4 **Cross Ash** Mons
33 K4 **Cross-at-Hand** Kent
147 J6 **Crosscanonby** Cumb
106 F5 **Crossdale Street** Norfk
123 G3 **Cross Flatts** C Brad
176 E2 **Crossford** Fife
175 L8 **Crossford** S Lans
177 K5 **Crossgatehall** E Loth
163 J1 **Crossgates** E Ayrs
176 F1 **Crossgates** Fife
124 B4 **Cross Gates** Leeds
134 F3 **Crossgates** N York
129 L6 **Crossgill** Lancs
123 L4 **Cross Green** Leeds
77 J4 **Cross Green** Suffk
77 K4 **Cross Green** Suffk
78 B4 **Cross Green** Suffk
51 H3 **Cross Hands** Carmth

163 L4 **Crosshands** E Ayrs
186 C7 **Crosshill** Fife
163 J7 **Crosshill** S Ayrs
163 K2 **Crosshouse** E Ayrs
83 K3 **Cross Houses** Shrops
20 D5 **Cross in Hand** E Susx
65 L3 **Cross Inn** Cerdgn
174 C2 **Cross Keys** Ag & B
37 K3 **Crosskeys** Caerph
230 F2 **Crosskirk** Highld
129 H2 **Crosslands** Cumb
17 G4 **Cross Lane** IoW
84 C4 **Cross Lane Head** Shrops
174 D5 **Crosslee** Rens
146 C2 **Crossmichael** D & G
216 E7 **Cross of Jackston** Abers
100 F4 **Cross o' th' hands** Derbys
206 B4 **Crossroads** Abers
206 E6 **Crossroads** Abers
92 E3 **Cross Street** Suffk
196 E5 **Crosston** Angus
113 H5 **Cross Town** Ches E
70 E2 **Crossway Green** Worcs
14 E5 **Crossways** Dorset
64 F6 **Crosswell** Pembks
129 J2 **Crosthwaite** Cumb
121 G6 **Croston** Lancs
92 F1 **Crostwick** Norfk
44 F3 **Crouch End** Gt Lon
28 B6 **Croucheston** Wilts
14 D1 **Crouch Hill** Dorset
73 G7 **Croughton** Nhants
216 F2 **Crovie** Abers
3 H4 **Crowan** Cnwll
32 K6 **Crowborough** E Susx
25 H4 **Crowcombe** Somset
114 C7 **Crowdecote** Derbys
114 B2 **Crowden** Derbys
114 D2 **Crow Edge** Barns
58 C7 **Crowell** Oxon
78 D3 **Crowfield** Suffk
178 F4 **Crowhill** E Loth
54 F3 **Crow Hill** Herefs
20 F3 **Crowhurst** E Susx
32 D4 **Crowhurst** Surrey
89 J2 **Crowland** Lincs
78 B1 **Crowland** Suffk
2 F5 **Crowlas** Cnwll
125 J7 **Crowle** N Linc
71 G4 **Crowle** Worcs
71 G3 **Crowle Green** Worcs
41 L3 **Crowmarsh Gifford** Oxon
78 F1 **Crown Corner** Suffk
6 C4 **Crownhill** C Plym
74 B6 **Crownhill Crematorium** M Keyn
92 C3 **Crownthorpe** Norfk
3 H5 **Crowntown** Cnwll
2 D5 **Crows-an-Wra** Cnwll
42 D7 **Crowthorne** Wokham
112 E6 **Crowton** Ches W
151 L2 **Croxdale** Dur
100 B5 **Croxden** Staffs
43 H2 **Croxley Green** Herts
75 J3 **Croxton** Cambs
126 D7 **Croxton** N Linc
91 K6 **Croxton** Norfk
106 B6 **Croxton** Norfk
99 H6 **Croxton** Staffs
102 D6 **Croxton Kerrial** Leics
213 J4 **Croy** Highld
175 J3 **Croy** N Lans
23 G4 **Croyde** Devon
75 K5 **Croydon** Cambs
44 F6 **Croydon** Gt Lon
44 F6 **Croydon Crematorium** Gt Lon
203 G7 **Crubenmore** Highld
83 H2 **Cruckmeole** Shrops
83 H2 **Cruckton** Shrops
217 K6 **Cruden Bay** Abers

98 F8 **Crudgington** Wrekin
39 L2 **Crudwell** Wilts
37 K2 **Crumlin** Caerph
5 K5 **Crumplehorn** Cnwll
113 J2 **Crumpsall** Manch
34 E5 **Crundale** Kent
49 K5 **Crunwear** Pembks
29 H1 **Crux Easton** Hants
50 F3 **Crwbin** Carmth
42 E2 **Cryers Hill** Bucks
65 G7 **Crymmych** Pembks
52 C6 **Crynant** Neath
45 G5 **Crystal Palace** Gt Lon
209 L3 **Cuaig** Highld
181 L4 **Cuan Ferry Village**
Ag & B
72 D2 **Cubbington** Warwks
4 C4 **Cubert** Cnwll
58 D4 **Cublington** Bucks
69 H6 **Cublington** Herefs
32 B7 **Cuckfield** W Susx
27 H6 **Cucklington** Somset
115 K7 **Cuckney** Notts
57 L7 **Cuddesdon** Oxon
58 C5 **Cuddington** Bucks
112 E7 **Cuddington** Ches W
98 C3 **Cuddington Heath**
Ches W
32 D2 **Cudham** Gt Lon
10 D8 **Cudliptown** Devon
15 K3 **Cudnell** Bmouth
124 B8 **Cudworth** Barns
13 J1 **Cudworth** Somset
59 M7 **Cuffley** Herts
191 J5 **Cuil** Highld
212 F3 **Culbokie** Highld
212 D6 **Culburnie** Highld
213 G5 **Culcabock** Highld
213 K4 **Culcharry** Highld
112 F5 **Culcheth** Warrtn
215 L7 **Culdrain** Abers
209 L6 **Culduie** Highld
77 J1 **Culford** Suffk
138 E2 **Culgaith** Cumb
41 J2 **Culham** Oxon
224 C2 **Culkein** Highld
224 D2 **Culkein Drumbeg**
Highld
39 L2 **Culkerton** Gloucs
215 L2 **Cullen** Moray
159 J7 **Cullercoats** N Tyne
206 E5 **Cullerlie** Abers
213 G2 **Cullicudden** Highld
123 G3 **Cullingworth** C Brad
199 G2 **Cuillin Hills** Highld
181 L5 **Cullipool House**
Ag & B
235 d2 **Cullivoe** Shet
213 H5 **Culloden** Highld
12 C2 **Cullompton** Devon
12 D2 **Cullompton Services**
Devon
25 H7 **Culm Davy** Devon
83 J6 **Culmington** Shrops
25 H8 **Culmstock** Devon
224 C7 **Culnacraig** Highld
146 D5 **Culnaightrie** D & G
209 H2 **Culnaknock** Highld
222 D3 **Culrain** Highld
176 D2 **Culross** Fife
163 H6 **Culroy** S Ayrs
216 C7 **Culsalmond** Abers
145 K5 **Culscadden** D & G
145 G5 **Culshabbin** D & G
235 b6 **Culswick** Shet
207 H1 **Cultercullen** Abers
207 G5 **Cults** C Aber
45 M7 **Culverstone Green**
Kent
103 G4 **Culverthorpe** Lincs
73 G5 **Culworth** Nhants
163 G7 **Culzean Castle &**
Country Park S Ayrs
175 K4 **Cumbernauld** N Lans
175 K3 **Cumbernauld Village**
N Lans

119 G6 **Cumberworth** Lincs
216 F4 **Cuminestown** Abers
179 G6 **Cumledge** Border
148 D4 **Cummersdale** Cumb
147 K2 **Cummertrees** D & G
214 E1 **Cummingston** Moray
164 B5 **Cumnock** E Ayrs
57 J7 **Cumnor** Oxon
148 F5 **Cumrew** Cumb
155 J5 **Cumrue** D & G
148 D4 **Cumwhinton** Cumb
148 E4 **Cumwhitton** Cumb
132 F5 **Cundall** N York
163 J2 **Cunninghamhead**
N Ayrs
235 C7 **Cunningsburgh** Shet
186 F4 **Cupar** Fife
186 F5 **Cupar Muir** Fife
114 E6 **Curbar** Derbys
17 G1 **Curbridge** Hants
57 G6 **Curbridge** Oxon
29 K8 **Curdridge** Hants
85 L5 **Curdworth** Warwks
25 L7 **Curland** Somset
41 J6 **Curridge** W Berk
177 G5 **Currie** C Edin
25 L6 **Curry Mallet** Somset
26 B6 **Curry Rivel** Somset
33 J5 **Curtisden Green** Kent
7 H5 **Curtisknowle** Devon
3 H6 **Cury** Cnwll
205 L3 **Cushnie** Abers
145 J7 **Cutcloy** D & G
24 E4 **Cutcombe** Somset
223 G4 **Cuthill** Highld
70 F2 **Cutnall Green** Worcs
56 C3 **Cutsdean** Gloucs
115 G6 **Cutthorpe** Derbys
42 A2 **Cuxham** Oxon
46 B6 **Cuxton** Medway
117 K2 **Cuxwold** Lincs
110 E6 **Cwm** Denbgs
36 B3 **Cwmafan** Neath
52 F7 **Cwmaman** Rhondd
50 B1 **Cwmbach** Carmth
68 D6 **Cwmbach** Powys
52 F7 **Cwmbach** Rhondd
68 B4 **Cwmbach Llechrhyd**
Powys
37 L2 **Cwmbran** Torfn
37 K2 **Cwmcarn** Caerph
54 C6 **Cwmcarvan** Mons
65 J6 **Cwm-cou** Cerdgn
53 H4 **Cwm Crawnon**
Powys
52 F7 **Cwmdare** Rhondd
53 J4 **Cwmdu** Powys
51 J6 **Cwmdu** Swans
65 L7 **Cwmduad** Carmth
36 D3 **Cwmfelin** Brdgnd
53 H7 **Cwmfelin** Myr Td
49 K4 **Cwmfelin Boeth**
Carmth
37 J3 **Cwmfelinfach** Caerph
50 E3 **Cwmffrwd** Carmth
52 C5 **Cwmgiedd** Powys
51 K4 **Cwmgorse** Carmth
51 H4 **Cwmgwili** Carmth
65 K6 **Cwmhiraeth** Carmth
81 J2 **Cwm Llinau** Powys
51 L3 **Cwmllynfell** Neath
51 G3 **Cwmmawr** Carmth
36 E2 **Cwmparc** Rhondd
65 K6 **Cwmpengraig**
Carmth
53 K6 **Cwmtillery** Blae G
109 H8 **Cwm-y-glo** Gwynd
81 H8 **Cwmystwyth** Cerdgn
66 C5 **Cwrt-newydd** Cerdgn
51 L5 **Cylibebyll** Neath
36 D2 **Cymer** Neath
36 F3 **Cymmer** Rhondd
67 H6 **Cynghordy** Carmth
36 C2 **Cynonville** Neath
97 G4 **Cynwyd** Denbgs
65 L8 **Cynwyl Elfed** Carmth

D

7 K3 **Daccombe** Devon
138 C2 **Dacre** Cumb
132 B7 **Dacre** N York
132 B6 **Dacre Banks** N York
149 M7 **Daddry Shield** Dur
73 J6 **Dadford** Bucks
86 E4 **Dadlington** Leics
45 J3 **Dagenham** Gt Lon
55 M6 **Daglingworth** Gloucs
59 G5 **Dagnall** Bucks
152 F2 **Dailly** S Ayrs
187 G4 **Dairsie** Fife
233 b8 **Dalabrog** W Isls
182 D5 **Dalavich** Ag & B
146 E3 **Dalbeattie** D & G
237 b5 **Dalby** IoM
133 K5 **Dalby** N York
194 F5 **Dalcapon** P & K
226 F7 **Dalchalm** Highld
201 L3 **Dalchreichart** Highld
184 F4 **Dalchruin** P & K
185 L2 **Dalcrue** P & K
12 D5 **Dalditch** Devon
101 H5 **Dale** Derbys
48 D6 **Dale** Pembks
190 E3 **Dalelia** Highld
163 H1 **Dalgarven** N Ayrs
177 G2 **Dalgety Bay** Fife
164 B6 **Dalgig** E Ayrs
185 G3 **Dalginross** P & K
194 F6 **Dalguise** P & K
230 C5 **Dalhalvaig** Highld
77 G3 **Dalham** Suffk
233 b8 **Daliburgh** W Isls
177 K5 **Dalkeith** Mdloth
214 D4 **Dallas** Moray
78 F4 **Dallinghoo** Suffk
20 D2 **Dallington** E Susx
73 K3 **Dallington** Nhants
183 H3 **Dalmally** Ag & B
184 C7 **Dalmary** Stirlg
153 K2 **Dalmellington** E Ayrs
176 F3 **Dalmeny** C Edin
203 H2 **Dalmigavie** Highld
203 H3 **Dalmigavie Lodge**
Highld
222 F7 **Dalmore** Highld
174 E4 **Dalmuir** W Duns
190 E3 **Dalnabreck** Highld
194 B3 **Dalnacardoch** P & K
203 K2 **Dalnahaitnach** Highld
193 K2 **Dalnaspidal** P & K
230 F7 **Dalnawillan Lodge**
Highld
194 C5 **Daloist** P & K
186 A6 **Dalqueich** P & K
153 G3 **Dalquhairn** S Ayrs
226 D6 **Dalreavoch Lodge**
Highld
174 B7 **Dalry** N Ayrs
163 J6 **Dalrymple** E Ayrs
175 L7 **Dalserf** S Lans
161 G6 **Dalsmeran** Ag & B
148 C5 **Dalston** Cumb
45 G3 **Dalston** Gt Lon
155 G5 **Dalswinton** D & G
155 K7 **Dalton** D & G
132 F4 **Dalton** N York
140 E5 **Dalton** N York
158 E7 **Dalton** Nthumb
128 F5 **Dalton-in-Furness**
Cumb
151 K5 **Dalton-le-Dale** Dur
141 H5 **Dalton-on-Tees**
N York
141 L2 **Dalton Piercy** Hartpl
165 G7 **Dalveich** D & G
184 D3 **Dalveich** Stirlg
202 F7 **Dalwhinnie** Highld
13 G3 **Dalwood** Devon
28 C7 **Damerham** Hants
93 J2 **Damgate** Norfk
61 J6 **Danbury** Essex

142 F5 **Danby** N York
141 H7 **Danby Wiske** N York
215 G5 **Dandaleith** Moray
177 J4 **Danderhall** Mdloth
113 L7 **Danebridge** Ches E
60 B4 **Dane End** Herts
32 D7 **Danehill** E Susx
87 H3 **Dane Hills** C Leic
34 E4 **Dane Street** Kent
216 D3 **Danshillock** Abers
178 C5 **Danskine** E Loth
45 K5 **Darenth** Kent
112 E5 **Daresbury** Halton
115 H1 **Darfield** Barns
34 E3 **Dargate** Kent
5 K3 **Darite** Cnwll
85 H4 **Darlaston** Wsall
85 H4 **Darlaston Green**
Wsall
132 C7 **Darley** N York
101 G5 **Darley Abbey** C Derb
100 E1 **Darley Bridge** Derbys
114 F8 **Darley Dale** Derbys
85 L8 **Darley Green** Solhll
59 J4 **Darleyhall** Herts
132 B7 **Darley Head** N York
72 B6 **Darlingscott** Warwks
141 H4 **Darlington** Darltn
141 G4 **Darlington**
Crematorium Darltn
116 C6 **Darlton** Notts
167 H3 **Darnick** Border
81 H3 **Darowen** Powys
216 E5 **Darra** Abers
9 G2 **Darracott** Devon
23 G4 **Darracott** Devon
158 E7 **Darras Hall** Nthumb
124 D6 **Darrington** Wakefd
79 J1 **Darsham** Suffk
26 E3 **Darshill** Somset
45 K5 **Dartford** Kent
7 H4 **Dartington** Devon
11 G8 **Dartmoor National**
Park Devon
7 K5 **Dartmouth** Devon
123 L7 **Darton** Barns
164 B2 **Darvel** E Ayrs
121 K6 **Darwen** Bl w D
43 G5 **Datchet** W & M
59 L4 **Datchworth** Herts
121 K8 **Daubhill** Bolton
214 F6 **Daugh of Kinermony**
Moray
39 M4 **Dauntsey** Wilts
214 C6 **Dava** Highld
112 F7 **Davenham** Ches W
73 H3 **Daventry** Nhants
177 G4 **Davidson's Mains**
C Edin
8 F7 **Davidstow** Cnwll
155 M2 **Davington** D & G
34 D3 **Davington Hill** Kent
216 E8 **Daviot** Abers
213 H6 **Daviot** Highld
213 H6 **Daviot House** Highld
215 K4 **Davoch of Grange**
Moray
31 K3 **Dawesgreen** Surrey
84 C2 **Dawley** Wrekin
12 B6 **Dawlish** Devon
12 C6 **Dawlish Warren**
Devon
110 B6 **Dawn** Conwy
101 L4 **Daybrook** Notts
56 E3 **Daylesford** Gloucs
35 K4 **Deal** Kent
136 E3 **Dean** Cumb
7 H3 **Dean** Devon
23 L2 **Dean** Devon
29 K7 **Dean** Hants
57 G4 **Dean** Oxon
26 F3 **Dean** Somset
45 L6 **Dean Bottom** Kent
166 F6 **Deanburnhaugh**
Border
7 G3 **Deancombe** Devon

57 J6 **Dean Court** Oxon
121 K8 **Deane** Bolton
29 K2 **Deane** Hants
122 F7 **Deanham** Kirk
27 M7 **Deanland** Dorset
7 H3 **Dean Prior** Devon
149 L3 **Deanraw** Nthumb
176 D5 **Deans** W Loth
136 F2 **Deanscales** Cumb
73 L6 **Deanshanger** Nhants
215 H4 **Deanshaugh** Moray
184 F6 **Deanston** Stirlg
147 J7 **Dearham** Cumb
78 F4 **Debach** Suffk
45 H2 **Debden** Essex
60 E2 **Debden** Essex
78 E2 **Debenham** Suffk
70 E5 **Deblin's Green** Worcs
176 E4 **Dechmont** W Loth
176 D4 **Dechmont Road**
          W Loth
57 J2 **Deddington** Oxon
62 C2 **Dedham** Essex
42 F5 **Dedworth** W & M
88 D5 **Deene** Nhants
88 D5 **Deenethorpe** Nhants
114 F3 **Deepcar** Sheff
89 G2 **Deeping Gate** C Pete
89 H2 **Deeping St James**
          Lincs
89 J1 **Deeping St Nicholas**
          Lincs
55 K3 **Deerhurst** Gloucs
71 G5 **Defford** Worcs
52 E3 **Defynnog** Powys
109 L5 **Deganwy** Conwy
182 A5 **Degnish** Ag & B
124 F2 **Deighton** C York
141 J6 **Deighton** N York
109 H8 **Deiniolen** Gwynd
8 E7 **Delabole** Cnwll
112 E7 **Delamere** Ches W
207 H2 **Delfrigs** Abers
214 D7 **Delliefure** Highld
18 A5 **Dell Quay** W Susx
204 E3 **Delnabo** Moray
214 E7 **Delnashaugh Inn**
          Moray
223 G6 **Delny** Highld
122 E8 **Delph** Oldham
150 E5 **Delves** Dur
195 H7 **Delvine** P & K
103 H5 **Dembleby** Lincs
115 J2 **Denaby** Donc
110 E7 **Denbigh** Denbgs
186 F4 **Denbrae** Fife
7 J3 **Denbury** Devon
101 H4 **Denby** Derbys
123 J8 **Denby Dale** Kirk
41 G3 **Denchworth** Oxon
128 F5 **Dendron** Cumb
185 K4 **Denfield** P & K
88 E7 **Denford** Nhants
62 B7 **Dengie** Essex
43 H3 **Denham** Bucks
77 H3 **Denham** Suffk
92 E8 **Denham** Suffk
43 H3 **Denham Green** Bucks
217 J4 **Denhead** Abers
187 G5 **Denhead** Fife
186 F2 **Denhead of Gray**
          C Dund
167 J5 **Denholm** Border
123 G4 **Denholme** C Brad
30 A8 **Denmead** Hants
207 H3 **Denmore** C Aber
79 G2 **Dennington** Suffk
175 L2 **Denny** Falk
175 L3 **Dennyloanhead** Falk
186 D4 **Den of Lindores** Fife
122 F2 **Denshaw** Oldham
206 F6 **Denside** Abers
35 G6 **Densole** Kent
77 H4 **Denston** Suffk
100 C4 **Denstone** Staffs
34 E3 **Denstroude** Kent

130 D3 **Dent** Cumb
89 G6 **Denton** Cambs
140 F4 **Denton** Darltn
19 L5 **Denton** E Susx
35 G5 **Denton** Kent
102 E6 **Denton** Lincs
123 H2 **Denton** N York
74 B3 **Denton** Nhants
93 G5 **Denton** Norfk
113 L3 **Denton** Tamesd
90 E3 **Denver** Norfk
169 J6 **Denwick** Nthumb
92 C4 **Deopham** Norfk
92 C4 **Deopham Green**
          Norfk
77 H3 **Depden** Suffk
45 G4 **Deptford** Gt Lon
28 A4 **Deptford** Wilts
101 G5 **Derby** C Derb
23 J5 **Derby** Devon
237 b7 **Derbyhaven** IoM
101 H6 **Derby South**
          Services Derbys
194 D5 **Derculich** P & K
92 B2 **Dereham** Norfk
53 H7 **Deri** Caerph
35 G5 **Derringstone** Kent
99 K7 **Derrington** Staffs
39 L6 **Derry Hill** Wilts
125 J8 **Derrythorpe** N Linc
105 H6 **Dersingham** Norfk
189 K6 **Dervaig** Ag & B
97 G3 **Derwen** Denbgs
80 F4 **Derwenlas** Powys
137 J3 **Derwent Water**
          Cumb
88 B6 **Desborough** Nhants
86 F3 **Desford** Leics
215 L3 **Deskford** Moray
33 K2 **Detling** Kent
54 C7 **Devauden** Mons
81 G7 **Devil's Bridge** Cerdgn
40 A7 **Devizes** Wilts
6 C5 **Devonport** C Plym
185 J7 **Devonside** Clacks
4 C7 **Devoran** Cnwll
177 K5 **Dewarton** Mdloth
14 E3 **Dewlish** Dorset
123 K6 **Dewsbury** Kirk
123 J6 **Dewsbury Moor**
          Crematorium Kirk
97 K8 **Deytheur** Powys
18 F2 **Dial Post** W Susx
16 E2 **Dibden** Hants
16 E2 **Dibden Purlieu** Hants
92 E6 **Dickleburgh** Norfk
56 B2 **Didbrook** Gloucs
41 K3 **Didcot** Oxon
41 K3 **Didcot Railway**
          Centre Oxon
75 H2 **Diddington** Cambs
83 K6 **Diddlebury** Shrops
18 A3 **Didling** W Susx
39 J3 **Didmarton** Gloucs
113 J3 **Didsbury** Manch
103 H2 **Digby** Lincs
218 C7 **Digg** Highld
122 F8 **Diggle** Oldham
112 C1 **Digmoor** Lancs
66 C4 **Dihewyd** Cerdgn
107 G7 **Dilham** Norfk
99 L4 **Dilhorne** Staffs
121 L4 **Dill Hall** Lancs
75 G2 **Dillington** Cambs
150 B3 **Dilston** Nthumb
27 K2 **Dilton** Wilts
27 J2 **Dilton Marsh** Wilts
69 H4 **Dilwyn** Herefs
94 E5 **Dinas** Gwynd
64 E6 **Dinas** Pembks
81 J1 **Dinas-Mawddwy**
          Gwynd
37 J6 **Dinas Powys** V Glam
26 E3 **Dinder** Somset
69 K6 **Dinedor** Herefs
54 C6 **Dingestow** Mons

111 K4 **Dingle** Lpool
87 L6 **Dingley** Nhants
212 E3 **Dingwall** Highld
205 K5 **Dinnet** Abers
158 F7 **Dinnington** N u Ty
115 K4 **Dinnington** Rothm
26 B8 **Dinnington** Somset
95 K1 **Dinorwic** Gwynd
58 C5 **Dinton** Bucks
28 A5 **Dinton** Wilts
155 K4 **Dinwoodie** D & G
9 J2 **Dinworthy** Devon
25 J6 **Dipford** Somset
161 K2 **Dippen** Ag & B
162 D5 **Dippen** N Ayrs
10 C7 **Dippertown** Devon
215 H3 **Dipple** Moray
152 E2 **Dipple** S Ayrs
7 G4 **Diptford** Devon
150 E4 **Dipton** Dur
178 B2 **Dirleton** E Loth
149 L5 **Dirt Pot** Nthumb
101 J7 **Diseworth** Leics
132 F5 **Dishforth** N York
113 L5 **Disley** Ches E
92 D7 **Diss** Norfk
136 D3 **Distington** Cumb
136 E3 **Distington Hall**
          Crematorium Cumb
28 C5 **Ditchampton** Wilts
169 H5 **Ditchburn** Nthumb
26 F4 **Ditcheat** Somset
93 G5 **Ditchingham** Norfk
19 J3 **Ditchling** E Susx
83 K2 **Ditherington** Shrops
39 J6 **Ditteridge** Wilts
7 K5 **Dittisham** Devon
112 D4 **Ditton** Halton
33 J2 **Ditton** Kent
76 F3 **Ditton Green** Cambs
83 L5 **Ditton Priors** Shrops
55 M2 **Dixton** Gloucs
54 D5 **Dixton** Mons
113 M1 **Dobcross** Oldham
5 K3 **Dobwalls** Cnwll
11 H7 **Doccombe** Devon
212 F6 **Dochgarroch** Highld
130 B5 **Docker** Lancs
105 J5 **Docking** Norfk
69 L3 **Docklow** Herefs
137 L3 **Dockray** Cumb
60 F7 **Doddinghurst** Essex
90 B5 **Doddington** Cambs
34 C4 **Doddington** Kent
116 E7 **Doddington** Lincs
168 E3 **Doddington** Nthumb
84 B7 **Doddington** Shrops
11 K7 **Doddiscombsleigh**
          Devon
98 E4 **Dodd's Green** Ches E
73 H3 **Dodford** Nhants
85 G8 **Dodford** Worcs
39 H4 **Dodington** S Glos
25 J4 **Dodington** Somset
98 A1 **Dodleston** Ches W
174 F7 **Dodside** E Rens
100 A5 **Dod's Leigh** Staffs
114 F1 **Dodworth** Barns
103 K2 **Dogdyke** Lincs
30 C2 **Dogmersfield** Hants
82 B2 **Dolanog** Powys
95 J4 **Dolbenmaen** Gwynd
81 K3 **Dolfach** Powys
82 C6 **Dolfor** Powys
109 L7 **Dolgarrog** Conwy
96 B8 **Dolgellau** Gwynd
226 F7 **Doll** Highld
185 K7 **Dollar** Clacks
185 K7 **Dollarfield** Clacks
111 H6 **Dolphin** Flints
129 L8 **Dolphinholme** Lancs
176 F8 **Dolphinton** S Lans
10 E3 **Dolton** Devon
110 B6 **Dolwen** Conwy
96 B3 **Dolwyddelan** Conwy
97 L8 **Domgay** Powys

115 L2 **Doncaster** Donc
125 G7 **Doncaster North**
          Services Donc
27 K6 **Donhead St Andrew**
          Wilts
27 K6 **Donhead St Mary**
          Wilts
177 G2 **Donibristle** Fife
25 G3 **Doniford** Somset
103 K5 **Donington** Lincs
118 C5 **Donington on Bain**
          Lincs
101 J7 **Donington Park**
          Services Leics
86 C2 **Donisthorpe** Leics
56 D3 **Donnington** Gloucs
83 L2 **Donnington** Shrops
41 J6 **Donnington** W Berk
18 B5 **Donnington** W Susx
84 C2 **Donnington** Wrekin
84 C2 **Donnington Wood**
          Wrekin
25 M8 **Donyatt** Somset
163 H5 **Doonfoot** S Ayrs
163 J6 **Doonholm** S Ayrs
204 D3 **Dorback Lodge**
          Highld
14 D4 **Dorchester** Dorset
41 L2 **Dorchester** Oxon
86 C4 **Dordon** Warwks
114 F5 **Dore** Sheff
212 F7 **Dores** Highld
31 K2 **Dorking** Surrey
32 D5 **Dormans Land** Surrey
69 L6 **Dormington** Herefs
71 H3 **Dormston** Worcs
42 F5 **Dorney** Bucks
200 D1 **Dornie** Highld
223 H4 **Dornoch** Highld
147 M2 **Dornock** D & G
230 F5 **Dorrery** Highld
85 L8 **Dorridge** Solhll
103 H2 **Dorrington** Lincs
83 J3 **Dorrington** Shrops
99 G4 **Dorrington** Shrops
71 K4 **Dorsington** Warwks
69 G6 **Dorstone** Herefs
58 B5 **Dorton** Bucks
237 d6 **Douglas** IoM
165 G4 **Douglas** S Lans
187 G2 **Douglas and Angus**
          C Dund
237 d5 **Douglas Borough**
          Crematorium IoM
165 G3 **Douglas Castle** S Lans
183 H7 **Douglas Pier** Ag & B
196 C6 **Douglastown** Angus
165 G3 **Douglas Water** S Lans
164 F3 **Douglas West** S Lans
26 F3 **Doulting** Somset
234 b5 **Dounby** Ork
221 L2 **Doune** Highld
184 F6 **Doune** Stirlg
152 E3 **Dounepark** S Ayrs
222 D4 **Dounie** Highld
6 D3 **Dousland** Devon
114 B6 **Dove Holes** Derbys
147 J7 **Dovenby** Cumb
35 J6 **Dover** Kent
35 J6 **Dover Castle** Kent
62 F2 **Dovercourt** Essex
70 F2 **Doverdale** Worcs
100 C5 **Doveridge** Derbys
31 L2 **Doversgreen** Surrey
194 F6 **Dowally** P & K
55 M4 **Dowdeswell** Gloucs
53 G6 **Dowlais** Myr Td
10 E3 **Dowland** Devon
26 A8 **Dowlish Wake**
          Somset
40 C2 **Down Ampney**
          Gloucs
5 L5 **Downderry** Cnwll
45 H7 **Downe** Gt Lon
39 J2 **Downend** Gloucs
38 F5 **Downend** S Glos

186 F2 **Downfield** C Dund
6 A2 **Downgate** Cnwll
46 B2 **Downham** Essex
45 H5 **Downham** Gt Lon
122 B2 **Downham** Lancs
90 E3 **Downham Market** Norfk
55 K4 **Down Hatherley** Gloucs
26 E6 **Downhead** Somset
27 G3 **Downhead** Somset
186 A2 **Downhill** P & K
140 E7 **Downholme** N York
207 H6 **Downies** Abers
42 D2 **Downley** Bucks
11 H4 **Down St Mary** Devon
19 J4 **Downs Crematorium** Br & H
43 J8 **Downside** Surrey
6 D6 **Down Thomas** Devon
16 C4 **Downton** Hants
28 D6 **Downton** Wilts
103 J6 **Dowsby** Lincs
39 G5 **Doynton** S Glos
37 K3 **Draethen** Caerph
164 F1 **Draffan** S Lans
116 B4 **Drakeholes** Notts
174 B7 **Drakemyre** N Ayrs
71 G5 **Drakes Broughton** Worcs
131 K8 **Draughton** N York
87 L7 **Draughton** Nhants
125 G5 **Drax** N York
72 F1 **Draycote** Warwks
101 H6 **Draycott** Derbys
71 L7 **Draycott** Gloucs
26 C2 **Draycott** Somset
100 D6 **Draycott in the Clay** Staffs
99 M4 **Draycott in the Moors** Staffs
17 J2 **Drayton** C Port
88 B5 **Drayton** Leics
92 E2 **Drayton** Norfk
41 J2 **Drayton** Oxon
72 E6 **Drayton** Oxon
26 B6 **Drayton** Somset
85 G7 **Drayton** Worcs
85 L4 **Drayton Bassett** Staffs
58 E5 **Drayton Beauchamp** Bucks
85 L4 **Drayton Manor Park** Staffs
58 D3 **Drayton Parslow** Bucks
41 L2 **Drayton St Leonard** Oxon
48 F5 **Dreen Hill** Pembks
51 G3 **Drefach** Carmth
65 K6 **Drefach** Carmth
66 C5 **Drefach** Cerdgn
163 J2 **Dreghorn** N Ayrs
35 H6 **Drellingore** Kent
178 B3 **Drem** E Loth
11 H6 **Drewsteignton** Devon
118 E6 **Driby** Lincs
134 F7 **Driffield** E R Yk
56 B7 **Driffield** Gloucs
2 D5 **Drift** Cnwll
136 E7 **Drigg** Cumb
123 J5 **Drighlington** Leeds
190 B5 **Drimnin** Highld
13 K2 **Drimpton** Dorset
191 J1 **Drimsallie** Highld
124 E2 **Dringhouses** C York
77 L3 **Drinkstone** Suffk
77 L3 **Drinkstone Green** Suffk
100 A6 **Drointon** Staffs
70 F2 **Droitwich** Worcs
186 B4 **Dron** P & K
115 G5 **Dronfield** Derbys
163 K5 **Drongan** E Ayrs
186 E1 **Dronley** Angus

14 E2 **Droop** Dorset
29 L7 **Droxford** Hants
113 K2 **Droylsden** Tamesd
97 G4 **Druid** Denbgs
48 E4 **Druidston** Pembks
191 L3 **Druimarbin** Highld
191 K7 **Druimavuic** Ag & B
172 C4 **Druimdrishaig** Ag & B
199 L7 **Druimindarroch** Highld
172 F3 **Drum** Ag & B
185 L7 **Drum** P & K
165 H2 **Drumalbin** S Lans
224 D3 **Drumbeg** Highld
216 B6 **Drumblade** Abers
144 C6 **Drumbreddon** D & G
210 B7 **Drumbuie** Highld
148 A3 **Drumburgh** Cumb
146 F4 **Drumburn** D & G
174 F4 **Drumchapel** C Glas
193 L5 **Drumchastle** P & K
164 C2 **Drumclog** S Lans
187 G6 **Drumeldrie** Fife
165 M3 **Drumelzier** Border
199 L3 **Drumfearn** Highld
206 D5 **Drumfrennie** Abers
196 C6 **Drumgley** Angus
203 J5 **Drumguish** Highld
214 E7 **Drumin** Moray
153 L3 **Drumjohn** D & G
153 G6 **Drumlamford** S Ayrs
206 C4 **Drumlasie** Abers
148 A5 **Drumleaning** Cumb
161 H5 **Drumlemble** Ag & B
197 J1 **Drumlithie** Abers
145 H6 **Drummoddie** D & G
144 D7 **Drummore** D & G
215 J5 **Drummuir** Moray
212 D7 **Drumnadrochit** Highld
144 D7 **Drumnaglaur** D & G
215 L4 **Drumnagorrach** Moray
154 F6 **Drumpark** D & G
224 E7 **Drumrunie Lodge** Highld
163 G6 **Drumshang** S Ayrs
209 G8 **Drumuie** Highld
204 B2 **Drumuillie** Highld
184 E6 **Drumvaich** Stirlg
186 B5 **Drunzie** P & K
138 F4 **Drybeck** Cumb
215 K2 **Drybridge** Moray
163 J3 **Drybridge** N Ayrs
54 F4 **Drybrook** Gloucs
167 J3 **Dryburgh** Border
102 D3 **Dry Doddington** Lincs
75 L3 **Dry Drayton** Cambs
174 E2 **Drymen** Stirlg
217 G5 **Drymuir** Abers
208 F7 **Drynoch** Highld
216 F2 **Dubford** Abers
225 J5 **Duchally** Highld
57 G6 **Ducklington** Oxon
76 C7 **Duddenhoe End** Essex
177 J4 **Duddingston** C Edin
88 E4 **Duddington** Nhants
25 K7 **Duddlestone** Somset
84 B6 **Duddlewick** Shrops
168 D2 **Duddo** Nthumb
112 D8 **Duddon** Ches W
97 M5 **Duddleston** Shrops
98 A5 **Duddleston Heath** Shrops
85 G5 **Dudley** Dudley
159 G2 **Dudley** N Tyne
85 G5 **Dudley Port** Sandw
15 K3 **Dudsbury** Dorset
101 G4 **Duffield** Derbys
36 C2 **Duffryn** Neath
215 H6 **Dufftown** Moray
214 E2 **Duffus** Moray
139 G3 **Dufton** Cumb
134 D6 **Duggleby** N York
210 B7 **Duirinish** Highld

199 L3 **Duisdalemore** Highld
191 K2 **Duisky** Highld
78 C6 **Duke Street** Suffk
113 L2 **Dukinfield** Tamesd
113 L2 **Dukinfield Crematorium** Tamesd
26 E3 **Dulcote** Somset
12 D2 **Dulford** Devon
194 C6 **Dull** P & K
175 K3 **Dullatur** N Lans
76 F3 **Dullingham** Cambs
76 F3 **Dullingham Ley** Cambs
204 B1 **Dulnain Bridge** Highld
75 H3 **Duloe** Bed
5 K4 **Duloe** Cnwll
24 E5 **Dulverton** Somset
45 G5 **Dulwich** Gt Lon
174 D4 **Dumbarton** W Duns
71 H7 **Dumbleton** Gloucs
155 G6 **Dumfries** D & G
174 F2 **Dumgoyne** Stirlg
29 L3 **Dummer** Hants
35 K2 **Dumpton** Kent
197 G4 **Dun** Angus
193 L5 **Dunalastair** P & K
173 K4 **Dunan** Ag & B
209 J8 **Dunan** Highld
193 G5 **Dunan** P & K
161 H7 **Dunaverty** Ag & B
25 L3 **Dunball** Somset
178 E3 **Dunbar** E Loth
227 L3 **Dunbeath** Highld
182 C2 **Dunbeg** Ag & B
185 G6 **Dunblane** Stirlg
186 E4 **Dunbog** Fife
212 F3 **Duncanston** Highld
216 B8 **Duncanstone** Abers
11 K7 **Dunchideock** Devon
72 F1 **Dunchurch** Warwks
155 G5 **Duncow** D & G
186 B5 **Duncrievie** P & K
18 C3 **Duncton** W Susx
186 F2 **Dundee** C Dund
186 F2 **Dundee Airport** C Dund
186 F2 **Dundee Crematorium** C Dund
26 C5 **Dundon** Somset
163 J3 **Dundonald** S Ayrs
220 E4 **Dundonnell** Highld
147 L5 **Dundraw** Cumb
201 L3 **Dundreggan** Highld
146 D5 **Dundrennan** D & G
38 E6 **Dundry** N Som
206 E4 **Dunecht** Abers
176 F2 **Dunfermline** Fife
176 F2 **Dunfermline Crematorium** Fife
40 C2 **Dunfield** Gloucs
164 D3 **Dungavel** S Lans
21 L3 **Dungeness** Kent
116 D6 **Dunham** Notts
112 C6 **Dunham-on-the-Hill** Ches W
70 F2 **Dunhampton** Worcs
113 H4 **Dunham Town** Traffd
113 G4 **Dunham Woodhouses** Traffd
117 G5 **Dunholme** Lincs
187 J5 **Dunino** Fife
175 L2 **Dunipace** Falk
195 G7 **Dunkeld** P & K
39 G3 **Dunkerton** BaNES
12 E2 **Dunkeswell** Devon
123 L2 **Dunkeswick** N York
34 E3 **Dunkirk** Kent
39 H4 **Dunk's S Glos
33 G3 **Dunk's Green** Kent
196 F3 **Dunlappie** Angus
70 E2 **Dunley** Worcs
174 D8 **Dunlop** E Ayrs
202 F2 **Dunmaglass** Highld
176 B1 **Dunmore** Falk
231 J2 **Dunnet** Highld
196 E6 **Dunnichen** Angus

185 L4 **Dunning** P & K
133 K8 **Dunnington** C York
126 E1 **Dunnington** E R Yk
71 J4 **Dunnington** Warwks
122 B5 **Dunnockshaw** Lancs
173 K3 **Dunoon** Ag & B
214 C5 **Dunphail** Moray
144 E4 **Dunragit** D & G
179 G7 **Duns** Border
103 J6 **Dunsby** Lincs
154 F5 **Dunscore** D & G
124 F8 **Dunscroft** Donc
142 D4 **Dunsdale** R & Cl
42 C5 **Dunsden Green** Oxon
9 J3 **Dunsdon** Devon
31 G4 **Dunsfold** Surrey
11 J6 **Dunsford** Devon
186 D5 **Dunshalt** Fife
217 J5 **Dunshillock** Abers
101 J1 **Dunsill** Notts
143 H5 **Dunsley** N York
84 F6 **Dunsley** Staffs
58 E6 **Dunsmore** Bucks
121 K1 **Dunsop Bridge** Lancs
59 G4 **Dunstable** C Beds
100 D7 **Dunstall** Staffs
169 K5 **Dunstan** Nthumb
24 F3 **Dunster** Somset
57 J3 **Duns Tew** Oxon
151 G3 **Dunston** Gatesd
117 H8 **Dunston** Lincs
92 F3 **Dunston** Norfk
99 L8 **Dunston** Staffs
6 E5 **Dunstone** Devon
7 G2 **Dunstone** Devon
124 F8 **Dunsville** Donc
126 D4 **Dunswell** E R Yk
176 E8 **Dunsyre** S Lans
6 B1 **Dunterton** Devon
55 L6 **Duntisbourne Abbots** Gloucs
55 M6 **Duntisbourne Rouse** Gloucs
14 D2 **Duntish** Dorset
174 E4 **Duntocher** W Duns
58 D3 **Dunton** Bucks
75 J5 **Dunton** C Beds
105 L6 **Dunton** Norfk
87 G5 **Dunton Bassett** Leics
32 F2 **Dunton Green** Kent
218 C6 **Duntulm** Highld
163 G6 **Dunure** S Ayrs
51 H6 **Dunvant** Swans
208 D5 **Dunvegan** Highld
79 K1 **Dunwich** Suffk
3 K5 **Durgan** Cnwll
151 G6 **Durham** Dur
151 G6 **Durham Cathedral** Dur
151 G6 **Durham Crematorium** Dur
151 H7 **Durham Services** Dur
141 J5 **Durham Tees Valley Airport** S on T
154 F2 **Durisdeer** D & G
154 F2 **Durisdeermill** D & G
25 L4 **Durleigh** Somset
29 K7 **Durley** Hants
40 E7 **Durley** Wilts
29 K7 **Durley Street** Hants
35 H3 **Durlock** Kent
35 J2 **Durlock** Kent
228 F3 **Durness** Highld
216 D8 **Durno** Abers
191 K5 **Duror** Highld
182 D5 **Durran** Ag & B
18 F5 **Durrington** W Susx
28 D3 **Durrington** Wilts
206 E6 **Durris** Abers
39 H2 **Dursley** Gloucs
55 G4 **Dursley Cross** Gloucs
25 L5 **Durston** Somset
15 G2 **Durweston** Dorset
73 K3 **Duston** Nhants
203 L1 **Duthil** Highld
112 E5 **Dutton** Ches W

76 C5 **Duxford** Cambs
57 G7 **Duxford** Oxon
76 C5 **Duxford Aircraft Museum** Cambs
109 L6 **Dwygyfylchi** Conwy
108 F7 **Dwyran** IoA
207 G3 **Dyce** C Aber
95 K7 **Dyffryn Ardudwy** Gwynd
52 D6 **Dyffryn Cellwen** Neath
103 J7 **Dyke** Lincs
214 B3 **Dyke** Moray
195 K5 **Dykehead** Angus
196 C4 **Dykehead** Angus
176 B6 **Dykehead** N Lans
184 D7 **Dykehead** Stirlg
197 H3 **Dykelands** Abers
195 K5 **Dykends** Angus
216 D5 **Dykeside** Abers
34 E8 **Dymchurch** Kent
55 G2 **Dymock** Gloucs
39 H5 **Dyrham** S Glos
186 E8 **Dysart** Fife
110 E5 **Dyserth** Denbgs

E

120 F2 **Eagland Hill** Lancs
116 E7 **Eagle** Lincs
141 K4 **Eaglescliffe** S on T
136 F2 **Eaglesfield** Cumb
155 M7 **Eaglesfield** D & G
175 G7 **Eaglesham** E Rens
121 L7 **Eagley** Bolton
102 A1 **Eakring** Notts
125 J7 **Ealand** N Linc
44 D4 **Ealing** Gt Lon
149 H4 **Eals** Nthumb
138 D2 **Eamont Bridge** Cumb
122 D2 **Earby** Lancs
84 C5 **Eardington** Shrops
69 H3 **Eardisland** Herefs
68 F5 **Eardisley** Herefs
98 A7 **Eardiston** Shrops
70 C2 **Eardiston** Worcs
89 L8 **Earith** Cambs
112 E3 **Earlestown** St Hel
42 C6 **Earley** Wokham
92 E2 **Earlham Crematorium** Norfk
208 F3 **Earlish** Highld
74 C2 **Earls Barton** Nhants
61 K3 **Earls Colne** Essex
71 G3 **Earls Common** Worcs
70 F6 **Earl's Croome** Worcs
86 D7 **Earlsdon** Covtry
187 H7 **Earlsferry** Fife
44 E5 **Earlsfield** Gt Lon
216 F7 **Earlsford** Abers
123 K6 **Earlsheaton** Kirk
86 F4 **Earl Shilton** Leics
78 F2 **Earl Soham** Suffk
114 C7 **Earl Sterndale** Derbys
167 J2 **Earlston** Border
163 K3 **Earlston** E Ayrs
32 B4 **Earlswood** Surrey
85 K8 **Earlswood** Warwks
17 M3 **Earnley** W Susx
159 H7 **Earsdon** N Tyne
158 F4 **Earsdon** Nthumb
93 G5 **Earsham** Norfk
18 C4 **Eartham** W Susx
142 C5 **Easby** N York
181 L4 **Easdale** Ag & B
30 E6 **Easebourne** W Susx
86 F7 **Easenhall** Warwks
30 F3 **Eashing** Surrey
58 B6 **Easington** Bucks
151 K6 **Easington** Dur
127 J6 **Easington** E R Yk
142 F4 **Easington** R & Cl
151 K6 **Easington Colliery** Dur

151 J5 **Easington Lane** Sundld
133 H5 **Easingwold** N York
196 B7 **Eassie and Nevay** Angus
37 G6 **East Aberthaw** V Glam
7 H6 **East Allington** Devon
24 D6 **East Anstey** Devon
17 H5 **East Ashey** IoW
17 M2 **East Ashling** W Susx
134 F3 **East Ayton** N York
117 K5 **East Barkwith** Lincs
33 J3 **East Barming** Kent
143 G5 **East Barnby** N York
44 F2 **East Barnet** Gt Lon
178 F3 **East Barns** E Loth
105 L5 **East Barsham** Norfk
106 E4 **East Beckham** Norfk
43 H5 **East Bedfont** Gt Lon
78 C7 **East Bergholt** Suffk
106 A8 **East Bilney** Norfk
20 A5 **East Blatchington** E Susx
151 J3 **East Boldon** S Tyne
16 D3 **East Boldre** Hants
141 H4 **Eastbourne** Darltn
20 C5 **Eastbourne** E Susx
20 D5 **Eastbourne Crematorium** E Susx
91 L2 **East Bradenham** Norfk
25 M2 **East Brent** Somset
79 J2 **Eastbridge** Suffk
102 B4 **East Bridgford** Notts
23 L5 **East Buckland** Devon
12 D5 **East Budleigh** Devon
122 F2 **Eastburn** C Brad
43 J2 **Eastbury** Herts
41 G5 **Eastbury** W Berk
116 D1 **East Butterwick** N Linc
131 J8 **Eastby** N York
176 E5 **East Calder** W Loth
92 E3 **East Carleton** Norfk
123 J2 **East Carlton** Leeds
88 B5 **East Carlton** Nhants
14 E5 **East Chaldon (Chaldon Herring)** Dorset
41 G3 **East Challow** Oxon
7 H7 **East Charleton** Devon
14 A2 **East Chelborough** Dorset
19 K3 **East Chiltington** E Susx
26 C8 **East Chinnock** Somset
28 C2 **East Chisenbury** Wilts
47 G5 **Eastchurch** Kent
31 H2 **East Clandon** Surrey
58 C3 **East Claydon** Bucks
26 D8 **East Coker** Somset
55 K6 **Eastcombe** Gloucs
25 J5 **East Combe** Somset
26 E3 **East Compton** Somset
7 J5 **East Cornworthy** Devon
43 J3 **Eastcote** Gt Lon
73 K4 **Eastcote** Nhants
85 L7 **Eastcote** Solhll
28 A1 **Eastcott** Wilts
125 G3 **East Cottingwith** E R Yk
39 L2 **Eastcourt** Wilts
40 E7 **Eastcourt** Wilts
16 F4 **East Cowes** IoW
125 G6 **East Cowick** E R Yk
141 H6 **East Cowton** N York
27 G3 **East Cranmore** Somset
20 B6 **East Dean** E Susx
54 F4 **East Dean** Gloucs
28 F6 **East Dean** Hants
18 B3 **East Dean** W Susx

116 C6 **East Drayton** Notts
45 G5 **East Dulwich** Gt Lon
38 E7 **East Dundry** N Som
126 C5 **East Ella** C KuH
46 F2 **Eastend** Essex
16 D3 **East End** Hants
41 H7 **East End** Hants
33 L6 **East End** Kent
57 H5 **East End** Oxon
26 F3 **East End** Somset
205 G6 **Easter Balmoral** Abers
38 E4 **Easter Compton** S Glos
213 H4 **Easter Dalziel** Highld
18 C5 **Eastergate** W Susx
175 J5 **Easterhouse** C Glas
177 H5 **Easter Howgate** Mdloth
212 E4 **Easter Kinkell** Highld
212 E5 **Easter Moniack** Highld
86 C7 **Eastern Green** Covtry
206 F4 **Easter Ord** Abers
187 J6 **Easter Pitkierie** Fife
235 c6 **Easter Skeld** Shet
168 A3 **Easter Softlaw** Border
28 A1 **Easterton** Wilts
28 D2 **East Everleigh** Wilts
33 J3 **East Farleigh** Kent
87 K6 **East Farndon** Nhants
116 D2 **East Ferry** Lincs
176 B5 **Eastfield** N Lans
135 G3 **Eastfield** N York
178 C3 **East Fortune** E Loth
41 G5 **East Garston** W Berk
150 B7 **Eastgate** Dur
106 D7 **Eastgate** Norfk
87 J2 **East Goscote** Leics
40 E7 **East Grafton** Wilts
28 E5 **East Grimstead** Wilts
32 D5 **East Grinstead** W Susx
21 J2 **East Guldeford** E Susx
73 J2 **East Haddon** Nhants
41 K3 **East Hagbourne** Oxon
126 E6 **East Halton** N Linc
45 H4 **East Ham** Gt Lon
42 D6 **Easthampstead Park Crematorium** Br For
69 H2 **Easthampton** Herefs
41 H2 **East Hanney** Oxon
61 J7 **East Hanningfield** Essex
124 C6 **East Hardwick** Wakefd
92 B6 **East Harling** Norfk
141 K7 **East Harlsey** N York
28 C5 **East Harnham** Wilts
26 E1 **East Harptree** BaNES
141 K4 **East Hartburn** S on T
30 D7 **East Harting** W Susx
27 L5 **East Hatch** Wilts
75 K4 **East Hatley** Cambs
132 B2 **East Hauxwell** N York
187 J1 **East Haven** Angus
103 K4 **East Heckington** Lincs
150 E6 **East Hedleyhope** Dur
227 H5 **East Helmsdale** Highld
41 J3 **East Hendred** Oxon
134 E4 **East Heslerton** N York
20 B3 **East Hoathly** E Susx
15 G5 **East Holme** Dorset
83 L4 **Easthope** Shrops
61 L4 **Easthorpe** Essex
26 E3 **East Horrington** Somset
31 H2 **East Horsley** Surrey
15 K4 **East Howe** Bmouth
25 M3 **East Huntspill** Somset
41 J4 **East Ilsley** W Berk
11 H3 **Eastington** Devon

55 H6 **Eastington** Gloucs
56 C5 **Eastington** Gloucs
118 E8 **East Keal** Lincs
40 C6 **East Kennett** Wilts
124 B2 **East Keswick** Leeds
175 H7 **East Kilbride** S Lans
118 D8 **East Kirkby** Lincs
14 F5 **East Knighton** Dorset
27 K5 **East Knoyle** Wilts
26 B7 **East Lambrook** Somset
122 B8 **East Lancashire Crematorium** Bury
154 E7 **Eastlands** D & G
35 J5 **East Langdon** Kent
87 K5 **East Langton** Leics
191 L5 **East Laroch** Highld
18 B4 **East Lavant** W Susx
18 C3 **East Lavington** W Susx
140 E5 **East Layton** N York
56 D6 **Eastleach Martin** Gloucs
56 D6 **Eastleach Turville** Gloucs
101 K7 **East Leake** Notts
11 G4 **East Leigh** Devon
23 H5 **Eastleigh** Devon
29 J7 **Eastleigh** Hants
105 K8 **East Lexham** Norfk
34 C4 **Eastling** Kent
178 D3 **East Linton** E Loth
41 H3 **East Lockinge** Oxon
116 C2 **East Lound** N Linc
15 G4 **East Lulworth** Dorset
134 E5 **East Lutton** N York
26 E5 **East Lydford** Somset
33 J2 **East Malling** Kent
30 D8 **East Marden** W Susx
116 C6 **East Markham** Notts
28 B7 **East Martin** Hants
122 D1 **East Marton** N York
30 B6 **East Meon** Hants
62 C5 **East Mersea** Essex
101 J7 *East Midlands Airport* Leics
43 J6 **East Molesey** Surrey
15 G4 **East Morden** Dorset
123 G3 **East Morton** C Brad
154 F3 **East Morton** D & G
133 L4 **East Ness** N York
17 J3 **Eastney** C Port
70 D6 **Eastnor** Herefs
87 L4 **East Norton** Leics
125 J7 **Eastoft** N Linc
7 J2 **East Ogwell** Devon
75 G1 **Easton** Cambs
148 B3 **Easton** Cumb
11 G6 **Easton** Devon
14 D7 **Easton** Dorset
29 K5 **Easton** Hants
102 F6 **Easton** Lincs
92 D2 **Easton** Norfk
26 D3 **Easton** Somset
79 G3 **Easton** Suffk
39 K6 **Easton** Wilts
39 K3 **Easton Grey** Wilts
38 D5 **Easton-in-Gordano** N Som
74 C3 **Easton Maudit** Nhants
88 E3 **Easton on the Hill** Nhants
40 D7 **Easton Royal** Wilts
27 J7 **East Orchard** Dorset
33 H4 **East Peckham** Kent
49 G6 **East Pennar** Pembks
26 E4 **East Pennard** Somset
75 G2 **East Perry** Cambs
7 H7 **East Portlemouth** Devon
7 G8 **East Prawle** Devon
18 E5 **East Preston** W Susx
14 D1 **East Pulham** Dorset
9 K2 **East Putford** Devon

25 H3 **East Quantoxhead** Somset
151 H5 **East Rainton** Sundld
118 C2 **East Ravendale** NE Lin
105 L7 **East Raynham** Norfk
89 K4 **Eastrea** Cambs
134 F5 **East Riding Crematorium** E R Yk
147 M2 **Eastriggs** D & G
124 B2 **East Rigton** Leeds
125 J4 **Eastrington** E R Yk
40 D2 **Eastrop** Swindn
141 K6 **East Rounton** N York
105 K6 **East Rudham** Norfk
106 E4 **East Runton** Norfk
107 H6 **East Ruston** Norfk
35 J4 **Eastry** Kent
178 B5 **East Saltoun** E Loth
44 D5 **East Sheen** Gt Lon
41 H5 **East Shefford** W Berk
116 C3 **East Stockwith** Lincs
15 G5 **East Stoke** Dorset
102 C3 **East Stoke** Notts
27 J6 **East Stour** Dorset
35 H3 **East Stourmouth** Kent
23 K6 **East Stowford** Devon
29 K4 **East Stratton** Hants
35 J5 **East Studdal** Kent
5 J3 **East Taphouse** Cnwll
23 G6 **East-the-Water** Devon
158 F3 **East Thirston** Nthumb
46 B5 **East Tilbury** Thurr
30 B5 **East Tisted** Hants
117 J5 **East Torrington** Lincs
92 C2 **East Tuddenham** Norfk
28 F5 **East Tytherley** Hants
39 L5 **East Tytherton** Wilts
11 J4 **East Village** Devon
38 E5 **Eastville** Bristl
104 C2 **Eastville** Lincs
83 K5 **East Wall** Shrops
91 G1 **East Walton** Norfk
26 D2 **East Water** Somset
10 F6 **East Week** Devon
102 C6 **Eastwell** Leics
28 F7 **East Wellow** Hants
186 E7 **East Wemyss** Fife
176 C5 **East Whitburn** W Loth
60 C5 **Eastwick** Herts
45 J5 **East Wickham** Gt Lon
49 J6 **East Williamston** Pembks
91 G1 **East Winch** Norfk
28 E5 **East Winterslow** Wilts
17 L3 **East Wittering** W Susx
131 L3 **East Witton** N York
122 E5 **Eastwood** Calder
101 J3 **Eastwood** Notts
46 D3 **Eastwood** Sthend
158 A5 **East Woodburn** Nthumb
41 H7 **East Woodhay** Hants
30 C4 **East Worldham** Hants
91 K5 **East Wretham** Norfk
9 H2 **East Youlstone** Devon
72 E2 **Eathorpe** Warwks
113 K7 **Eaton** Ches E
112 E8 **Eaton** Ches W
102 D6 **Eaton** Leics
92 E3 **Eaton** Norfk
116 B6 **Eaton** Notts
57 H7 **Eaton** Oxon
85 K5 **Eaton** Shrops
58 F4 **Eaton Bray** C Beds
83 L3 **Eaton Constantine** Shrops
58 F4 **Eaton Green** C Beds
56 E7 **Eaton Hastings** Oxon

83 K3 **Eaton Mascott** Shrops
75 H3 **Eaton Socon** Cambs
98 F7 **Eaton upon Tern** Shrops
134 D3 **Ebberston** N York
27 M6 **Ebbesborne Wake** Wilts
53 J6 **Ebbw Vale** Blae G
150 D4 **Ebchester** Dur
12 C5 **Ebford** Devon
55 J6 **Ebley** Gloucs
98 C3 **Ebnal** Ches W
71 L6 **Ebrington** Gloucs
41 J8 **Ecchinswell** Hants
178 F5 **Ecclaw** Border
155 L7 **Ecclefechan** D & G
168 A2 **Eccles** Border
46 B7 **Eccles** Kent
113 H2 **Eccles** Salfd
114 F5 **Ecclesall** Sheff
113 H3 **Eccles Crematorium** Salfd
115 G3 **Ecclesfield** Sheff
99 J6 **Eccleshall** Staffs
123 H4 **Eccleshill** C Brad
176 E4 **Ecclesmachan** W Loth
92 B5 **Eccles Road** Norfk
112 B8 **Eccleston** Ches W
121 G6 **Eccleston** Lancs
112 C3 **Eccleston** St Hel
206 E4 **Echt** Abers
167 L4 **Eckford** Border
115 H5 **Eckington** Derbys
71 G6 **Eckington** Worcs
74 B2 **Ecton** Nhants
114 C4 **Edale** Derbys
234 d4 **Eday** Ork
234 d4 *Eday Airport* Ork
19 H4 **Edburton** W Susx
222 F4 **Edderton** Highld
177 H8 **Eddleston** Border
175 J7 **Eddlewood** S Lans
32 D4 **Edenbridge** Kent
122 B6 **Edenfield** Lancs
138 E2 **Edenhall** Cumb
103 H7 **Edenham** Lincs
45 G4 **Eden Park** Gt Lon
5 G5 **Eden Project** Cnwll
114 E7 **Edensor** Derbys
183 K8 **Edentaggart** Ag & B
115 L1 **Edenthorpe** Donc
94 E5 **Edern** Gwynd
85 J6 **Edgbaston** Birm
58 B4 **Edgcott** Bucks
24 D4 **Edgcott** Somset
55 J6 **Edge** Gloucs
83 H2 **Edge** Shrops
106 C5 **Edgefield** Norfk
106 D5 **Edgefield Green** Norfk
123 H6 **Edgerton** Kirk
55 L6 **Edgeworth** Gloucs
99 G8 **Edgmond** Wrekin
83 H6 **Edgton** Shrops
44 D2 **Edgware** Gt Lon
121 L6 **Edgworth** Bl w D
208 E4 **Edinbane** Highld
177 H4 **Edinburgh** C Edin
176 F4 *Edinburgh Airport* C Edin
177 H4 **Edinburgh Castle** C Edin
177 H4 **Edinburgh Royal Botanic Gardens** C Edin
177 G4 **Edinburgh Zoo** C Edin
86 B2 **Edingale** Staffs
146 E3 **Edingham** D & G
102 A2 **Edingley** Notts
107 G6 **Edingthorpe** Norfk
107 G6 **Edingthorpe Green** Norfk
179 J7 **Edington** Border
158 E5 **Edington** Nthumb
26 B4 **Edington** Somset

27 L2 **Edington** Wilts
26 B3 **Edington Burtle** Somset
26 A2 **Edingworth** Somset
25 L2 **Edithmead** Somset
88 D3 **Edith Weston** Rutlnd
58 F4 **Edlesborough** Bucks
169 G7 **Edlingham** Nthumb
118 C7 **Edlington** Lincs
15 K1 **Edmondsham** Dorset
151 G5 **Edmondsley** Dur
102 E8 **Edmondthorpe** Leics
45 G2 **Edmonton** Gt Lon
150 C5 **Edmundbyers** Dur
167 L2 **Ednam** Border
194 D6 **Edradynate** P & K
179 H7 **Edrom** Border
98 D6 **Edstaston** Shrops
71 L3 **Edstone** Warwks
101 L5 **Edwalton** Notts
115 L7 **Edwinstowe** Notts
75 J6 **Edworth** C Beds
70 B3 **Edwyn Ralph** Herefs
196 F3 **Edzell** Angus
197 G3 **Edzell Woods** Abers
36 B2 **Efail-fach** Neath
37 G4 **Efail Isaf** Rhondd
94 F5 **Efailnewydd** Gwynd
49 K3 **Efailwen** Carmth
97 H2 **Efenechtyd** Denbgs
156 B4 **Effgill** D & G
31 J2 **Effingham** Surrey
6 D4 **Efford Crematorium** C Plym
121 K7 **Egerton** Bolton
34 B5 **Egerton** Kent
6 D4 **Eggbuckland** C Plym
11 G3 **Eggesford** Devon
58 F3 **Eggington** C Beds
100 E6 **Egginton** Derbys
141 K4 **Egglescliffe** S on T
140 C3 **Eggleston** Dur
43 G6 **Egham** Surrey
88 C3 **Egleton** Rutlnd
169 G5 **Eglingham** Nthumb
4 F2 **Egloshayle** Cnwll
9 H7 **Egloskerry** Cnwll
109 M7 **Eglwysbach** Conwy
98 C4 **Eglwys Cross** Wrexhm
65 G6 **Eglwyswrw** Pembks
116 B7 **Egmanton** Notts
136 D5 **Egremont** Cumb
111 K3 **Egremont** Wirral
143 G6 **Egton** N York
143 G6 **Egton Bridge** N York
42 F3 **Egypt** Bucks
199 G7 **Eigg** Highld
61 M3 **Eight Ash Green** Essex
200 C2 **Eilanreach** Highld
67 J2 **Elan Valley** Powys
67 K2 **Elan Village** Powys
38 E3 **Elberton** S Glos
6 D5 **Elburton** C Plym
40 C4 **Elcombe** Swindn
55 H2 **Eldersfield** Worcs
174 E5 **Elderslie** Rens
141 G2 **Eldon** Dur
206 F7 **Elfhill** Abers
85 L2 **Elford** Staffs
214 F2 **Elgin** Moray
199 H3 **Elgol** Highld
35 G6 **Elham** Kent
187 H7 **Elie** Fife
108 D4 **Elim** IoA
29 G8 **Eling** Hants
116 B6 **Elkesley** Notts
55 L5 **Elkstone** Gloucs
216 C3 **Ella** Abers
7 L3 **Ellacombe** Torbay
181 L4 **Ellanbeich** Ag & B
123 G6 **Elland** Calder
172 C3 **Ellary** Ag & B
100 C4 **Ellastone** Staffs
129 K7 **Ellel** Lancs
178 F6 **Ellemford** Border

99 J7 **Ellenhall** Staffs
31 H4 **Ellen's Green** Surrey
141 K7 **Ellerbeck** N York
143 G4 **Ellerby** N York
98 F7 **Ellerdine Heath** Wrekin
191 K6 **Elleric** Ag & B
125 L5 **Ellerker** E R Yk
125 G3 **Ellerton** E R Yk
141 G7 **Ellerton** N York
58 D6 **Ellesborough** Bucks
98 B5 **Ellesmere** Shrops
111 L6 **Ellesmere Port** Ches W
93 H5 **Ellingham** Norfk
169 H4 **Ellingham** Nthumb
132 B3 **Ellingstring** N York
75 H1 **Ellington** Cambs
159 G4 **Ellington** Nthumb
27 J3 **Elliots Green** Somset
29 M3 **Ellisfield** Hants
209 H2 **Ellishader** Highld
86 E2 **Ellistown** Leics
217 H7 **Ellon** Abers
148 D7 **Ellonby** Cumb
126 B5 **Elloughton** E R Yk
54 E6 **Ellwood** Gloucs
90 C3 **Elm** Cambs
70 F2 **Elmbridge** Worcs
76 C6 **Elmdon** Essex
85 L6 **Elmdon** Solhll
45 G6 **Elmers End** Gt Lon
86 F4 **Elmesthorpe** Leics
85 K2 **Elmhurst** Staffs
71 H6 **Elmley Castle** Worcs
70 F1 **Elmley Lovett** Worcs
55 H5 **Elmore** Gloucs
55 H5 **Elmore Back** Gloucs
45 K3 **Elm Park** Gt Lon
78 C5 **Elmsett** Suffk
62 C3 **Elmstead Market** Essex
34 F5 **Elmsted Court** Kent
35 H3 **Elmstone** Kent
55 K3 **Elmstone Hardwicke** Gloucs
134 F7 **Elmswell** E R Yk
78 B2 **Elmswell** Suffk
115 J6 **Elmton** Derbys
224 F6 **Elphin** Highld
177 K4 **Elphinstone** E Loth
206 F4 **Elrick** Abers
145 G5 **Elrig** D & G
149 L3 **Elrington** Nthumb
158 B4 **Elsdon** Nthumb
60 E3 **Elsenham** Essex
57 K6 **Elsfield** Oxon
126 C7 **Elsham** N Linc
92 C1 **Elsing** Norfk
122 D2 **Elslack** N York
17 H3 **Elson** Hants
165 K2 **Elsrickle** S Lans
30 E3 **Elstead** Surrey
30 D7 **Elsted** W Susx
103 H7 **Elsthorpe** Lincs
102 C3 **Elston** Notts
74 F5 **Elstow** Bed
44 D2 **Elstree** Herts
126 F4 **Elstronwick** E R Yk
120 F3 **Elswick** Lancs
151 G3 **Elswick** N u Ty
75 K2 **Elsworth** Cambs
137 K6 **Elterwater** Cumb
45 H5 **Eltham** Gt Lon
45 J5 **Eltham Crematorium** Gt Lon
75 J3 **Eltisley** Cambs
88 F5 **Elton** Cambs
112 C6 **Elton** Ches W
100 E1 **Elton** Derbys
69 J1 **Elton** Herefs
102 C5 **Elton** Notts
141 J4 **Elton** S on T
150 D3 **Eltringham** Nthumb
165 J6 **Elvanfoot** S Lans
101 H6 **Elvaston** Derbys

91 J7 **Elveden** Suffk
30 D1 **Elvetham Heath** Hants
178 A4 **Elvingston** E Loth
125 G2 **Elvington** C York
35 H5 **Elvington** Kent
141 K2 **Elwick** Hartpl
99 H1 **Elworth** Ches E
25 G4 **Elworthy** Somset
90 D7 **Ely** Cambs
37 H5 **Ely** Cardif
74 C5 **Emberton** M Keyn
137 G2 **Embleton** Cumb
169 J5 **Embleton** Nthumb
223 H3 **Embo** Highld
26 E2 **Emborough** Somset
223 H3 **Embo Street** Highld
131 J8 **Embsay** N York
16 C2 **Emery Down** Hants
123 K7 **Emley** Kirk
58 C7 **Emmington** Oxon
90 C3 **Emneth** Norfk
90 D3 **Emneth Hungate** Norfk
88 D2 **Empingham** Rutlnd
30 C5 **Empshott** Hants
83 K2 **Emstrey Crematorium** Shrops
17 K2 **Emsworth** Hants
41 H7 **Enborne** W Berk
41 H7 **Enborne Row** W Berk
87 G4 **Enderby** Leics
129 L3 **Endmoor** Cumb
99 L2 **Endon** Staffs
99 L2 **Endon Bank** Staffs
60 B7 **Enfield** Gt Lon
60 B7 **Enfield Crematorium** Gt Lon
60 B7 **Enfield Lock** Gt Lon
60 B7 **Enfield Wash** Gt Lon
28 C2 **Enford** Wilts
39 G4 **Engine Common** S Glos
41 L6 **Englefield** W Berk
43 G6 **Englefield Green** Surrey
54 E5 **English Bicknor** Gloucs
39 G7 **Englishcombe** BaNES
98 C6 **English Frankton** Shrops
29 G2 **Enham-Alamein** Hants
25 K4 **Enmore** Somset
27 J6 **Enmore Green** Dorset
136 E4 **Ennerdale Bridge** Cumb
195 G4 **Enochdhu** P & K
189 J6 **Ensay** Ag & B
15 K3 **Ensbury** Bmouth
83 H1 **Ensdon** Shrops
57 G3 **Enstone** Oxon
154 E2 **Enterkinfoot** D & G
84 E6 **Enville** Staffs
233 b9 **Eolaigearraidh** W Isls
55 H5 **Epney** Gloucs
101 M3 **Epperstone** Notts
60 D7 **Epping** Essex
60 C6 **Epping Green** Essex
60 C6 **Epping Upland** Essex
140 F5 **Eppleby** N York
44 E7 **Epsom** Surrey
72 D6 **Epwell** Oxon
116 C2 **Epworth** N Linc
97 M4 **Erbistock** Wrexhm
85 K5 **Erdington** Birm
32 F6 **Eridge Green** E Susx
172 E4 **Erines** Ag & B
191 H7 **Eriska** Ag & B
233 c9 **Eriskay** W Isls
91 G7 **Eriswell** Suffk
45 K4 **Erith** Gt Lon
27 L2 **Erlestoke** Wilts
6 F5 **Ermington** Devon
106 E6 **Erpingham** Norfk
202 E2 **Errogie** Highld

186 D3 **Errol** P & K
174 E4 **Erskine** Rens
144 B2 **Ervie** D & G
78 F7 **Erwarton** Suffk
68 C6 **Erwood** Powys
141 H5 **Eryholme** N York
97 J2 **Eryrys** Denbgs
140 F2 **Escomb** Dur
124 F2 **Escrick** N York
81 G3 **Esgairgeiliog** Powys
150 F6 **Esh** Dur
43 J7 **Esher** Surrey
158 F3 **Eshott** Nthumb
150 F6 **Esh Winning** Dur
212 C6 **Eskadale** Highld
177 J5 **Eskbank** Mdloth
137 G6 **Eskdale Green** Cumb
156 A3 **Eskdalemuir** D & G
120 E3 **Esprick** Lancs
88 F2 **Essendine** Rutlnd
59 L6 **Essendon** Herts
213 G6 **Essich** Highld
85 G3 **Essington** Staffs
217 H7 **Esslemont** Abers
142 C4 **Eston** R & Cl
168 D2 **Etal** Nthumb
40 B7 **Etchilhampton** Wilts
33 J7 **Etchingham** E Susx
34 F6 **Etchinghill** Kent
100 B8 **Etchinghill** Staffs
42 F5 **Eton** W & M
42 F5 **Eton Wick** W & M
99 K3 **Etruria** C Stke
203 G6 **Etteridge** Highld
139 K2 **Ettersgill** Dur
99 G1 **Ettiley Heath** Ches E
85 G4 **Ettingshall** Wolves
72 C5 **Ettington** Warwks
89 G3 **Etton** C Pete
126 B2 **Etton** E R Yk
166 D6 **Ettrick** Border
166 F4 **Ettrickbridge** Border
166 C6 **Ettrickhill** Border
100 F6 **Etwall** Derbys
91 K7 **Euston** Suffk
121 H6 **Euxton** Lancs
212 F2 **Evanton** Highld
103 H3 **Evedon** Lincs
223 G4 **Evelix** Highld
68 F3 **Evenjobb** Powys
73 H7 **Evenley** Nhants
56 E3 **Evenlode** Gloucs
140 E3 **Evenwood** Dur
26 F4 **Evercreech** Somset
125 J3 **Everingham** E R Yk
28 D2 **Everleigh** Wilts
59 G2 **Eversholt** C Beds
14 B2 **Evershot** Dorset
42 C7 **Eversley** Hants
42 C7 **Eversley Cross** Hants
125 L4 **Everthorpe** E R Yk
75 H4 **Everton** C Beds
16 C4 **Everton** Hants
111 K3 **Everton** Lpool
116 B4 **Everton** Notts
156 C6 **Evertown** D & G
70 C5 **Evesbatch** Herefs
71 J5 **Evesham** Worcs
87 J3 **Evington** C Leic
114 F3 **Ewden Village** Sheff
44 F7 **Ewell** Surrey
35 H6 **Ewell Minnis** Kent
41 M3 **Ewelme** Oxon
40 A2 **Ewen** Gloucs
36 D5 **Ewenny** V Glam
103 J3 **Ewerby** Lincs
158 D4 **Ewesley** Nthumb
31 H4 **Ewhurst** Surrey
20 F2 **Ewhurst Green** E Susx
31 H4 **Ewhurst Green** Surrey
111 J7 **Ewloe** Flints
10 C6 **Eworthy** Devon
30 D2 **Ewshot** Hants
54 B3 **Ewyas Harold** Herefs
10 E4 **Exbourne** Devon

24 E6 **Exbridge** Somset
16 E3 **Exbury** Hants
132 D3 **Exelby** N York
11 L6 **Exeter** Devon
12 C4 **Exeter Airport** Devon
12 B4 **Exeter & Devon Crematorium** Devon
12 C4 **Exeter Services** Devon
24 D4 **Exford** Somset
83 J3 **Exfordsgreen** Shrops
71 K4 **Exhall** Warwks
86 D6 **Exhall** Warwks
42 A4 **Exlade Street** Oxon
12 B5 **Exminster** Devon
24 D4 **Exmoor National Park**
12 C6 **Exmouth** Devon
76 E2 **Exning** Suffk
35 G5 **Exted** Kent
12 C5 **Exton** Devon
29 L7 **Exton** Hants
88 D2 **Exton** Rutlnd
24 E5 **Exton** Somset
11 K6 **Exwick** Devon
114 E6 **Eyam** Derbys
73 G4 **Eydon** Nhants
89 J3 **Eye** C Pete
69 J2 **Eye** Herefs
92 D8 **Eye** Suffk
179 K5 **Eyemouth** Border
75 J5 **Eyeworth** C Beds
33 L3 **Eyhorne Street** Kent
79 G4 **Eyke** Suffk
75 H3 **Eynesbury** Cambs
45 K6 **Eynsford** Kent
57 H6 **Eynsham** Oxon
13 L4 **Eype** Dorset
208 F4 **Eyre** Highld
35 H5 **Eythorne** Kent
69 J3 **Eyton** Herefs
83 G6 **Eyton** Shrops
98 C7 **Eyton** Shrops
83 L3 **Eyton on Severn** Shrops
84 B1 **Eyton upon the Weald Moors** Wrekin

F

41 H8 **Faccombe** Hants
141 L6 **Faceby** N York
82 B1 **Fachwen** Powys
98 E3 **Faddiley** Ches E
133 K2 **Fadmoor** N York
51 K5 **Faerdre** Swans
174 F4 **Faifley** W Duns
38 D6 **Failand** N Som
163 L4 **Failford** S Ayrs
113 K2 **Failsworth** Oldham
80 E2 **Fairbourne** Gwynd
124 D5 **Fairburn** N York
114 B6 **Fairfield** Derbys
85 G7 **Fairfield** Worcs
56 D7 **Fairford** Gloucs
146 F4 **Fairgirth** D & G
120 D5 **Fairhaven** Lancs
235 e7 **Fair Isle** Shet
30 F2 **Fairlands** Surrey
173 L7 **Fairlie** N Ayrs
21 G4 **Fairlight** E Susx
12 E3 **Fairmile** Devon
43 J7 **Fairmile** Surrey
167 G3 **Fairnilee** Border
29 J7 **Fair Oak** Hants
99 H6 **Fairoak** Staffs
42 A7 **Fair Oak Green** Hants
45 L7 **Fairseat** Kent
61 J5 **Fairstead** Essex
105 G8 **Fairstead** Norfk
32 E7 **Fairwarp** E Susx
37 H5 **Fairwater** Cardif
22 F6 **Fairy Cross** Devon
105 L6 **Fakenham** Norfk

91 K7 **Fakenham Magna** Suffk
177 L6 **Fala** Mdloth
177 L6 **Fala Dam** Mdloth
177 L7 **Falahill** Border
117 H5 **Faldingworth** Lincs
236 e7 **Faldouet** Jersey
39 G2 **Falfield** S Glos
79 G6 **Falkenham** Suffk
176 B3 **Falkirk** Falk
186 D6 **Falkland** Fife
165 J2 **Fallburn** S Lans
185 H8 **Fallin** Stirlg
169 J5 **Falloden** Nthumb
113 J3 **Fallowfield** Manch
150 B2 **Fallowfield** Nthumb
182 E5 **Falls of Blarghour** Ag & B
19 K4 **Falmer** E Susx
3 K5 **Falmouth** Cnwll
156 D2 **Falnash** Border
134 F2 **Falsgrave** N York
157 J5 **Falstone** Nthumb
228 B5 **Fanagmore** Highld
59 G3 **Fancott** C Beds
212 D5 **Fanellan** Highld
142 C7 **Fangdale Beck** N York
134 B8 **Fangfoss** E R Yk
189 K7 **Fanmore** Ag & B
211 K2 **Fannich Lodge** Highld
167 J2 **Fans** Border
74 C7 **Far Bletchley** M Keyn
89 H5 **Farcet** Cambs
73 L3 **Far Cotton** Nhants
17 H2 **Fareham** Hants
137 J7 **Far End** Cumb
85 J2 **Farewell** Staffs
55 H7 **Far Green** Gloucs
40 F2 **Faringdon** Oxon
121 H5 **Farington** Lancs
185 L1 **Farkhill** P & K
148 F3 **Farlam** Cumb
38 D6 **Farleigh** N Som
32 C2 **Farleigh** Surrey
39 J8 **Farleigh Hungerford** Somset
29 L3 **Farleigh Wallop** Hants
119 G6 **Farlesthorpe** Lincs
129 L4 **Farleton** Cumb
130 B6 **Farleton** Lancs
100 B4 **Farley** Staffs
28 E5 **Farley** Wilts
77 G4 **Farley Green** Suffk
31 H3 **Farley Green** Surrey
42 C7 **Farley Hill** Wokham
55 H5 **Farleys End** Gloucs
17 J2 **Farlington** C Port
133 J6 **Farlington** N York
84 B7 **Farlow** Shrops
38 F7 **Farmborough** BaNES
56 B3 **Farmcote** Gloucs
66 E5 **Farmers** Carmth
56 C5 **Farmington** Gloucs
57 J6 **Farmoor** Oxon
112 D2 **Far Moor** Wigan
215 L4 **Farmtown** Moray
45 H7 **Farnborough** Gt Lon
30 E2 **Farnborough** Hants
41 H4 **Farnborough** W Berk
72 E5 **Farnborough** Warwks
30 E1 **Farnborough Park** Hants
30 E1 **Farnborough Street** Hants
31 G3 **Farncombe** Surrey
74 D2 **Farndish** Bed
98 B2 **Farndon** Ches W
102 C3 **Farndon** Notts
169 K2 **Farne Islands** Nthumb
197 G5 **Farnell** Angus
27 L7 **Farnham** Dorset
60 D3 **Farnham** Essex
132 E7 **Farnham** N York
79 H3 **Farnham** Suffk

30 D3 **Farnham** Surrey
42 F4 **Farnham Common** Bucks
42 F4 **Farnham Royal** Bucks
45 K6 **Farningham** Kent
123 K4 **Farnley** Leeds
123 J2 **Farnley** Leeds
123 H7 **Farnley Tyas** Kirk
101 M2 **Farnsfield** Notts
113 G1 **Farnworth** Bolton
112 D4 **Farnworth** Halton
55 L7 **Far Oakridge** Gloucs
203 K5 **Farr** Highld
213 G7 **Farr** Highld
229 L3 **Farr** Highld
202 E2 **Farraline** Highld
12 C4 **Farringdon** Devon
26 F1 **Farrington Gurney** BaNES
137 K7 **Far Sawrey** Cumb
73 G6 **Farthinghoe** Nhants
73 H4 **Farthingstone** Nhants
118 C6 **Far Thorpe** Lincs
123 H6 **Fartown** Kirk
123 J4 **Fartown** Leeds
191 K6 **Fasnacloich** Ag & B
211 L8 **Fasnakyle** Highld
191 K2 **Fassfern** Highld
151 H4 **Fatfield** Sundld
176 C6 **Fauldhouse** W Loth
61 J5 **Faulkbourne** Essex
27 H1 **Faulkland** Somset
98 E6 **Fauls** Shrops
34 D3 **Faversham** Kent
132 F5 **Fawdington** N York
151 G2 **Fawdon** N u Ty
45 L6 **Fawkham Green** Kent
57 G4 **Fawler** Oxon
42 C3 **Fawley** Bucks
16 F2 **Fawley** Hants
41 H4 **Fawley** W Berk
125 K5 **Faxfleet** E R Yk
31 K5 **Faygate** W Susx
111 K3 **Fazakerley** Lpool
85 L3 **Fazeley** Staffs
132 B4 **Fearby** N York
223 H6 **Fearn** Highld
194 B7 **Fearnan** P & K
210 B3 **Fearnbeg** Highld
209 L3 **Fearnmore** Highld
172 F3 **Fearnoch** Ag & B
85 G3 **Featherstone** Staffs
124 C6 **Featherstone** Wakefd
71 H3 **Feckenham** Worcs
61 L4 **Feering** Essex
140 C7 **Feetham** N York
32 C5 **Felbridge** Surrey
106 E5 **Felbrigg** Norfk
32 C5 **Felcourt** Surrey
51 G2 **Felindre** Carmth
65 K6 **Felindre** Carmth
82 D7 **Felindre** Powys
51 J5 **Felindre** Swans
64 F6 **Felindre Farchog** Pembks
51 G2 **Felin gwm Isaf** Carmth
51 G1 **Felin gwm Uchaf** Carmth
133 G4 **Felixkirk** N York
79 G7 **Felixstowe** Suffk
151 G3 **Felling** Gatesd
74 E3 **Felmersham** Bed
106 F6 **Felmingham** Norfk
18 C5 **Felpham** W Susx
77 L3 **Felsham** Suffk
61 G4 **Felsted** Essex
43 J5 **Feltham** Gt Lon
43 H6 **Felthamhill** Surrey
106 E8 **Felthorpe** Norfk
69 L5 **Felton** Herefs
38 D7 **Felton** N Som
158 F3 **Felton** Nthumb
98 B8 **Felton Butler** Shrops
91 G5 **Feltwell** Norfk

122 C3 **Fence** Lancs
115 H4 **Fence** Rothm
132 D2 **Fencote** N York
57 L5 **Fencott** Oxon
104 D1 **Fendike Corner** Lincs
76 C3 **Fen Ditton** Cambs
75 L2 **Fen Drayton** Cambs
121 J5 **Feniscowles** Bl w D
12 E3 **Feniton** Devon
84 D6 **Fenn Green** Shrops
46 D5 **Fenn Street** Medway
100 D3 **Fenny Bentley** Derbys
12 E3 **Fenny Bridges** Devon
72 E4 **Fenny Compton** Warwks
86 D4 **Fenny Drayton** Leics
75 K2 **Fenstanton** Cambs
92 B4 **Fen Street** Norfk
99 K4 **Fenton** C Stke
89 K7 **Fenton** Cambs
148 E4 **Fenton** Cumb
102 E3 **Fenton** Lincs
116 D6 **Fenton** Lincs
116 C5 **Fenton** Notts
168 E3 **Fenton** Nthumb
178 B3 **Fenton Barns** E Loth
124 F7 **Fenwick** Donc
163 L2 **Fenwick** E Ayrs
158 D7 **Fenwick** Nthumb
169 G2 **Fenwick** Nthumb
4 C7 **Feock** Cnwll
171 H4 **Feolin Ferry** Ag & B
163 J2 **Fergushill** N Ayrs
208 B4 **Feriniquarrie** Highld
196 D4 **Fern** Angus
36 F2 **Ferndale** Rhondd
15 K3 **Ferndown** Dorset
214 B5 **Ferness** Highld
40 F3 **Fernham** Oxon
70 F3 **Fernhill Heath** Worcs
30 E5 **Fernhurst** W Susx
186 E4 **Fernie** Fife
175 K7 **Ferniegair** S Lans
208 F7 **Fernilea** Highld
114 A5 **Fernilee** Derbys
102 D3 **Fernwood** Notts
132 E7 **Ferrensby** N York
199 K4 **Ferrindonald** Highld
18 F5 **Ferring** W Susx
124 D6 **Ferrybridge Services** Wakefd
197 H5 **Ferryden** Angus
141 H2 **Ferryhill** Dur
223 G4 **Ferry Point** Highld
50 D4 **Ferryside** Carmth
223 G4 **Ferrytown** Highld
92 C6 **Fersfield** Norfk
192 F2 **Fersit** Highld
203 K4 **Feshiebridge** Highld
31 J1 **Fetcham** Surrey
235 e2 **Fetlar** Shet
217 J4 **Fetterangus** Abers
197 G2 **Fettercairn** Abers
132 B8 **Fewston** N York
51 J2 **Ffairfach** Carmth
67 G2 **Ffair Rhos** Cerdgn
96 A4 **Ffestiniog** Gwynd
95 L4 **Ffestiniog Railway** Gwynd
51 H5 **Fforest** Carmth
51 J6 **Fforest Fach** Swans
65 L5 **Ffostrasol** Cerdgn
97 L2 **Ffrith** Flints
111 G5 **Ffynnongroyw** Flints
225 K3 **Fiag Lodge** Highld
32 C2 **Fickleshole** Surrey
55 L2 **Fiddington** Gloucs
25 K4 **Fiddington** Somset
27 J8 **Fiddleford** Dorset
4 C7 **Fiddlers Green** Cnwll
100 A5 **Field** Staffs
129 J3 **Field Broughton** Cumb
106 B5 **Field Dalling** Norfk
86 F2 **Field Head** Leics

27 H6 **Fifehead Magdalen** Dorset
14 E1 **Fifehead Neville** Dorset
14 E1 **Fifehead St Quintin** Dorset
215 J4 **Fife Keith** Moray
56 E4 **Fifield** Oxon
42 E5 **Fifield** W & M
28 D3 **Figheldean** Wilts
93 K2 **Filby** Norfk
135 H4 **Filey** N York
74 C5 **Filgrave** M Keyn
56 E6 **Filkins** Oxon
23 K5 **Filleigh** Devon
116 F4 **Fillingham** Lincs
86 C6 **Fillongley** Warwks
38 E5 **Filton** S Glos
134 D7 **Fimber** E R Yk
196 D5 **Finavon** Angus
91 G3 **Fincham** Norfk
42 D7 **Finchampstead** Wokham
182 C6 **Fincharn** Ag & B
30 C8 **Finchdean** Hants
61 G2 **Finchingfield** Essex
44 F2 **Finchley** Gt Lon
100 F6 **Findern** Derbys
214 C2 **Findhorn** Moray
213 J8 **Findhorn Bridge** Highld
215 K2 **Findochty** Moray
185 L4 **Findo Gask** P & K
207 H6 **Findon** Abers
18 F4 **Findon** W Susx
212 F3 **Findon Mains** Highld
206 B4 **Findrack House** Abers
74 D1 **Finedon** Nhants
186 C4 **Fingask** P & K
42 C3 **Fingest** Bucks
132 B2 **Finghall** N York
164 E6 **Fingland** D & G
35 J4 **Finglesham** Kent
62 B4 **Fingringhoe** Essex
184 C1 **Finlarig** Stirlg
57 M2 **Finmere** Oxon
193 H5 **Finnart** P & K
78 C1 **Finningham** Suffk
116 A2 **Finningley** Donc
232 d5 **Finsbay** W Isls
71 H1 **Finstall** Worcs
129 H2 **Finsthwaite** Cumb
57 G5 **Finstock** Oxon
234 b6 **Finstown** Ork
216 E4 **Fintry** Abers
175 H2 **Fintry** Stirlg
206 B6 **Finzean** Abers
180 D3 **Fionnphort** Ag & B
232 d5 **Fionnsbhagh** W Isls
130 C2 **Firbank** Cumb
115 K4 **Firbeck** Rothm
132 D3 **Firby** N York
134 B6 **Firby** N York
19 M4 **Firle** E Susx
118 F8 **Firsby** Lincs
150 E7 **Fir Tree** Dur
17 G4 **Fishbourne** IoW
18 A5 **Fishbourne** W Susx
18 A5 **Fishbourne Roman Palace** W Susx
141 J2 **Fishburn** Dur
185 J7 **Fishcross** Clacks
216 C7 **Fisherford** Abers
177 K4 **Fisherrow** E Loth
29 J7 **Fisher's Pond** Hants
213 H4 **Fisherton** Highld
163 H6 **Fisherton** S Ayrs
27 M4 **Fisherton de la Mere** Wilts
64 D6 **Fishguard** Pembks
125 G7 **Fishlake** Donc
190 D7 **Fishnish Pier** Ag & B
38 F5 **Fishponds** Bristl
104 B4 **Fishtoft** Lincs
104 A3 **Fishtoft Drove** Lincs

208 E7 **Fiskavaig** Highld
117 H6 **Fiskerton** Lincs
102 C3 **Fiskerton** Notts
28 D2 **Fittleton** Wilts
18 D2 **Fittleworth** W Susx
98 C8 **Fitz** Shrops
25 H5 **Fitzhead** Somset
124 C7 **Fitzwilliam** Wakefd
19 M2 **Five Ash Down** E Susx
32 F7 **Five Ashes** E Susx
26 A6 **Fivehead** Somset
9 G8 **Fivelanes** Cnwll
33 H4 **Five Oak Green** Kent
236 d7 **Five Oaks** Jersey
31 H5 **Five Oaks** W Susx
42 E3 **Flackwell Heath** Bucks
71 H5 **Fladbury** Worcs
235 c6 **Fladdabister** Shet
114 C7 **Flagg** Derbys
135 K5 **Flamborough** E R Yk
135 K5 **Flamborough Head** E R Yk
134 B4 **Flamingo Land Theme Park** N York
59 H5 **Flamstead** Herts
18 C5 **Flansham** W Susx
123 L6 **Flanshaw** Wakefd
131 H7 **Flasby** N York
114 A7 **Flash** Staffs
208 E4 **Flashader** Highld
59 G7 **Flaunden** Herts
102 C4 **Flawborough** Notts
133 G6 **Flawith** N York
38 D6 **Flax Bourton** N Som
132 F7 **Flaxby** N York
55 G5 **Flaxley** Gloucs
25 H4 **Flaxpool** Somset
133 K6 **Flaxton** N York
87 J5 **Fleckney** Leics
73 G2 **Flecknoe** Warwks
116 D6 **Fledborough** Notts
14 C6 **Fleet** Dorset
30 D2 **Fleet** Hants
104 C7 **Fleet** Lincs
104 C7 **Fleet Hargate** Lincs
30 D1 **Fleet Services** Hants
120 D2 **Fleetwood** Lancs
36 F6 **Flemingston** V Glam
175 H6 **Flemington** S Lans
77 J1 **Flempton** Suffk
147 L6 **Fletchertown** Cumb
19 L2 **Fletching** E Susx
9 G4 **Flexbury** Cnwll
30 F2 **Flexford** Surrey
147 H7 **Flimby** Cumb
33 J6 **Flimwell** E Susx
111 H6 **Flint** Flints
102 C4 **Flintham** Notts
126 F4 **Flinton** E R Yk
105 H6 **Flitcham** Norfk
74 F7 **Flitton** C Beds
74 F7 **Flitwick** C Beds
125 K7 **Flixborough** N Linc
125 K7 **Flixborough Stather** N Linc
135 G4 **Flixton** N York
93 G6 **Flixton** Suffk
113 H3 **Flixton** Traffd
123 J7 **Flockton** Kirk
123 K7 **Flockton Green** Kirk
218 C6 **Flodigarry** Highld
129 H4 **Flookburgh** Cumb
92 E4 **Flordon** Norfk
73 J3 **Flore** Nhants
78 C5 **Flowton** Suffk
3 L4 **Flushing** Cnwll
12 E4 **Fluxton** Devon
71 H4 **Flyford Flavell** Worcs
46 B8 **Fobbing** Thurr
215 H3 **Fochabers** Moray
53 H6 **Fochriw** Caerph
125 K6 **Fockerby** N Linc
26 E5 **Foddington** Somset
81 L2 **Foel** Powys
125 H3 **Foggathorpe** E R Yk

179 G8 **Fogo** Border
214 F3 **Fogwatt** Moray
228 B5 **Foindle** Highld
195 J4 **Folda** Angus
100 B5 **Fole** Staffs
86 D6 **Foleshill** Covtry
26 F8 **Folke** Dorset
35 H7 **Folkestone** Kent
103 H5 **Folkingham** Lincs
20 B5 **Folkington** E Susx
89 G5 **Folksworth** Cambs
135 G4 **Folkton** N York
216 D7 **Folla Rule** Abers
132 E8 **Follifoot** N York
10 E5 **Folly Gate** Devon
27 L5 **Fonthill Bishop** Wilts
27 L5 **Fonthill Gifford** Wilts
27 K7 **Fontmell Magna** Dorset
27 J8 **Fontmell Parva** Dorset
18 C4 **Fontwell** W Susx
114 D6 **Foolow** Derbys
205 H3 **Forbestown** Abers
140 F5 **Forcett** N York
182 C6 **Ford** Ag & B
58 C6 **Ford** Bucks
115 H5 **Ford** Derbys
22 F6 **Ford** Devon
56 C3 **Ford** Gloucs
168 E2 **Ford** Nthumb
25 H5 **Ford** Somset
100 B2 **Ford** Staffs
18 D5 **Ford** W Susx
39 J5 **Ford** Wilts
32 F5 **Fordcombe** Kent
177 G2 **Fordell** Fife
82 E4 **Forden** Powys
61 G5 **Ford End** Essex
7 H3 **Forder Green** Devon
76 F1 **Fordham** Cambs
61 L3 **Fordham** Essex
90 E4 **Fordham** Norfk
28 D8 **Fordingbridge** Hants
135 G4 **Fordon** E R Yk
197 J2 **Fordoun** Abers
61 L3 **Fordstreet** Essex
25 J7 **Ford Street** Somset
35 G3 **Fordwich** Kent
216 B2 **Fordyce** Abers
99 L7 **Forebridge** Staffs
236 c4 **Forest** Guern
122 B1 **Forest Becks** Lancs
113 L6 **Forest Chapel** Ches E
45 H3 **Forest Gate** Gt Lon
31 J3 **Forest Green** Surrey
151 G2 **Forest Hall** N Tyne
45 G5 **Forest Hill** Gt Lon
57 L6 **Forest Hill** Oxon
132 E7 **Forest Lane Head** N York
185 K8 **Forest Mill** Clacks
54 F5 **Forest of Dean** Gloucs
45 J2 **Forest Park Crematorium** Gt Lon
32 D6 **Forest Row** E Susx
30 C8 **Forestside** W Susx
196 D6 **Forfar** Angus
186 A4 **Forgandenny** P & K
37 L2 **Forge Hammer** Torfn
215 J4 **Forgie** Moray
215 J4 **Forgieside** Moray
216 B5 **Forgue** Abers
111 J1 **Formby** Sefton
92 D5 **Forncett End** Norfk
92 E5 **Forncett St Mary** Norfk
92 E5 **Forncett St Peter** Norfk
77 J2 **Fornham All Saints** Suffk
77 J2 **Fornham St Martin** Suffk
213 L4 **Fornighty** Highld
214 C3 **Forres** Moray

99 L4 **Forsbrook** Staffs
227 M2 **Forse** Highld
230 C6 **Forsinard** Highld
202 B4 **Fort Augustus** Highld
185 L4 **Forteviot** P & K
176 C7 **Forth** S Lans
55 K2 **Forthampton** Gloucs
194 B6 **Fortingall** P & K
29 H3 **Forton** Hants
121 G1 **Forton** Lancs
83 H1 **Forton** Shrops
13 J2 **Forton** Somset
99 H7 **Forton** Staffs
216 C5 **Fortrie** Abers
213 H3 **Fortrose** Highld
14 D7 **Fortuneswell** Dorset
191 L2 **Fort William** Highld
60 B7 **Forty Hill** Gt Lon
40 F8 **Fosbury** Wilts
56 E4 **Foscot** Oxon
104 A5 **Fosdyke** Lincs
194 C5 **Foss** P & K
56 B5 **Fossebridge** Gloucs
60 D6 **Foster Street** Essex
100 D6 **Foston** Derbys
87 H4 **Foston** Leics
102 E4 **Foston** Lincs
133 L6 **Foston** N York
135 H7 **Foston on the Wolds** E R Yk
118 D3 **Fotherby** Lincs
88 F5 **Fotheringhay** Nhants
235 a6 **Foula** Shet
179 J7 **Foulden** Border
91 H4 **Foulden** Norfk
86 B4 **Foul End** Warwks
47 G2 **Foulness Island** Essex
236 d3 **Foulon Vale Crematorium** Guern
122 D3 **Foulridge** Lancs
106 B7 **Foulsham** Norfk
177 L8 **Fountainhall** Border
78 B1 **Four Ashes** Suffk
97 K8 **Four Crosses** Powys
32 E4 **Four Elms** Kent
25 K4 **Four Forks** Somset
90 C1 **Four Gotes** Cambs
3 J4 **Four Lanes** Cnwll
30 A4 **Four Marks** Hants
108 C5 **Four Mile Bridge** IoA
86 B7 **Four Oaks** Solhll
223 H3 **Fourpenny** Highld
50 F4 **Four Roads** Carmth
149 M2 **Fourstones** Nthumb
33 K7 **Four Throws** Kent
76 D5 **Fourwentways Services** Cambs
28 A5 **Fovant** Wilts
207 H2 **Foveran** Abers
5 H5 **Fowey** Cnwll
33 J4 **Fowlhall** Kent
186 E2 **Fowlis** Angus
185 J3 **Fowlis Wester** P & K
76 B5 **Fowlmere** Cambs
69 L7 **Fownhope** Herefs
174 E6 **Foxbar** Rens
27 G1 **Foxcote** Somset
237 D5 **Foxdale** IoM
77 J5 **Foxearth** Essex
128 F3 **Foxfield** Cumb
4 F5 **Foxhole** Cnwll
134 F5 **Foxholes** N York
106 C7 **Foxley** Norfk
100 B3 **Foxt** Staffs
76 B5 **Foxton** Cambs
87 K5 **Foxton** Leics
141 K7 **Foxton** N York
84 B7 **Foxwood** Shrops
54 E3 **Foy** Herefs
202 D2 **Foyers** Highld
213 L4 **Foynesfield** Highld
4 E4 **Fraddon** Cnwll
85 L2 **Fradley** Staffs
99 M6 **Fradswell** Staffs
135 J7 **Fraisthorpe** E R Yk
20 A2 **Framfield** E Susx

92 F3 **Framingham Earl** Norfk
92 F3 **Framingham Pigot** Norfk
79 G2 **Framlingham** Suffk
14 C4 **Frampton** Dorset
104 B5 **Frampton** Lincs
38 F4 **Frampton Cotterell** S Glos
55 L7 **Frampton Mansell** Gloucs
55 H6 **Frampton on Severn** Gloucs
78 E3 **Framsden** Suffk
151 G6 **Framwellgate Moor** Dur
121 J3 **Frances Green** Lancs
84 E7 **Franche** Worcs
111 H4 **Frankby** Wirral
85 H7 **Frankley** Worcs
85 H7 **Frankley Services** Worcs
72 E1 **Frankton** Warwks
33 G6 **Frant** E Susx
217 J2 **Fraserburgh** Abers
62 C4 **Frating** Essex
62 C4 **Frating Green** Essex
17 J3 **Fratton** C Port
6 B5 **Freathy** Cnwll
76 F1 **Freckenham** Suffk
120 F5 **Freckleton** Lancs
102 D7 **Freeby** Leics
29 J2 **Freefolk** Hants
57 H5 **Freeland** Oxon
93 J3 **Freethorpe** Norfk
93 J3 **Freethorpe Common** Norfk
104 B4 **Freiston** Lincs
23 H5 **Fremington** Devon
140 D7 **Fremington** N York
38 F5 **Frenchay** S Glos
194 C5 **Frenich** P & K
30 D3 **Frensham** Surrey
120 C8 **Freshfield** Sefton
39 H7 **Freshford** Wilts
16 D5 **Freshwater** IoW
92 F7 **Fressingfield** Suffk
78 E6 **Freston** Suffk
231 L3 **Freswick** Highld
55 G6 **Fretherne** Gloucs
106 F8 **Frettenham** Norfk
186 E6 **Freuchie** Fife
49 G5 **Freystrop** Pembks
85 H4 **Friar Park** Sandw
90 C3 **Friday Bridge** Cambs
79 H3 **Friday Street** Suffk
134 D7 **Fridaythorpe** E R Yk
44 F2 **Friern Barnet** Gt Lon
188 F5 **Friesland Bay** Ag & B
117 H5 **Friesthorpe** Lincs
102 F3 **Frieston** Lincs
42 D3 **Frieth** Bucks
41 H2 **Frilford** Oxon
41 K5 **Frilsham** W Berk
42 E8 **Frimley** Surrey
46 C6 **Frindsbury** Medway
105 H5 **Fring** Norfk
57 L3 **Fringford** Oxon
34 B4 **Frinsted** Kent
62 F4 **Frinton-on-Sea** Essex
196 F6 **Friockheim** Angus
102 B8 **Frisby on the Wreake** Leics
104 D2 **Friskney** Lincs
20 B6 **Friston** E Susx
79 J3 **Friston** Suffk
101 G3 **Fritchley** Derbys
28 E8 **Fritham** Hants
23 G7 **Frithelstock** Devon
23 G7 **Frithelstock Stone** Devon
104 A3 **Frithville** Lincs
33 K5 **Frittenden** Kent
7 J6 **Frittiscombe** Devon
92 F5 **Fritton** Norfk
93 K4 **Fritton** Norfk

57 K3 **Fritwell** Oxon
123 H4 **Frizinghall** C Brad
136 E4 **Frizington** Cumb
55 H7 **Frocester** Gloucs
83 K3 **Frodesley** Shrops
112 D6 **Frodsham** Ches W
168 B4 **Frogden** Border
76 B5 **Frog End** Cambs
114 E6 **Froggatt** Derbys
100 A3 **Froghall** Staffs
7 H7 **Frogmore** Devon
89 H2 **Frognall** Lincs
70 E2 **Frog Pool** Worcs
6 A3 **Frogwell** Cnwll
87 G5 **Frolesworth** Leics
27 H2 **Frome** Somset
14 B2 **Frome St Quintin** Dorset
70 C5 **Fromes Hill** Herefs
108 F7 **Froncysyllte** Denbgs
96 D5 **Fron-goch** Gwynd
97 L4 **Fron Isaf** Wrexhm
150 C7 **Frosterley** Dur
40 F6 **Froxfield** Wilts
30 B6 **Froxfield Green** Hants
29 H7 **Fryern Hill** Hants
61 G7 **Fryerning** Essex
190 C6 **Fuinary** Highld
102 F3 **Fulbeck** Lincs
76 D4 **Fulbourn** Cambs
56 E5 **Fulbrook** Oxon
29 J5 **Fulflood** Hants
124 F2 **Fulford** C York
25 K5 **Fulford** Somset
99 L5 **Fulford** Staffs
44 E5 **Fulham** Gt Lon
19 H4 **Fulking** W Susx
163 H2 **Fullarton** N Ayrs
61 H5 **Fuller Street** Essex
29 G4 **Fullerton** Hants
118 D6 **Fulletby** Lincs
72 C5 **Fullready** Warwks
134 B7 **Full Sutton** E R Yk
174 E7 **Fullwood** E Ayrs
43 G4 **Fulmer** Bucks
106 B6 **Fulmodeston** Norfk
117 H5 **Fulnetby** Lincs
103 L7 **Fulney** Lincs
118 D3 **Fulstow** Lincs
151 J3 **Fulwell** Sundld
121 H4 **Fulwood** Lancs
114 F4 **Fulwood** Sheff
92 D4 **Fundenhall** Norfk
17 L2 **Funtington** W Susx
184 F3 **Funtullich** P & K
13 H2 **Furley** Devon
182 E7 **Furnace** Ag & B
51 G5 **Furnace** Carmth
114 A5 **Furness Vale** Derbys
60 C3 **Furneux Pelham** Herts
28 F7 **Furzley** Hants
28 F3 **Fyfield** Essex
28 F3 **Fyfield** Hants
57 H7 **Fyfield** Oxon
40 C6 **Fyfield** Wilts
40 D7 **Fyfield** Wilts
143 J6 **Fylingthorpe** N York
30 D6 **Fyning** W Susx
216 E6 **Fyvie** Abers

G

174 E7 **Gabroc Hill** E Ayrs
87 K2 **Gaddesby** Leics
59 H5 **Gaddesden Row** Herts
163 K5 **Gadgirth** S Ayrs
38 F2 **Gaer-llwyd** Mons
108 F7 **Gaerwen** IoA
163 H3 **Gailes** N Ayrs
85 G2 **Gailey** Staffs
140 F4 **Gainford** Dur
116 D4 **Gainsborough** Lincs

77 G7 **Gainsford End** Essex
219 J6 **Gairloch** Highld
201 J8 **Gairlochy** Highld
186 B7 **Gairneybridge** P & K
148 C5 **Gaitsgill** Cumb
167 G3 **Galashiels** Border
129 K7 **Galgate** Lancs
26 F5 **Galhampton** Somset
182 B3 **Gallanach** Ag & B
186 E8 **Gallatown** Fife
61 H7 **Galleywood** Essex
202 E7 **Gallovie** Highld
153 J5 **Galloway Forest Park**
196 D7 **Gallowfauld** Angus
186 B1 **Gallowhill** P & K
200 C2 **Galltair** Highld
7 G7 **Galmpton** Devon
7 K5 **Galmpton** Torbay
132 C5 **Galphay** N York
163 L3 **Galston** E Ayrs
149 G6 **Gamblesby** Cumb
75 J4 **Gamlingay** Cambs
75 J4 **Gamlingay Great Heath** Cambs
216 F2 **Gamrie** Abers
101 L5 **Gamston** Notts
116 B6 **Gamston** Notts
182 B2 **Ganavan Bay** Ag & B
96 B7 **Ganllwyd** Gwynd
196 F3 **Gannachy** Angus
126 E4 **Ganstead** E R Yk
133 L5 **Ganthorpe** N York
134 F4 **Ganton** N York
215 H4 **Garbity** Moray
92 B7 **Garboldisham** Norfk
205 G4 **Garchory** Abers
42 D6 **Gardeners Green** Wokham
216 F2 **Gardenstown** Abers
114 E2 **Garden Village** Sheff
235 C5 **Garderhouse** Shet
27 H4 **Gare Hill** Somset
173 L1 **Garelochhead** Ag & B
41 H2 **Garford** Oxon
124 B4 **Garforth** Leeds
131 H8 **Gargrave** N York
184 F8 **Gargunnock** Stirlg
92 E6 **Garlic Street** Norfk
145 K5 **Garlieston** D & G
35 J2 **Garlinge** Kent
34 F4 **Garlinge Green** Kent
206 E4 **Garlogie** Abers
216 F4 **Garmond** Abers
215 H2 **Garmouth** Moray
83 L3 **Garmston** Shrops
95 J4 **Garn-Dolbenmaen** Gwynd
175 J5 **Garnkirk** N Lans
232 g2 **Garrabost** W Isls
164 B5 **Garrallan** E Ayrs
3 J6 **Garras** Cnwll
95 K4 **Garreg** Gwynd
149 J6 **Garrigill** Cumb
153 M6 **Garroch** D & G
144 D7 **Garrochtrie** D & G
173 J7 **Garrochty** Ag & B
209 H2 **Garros** Highld
130 E2 **Garsdale Head** Cumb
39 L3 **Garsdon** Wilts
99 L5 **Garshall Green** Staffs
57 L7 **Garsington** Oxon
121 G2 **Garstang** Lancs
59 J7 **Garston** Herts
112 B5 **Garston** Lpool
171 G6 **Gartachossan** Ag & B
175 J5 **Gartcosh** N Lans
67 K5 **Garth** Powys
97 K4 **Garth** Wrexhm
175 H5 **Garth** C Glas
82 E4 **Garthmyl** Powys
102 D7 **Garthorpe** Leics
125 K6 **Garthorpe** N Linc
80 E6 **Garth Penrhyncoch** Cerdgn
138 D7 **Garth Row** Cumb

215 L7 **Gartly** Abers
184 C7 **Gartmore** Stirlg
175 K5 **Gartness** N Lans
174 F2 **Gartness** Stirlg
174 D2 **Gartocharn** W Duns
127 G4 **Garton** E R Yk
134 F7 **Garton-on-the-Wolds** E R Yk
227 H5 **Gartymore** Highld
178 D4 **Garvald** E Loth
191 J2 **Garvan** Highld
171 G1 **Garvard** Ag & B
212 D5 **Garve** Highld
181 K5 **Garvellachs** Ag & B
92 B3 **Garvestone** Norfk
174 B4 **Garvock** Inver
54 C4 **Garway** Herefs
232 f3 **Garyvard** W Isls
27 H5 **Gasper** Wilts
39 K6 **Gastard** Wilts
91 L7 **Gasthorpe** Norfk
60 D5 **Gaston Green** Essex
16 F5 **Gatcombe** IoW
116 D5 **Gate Burton** Lincs
124 E5 **Gateforth** N York
163 K3 **Gatehead** E Ayrs
133 L7 **Gate Helmsley** N York
157 K4 **Gatehouse** Nthumb
145 M4 **Gatehouse of Fleet** D & G
106 A7 **Gateley** Norfk
132 E3 **Gatenby** N York
168 B5 **Gateshaw** Border
151 G3 **Gateshead** Gatesd
196 D7 **Gateside** Angus
174 E6 **Gateside** E Rens
186 C5 **Gateside** Fife
174 C7 **Gateside** N Ayrs
154 F2 **Gateslack** D & G
113 J4 **Gatley** Stockp
167 H3 **Gattonside** Border
32 B5 **Gatwick Airport** W Susx
87 K4 **Gaulby** Leics
186 F3 **Gauldry** Fife
195 K6 **Gauldswell** P & K
117 K6 **Gautby** Lincs
179 G7 **Gavinton** Border
58 B2 **Gawcott** Bucks
113 K7 **Gawsworth** Ches E
130 D3 **Gawthrop** Cumb
129 G3 **Gawthwaite** Cumb
72 D4 **Gaydon** Warwks
74 B5 **Gayhurst** M Keyn
131 G2 **Gayle** N York
140 E5 **Gayles** N York
73 K4 **Gayton** Nhants
105 H8 **Gayton** Norfk
99 M6 **Gayton** Staffs
118 F5 **Gayton le Marsh** Lincs
105 H8 **Gayton Thorpe** Norfk
105 G7 **Gaywood** Norfk
77 G2 **Gazeley** Suffk
232 f3 **Gearraidh Bhaird** W Isls
208 D3 **Geary** Highld
77 L3 **Gedding** Suffk
88 C6 **Geddington** Nhants
101 L4 **Gedling** Notts
104 C7 **Gedney** Lincs
104 C7 **Gedney Broadgate** Lincs
104 D6 **Gedney Drove End** Lincs
104 C7 **Gedney Dyke** Lincs
89 L2 **Gedney Hill** Lincs
88 E3 **Geeston** Rutlnd
93 H5 **Geldeston** Norfk
110 F8 **Gellifor** Denbgs
37 H2 **Gelligaer** Caerph
95 M4 **Gellilydan** Gwynd
51 K5 **Gellinudd** Neath
195 H8 **Gellyburn** P & K
50 C2 **Gellywen** Carmth
146 D3 **Gelston** D & G
102 E4 **Gelston** Lincs

135 H7 **Gembling** E R Yk
85 J2 **Gentleshaw** Staffs
156 B4 **Georgefield** D & G
43 G4 **George Green** Bucks
23 G4 **Georgeham** Devon
231 H4 **Georgemas Junction Station** Highld
23 L6 **George Nympton** Devon
234 b5 **Georth** Ork
10 C6 **Germansweek** Devon
4 D8 **Gerrans** Cnwll
43 G3 **Gerrards Cross** Bucks
142 E5 **Gerrick** R & Cl
77 J6 **Gestingthorpe** Essex
82 E2 **Geuffordd** Powys
45 K3 **Gidea Park** Gt Lon
175 G6 **Giffnock** E Rens
178 C5 **Gifford** E Loth
186 E5 **Giffordtown** Fife
130 F6 **Giggleswick** N York
171 L7 **Gigha** Ag & B
125 K5 **Gilberdyke** E R Yk
178 B5 **Gilchriston** E Loth
147 K7 **Gilcrux** Cumb
123 K5 **Gildersome** Leeds
115 K4 **Gildingwells** Rothm
151 H6 **Gilesgate Moor** Dur
36 F6 **Gileston** V Glam
53 J7 **Gilfach** Caerph
36 F3 **Gilfach Goch** Brdgnd
65 L3 **Gilfachrheda** Cerdgn
136 E3 **Gilgarran** Cumb
133 K2 **Gillamoor** N York
208 D3 **Gillen** Highld
155 K4 **Gillesbie** D & G
133 J4 **Gilling East** N York
27 J6 **Gillingham** Dorset
46 C6 **Gillingham** Medway
93 J5 **Gillingham** Norfk
140 F6 **Gilling West** N York
231 J4 **Gillock** Highld
231 K2 **Gills** Highld
166 E5 **Gilmanscleuch** Border
177 J5 **Gilmerton** C Edin
185 J3 **Gilmerton** P & K
140 C5 **Gilmonby** Dur
87 H6 **Gilmorton** Leics
87 H3 **Gilroes Crematorium** C Leic
149 G2 **Gilsland** Nthumb
177 L6 **Gilston** Border
60 D5 **Gilston** Herts
53 K5 **Gilwern** Mons
107 G5 **Gimingham** Norfk
78 C2 **Gipping** Suffk
103 M3 **Gipsey Bridge** Lincs
163 J2 **Girdle Toll** N Ayrs
235 C5 **Girlsta** Shet
141 J5 **Girsby** N York
146 A4 **Girthon** D & G
76 B3 **Girton** Cambs
116 D7 **Girton** Notts
152 E3 **Girvan** S Ayrs
122 C2 **Gisburn** Lancs
93 K5 **Gisleham** Suffk
78 C1 **Gislingham** Suffk
92 D6 **Gissing** Norfk
12 E3 **Gittisham** Devon
68 E4 **Gladestry** Powys
177 M4 **Gladsmuir** E Loth
51 K5 **Glais** Swans
143 G6 **Glaisdale** N York
196 C6 **Glamis** Angus
51 J3 **Glanaman** Carmth
106 C4 **Glandford** Norfk
49 K2 **Glandwr** Pembks
80 F4 **Glandyfi** Cerdgn
36 D3 **Glanllynfi** Brdgnd
169 G6 **Glanton** Nthumb
14 D2 **Glanvilles Wootton** Dorset
111 G5 **Glan-y-don** Flints
88 E5 **Glapthorn** Nhants
115 J7 **Glapwell** Derbys

68 D6 **Glasbury** Powys
68 D4 **Glascwm** Powys
96 E3 **Glasfryn** Conwy
175 G5 **Glasgow** C Glas
174 E5 *Glasgow Airport* Rens
175 G5 **Glasgow Science Centre** C Glas
109 H7 **Glasinfryn** Gwynd
199 L6 **Glasnacardoch Bay** Highld
199 H3 **Glasnakille** Highld
175 J8 **Glassford** S Lans
55 G4 **Glasshouse** Gloucs
132 B6 **Glasshouses** N York
148 A3 **Glasson** Cumb
129 K7 **Glasson** Lancs
149 G7 **Glassonby** Cumb
196 F6 **Glasterlaw** Angus
88 C4 **Glaston** Rutlnd
26 D4 **Glastonbury** Somset
89 H6 **Glatton** Cambs
113 C3 **Glazebrook** Warrtn
112 F3 **Glazebury** Warrtn
84 C5 **Glazeley** Shrops
128 F5 **Gleaston** Cumb
202 D2 **Glebe** Highld
123 L3 **Gledhow** Leeds
146 B5 **Gledpark** D & G
97 L5 **Gledrid** Shrops
77 J5 **Glemsford** Suffk
215 G6 **Glenallachie** Highld
199 K6 **Glenancross** Highld
190 B7 **Glenaros House** Ag & B
237 d3 **Glen Auldyn** IoM
161 H3 **Glenbarr** Ag & B
216 B4 **Glenbarry** Abers
190 C4 **Glenbeg** Highld
214 C8 **Glenbeg** Highld
197 J1 **Glenbervie** Abers
175 J5 **Glenboig** N Lans
190 C4 **Glenborrodale** Highld
183 G7 **Glenbranter** Ag & B
165 K5 **Glenbreck** Border
198 F2 **Glenbrittle House** Highld
164 E4 **Glenbuck** E Ayrs
196 B4 **Glencally** Angus
147 H2 **Glencaple** D & G
211 G4 **Glencarron Lodge** Highld
186 C3 **Glencarse** P & K
192 B6 **Glenceitlein** Highld
204 E8 **Glen Clunie Lodge** Abers
191 L5 **Glencoe** Highld
165 L4 **Glencothe** Border
186 C7 **Glencraig** Fife
154 D4 **Glencrosh** D & G
208 B4 **Glendale** Highld
173 G2 **Glendaruel** Ag & B
185 K6 **Glendevon** P & K
202 C4 **Glendoe Lodge** Highld
186 C3 **Glendoick** P & K
186 D4 **Glenduckie** Fife
185 J5 **Gleneagles** P & K
185 J5 **Gleneagles Hotel** P & K
170 F7 **Glenegedale** Ag & B
200 C4 **Glenelg** Highld
214 C5 **Glenerney** Moray
186 B5 **Glenfarg** P & K
203 K6 **Glenfeshie Lodge** Highld
87 G3 **Glenfield** Leics
191 H1 **Glenfinnan** Highld
201 K7 **Glenfintaig Lodge** Highld
186 C4 **Glenfoot** P & K
183 H4 **Glenfyne Lodge** Ag & B
174 C7 **Glengarnock** N Ayrs
231 G2 **Glengolly** Highld
189 K5 **Glengorm Castle** Ag & B

209 G5 **Glengrasco** Highld
165 L3 **Glenholm** Border
154 A5 **Glenhoul** D & G
195 K4 **Glenisla** Angus
173 K3 **Glenkin** Ag & B
205 K3 **Glenkindie** Abers
214 F8 **Glenlivet** Moray
146 C3 **Glenlochar** D & G
186 C6 **Glenlomond** P & K
144 E4 **Glenluce** D & G
173 J2 **Glenmassen** Ag & B
175 K5 **Glenmavis** N Lans
237 D5 **Glen Maye** IoM
209 G6 **Glenmore** Highld
204 B4 **Glenmore Lodge**
    Highld
192 B3 **Glen Nevis House**
    Highld
185 H7 **Glenochil** Clacks
87 H4 **Glen Parva** Leics
196 C4 **Glenquiech** Angus
172 E5 **Glenralloch** Ag & B
137 L4 **Glenridding** Cumb
186 D7 **Glenrothes** Fife
185 K1 **Glenshee** P & K
202 E6 **Glenshero Lodge**
    Highld
173 J3 **Glenstriven** Ag & B
117 G4 **Glentham** Lincs
203 J6 **Glentromie Lodge**
    Highld
153 J6 **Glen Trool Lodge**
    D & G
153 H6 **Glentrool Village**
    D & G
203 G6 **Glentruim House**
    Highld
116 F4 **Glentworth** Lincs
190 D2 **Glenuig** Highld
191 K6 **Glenure** Ag & B
209 G6 **Glenvarragill** Highld
237 C5 **Glen Vine** IoM
152 E7 **Glenwhilly** D & G
164 F4 **Glespin** S Lans
54 E4 **Glewstone** Herefs
89 H3 **Glinton** C Pete
87 L4 **Glooston** Leics
114 B3 **Glossop** Derbys
159 G2 **Gloster Hill** Nthumb
55 J4 **Gloucester** Gloucs
55 J5 **Gloucester**
    Crematorium Gloucs
55 K4 **Gloucestershire**
    Airport Gloucs
122 F2 **Glusburn** N York
227 H2 **Glutt Lodge** Highld
57 H4 **Glympton** Oxon
65 K5 **Glynarthen** Cerdgn
97 J5 **Glyn Ceiriog** Wrexhm
52 D7 **Glyncorrwg** Neath
19 L4 **Glynde** E Susx
97 J4 **Glyndyfrdwy** Denbgs
52 D6 **Glynneath** Neath
5 H3 **Glynn Valley**
    Crematorium Cnwll
37 H3 **Glyntaff**
    Crematorium Rhondd
52 D5 **Glyntawe** Powys
65 K6 **Glynteg** Carmth
99 J7 **Gnosall** Staffs
99 J7 **Gnosall Heath** Staffs
87 L4 **Goadby** Leics
102 C7 **Goadby Marwood**
    Leics
40 A5 **Goatacre** Wilts
182 E7 **Goatfield** Ag & B
26 F7 **Goathill** Dorset
143 H6 **Goathland** N York
25 K5 **Goathurst** Somset
97 L5 **Gobowen** Shrops
30 F3 **Godalming** Surrey
33 L6 **Goddard's Green**
    Kent
75 J1 **Godmanchester**
    Cambs
14 C3 **Godmanstone** Dorset

34 E5 **Godmersham** Kent
26 C3 **Godney** Somset
3 G5 **Godolphin Cross**
    Cnwll
51 L4 **Godre'r-graig** Neath
17 G6 **Godshill** IoW
32 C3 **Godstone** Surrey
53 L6 **Goetre** Mons
60 B7 **Goff's Oak** Herts
53 K5 **Gofilon** Mons
177 G4 **Gogar** C Edin
80 F7 **Goginan** Cerdgn
95 J4 **Golan** Gwynd
5 H5 **Golant** Cnwll
5 M2 **Golberdon** Cnwll
112 E3 **Golborne** Wigan
123 G7 **Golcar** Kirk
38 A4 **Goldcliff** Newpt
33 H4 **Golden Green** Kent
30 D3 **Golden Pot** Hants
44 E3 **Golders Green** Gt Lon
44 E3 **Golders Green**
    Crematorium Gt Lon
61 L6 **Goldhanger** Essex
74 F4 **Goldington** Bed
132 F7 **Goldsborough** N York
143 H4 **Goldsborough** N York
2 F5 **Goldsithney** Cnwll
43 G8 **Goldsworth Park**
    Surrey
115 J2 **Goldthorpe** Barns
22 F6 **Goldworthy** Devon
213 J4 **Gollanfield** Highld
223 H2 **Golspie** Highld
28 D4 **Gomeldon** Wilts
31 H2 **Gomshall** Surrey
102 B3 **Gonalston** Notts
102 E5 **Gonerby Hill Foot**
    Lincs
235 C4 **Gonfirth** Shet
60 F5 **Good Easter** Essex
91 H3 **Gooderstone** Norfk
23 J5 **Goodleigh** Devon
125 K2 **Goodmanham** E R Yk
45 J3 **Goodmayes** Gt Lon
34 D3 **Goodnestone** Kent
35 H4 **Goodnestone** Kent
54 E4 **Goodrich** Herefs
54 E4 **Goodrich Castle**
    Herefs
7 K4 **Goodrington** Torbay
122 B5 **Goodshaw Fold** Lancs
64 C6 **Goodwick** Pembks
29 G3 **Goodworth Clatford**
    Hants
125 H5 **Goole** E R Yk
71 H4 **Goom's Hill** Worcs
3 J2 **Goonbell** Cnwll
3 K1 **Goonhavern** Cnwll
3 J2 **Goonvrea** Cnwll
206 E8 **Goosecruives** Abers
11 G6 **Gooseford** Devon
62 D3 **Goose Green** Essex
38 F5 **Goose Green** S Glos
41 G3 **Goosey** Oxon
121 H3 **Goosnargh** Lancs
113 H7 **Goostrey** Ches E
38 D5 **Gordano Services**
    N Som
167 K2 **Gordon** Border
166 D4 **Gordon Arms Hotel**
    Border
216 B3 **Gordonstown** Abers
216 D6 **Gordonstown** Abers
177 K6 **Gorebridge** Mdloth
90 B2 **Gorefield** Cambs
40 C8 **Gores** Wilts
236 e7 **Gorey** Jersey
41 L4 **Goring** Oxon
18 F5 **Goring-by-Sea** W Susx
93 L3 **Gorleston on Sea**
    Norfk
85 G5 **Gornal Wood**
    Crematorium Dudley
216 E3 **Gorrachie** Abers
4 F7 **Gorran** Cnwll

4 F7 **Gorran Haven** Cnwll
111 G6 **Gorsedd** Flints
40 D3 **Gorse Hill** Swindn
51 H5 **Gorseinon** Swans
66 C4 **Gorsgoch** Cerdgn
51 H3 **Gorslas** Carmth
55 G3 **Gorsley** Gloucs
54 F3 **Gorsley Common**
    Herefs
212 B2 **Gorstan** Highld
100 C6 **Gorsty Hill** Staffs
181 L2 **Gorten** Ag & B
202 E2 **Gorthleck** Highld
113 K3 **Gorton** Manch
78 D4 **Gosbeck** Suffk
103 L6 **Gosberton** Lincs
61 J3 **Gosfield** Essex
136 E6 **Gosforth** Cumb
151 G2 **Gosforth** N u Ty
84 F5 **Gospel End** Staffs
17 H3 **Gosport** Hants
55 H7 **Gossington** Gloucs
101 K6 **Gotham** Notts
55 L3 **Gotherington** Gloucs
25 K5 **Gotton** Somset
33 J5 **Goudhurst** Kent
118 C5 **Goulceby** Lincs
216 E6 **Gourdas** Abers
186 F2 **Gourdie** C Dund
197 K3 **Gourdon** Abers
173 L3 **Gourock** Inver
174 F5 **Govan** C Glas
7 H6 **Goveton** Devon
124 F6 **Gowdall** E R Yk
212 D3 **Gower** Highld
51 G7 **Gower** Swans
51 H6 **Gowerton** Swans
176 E1 **Gowkhall** Fife
126 F2 **Goxhill** E R Yk
126 D6 **Goxhill** N Linc
232 f3 **Grabhair** W Isls
18 C3 **Graffham** W Susx
75 H2 **Grafham** Cambs
31 G3 **Grafham** Surrey
132 F6 **Grafton** N York
57 H2 **Grafton** Oxon
98 B8 **Grafton** Shrops
71 H6 **Grafton** Worcs
71 G4 **Grafton Flyford**
    Worcs
73 L5 **Grafton Regis** Nhants
88 D7 **Grafton Underwood**
    Nhants
34 B5 **Grafty Green** Kent
109 M6 **Graig** Conwy
97 J2 **Graig-fechan** Denbgs
46 E5 **Grain** Medway
118 C2 **Grainsby** Lincs
118 E3 **Grainthorpe** Lincs
4 E6 **Grampound** Cnwll
4 E5 **Grampound Road**
    Cnwll
233 c5 **Gramsdal** W Isls
233 c6 **Gramsdale** W Isls
58 C3 **Granborough** Bucks
102 C5 **Granby** Notts
72 F2 **Grandborough**
    Warwks
236 d7 **Grand Chemins**
    Jersey
236 c2 **Grandes Rocques**
    Guern
101 H7 **Grand Prix Collection**
    Donington Leics
194 E5 **Grandtully** P & K
137 H4 **Grange** Cumb
46 D6 **Grange** Medway
186 D3 **Grange** P & K
215 K4 **Grange Crossroads**
    Moray
214 C3 **Grange Hall** Moray
165 J2 **Grangehall** S Lans
45 H2 **Grange Hill** Essex
100 E2 **Grangemill** Derbys
123 J7 **Grange Moor** Kirk
176 C3 **Grangemouth** Falk

186 D4 **Grange of Lindores**
    Fife
129 J4 **Grange-over-Sands**
    Cumb
176 D3 **Grangepans** Falk
142 C3 **Grangetown** R & Cl
151 K4 **Grangetown** Sundld
151 G4 **Grange Villa** Dur
135 H7 **Gransmoor** E R Yk
64 C7 **Granston** Pembks
76 B4 **Grantchester** Cambs
102 E5 **Grantham** Lincs
102 F5 **Grantham**
    Crematorium Lincs
102 E5 **Grantham North**
    Services Lincs
177 H3 **Granton** C Edin
214 C8 **Grantown-on-Spey**
    Highld
179 G5 **Grantshouse** Border
117 H1 **Grasby** Lincs
137 K5 **Grasmere** Cumb
113 L1 **Grasscroft** Oldham
114 L4 **Grassendale** Lpool
131 J6 **Grassington** N York
115 H7 **Grassmoor** Derbys
116 C7 **Grassthorpe** Notts
28 F3 **Grateley** Hants
75 J2 **Graveley** Cambs
59 L3 **Graveley** Herts
34 E3 **Graveney** Kent
46 A5 **Gravesend** Kent
232 f3 **Gravir** W Isls
116 F3 **Grayingham** Lincs
138 E7 **Grayrigg** Cumb
45 L4 **Grays** Thurr
30 E4 **Grayshott** Hants
30 E4 **Grayswood** Surrey
115 H3 **Greasbrough** Rothm
111 H4 **Greasby** Wirral
101 J3 **Greasley** Notts
76 D5 **Great Abington**
    Cambs
88 D7 **Great Addington**
    Nhants
71 K3 **Great Alne** Warwks
111 K1 **Great Altcar** Lancs
60 B5 **Great Amwell** Herts
138 F5 **Great Asby** Cumb
78 B2 **Great Ashfield** Suffk
142 C5 **Great Ayton** N York
61 H6 **Great Baddow** Essex
39 J4 **Great Badminton**
    S Glos
61 G2 **Great Bardfield** Essex
75 G4 **Great Barford** Bed
85 J4 **Great Barr** Sandw
56 E5 **Great Barrington**
    Gloucs
112 C7 **Great Barrow** Ches W
77 K2 **Great Barton** Suffk
134 B4 **Great Barugh** N York
158 C6 **Great Bavington**
    Nthumb
78 F5 **Great Bealings** Suffk
40 F7 **Great Bedwyn** Wilts
62 D4 **Great Bentley** Essex
74 B3 **Great Billing** Nhants
105 J6 **Great Bircham** Norfk
78 D4 **Great Blakenham**
    Suffk
138 C2 **Great Blencow** Cumb
98 F7 **Great Bolas** Wrekin
31 J1 **Great Bookham**
    Surrey
72 F5 **Great Bourton** Oxon
87 L5 **Great Bowden** Leics
76 F4 **Great Bradley** Suffk
61 K5 **Great Braxted** Essex
78 C4 **Great Bricett** Suffk
58 E3 **Great Brickhill** Bucks
99 K6 **Great Bridgeford**
    Staffs
73 J2 **Great Brington**
    Nhants
62 C3 **Great Bromley** Essex

136 E2 Great Broughton Cumb
142 C6 Great Broughton N York
112 F6 Great Budworth Ches W
141 H4 Great Burdon Darltn
46 B2 Great Burstead Essex
142 B6 Great Busby N York
118 E4 Great Carlton Lincs
88 E2 Great Casterton Rutlnd
39 K7 Great Chalfield Wilts
34 C6 Great Chart Kent
84 E1 Great Chatwell Staffs
76 D6 Great Chesterford Essex
27 M1 Great Cheverell Wilts
76 B6 Great Chishill Cambs
62 E5 Great Clacton Essex
136 E2 Great Clifton Cumb
126 F8 Great Coates NE Lin
71 G6 Great Comberton Worcs
148 E4 Great Corby Cumb
77 K6 Great Cornard Suffk
126 F3 Great Cowden E R Yk
40 F2 Great Coxwell Oxon
88 B7 Great Cransley Nhants
91 J3 Great Cressingham Norfk
137 J3 Great Crosthwaite Cumb
100 D5 Great Cubley Derbys
173 K6 Great Cumbrae Island N Ayrs
87 L2 Great Dalby Leics
74 C2 Great Doddington Nhants
91 K1 Great Dunham Norfk
61 G4 Great Dunmow Essex
28 C4 Great Durnford Wilts
60 F3 Great Easton Essex
88 B5 Great Easton Leics
120 F3 Great Eccleston Lancs
92 B4 Great Ellingham Norfk
27 H2 Great Elm Somset
73 H3 Great Everdon Nhants
75 L4 Great Eversden Cambs
78 B3 Great Finborough Suffk
88 F2 Greatford Lincs
91 K2 Great Fransham Norfk
59 G5 Great Gaddesden Herts
100 B4 Greatgate Staffs
89 G6 Great Gidding Cambs
134 C8 Great Givendale E R Yk
79 H3 Great Glemham Suffk
87 J4 Great Glen Leics
102 E5 Great Gonerby Lincs
75 J4 Great Gransden Cambs
75 K5 Great Green Cambs
77 K4 Great Green Suffk
134 B4 Great Habton N York
103 J4 Great Hale Lincs
60 E4 Great Hallingbury Essex
30 C5 Greatham Hants
141 L2 Greatham Hartpl
18 E3 Greatham W Susx
58 D7 Great Hampden Bucks
74 C1 Great Harrowden Nhants
121 L4 Great Harwood Lancs
57 M7 Great Haseley Oxon
126 F3 Great Hatfield E R Yk

99 M7 Great Haywood Staffs
124 E6 Great Heck N York
77 K6 Great Henny Essex
39 K8 Great Hinton Wilts
91 L5 Great Hockham Norfk
62 E4 Great Holland Essex
42 E6 Great Hollands Br For
62 B2 Great Horkesley Essex
60 C3 Great Hormead Herts
123 H4 Great Horton C Brad
58 C2 Great Horwood Bucks
115 H1 Great Houghton Barns
73 L3 Great Houghton Nhants
114 D6 Great Hucklow Derbys
135 H7 Great Kelk E R Yk
58 D6 Great Kimble Bucks
42 E2 Great Kingshill Bucks
137 J6 Great Langdale Cumb
141 H7 Great Langton N York
61 H4 Great Leighs Essex
126 E8 Great Limber Lincs
74 C6 Great Linford M Keyn
77 K1 Great Livermere Suffk
114 D6 Great Longstone Derbys
151 H5 Great Lumley Dur
70 D5 Great Malvern Worcs
77 J7 Great Maplestead Essex
120 D4 Great Marton Bpool
105 J7 Great Massingham Norfk
57 L7 Great Milton Oxon
58 E7 Great Missenden Bucks
121 K3 Great Mitton Lancs
35 K4 Great Mongeham Kent
92 E5 Great Moulton Norfk
139 H4 Great Musgrave Cumb
98 B8 Great Ness Shrops
61 H4 Great Notley Essex
54 B6 Great Oak Mons
62 E3 Great Oakley Essex
88 C6 Great Oakley Nhants
59 J3 Great Offley Herts
139 G4 Great Ormside Cumb
148 B4 Great Orton Cumb
133 G6 Great Ouseburn N York
87 K6 Great Oxendon Nhants
61 G6 Great Oxney Green Essex
75 H2 Great Paxton Cambs
120 E4 Great Plumpton Lancs
93 G2 Great Plumstead Norfk
102 F6 Great Ponton Lincs
124 B5 Great Preston Leeds
89 J7 Great Raveley Cambs
56 D5 Great Rissington Gloucs
56 F2 Great Rollright Oxon
106 A6 Great Ryburgh Norfk
168 F6 Great Ryle Nthumb
83 J3 Great Ryton Shrops
61 H3 Great Saling Essex
148 F7 Great Salkeld Cumb
76 F7 Great Sampford Essex
111 K7 Great Saughall Ches W
41 G5 Great Shefford W Berk

76 C4 Great Shelford Cambs
141 H6 Great Smeaton N York
105 M5 Great Snoring Norfk
39 L4 Great Somerford Wilts
99 G6 Great Soudley Shrops
141 H3 Great Stainton Darltn
46 E2 Great Stambridge Essex
75 G2 Great Staughton Cambs
118 F8 Great Steeping Lincs
38 F4 Great Stoke S Glos
21 L2 Greatstone-on-Sea Kent
138 D3 Great Strickland Cumb
89 J8 Great Stukeley Cambs
117 K6 Great Sturton Lincs
158 B6 Great Swinburne Nthumb
57 H3 Great Tew Oxon
61 L3 Great Tey Essex
23 H7 Great Torrington Devon
158 C3 Great Tosson Nthumb
61 K5 Great Totham Essex
61 L5 Great Totham Essex
129 G5 Great Urswick Cumb
46 F3 Great Wakering Essex
77 K5 Great Waldingfield Suffk
105 M5 Great Walsingham Norfk
61 H5 Great Waltham Essex
45 L2 Great Warley Essex
71 H7 Great Washbourne Gloucs
11 G7 Great Weeke Devon
88 D5 Great Weldon Nhants
78 C6 Great Wenham Suffk
158 C7 Great Whittington Nthumb
62 A5 Great Wigborough Essex
76 D3 Great Wilbraham Cambs
28 B4 Great Wishford Wilts
55 K5 Great Witcombe Gloucs
70 D2 Great Witley Worcs
72 B7 Great Wolford Warwks
73 G6 Greatworth Nhants
77 G5 Great Wratting Suffk
59 K3 Great Wymondley Herts
85 H3 Great Wyrley Staffs
93 L3 Great Yarmouth Norfk
93 K3 Great Yarmouth Crematorium Norfk
77 H6 Great Yeldham Essex
176 C6 Greenburn W Loth
60 B2 Green End Herts
60 B4 Green End Herts
173 M1 Greenfield Ag & B
74 F7 Greenfield C Beds
111 H6 Greenfield Flints
201 J5 Greenfield Highld
113 M2 Greenfield Oldham
43 J4 Greenford Gt Lon
175 K4 Greengairs N Lans
123 J3 Greengates C Brad
120 E4 Greenhalgh Lancs
25 G7 Greenham Somset
133 G7 Green Hammerton N York
157 K5 Greenhaugh Nthumb
149 H3 Greenhead Nthumb
85 H2 Green Heath Staffs
155 J6 Greenhill D & G
175 L3 Greenhill Falk

47 K6 Greenhill Kent
165 H3 Greenhill S Lans
45 L5 Greenhithe Kent
164 B3 Greenholm E Ayrs
167 H5 Greenhouse Border
131 L6 Greenhow Hill N York
231 J3 Greenland Highld
115 H4 Greenland Sheff
167 L1 Greenlaw Border
155 H6 Greenlea D & G
185 H6 Greenloaning P & K
122 B7 Greenmount Bury
174 B3 Greenock Inver
129 G3 Greenodd Cumb
26 E2 Green Ore Somset
138 C6 Green Quarter Cumb
165 K2 Greenshields S Lans
150 E3 Greenside Gatesd
123 H7 Greenside Kirk
73 J4 Greens Norton Nhants
62 B3 Greenstead Essex
61 K3 Greenstead Green Essex
59 K7 Green Street Herts
60 D4 Green Street Herts
45 L6 Green Street Green Kent
60 C4 Green Tye Herts
25 L6 Greenway Somset
45 G4 Greenwich Gt Lon
56 B3 Greet Gloucs
69 L1 Greete Shrops
118 D7 Greetham Lincs
88 D2 Greetham Rutlnd
123 G6 Greetland Calder
26 B4 Greinton Somset
237 b6 Grenaby IoM
74 C3 Grendon Nhants
86 C4 Grendon Warwks
58 B4 Grendon Underwood Bucks
115 G3 Grenoside Sheff
114 F3 Grenoside Crematorium Sheff
232 e4 Greosabhagh W Isls
97 M2 Gresford Wrexhm
106 E5 Gresham Norfk
208 E4 Greshornish House Hotel Highld
91 L1 Gressenhall Norfk
91 L1 Gressenhall Green Norfk
130 B5 Gressingham Lancs
140 D5 Greta Bridge Dur
148 B2 Gretna D & G
148 B2 Gretna Green D & G
148 B2 Gretna Services D & G
56 A2 Gretton Gloucs
88 C5 Gretton Nhants
83 K4 Gretton Shrops
132 C4 Grewelthorpe N York
155 J4 Greyrigg D & G
42 B4 Greys Green Oxon
136 E2 Greysouthen Cumb
138 B2 Greystoke Cumb
196 E7 Greystone Angus
30 B2 Greywell Hants
86 D5 Griff Warwks
53 L7 Griffithstown Torfn
121 J7 Grimeford Village Lancs
115 G4 Grimesthorpe Sheff
124 C8 Grimethorpe Barns
70 E3 Grimley Worcs
163 H7 Grimmet S Ayrs
118 E4 Grimoldby Lincs
98 A7 Grimpo Shrops
121 H4 Grimsargh Lancs
127 G7 Grimsby NE Lin
118 C1 Grimsby Crematorium NE Lin
73 J4 Grimscote Nhants
9 H4 Grimscott Cnwll
232 f3 Grimshader W Isls
103 H7 Grimsthorpe Lincs

102 B7 **Grimston** Leics
105 H7 **Grimston** Norfk
14 C4 **Grimstone** Dorset
77 L2 **Grimstone End** Suffk
135 H5 **Grindale** E R Yk
114 E6 **Grindleford** Derbys
121 L2 **Grindleton** Lancs
98 D4 **Grindley Brook**
Shrops
114 D6 **Grindlow** Derbys
100 B2 **Grindon** Staffs
151 J4 **Grindon** Sundld
116 C4 **Gringley on the Hill**
Notts
148 C4 **Grinsdale** Cumb
98 D7 **Grinshill** Shrops
140 D7 **Grinton** N York
232 f3 **Griomaisiader** W Isls
233 c6 **Griomsaigh** W Isls
188 F4 **Grishipoll** Ag & B
135 H3 **Gristhorpe** N York
91 L4 **Griston** Norfk
234 d6 **Gritley** Ork
40 B4 **Grittenham** Wilts
39 K4 **Grittleton** Wilts
128 F3 **Grizebeck** Cumb
137 K7 **Grizedale** Cumb
87 G3 **Groby** Leics
110 D8 **Groes** Conwy
37 G4 **Groes-faen** Rhondd
95 H2 **Groeslon** Gwynd
37 H3 **Groes-Wen** Caerph
233 b7 **Grogarry** W Isls
161 K1 **Grogport** Ag & B
233 b7 **Groigearraidh** W Isls
110 F5 **Gronant** Flints
32 F5 **Groombridge** E Susx
232 e4 **Grosebay** W Isls
54 B3 **Grosmont** Mons
143 H6 **Grosmont** N York
77 L6 **Groton** Suffk
236 e7 **Grouville** Jersey
116 C5 **Grove** Notts
41 H3 **Grove** Oxon
33 K3 **Grove Green** Kent
45 H5 **Grove Park** Gt Lon
51 H5 **Grovesend** Swans
219 L4 **Gruinard** Highld
170 F5 **Gruinart** Ag & B
208 F8 **Grula** Highld
190 B7 **Gruline** Ag & B
78 F4 **Grundisburgh** Suffk
235 c5 **Gruting** Shet
192 B7 **Gualachulain** Highld
187 G4 **Guardbridge** Fife
70 E5 **Guarlford** Worcs
194 F6 **Guay** P & K
236 c3 *Guernsey Airport*
Guern
21 G3 **Guestling Green**
E Susx
21 G3 **Guestling Thorn**
E Susx
106 C6 **Guestwick** Norfk
121 K5 **Guide** Bl w D
159 G5 **Guide Post** Nthumb
75 K5 **Guilden Morden**
Cambs
112 C7 **Guilden Sutton**
Ches W
31 G2 **Guildford** Surrey
31 G3 **Guildford**
Crematorium Surrey
186 B2 **Guildtown** P & K
87 J8 **Guilsborough** Nhants
82 E2 **Guilsfield** Powys
163 J7 **Guiltreehill** S Ayrs
23 J4 **Guineaford** Devon
142 D4 **Guisborough** R & Cl
123 J3 **Guiseley** Leeds
106 B7 **Guist** Norfk
56 C3 **Guiting Power** Gloucs
178 B2 **Gullane** E Loth
2 E5 **Gulval** Cnwll
6 C2 **Gulworthy** Devon
49 J7 **Gumfreston** Pembks

87 K5 **Gumley** Leics
102 E7 **Gunby** Lincs
118 F7 **Gunby** Lincs
29 L5 **Gundleton** Hants
20 C3 **Gun Hill** E Susx
23 K5 **Gunn** Devon
139 L7 **Gunnerside** N York
158 A7 **Gunnerton** Nthumb
125 K7 **Gunness** N Linc
6 C2 **Gunnislake** Cnwll
235 d6 **Gunnista** Shet
116 D3 **Gunthorpe** N Linc
106 B5 **Gunthorpe** Norfk
102 B4 **Gunthorpe** Notts
3 H6 **Gunwalloe** Cnwll
16 F4 **Gurnard** IoW
26 F2 **Gurney Slade** Somset
52 B6 **Gurnos** Powys
15 J1 **Gussage All Saints**
Dorset
27 L8 **Gussage St Andrew**
Dorset
15 J1 **Gussage St Michael**
Dorset
35 J5 **Guston** Kent
235 d2 **Gutcher** Shet
196 F6 **Guthrie** Angus
90 B3 **Guyhirn** Cambs
158 F2 **Guyzance** Nthumb
110 F5 **Gwaenysgor** Flints
108 E6 **Gwalchmai** IoA
51 K3 **Gwaun-Cae-Gurwen**
Carmth
3 J6 **Gweek** Cnwll
68 B6 **Gwenddwr** Powys
3 J4 **Gwennap** Cnwll
37 L2 **Gwent Crematorium**
Mons
111 H7 **Gwernaffield** Flints
54 B7 **Gwernesney** Mons
66 C7 **Gwernogle** Carmth
111 H8 **Gwernymynydd**
Flints
110 F5 **Gwespyr** Flints
3 G4 **Gwinear** Cnwll
3 G3 **Gwithian** Cnwll
97 G3 **Gwyddelwern**
Denbgs
66 B7 **Gwyddgrug** Carmth
96 D1 **Gwytherin** Conwy

H

83 H3 **Habberley** Shrops
84 E7 **Habberley** Worcs
122 B4 **Habergham** Lancs
119 G7 **Habertoft** Lincs
126 E7 **Habrough** NE Lin
103 J7 **Hacconby** Lincs
103 G5 **Haceby** Lincs
79 G3 **Hacheston** Suffk
44 F6 **Hackbridge** Gt Lon
115 H5 **Hackenthorpe** Sheff
92 C3 **Hackford** Norfk
132 C2 **Hackforth** N York
234 C5 **Hackland** Ork
74 B4 **Hackleton** Nhants
35 J4 **Hackling** Kent
134 F2 **Hackness** N York
45 G3 **Hackney** Gt Lon
117 G5 **Hackthorn** Lincs
138 D3 **Hackthorpe** Cumb
168 B3 **Hadden** Border
58 C6 **Haddenham** Bucks
90 C7 **Haddenham** Cambs
178 B4 **Haddington** E Loth
116 E8 **Haddington** Lincs
93 J4 **Haddiscoe** Norfk
216 F6 **Haddo** Abers
89 G5 **Haddon** Cambs
114 A3 **Hadfield** Derbys
60 C4 **Hadham Ford** Herts
46 D3 **Hadleigh** Essex
78 B6 **Hadleigh** Suffk
70 F2 **Hadley** Worcs

84 C2 **Hadley** Wrekin
100 C7 **Hadley End** Staffs
44 E1 **Hadley Wood** Gt Lon
33 H3 **Hadlow** Kent
20 B2 **Hadlow Down** E Susx
98 D7 **Hadnall** Shrops
76 D5 **Hadstock** Essex
71 G3 **Hadzor** Worcs
235 c5 **Haggersta** Shet
168 F2 **Haggerston** Nthumb
175 L3 **Haggs** Falk
69 L6 **Hagley** Herefs
85 G7 **Hagley** Worcs
118 D7 **Hagworthingham**
Lincs
136 E5 **Haile** Cumb
57 G5 **Hailey** Oxon
20 C4 **Hailsham** E Susx
75 H3 **Hail Weston** Cambs
45 J2 **Hainault** Gt Lon
106 F8 **Hainford** Norfk
117 K5 **Hainton** Lincs
135 H6 **Haisthorpe** E R Yk
48 F6 **Hakin** Pembks
102 B2 **Halam** Notts
176 F1 **Halbeath** Fife
24 E3 **Halberton** Devon
231 J4 **Halcro** Highld
129 K4 **Hale** Cumb
112 C5 **Hale** Halton
28 D7 **Hale** Hants
30 D2 **Hale** Surrey
113 H4 **Hale** Traffd
20 B3 **Hale Green** E Susx
93 H4 **Hales** Norfk
99 G5 **Hales** Staffs
85 G6 **Halesowen** Dudley
34 F3 **Hales Place** Kent
33 H4 **Hale Street** Kent
93 H7 **Halesworth** Suffk
112 C4 **Halewood** Knows
7 J2 **Halford** Devon
72 C5 **Halford** Warwks
84 E5 **Halfpenny Green**
Staffs
83 G2 **Halfway House**
Shrops
46 F5 **Halfway Houses** Kent
123 G5 **Halifax** Calder
231 G4 **Halkirk** Highld
111 H7 **Halkyn** Flints
174 D7 **Hall** E Rens
20 A3 **Halland** E Susx
87 L4 **Hallaton** Leics
38 F8 **Hallatrow** BaNES
149 G3 **Hallbankgate** Cumb
137 H7 **Hall Dunnerdale**
Cumb
38 D4 **Hallen** S Glos
151 H6 **Hallgarth** Dur
176 B3 **Hall Glen** Falk
85 K7 **Hall Green** Birm
208 D3 **Hallin** Highld
46 B7 **Halling** Medway
118 D4 **Hallington** Lincs
158 C6 **Hallington** Nthumb
121 K7 **Halliwell** Bolton
102 B3 **Halloughton** Notts
70 E3 **Hallow** Worcs
7 J7 **Hallsands** Devon
59 L3 **Hall's Green** Herts
166 B2 **Hallyne** Border
55 G7 **Halmore** Gloucs
18 B4 **Halnaker** W Susx
120 E7 **Halsall** Lancs
73 H6 **Halse** Nhants
25 H5 **Halse** Somset
2 E4 **Halsetown** Cnwll
127 G5 **Halsham** E R Yk
61 K2 **Halstead** Essex
45 J7 **Halstead** Kent
87 L3 **Halstead** Leics
14 A2 **Halstock** Dorset
126 C4 **Haltemprice**
Crematorium E R Yk
118 C8 **Haltham** Lincs

58 E6 **Halton** Bucks
129 K6 **Halton** Lancs
123 L4 **Halton** Leeds
150 C2 **Halton** Nthumb
97 L4 **Halton** Wrexhm
131 K8 **Halton East** N York
131 G4 **Halton Gill** N York
118 F7 **Halton Holegate**
Lincs
149 H4 **Halton Lea Gate**
Nthumb
150 C2 **Halton Shields**
Nthumb
130 F8 **Halton West** N York
149 J3 **Haltwhistle** Nthumb
93 J3 **Halvergate** Norfk
7 H5 **Halwell** Devon
10 C5 **Halwill** Devon
10 C5 **Halwill Junction**
Devon
13 G3 **Ham** Devon
55 G7 **Ham** Gloucs
44 D5 **Ham** Gt Lon
35 J4 **Ham** Kent
25 L6 **Ham** Somset
41 G7 **Ham** Wilts
42 C3 **Hambleden** Bucks
29 M7 **Hambledon** Hants
30 F4 **Hambledon** Surrey
16 F2 **Hamble-le-Rice** Hants
120 E3 **Hambleton** Lancs
124 E4 **Hambleton** N York
26 B6 **Hambridge** Somset
17 L2 **Hambrook** W Susx
118 D7 **Hameringham** Lincs
89 G7 **Hamerton** Cambs
71 H2 **Ham Green** Worcs
175 J7 **Hamilton** S Lans
175 J6 **Hamilton Services**
S Lans
14 B2 **Hamlet** Dorset
44 E4 **Hammersmith** Gt Lon
85 J3 **Hammerwich** Staffs
27 J8 **Hammoon** Dorset
235 c6 **Hamnavoe** Shet
20 C5 **Hampden Park** E Susx
56 C5 **Hampnett** Gloucs
124 D7 **Hampole** Donc
15 K3 **Hampreston** Dorset
44 E3 **Hampstead** Gt Lon
41 K5 **Hampstead Norrey's**
W Berk
132 C7 **Hampsthwaite**
N York
89 H5 **Hampton** C Pete
43 J6 **Hampton** Gt Lon
47 K6 **Hampton** Kent
84 D6 **Hampton** Shrops
40 D3 **Hampton** Swindn
71 H5 **Hampton** Worcs
69 L6 **Hampton Bishop**
Herefs
44 D6 **Hampton Court**
Palace & Gardens
Gt Lon
98 D3 **Hampton Heath**
Ches W
86 B7 **Hampton in Arden**
Solhll
70 F2 **Hampton Lovett**
Worcs
72 B3 **Hampton Lucy**
Warwks
72 C2 **Hampton Magna**
Warwks
57 J5 **Hampton Poyle** Oxon
44 D6 **Hampton Wick** Gt Lon
28 E7 **Hamptworth** Wilts
19 L3 **Hamsey** E Susx
100 C8 **Hamstall Ridware**
Staffs
41 H7 **Hamstead Marshall**
W Berk
140 E2 **Hamsterley** Dur
150 E4 **Hamsterley** Dur
34 D7 **Hamstreet** Kent

26 D4 **Ham Street** Somset
15 J4 **Hamworthy** Poole
100 D6 **Hanbury** Staffs
71 G2 **Hanbury** Worcs
99 J4 **Hanchurch** Staffs
228 A6 **Handa Island** Highld
12 D4 **Hand and Pen** Devon
112 B7 **Handbridge** Ches W
31 L5 **Handcross** W Susx
113 J5 **Handforth** Ches E
98 C2 **Handley** Ches W
101 G1 **Handley** Derbys
85 J5 **Handsworth** Birm
115 H4 **Handsworth** Sheff
123 K6 **Hanging Heaton** Kirk
87 L8 **Hanging Houghton** Nhants
28 B4 **Hanging Langford** Wilts
19 H4 **Hangleton** Br & H
38 F6 **Hanham** S Glos
98 F4 **Hankelow** Ches E
39 L3 **Hankerton** Wilts
99 K3 **Hanley** C Stke
99 K3 **Hanley** C Stke
70 E6 **Hanley Castle** Worcs
70 B2 **Hanley Child** Worcs
70 E6 **Hanley Swan** Worcs
70 C2 **Hanley William** Worcs
131 G7 **Hanlith** N York
98 C4 **Hanmer** Wrexhm
23 J5 **Hannaford** Devon
29 K1 **Hannington** Hants
74 B1 **Hannington** Nhants
40 D2 **Hannington** Swindn
40 D2 **Hannington Wick** Swindn
74 B5 **Hanslope** M Keyn
103 H7 **Hanthorpe** Lincs
44 D4 **Hanwell** Gt Lon
72 E5 **Hanwood** Shrops
83 J2 **Hanworth** Gt Lon
43 J6 **Hanworth** Norfk
106 E5 **Hanworth** Norfk
165 G3 **Happendon** S Lans
165 G3 **Happendon Services** S Lans
107 H6 **Happisburgh** Norfk
107 H6 **Happisburgh Common** Norfk
112 C6 **Hapsford** Ches W
122 B4 **Hapton** Lancs
92 E4 **Hapton** Norfk
7 H4 **Harberton** Devon
7 H5 **Harbertonford** Devon
34 F3 **Harbledown** Kent
85 H6 **Harborne** Birm
86 F7 **Harborough Magna** Warwks
158 B2 **Harbottle** Nthumb
7 G4 **Harbourneford** Devon
72 D3 **Harbury** Warwks
102 C6 **Harby** Leics
116 E7 **Harby** Notts
11 K8 **Harcombe** Devon
12 F4 **Harcombe** Devon
13 J4 **Harcombe Bottom** Devon
123 G3 **Harden** C Brad
85 H4 **Harden** Wsall
39 K5 **Hardenhuish** Wilts
206 E5 **Hardgate** Abers
146 E2 **Hardgate** D & G
174 F4 **Hardgate** W Duns
18 E3 **Hardham** W Susx
92 C3 **Hardingham** Norfk
73 L3 **Hardingstone** Nhants
27 H2 **Hardington** Somset
13 M1 **Hardington Mandeville** Somset
13 M1 **Hardington Marsh** Somset
26 D8 **Hardington Moor** Somset
22 C7 **Hardisworthy** Devon

16 E2 **Hardley** Hants
93 H4 **Hardley Street** Norfk
131 G2 **Hardraw** N York
115 H8 **Hardstoft** Derbys
17 H3 **Hardway** Hants
27 G5 **Hardway** Somset
58 D4 **Hardwick** Bucks
75 L3 **Hardwick** Cambs
74 B1 **Hardwick** Nhants
92 F5 **Hardwick** Norfk
57 G6 **Hardwick** Oxon
57 L3 **Hardwick** Oxon
55 H5 **Hardwicke** Gloucs
55 K3 **Hardwicke** Gloucs
61 M4 **Hardy's Green** Essex
118 D7 **Hareby** Lincs
123 G4 **Hare Croft** C Brad
43 H3 **Harefield** Gt Lon
62 D3 **Hare Green** Essex
42 D5 **Hare Hatch** Wokham
100 D5 **Harehill** Derbys
123 L4 **Harehills** Leeds
167 H5 **Harelaw** Border
156 D6 **Harelaw** D & G
55 J6 **Harescombe** Gloucs
55 J6 **Haresfield** Gloucs
29 J5 **Harestock** Hants
60 C6 **Hare Street** Essex
60 C3 **Hare Street** Herts
123 L2 **Harewood** Leeds
54 D3 **Harewood End** Herefs
6 F4 **Harford** Devon
98 C1 **Hargrave** Ches W
74 F1 **Hargrave** Nhants
77 H3 **Hargrave Green** Suffk
78 E7 **Harkstead** Suffk
86 B2 **Harlaston** Staffs
102 E6 **Harlaxton** Lincs
95 K6 **Harlech** Gwynd
83 K1 **Harlescott** Shrops
44 E4 **Harlesden** Gt Lon
115 J6 **Harlesthorpe** Derbys
7 J6 **Harleston** Devon
92 F6 **Harleston** Norfk
78 B3 **Harleston** Suffk
73 K2 **Harlestone** Nhants
122 C4 **Harle Syke** Lancs
115 G2 **Harley** Rothm
83 L3 **Harley** Shrops
59 G2 **Harlington** C Beds
115 J2 **Harlington** Donc
43 H5 **Harlington** Gt Lon
208 D6 **Harlosh** Highld
60 D6 **Harlow** Essex
150 D2 **Harlow Hill** Nthumb
125 H3 **Harlthorpe** E R Yk
76 B4 **Harlton** Cambs
4 D2 **Harlyn** Cnwll
15 J6 **Harman's Cross** Dorset
131 L2 **Harmby** N York
59 L5 **Harmer Green** Herts
98 C7 **Harmer Hill** Shrops
116 F8 **Harmston** Lincs
83 L3 **Harnage** Shrops
56 B7 **Harnhill** Gloucs
45 K2 **Harold Hill** Gt Lon
48 E4 **Haroldston West** Pembks
235 e1 **Haroldswick** Shet
45 K3 **Harold Wood** Gt Lon
133 K3 **Harome** N York
59 J5 **Harpenden** Herts
12 E4 **Harpford** Devon
135 H7 **Harpham** E R Yk
105 J7 **Harpley** Norfk
70 C3 **Harpley** Worcs
73 K3 **Harpole** Nhants
231 G4 **Harpsdale** Highld
116 F4 **Harpswell** Lincs
113 K2 **Harpurhey** Manch
148 D4 **Harraby** Cumb
23 J6 **Harracott** Devon
199 K2 **Harrapool** Highld
185 K2 **Harrietfield** P & K

33 L3 **Harrietsham** Kent
44 F3 **Harringay** Gt Lon
136 D3 **Harrington** Cumb
118 E6 **Harrington** Lincs
87 L7 **Harrington** Nhants
88 D4 **Harringworth** Nhants
232 d4 **Harris** W Isls
132 D8 **Harrogate** N York
132 E8 **Harrogate Crematorium** N York
74 D3 **Harrold** Bed
44 D3 **Harrow** Gt Lon
6 B2 **Harrowbarrow** Cnwll
77 J4 **Harrow Green** Suffk
44 D3 **Harrow on the Hill** Gt Lon
44 D3 **Harrow Weald** Gt Lon
76 B4 **Harston** Cambs
102 D6 **Harston** Leics
125 J3 **Harswell** E R Yk
151 L7 **Hart** Hartpl
158 D5 **Hartburn** Nthumb
77 J4 **Hartest** Suffk
32 E6 **Hartfield** E Susx
89 J8 **Hartford** Cambs
112 F6 **Hartford** Ches W
42 C8 **Hartfordbridge** Hants
61 G4 **Hartford End** Essex
140 F6 **Hartforth** N York
27 J7 **Hartgrove** Dorset
98 D2 **Harthill** Ches W
176 B5 **Harthill** N Lans
115 J5 **Harthill** Rothm
100 C1 **Hartington** Derbys
22 D6 **Hartland** Devon
22 C6 **Hartland Quay** Devon
70 E1 **Hartlebury** Worcs
151 L7 **Hartlepool** Hartpl
142 B2 **Hartlepool Crematorium** Hartpl
139 H5 **Hartley** Cumb
33 K6 **Hartley** Kent
45 L6 **Hartley** Kent
42 B8 **Hartley Wespall** Hants
30 C1 **Hartley Wintney** Hants
46 D7 **Hartlip** Kent
133 L6 **Harton** N York
151 J2 **Harton** S Tyne
55 J3 **Hartpury** Gloucs
123 J6 **Hartshead** Kirk
123 H5 **Hartshead Moor Services** Calder
99 K4 **Hartshill** C Stke
86 D5 **Hartshill** Warwks
100 F7 **Hartshorne** Derbys
73 L4 **Hartwell** Nhants
132 C6 **Hartwith** N York
175 L6 **Hartwood** N Lans
166 F4 **Hartwoodmyres** Border
46 A7 **Harvel** Kent
71 J5 **Harvington** Worcs
84 F8 **Harvington** Worcs
116 B3 **Harwell** Notts
41 J3 **Harwell** Oxon
62 F2 **Harwich** Essex
143 K7 **Harwood Dale** N York
59 L4 **Harwood Park Crematorium** Herts
115 L3 **Harworth** Notts
85 G6 **Hasbury** Dudley
31 G4 **Hascombe** Surrey
87 K7 **Haselbech** Nhants
13 L1 **Haselbury Plucknett** Somset
72 B2 **Haseley** Warwks
71 K3 **Haselor** Warwks
55 J3 **Hasfield** Gloucs
120 E8 **Haskayne** Lancs
78 F4 **Hasketon** Suffk
30 E5 **Haslemere** Surrey
122 B6 **Haslingden** Lancs
76 B4 **Haslingfield** Cambs
99 G2 **Haslington** Ches E

93 H3 **Hassingham** Norfk
19 J3 **Hassocks** W Susx
114 E6 **Hassop** Derbys
231 K5 **Haster** Highld
34 E5 **Hastingleigh** Kent
21 G4 **Hastings** E Susx
21 G3 **Hastings Borough Crematorium** E Susx
60 D6 **Hastingwood** Essex
58 F6 **Hastoe** Herts
151 J6 **Haswell** Dur
151 J6 **Haswell Plough** Dur
25 L7 **Hatch Beauchamp** Somset
43 J3 **Hatch End** Gt Lon
112 D6 **Hatchmere** Ches W
117 K2 **Hatcliffe** NE Lin
125 G8 **Hatfield** Donc
69 L3 **Hatfield** Herefs
59 L6 **Hatfield** Herts
60 E5 **Hatfield Broad Oak** Essex
60 E5 **Hatfield Heath** Essex
61 J5 **Hatfield Peverel** Essex
125 G8 **Hatfield Woodhouse** Donc
41 G2 **Hatford** Oxon
29 G2 **Hatherden** Hants
10 D4 **Hatherleigh** Devon
101 J7 **Hathern** Leics
56 D6 **Hatherop** Gloucs
114 E5 **Hathersage** Derbys
114 E5 **Hathersage Booths** Derbys
99 G3 **Hatherton** Ches E
85 G2 **Hatherton** Staffs
75 K4 **Hatley St George** Cambs
6 B4 **Hatt** Cnwll
113 M3 **Hattersley** Tamesd
217 K6 **Hatton** Abers
196 D7 **Hatton** Angus
100 E6 **Hatton** Derbys
43 J5 **Hatton** Gt Lon
117 K6 **Hatton** Lincs
83 J5 **Hatton** Shrops
112 E5 **Hatton** Warrtn
72 B2 **Hatton** Warwks
206 F3 **Hatton of Fintray** Abers
163 L4 **Haugh** E Ayrs
118 D5 **Haugham** Lincs
175 G3 **Haughhead** E Duns
78 B3 **Haughley** Suffk
78 B2 **Haughley Green** Suffk
215 J6 **Haugh of Glass** Moray
146 E2 **Haugh of Urr** D & G
84 D2 **Haughton** Shrops
98 B6 **Haughton** Shrops
99 K7 **Haughton** Staffs
141 H4 **Haughton le Skerne** Darltn
98 E2 **Haughton Moss** Ches E
60 B4 **Haultwick** Herts
86 B2 **Haunton** Staffs
76 B4 **Hauxton** Cambs
17 K2 **Havant** Hants
17 G4 **Havenstreet** IoW
124 B7 **Havercroft** Wakefd
48 F4 **Haverfordwest** Pembks
76 F5 **Haverhill** Suffk
128 E4 **Haverigg** Cumb
45 K2 **Havering-atte-Bower** Gt Lon
74 B6 **Haversham** M Keyn
129 H3 **Haverthwaite** Cumb
38 C7 **Havyat** N Som
111 J7 **Hawarden** Flints
61 J4 **Hawbush Green** Essex
65 K6 **Hawen** Cerdgn
131 G2 **Hawes** N York
92 F4 **Hawe's Green** Norfk

70 E3 **Hawford** Worcs
167 G6 **Hawick** Border
13 J3 **Hawkchurch** Devon
77 H4 **Hawkedon** Suffk
27 K2 **Hawkeridge** Wilts
39 H3 **Hawkesbury** S Glos
39 H3 **Hawkesbury Upton** S Glos
33 K6 **Hawkhurst** Kent
35 G6 **Hawkinge** Kent
35 G6 **Hawkinge Crematorium** Kent
30 C5 **Hawkley** Hants
24 D5 **Hawkridge** Somset
137 K7 **Hawkshead** Cumb
137 K7 **Hawkshead Hill** Cumb
165 G2 **Hawksland** S Lans
61 G2 **Hawkspur Green** Essex
98 E6 **Hawkstone** Shrops
131 H5 **Hawkswick** N York
123 H3 **Hawksworth** Leeds
102 C4 **Hawksworth** Notts
46 E2 **Hawkwell** Essex
42 E8 **Hawley** Hants
56 B4 **Hawling** Gloucs
133 H2 **Hawnby** N York
122 F3 **Haworth** C Brad
77 J3 **Hawstead** Suffk
151 K5 **Hawthorn** Dur
103 K2 **Hawthorn Hill** Lincs
102 C3 **Hawton** Notts
133 J7 **Haxby** C York
116 C2 **Haxey** N Linc
39 G7 **Haycombe Crematorium** BaNES
112 E3 **Haydock** St Hel
149 L3 **Haydon Bridge** Nthumb
40 C3 **Haydon Wick** Swindn
43 J4 **Hayes** Gt Lon
45 H6 **Hayes** Gt Lon
43 H4 **Hayes End** Gt Lon
182 F3 **Hayfield** Ag & B
114 B4 **Hayfield** Derbys
196 E7 **Hayhillock** Angus
2 F4 **Hayle** Cnwll
85 G6 **Hayley Green** Dudley
17 K3 **Hayling Island** Hants
11 H7 **Hayne** Devon
74 F6 **Haynes (Church End)** C Beds
75 G6 **Haynes (Northwood End)** C Beds
75 G6 **Haynes (Silver End)** C Beds
74 F6 **Haynes (West End)** C Beds
68 E6 **Hay-on-Wye** Powys
48 F3 **Hayscastle** Pembks
48 F3 **Hayscastle Cross** Pembks
60 C3 **Hay Street** Herts
147 K6 **Hayton** Cumb
148 E4 **Hayton** Cumb
125 J2 **Hayton** E R Yk
116 B5 **Hayton** Notts
7 H1 **Haytor Vale** Devon
9 K3 **Haytown** Devon
19 J2 **Haywards Heath** W Susx
124 E7 **Haywood** Donc
165 G1 **Hazelbank** S Lans
14 E2 **Hazelbury Bryan** Dorset
61 K7 **Hazeleigh** Essex
113 L4 **Hazel Grove** Stockp
186 E3 **Hazelton Walls** Fife
101 G4 **Hazelwood** Derbys
42 E2 **Hazlemere** Bucks
159 G7 **Hazlerigg** N u Ty
56 B4 **Hazleton** Gloucs
105 G5 **Heacham** Norfk
29 J5 **Headbourne Worthy** Hants

33 L4 **Headcorn** Kent
123 K4 **Headingley** Leeds
57 K6 **Headington** Oxon
140 F4 **Headlam** Dur
176 B6 **Headlesscross** N Lans
71 J2 **Headless Cross** Worcs
30 D4 **Headley** Hants
41 K7 **Headley** Hants
31 K1 **Headley** Surrey
30 D4 **Headley Down** Hants
116 C6 **Headon** Notts
175 J8 **Heads** S Lans
148 E4 **Heads Nook** Cumb
101 G3 **Heage** Derbys
124 D2 **Healaugh** N York
140 C7 **Healaugh** N York
113 J4 **Heald Green** Stockp
25 K7 **Heale** Somset
26 B6 **Heale** Somset
132 B4 **Healey** N York
150 D5 **Healeyfield** Dur
126 F7 **Healing** NE Lin
2 E5 **Heamoor** Cnwll
101 H3 **Heanor** Derbys
23 H4 **Heanton Punchardon** Devon
116 E4 **Heapham** Lincs
86 E5 **Heart of England Crematorium** Warwks
176 B5 *Heart of Scotland Services* N Lans
24 B5 **Heasley Mill** Devon
199 K2 **Heast** Highld
115 J7 **Heath** Derbys
123 L6 **Heath** Wakefd
58 F3 **Heath and Reach** C Beds
100 D1 **Heathcote** Derbys
86 E2 **Heather** Leics
20 C2 **Heathfield** E Susx
25 J6 **Heathfield** Somset
71 J1 **Heath Green** Worcs
155 H6 **Heath Hall** D & G
85 H2 **Heath Hayes & Wimblebury** Staffs
84 D2 **Heath Hill** Shrops
43 H5 *Heathrow Airport* Gt Lon
84 E5 **Heathton** Shrops
85 G4 **Heath Town** Wolves
100 B6 **Heatley** Staffs
113 G4 **Heatley** Warrtn
123 H4 **Heaton** C Brad
151 G2 **Heaton** N u Ty
113 L8 **Heaton** Staffs
120 E7 **Heaton's Bridge** Lancs
33 G2 **Heaverham** Kent
12 B4 **Heavitree** Devon
151 H3 **Hebburn** S Tyne
131 J6 **Hebden** N York
122 E5 **Hebden Bridge** Calder
60 A4 **Hebing End** Herts
49 K3 **Hebron** Carmth
158 F4 **Hebron** Nthumb
42 B7 **Heckfield** Hants
92 E7 **Heckfield Green** Suffk
61 M4 **Heckfordbridge** Essex
103 J4 **Heckington** Lincs
123 J5 **Heckmondwike** Kirk
39 M6 **Heddington** Wilts
150 E2 **Heddon-on-the-Wall** Nthumb
93 G5 **Hedenham** Norfk
29 J8 **Hedge End** Hants
42 F3 **Hedgerley** Bucks
25 L5 **Hedging** Somset
150 D3 **Hedley on the Hill** Nthumb
85 H2 **Hednesford** Staffs
126 F5 **Hedon** E R Yk
42 E3 **Hedsor** Bucks
235 c5 **Heglibister** Shet
141 G3 **Heighington** Darltn
117 G7 **Heighington** Lincs

70 D1 **Heightington** Worcs
167 L4 **Heiton** Border
12 C2 **Hele** Devon
23 H3 **Hele** Devon
174 B2 **Helensburgh** Ag & B
163 K3 **Helenton** S Ayrs
3 K6 **Helford** Cnwll
3 K6 **Helford Passage** Cnwll
105 K7 **Helhoughton** Norfk
76 F6 **Helions Bumpstead** Essex
5 G2 **Helland** Cnwll
9 H6 **Hellescott** Cnwll
92 E2 **Hellesdon** Norfk
73 G3 **Hellidon** Nhants
131 G7 **Hellifield** N York
20 C4 **Hellingly** E Susx
158 F3 **Helm** Nthumb
73 H5 **Helmdon** Nhants
123 G7 **Helme** Kirk
78 E3 **Helmingham** Suffk
227 H5 **Helmsdale** Highld
122 B6 **Helmshore** Lancs
133 J3 **Helmsley** N York
133 G5 **Helperby** N York
134 E5 **Helperthorpe** N York
103 J4 **Helpringham** Lincs
89 G3 **Helpston** C Pete
112 C6 **Helsby** Ches W
3 H5 **Helston** Cnwll
8 E8 **Helstone** Cnwll
138 D3 **Helton** Cumb
59 H6 **Hemel Hempstead** Herts
6 E4 **Hemerdon** Devon
125 G4 **Hemingbrough** N York
118 C6 **Hemingby** Lincs
75 K1 **Hemingford Abbots** Cambs
75 K1 **Hemingford Grey** Cambs
78 D4 **Hemingstone** Suffk
101 J6 **Hemington** Leics
88 F6 **Hemington** Nhants
27 G2 **Hemington** Somset
79 G6 **Hemley** Suffk
142 B4 **Hemlington** Middsb
92 F5 **Hempnall** Norfk
92 F5 **Hempnall Green** Norfk
214 D2 **Hempriggs** Moray
76 F6 **Hempstead** Essex
106 D5 **Hempstead** Norfk
107 J6 **Hempstead** Norfk
105 L6 **Hempton** Norfk
57 H2 **Hempton** Oxon
107 K8 **Hemsby** Norfk
116 F4 **Hemswell** Lincs
116 F4 **Hemswell Cliff** Lincs
124 C7 **Hemsworth** Wakefd
25 H8 **Hemyock** Devon
167 L3 **Hendersyde Park** Border
44 E3 **Hendon** Gt Lon
151 K4 **Hendon** Sundld
44 E2 **Hendon Crematorium** Gt Lon
51 H5 **Hendy** Carmth
19 G3 **Henfield** W Susx
37 K2 **Hengoed** Caerph
68 E4 **Hengoed** Powys
77 J2 **Hengrave** Suffk
60 E3 **Henham** Essex
82 C2 **Heniarth** Powys
25 L6 **Henlade** Somset
14 D2 **Henley** Dorset
26 B5 **Henley** Somset
78 E4 **Henley** Suffk
30 E6 **Henley** W Susx
71 L2 **Henley-in-Arden** Warwks
42 C4 **Henley-on-Thames** Oxon
20 E3 **Henley's Down** E Susx

65 K6 **Henllan** Cerdgn
110 E7 **Henllan** Denbgs
37 K3 **Henllys** Torfn
75 H6 **Henlow** C Beds
11 J8 **Hennock** Devon
77 K6 **Henny Street** Essex
109 L6 **Henryd** Conwy
49 H3 **Henry's Moat (Castell Hendre)** Pembks
124 F5 **Hensall** N York
149 K3 **Henshaw** Nthumb
136 D4 **Hensingham** Cumb
93 K6 **Henstead** Suffk
29 J6 **Hensting** Hants
27 G7 **Henstridge** Somset
27 G7 **Henstridge Ash** Somset
58 C7 **Henton** Oxon
26 C3 **Henton** Somset
70 E4 **Henwick** Worcs
5 L2 **Henwood** Cnwll
36 E4 **Heol-y-Cyw** Brdgnd
158 C2 **Hepple** Nthumb
158 F5 **Hepscott** Nthumb
122 E5 **Heptonstall** Calder
114 D1 **Hepworth** Kirk
92 B8 **Hepworth** Suffk
48 E6 **Herbrandston** Pembks
69 K6 **Hereford** Herefs
69 J6 **Hereford Crematorium** Herefs
35 K2 **Hereson** Kent
218 B7 **Heribusta** Highld
177 L7 **Heriot** Border
177 G4 **Hermiston** C Edin
156 E3 **Hermitage** Border
14 C2 **Hermitage** Dorset
41 J5 **Hermitage** W Berk
65 K7 **Hermon** Carmth
49 L2 **Hermon** Pembks
47 K6 **Herne** Kent
47 K6 **Herne Bay** Kent
44 F5 **Herne Hill** Gt Lon
33 H4 **Herne Pound** Kent
34 E3 **Hernhill** Kent
5 K4 **Herodsfoot** Cnwll
152 D5 **Heronsford** S Ayrs
30 A3 **Herriard** Hants
93 K4 **Herringfleet** Suffk
77 G1 **Herringswell** Suffk
115 J2 **Herringthorpe** Rothm
151 H4 **Herrington** Sundld
35 G3 **Hersden** Kent
43 J7 **Hersham** Surrey
20 D3 **Herstmonceux** E Susx
234 c7 **Herston** Ork
60 B5 **Hertford** Herts
60 B5 **Hertford Heath** Herts
60 A5 **Hertingfordbury** Herts
120 F5 **Hesketh Bank** Lancs
121 J3 **Hesketh Lane** Lancs
148 C7 **Hesket Newmarket** Cumb
151 K7 **Hesleden** Dur
124 F1 **Heslington** C York
133 H8 **Hessay** C York
5 L4 **Hessenford** Cnwll
77 L3 **Hessett** Suffk
126 C5 **Hessle** E R Yk
124 C6 **Hessle** Wakefd
129 K6 **Hest Bank** Lancs
43 J5 **Heston** Gt Lon
43 J5 *Heston Services* Gt Lon
234 b5 **Hestwall** Ork
111 J5 **Heswall** Wirral
57 L3 **Hethe** Oxon
92 D3 **Hethersett** Norfk
148 E2 **Hethersgill** Cumb
168 D4 **Hethpool** Nthumb
151 G7 **Hett** Dur
131 H7 **Hetton** N York

151 J5 **Hetton-le-Hole** Sundld
158 D7 **Heugh** Nthumb
205 J3 **Heughhead** Abers
179 H6 **Heugh Head** Border
93 G8 **Heveningham** Suffk
32 E4 **Hever** Kent
129 K3 **Heversham** Cumb
106 E7 **Hevingham** Norfk
4 F6 **Hewas Water** Cnwll
54 E7 **Hewelsfield** Gloucs
13 K2 **Hewish** Somset
13 J2 **Hewood** Dorset
150 B3 **Hexham** Nthumb
45 K6 **Hextable** Kent
115 K2 **Hexthorpe** Donc
59 J2 **Hexton** Herts
9 K8 **Hexworthy** Cnwll
6 F2 **Hexworthy** Devon
61 G7 **Heybridge** Essex
61 K6 **Heybridge** Essex
6 D6 **Heybrook Bay** Devon
76 B6 **Heydon** Cambs
106 D6 **Heydon** Norfk
103 G5 **Heydour** Lincs
188 C7 **Heylipoll** Ag & B
235 C3 **Heylor** Shet
129 J7 **Heysham** Lancs
18 B3 **Heyshott** W Susx
27 L3 **Heytesbury** Wilts
57 G3 **Heythrop** Oxon
122 C7 **Heywood** Rochdl
27 K2 **Heywood** Wilts
116 F2 **Hibaldstow** N Linc
115 J1 **Hickleton** Donc
107 J7 **Hickling** Norfk
102 B6 **Hickling** Notts
107 J7 **Hickling Green** Norfk
31 L7 **Hickstead** W Susx
71 L6 **Hidcote Bartrim** Gloucs
71 L6 **Hidcote Boyce** Gloucs
124 C6 **High Ackworth** Wakefd
114 F1 **Higham** Barns
101 H2 **Higham** Derbys
33 G4 **Higham** Kent
46 B5 **Higham** Kent
122 B3 **Higham** Lancs
77 H2 **Higham** Suffk
78 B7 **Higham** Suffk
158 E6 **Higham Dykes** Nthumb
74 D2 **Higham Ferrers** Nhants
59 J2 **Higham Gobion** C Beds
45 G3 **Higham Hill** Gt Lon
86 E4 **Higham on the Hill** Leics
10 C4 **Highampton** Devon
45 H2 **Highams Park** Gt Lon
144 C6 **High Ardwell** D & G
154 F5 **High Auldgirth** D & G
148 F6 **High Bankhill** Cumb
60 C7 **High Beach** Essex
130 C5 **High Bentham** N York
23 J7 **High Bickington** Devon
130 B4 **High Biggins** Cumb
175 J6 **High Blantyre** S Lans
175 L3 **High Bonnybridge** Falk
23 L5 **High Bray** Devon
25 L3 **Highbridge** Somset
32 C7 **Highbrook** W Susx
33 G5 **High Brooms** Kent
123 J7 **Highburton** Kirk
44 F3 **Highbury** Gt Lon
27 G2 **Highbury** Somset
130 C4 **High Casterton** Cumb
133 L8 **High Catton** E R Yk
41 H8 **Highclere** Hants
16 B4 **Highcliffe** Dorset
141 G4 **High Coniscliffe** Darltn

148 E3 **High Crosby** Cumb
163 K1 **High Cross** E Ayrs
30 B6 **High Cross** Hants
60 B4 **High Cross** Herts
71 L2 **High Cross** Warwks
144 D7 **High Drummore** D & G
60 F5 **High Easter** Essex
132 B3 **High Ellington** N York
14 E2 **Higher Ansty** Dorset
121 G4 **Higher Bartle** Lancs
14 D4 **Higher Bockhampton** Dorset
7 L5 **Higher Brixham** Torbay
98 E8 **Higher Ercall** Wrekin
13 K1 **Higher Chillington** Somset
113 G2 **Higher Folds** Wigan
7 L3 **Higher Gabwell** Devon
129 J7 **Higher Heysham** Lancs
113 G3 **Higher Irlam** Salfd
97 L1 **Higher Kinnerton** Flints
23 J4 **Higher Muddiford** Devon
121 G5 **Higher Penwortham** Lancs
4 C6 **Higher Town** Cnwll
4 F4 **Higher Town** Cnwll
2 b1 **Higher Town** IoS
121 H5 **Higher Walton** Lancs
112 E4 **Higher Walton** Warrtn
13 H2 **Higher Wambrook** Somset
14 D4 **Higher Waterston** Dorset
121 J6 **Higher Wheelton** Lancs
112 F5 **Higher Whitley** Ches W
14 B3 **Higher Wraxhall** Dorset
98 C4 **Higher Wych** Ches W
140 F2 **High Etherley** Dur
150 E3 **Highfield** Gatesd
174 C7 **Highfield** N Ayrs
61 J3 **High Garrett** Essex
44 F3 **Highgate** Gt Lon
132 C5 **High Grantley** N York
92 B3 **High Green** Norfk
92 E5 **High Green** Norfk
115 G3 **High Green** Sheff
70 F5 **High Green** Worcs
34 B7 **High Halden** Kent
46 C5 **High Halstow** Medway
26 B5 **High Ham** Somset
132 D7 **High Harrogate** N York
98 E7 **High Hatton** Shrops
159 G2 **High Hauxley** Nthumb
143 J5 **High Hawsker** N York
148 E6 **High Hesket** Cumb
123 K8 **High Hoyland** Barns
32 E7 **High Hurstwood** E Susx
134 B5 **High Hutton** N York
147 M7 **High Ireby** Cumb
133 H4 **High Kilburn** N York
140 E3 **High Lands** Dur
203 J4 **Highland Wildlife Park** Highld
115 H5 **Highlane** Derbys
113 L4 **High Lane** Stockp
3 G4 **High Lanes** Cnwll
55 H4 **Highleadon** Gloucs
113 G5 **High Legh** Ches E
18 A6 **Highleigh** W Susx
141 K5 **High Leven** S on T
84 D6 **Highley** Shrops
38 F8 **High Littleton** BaNES
137 G3 **High Lorton** Cumb

116 D7 **High Marnham** Notts
115 K2 **High Melton** Donc
150 D3 **High Mickley** Nthumb
42 B4 **Highmoor** Oxon
42 B4 **Highmoor Cross** Oxon
55 H4 **Highnam** Gloucs
151 J4 **High Newport** Sundld
129 J3 **High Newton** Cumb
129 G2 **High Nibthwaite** Cumb
99 H7 **High Offley** Staffs
60 E7 **High Ongar** Essex
84 E1 **High Onn** Staffs
62 C4 **High Park Corner** Essex
163 L7 **High Pennyvenie** E Ayrs
60 F4 **High Roding** Essex
18 F4 **High Salvington** W Susx
150 E3 **High Spen** Gatesd
34 B3 **Highsted** Kent
4 F5 **Highstreet** Cnwll
34 E3 **Highstreet** Kent
79 J4 **High Street** Suffk
31 G4 **Highstreet Green** Surrey
155 J6 **Hightae** D & G
111 J2 **Hightown** Sefton
77 L4 **Hightown Green** Suffk
118 C7 **High Toynton** Lincs
158 C2 **High Trewhitt** Nthumb
151 G4 **High Urpeth** Dur
176 D2 **High Valleyfield** Fife
7 J2 **Highweek** Devon
44 E2 **Highwood Hill** Gt Lon
40 D2 **Highworth** Swindn
137 K7 **High Wray** Cumb
60 D5 **High Wych** Herts
42 E2 **High Wycombe** Bucks
91 J4 **Hilborough** Norfk
40 C8 **Hilcott** Wilts
32 F4 **Hildenborough** Kent
33 G4 **Hilden Park** Kent
76 D5 **Hildersham** Cambs
99 L5 **Hilderstone** Staffs
135 J6 **Hilderthorpe** E R Yk
14 C2 **Hilfield** Dorset
90 E4 **Hilgay** Norfk
38 F2 **Hill** S Glos
72 F2 **Hill** Warwks
124 D5 **Hillam** N York
30 C6 **Hill Brow** Hants
15 J3 **Hillbutts** Dorset
99 H5 **Hill Chorlton** Staffs
100 F3 **Hillclifflane** Derbys
25 H6 **Hill Common** Somset
104 B3 **Hilldyke** Lincs
176 F2 **Hillend** Fife
185 L7 **Hill End** Fife
70 F6 **Hill End** Gloucs
177 H5 **Hillend** Mdloth
175 L5 **Hillend** N Lans
58 B3 **Hillesden** Bucks
39 H3 **Hillesley** Gloucs
25 J6 **Hillfarrance** Somset
46 D7 **Hill Green** Kent
216 B7 **Hillhead** Abers
17 G2 **Hill Head** Hants
165 J2 **Hillhead** S Lans
217 K5 **Hillhead of Cocklaw** Abers
231 H5 **Hilliclay** Highld
43 H4 **Hillingdon** Gt Lon
174 F5 **Hillington** C Glas
105 H7 **Hillington** Norfk
87 G8 **Hillmorton** Warwks
176 F1 **Hill of Beath** Fife
223 H5 **Hill of Fearn** Highld
186 F5 **Hill of Tarvit** Fife
146 D3 **Hillowton** D & G
100 B8 **Hill Ridware** Staffs
207 H5 **Hillside** Abers

197 H4 **Hillside** Angus
123 H6 **Hill Side** Kirk
115 J7 **Hills Town** Derbys
29 G7 **Hillstreet** Hants
235 C3 **Hillswick** Shet
123 L7 **Hill Top** Wakefd
235 c8 **Hillwell** Shet
40 A5 **Hilmarton** Wilts
39 K8 **Hilperton** Wilts
17 J2 **Hilsea** C Port
127 G4 **Hilston** E R Yk
179 H7 **Hilton** Border
75 K2 **Hilton** Cambs
139 G3 **Hilton** Cumb
100 E6 **Hilton** Derbys
14 E2 **Hilton** Dorset
140 F3 **Hilton** Dur
223 J6 **Hilton** Highld
141 K5 **Hilton** S on T
84 D4 **Hilton** Shrops
85 G3 **Hilton Park Services** Staffs
71 G3 **Himbleton** Worcs
84 F5 **Himley** Staffs
129 L3 **Hincaster** Cumb
44 D6 **Hinchley Wood** Surrey
86 E5 **Hinckley** Leics
92 B7 **Hinderclay** Suffk
143 G4 **Hinderwell** N York
30 E4 **Hindhead** Surrey
112 F1 **Hindley** Wigan
70 F3 **Hindlip** Worcs
106 C6 **Hindolveston** Norfk
27 K5 **Hindon** Wilts
106 B5 **Hindringham** Norfk
92 B3 **Hingham** Norfk
99 G7 **Hinstock** Shrops
78 C5 **Hintlesham** Suffk
69 G6 **Hinton** Herefs
39 G5 **Hinton** S Glos
83 H2 **Hinton** Shrops
29 L6 **Hinton Ampner** Hants
26 E1 **Hinton Blewett** BaNES
39 H8 **Hinton Charterhouse** BaNES
73 H6 **Hinton-in-the-Hedges** Nhants
15 J2 **Hinton Martell** Dorset
71 H6 **Hinton on the Green** Worcs
40 E4 **Hinton Parva** Swindn
26 B8 **Hinton St George** Somset
27 H7 **Hinton St Mary** Dorset
57 G7 **Hinton Waldrist** Oxon
85 L3 **Hints** Staffs
74 D3 **Hinwick** Bed
34 D6 **Hinxhill** Kent
76 C5 **Hinxton** Cambs
75 J6 **Hinxworth** Herts
123 H5 **Hipperholme** Calder
140 F7 **Hipswell** N York
206 D5 **Hirn** Abers
97 G7 **Hirnant** Powys
159 G5 **Hirst** Nthumb
124 F5 **Hirst Courtney** N York
52 E6 **Hirwaun** Rhondd
23 J6 **Hiscott** Devon
76 B2 **Histon** Cambs
78 B4 **Hitcham** Suffk
78 B4 **Hitcham Causeway** Suffk
78 B4 **Hitcham Street** Suffk
59 K3 **Hitchin** Herts
45 H5 **Hither Green** Gt Lon
11 H5 **Hittisleigh** Devon
125 J4 **Hive** E R Yk
100 A7 **Hixon** Staffs
35 H3 **Hoaden** Kent
100 C7 **Hoar Cross** Staffs
54 D3 **Hoarwithy** Herefs
47 K7 **Hoath** Kent
82 F7 **Hobarris** Shrops

167 J7 **Hobkirk** Border
150 F4 **Hobson** Dur
102 A8 **Hoby** Leics
92 C2 **Hockering** Norfk
102 B2 **Hockerton** Notts
46 D2 **Hockley** Essex
85 L8 **Hockley Heath** Solhll
58 F3 **Hockliffe** C Beds
91 G6 **Hockwold cum Wilton** Norfk
25 G7 **Hockworthy** Devon
60 B6 **Hoddesdon** Herts
121 L6 **Hoddlesden** Bl w D
155 L7 **Hoddom Cross** D & G
155 K7 **Hoddom Mains** D & G
49 H7 **Hodgeston** Pembks
98 E6 **Hodnet** Shrops
115 L4 **Hodsock** Notts
45 L7 **Hodsoll Street** Kent
40 D4 **Hodson** Swindn
115 K6 **Hodthorpe** Derbys
92 B1 **Hoe** Norfk
34 D4 **Hogben's Hill** Kent
58 D3 **Hoggeston** Bucks
86 B5 **Hoggrill's End** Warwks
121 J5 **Hoghton** Lancs
100 E3 **Hognaston** Derbys
119 H6 **Hogsthorpe** Lincs
104 B7 **Holbeach** Lincs
104 B6 **Holbeach Bank** Lincs
104 B6 **Holbeach Clough** Lincs
89 K2 **Holbeach Drove** Lincs
104 C6 **Holbeach Hurn** Lincs
104 B8 **Holbeach St Johns** Lincs
104 C6 **Holbeach St Mark's** Lincs
104 C6 **Holbeach St Matthew** Lincs
115 K6 **Holbeck** Notts
71 H3 **Holberrow Green** Worcs
6 F5 **Holbeton** Devon
44 F4 **Holborn** Gt Lon
101 G4 **Holbrook** Derbys
78 E6 **Holbrook** Suffk
86 D6 **Holbrooks** Covtry
16 E2 **Holbury** Hants
12 B7 **Holcombe** Devon
26 F2 **Holcombe** Somset
25 G7 **Holcombe Rogus** Devon
73 L1 **Holcot** Nhants
122 B1 **Holden** Lancs
73 K2 **Holdenby** Nhants
61 G3 **Holder's Green** Essex
83 L5 **Holdgate** Shrops
103 H3 **Holdingham** Lincs
13 J2 **Holditch** Dorset
10 B4 **Holemoor** Devon
25 J3 **Holford** Somset
124 E1 **Holgate** C York
129 H4 **Holker** Cumb
105 L4 **Holkham** Norfk
105 L4 **Holkham Hall** Norfk
9 K4 **Hollacombe** Devon
103 L3 **Holland Fen** Lincs
62 E5 **Holland-on-Sea** Essex
234 e3 **Hollandstoun** Ork
148 A2 **Hollee** D & G
79 H5 **Hollesley** Suffk
7 K4 **Hollicombe** Torbay
33 L3 **Hollingbourne** Kent
19 J4 **Hollingbury** Br & H
58 E3 **Hollingdon** Bucks
100 E5 **Hollington** Derbys
100 B5 **Hollington** Staffs
114 A3 **Hollingworth** Tamesd
114 B7 **Hollinsclough** Staffs
115 G5 **Hollins End** Sheff
113 G4 **Hollins Green** Warrtn
84 C2 **Hollinswood** Wrekin
113 K2 **Hollinwood Crematorium** Oldham
10 F3 **Hollocombe** Devon

100 F2 **Holloway** Derbys
44 F3 **Holloway** Gt Lon
73 K1 **Hollowell** Nhants
112 C7 **Hollowmoor Heath** Ches W
156 C6 **Hollows** D & G
53 J7 **Hollybush** Caerph
163 K6 **Hollybush** E Ayrs
70 D6 **Hollybush** Herefs
70 F6 **Holly Green** Worcs
127 H5 **Hollym** E R Yk
114 C1 **Holmbridge** Kirk
31 J3 **Holmbury St Mary** Surrey
5 G5 **Holmbush** Cnwll
99 K7 **Holmcroft** Staffs
89 H6 **Holme** Cambs
129 L4 **Holme** Cumb
114 C1 **Holme** Kirk
132 E3 **Holme** N York
102 D2 **Holme** Notts
122 C5 **Holme Chapel** Lancs
124 E3 **Holme Green** N York
91 K3 **Holme Hale** Norfk
69 L7 **Holme Lacy** Herefs
69 G4 **Holme Marsh** Herefs
105 H4 **Holme next the Sea** Norfk
126 B2 **Holme on the Wolds** E R Yk
101 L5 **Holme Pierrepont** Notts
69 K6 **Holmer** Herefs
42 E2 **Holmer Green** Bucks
147 J5 **Holme St Cuthbert** Cumb
113 H7 **Holmes Chapel** Ches E
114 F6 **Holmesfield** Derbys
120 F6 **Holmeswood** Lancs
32 B3 **Holmethorpe** Surrey
125 J3 **Holme upon Spalding Moor** E R Yk
115 H7 **Holmewood** Derbys
123 H8 **Holmfirth** Kirk
164 B5 **Holmhead** E Ayrs
127 J5 **Holmpton** E R Yk
136 E7 **Holmrook** Cumb
163 J2 **Holmsford Bridge Crematorium** N Ayrs
150 F5 **Holmside** Dur
7 G3 **Holne** Devon
14 C1 **Holnest** Dorset
24 E3 **Holnicote** Somset
9 J4 **Holsworthy** Devon
9 K3 **Holsworthy Beacon** Devon
15 J2 **Holt** Dorset
106 C5 **Holt** Norfk
39 K7 **Holt** Wilts
70 E3 **Holt** Worcs
98 B2 **Holt** Wrexhm
133 K8 **Holtby** C York
71 J1 **Holt End** Worcs
70 E2 **Holt Heath** Worcs
57 L6 **Holton** Oxon
27 G6 **Holton** Somset
93 J7 **Holton** Suffk
117 J5 **Holton cum Beckering** Lincs
118 C2 **Holton le Clay** Lincs
117 H3 **Holton le Moor** Lincs
78 C6 **Holton St Mary** Suffk
14 D1 **Holwell** Dorset
59 K2 **Holwell** Herts
102 B7 **Holwell** Leics
56 E6 **Holwell** Oxon
139 K2 **Holwick** Dur
30 B4 **Holybourne** Hants
108 C5 **Holyhead** IoA
108 C5 **Holy Island** IoA
169 H2 **Holy Island** Nthumb
169 H2 **Holy Island** Nthumb
115 G7 **Holymoorside** Derbys
42 E5 **Holyport** W & M
158 B2 **Holystone** Nthumb

175 K6 **Holytown** N Lans
59 G5 **Holywell** C Beds
75 L1 **Holywell** Cambs
4 B4 **Holywell** Cnwll
14 B2 **Holywell** Dorset
111 G6 **Holywell** Flints
123 G6 **Holywell Green** Calder
25 H7 **Holywell Lake** Somset
91 G7 **Holywell Row** Suffk
155 G6 **Holywood** D & G
155 G6 **Holywood Village** D & G
84 B3 **Homer** Shrops
111 K2 **Homer Green** Sefton
93 G6 **Homersfield** Suffk
28 C6 **Homington** Wilts
71 K5 **Honeybourne** Worcs
10 F4 **Honeychurch** Devon
40 C7 **Honeystreet** Wilts
77 L7 **Honey Tye** Suffk
86 B8 **Honiley** Warwks
107 G6 **Honing** Norfk
92 D2 **Honingham** Norfk
102 F4 **Honington** Lincs
91 K8 **Honington** Suffk
72 C6 **Honington** Warwks
12 F3 **Honiton** Devon
123 H7 **Honley** Kirk
45 G5 **Honor Oak Crematorium** Gt Lon
6 D5 **Hooe** C Plym
20 E4 **Hooe** E Susx
113 G5 **Hoo Green** Ches E
120 D3 **Hoohill** Bpool
125 H5 **Hook** E R Yk
44 D7 **Hook** Gt Lon
30 B1 **Hook** Hants
49 G5 **Hook** Pembks
40 B4 **Hook** Wilts
14 A3 **Hooke** Dorset
33 H6 **Hook Green** Kent
45 L6 **Hook Green** Kent
57 G2 **Hook Norton** Oxon
11 K5 **Hookway** Devon
32 B3 **Hooley** Surrey
46 C5 **Hoo St Werburgh** Medway
115 K3 **Hooton Levitt** Rothm
124 D8 **Hooton Pagnell** Donc
115 J3 **Hooton Roberts** Rothm
114 D5 **Hope** Derbys
7 G7 **Hope** Devon
97 L2 **Hope** Flints
83 L8 **Hope** Shrops
100 C2 **Hope** Staffs
83 J5 **Hope Bowdler** Shrops
166 D6 **Hopehouse** Border
214 E1 **Hopeman** Moray
54 F4 **Hope Mansell** Herefs
83 H6 **Hopesay** Shrops
69 K4 **Hope under Dinmore** Herefs
133 K8 **Hopgrove** C York
132 F7 **Hopperton** N York
84 D5 **Hopstone** Shrops
100 E2 **Hopton** Derbys
99 L7 **Hopton** Staffs
92 B7 **Hopton** Suffk
83 K7 **Hopton Cangeford** Shrops
83 G7 **Hopton Castle** Shrops
83 H7 **Hoptonheath** Shrops
93 L4 **Hopton on Sea** Norfk
84 B7 **Hopton Wafers** Shrops
85 L3 **Hopwas** Staffs
85 J7 **Hopwood** Worcs
85 J8 **Hopwood Park Services** Worcs
20 C3 **Horam** E Susx
103 J5 **Horbling** Lincs
123 K6 **Horbury** Wakefd
151 K6 **Horden** Dur
16 C4 **Hordle** Hants

98 B6 **Hordley** Shrops
38 E5 **Horfield** Bristl
92 E8 **Horham** Suffk
62 B3 **Horkesley Heath** Essex
126 B6 **Horkstow** N Linc
72 E5 **Horley** Oxon
32 B5 **Horley** Surrey
26 E5 **Hornblotton Green** Somset
130 B5 **Hornby** Lancs
132 C2 **Hornby** N York
141 J6 **Hornby** N York
118 C7 **Horncastle** Lincs
45 K3 **Hornchurch** Gt Lon
179 J7 **Horncliffe** Nthumb
179 J8 **Horndean** Border
30 B8 **Horndean** Hants
10 D8 **Horndon** Devon
46 A4 **Horndon on the Hill** Thurr
32 C4 **Horne** Surrey
24 D3 **Horner** Somset
107 H8 **Horning** Norfk
88 B4 **Horninghold** Leics
100 E7 **Horninglow** Staffs
76 C3 **Horningsea** Cambs
27 J3 **Horningsham** Wilts
105 M7 **Horningtoft** Norfk
22 F6 **Horns Cross** Devon
126 F2 **Hornsea** E R Yk
44 F3 **Hornsey** Gt Lon
72 E5 **Hornton** Oxon
235 d2 **Horra** Shet
6 D2 **Horrabridge** Devon
7 H2 **Horridge** Devon
77 J3 **Horringer** Suffk
121 L2 **Horrocksford** Lancs
6 B2 **Horsebridge** Devon
20 C4 **Horsebridge** E Susx
29 G5 **Horsebridge** Hants
83 G3 **Horsebridge** Shrops
84 C3 **Horsehay** Wrekin
76 E5 **Horseheath** Cambs
131 K4 **Horsehouse** N York
43 G8 **Horsell** Surrey
98 C4 **Horseman's Green** Wrexhm
107 K7 **Horsey** Norfk
25 L4 **Horsey** Somset
92 E1 **Horsford** Norfk
123 J3 **Horsforth** Leeds
31 K5 **Horsham** W Susx
70 D3 **Horsham** Worcs
92 E1 **Horsham St Faith** Norfk
117 K7 **Horsington** Lincs
27 G6 **Horsington** Somset
101 G4 **Horsley** Derbys
39 J2 **Horsley** Gloucs
150 D2 **Horsley** Nthumb
157 L3 **Horsley** Nthumb
62 D3 **Horsleycross Street** Essex
167 H5 **Horsleyhill** Border
101 H4 **Horsley Woodhouse** Derbys
33 J5 **Horsmonden** Kent
57 L6 **Horspath** Oxon
106 F8 **Horstead** Norfk
32 C7 **Horsted Keynes** W Susx
58 F4 **Horton** Bucks
15 J2 **Horton** Dorset
122 C1 **Horton** Lancs
74 B4 **Horton** Nhants
39 H4 **Horton** S Glos
25 L7 **Horton** Somset
99 L2 **Horton** Staffs
50 F7 **Horton** Swans
43 G5 **Horton** W & M
40 B7 **Horton** Wilts
84 C1 **Horton** Wrekin
57 L5 **Horton-cum-Studley** Oxon
98 C3 **Horton Green** Ches W

130 F5 **Horton in Ribblesdale** N York
45 K6 **Horton Kirby** Kent
121 J7 **Horwich** Bolton
23 H6 **Horwood** Devon
166 F6 **Hoscote** Border
102 B6 **Hose** Leics
185 H3 **Hosh** P & K
235 C7 **Hoswick** Shet
125 L4 **Hotham** E R Yk
34 C5 **Hothfield** Kent
101 L7 **Hoton** Leics
157 K5 **Hott** Nthumb
99 G3 **Hough** Ches E
102 E4 **Hougham** Lincs
112 C4 **Hough Green** Halton
102 F3 **Hough-on-the-Hill** Lincs
75 K1 **Houghton** Cambs
29 G5 **Houghton** Hants
49 G6 **Houghton** Pembks
18 D4 **Houghton** W Susx
74 F6 **Houghton Conquest** C Beds
21 H2 **Houghton Green** E Susx
151 H5 **Houghton-le-Spring** Sundld
87 J3 **Houghton on the Hill** Leics
59 G4 **Houghton Regis** C Beds
105 L5 **Houghton St Giles** Norfk
42 B8 **Hound Green** Hants
178 D8 **Houndslow** Border
179 H5 **Houndwood** Border
43 J5 **Hounslow** Gt Lon
213 L4 **Househill** Highld
123 J6 **Houses Hill** Kirk
149 K2 **Housesteads Roman Fort** Nthumb
207 G1 **Housieside** Abers
174 D5 **Houston** Rens
227 K2 **Houstry** Highld
234 b6 **Houton** Ork
19 J5 **Hove** Br & H
102 B3 **Hoveringham** Notts
107 G8 **Hoveton** Norfk
133 K4 **Hovingham** N York
54 E3 **How Caple** Herefs
125 H5 **Howden** E R Yk
150 E7 **Howden-le-Wear** Dur
231 K3 **Howe** Highld
132 E4 **Howe** N York
92 F4 **Howe** Norfk
112 F2 **Howe Bridge Crematorium** Wigan
61 J7 **Howe Green** Essex
61 K7 **Howegreen** Essex
103 J4 **Howell** Lincs
216 E5 **Howe of Teuchar** Abers
147 L2 **Howes** D & G
61 H5 **Howe Street** Essex
77 G7 **Howe Street** Essex
68 B3 **Howey** Powys
136 D3 **Howgate** Cumb
177 H6 **Howgate** Mdloth
169 K5 **Howick** Nthumb
140 D3 **Howle** Dur
99 G7 **Howle** Wrekin
54 E4 **Howle Hill** Herefs
76 E7 **Howlett End** Essex
13 H1 **Howley** Somset
148 E4 **How Mill** Cumb
233 b7 **Howmore** W Isls
168 B5 **Hownam** Border
117 H2 **Howsham** N Linc
133 L6 **Howsham** N York
168 D3 **Howtel** Nthumb
174 D6 **Howwood** Rens
92 E7 **Hoxne** Suffk
234 b7 **Hoy** Ork
111 H4 **Hoylake** Wirral

115 G2 **Hoyland Nether** Barns
114 E1 **Hoyland Swaine** Barns
48 E6 **Hubberston** Pembks
123 K2 **Huby** N York
133 J6 **Huby** N York
55 K4 **Hucclecote** Gloucs
33 L2 **Hucking** Kent
101 K3 **Hucknall** Notts
123 H7 **Huddersfield** Kirk
123 H6 **Huddersfield Crematorium** Kirk
71 G3 **Huddington** Worcs
140 E7 **Hudswell** N York
134 D7 **Huggate** E R Yk
42 E2 **Hughenden Valley** Bucks
83 L4 **Hughley** Shrops
2 b2 **Hugh Town** IoS
10 D3 **Huish** Devon
40 C7 **Huish** Wilts
25 G5 **Huish Champflower** Somset
26 B6 **Huish Episcopi** Somset
58 D5 **Hulcott** Bucks
12 C5 **Hulham** Devon
100 E3 **Hulland** Derbys
100 E3 **Hulland Ward** Derbys
39 K4 **Hullavington** Wilts
46 D2 **Hullbridge** Essex
113 J3 **Hulme** Manch
99 L4 **Hulme** Staffs
112 E4 **Hulme** Warrtn
100 C2 **Hulme End** Staffs
113 J7 **Hulme Walfield** Ches E
16 E5 **Hulverstone** IoW
93 K6 **Hulver Street** Suffk
126 D7 *Humberside Airport* N Linc
118 D1 **Humberston** NE Lin
87 J3 **Humberstone** C Leic
178 B5 **Humbie** E Loth
126 F4 **Humbleton** E R Yk
103 G6 **Humby** Lincs
167 L2 **Hume** Border
158 A7 **Humshaugh** Nthumb
231 L2 **Huna** Highld
87 G4 **Huncote** Leics
167 K5 **Hundalee** Border
140 C3 **Hunderthwaite** Dur
118 E7 **Hundleby** Lincs
49 G7 **Hundleton** Pembks
77 G5 **Hundon** Suffk
120 F6 **Hundred End** Lancs
68 C4 **Hundred House** Powys
87 K3 **Hungarton** Leics
25 G4 **Hungerford** Somset
41 G6 **Hungerford** W Berk
41 G6 **Hungerford Newtown** W Berk
69 J7 **Hungerstone** Herefs
135 H4 **Hunmanby** N York
72 D2 **Hunningham** Warwks
73 K3 **Hunsbury Hill** Nhants
60 C5 **Hunsdon** Herts
132 F8 **Hunsingore** N York
123 L4 **Hunslet** Leeds
149 L2 **Hunsonby** Cumb
105 G4 **Hunstanton** Norfk
150 B5 **Hunstanworth** Dur
99 G4 **Hunsterson** Ches E
77 L2 **Hunston** Suffk
18 B5 **Hunston** W Susx
38 F7 **Hunstrete** BaNES
123 J5 **Hunsworth** Kirk
173 K3 **Hunter's Quay** Ag & B
25 M6 **Huntham** Somset
196 D3 **Hunthill Lodge** Angus
89 J8 **Huntingdon** Cambs
93 G8 **Huntingfield** Suffk
133 J7 **Huntington** C York
112 B8 **Huntington** Ches W

178 B4 **Huntington** E Loth
68 E4 **Huntington** Herefs
85 H2 **Huntington** Staffs
55 G4 **Huntley** Gloucs
215 L6 **Huntly** Abers
33 J4 **Hunton** Kent
132 B2 **Hunton** N York
24 E3 **Huntscott** Somset
24 F7 **Huntsham** Devon
23 H6 **Huntshaw** Devon
25 L3 **Huntspill** Somset
25 K5 **Huntstile** Somset
25 L4 **Huntworth** Somset
140 F2 **Hunwick** Dur
106 C5 **Hunworth** Norfk
28 D5 **Hurdcott** Wilts
113 L6 **Hurdsfield** Ches E
42 D4 **Hurley** W & M
86 B4 **Hurley** Warwks
86 B4 **Hurley Common** Warwks
163 L3 **Hurlford** E Ayrs
15 L3 **Hurn** Dorset
29 H6 **Hursley** Hants
42 C5 **Hurst** Wokham
29 H3 **Hurstbourne Priors** Hants
29 G2 **Hurstbourne Tarrant** Hants
33 J7 **Hurst Green** E Susx
62 C5 **Hurst Green** Essex
121 K3 **Hurst Green** Lancs
32 D3 **Hurst Green** Surrey
19 J3 **Hurstpierpoint** W Susx
122 C4 **Hurstwood** Lancs
234 C6 **Hurtiso** Ork
141 H5 **Hurworth-on-Tees** Darltn
141 H5 **Hurworth Place** Darltn
87 J6 **Husbands Bosworth** Leics
74 D7 **Husborne Crawley** C Beds
133 H4 **Husthwaite** N York
115 G5 **Hutcliffe Wood Crematorium** Sheff
101 J2 **Huthwaite** Notts
119 G6 **Huttoft** Lincs
179 J7 **Hutton** Border
134 F8 **Hutton** E R Yk
45 M2 **Hutton** Essex
121 G5 **Hutton** Lancs
37 M8 **Hutton** N Som
141 H7 **Hutton Bonville** N York
134 F3 **Hutton Buscel** N York
132 E5 **Hutton Conyers** N York
126 C1 **Hutton Cranswick** E R Yk
148 D7 **Hutton End** Cumb
151 K7 **Hutton Henry** Dur
133 L2 **Hutton-le-Hole** N York
142 D4 **Hutton Lowcross** R & Cl
140 E5 **Hutton Magna** Dur
130 B4 **Hutton Roof** Cumb
148 C7 **Hutton Roof** Cumb
141 K6 **Hutton Rudby** N York
133 G4 **Hutton Sessay** N York
124 D1 **Hutton Wandesley** N York
12 B3 **Huxham** Devon
98 D1 **Huxley** Ches W
112 C4 **Huyton** Knows
128 D2 **Hycemoor** Cumb
113 L3 **Hyde** Tamesd
58 F7 **Hyde Heath** Bucks
99 K8 **Hyde Lea** Staffs
165 H2 **Hyndford Bridge** S Lans
188 C8 **Hynish** Ag & B
82 F5 **Hyssington** Powys

16 E2 **Hythe** Hants
34 F7 **Hythe** Kent
43 G6 **Hythe End** W & M

I

14 E2 **Ibberton** Dorset
100 E2 **Ible** Derbys
15 L1 **Ibsley** Hants
86 E2 **Ibstock** Leics
42 C2 **Ibstone** Bucks
29 G2 **Ibthorpe** Hants
143 H5 **Iburndale** N York
29 K1 **Ibworth** Hants
91 J4 **Ickburgh** Norfk
43 H3 **Ickenham** Gt Lon
57 M6 **Ickford** Bucks
35 G3 **Ickham** Kent
59 K2 **Ickleford** Herts
21 H3 **Icklesham** E Susx
76 C5 **Ickleton** Cambs
91 H3 **Icklingham** Suffk
122 E2 **Ickornshaw** N York
75 G5 **Ickwell Green** C Beds
77 J3 **Ickworth** Suffk
56 E4 **Icomb** Gloucs
56 E4 **Idbury** Oxon
10 E3 **Iddesleigh** Devon
11 K6 **Ide** Devon
7 K1 **Ideford** Devon
32 E3 **Ide Hill** Kent
21 H2 **Iden** E Susx
33 J5 **Iden Green** Kent
33 K6 **Iden Green** Kent
123 H3 **Idle** C Brad
4 C6 **Idless** Cnwll
72 C5 **Idlicote** Warwks
28 D4 **Idmiston** Wilts
50 E3 **Idole** Carmth
100 F3 **Idridgehay** Derbys
208 F2 **Idrigill** Highld
40 E4 **Idstone** Oxon
57 K7 **Iffley** Oxon
31 L4 **Ifield** W Susx
31 G5 **Ifold** W Susx
15 L4 **Iford** Bmouth
19 L4 **Iford** E Susx
38 C3 **Ifton** Mons
98 E5 **Ightfield** Shrops
33 G2 **Ightham** Kent
79 J4 **Iken** Suffk
100 C3 **Ilam** Staffs
26 D6 **Ilchester** Somset
168 F5 **Ilderton** Nthumb
45 H3 **Ilford** Gt Lon
26 A7 **Ilford** Somset
23 H2 **Ilfracombe** Devon
101 J4 **Ilkeston** Derbys
93 H6 **Ilketshall St Andrew** Suffk
93 H6 **Ilketshall St Margaret** Suffk
123 G2 **Ilkley** C Brad
5 L1 **Illand** Cnwll
85 H7 **Illey** Dudley
3 H3 **Illogan** Cnwll
87 K4 **Illston on the Hill** Leics
58 C6 **Ilmer** Bucks
72 B5 **Ilmington** Warwks
26 A8 **Ilminster** Somset
7 H2 **Ilsington** Devon
51 H7 **Ilston** Swans
132 B4 **Ilton** N York
25 M7 **Ilton** Somset
161 L2 **Imachar** N Ayrs
126 F7 **Immingham** NF Lin
126 F7 **Immingham Dock** NE Lin
76 C2 **Impington** Cambs
112 C6 **Ince** Ches W
111 K2 **Ince Blundell** Sefton
112 E1 **Ince-in-Makerfield** Wigan

221 K7 **Inchbae Lodge Hotel** Highld
196 F4 **Inchbare** Angus
215 G4 **Inchberry** Moray
211 G3 **Incheril** Highld
174 E5 **Inchinnan** Rens
201 J5 **Inchlaggan** Highld
186 D3 **Inchmichael** P & K
202 B3 **Inchnacardoch Hotel** Highld
224 F4 **Inchnadamph** Highld
186 D2 **Inchture** P & K
211 K6 **Inchvuilt** Highld
186 C4 **Inchyra** P & K
4 E4 **Indian Queens** Cnwll
61 G7 **Ingatestone** Essex
114 E1 **Ingbirchworth** Barns
99 L7 **Ingestre** Staffs
116 F5 **Ingham** Lincs
107 H7 **Ingham** Norfk
77 J1 **Ingham** Suffk
107 H6 **Ingham Corner** Norfk
101 G6 **Ingleby** Derbys
141 K6 **Ingleby Arncliffe** N York
141 K4 **Ingleby Barwick** S on T
142 C6 **Ingleby Greenhow** N York
10 E4 **Ingleigh Green** Devon
39 G7 **Inglesbatch** BaNES
56 D7 **Inglesham** Swindn
147 G2 **Ingleston** D & G
140 F3 **Ingleton** Dur
130 D5 **Ingleton** N York
121 H3 **Inglewhite** Lancs
158 C7 **Ingoe** Nthumb
121 G4 **Ingol** Lancs
105 G6 **Ingoldisthorpe** Norfk
119 H7 **Ingoldmells** Lincs
103 G6 **Ingoldsby** Lincs
168 F6 **Ingram** Nthumb
45 M2 **Ingrave** Essex
122 F3 **Ingrow** C Brad
138 C7 **Ings** Cumb
38 E3 **Ingst** S Glos
88 E2 **Ingthorpe** Rutlnd
106 E6 **Ingworth** Norfk
71 H3 **Inkberrow** Worcs
217 H6 **Inkhorn** Abers
41 G7 **Inkpen** W Berk
231 J2 **Inkstack** Highld
173 K4 **Innellan** Ag & B
166 E3 **Innerleithen** Border
186 F7 **Innerleven** Fife
144 C3 **Innermessan** D & G
178 F4 **Innerwick** E Loth
215 G2 **Innesmill** Moray
216 C8 **Insch** Abers
203 J5 **Insh** Highld
120 F3 **Inskip** Lancs
23 G5 **Instow** Devon
115 H5 **Intake** Sheff
204 F6 **Inver** Abers
223 J5 **Inver** Highld
194 F7 **Inver** P & K
190 F1 **Inverailort** Highld
210 C3 **Inveralligin** Highld
217 K2 **Inverallochy** Abers
222 D2 **Inveran** Highld
182 F5 **Inveraray** Ag & B
209 J7 **Inverarish** Highld
196 D7 **Inverarity** Angus
183 K4 **Inverarnan** Stirlg
219 J4 **Inverasdale** Highld
182 E2 **Inverawe** Ag & B
183 K7 **Inverbeg** Ag & B
197 K2 **Inverbervie** Abers
216 C2 **Inver-boyndie** Abers
191 K6 **Invercreran House Hotel** Ag & B
203 L3 **Inverdruie** Highld
177 K4 **Inveresk** E Loth
182 E1 **Inveresragan** Ag & B
219 K5 **Inverewe Garden** Highld

204 D7 **Inverey** Abers
202 D2 **Inverfarigaig** Highld
191 J7 **Inverfolla** Ag & B
201 L5 **Invergarry** Highld
184 F2 **Invergeldie** P & K
201 K7 **Invergloy** Highld
222 F7 **Invergordon** Highld
186 F2 **Invergowrie** P & K
200 B4 **Inverguseran** Highld
193 L5 **Inverhadden** P & K
183 L3 **Inverherive Hotel** Stirlg
200 B5 **Inverie** Highld
182 E4 **Inverinan** Ag & B
200 E2 **Inverinate** Highld
197 G6 **Inverkeilor** Angus
176 F2 **Inverkeithing** Fife
216 C5 **Inverkeithny** Abers
173 L4 **Inverkip** Inver
224 C4 **Inverkirkaig** Highld
220 F4 **Inverlael** Highld
192 E1 **Inverlair** Highld
182 C6 **Inverliever Lodge** Ag & B
183 H2 **Inverlochy** Ag & B
196 D1 **Invermark** Angus
215 J6 **Invermarkie** Abers
202 C3 **Invermoriston** Highld
229 L4 **Invernaver** Highld
213 G5 **Inverness** Highld
212 F5 **Inverness Crematorium** Highld
213 J4 *Inverness Dalcross Airport* Highld
183 G7 **Invernoaden** Ag & B
192 D7 **Inveroran Hotel** Ag & B
196 C5 **Inverquharity** Angus
217 J5 **Inverquhomery** Abers
201 K8 **Inverroy** Highld
191 J4 **Inversanda** Highld
200 E2 **Invershiel** Highld
222 D3 **Invershin** Highld
231 J8 **Invershore** Highld
183 K5 **Inversnaid Hotel** Stirlg
217 L5 **Inverugie** Abers
185 K5 **Inveruglas** Ag & B
203 J5 **Inveruglass** Highld
206 E2 **Inverurie** Abers
10 E5 **Inwardleigh** Devon
61 L4 **Inworth** Essex
233 b7 **Iochdar** W Isls
180 D3 **Iona** Ag & B
30 D6 **Iping** W Susx
7 J3 **Ippleden** Devon
41 M4 **Ipsden** Oxon
100 A3 **Ipstones** Staffs
78 E5 **Ipswich** Suffk
78 E5 **Ipswich Crematorium** Suffk
111 J5 **Irby** Wirral
118 F8 **Irby in the Marsh** Lincs
117 K1 **Irby upon Humber** NE Lin
74 D2 **Irchester** Nhants
147 M7 **Ireby** Cumb
130 C4 **Ireby** Lancs
128 F4 **Ireleth** Cumb
149 L7 **Ireshopeburn** Dur
100 F3 **Ireton Wood** Derbys
113 G3 **Irlam** Salfd
103 G7 **Irnham** Lincs
39 G4 **Iron Acton** S Glos
84 C3 **Ironbridge** Wrekin
84 C3 **Ironbridge Gorge Museums** Wrekin
154 B6 **Ironmacannie** D & G
101 H3 **Ironville** Derbys
107 H7 **Irstead** Norfk
148 E3 **Irthington** Cumb
74 D1 **Irthlingborough** Nhants
134 F3 **Irton** N York

163 H2 **Irvine** N Ayrs
163 H2 **Irvine Maritime Centre** N Ayrs
230 E3 **Isauld** Highld
235 C2 **Isbister** Shet
235 d4 **Isbister** Shet
19 L3 **Isfield** E Susx
88 C8 **Isham** Nhants
30 C3 **Isington** Hants
171 G4 **Islay** Ag & B
170 F7 *Islay Airport* Ag & B
26 A7 **Isle Abbotts** Somset
26 A7 **Isle Brewers** Somset
90 F8 **Isleham** Cambs
45 G4 **Isle of Dogs** Gt Lon
46 E5 **Isle of Grain** Medway
232 f2 **Isle of Lewis** W Isls
237 c4 **Isle of Man** IoM
237 b7 *Isle of Man Ronaldsway Airport* IoM
181 J1 **Isle of Mull** Ag & B
15 J5 **Isle of Purbeck** Dorset
46 F6 **Isle of Sheppey** Kent
208 F6 **Isle of Skye** Highld
35 J2 **Isle of Thanet** Kent
128 E6 **Isle of Walney** Cumb
145 K7 **Isle of Whithorn** D & G
17 G5 **Isle of Wight** IoW
17 G4 **Isle of Wight Crematorium** IoW
199 L3 **Isleornsay** Highld
2 b2 *Isles of Scilly St Mary's Airport* IoS
155 G7 **Islesteps** D & G
44 D5 **Isleworth** Gt Lon
101 H7 **Isley Walton** Leics
232 d3 **Islibhig** W Isls
44 F3 **Islington** Gt Lon
44 F2 **Islington Crematorium** Gt Lon
88 E7 **Islip** Nhants
57 K5 **Islip** Oxon
232 d3 **Islivig** W Isls
83 L2 **Isombridge** Wrekin
29 K5 **Itchen Abbas** Hants
29 K5 **Itchen Stoke** Hants
31 J5 **Itchingfield** W Susx
106 D6 **Itteringham** Norfk
11 G5 **Itton** Devon
38 C2 **Itton** Mons
38 C2 **Itton Common** Mons
148 D6 **Ivegill** Cumb
43 G4 **Iver** Bucks
43 G4 **Iver Heath** Bucks
150 E5 **Iveston** Dur
58 F5 **Ivinghoe** Bucks
58 F4 **Ivinghoe Aston** Bucks
69 J3 **Ivington** Herefs
6 F5 **Ivybridge** Devon
21 K1 **Ivychurch** Kent
33 G3 **Ivy Hatch** Kent
46 E6 **Iwade** Kent
27 K8 **Iwerne Courtney or Shroton** Dorset
27 K8 **Iwerne Minster** Dorset
77 L1 **Ixworth** Suffk
91 K8 **Ixworth Thorpe** Suffk

J
12 C4 **Jack-in-the-Green** Devon
175 G7 **Jackton** S Lans
9 G5 **Jacobstow** Cnwll
10 E4 **Jacobstowe** Devon
49 H7 **Jameston** Pembks
212 D3 **Jamestown** Highld
174 D3 **Jamestown** W Duns
227 L3 **Janetstown** Highld
231 L5 **Janets-town** Highld
155 J5 **Jardine Hall** D & G

151 H3 **Jarrow** S Tyne
61 H3 **Jasper's Green** Essex
175 L4 **Jawcraig** Falk
62 D5 **Jaywick** Essex
167 K5 **Jedburgh** Border
49 J6 **Jeffreyston** Pembks
213 H2 **Jemimaville** Highld
236 d4 **Jerbourg** Guern
236 b7 *Jersey Airport* Jersey
236 c7 **Jersey Crematorium** Jersey
151 G2 **Jesmond** N u Ty
20 B5 **Jevington** E Susx
59 H5 **Jockey End** Herts
148 D7 **Johnby** Cumb
112 B5 *John Lennon Airport* Lpool
231 L2 **John o' Groats** Highld
197 J3 **Johnshaven** Abers
48 F5 **Johnston** Pembks
155 M3 **Johnstone** D & G
174 D5 **Johnstone** Rens
155 J4 **Johnstonebridge** D & G
50 E2 **Johnstown** Carmth
97 L4 **Johnstown** Wrexhm
177 J4 **Joppa** C Edin
66 D2 **Joppa** Cerdgn
163 K5 **Joppa** S Ayrs
64 C7 **Jordanston** Pembks
45 K5 **Joyden's Wood** Kent
150 B3 **Juniper** Nthumb
177 G5 **Juniper Green** C Edin
171 J2 **Jura** Ag & B
237 c2 **Jurby** IoM

K
139 H5 **Kaber** Cumb
165 J1 **Kaimend** S Lans
173 G4 **Kames** Ag & B
164 D4 **Kames** E Ayrs
4 C7 **Kea** Cnwll
125 K2 **Keadby** N Linc
104 B3 **Keal Cotes** Lincs
113 H1 **Kearsley** Bolton
158 C6 **Kearsley** Nthumb
35 H6 **Kearsney** Kent
130 B4 **Kearstwick** Cumb
77 G5 **Kedington** Suffk
100 F4 **Kedleston** Derbys
126 E8 **Keelby** Lincs
99 J4 **Keele** Staffs
99 J4 **Keele Services** Staffs
123 G4 **Keelham** C Brad
48 F4 **Keeston** Pembks
39 L8 **Keevil** Wilts
101 J7 **Kegworth** Leics
3 G3 **Kehelland** Cnwll
206 B2 **Keig** Abers
122 F3 **Keighley** C Brad
122 F3 **Keighley Crematorium** C Brad
185 J8 **Keilarsbrae** Clacks
185 K3 **Keillour** P & K
204 E6 **Keiloch** Abers
171 K5 **Keils** Ag & B
26 D5 **Keinton Mandeville** Somset
154 E4 **Keir Mill** D & G
139 G3 **Keisley** Cumb
231 L4 **Keiss** Highld
215 J4 **Keith** Moray
195 K8 **Keithick** P & K
196 F4 **Keithock** Angus
212 E3 **Keithtown** Highld
122 D2 **Kelbrook** Lancs
173 L6 **Kelburn** N Ayrs
103 G4 **Kelby** Lincs
139 K6 **Keld** N York
124 F3 **Kelfield** N York
102 C2 **Kelham** Notts
147 K2 **Kelhead** D & G
120 E5 **Kellamergh** Lancs
187 G1 **Kellas** Angus

214 E4 **Kellas** Moray
7 J7 **Kellaton** Devon
106 C4 **Kelling** Norfk
124 E5 **Kellington** N York
151 J7 **Kelloe** Dur
164 E6 **Kelloholm** D & G
9 K8 **Kelly** Devon
87 K7 **Kelmarsh** Nhants
56 E7 **Kelmscott** Oxon
79 H2 **Kelsale** Suffk
112 D7 **Kelsall** Ches W
75 K7 **Kelshall** Herts
147 L5 **Kelsick** Cumb
167 L3 **Kelso** Border
115 G8 **Kelstedge** Derbys
118 C4 **Kelstern** Lincs
39 G6 **Kelston** BaNES
194 B6 **Keltneyburn** P & K
155 H7 **Kelton** D & G
186 B8 **Kelty** Fife
61 K4 **Kelvedon** Essex
60 F7 **Kelvedon Hatch** Essex
2 C5 **Kelynack** Cnwll
187 G4 **Kemback** Fife
84 D3 **Kemberton** Shrops
39 M2 **Kemble** Gloucs
71 G6 **Kemerton** Worcs
53 M6 **Kemeys Commander** Mons
206 E3 **Kemnay** Abers
54 F3 **Kempley** Gloucs
55 G3 **Kempley Green** Gloucs
70 F5 **Kempsey** Worcs
40 D2 **Kempsford** Gloucs
29 L2 **Kempshott** Hants
74 F5 **Kempston** Bed
83 G6 **Kempton** Shrops
19 J5 **Kemp Town** Br & H
32 F2 **Kemsing** Kent
34 C7 **Kenardington** Kent
69 J6 **Kenchester** Herefs
56 E6 **Kencot** Oxon
129 L2 **Kendal** Cumb
36 C4 **Kenfig** Brdgnd
72 C1 **Kenilworth** Warwks
32 B2 **Kenley** Gt Lon
84 C1 **Kenley** Shrops
210 B3 **Kenmore** Highld
194 B7 **Kenmore** P & K
11 L7 **Kenn** Devon
38 B6 **Kenn** N Som
172 D5 **Kennacraig** Ag & B
11 J4 **Kennerleigh** Devon
111 L2 **Kennessee Green** Sefton
176 C1 **Kennet** Clacks
215 L8 **Kennethmont** Abers
77 G2 **Kennett** Cambs
11 L7 **Kennford** Devon
92 C6 **Kenninghall** Norfk
34 D5 **Kennington** Kent
57 K7 **Kennington** Oxon
186 F6 **Kennoway** Fife
25 L7 **Kenny** Somset
90 F7 **Kennyhill** Suffk
134 C6 **Kennythorpe** N York
188 C6 **Kenovay** Ag & B
208 F4 **Kensaleyre** Highld
44 E4 **Kensington** Gt Lon
59 G4 **Kensworth Common** C Beds
191 K5 **Kentallen** Highld
33 G5 **Kent and Sussex Crematorium** Kent
54 B3 **Kentchurch** Herefs
77 G2 **Kentford** Suffk
35 J2 *Kent International Airport* Kent
12 D2 **Kentisbeare** Devon
23 K3 **Kentisbury** Devon
44 F3 **Kentish Town** Gt Lon
138 C6 **Kentmere** Cumb
12 B5 **Kenton** Devon
44 D3 **Kenton** Gt Lon

150 F2 **Kenton** N u Ty
78 E2 **Kenton** Suffk
190 D3 **Kentra** Highld
55 H4 **Kent's Green** Gloucs
28 F6 **Kent's Oak** Hants
4 C6 **Kenwyn** Cnwll
228 F3 **Keoldale** Highld
200 F1 **Keppoch** Highld
133 G2 **Kepwick** N York
86 D6 **Keresley** Covtry
182 B2 **Kerrera** Ag & B
2 D5 **Kerris** Cnwll
82 D5 **Kerry** Powys
173 J6 **Kerrycroy** Ag & B
116 B8 **Kersall** Notts
12 D5 **Kersbrook** Devon
78 B5 **Kersey** Suffk
232 f3 **Kershader** W Isls
12 D2 **Kerswell** Devon
70 F5 **Kerswell Green** Worcs
78 F5 **Kesgrave** Suffk
93 L6 **Kessingland** Suffk
4 F6 **Kestle** Cnwll
4 D4 **Kestle Mill** Cnwll
45 H7 **Keston** Gt Lon
137 J3 **Keswick** Cumb
92 E3 **Keswick** Norfk
118 E6 **Ketsby** Lincs
88 C7 **Kettering** Nhants
88 C7 **Kettering Crematorium** Nhants
92 E3 **Ketteringham** Norfk
195 K8 **Kettins** P & K
77 L4 **Kettlebaston** Suffk
186 E6 **Kettlebridge** Fife
86 B3 **Kettlebrook** Staffs
78 F3 **Kettleburgh** Suffk
155 K6 **Kettleholm** D & G
113 M5 **Kettleshulme** Ches E
132 C7 **Kettlesing** N York
132 C7 **Kettlesing Bottom** N York
106 A6 **Kettlestone** Norfk
116 D6 **Kettlethorpe** Lincs
234 d4 **Kettletoft** Ork
131 H5 **Kettlewell** N York
88 E3 **Ketton** Rutlnd
44 D5 **Kew** Gt Lon
44 D5 **Kew Gardens** Gt Lon
37 M7 **Kewstoke** N Som
125 L1 **Kexby** C York
116 E4 **Kexby** Lincs
113 K8 **Key Green** Ches E
87 J3 **Keyham** Leics
16 C4 **Keyhaven** Hants
127 G5 **Keyingham** E R Yk
19 J3 **Keymer** W Susx
38 F6 **Keynsham** BaNES
74 F3 **Keysoe** Bed
74 F3 **Keysoe Row** Bed
88 F7 **Keyston** Cambs
101 L6 **Keyworth** Notts
151 G4 **Kibblesworth** Gatesd
87 K5 **Kibworth Beauchamp** Leics
87 K5 **Kibworth Harcourt** Leics
45 H5 **Kidbrooke** Gt Lon
84 E7 **Kidderminster** Worcs
57 J5 **Kidlington** Oxon
42 B5 **Kidmore End** Oxon
145 J7 **Kidsdale** D & G
99 J2 **Kidsgrove** Staffs
50 E4 **Kidwelly** Carmth
191 H8 **Kiel Crofts** Ag & B
157 G4 **Kielder** Nthumb
171 H5 **Kiells** Ag & B
199 K4 **Kilbarchan** Rens
8 E4 **Kilbeg** Highld
172 C5 **Kilberry** Ag & B
174 C7 **Kilbirnie** N Ayrs
173 H5 **Kilbride** Ag & B
182 B3 **Kilbride** Ag & B
214 D3 **Kilbuiack** Moray
101 G4 **Kilburn** Derbys

44 E4 **Kilburn** Gt Lon
133 H4 **Kilburn** N York
87 J4 **Kilby** Leics
172 D6 **Kilchamaig** Ag & B
173 J7 **Kilchattan** Ag & B
180 E7 **Kilchattan** Ag & B
191 G8 **Kilcheran** Ag & B
189 L4 **Kilchoan** Highld
170 D5 **Kilchoman** Ag & B
182 E3 **Kilchrenan** Ag & B
187 H6 **Kilconquhar** Fife
55 G3 **Kilcot** Gloucs
212 E4 **Kilcoy** Highld
173 L3 **Kilcreggan** Ag & B
142 D5 **Kildale** N York
161 J5 **Kildalloig** Ag & B
223 G6 **Kildary** Highld
173 G5 **Kildavaig** Ag & B
173 H5 **Kildavanan** Ag & B
227 G4 **Kildonan** Highld
162 D5 **Kildonan** N Ayrs
226 F4 **Kildonan Lodge** Highld
199 G7 **Kildonnan** Highld
144 C4 **Kildrochet House** D & G
205 K2 **Kildrummy** Abers
122 F2 **Kildwick** N York
172 F3 **Kilfinan** Ag & B
201 K6 **Kilfinnan** Highld
49 J6 **Kilgetty** Pembks
152 F2 **Kilgrammie** S Ayrs
38 C2 **Kilgwrrwg Common** Mons
135 G6 **Kilham** E R Yk
188 B7 **Kilkenneth** Ag & B
161 H4 **Kilkenzie** Ag & B
161 J5 **Kilkerran** Ag & B
9 H3 **Kilkhampton** Cnwll
115 J5 **Killamarsh** Derbys
51 H6 **Killay** Swans
174 F2 **Killearn** Stirlg
213 G3 **Killen** Highld
140 F3 **Killerby** Darltn
12 C3 **Killerton** Devon
193 J5 **Killichonan** P & K
192 D1 **Killiechonate** Highld
190 B7 **Killiechronan** Ag & B
194 E4 **Killiecrankie** P & K
210 E7 **Killilan** Highld
231 K4 **Killimster** Highld
184 C2 **Killin** Stirlg
132 D7 **Killinghall** N York
130 C2 **Killington** Cumb
130 B2 *Killington Lake Services* Cumb
159 G7 **Killingworth** N Tyne
167 G1 **Killochyett** Border
174 C4 **Kilmacolm** Inver
184 D5 **Kilmahog** Stirlg
182 A8 **Kilmahumaig** Ag & B
218 C6 **Kilmaluag** Highld
186 F3 **Kilmany** Fife
163 K2 **Kilmarnock** E Ayrs
182 B7 **Kilmartin** Ag & B
163 K2 **Kilmaurs** E Ayrs
182 B5 **Kilmelford** Ag & B
27 G2 **Kilmersdon** Somset
29 L6 **Kilmeston** Hants
161 H5 **Kilmichael** Ag & B
182 B8 **Kilmichael Glassary** Ag & B
172 D2 **Kilmichael of Inverlussa** Ag & B
13 H3 **Kilmington** Devon
27 H4 **Kilmington** Wilts
27 H4 **Kilmington Common** Wilts
27 H4 **Kilmington Street** Wilts
212 D5 **Kilmorack** Highld
182 C3 **Kilmore** Ag & B
199 K4 **Kilmore** Highld
172 C4 **Kilmory** Ag & B
190 B3 **Kilmory** Highld
162 B5 **Kilmory** N Ayrs

208 D5 **Kilmuir** Highld
213 G4 **Kilmuir** Highld
218 B7 **Kilmuir** Highld
223 G6 **Kilmuir** Highld
173 K3 **Kilmun** Ag & B
170 F4 **Kilnave** Ag & B
176 B8 **Kilncadzow** S Lans
33 J6 **Kilndown** Kent
182 B3 **Kilninver** Ag & B
150 C4 **Kiln Pit Hill** Nthumb
127 J7 **Kilnsea** E R Yk
131 H6 **Kilnsey** N York
126 C1 **Kilnwick** E R Yk
180 E7 **Kiloran** Ag & B
162 A4 **Kilpatrick** N Ayrs
54 C3 **Kilpeck** Herefs
125 J5 **Kilpin** E R Yk
187 J6 **Kilrenny** Fife
73 H1 **Kilsby** Nhants
186 C3 **Kilspindie** P & K
144 D7 **Kilstay** D & G
175 J3 **Kilsyth** N Lans
212 D6 **Kiltarlity** Highld
142 E4 **Kilton** R & Cl
142 E4 **Kilton Thorpe** R & Cl
218 B7 **Kilvaxter** Highld
25 H3 **Kilve** Somset
102 D4 **Kilvington** Notts
163 H2 **Kilwinning** N Ayrs
92 C3 **Kimberley** Norfk
101 J4 **Kimberley** Notts
115 H3 **Kimberworth** Rothm
151 G5 **Kimblesworth** Dur
75 G2 **Kimbolton** Cambs
69 K3 **Kimbolton** Herefs
87 H6 **Kimcote** Leics
15 H6 **Kimmeridge** Dorset
28 F3 **Kimpton** Hants
59 K4 **Kimpton** Herts
226 F3 **Kinbrace** Highld
185 G6 **Kinbuck** Stirlg
187 G3 **Kincaple** Fife
176 C2 **Kincardine** Fife
222 E4 **Kincardine** Highld
206 B5 **Kincardine O'Neil** Abers
195 J8 **Kinclaven** P & K
207 H5 **Kincorth** C Aber
214 C3 **Kincorth House** Moray
203 K4 **Kincraig** Highld
194 F6 **Kincraigie** P & K
194 F6 **Kindallachan** P & K
172 B7 **Kinerarach** Ag & B
56 C3 **Kineton** Gloucs
72 D4 **Kineton** Warwks
186 C3 **Kinfauns** P & K
173 J6 **Kingarth** Ag & B
81 G3 *King Arthur's Labyrinth* Gwynd
207 G5 **Kingcausie** Abers
54 B6 **Kingcoed** Mons
117 H3 **Kingerby** Lincs
56 E3 **Kingham** Oxon
155 G7 **Kingholm Quay** D & G
177 H2 **Kinghorn** Fife
186 D7 **Kinglassie** Fife
196 B5 **Kingoldrum** Angus
186 E2 **Kingoodie** P & K
6 C5 **Kingsand** Cnwll
187 K5 **Kingsbarns** Fife
7 H6 **Kingsbridge** Devon
24 F4 **Kingsbridge** Somset
85 K1 **King's Bromley** Staffs
208 F4 **Kingsburgh** Highld
44 D3 **Kingsbury** Gt Lon
86 B4 **Kingsbury** Warwks
26 B7 **Kingsbury Episcopi** Somset
54 E3 **King's Caple** Herefs
41 K8 **Kingsclere** Hants
88 E4 **King's Cliffe** Nhants
39 J2 **Kingscote** Gloucs
23 H7 **Kingscott** Devon
71 J3 **King's Coughton** Warwks

162 D4 **Kingscross** N Ayrs
26 D6 **Kingsdon** Somset
35 K5 **Kingsdown** Kent
40 D3 **Kingsdown** Swindn
39 J6 **Kingsdown** Wilts
40 D3 **Kingsdown Crematorium** Swindn
176 F1 **Kingseat** Fife
58 C6 **Kingsey** Bucks
31 K4 **Kingsfold** W Susx
206 F4 **Kingsford** C Aber
174 E8 **Kingsford** E Ayrs
35 K1 **Kingsgate** Kent
77 K3 **Kingshall Street** Suffk
85 J7 **King's Heath** Birm
33 H3 **Kings Hill** Kent
85 H4 **King's Hill** Wsall
192 D5 **Kings House Hotel** Highld
184 C4 **Kingshouse Hotel** Stirlg
7 K3 **Kingskerswell** Devon
186 E5 **Kingskettle** Fife
69 J3 **Kingsland** Herefs
108 C5 **Kingsland** IoA
59 H7 **Kings Langley** Herts
112 D6 **Kingsley** Ches W
30 C4 **Kingsley** Hants
100 A3 **Kingsley** Staffs
30 E5 **Kingsley Green** W Susx
73 L3 **Kingsley Park** Nhants
104 F8 **King's Lynn** Norfk
138 E3 **Kings Meaburn** Cumb
236 c3 **King's Mills** Guern
196 D6 **Kingsmuir** Angus
166 C2 **Kings Muir** Border
187 J5 **Kingsmuir** Fife
86 F7 **Kings Newnham** Warwks
34 D6 **Kingsnorth** Kent
85 J7 **King's Norton** Birm
87 K4 **King's Norton** Leics
23 L7 **King's Nympton** Devon
69 J4 **King's Pyon** Herefs
89 J7 **Kings Ripton** Cambs
29 G5 **King's Somborne** Hants
14 D1 **King's Stag** Dorset
55 J7 **King's Stanley** Gloucs
72 F7 **King's Sutton** Nhants
85 J4 **Kingstanding** Birm
7 K2 **Kingsteignton** Devon
54 D2 **Kingsthorne** Herefs
73 L2 **Kingsthorpe** Nhants
75 L4 **Kingston** Cambs
6 A2 **Kingston** Cnwll
6 F6 **Kingston** Devon
14 E1 **Kingston** Dorset
15 H6 **Kingston** Dorset
178 C3 **Kingston** E Loth
16 F6 **Kingston** IoW
35 G4 **Kingston** Kent
57 H7 **Kingston Bagpuize** Oxon
58 C7 **Kingston Blount** Oxon
27 J4 **Kingston Deverill** Wilts
69 H7 **Kingstone** Herefs
26 B8 **Kingstone** Somset
100 B6 **Kingstone** Staffs
40 F3 **Kingston Lisle** Oxon
19 K4 **Kingston near Lewes** E Susx
101 J6 **Kingston on Soar** Notts
215 H2 **Kingston on Spey** Moray
14 B4 **Kingston Russell** Dorset
25 K5 **Kingston St Mary** Somset
38 B6 **Kingston Seymour** N Som

126 D5 **Kingston upon Hull** C KuH
44 D6 **Kingston upon Thames** Gt Lon
44 D6 **Kingston upon Thames Crematorium** Gt Lon
59 K4 **King's Walden** Herts
7 K5 **Kingswear** Devon
207 G4 **Kingswells** C Aber
38 D5 **Kings Weston** Bristl
84 F5 **Kingswinford** Dudley
58 B4 **Kingswood** Bucks
39 H3 **Kingswood** Gloucs
38 F5 **Kingswood** S Glos
25 H4 **Kingswood** Somset
31 L1 **Kingswood** Surrey
71 L1 **Kingswood** Warwks
84 E3 **Kingswood Common** Staffs
29 J5 **Kings Worthy** Hants
117 J6 **Kingthorpe** Lincs
68 F3 **Kington** Herefs
38 F3 **Kington** S Glos
71 H4 **Kington** Worcs
39 L5 **Kington Langley** Wilts
27 H6 **Kington Magna** Dorset
39 K5 **Kington St Michael** Wilts
203 H5 **Kingussie** Highld
26 D5 **Kingweston** Somset
217 H7 **Kinharrachie** Abers
147 G2 **Kinharvie** D & G
185 J4 **Kinkell Bridge** P & K
217 J6 **Kinknockie** Abers
177 G5 **Kinleith** C Edin
84 C7 **Kinlet** Shrops
198 F5 **Kinloch** Highld
225 H2 **Kinloch** Highld
229 H5 **Kinloch** Highld
195 J7 **Kinloch** P & K
195 L7 **Kinloch** P & K
184 B6 **Kinlochard** Stirlg
228 C4 **Kinlochbervie** Highld
191 J1 **Kinlocheil** Highld
210 F3 **Kinlochewe** Highld
200 E4 **Kinloch Hourn** Highld
202 E7 **Kinlochlaggan** Highld
192 C4 **Kinlochleven** Highld
190 E2 **Kinlochmoidart** Highld
200 B8 **Kinlochnanuagh** Highld
193 L5 **Kinloch Rannoch** P & K
214 C3 **Kinloss** Moray
110 D5 **Kinmel Bay** Conwy
206 F2 **Kinmuck** Abers
207 G2 **Kinmundy** Abers
160 B2 **Kinnabus** Ag & B
217 H5 **Kinnadie** Abers
194 F5 **Kinnaird** P & K
197 G5 **Kinnaird Castle** Angus
214 F1 **Kinneddar** Moray
197 K2 **Kinneff** Abers
155 H2 **Kinnelhead** D & G
196 F6 **Kinnell** Angus
97 M7 **Kinnerley** Shrops
69 G5 **Kinnersley** Herefs
70 F5 **Kinnersley** Worcs
68 E2 **Kinnerton** Powys
186 C6 **Kinnesswood** P & K
140 D3 **Kinninvie** Dur
196 B5 **Kinnordy** Angus
102 B6 **Kinoulton** Notts
186 B6 **Kinross** P & K
186 C2 **Kinrossie** P & K
186 B6 **Kinross Services** P & K
69 G2 **Kinsham** Herefs
71 G7 **Kinsham** Worcs
124 C7 **Kinsley** Wakefd
15 K3 **Kinson** Bmouth
200 F2 **Kintail** Highld

41 G6 **Kintbury** W Berk
214 B3 **Kintessack** Moray
186 B6 **Kintillo** P & K
83 H8 **Kinton** Herefs
98 A8 **Kinton** Shrops
206 E3 **Kintore** Abers
171 H7 **Kintour** Ag & B
170 F7 **Kintra** Ag & B
180 D3 **Kintra** Ag & B
182 B6 **Kintraw** Ag & B
161 J2 **Kintyre** Ag & B
203 L2 **Kinveachy** Highld
84 E6 **Kinver** Staffs
124 C4 **Kippax** Leeds
184 E7 **Kippen** Stirlg
146 E4 **Kippford or Scaur** D & G
33 H5 **Kipping's Cross** Kent
234 b6 **Kirbister** Ork
93 G3 **Kirby Bedon** Norfk
102 B8 **Kirby Bellars** Leics
93 H5 **Kirby Cane** Norfk
62 F4 **Kirby Cross** Essex
87 G3 **Kirby Fields** Leics
134 D6 **Kirby Grindalythe** N York
132 F5 **Kirby Hill** N York
140 E6 **Kirby Hill** N York
133 G3 **Kirby Knowle** N York
62 F4 **Kirby le Soken** Essex
134 B4 **Kirby Misperton** N York
87 G3 **Kirby Muxloe** Leics
141 K7 **Kirby Sigston** N York
134 C7 **Kirby Underdale** E R Yk
132 E3 **Kirby Wiske** N York
31 G6 **Kirdford** W Susx
231 K4 **Kirk** Highld
235 d2 **Kirkabister** Shet
146 A5 **Kirkandrews** D & G
148 C4 **Kirkandrews upon Eden** Cumb
148 B4 **Kirkbampton** Cumb
147 G3 **Kirkbean** D & G
124 F7 **Kirk Bramwith** Donc
147 M4 **Kirkbride** Cumb
196 E7 **Kirkbuddo** Angus
156 D2 **Kirkburn** Border
134 F7 **Kirkburn** E R Yk
123 J7 **Kirkburton** Kirk
111 L2 **Kirkby** Knows
117 H3 **Kirkby** Lincs
142 C6 **Kirkby** N York
141 G7 **Kirkby Fleetham** N York
103 H2 **Kirkby Green** Lincs
101 J2 **Kirkby in Ashfield** Notts
128 F3 **Kirkby-in-Furness** Cumb
103 J4 **Kirkby la Thorpe** Lincs
130 B4 **Kirkby Lonsdale** Cumb
131 G7 **Kirkby Malham** N York
86 F4 **Kirkby Mallory** Leics
132 C5 **Kirkby Malzeard** N York
133 L3 **Kirkbymoorside** N York
118 C8 **Kirkby on Bain** Lincs
123 L2 **Kirkby Overblow** N York
139 H5 **Kirkby Stephen** Cumb
138 F3 **Kirkby Thore** Cumb
103 H6 **Kirkby Underwood** Lincs
124 D3 **Kirkby Wharf** N York
186 D8 **Kirkcaldy** Fife
186 D8 **Kirkcaldy Crematorium** Fife
148 F2 **Kirkcambeck** Cumb
146 B5 **Kirkchrist** D & G

144 B2 **Kirkcolm** D & G
164 E6 **Kirkconnel** D & G
146 B3 **Kirkconnell** D & G
147 G2 **Kirkconnell** D & G
145 G3 **Kirkcowan** D & G
146 B5 **Kirkcudbright** D & G
111 K3 **Kirkdale** Lpool
124 B1 **Kirk Deighton** N York
126 C5 **Kirk Ella** E R Yk
165 G2 **Kirkfieldbank** S Lans
146 F2 **Kirkgunzeon** D & G
101 J4 **Kirk Hallam** Derbys
120 F4 **Kirkham** Lancs
134 B6 **Kirkham** N York
123 K6 **Kirkhamgate** Wakefd
133 G7 **Kirk Hammerton** N York
149 H5 **Kirkhaugh** Nthumb
123 H6 **Kirkheaton** Kirk
158 C6 **Kirkheaton** Nthumb
212 E5 **Kirkhill** Highld
165 J7 **Kirkhope** S Lans
199 H2 **Kirkibost** Highld
195 L7 **Kirkinch** P & K
145 J5 **Kirkinner** D & G
175 H4 **Kirkintilloch** E Duns
100 E3 **Kirk Ireton** Derbys
136 E4 **Kirkland** Cumb
154 E4 **Kirkland** D & G
155 H4 **Kirkland** D & G
164 E6 **Kirkland** D & G
100 F5 **Kirk Langley** Derbys
142 D3 **Kirkleatham** R & Cl
141 K5 **Kirklevington** S on T
93 L5 **Kirkley** Suffk
132 D4 **Kirklington** N York
102 B2 **Kirklington** Notts
148 D2 **Kirklinton** Cumb
176 F4 **Kirkliston** C Edin
145 K4 **Kirkmabreck** D & G
144 D7 **Kirkmaiden** D & G
141 G2 **Kirk Merrington** Dur
237 C4 **Kirk Michael** IoM
195 H4 **Kirkmichael** P & K
163 J7 **Kirkmichael** S Ayrs
164 F2 **Kirkmuirhill** S Lans
168 D4 **Kirknewton** Nthumb
176 F5 **Kirknewton** W Loth
215 L7 **Kirkney** Abers
175 L5 **Kirk of Shotts** N Lans
148 F6 **Kirkoswald** Cumb
163 G7 **Kirkoswald** S Ayrs
154 F4 **Kirkpatrick** D & G
154 D7 **Kirkpatrick Durham** D & G
156 B7 **Kirkpatrick-Fleming** D & G
124 F8 **Kirk Sandall** Donc
128 D4 **Kirksanton** Cumb
124 D7 **Kirk Smeaton** N York
123 K4 **Kirkstall** Leeds
103 K1 **Kirkstead** Lincs
215 L7 **Kirkstile** Abers
156 C4 **Kirkstile** D & G
231 L2 **Kirkstyle** Highld
124 B6 **Kirkthorpe** Wakefd
206 C1 **Kirkton** Abers
155 G6 **Kirkton** D & G
186 F3 **Kirkton** Fife
210 C8 **Kirkton** Highld
210 D6 **Kirkton** Highld
185 K4 **Kirkton** P & K
166 C2 **Kirkton Manor** Border
195 L6 **Kirkton of Airlie** Angus
196 B8 **Kirkton of Auchterhouse** Angus
213 K5 **Kirkton of Barevan** Highld
186 C2 **Kirkton of Collace** P & K
205 J3 **Kirkton of Glenbuchat** Abers
217 J7 **Kirkton of Logie Buchan** Abers

Kirkton of Menmuir - Langton 281

196 E4 **Kirkton of Menmuir** Angus
196 E8 **Kirkton of Monikie** Angus
216 D7 **Kirkton of Rayne** Abers
206 F4 **Kirkton of Skene** Abers
186 F1 **Kirkton of Strathmartine** Angus
196 C8 **Kirkton of Tealing** Angus
206 C3 **Kirkton of Tough** Abers
217 J2 **Kirktown** Abers
217 K4 **Kirktown** Abers
216 D3 **Kirktown of Alvah** Abers
206 F1 **Kirktown of Bourtie** Abers
206 F7 **Kirktown of Fetteresso** Abers
215 H6 **Kirktown of Mortlach** Moray
217 K8 **Kirktown of Slains** Abers
165 M1 **Kirkurd** Border
234 c6 **Kirkwall** Ork
234 c6 *Kirkwall Airport* Ork
158 C5 **Kirkwhelpington** Nthumb
168 C4 **Kirk Yetholm** Border
126 D7 **Kirmington** N Linc
117 K3 **Kirmond le Mire** Lincs
173 K3 **Kirn** Ag & B
196 C5 **Kirriemuir** Angus
93 G4 **Kirstead Green** Norfk
155 M7 **Kirtlebridge** D & G
77 G3 **Kirtling** Cambs
76 F4 **Kirtling Green** Cambs
57 J4 **Kirtlington** Oxon
229 M3 **Kirtomy** Highld
104 A5 **Kirton** Lincs
116 B7 **Kirton** Notts
78 F6 **Kirton** Suffk
174 D4 **Kirtonhill** W Duns
116 F2 **Kirton in Lindsey** N Linc
145 J4 **Kirwaugh** D & G
210 C6 **Kishorn** Highld
73 K3 **Kislingbury** Nhants
25 G6 **Kittisford** Somset
207 H4 **Kittybrewster** C Aber
54 C2 **Kivernoll** Herefs
115 J5 **Kiveton Park** Rothm
116 D5 **Knaith** Lincs
27 J6 **Knap Corner** Dorset
42 F8 **Knaphill** Surrey
25 L6 **Knapp** Somset
124 E1 **Knapton** C York
134 D4 **Knapton** N York
107 G5 **Knapton** Norfk
75 K2 **Knapwell** Cambs
132 E7 **Knaresborough** N York
149 H4 **Knarsdale** Nthumb
217 G5 **Knaven** Abers
132 F2 **Knayton** N York
59 L4 **Knebworth** Herts
125 H5 **Knedlington** E R Yk
116 B8 **Kneesall** Notts
75 L5 **Kneesworth** Cambs
102 B4 **Kneeton** Notts
50 F7 **Knelston** Swans
99 L5 **Knenhall** Staffs
72 E4 **Knightcote** Warwks
99 J7 **Knightley** Staffs
87 H4 **Knighton** C Leic
14 C1 **Knighton** Dorset
82 F8 **Knighton** Powys
25 J3 **Knighton** Somset
99 G4 **Knighton** Staffs
99 H6 **Knighton** Staffs
70 B1 **Knighton on Teme** Worcs
70 D4 **Knightwick** Worcs
68 F3 **Knill** Herefs
102 D6 **Knipton** Leics
100 E3 **Kniveton** Derbys
138 F2 **Knock** Cumb
199 K4 **Knock** Highld
215 L4 **Knock** Moray
232 g2 **Knock** W Isls
227 K3 **Knockally** Highld
224 F6 **Knockan** Highld
214 F6 **Knockando** Moray
212 E5 **Knockbain** Highld
212 F3 **Knockbain** Highld
173 L5 **Knock Castle** N Ayrs
231 H4 **Knockdee** Highld
173 J4 **Knockdow** Ag & B
39 J3 **Knockdown** Wilts
153 G3 **Knockeen** S Ayrs
162 D4 **Knockenkelly** N Ayrs
163 K2 **Knockentiber** E Ayrs
32 E2 **Knockholt** Kent
32 E2 **Knockholt Pound** Kent
97 M7 **Knockin** Shrops
163 K2 **Knockinlaw** E Ayrs
144 B3 **Knocknain** D & G
171 K4 **Knockrome** Ag & B
237 b4 **Knocksharry** IoM
153 M5 **Knocksheen** D & G
154 D7 **Knockvennie Smithy** D & G
79 J3 **Knodishall** Suffk
79 J3 **Knodishall Common** Suffk
26 C6 **Knole** Somset
113 J5 **Knolls Green** Ches E
98 B5 **Knolton** Wrexhm
27 L3 **Knook** Wilts
88 B2 **Knossington** Leics
120 E2 **Knott End-on-Sea** Lancs
74 E2 **Knotting** Bed
74 E3 **Knotting Green** Bed
124 D5 **Knottingley** Wakefd
112 B3 **Knotty Ash** Lpool
83 L7 **Knowbury** Shrops
153 G7 **Knowe** D & G
154 A4 **Knowehead** D & G
163 G6 **Knoweside** S Ayrs
38 E6 **Knowle** Bristl
11 H5 **Knowle** Devon
12 C2 **Knowle** Devon
12 D6 **Knowle** Devon
23 H4 **Knowle** Devon
83 L8 **Knowle** Shrops
85 L7 **Knowle** Solhll
24 E3 **Knowle** Somset
148 D4 **Knowlefield** Cumb
121 J3 **Knowle Green** Lancs
13 J1 **Knowle St Giles** Somset
42 D4 **Knowl Hill** W & M
112 C3 **Knowsley** Knows
112 C3 **Knowsley Safari Park** Knows
24 C6 **Knowstone** Devon
33 K5 **Knox Bridge** Kent
82 F8 **Knucklas** Powys
74 D2 **Knuston** Nhants
113 H5 **Knutsford** Ches E
113 G6 **Knutsford Services** Ches E
122 F6 **Krumlin** Calder
3 J7 **Kuggar** Cnwll
200 B1 **Kyleakin** Highld
210 B8 **Kyle of Lochalsh** Highld
200 B2 **Kylerhea** Highld
224 F2 **Kylesku** Highld
200 C6 **Kylesmorar** Highld
232 e4 **Kyles Scalpay** W Isls
224 F2 **Kylestrome** Highld
84 C1 **Kynnersley** Wrekin
69 L2 **Kyrewood** Worcs

L

232 f3 **Lacasaigh** W Isls
232 f2 **Lacasdal** W Isls
117 K1 **Laceby** NE Lin
58 D7 **Lacey Green** Bucks
113 G6 **Lach Dennis** Ches W
77 H1 **Lackford** Suffk
77 H1 **Lackford Green** Suffk
39 K6 **Lacock** Wilts
72 E3 **Ladbroke** Warwks
33 J4 **Laddingford** Kent
4 D5 **Ladock** Cnwll
234 d4 **Lady** Ork
186 E5 **Ladybank** Fife
165 H4 **Ladygill** S Lans
128 E3 **Lady Hall** Cumb
179 J8 **Ladykirk** Border
85 J6 **Ladywood** Birm
70 F3 **Ladywood** Worcs
236 e1 **La Fontenelle** Guern
154 F5 **Lag** D & G
190 D4 **Laga** Highld
160 C1 **Lagavulin** Ag & B
162 B5 **Lagg** N Ayrs
201 L6 **Laggan** Highld
202 F6 **Laggan** Highld
236 b5 **La Greve de Lecq** Jersey
228 F4 **Laid** Highld
219 L3 **Laide** Highld
199 G7 **Laig** Highld
174 E8 **Laigh Clunch** E Ayrs
163 L2 **Laigh Fenwick** E Ayrs
164 C5 **Laigh Glenmuir** E Ayrs
175 J7 **Laighstonehall** S Lans
46 B3 **Laindon** Essex
225 M7 **Lairg** Highld
123 J4 **Laisterdyke** C Brad
17 H5 **Lake** IoW
15 J4 **Lake** Poole
28 C4 **Lake** Wilts
137 H5 **Lake District National Park** Cumb
91 G6 **Lakenheath** Suffk
90 D4 **Lakesend** Norfk
36 D4 **Laleston** Brdgnd
177 G7 **Lamancha** Border
77 K7 **Lamarsh** Essex
106 F7 **Lamas** Norfk
167 L2 **Lambden** Border
33 H6 **Lamberhurst** Kent
33 H6 **Lamberhurst Down** Kent
179 K6 **Lamberton** Border
44 F4 **Lambeth** Gt Lon
44 F5 **Lambeth Crematorium** Gt Lon
77 G4 **Lambfair Green** Suffk
101 M4 **Lambley** Notts
149 H4 **Lambley** Nthumb
40 F5 **Lambourn** W Berk
45 J2 **Lambourne End** Essex
31 L4 **Lambs Green** W Susx
6 C1 **Lamerton** Devon
151 G4 **Lamesley** Gatesd
165 J3 **Lamington** S Lans
162 C3 **Lamlash** N Ayrs
148 D7 **Lamonby** Cumb
2 E6 **Lamorna** Cnwll
4 D7 **Lamorran** Cnwll
66 D5 **Lampeter** Cerdgn
49 K5 **Lampeter Velfrey** Pembks
49 H7 **Lamphey** Pembks
136 F3 **Lamplugh** Cumb
87 L8 **Lamport** Nhants
26 F4 **Lamyatt** Somset
165 G2 **Lanark** S Lans
129 K7 **Lancaster** Lancs
129 K6 **Lancaster & Morecambe Crematorium** Lancs
121 G1 **Lancaster Services (Forton)** Lancs
150 F5 **Lanchester** Dur
19 G5 **Lancing** W Susx
236 d1 **L'Ancresse** Guern
76 C2 **Landbeach** Cambs
23 G6 **Landcross** Devon
206 E4 **Landerberry** Abers
28 E7 **Landford** Wilts
227 L2 **Land-hallow** Highld
111 J4 **Landican Crematorium** Wirral
50 F6 **Landimore** Swans
23 J5 **Landkey** Devon
51 J6 **Landore** Swans
6 B4 **Landrake** Cnwll
2 C6 **Land's End** Cnwll
2 C5 *Land's End Airport* Cnwll
6 C4 **Landulph** Cnwll
4 C4 **Lane** Cnwll
9 G7 **Laneast** Cnwll
42 D3 **Lane End** Bucks
27 J3 **Lane End** Wilts
100 E5 **Lane Ends** Derbys
128 D2 **Lane End Waberthwaite** Cumb
116 D6 **Laneham** Notts
140 E5 **Lane Head** Dur
149 L6 **Lanehead** Dur
25 K6 **Langaller** Somset
102 B5 **Langar** Notts
174 D4 **Langbank** Rens
123 G1 **Langbar** N York
130 F6 **Langcliffe** N York
134 E2 **Langdale End** N York
16 E2 **Langdown** Hants
186 E6 **Langdyke** Fife
62 B4 **Langenhoe** Essex
75 H6 **Langford** C Beds
12 D2 **Langford** Devon
61 K6 **Langford** Essex
102 D2 **Langford** Notts
56 E7 **Langford** Oxon
25 H6 **Langford Budville** Somset
62 B2 **Langham** Essex
106 B4 **Langham** Norfk
88 B2 **Langham** Rutlnd
77 L1 **Langham** Suffk
121 K4 **Langho** Lancs
156 C5 **Langholm** D & G
167 H3 **Langlee** Border
16 F3 **Langley** Hants
59 K4 **Langley** Herts
33 K3 **Langley** Kent
149 L3 **Langley** Nthumb
43 G5 **Langley** Slough
25 G5 **Langley** Somset
30 D5 **Langley** W Susx
71 L3 **Langley** Warwks
39 L5 **Langley Burrell** Wilts
61 L4 **Langley Green** Essex
25 G5 **Langley Marsh** Somset
150 F6 **Langley Park** Dur
93 H3 **Langley Street** Norfk
76 C7 **Langley Upper Green** Essex
20 D5 **Langney** E Susx
115 L4 **Langold** Notts
9 J7 **Langore** Cnwll
26 B6 **Langport** Somset
103 L3 **Langrick** Lincs
39 H6 **Langridge** BaNES
147 K5 **Langrigg** Cumb
30 B6 **Langrish** Hants
114 E2 **Langsett** Barns
185 G5 **Langside** P & K
17 K2 **Langstone** Hants
132 C2 **Langthorne** N York
132 F6 **Langthorpe** N York
140 C6 **Langthwaite** N York
134 F6 **Langtoft** E R Yk
89 G2 **Langtoft** Lincs
140 F4 **Langton** Dur

118 C7 **Langton** Lincs
118 E7 **Langton** Lincs
134 C6 **Langton** N York
117 J6 **Langton by Wragby** Lincs
32 F5 **Langton Green** Kent
14 C6 **Langton Herring** Dorset
15 J6 **Langton Matravers** Dorset
10 C2 **Langtree** Devon
148 F7 **Langwathby** Cumb
227 K4 **Langwell House** Highld
115 K7 **Langwith** Derbys
115 K7 **Langwith Junction** Derbys
117 H6 **Langworth** Lincs
5 H3 **Lanhydrock House & Gardens** Cnwll
5 G3 **Lanivet** Cnwll
5 G4 **Lanlivery** Cnwll
3 J4 **Lanner** Cnwll
5 J4 **Lanreath** Cnwll
5 J5 **Lansallos** Cnwll
8 E7 **Lanteglos** Cnwll
5 J5 **Lanteglos Highway** Cnwll
167 J5 **Lanton** Border
168 D3 **Lanton** Nthumb
11 H3 **Lapford** Devon
160 C1 **Laphroaig** Ag & B
84 F2 **Lapley** Staffs
71 L1 **Lapworth** Warwks
190 E6 **Larachbeg** Highld
176 B3 **Larbert** Falk
216 B7 **Largie** Abers
172 F2 **Largiemore** Ag & B
187 H5 **Largoward** Fife
173 L6 **Largs** N Ayrs
162 D5 **Largybeg** N Ayrs
162 D4 **Largymore** N Ayrs
173 L4 **Larkfield** Inver
33 J2 **Larkfield** Kent
175 K7 **Larkhall** S Lans
28 C3 **Larkhill** Wilts
92 B5 **Larling** Norfk
236 e8 **La Rocque** Jersey
140 C4 **Lartington** Dur
30 A3 **Lasham** Hants
186 B8 **Lassodie** Fife
177 J5 **Lasswade** Mdloth
133 L2 **Lastingham** N York
61 L7 **Latchingdon** Essex
6 B2 **Latchley** Cnwll
74 C5 **Lathbury** M Keyn
227 L2 **Latheron** Highld
227 L3 **Latheronwheel** Highld
187 H5 **Lathones** Fife
59 G7 **Latimer** Bucks
38 F4 **Latteridge** S Glos
27 G6 **Lattiford** Somset
40 C2 **Latton** Wilts
178 C8 **Lauder** Border
50 C4 **Laugharne** Carmth
116 D6 **Laughterton** Lincs
20 A3 **Laughton** E Susx
87 J5 **Laughton** Leics
103 H6 **Laughton** Lincs
116 D3 **Laughton** Lincs
115 K4 **Laughton-en-le-Morthen** Rothm
9 H4 **Launcells** Cnwll
9 J7 **Launceston** Cnwll
57 L4 **Launton** Oxon
197 H3 **Laurencekirk** Abers
146 B3 **Laurieston** D & G
176 B3 **Laurieston** Falk
74 D4 **Lavendon** M Keyn
77 K5 **Lavenham** Suffk
37 J6 **Lavernock** V Glam
148 E3 **Laversdale** Cumb
28 D5 **Laverstock** Wilts
29 J2 **Laverstoke** Hants
71 J7 **Laverton** Gloucs

132 C5 **Laverton** N York
27 H2 **Laverton** Somset
236 d4 **La Villette** Guern
98 A2 **Lavister** Wrexhm
175 L7 **Law** S Lans
193 L7 **Lawers** P & K
62 C2 **Lawford** Essex
25 H4 **Lawford** Somset
186 A3 **Lawgrove** P & K
175 L7 **Law Hill** S Lans
9 J7 **Lawhitton** Cnwll
130 E6 **Lawkland** N York
123 K3 **Lawns Wood Crematorium** Leeds
49 H6 **Lawrenny** Pembks
77 K4 **Lawshall** Suffk
232 f3 **Laxay** W Isls
232 f2 **Laxdale** W Isls
237 d4 **Laxey** IoM
93 G8 **Laxfield** Suffk
228 C6 **Laxford Bridge** Highld
235 d4 **Laxo** Shet
125 J5 **Laxton** E R Yk
88 D4 **Laxton** Nhants
116 B7 **Laxton** Notts
122 F3 **Laycock** C Brad
61 M4 **Layer Breton** Essex
62 A4 **Layer-de-la-Haye** Essex
61 L4 **Layer Marney** Essex
78 B6 **Layham** Suffk
13 K2 **Laymore** Dorset
125 H3 **Laytham** E R Yk
147 M4 **Laythes** Cumb
148 F6 **Lazonby** Cumb
101 G2 **Lea** Derbys
54 F4 **Lea** Herefs
116 D4 **Lea** Lincs
83 G5 **Lea** Shrops
39 L3 **Lea** Wilts
212 F5 **Leachkin** Highld
177 H7 **Leadburn** Border
102 F3 **Leadenham** Lincs
60 F5 **Leaden Roding** Essex
150 E5 **Leadgate** Dur
165 G6 **Leadhills** S Lans
56 F5 **Leafield** Oxon
59 H4 **Leagrave** Luton
104 C3 **Leake Common Side** Lincs
142 F5 **Lealholm** N York
209 H3 **Lealt** Highld
86 B5 **Lea Marston** Warwks
72 F2 **Leamington Hastings** Warwks
72 D2 **Leamington Spa** Warwks
20 C4 **Leap Cross** E Susx
129 K3 **Leasgill** Cumb
103 H3 **Leasingham** Lincs
141 G2 **Leasingthorne** Dur
31 K1 **Leatherhead** Surrey
123 J2 **Leathley** N York
98 C8 **Leaton** Shrops
34 D4 **Leaveland** Kent
77 L6 **Leavenheath** Suffk
134 C6 **Leavening** N York
45 H7 **Leaves Green** Gt Lon
135 G3 **Lebberston** N York
236 c4 **Le Bourg** Guern
56 E7 **Lechlade on Thames** Gloucs
170 E5 **Lecht Gruinart** Ag & B
130 C4 **Leck** Lancs
193 L7 **Leckbuie** P & K
29 G4 **Leckford** Hants
73 K6 **Leckhampstead** Bucks
41 H5 **Leckhampstead** W Berk
41 H5 **Leckhampstead Thicket** W Berk
55 L4 **Leckhampton** Gloucs
220 F4 **Leckmelm** Highld
126 C2 **Leconfield** E R Yk

191 H8 **Ledaig** Ag & B
58 E4 **Ledburn** Bucks
70 C6 **Ledbury** Herefs
69 H4 **Ledgemoor** Herefs
224 F6 **Ledmore Junction** Highld
124 C4 **Ledsham** Leeds
124 C5 **Ledston** Leeds
57 H3 **Ledwell** Oxon
23 H3 **Lee** Devon
45 H5 **Lee** Gt Lon
83 J4 **Leebotwood** Shrops
98 D6 **Lee Brockhurst** Shrops
128 C5 **Leece** Cumb
46 B3 **Lee Chapel** Essex
58 E6 **Lee Clump** Bucks
33 L3 **Leeds** Kent
123 K4 **Leeds** Leeds
123 J3 **Leeds Bradford Airport** Leeds
33 L3 **Leeds Castle** Kent
3 G4 **Leedstown** Cnwll
99 M2 **Leek** Staffs
72 C2 **Leek Wootton** Warwks
6 E5 **Lee Mill** Devon
132 D2 **Leeming** N York
132 D2 **Leeming Bar** N York
17 G3 **Lee-on-the-Solent** Hants
100 C5 **Lees** Derbys
113 L2 **Lees** Oldham
100 E5 **Lees Green** Derbys
87 L2 **Leesthorpe** Leics
97 K1 **Leeswood** Flints
186 C3 **Leetown** P & K
112 F6 **Leftwich** Ches W
118 E5 **Legbourne** Lincs
167 J2 **Legerwood** Border
42 F5 **Legoland** W & M
117 J4 **Legsby** Lincs
87 H3 **Leicester** C Leic
87 G3 **Leicester Forest East** Leics
87 G3 **Leicester Forest East Services** Leics
86 F2 **Leicester (Markfield) Services** Leics
14 C2 **Leigh** Dorset
55 K3 **Leigh** Gloucs
32 F4 **Leigh** Kent
31 L3 **Leigh** Surrey
112 F2 **Leigh** Wigan
40 B3 **Leigh** Wilts
70 D4 **Leigh** Worcs
46 D4 **Leigh Beck** Essex
39 K5 **Leigh Delamere** Wilts
39 K5 **Leigh Delamere Services** Wilts
34 B7 **Leigh Green** Kent
175 H7 **Leigh Knoweglass** S Lans
46 D3 **Leigh-on-Sea** Sthend
15 J3 **Leigh Park** Dorset
70 D4 **Leigh Sinton** Worcs
85 J3 **Leighswood** Wsall
39 J3 **Leighterton** Gloucs
82 E3 **Leighton** Powys
84 B3 **Leighton** Shrops
89 G7 **Leighton Bromswold** Cambs
58 F3 **Leighton Buzzard** C Beds
27 G3 **Leigh upon Mendip** Somset
38 E6 **Leigh Woods** N Som
69 J2 **Leinthall Earls** Herefs
69 J1 **Leinthall Starkes** Herefs
69 H8 **Leintwardine** Herefs
87 G5 **Leire** Leics
79 J3 **Leiston** Suffk
195 L7 **Leitfie** P & K
177 H3 **Leith** C Edin
168 B1 **Leitholm** Border

2 F4 **Lelant** Cnwll
126 F4 **Lelley** E R Yk
168 B3 **Lempitlaw** Border
232 f3 **Lemreway** W Isls
59 L5 **Lemsford** Herts
71 J5 **Lenchwick** Worcs
152 D4 **Lendalfoot** S Ayrs
184 C6 **Lendrick** Stirlg
217 L6 **Lendrum Terrace** Abers
34 B4 **Lenham** Kent
34 B5 **Lenham Heath** Kent
202 D1 **Lenie** Highld
168 C2 **Lennel** Border
146 A5 **Lennox Plunton** D & G
175 H3 **Lennoxtown** E Duns
101 K5 **Lenton** C Nott
103 G6 **Lenton** Lincs
106 D8 **Lenwade** Norfk
175 H4 **Lenzie** E Duns
205 L4 **Leochel-Cushnie** Abers
69 K3 **Leominster** Herefs
55 J7 **Leonard Stanley** Gloucs
208 B4 **Lephin** Highld
134 B7 **Leppington** N York
123 J7 **Lepton** Kirk
236 b3 **L'Eree** Guern
5 J4 **Lerryn** Cnwll
235 d6 **Lerwick** Shet
169 J6 **Lesbury** Nthumb
206 B1 **Leslie** Abers
186 D6 **Leslie** Fife
164 F2 **Lesmahagow** S Lans
8 F6 **Lesnewth** Cnwll
236 d2 **Les Quartiers** Guern
236 b7 **Les Quennevais** Jersey
107 H6 **Lessingham** Norfk
147 L5 **Lessonhall** Cumb
144 B3 **Leswalt** D & G
236 a6 **L'Etacq** Jersey
43 J2 **Letchmore Heath** Herts
59 L2 **Letchworth Garden City** Herts
41 G4 **Letcombe Bassett** Oxon
41 G3 **Letcombe Regis** Oxon
196 E6 **Letham** Angus
167 K7 **Letham** Border
176 B2 **Letham** Falk
186 E4 **Letham** Fife
197 G7 **Letham Grange** Angus
195 H7 **Lethendy** P & K
206 B2 **Lethenty** Abers
216 F6 **Lethenty** Abers
78 F3 **Letheringham** Suffk
106 C5 **Letheringsett** Norfk
219 L7 **Letterewe** Highld
200 D2 **Letterfearn** Highld
201 K6 **Letterfinlay Lodge Hotel** Highld
199 M7 **Lettermorar** Highld
220 F4 **Letters** Highld
165 H5 **Lettershaw** S Lans
48 F2 **Letterston** Pembks
204 C2 **Lettoch** Highld
214 D7 **Lettoch** Highld
69 G5 **Letton** Herefs
59 M5 **Letty Green** Herts
115 K4 **Letwell** Rothm
187 G3 **Leuchars** Fife
232 f3 **Leumrabhagh** W Isls
232 f3 **Leurbost** W Isls
84 F1 **Levedale** Staffs
126 D2 **Leven** E R Yk
186 F7 **Leven** Fife
129 K3 **Levens** Cumb
60 B4 **Levens Green** Herts
113 K3 **Levenshulme** Manch
235 c7 **Levenwick** Shet
232 d5 **Leverburgh** W Isls

90 C2 **Leverington** Cambs
59 H6 **Leverstock Green** Herts
104 C3 **Leverton** Lincs
236 C2 **Le Villocq** Guern
78 F6 **Levington** Suffk
134 C2 **Levisham** N York
56 F6 **Lew** Oxon
9 H8 **Lewannick** Cnwll
10 C7 **Lewdown** Devon
19 L4 **Lewes** E Susx
48 F3 **Leweston** Pembks
45 G5 **Lewisham** Gt Lon
45 H5 **Lewisham Crematorium** Gt Lon
212 D8 **Lewiston** Highld
36 E3 **Lewistown** Brdgnd
42 B2 **Lewknor** Oxon
34 C3 **Lewson Street** Kent
10 C7 **Lewtrenchard** Devon
62 A3 **Lexden** Essex
25 K4 **Lexworthy** Somset
33 H2 **Leybourne** Kent
131 L2 **Leyburn** N York
59 K3 **Leygreen** Herts
59 G7 **Ley Hill** Bucks
121 H6 **Leyland** Lancs
206 E3 **Leylodge** Abers
217 J4 **Leys** Abers
195 K8 **Leys** P & K
47 G6 **Leysdown-on-Sea** Kent
196 F6 **Leysmill** Angus
196 C6 **Leys of Cossans** Angus
69 L2 **Leysters** Herefs
45 G3 **Leyton** Gt Lon
45 H3 **Leytonstone** Gt Lon
5 M1 **Lezant** Cnwll
215 G3 **Lhanbryde** Moray
52 F3 **Libanus** Powys
165 J2 **Libberton** S Lans
177 J4 **Liberton** C Edin
85 K2 **Lichfield** Staffs
85 H7 **Lickey** Worcs
85 H8 **Lickey End** Worcs
30 F6 **Lickfold** W Susx
190 F4 **Liddesdale** Highld
40 E4 **Liddington** Swindn
77 G3 **Lidgate** Suffk
74 E6 **Lidlington** C Beds
186 E2 **Liff** Angus
85 J7 **Lifford** Birm
9 K7 **Lifton** Devon
9 K7 **Liftondown** Devon
72 D4 **Lighthorne** Warwks
72 D4 **Lighthorne Heath** Warwks
42 F7 **Lightwater** Surrey
87 H7 **Lilbourne** Nhants
84 D1 **Lilleshall** Wrekin
59 J3 **Lilley** Herts
167 H4 **Lilliesleaf** Border
73 K6 **Lillingstone Dayrell** Bucks
73 K6 **Lillingstone Lovell** Bucks
26 F8 **Lillington** Dorset
15 K4 **Lilliput** Poole
25 J3 **Lilstock** Somset
59 H3 **Limbury** Luton
175 J7 **Limekilnburn** S Lans
176 E2 **Limekilns** Fife
176 B4 **Limerigg** Falk
16 E6 **Limerstone** IoW
55 J2 **Lime Street** Worcs
26 D6 **Limington** Somset
164 C4 **Limmerhaugh** E Ayrs
93 H3 **Limpenhoe** Norfk
39 H7 **Limpley Stoke** Wilts
32 D3 **Limpsfield** Surrey
32 D3 **Limpsfield Chart** Surrey
101 K3 **Linby** Notts
30 E5 **Linchmere** W Susx
155 G6 **Lincluden** D & G

116 F7 **Lincoln** Lincs
117 G7 **Lincoln Crematorium** Lincs
70 E2 **Lincomb** Worcs
129 J4 **Lindale** Cumb
128 F4 **Lindal in Furness** Cumb
32 C7 **Lindfield** W Susx
30 D4 **Lindford** Hants
123 G6 **Lindley** Kirk
123 J2 **Lindley Green** N York
70 C2 **Lindridge** Worcs
61 G3 **Lindsell** Essex
77 L5 **Lindsey** Suffk
78 B5 **Lindsey Tye** Suffk
142 E4 **Lingdale** R & Cl
69 G2 **Lingen** Herefs
32 C4 **Lingfield** Surrey
93 H2 **Lingwood** Norfk
218 B7 **Linicro** Highld
55 J2 **Linkend** Worcs
41 G8 **Linkenholt** Hants
5 L2 **Linkinhorne** Cnwll
177 J1 **Linktown** Fife
214 F3 **Linkwood** Moray
83 G5 **Linley** Shrops
70 C4 **Linley Green** Herefs
176 D3 **Linlithgow** W Loth
222 D2 **Linsidemore** Highld
58 E3 **Linslade** C Beds
93 G7 **Linstead Parva** Suffk
148 D4 **Linstock** Cumb
85 H8 **Linthurst** Worcs
123 G7 **Linthwaite** Kirk
179 H6 **Lintlaw** Border
215 L2 **Lintmill** Moray
168 B4 **Linton** Border
76 E5 **Linton** Cambs
86 C1 **Linton** Derbys
54 F3 **Linton** Herefs
33 K3 **Linton** Kent
124 B2 **Linton** Leeds
131 J6 **Linton** N York
54 F3 **Linton Hill** Herefs
133 G7 **Linton-on-Ouse** N York
117 J4 **Linwood** Lincs
174 E5 **Linwood** Rens
233 b7 **Lionacleit** W Isls
232 g1 **Lional** W Isls
30 D5 **Liphook** Hants
111 J3 **Liscard** Wirral
24 D5 **Liscombe** Somset
5 K3 **Liskeard** Cnwll
191 G7 **Lismore** Ag & B
30 C5 **Liss** Hants
135 H7 **Lissett** E R Yk
117 J5 **Lissington** Lincs
37 J4 **Lisvane** Cardif
37 M3 **Liswerry** Newpt
105 L8 **Litcham** Norfk
73 J4 **Litchborough** Nhants
29 J4 **Litchfield** Hants
111 K2 **Litherland** Sefton
75 K6 **Litlington** Cambs
20 B5 **Litlington** E Susx
76 D5 **Little Abington** Cambs
88 D8 **Little Addington** Nhants
145 J5 **Little Airies** D & G
71 K3 **Little Alne** Warwks
111 J1 **Little Altcar** Sefton
60 B5 **Little Amwell** Herts
85 K4 **Little Aston** Staffs
142 C5 **Little Ayton** N York
61 J6 **Little Baddow** Essex
39 J4 **Little Badminton** S Glos
148 A4 **Little Bampton** Cumb
61 G2 **Little Bardfield** Essex
75 H3 **Little Barford** Bed
106 D5 **Little Barningham** Norfk
56 D5 **Little Barrington** Gloucs

112 C7 **Little Barrow** Ches W
158 C6 **Little Bavington** Nthumb
40 F7 **Little Bedwyn** Wilts
62 D3 **Little Bentley** Essex
59 M6 **Little Berkhamsted** Herts
74 B3 **Little Billing** Nhants
58 F4 **Little Billington** C Beds
54 D2 **Little Birch** Herefs
78 D5 **Little Blakenham** Suffk
148 E7 **Little Blencow** Cumb
31 G7 **Little Bognor** W Susx
100 F2 **Little Bolehill** Derbys
113 G4 **Little Bollington** Ches E
31 J1 **Little Bookham** Surrey
116 D5 **Littleborough** Notts
122 D7 **Littleborough** Rochdl
35 G3 **Littlebourne** Kent
72 F5 **Little Bourton** Oxon
77 G4 **Little Bradley** Suffk
61 K5 **Little Braxted** Essex
196 F4 **Little Brechin** Angus
14 B5 **Littlebredy** Dorset
58 E2 **Little Brickhill** M Keyn
73 J2 **Little Brington** Nhants
62 C3 **Little Bromley** Essex
112 E7 **Little Budworth** Ches W
212 F4 **Littleburn** Highld
46 A2 **Little Burstead** Essex
76 D6 **Littlebury** Essex
76 C6 **Littlebury Green** Essex
103 G8 **Little Bytham** Lincs
118 E4 **Little Carlton** Lincs
88 E2 **Little Casterton** Rutlnd
118 E5 **Little Cawthorpe** Lincs
42 C5 **Little Chalfont** Bucks
34 C5 **Little Chart** Kent
76 D6 **Little Chesterford** Essex
27 M2 **Little Cheverell** Wilts
76 B6 **Little Chishill** Cambs
62 E4 **Little Clacton** Essex
136 E2 **Little Clifton** Cumb
71 G5 **Little Comberton** Worcs
20 E4 **Little Common** E Susx
56 E3 **Little Compton** Warwks
77 K6 **Little Cornard** Suffk
69 L4 **Little Cowarne** Herefs
40 F7 **Little Coxwell** Oxon
132 C2 **Little Crakehall** N York
91 K4 **Little Cressingham** Norfk
111 K2 **Little Crosby** Sefton
100 D5 **Little Cubley** Derbys
87 L2 **Little Dalby** Leics
54 F5 **Littledean** Gloucs
54 D2 **Little Dewchurch** Herefs
76 F3 **Little Ditton** Cambs
90 D6 **Little Downham** Cambs
134 F7 **Little Driffield** E R Yk
91 K2 **Little Dunham** Norfk
195 G7 **Little Dunkeld** P & K
61 G4 **Little Dunmow** Essex
28 C5 **Little Durnford** Wilts
60 F3 **Little Easton** Essex
101 G4 **Little Eaton** Derbys
92 B4 **Little Ellingham** Norfk
73 H3 **Little Everdon** Nhants
75 L4 **Little Eversden** Cambs

56 E7 **Little Faringdon** Oxon
132 D2 **Little Fencote** N York
124 D4 **Little Fenton** N York
91 K2 **Little Fransham** Norfk
59 G5 **Little Gaddesden** Herts
79 H3 **Little Glemham** Suffk
55 G3 **Little Gorsley** Herefs
75 J4 **Little Gransden** Cambs
27 G2 **Little Green** Somset
118 D3 **Little Grimsby** Lincs
60 C4 **Little Hadham** Herts
103 J4 **Little Hale** Lincs
101 J4 **Little Hallam** Derbys
60 D4 **Little Hallingbury** Essex
12 D6 **Littleham** Devon
23 G6 **Littleham** Devon
18 D5 **Littlehampton** W Susx
74 C1 **Little Harrowden** Nhants
57 M7 **Little Haseley** Oxon
48 E5 **Little Haven** Pembks
31 K5 **Littlehaven** W Susx
85 K3 **Little Hay** Staffs
100 A7 **Little Haywood** Staffs
7 J4 **Littlehempston** Devon
69 K2 **Little Hereford** Herefs
62 A2 **Little Horkesley** Essex
60 C3 **Little Hormead** Herts
19 M3 **Little Horsted** E Susx
123 H4 **Little Horton** C Brad
58 C2 **Little Horwood** Bucks
115 H1 **Little Houghton** Barns
74 B3 **Little Houghton** Nhants
114 D5 **Little Hucklow** Derbys
133 G4 **Little Hutton** N York
74 C2 **Little Irchester** Nhants
27 H3 **Little Keyford** Somset
58 D6 **Little Kimble** Bucks
72 D4 **Little Kineton** Warwks
58 E7 **Little Kingshill** Bucks
146 E3 **Little Knox** D & G
137 J6 **Little Langdale** Cumb
28 B4 **Little Langford** Wilts
112 F6 **Little Leigh** Ches W
61 H5 **Little Leighs** Essex
121 L8 **Little Lever** Bolton
74 B5 **Little Linford** M Keyn
26 C6 **Little Load** Somset
20 C2 **Little London** E Susx
29 G2 **Little London** Hants
41 L8 **Little London** Hants
114 D6 **Little Longstone** Derbys
70 D6 **Little Malvern** Worcs
77 J7 **Little Maplestead** Essex
70 C7 **Little Marcle** Herefs
42 E3 **Little Marlow** Bucks
105 J7 **Little Massingham** Norfk
92 E3 **Little Melton** Norfk
205 H6 **Littlemill** Abers
213 L4 **Littlemill** Highld
53 L7 **Little Mill** Mons
57 L7 **Little Milton** Oxon
58 F7 **Little Missenden** Bucks
57 K7 **Littlemore** Oxon
139 H5 **Little Musgrave** Cumb
98 B8 **Little Ness** Shrops
49 G2 **Little Newcastle** Pembks
140 E4 **Little Newsham** Dur
26 C7 **Little Norton** Somset
62 F3 **Little Oakley** Essex

88 C6 **Little Oakley** Nhants
148 C4 **Little Orton** Cumb
101 G5 **Littleover** C Derb
86 B6 **Little Packington** Warwks
75 H3 **Little Paxton** Cambs
4 E2 **Little Petherick** Cnwll
93 G2 **Little Plumstead** Norfk
102 F6 **Little Ponton** Lincs
90 E6 **Littleport** Cambs
73 H4 **Little Preston** Nhants
89 J7 **Little Raveley** Cambs
125 J6 **Little Reedness** E R Yk
132 F8 **Little Ribston** N York
56 D4 **Little Rissington** Gloucs
56 F3 **Little Rollright** Oxon
106 A6 **Little Ryburgh** Norfk
148 F7 **Little Salkeld** Cumb
76 F7 **Little Sampford** Essex
111 K7 **Little Saughall** Ches W
77 H2 **Little Saxham** Suffk
212 B3 **Little Scatwell** Highld
76 C4 **Little Shelford** Cambs
120 E3 **Little Singleton** Lancs
125 G3 **Little Skipwith** N York
124 D6 **Little Smeaton** N York
106 A6 **Little Snoring** Norfk
39 H4 **Little Sodbury** S Glos
29 G5 **Little Somborne** Hants
39 L4 **Little Somerford** Wilts
99 G6 **Little Soudley** Shrops
141 J3 **Little Stainton** Darltn
112 B6 **Little Stanney** Ches W
75 G3 **Little Staughton** Bed
118 F8 **Little Steeping** Lincs
99 K6 **Little Stoke** Staffs
21 L2 **Littlestone-on-Sea** Kent
78 D3 **Little Stonham** Suffk
87 J4 **Little Stretton** Leics
83 J5 **Little Stretton** Shrops
138 E4 **Little Strickland** Cumb
89 H7 **Little Stukeley** Cambs
99 J6 **Little Sugnall** Staffs
158 B6 **Little Swinburne** Nthumb
146 C4 **Little Sypland** D & G
57 G3 **Little Tew** Oxon
61 L4 **Little Tey** Essex
90 D7 **Little Thetford** Cambs
151 K6 **Little Thorpe** Dur
87 G4 **Littlethorpe** Leics
132 E5 **Littlethorpe** N York
77 G4 **Little Thurlow Green** Suffk
45 L4 **Little Thurrock** Thurr
196 B6 **Littleton** Angus
112 C7 **Littleton** Ches W
146 B4 **Littleton** D & G
29 J5 **Littleton** Hants
26 C5 **Littleton** Somset
43 H6 **Littleton** Surrey
39 J4 **Littleton Drew** Wilts
38 E3 **Littleton-on-Severn** S Glos
27 M2 **Littleton Pannell** Wilts
10 D2 **Little Torrington** Devon
151 H6 **Littletown** Dur
121 K4 **Little Town** Lancs
128 F5 **Little Urswick** Cumb
46 F3 **Little Wakering** Essex
76 D6 **Little Walden** Essex
77 K5 **Little Waldingfield** Suffk
105 M5 **Little Walsingham** Norfk
61 H5 **Little Waltham** Essex

55 M2 **Little Washbourne** Gloucs
126 B4 **Little Weighton** E R Yk
88 D5 **Little Weldon** Nhants
78 C6 **Little Wenham** Suffk
84 B3 **Little Wenlock** Wrekin
26 F6 **Little Weston** Somset
17 H4 **Little Whitefield** IoW
42 D4 **Littlewick Green** W & M
76 D3 **Little Wilbraham** Cambs
55 K5 **Little Witcombe** Gloucs
70 D2 **Little Witley** Worcs
41 K2 **Little Wittenham** Oxon
72 C7 **Little Wolford** Warwks
44 F7 **Little Woodcote** Gt Lon
40 F2 **Littleworth** Oxon
99 L7 **Littleworth** Staffs
70 F4 **Littleworth** Worcs
77 G5 **Little Wratting** Suffk
74 D2 **Little Wymington** Bed
59 K3 **Little Wymondley** Herts
85 H3 **Little Wyrley** Staffs
77 H6 **Little Yeldham** Essex
61 H4 **Littley Green** Essex
114 D6 **Litton** Derbys
131 G5 **Litton** N York
26 E1 **Litton** Somset
14 A4 **Litton Cheney** Dorset
232 f3 **Liurbost** W Isls
111 K4 **Liverpool** Lpool
123 J5 **Liversedge** Kirk
7 J2 **Liverton** Devon
142 F4 **Liverton** R & Cl
176 E5 **Livingston** W Loth
176 E5 **Livingston Village** W Loth
111 G7 **Lixwm** Flints
3 J8 **Lizard** Cnwll
95 G4 **Llanaelhaearn** Gwynd
66 F1 **Llanafan** Cerdgn
67 L4 **Llanafan-Fawr** Powys
109 G4 **Llanallgo** IoA
97 J6 **Llanarmon Dyffryn Ceiriog** Wrexhm
97 J2 **Llanarmon-yn-Ial** Denbgs
65 L3 **Llanarth** Cerdgn
54 B5 **Llanarth** Mons
51 G2 **Llanarthne** Carmth
110 F5 **Llanasa** Flints
80 E7 **Llanbadarn Fawr** Cerdgn
82 C7 **Llanbadarn Fynydd** Powys
54 B7 **Llanbadoc** Mons
38 B3 **Llanbeder** Newpt
95 K7 **Llanbedr** Gwynd
53 K4 **Llanbedr** Powys
97 H2 **Llanbedr-Dyffryn-Clwyd** Denbgs
109 G5 **Llanbedrgoch** IoA
94 F6 **Llanbedrog** Gwynd
109 L7 **Llanbedr-y-Cennin** Conwy
95 K1 **Llanberis** Gwynd
82 C8 **Llanbethery** V Glam
36 F5 **Llanblethian** V Glam
49 L3 **Llanboidy** Carmth
37 J3 **Llanbradach** Caerph
81 J3 **Llanbrynmair** Powys
37 G6 **Llancadle** V Glam
37 G6 **Llancarfan** V Glam
54 D4 **Llancloudy** Herefs
37 J5 **Llandaff** Cardif
95 K6 **Llandanwg** Gwynd
109 G7 **Llanddaniel Fab** IoA
51 G3 **Llanddarog** Carmth

66 D1 **Llanddeiniol** Cerdgn
109 H7 **Llanddeiniolen** Gwynd
96 F5 **Llandderfel** Gwynd
108 D4 **Llanddeusant** IoA
53 G2 **Llanddew** Powys
50 F7 **Llanddewi** Swans
66 F4 **Llanddewi Brefi** Cerdgn
53 M5 **Llanddewi Rhydderch** Mons
49 K4 **Llanddewi Velfrey** Pembks
68 C2 **Llanddewi Ystradenni** Powys
109 M8 **Llanddoget** Conwy
109 H5 **Llanddona** IoA
50 B3 **Llanddowror** Carmth
110 C6 **Llanddulas** Conwy
95 K7 **Llanddwywe** Gwynd
109 G5 **Llanddyfnan** IoA
53 H3 **Llandefaelog-Tre'r-Graig** Powys
68 C7 **Llandefalle** Powys
109 H6 **Llandegfan** IoA
97 J3 **Llandegla** Denbgs
68 D2 **Llandegley** Powys
37 M2 **Llandegveth** Mons
51 J2 **Llandeilo** Carmth
68 C5 **Llandeilo Graban** Powys
48 E3 **Llandeloy** Pembks
54 B7 **Llandenny** Mons
38 B3 **Llandevaud** Newpt
38 B3 **Llandevenny** Mons
82 B5 **Llandinam** Powys
49 J3 **Llandissilio** Pembks
54 D7 **Llandogo** Mons
36 F6 **Llandough** V Glam
37 J5 **Llandough** V Glam
67 G7 **Llandovery** Carmth
36 E5 **Llandow** V Glam
66 F6 **Llandre** Carmth
80 E6 **Llandre** Cerdgn
49 J2 **Llandre Isaf** Pembks
97 G5 **Llandrillo** Denbgs
110 B5 **Llandrillo-yn-Rhos** Conwy
68 B3 **Llandrindod Wells** Powys
97 L8 **Llandrinio** Powys
109 L5 **Llandudno** Conwy
109 M6 **Llandudno Junction** Conwy
67 J6 **Llandulas** Powys
95 H2 **Llandwrog** Gwynd
51 J3 **Llandybie** Carmth
50 E3 **Llandyfaelog** Carmth
65 K6 **Llandyfriog** Cerdgn
109 H7 **Llandygai** Gwynd
65 H5 **Llandygwydd** Cerdgn
110 F8 **Llandyrnog** Denbgs
82 E4 **Llandyssil** Powys
65 L6 **Llandysul** Cerdgn
37 K4 **Llanedeyrn** Cardif
68 B6 **Llaneglwys** Powys
80 D3 **Llanegryn** Gwynd
51 G2 **Llanegwad** Carmth
108 F3 **Llaneilian** IoA
110 B6 **Llanelian-yn-Rhôs** Conwy
97 H3 **Llanelidan** Denbgs
68 D7 **Llanelieu** Powys
53 L5 **Llanellen** Mons
51 G5 **Llanelli** Carmth
51 G5 **Llanelli Crematorium** Carmth
96 A8 **Llanelltyd** Gwynd
82 E4 **Llanelwedd** Powys
95 K7 **Llanenddwyn** Gwynd
94 E6 **Llanengan** Gwynd
108 E5 **Llanerchymedd** IoA
82 B2 **Llanerfyl** Powys
108 D5 **Llanfachraeth** IoA
96 B7 **Llanfachreth** Gwynd
108 D6 **Llanfaelog** IoA

94 D6 **Llanfaelrhys** Gwynd
108 D4 **Llanfaethlu** IoA
95 K6 **Llanfair** Gwynd
82 C3 **Llanfair Caereinion** Powys
66 E4 **Llanfair Clydogau** Cerdgn
97 H2 **Llanfair Dyffryn Clwyd** Denbgs
109 K6 **Llanfairfechan** Conwy
109 G7 **Llanfair-is-gaer** Gwynd
109 G6 **Llanfair P G** IoA
110 C7 **Llanfair Talhaiarn** Conwy
82 E7 **Llanfair Waterdine** Shrops
108 F7 **Llanfair-y-Cwmwd** IoA
108 D4 **Llanfairynghornwy** IoA
108 C6 **Llanfair-yn-Neubwll** IoA
49 K4 **Llanfallteg** Carmth
49 K4 **Llanfallteg West** Carmth
80 D7 **Llanfarian** Cerdgn
97 J7 **Llanfechain** Powys
108 E3 **Llanfechell** IoA
97 J1 **Llanferres** Denbgs
66 B6 **Llanfihangel-ar-arth** Carmth
96 F3 **Llanfihangel Glyn Myfyr** Conwy
67 K7 **Llanfihangel Nant Bran** Powys
68 D2 **Llanfihangel Rhydithon** Powys
38 C3 **Llanfihangel Rogiet** Mons
80 F7 **Llanfihangel-y-Creuddyn** Cerdgn
82 C1 **Llanfihangel-yng-Ngwynfa** Powys
108 D6 **Llanfihangel yn Nhowyn** IoA
95 K5 **Llanfihangel-y-traethau** Gwynd
53 H2 **Llanfilo** Powys
53 L5 **Llanfoist** Mons
96 E5 **Llanfor** Gwynd
37 L2 **Llanfrechfa** Torfn
53 G3 **Llanfrynach** Powys
97 H2 **Llanfwrog** Denbgs
108 C5 **Llanfwrog** IoA
97 H8 **Llanfyllin** Powys
66 D8 **Llanfynydd** Carmth
97 L2 **Llanfynydd** Flints
49 L2 **Llanfyrnach** Pembks
81 L2 **Llangadfan** Powys
66 F8 **Llangadog** Carmth
108 E7 **Llangadwaladr** IoA
108 F7 **Llangaffo** IoA
67 K5 **Llangammarch Wells** Powys
36 E5 **Llangan** V Glam
54 D4 **Llangarron** Herefs
51 H2 **Llangathen** Carmth
53 K4 **Llangattock** Powys
54 A4 **Llangattock Lingoed** Mons
97 J7 **Llangedwyn** Powys
108 F6 **Llangefni** IoA
36 E3 **Llangeinor** Brdgnd
108 F7 **Llangeinwen** IoA
66 E3 **Llangeitho** Cerdgn
65 L6 **Llangeler** Carmth
80 D3 **Llangelynin** Gwynd
50 F3 **Llangendeirne** Carmth
51 H5 **Llangennech** Carmth
50 F7 **Llangennith** Swans
110 B7 **Llangernyw** Conwy
94 E6 **Llangian** Gwynd
64 C7 **Llangloffan** Pembks

49 K3 **Llanglydwen** Carmth
109 J5 **Llangoed** IoA
97 K4 **Llangollen** Denbgs
49 J3 **Llangolman** Pembks
53 H3 **Llangors** Powys
96 D6 **Llangower** Gwynd
65 K4 **Llangranog** Cerdgn
108 F6 **Llangristiolus** IoA
54 D4 **Llangrove** Herefs
68 E1 **Llangunllo** Powys
50 E2 **Llangunnor** Carmth
81 K7 **Llangurig** Powys
96 F4 **Llangwm** Conwy
54 B7 **Llangwm** Mons
49 G5 **Llangwm** Pembks
94 D6 **Llangwnnadl** Gwynd
66 D1 **Llangwyryfon**
    Cerdgn
66 E4 **Llangybi** Cerdgn
95 G4 **Llangybi** Gwynd
38 A2 **Llangybi** Mons
110 F8 **Llangynhafal** Denbgs
53 J4 **Llangynidr** Powys
50 B2 **Llangynin** Carmth
50 D3 **Llangynog** Carmth
97 G7 **Llangynog** Powys
36 D3 **Llangynwyd** Brdgnd
53 H3 **Llanhamlach** Powys
36 F4 **Llanharan** Rhondd
36 F4 **Llanharry** Rhondd
38 A2 **Llanhennock** Mons
53 K7 **Llanhilleth** Blae G
81 K6 **Llanidloes** Powys
94 E5 **Llaniestyn** Gwynd
68 E6 **Llanigon** Powys
80 E8 **Llanilar** Cerdgn
36 F4 **Llanilid** Rhondd
65 L3 **Llanina** Cerdgn
37 J4 **Llanishen** Cardif
54 C7 **Llanishen** Mons
109 J7 **Llanllechid** Gwynd
54 B7 **Llanllowell** Mons
82 B3 **Llanllugan** Powys
50 E2 **Llanllwch** Carmth
82 C5 **Llanllwchaiarn** Powys
66 C6 **Llanllwni** Carmth
95 H3 **Llanllyfni** Gwynd
50 F6 **Llanmadoc** Swans
38 B3 **Llanmaes** V Glam
38 B3 **Llanmartin** Newpt
50 B4 **Llanmiloe** Carmth
110 D7 **Llannefydd** Conwy
51 G4 **Llannon** Carmth
94 F5 **Llannor** Gwynd
66 C2 **Llanon** Cerdgn
53 L6 **Llanover** Mons
65 L8 **Llanpumsaint** Carmth
97 H7 **Llanrhaeadr-ym-**
    Mochnant Powys
48 D2 **Llanrhian** Pembks
50 F6 **Llanrhidian** Swans
96 B1 **Llanrhychwyn** Conwy
108 D4 **Llanrhyddlad** IoA
66 C1 **Llanrhystud** Cerdgn
54 C4 **Llanrothal** Herefs
109 G8 **Llanrug** Gwynd
37 K4 **Llanrumney** Cardif
96 C1 **Llanrwst** Conwy
66 C4 **Llansadurnen** Carmth
66 F7 **Llansadwrn** Carmth
109 H6 **Llansadwrn** IoA
50 E4 **Llansaint** Carmth
51 K6 **Llansamlet** Swans
109 M6 **Llansanffraid Glan**
    Conwy Conwy
110 C7 **Llansannan** Conwy
53 H4 **Llansantffraed** Powys
67 L2 **Llansantffraed-**
    Cwmdeuddwr Powys
68 C4 **Llansantffraed-in-**
    Elvel Powys
66 C2 **Llansantffraid**
    Cerdgn
97 K7 **Llansantffraid-ym-**
    Mechain Powys
66 E7 **Llansawel** Carmth

97 K6 **Llansilin** Powys
54 C7 **Llansoy** Mons
52 F3 **Llanspyddid** Powys
48 F6 **Llanstadwell** Pembks
50 D4 **Llansteffan** Carmth
37 L2 **Llantarnam** Torfn
49 K5 **Llanteg** Pembks
53 M5 **Llanthewy Skirrid**
    Mons
53 L3 **Llanthony** Mons
54 B5 **Llantilio-Crossenny**
    Mons
53 L5 **Llantilio Pertholey**
    Mons
38 B2 **Llantrisant** Mons
37 G4 **Llantrisant** Rhondd
37 G6 **Llantrithyd** V Glam
37 G3 **Llantwit Fardre**
    Rhondd
36 F6 **Llantwit Major**
    V Glam
96 D6 **Llanuwchllyn** Gwynd
38 B3 **Llanvaches** Newpt
38 C3 **Llanvair Discoed**
    Mons
54 A5 **Llanvapley** Mons
54 A5 **Llanvetherine** Mons
53 L4 **Llanvihangel**
    Crucorney Mons
96 F8 **Llanwddyn** Powys
66 C5 **Llanwenog** Cerdgn
38 A3 **Llanwern** Newpt
50 C1 **Llanwinio** Carmth
95 H2 **Llanwnda** Gwynd
64 C6 **Llanwnda** Pembks
66 C5 **Llanwnnen** Cerdgn
82 B5 **Llanwnog** Powys
66 F7 **Llanwrda** Carmth
81 H3 **Llanwrin** Powys
67 L2 **Llanwrthwl** Powys
67 J5 **Llanwrtyd Wells**
    Powys
82 C4 **Llanwyddelan** Powys
97 K7 **Llanyblodwel** Shrops
50 D3 **Llanybri** Carmth
66 C5 **Llanybydder** Carmth
49 J3 **Llanycefn** Pembks
64 D7 **Llanychaer Bridge**
    Pembks
96 D8 **Llanymawddwy**
    Gwynd
97 K7 **Llanymynech** Powys
108 D5 **Llanynghenedl** IoA
110 F8 **Llanynys** Denbgs
68 B3 **Llanyre** Powys
95 H5 **Llanystumdwy**
    Gwynd
53 H3 **Llanywern** Powys
49 H4 **Llawhaden** Pembks
81 K5 **Llawrglyn** Powys
97 M2 **Llay** Wrexhm
53 H6 **Llechrhyd** Caerph
65 H5 **Llechryd** Cerdgn
66 E1 **Lledrod** Cerdgn
94 E5 **Lleyn Peninsula**
94 F4 **Llithfaen** Gwynd
111 G6 **Lloc** Flints
68 D6 **Llowes** Powys
52 F6 **Llwydcoed** Rhondd
52 F6 **Llwydcoed**
    Crematorium Rhondd
82 B1 **Llwydiarth** Powys
66 B3 **Llwyncelyn** Cerdgn
65 L4 **Llwyndafydd** Cerdgn
80 D2 **Llwyngwril** Gwynd
97 K5 **Llwynmawr** Wrexhm
36 F2 **Llwynypia** Rhondd
97 L7 **Llynclys** Shrops
108 E5 **Llynfaes** IoA
110 B6 **Llysfaen** Conwy
68 C6 **Llyswen** Powys
36 E5 **Llysworney** V Glam
49 H3 **Llys-y-frân** Pembks
52 D3 **Llywel** Powys
176 C3 **Loan** Falk

177 J5 **Loanhead** Mdloth
147 G4 **Loaningfoot** D & G
163 J3 **Loans** S Ayrs
10 C7 **Lobhillcross** Devon
200 B8 **Lochailort** Highld
190 D7 **Lochaline** Highld
144 C4 **Lochans** D & G
155 H6 **Locharbriggs** D & G
182 D3 **Lochavich** Ag & B
183 G2 **Lochawe** Ag & B
233 C8 **Loch Baghasdail**
    W Isls
233 C8 **Lochboisdale** W Isls
181 J3 **Lochbuie** Ag & B
210 D6 **Lochcarron** Highld
181 L2 **Lochdon** Ag & B
181 L2 **Lochdonhead** Ag & B
172 D3 **Lochead** Ag & B
184 D3 **Lochearnhead** Stirlg
186 F2 **Lochee** C Dund
191 K2 **Locheilside Station**
    Highld
212 F6 **Lochend** Highld
233 c6 **Locheport** W Isls
233 c6 **Loch Euphoirt** W Isls
154 F7 **Lochfoot** D & G
172 F1 **Lochgair** Ag & B
186 C8 **Lochgelly** Fife
172 E2 **Lochgilphead** Ag & B
183 H6 **Lochgoilhead** Ag & B
186 D5 **Lochieheads** Fife
215 G2 **Lochill** Moray
214 B7 **Lochindorb Lodge**
    Highld
224 D4 **Lochinver** Highld
183 L8 **Loch Lomond**
211 L2 **Lochluichart** Highld
155 J5 **Lochmaben** D & G
233 c6 **Lochmaddy** W Isls
219 L7 **Loch Maree Hotel**
    Highld
233 c6 **Loch nam Madadh**
    W Isls
202 K1 **Loch Ness** Highld
186 C7 **Lochore** Fife
172 F7 **Lochranza** N Ayrs
197 H4 **Lochside** Abers
155 G6 **Lochside** D & G
213 J4 **Lochside** Highld
223 J5 **Lochslin** Highld
152 F6 **Lochton** S Ayrs
196 E4 **Lochty** Angus
187 H5 **Lochty** Fife
190 F5 **Lochuisge** Highld
174 C6 **Lochwinnoch** Rens
155 J3 **Lochwood** D & G
5 G4 **Lockengate** Cnwll
155 K5 **Lockerbie** D & G
40 C5 **Lockeridge** Wilts
28 F6 **Lockerley** Hants
38 A8 **Locking** N Som
112 F3 **Locking Stumps**
    Warrtn
126 B2 **Lockington** E R Yk
99 G6 **Lockleywood** Shrops
45 H6 **Locksbottom** Gt Lon
17 G2 **Locks Heath** Hants
134 C2 **Lockton** N York
87 L3 **Loddington** Leics
88 B7 **Loddington** Nhants
7 G6 **Loddiswell** Devon
93 H4 **Loddon** Norfk
76 D3 **Lode** Cambs
85 L7 **Lode Heath** Solhll
13 L4 **Loders** Dorset
85 H6 **Lodge Hill**
    Crematorium Birm
30 F6 **Lodsworth** W Susx
123 L5 **Lofthouse** Leeds
131 L5 **Lofthouse** N York
123 L5 **Lofthouse Gate**
    Wakefd
142 F4 **Loftus** R & Cl
164 C6 **Logan** E Ayrs
176 C6 **Loganlea** W Loth
99 G5 **Loggerheads** Staffs

197 H4 **Logie** Angus
186 F4 **Logie** Fife
214 C4 **Logie** Moray
205 K4 **Logie Coldstone**
    Abers
216 C6 **Logie Newton** Abers
197 G4 **Logie Pert** Angus
194 F5 **Logierait** P & K
217 H8 **Logierieve** Abers
49 K3 **Login** Carmth
75 C7 **Lolworth** Cambs
209 L4 **Lonbain** Highld
125 K2 **Londesborough**
    E R Yk
44 F4 **London** Gt Lon
4 F6 **London Apprentice**
    Cnwll
59 K7 **London Colney** Herts
132 D3 **Londonderry** N York
44 D2 **London Gateway**
    Services Gt Lon
102 F5 **Londonthorpe** Lincs
219 K6 **Londubh** Highld
219 J6 **Lonemore** Highld
38 D6 **Long Ashton** N Som
84 D8 **Long Bank** Worcs
102 D4 **Long Bennington**
    Lincs
151 G2 **Longbenton** N Tyne
56 D3 **Longborough** Gloucs
14 B4 **Long Bredy** Dorset
85 H7 **Longbridge** Birm
27 K4 **Longbridge Deverill**
    Wilts
73 J2 **Long Buckby** Nhants
26 F8 **Longburton** Dorset
102 B6 **Long Clawson** Leics
100 E5 **Longcliffe** Derbys
7 J4 **Longcombe** Devon
99 J7 **Long Compton** Staffs
56 F2 **Long Compton**
    Warwks
40 F3 **Longcot** Oxon
58 B6 **Long Crendon** Bucks
15 J1 **Long Crichel** Dorset
83 J3 **Longden** Shrops
44 D6 **Long Ditton** Surrey
85 J2 **Longdon** Staffs
70 E7 **Longdon** Worcs
85 J2 **Longdon Green** Staffs
84 B1 **Longdon upon Tern**
    Wrekin
11 K6 **Longdown** Devon
3 J4 **Longdowns** Cnwll
115 H7 **Long Duckmanton**
    Derbys
101 J5 **Long Eaton** Derbys
45 L6 **Longfield** Kent
86 D6 **Longford** Covtry
100 E5 **Longford** Derbys
55 J4 **Longford** Gloucs
98 F5 **Longford** Shrops
99 G8 **Longford** Wrekin
186 E2 **Longforgan** P & K
178 E6 **Longformacus**
    Border
158 E3 **Longframlington**
    Nthumb
112 C7 **Long Green** Ches W
55 J2 **Long Green** Worcs
15 K3 **Longham** Dorset
91 H7 **Longham** Norfk
57 H5 **Long Hanborough**
    Oxon
217 L6 **Longhaven** Abers
158 F4 **Longhirst** Nthumb
55 G4 **Longhope** Gloucs
234 b7 **Longhope** Ork
158 E4 **Longhorsley** Nthumb
169 J6 **Longhoughton**
    Nthumb
72 E2 **Long Itchington**
    Warwks
100 E5 **Longlane** Derbys
86 F7 **Long Lawford**
    Warwks

27 J3 **Longleat Safari Park** Wilts
55 J4 **Longlevens** Gloucs
195 L7 **Longleys** P & K
26 C6 **Long Load** Somset
216 E2 **Longmanhill** Abers
58 E5 **Long Marston** Herts
124 D1 **Long Marston** N York
71 L5 **Long Marston** Warwks
138 F3 **Long Marton** Cumb
77 J5 **Long Melford** Suffk
30 C5 **Longmoor Camp** Hants
214 F3 **Longmorn** Moray
113 K6 **Longmoss** Ches E
39 K3 **Long Newnton** Gloucs
167 J4 **Longnewton** Border
178 B5 **Long Newton** E Loth
141 J4 **Longnewton** S on T
55 H5 **Longney** Gloucs
177 L3 **Longniddry** E Loth
83 J4 **Longnor** Shrops
114 C3 **Longnor** Staffs
29 H3 **Longparish** Hants
130 F7 **Long Preston** N York
121 J3 **Longridge** Lancs
176 C5 **Longridge** W Loth
175 L4 **Longriggend** N Lans
126 E3 **Long Riston** E R Yk
2 E5 **Longrock** Cnwll
99 L2 **Longsdon** Staffs
217 K5 **Longside** Abers
76 B2 **Longstanton** Cambs
29 G4 **Longstock** Hants
75 J4 **Longstowe** Cambs
92 E5 **Long Stratton** Norfk
74 B5 **Long Street** M Keyn
28 C2 **Longstreet** Wilts
30 C3 **Long Sutton** Hants
104 C7 **Long Sutton** Lincs
26 C6 **Long Sutton** Somset
89 H4 **Longthorpe** C Pete
78 B2 **Long Thurlow** Suffk
138 B3 **Longthwaite** Cumb
99 K4 **Longton** C Stke
121 G5 **Longton** Lancs
148 C2 **Longtown** Cumb
53 L3 **Longtown** Herefs
236 d7 **Longueville** Jersey
83 K5 **Longville in the Dale** Shrops
84 B1 **Long Waste** Wrekin
101 J7 **Long Whatton** Leics
58 C6 **Longwick** Bucks
41 K2 **Long Wittenham** Oxon
158 D4 **Longwitton** Nthumb
146 C3 **Longwood** D & G
57 G7 **Longworth** Oxon
178 C3 **Longyester** E Loth
217 J3 **Lonmay** Abers
208 D5 **Lonmore** Highld
5 K5 **Looe** Cnwll
33 K3 **Loose** Kent
58 D7 **Loosley Row** Bucks
216 B4 **Lootcherbrae** Abers
26 B8 **Lopen** Somset
98 C6 **Loppington** Shrops
46 C7 **Lords Wood** Medway
195 J6 **Lornty** P & K
101 H3 **Loscoe** Derbys
214 F1 **Lossiemouth** Moray
4 F6 **Lost Gardens of Heligan** Cnwll
113 G6 **Lostock Gralam** Ches W
113 G6 **Lostock Green** Ches W
5 H4 **Lostwithiel** Cnwll
227 G6 **Lothbeg** Highld
122 E2 **Lothersdale** N York
227 G6 **Lothmore** Highld
42 E3 **Loudwater** Bucks
101 K8 **Loughborough** Leics

101 K8 **Loughborough Crematorium** Leics
51 H6 **Loughor** Swans
45 H2 **Loughton** Essex
74 B6 **Loughton** M Keyn
84 B6 **Loughton** Shrops
103 H8 **Lound** Lincs
116 B4 **Lound** Notts
93 K4 **Lound** Suffk
101 G8 **Lount** Leics
118 D4 **Louth** Lincs
122 B5 **Love Clough** Lancs
30 B8 **Lovedean** Hants
28 E7 **Lover** Wilts
115 L2 **Loversall** Donc
61 G6 **Loves Green** Essex
49 J5 **Loveston** Pembks
26 E5 **Lovington** Somset
124 C6 **Low Ackworth** Wakefd
144 B2 **Low Barbeth** D & G
130 C5 **Low Bentham** N York
130 B4 **Low Biggins** Cumb
138 E6 **Low Borrowbridge** Cumb
114 E3 **Low Bradfield** Sheff
122 F2 **Low Bradley** N York
116 C2 **Low Burnham** N Linc
136 D3 **Lowca** Cumb
133 L8 **Low Catton** E R Yk
148 D3 **Low Crosby** Cumb
102 A3 **Lowdham** Notts
141 J5 **Low Dinsdale** Darltn
124 E5 **Low Eggborough** N York
132 C3 **Low Ellington** N York
25 J4 **Lower Aisholt** Somset
14 E2 **Lower Ansty** Dorset
55 J3 **Lower Apperley** Gloucs
11 J7 **Lower Ashton** Devon
42 C4 **Lower Assendon** Oxon
121 G4 **Lower Bartle** Lancs
41 L5 **Lower Basildon** W Berk
31 L6 **Lower Beeding** W Susx
88 E5 **Lower Benefield** Nhants
71 H2 **Lower Bentley** Worcs
72 F4 **Lower Boddington** Nhants
30 D3 **Lower Bourne** Surrey
72 C6 **Lower Brailes** Warwks
199 L2 **Lower Breakish** Highld
70 E3 **Lower Broadheath** Worcs
69 G4 **Lower Broxwood** Herefs
69 K6 **Lower Bullingham** Herefs
28 D7 **Lower Burgate** Hants
75 H5 **Lower Caldecote** C Beds
55 H7 **Lower Cam** Gloucs
68 B7 **Lower Chapel** Powys
27 L5 **Lower Chicksgrove** Wilts
28 F2 **Lower Chute** Wilts
45 G3 **Lower Clapton** Gt Lon
85 G7 **Lower Clent** Worcs
123 J8 **Lower Cumberworth** Kirk
74 F2 **Lower Dean** Bed
210 C3 **Lower Diabaig** Highld
20 B4 **Lower Dicker** E Susx
83 G6 **Lower Down** Shrops
133 G6 **Lower Dunsforth** N York
70 B5 **Lower Egleton** Herefs
74 D6 **Lower End** M Keyn
35 H5 **Lower Eythorne** Kent
38 D5 **Lower Failand** N Som

30 B4 **Lower Farringdon** Hants
43 H6 **Lower Feltham** Gt Lon
30 C3 **Lower Froyle** Hants
7 L2 **Lower Gabwell** Devon
222 D4 **Lower Gledfield** Highld
26 C3 **Lower Godney** Somset
75 G7 **Lower Gravenhurst** C Beds
32 F5 **Lower Green** Kent
33 G5 **Lower Green** Kent
43 H6 **Lower Halliford** Surrey
46 E6 **Lower Halstow** Kent
15 J4 **Lower Hamworthy** Poole
34 F4 **Lower Hardres** Kent
58 C5 **Lower Hartwell** Bucks
68 F4 **Lower Hergest** Herefs
57 J3 **Lower Heyford** Oxon
123 H7 **Lower Houses** Kirk
113 G3 **Lower Irlam** Salfd
160 A2 **Lower Killeyan** Ag & B
38 C7 **Lower Langford** N Som
187 G6 **Lower Largo** Fife
100 A5 **Lower Leigh** Staffs
23 K4 **Lower Loxhore** Devon
54 E5 **Lower Lydbrook** Gloucs
69 H2 **Lower Lye** Herefs
37 K3 **Lower Machen** Newpt
25 J4 **Lower Merridge** Somset
73 G6 **Lower Middleton Cheney** Nhants
71 H5 **Lower Moor** Worcs
38 F3 **Lower Morton** S Glos
60 C6 **Lower Nazeing** Essex
37 J6 **Lower Penarth** V Glam
84 F4 **Lower Penn** Staffs
113 H6 **Lower Peover** Ches E
71 L5 **Lower Quinton** Warwks
78 C6 **Lower Raydon** Suffk
25 G4 **Lower Roadwater** Somset
39 L4 **Lower Seagry** Wilts
74 E6 **Lower Shelton** C Beds
42 C4 **Lower Shiplake** Oxon
72 F3 **Lower Shuckburgh** Warwks
56 D4 **Lower Slaughter** Gloucs
35 H6 **Lower Standen** Kent
39 L4 **Lower Stanton St Quintin** Wilts
46 D5 **Lower Stoke** Medway
38 F2 **Lower Stone** Gloucs
91 L5 **Lower Stow Bedon** Norfk
106 F5 **Lower Street** Norfk
78 D4 **Lower Street** Suffk
16 F1 **Lower Swanwick** Hants
56 D3 **Lower Swell** Gloucs
100 A5 **Lower Tean** Staffs
7 G2 **Lower Town** Devon
64 D6 **Lower Town** Pembks
72 D5 **Lower Town** Pembks
11 K8 **Lower Upcott** Devon
29 K7 **Lower Upham** Hants
26 B2 **Lower Weare** Somset
68 F4 **Lower Welson** Herefs
71 G6 **Lower Westmancote** Worcs
27 H3 **Lower Whatley** Somset

112 E5 **Lower Whitley** Ches W
29 M4 **Lower Wield** Hants
20 C5 **Lower Willingdon** E Susx
113 J7 **Lower Withington** Ches E
28 C4 **Lower Woodford** Wilts
14 B3 **Lower Wraxhall** Dorset
87 K3 **Lowesby** Leics
93 L5 **Lowestoft** Suffk
137 G3 **Loweswater** Cumb
151 G3 **Low Fell** Gatesd
31 L4 **Lowfield Heath** W Susx
174 E2 **Low Gartachorrans** Stirlg
132 C5 **Low Grantley** N York
26 B5 **Low Ham** Somset
132 D7 **Low Harrogate** N York
148 E5 **Low Hesket** Cumb
134 B6 **Low Hutton** N York
88 E7 **Lowick** Nhants
168 F2 **Lowick** Nthumb
129 G3 **Lowick Green** Cumb
137 G3 **Low Lorton** Cumb
116 D7 **Low Marnham** Notts
142 E7 **Low Mill** N York
151 H5 **Low Moorsley** Sundld
136 D3 **Low Moresby** Cumb
129 J3 **Low Newton** Cumb
149 G3 **Low Row** Cumb
140 B7 **Low Row** N York
144 B2 **Low Salchrie** D & G
125 L7 **Low Santon** N Linc
71 L2 **Lowsonford** Warwks
92 E4 **Low Tharston** Norfk
138 D3 **Lowther** Cumb
135 G7 **Lowthorpe** E R Yk
25 J7 **Lowton** Somset
176 D2 **Low Torry** Fife
141 J5 **Low Worsall** N York
137 K6 **Low Wray** Cumb
11 L2 **Loxbeare** Devon
31 G4 **Loxhill** Surrey
23 K4 **Loxhore** Devon
72 C4 **Loxley** Warwks
26 A1 **Loxton** N Som
31 H5 **Loxwood** W Susx
229 J6 **Loyal Lodge** Highld
87 K6 **Lubenham** Leics
24 E3 **Luccombe** Somset
17 H6 **Luccombe Village** IoW
169 H4 **Lucker** Nthumb
6 B2 **Luckett** Cnwll
77 J7 **Lucking Street** Essex
39 J4 **Luckington** Wilts
24 E4 **Luckwell Bridge** Somset
69 J2 **Lucton** Herefs
233 b9 **Ludag** W Isls
118 D3 **Ludborough** Lincs
6 F5 **Ludbrook** Devon
49 K5 **Ludchurch** Pembks
122 F5 **Luddenden** Calder
122 F5 **Luddenden Foot** Calder
46 A6 **Luddesdown** Kent
125 J7 **Luddington** N Linc
71 L4 **Luddington** Warwks
89 G6 **Luddington in the Brook** Nhants
117 K4 **Ludford** Lincs
83 K8 **Ludford** Shrops
58 A4 **Ludgershall** Bucks
28 E2 **Ludgershall** Wilts
2 E5 **Ludgvan** Cnwll
107 H8 **Ludham** Norfk
83 K7 **Ludlow** Shrops
26 B8 **Ludney** Somset
27 K6 **Ludwell** Wilts
151 J6 **Ludworth** Dur

178 B3 **Luffness** E Loth
164 C5 **Lugar** E Ayrs
178 D4 **Luggate Burn** E Loth
175 K4 **Luggiebank** N Lans
174 D7 **Lugton** E Ayrs
69 K6 **Lugwardine** Herefs
209 J8 **Luib** Highld
181 L5 **Luing** Ag & B
69 H6 **Lulham** Herefs
86 B2 **Lullington** Derbys
27 H2 **Lullington** Somset
38 D7 **Lulsgate Bottom** N Som
70 D4 **Lulsley** Worcs
122 F6 **Lumb** Calder
122 C5 **Lumb** Lancs
124 D4 **Lumby** N York
175 H4 **Lumloch** E Duns
206 B4 **Lumphanan** Abers
186 C8 **Lumphinnans** Fife
205 K2 **Lumsden** Abers
197 H6 **Lunan** Angus
196 D6 **Lunanhead** Angus
186 A2 **Luncarty** P & K
126 B2 **Lund** E R Yk
125 G4 **Lund** N York
11 L8 **Lundie** Angus
187 G6 **Lundin Links** Fife
187 G6 **Lundin Mill** Fife
22 B3 **Lundy** Devon
181 L5 **Lunga** Ag & B
235 d4 **Lunna** Shet
33 J2 **Lunsford** Kent
20 E4 **Lunsford's Cross** E Susx
111 K2 **Lunt** Sefton
12 F2 **Luppitt** Devon
123 L6 **Lupset** Wakefd
129 L4 **Lupton** Cumb
7 J4 **Lurgashall** W Susx
11 L2 **Lurley** Devon
7 J4 **Luscombe** Devon
183 L8 **Luss** Ag & B
171 L2 **Lussagiven** Ag & B
208 D3 **Lusta** Highld
11 H8 **Lustleigh** Devon
69 J2 **Luston** Herefs
197 G3 **Luthermuir** Abers
186 E4 **Luthrie** Fife
7 K1 **Luton** Devon
12 D2 **Luton** Devon
59 H4 **Luton** Luton
46 C6 **Luton** Medway
59 J4 *Luton Airport* Luton
87 G6 **Lutterworth** Leics
6 E4 **Lutton** Devon
7 G4 **Lutton** Devon
104 C7 **Lutton** Lincs
89 G6 **Lutton** Nhants
24 F4 **Luxborough** Somset
2 C1 **Luxulyan** Cnwll
231 J7 **Lybster** Highld
83 G6 **Lydbury North** Shrops
21 K2 **Lydd** Kent
21 L2 *Lydd Airport* Kent
35 H5 **Lydden** Kent
35 K2 **Lydden** Kent
88 C4 **Lyddington** Rutlnd
25 H5 **Lydeard St Lawrence** Somset
10 D7 **Lydford** Devon
26 E5 **Lydford on Fosse** Somset
122 D5 **Lydgate** Calder
83 G5 **Lydham** Shrops
40 C3 **Lydiard Millicent** Wilts
40 C4 **Lydiard Tregoze** Swindn
111 K2 **Lydiate** Sefton
85 H7 **Lydiate Ash** Worcs
27 H8 **Lydlinch** Dorset
54 F7 **Lydney** Gloucs
49 J7 **Lydstep** Pembks
85 G6 **Lye** Dudley
32 F6 **Lye Green** E Susx
71 L2 **Lye Green** Warwks

27 J3 **Lye's Green** Wilts
41 H2 **Lyford** Oxon
34 F6 **Lymbridge Green** Kent
13 J4 **Lyme Regis** Dorset
34 F6 **Lyminge** Kent
16 C4 **Lymington** Hants
18 D5 **Lyminster** W Susx
113 G4 **Lymm** Warrtn
112 F4 **Lymm Services** Warrtn
34 F7 **Lympne** Kent
25 M1 **Lympsham** Somset
12 C5 **Lympstone** Devon
203 J5 **Lynchat** Highld
92 D3 **Lynch Green** Norfk
16 C2 **Lyndhurst** Hants
88 C3 **Lyndon** Rutlnd
166 B2 **Lyne** Border
43 G7 **Lyne** Surrey
98 C6 **Lyneal** Shrops
56 F4 **Lyneham** Oxon
40 A5 **Lyneham** Wilts
40 A5 *Lyneham Airport* Wilts
206 E4 **Lyne of Skene** Abers
234 b7 **Lyness** Ork
106 C8 **Lyng** Norfk
25 M5 **Lyng** Somset
23 L2 **Lynmouth** Devon
214 F7 **Lynn of Shenval** Moray
34 C3 **Lynsted** Kent
23 L2 **Lynton** Devon
14 C2 **Lyon's Gate** Dorset
69 G4 **Lyonshall** Herefs
15 H4 **Lytchett Matravers** Dorset
15 H4 **Lytchett Minster** Dorset
231 K3 **Lyth** Highld
120 E5 **Lytham** Lancs
120 D5 **Lytham St Anne's** Lancs
143 H5 **Lythe** N York
230 F3 **Lythmore** Highld

M

3 K4 **Mabe Burnthouse** Cnwll
119 G2 **Mablethorpe** Lincs
113 K6 **Macclesfield** Ches E
113 K6 **Macclesfield Crematorium** Ches E
216 D2 **Macduff** Abers
161 J7 **Macharioch** Ag & B
37 K3 **Machen** Caerph
162 A3 **Machrie** N Ayrs
161 G5 **Machrihanish** Ag & B
180 E8 **Machrins** Ag & B
81 G4 **Machynlleth** Powys
51 G5 **Machynys** Carmth
100 F5 **Mackworth** Derbys
177 L4 **Macmerry** E Loth
185 K3 **Madderty** P & K
176 C3 **Maddiston** Falk
99 H4 **Madeley** Staffs
84 C3 **Madeley** Wrekin
76 B3 **Madingley** Cambs
69 H6 **Madley** Herefs
70 E5 **Madresfield** Worcs
2 E5 **Madron** Cnwll
49 J3 **Maenclochog** Pembks
36 F5 **Maendy** V Glam
95 L4 **Maentwrog** Gwynd
65 L3 **Maen-y-groes** Cerdgn
99 H5 **Maer** Staffs
36 F2 **Maerdy** Rhondd
97 L7 **Maesbrook** Shrops
97 L7 **Maesbury** Shrops
97 L7 **Maesbury Marsh** Shrops
65 K5 **Maesllyn** Cerdgn
36 D3 **Maesteg** Brdgnd

51 H3 **Maesybont** Carmth
37 J2 **Maesycwmmer** Caerph
215 H5 **Maggieknockater** Moray
20 C4 **Magham Down** E Susx
111 K2 **Maghull** Sefton
87 G6 **Magna Park** Leics
38 B3 **Magor** Mons
38 B3 *Magor Services* Mons
32 B6 **Maidenbower** W Susx
27 J4 **Maiden Bradley** Wilts
7 L3 **Maidencombe** Torbay
13 H4 **Maidenhayne** Devon
38 E6 **Maiden Head** N Som
42 E4 **Maidenhead** W & M
14 B3 **Maiden Newton** Dorset
163 G7 **Maidens** S Ayrs
42 E5 **Maiden's Green** Br For
118 D5 **Maidenwell** Lincs
49 G7 **Maiden Wells** Pembks
73 H4 **Maidford** Nhants
73 K7 **Maids Moreton** Bucks
33 K3 **Maidstone** Kent
33 L3 *Maidstone Services* Kent
87 L7 **Maidwell** Nhants
235 d6 **Mail** Shet
37 L3 **Maindee** Newpt
234 c6 **Mainland** Ork
235 c5 **Mainland** Shet
141 H2 **Mainsforth** Dur
196 E4 **Mains of Balhall** Angus
197 G2 **Mains of Balnakettle** Abers
214 D7 **Mains of Dalvey** Highld
197 H2 **Mains of Haulkerton** Abers
215 K8 **Mains of Lesmoir** Abers
147 G4 **Mainsriddle** D & G
82 F6 **Mainstone** Shrops
55 J4 **Maisemore** Gloucs
101 G4 **Makeney** Derbys
7 G7 **Malborough** Devon
61 K6 **Maldon** Essex
131 G6 **Malham** N York
209 G2 **Maligar** Highld
199 L6 **Mallaig** Highld
199 L5 **Mallaigvaig** Highld
177 G5 **Malleny Mills** C Edin
108 E7 **Malltraeth** IoA
81 J2 **Mallwyd** Gwynd
39 L3 **Malmesbury** Wilts
24 C2 **Malmsmead** Devon
98 C3 **Malpas** Ches W
4 D7 **Malpas** Cnwll
37 L3 **Malpas** Newpt
115 K3 **Maltby** Rothm
141 L5 **Maltby** S on T
118 F5 **Maltby le Marsh** Lincs
34 B6 **Maltman's Hill** Kent
134 C5 **Malton** N York
70 D5 **Malvern Hills** Worcs
70 E5 **Malvern Link** Worcs
70 D6 **Malvern Wells** Worcs
70 C1 **Mamble** Worcs
53 L7 **Mamhilad** Mons
3 K6 **Manaccan** Cnwll
82 C3 **Manafon** Powys
232 d5 **Manais** W Isls
11 H8 **Manaton** Devon
118 E4 **Manby** Lincs
86 D4 **Mancetter** Warwks
113 J3 **Manchester** Manch
113 J5 *Manchester Airport* Manch
111 K7 **Mancot** Flints
201 L5 **Mandally** Highld
179 G7 **Manderston House** Border

90 C5 **Manea** Cambs
85 K4 **Maney** Birm
140 F4 **Manfield** N York
38 F5 **Mangotsfield** S Glos
232 d5 **Manish** W Isls
112 D7 **Manley** Ches W
53 J7 **Manmoel** Caerph
188 C7 **Mannel** Ag & B
40 C8 **Manningford Bohune** Wilts
40 C8 **Manningford Bruce** Wilts
123 H4 **Manningham** C Brad
31 K5 **Manning's Heath** W Susx
15 K2 **Mannington** Dorset
62 D2 **Manningtree** Essex
207 H4 **Mannofield** C Aber
49 H7 **Manorbier** Pembks
49 H7 **Manorbier Newton** Pembks
167 K3 **Manorhill** Border
64 C7 **Manorowen** Pembks
45 H3 **Manor Park** Gt Lon
45 H4 **Manor Park Crematorium** Gt Lon
69 H5 **Mansell Gamage** Herefs
69 H5 **Mansell Lacy** Herefs
164 C6 **Mansfield** E Ayrs
101 K1 **Mansfield** Notts
101 K2 **Mansfield & District Crematorium** Notts
115 K8 **Mansfield Woodhouse** Notts
27 J7 **Manston** Dorset
35 J2 **Manston** Kent
124 B4 **Manston** Leeds
15 J2 **Manswood** Dorset
88 F1 **Manthorpe** Lincs
116 F2 **Manton** N Linc
88 C3 **Manton** Rutlnd
40 D6 **Manton** Wilts
60 D3 **Manuden** Essex
26 F6 **Maperton** Somset
102 B1 **Maplebeck** Notts
42 A5 **Mapledurham** Oxon
30 B2 **Mapledurwell** Hants
31 K6 **Maplehurst** W Susx
45 K7 **Maplescombe** Kent
100 D3 **Mapleton** Derbys
101 H4 **Mapperley** Derbys
101 L4 **Mapperley Park** C Nott
13 L3 **Mapperton** Dorset
71 J2 **Mappleborough Green** Warwks
126 F2 **Mappleton** E R Yk
123 L7 **Mapplewell** Barns
14 E2 **Mappowder** Dorset
4 C5 **Marazanvose** Cnwll
2 F5 **Marazion** Cnwll
98 E4 **Marbury** Ches E
90 B4 **March** Cambs
165 J6 **March** S Lans
41 J2 **Marcham** Oxon
98 E6 **Marchamley** Shrops
100 C6 **Marchington** Staffs
94 F7 **Marchros** Gwynd
98 A3 **Marchwiel** Wrexhm
16 D1 **Marchwood** Hants
36 E6 **Marcross** V Glam
69 K5 **Marden** Herefs
33 J4 **Marden** Kent
40 C8 **Marden** Wilts
33 K5 **Marden Thorn** Kent
53 L5 **Mardy** Mons
103 L1 **Mareham le Fen** Lincs
118 C7 **Mareham on the Hill** Lincs
18 E3 **Marehill** W Susx
19 M2 **Maresfield** E Susx
126 E5 **Marfleet** C KuH
98 A2 **Marford** Wrexhm

36 B3	**Margam** Neath
36 C4	**Margam Crematorium** Neath
27 J7	**Margaret Marsh** Dorset
61 G7	**Margaretting** Essex
61 G7	**Margaretting Tye** Essex
35 K1	**Margate** Kent
162 B3	**Margnaheglish** N Ayrs
145 M5	**Margrie** D & G
142 E4	**Margrove Park** R & Cl
91 G2	**Marham** Norfk
9 G4	**Marhamchurch** Cnwll
89 C3	**Marholm** C Pete
24 B6	**Mariansleigh** Devon
46 F5	**Marine Town** Kent
206 D4	**Marionburgh** Abers
209 H2	**Marishader** Highld
6 C3	**Maristow** Devon
155 J5	**Marjoriebanks** D & G
26 B2	**Mark** Somset
32 E5	**Markbeech** Kent
119 G5	**Markby** Lincs
33 G6	**Mark Cross** E Susx
100 F5	**Markeaton Crematorium** C Derb
86 E3	**Market Bosworth** Leics
89 G2	**Market Deeping** Lincs
98 F5	**Market Drayton** Shrops
87 K6	**Market Harborough** Leics
28 A1	**Market Lavington** Wilts
88 C1	**Market Overton** Rutlnd
117 J4	**Market Rasen** Lincs
118 C5	**Market Stainton** Lincs
115 K7	**Market Warsop** Notts
125 K6	**Market Weighton** E R Yk
92 B7	**Market Weston** Suffk
86 F2	**Markfield** Leics
53 J7	**Markham** Caerph
116 B6	**Markham Moor** Notts
186 E6	**Markinch** Fife
132 D6	**Markington** N York
178 C3	**Markle** E Loth
38 F7	**Marksbury** BaNES
61 L4	**Marks Tey** Essex
59 H5	**Markyate** Herts
40 D6	**Marlborough** Wilts
71 K4	**Marlcliff** Warwks
7 K3	**Marldon** Devon
79 G3	**Marlesford** Suffk
92 D2	**Marlingford** Norfk
48 D5	**Marloes** Pembks
42 D3	**Marlow** Bucks
42 D3	**Marlow Bottom** Bucks
32 D4	**Marlpit Hill** Kent
27 H7	**Marnhull** Dorset
113 L4	**Marple** Stockp
115 K1	**Marr** Donc
140 D7	**Marrick** N York
122 F7	**Marsden** Kirk
151 J3	**Marsden** S Tyne
59 K6	**Marshalswick** Herts
106 E7	**Marsham** Norfk
57 K7	**Marsh Baldon** Oxon
35 J3	**Marshborough** Kent
83 J5	**Marshbrook** Shrops
118 E2	**Marshchapel** Lincs
59 H3	**Marsh Farm** Luton
37 K4	**Marshfield** Newpt
39 H5	**Marshfield** S Glos
8 F6	**Marshgate** Cnwll
57 M4	**Marsh Gibbon** Bucks
12 D4	**Marsh Green** Devon
32 D4	**Marsh Green** Kent
90 D2	**Marshland St James** Norfk
115 H5	**Marsh Lane** Derbys
24 F3	**Marsh Street** Somset
13 J3	**Marshwood** Dorset
140 D6	**Marske** N York
142 D3	**Marske-by-the-Sea** R & Cl
69 G3	**Marston** Herefs
102 E4	**Marston** Lincs
57 K6	**Marston** Oxon
99 L6	**Marston** Staffs
27 L1	**Marston** Wilts
85 L6	**Marston Green** Solhll
26 E6	**Marston Magna** Somset
40 C2	**Marston Meysey** Wilts
100 C5	**Marston Montgomery** Derbys
74 E6	**Marston Moretaine** C Beds
100 E6	**Marston on Dove** Derbys
73 G6	**Marston St Lawrence** Nhants
87 K6	**Marston Trussell** Nhants
54 D4	**Marstow** Herefs
58 F5	**Marsworth** Bucks
40 F7	**Marten** Wilts
113 J6	**Marthall** Ches E
107 J8	**Martham** Norfk
28 B7	**Martin** Hants
35 J5	**Martin** Kent
103 J1	**Martin** Lincs
118 C7	**Martin** Lincs
23 L2	**Martinhoe** Devon
70 F3	**Martin Hussingtree** Worcs
14 C5	**Martinstown** Dorset
78 F5	**Martlesham** Suffk
78 F5	**Martlesham Heath** Suffk
49 H5	**Martletwy** Pembks
70 D3	**Martley** Worcs
26 C7	**Martock** Somset
113 J7	**Marton** Ches E
126 F3	**Marton** E R Yk
116 D5	**Marton** Lincs
142 B4	**Marton** Middsb
132 F6	**Marton** N York
134 B3	**Marton** N York
82 F3	**Marton** Shrops
72 E2	**Marton** Warwks
132 E5	**Marton-le-Moor** N York
29 K5	**Martyr Worthy** Hants
234 H4	**Marwick** Ork
23 H4	**Marwood** Devon
212 D4	**Marybank** Highld
212 E3	**Maryburgh** Highld
207 G5	**Maryculter** Abers
179 G6	**Marygold** Border
175 G4	**Maryhill** C Glas
197 H3	**Marykirk** Abers
44 F4	**Marylebone** Gt Lon
121 H8	**Marylebone** Wigan
214 F6	**Marypark** Moray
147 H7	**Maryport** Cumb
144 D7	**Maryport** D & G
10 C7	**Marystow** Devon
6 D1	**Mary Tavy** Devon
197 H5	**Maryton** Angus
206 B6	**Marywell** Abers
207 H5	**Marywell** Abers
197 H7	**Marywell** Angus
132 C4	**Masham** N York
130 C4	**Masongill** N York
163 J5	**Masonhill Crematorium** S Ayrs
115 J6	**Mastin Moor** Derbys
60 E5	**Matching Green** Essex
60 E5	**Matching Tye** Essex
158 C7	**Matfen** Nthumb
33 H5	**Matfield** Kent
38 D3	**Mathern** Mons
70 D5	**Mathon** Herefs
48 E2	**Mathry** Pembks
106 D5	**Matlask** Norfk
100 F1	**Matlock** Derbys
100 F2	**Matlock Bath** Derbys
55 J5	**Matson** Gloucs
116 B4	**Mattersey** Notts
42 B8	**Mattingley** Hants
92 C2	**Mattishall** Norfk
92 C2	**Mattishall Burgh** Norfk
163 L4	**Mauchline** E Ayrs
217 H5	**Maud** Abers
236 d6	**Maufant** Jersey
56 D3	**Maugersbury** Gloucs
237 e3	**Maughold** IoM
212 C6	**Mauld** Highld
74 F6	**Maulden** C Beds
138 F4	**Maulds Meaburn** Cumb
132 E3	**Maunby** N York
25 G5	**Maundown** Somset
93 K2	**Mautby** Norfk
85 J1	**Mavesyn Ridware** Staffs
118 E7	**Mavis Enderby** Lincs
147 J5	**Mawbray** Cumb
121 G7	**Mawdesley** Lancs
36 C4	**Mawdlam** Brdgnd
3 J6	**Mawgan** Cnwll
4 D3	**Mawgan Porth** Cnwll
3 J3	**Mawla** Cnwll
3 K5	**Mawnan** Cnwll
3 K5	**Mawnan Smith** Cnwll
88 B7	**Mawsley** Nhants
89 G2	**Maxey** C Pete
86 B6	**Maxstoke** Warwks
34 F5	**Maxted Street** Kent
167 J4	**Maxton** Border
35 J6	**Maxton** Kent
155 G6	**Maxwell Town** D & G
9 H6	**Maxworthy** Cnwll
99 J3	**May Bank** Staffs
163 H7	**Maybole** S Ayrs
43 G8	**Maybury** Surrey
33 G7	**Mayfield** E Susx
177 K5	**Mayfield** Mdloth
100 D4	**Mayfield** Staffs
31 G1	**Mayford** Surrey
55 G4	**May Hill** Gloucs
61 L7	**Mayland** Essex
61 L7	**Maylandsea** Essex
20 C3	**Maynard's Green** E Susx
93 J4	**Maypole Green** Norfk
77 K3	**Maypole Green** Suffk
39 G8	**Meadgate** BaNES
58 D6	**Meadle** Bucks
151 G6	**Meadowfield** Dur
9 K8	**Meadwell** Devon
123 K3	**Meanwood** Leeds
26 C3	**Meare** Somset
25 L6	**Meare Green** Somset
25 M6	**Meare Green** Somset
174 F7	**Mearns** E Rens
74 B2	**Mears Ashby** Nhants
86 D2	**Measham** Leics
129 J4	**Meathop** Cumb
6 D3	**Meavy** Devon
88 B5	**Medbourne** Leics
9 H2	**Meddon** Devon
115 L7	**Meden Vale** Notts
42 D4	**Medmenham** Bucks
150 E4	**Medomsley** Dur
30 A4	**Medstead** Hants
46 C7	**Medway Crematorium** Kent
46 D7	**Medway Services** Medway
99 M1	**Meerbrook** Staffs
60 C2	**Meesden** Herts
10 E3	**Meeth** Devon
107 G6	**Meeting House Hill** Norfk
50 C2	**Meidrim** Carmth
82 D2	**Meifod** Powys
195 L7	**Meigle** P & K
164 F6	**Meikle Carco** D & G
175 J7	**Meikle Earnock** S Lans
173 H6	**Meikle Kilmory** Ag & B
195 G8	**Meikle Obney** P & K
195 J7	**Meikleour** P & K
216 D7	**Meikle Wartle** Abers
50 F4	**Meinciau** Carmth
99 L4	**Meir** C Stke
75 L5	**Melbourn** Cambs
101 G7	**Melbourne** Derbys
125 H2	**Melbourne** E R Yk
27 K7	**Melbury Abbas** Dorset
14 B2	**Melbury Bubb** Dorset
14 B2	**Melbury Osmond** Dorset
74 E2	**Melchbourne** Bed
14 E2	**Melcombe Bingham** Dorset
10 E6	**Meldon** Devon
158 E5	**Meldon** Nthumb
75 L5	**Meldreth** Cambs
184 F7	**Meldrum** Stirlg
182 B5	**Melfort** Ag & B
196 E5	**Melgund Castle** Angus
110 E5	**Meliden** Denbgs
97 G3	**Melin-y-wig** Denbgs
138 D3	**Melkinthorpe** Cumb
149 J3	**Melkridge** Nthumb
39 K7	**Melksham** Wilts
130 B5	**Melling** Lancs
111 L2	**Melling** Sefton
92 C8	**Mellis** Suffk
219 K3	**Mellon Charles** Highld
219 K3	**Mellon Udrigle** Highld
121 J4	**Mellor** Lancs
113 M4	**Mellor** Stockp
121 J4	**Mellor Brook** Lancs
27 G2	**Mells** Somset
149 G7	**Melmerby** Cumb
131 K3	**Melmerby** N York
132 K4	**Melmerby** N York
229 J3	**Melness** Highld
13 L3	**Melplash** Dorset
167 H4	**Melrose** Border
234 b7	**Melsetter** Ork
140 F5	**Melsonby** N York
123 G7	**Meltham** Kirk
126 B5	**Melton** E R Yk
79 G4	**Melton** Suffk
106 C6	**Melton Constable** Norfk
102 C8	**Melton Mowbray** Leics
126 D7	**Melton Ross** N Linc
219 H4	**Melvaig** Highld
83 G1	**Melverley** Shrops
230 C3	**Melvich** Highld
13 H2	**Membury** Devon
40 F5	**Membury Services** W Berk
217 H2	**Memsie** Abers
196 C5	**Memus** Angus
109 H6	**Menai Bridge** IoA
92 F6	**Mendham** Suffk
26 D2	**Mendip Hills**
78 D2	**Mendlesham** Suffk
78 D2	**Mendlesham Green** Suffk
5 L4	**Menheniot** Cnwll
164 F7	**Mennock** D & G
123 H2	**Menston** C Brad
185 H7	**Menstrie** Clacks
58 E4	**Mentmore** Bucks
200 C7	**Meoble** Highld
83 J2	**Meole Brace** Shrops
29 L7	**Meonstoke** Hants
45 M6	**Meopham** Kent
90 B7	**Mepal** Cambs
75 G7	**Meppershall** C Beds
113 G5	**Mere** Ches E
27 J5	**Mere** Wilts
120 F6	**Mere Brow** Lancs
122 C4	**Mereclough** Lancs

33 H3 **Mereworth** Kent
86 B6 **Meriden** Solhll
208 F7 **Merkadale** Highld
15 J3 **Merley** Poole
48 F7 **Merrion** Pembks
26 C8 **Merriott** Somset
31 G2 **Merrow** Surrey
43 J2 **Merry Hill** Herts
84 F4 **Merryhill** Wolves
5 L3 **Merrymeet** Cnwll
62 B5 **Mersea Island** Essex
34 E6 **Mersham** Kent
32 B3 **Merstham** Surrey
18 B5 **Merston** W Susx
17 G5 **Merstone** IoW
67 L6 **Merthyr Cynog** Powys
36 D5 **Merthyr Mawr** Brdgnd
53 G6 **Merthyr Tydfil** Myr Td
53 G7 **Merthyr Vale** Myr Td
10 D3 **Merton** Devon
44 E6 **Merton** Gt Lon
91 K4 **Merton** Norfk
57 L4 **Merton** Oxon
24 B7 **Meshaw** Devon
61 L4 **Messing** Essex
116 E2 **Messingham** N Linc
93 G7 **Metfield** Suffk
6 B3 **Metherell** Cnwll
103 H1 **Metheringham** Lincs
186 F7 **Methil** Fife
186 F7 **Methilhill** Fife
124 B5 **Methley** Leeds
217 G6 **Methlick** Abers
185 L3 **Methven** P & K
91 G4 **Methwold** Norfk
91 G4 **Methwold Hythe** Norfk
93 H5 **Mettingham** Suffk
106 E5 **Metton** Norfk
4 F6 **Mevagissey** Cnwll
115 J2 **Mexborough** Donc
231 K2 **Mey** Highld
94 D6 **Meyllteyrn** Gwynd
56 C7 **Meysey Hampton** Gloucs
232 d2 **Miabhig** W Isls
232 d2 **Miavaig** W Isls
54 D3 **Michaelchurch** Herefs
69 G7 **Michaelchurch Escley** Herefs
37 K4 **Michaelstone-y-Fedw** Newpt
37 J5 **Michaelston-le-Pit** V Glam
5 G1 **Michaelstow** Cnwll
39 G2 **Michaelwood Services** Gloucs
29 K4 **Micheldever** Hants
29 K3 **Micheldever Station** Hants
29 G6 **Michelmersh** Hants
78 D3 **Mickfield** Suffk
115 K3 **Micklebring** Donc
143 G5 **Mickleby** N York
124 C4 **Micklefield** Leeds
31 K2 **Mickleham** Surrey
100 F5 **Mickleover** C Derb
140 B3 **Mickleton** Dur
71 L5 **Mickleton** Gloucs
124 B5 **Mickletown** Leeds
112 C7 **Mickle Trafford** Ches W
132 C4 **Mickley** N York
77 J3 **Mickley Green** Suffk
150 D3 **Mickley Square** Nthumb
217 H2 **Mid Ardlaw** Abers
234 c4 **Midbea** Ork
206 C5 **Mid Beltie** Abers
176 E5 **Mid Calder** W Loth
231 K7 **Mid Clyth** Highld
216 C3 **Mid Culbeuchly** Abers
57 J3 **Middle Aston** Oxon
57 H3 **Middle Barton** Oxon

155 L6 **Middlebie** D & G
194 D3 **Middlebridge** P & K
26 C8 **Middle Chinnock** Somset
58 B3 **Middle Claydon** Bucks
131 L3 **Middleham** N York
115 H6 **Middle Handley** Derbys
39 J6 **Middlehill** Wilts
83 K5 **Middlehope** Shrops
172 F1 **Middle Kames** Ag & B
71 J5 **Middle Littleton** Worcs
14 C2 **Middlemarsh** Dorset
100 C4 **Middle Mayfield** Staffs
117 H4 **Middle Rasen** Lincs
7 K2 **Middle Rocombe** Devon
141 L4 **Middlesbrough** Middsb
129 L2 **Middleshaw** Cumb
131 K5 **Middlesmoor** N York
46 D5 **Middle Stoke** Medway
141 G2 **Middlestone** Dur
123 K6 **Middlestown** Wakefd
167 K2 **Middlethird** Border
188 B7 **Middleton** Ag & B
100 F2 **Middleton** Derbys
114 D8 **Middleton** Derbys
77 K6 **Middleton** Essex
29 H3 **Middleton** Hants
69 K1 **Middleton** Herefs
123 L5 **Middleton** Leeds
123 G2 **Middleton** N York
134 B3 **Middleton** N York
88 B5 **Middleton** Nhants
90 F1 **Middleton** Norfk
158 D5 **Middleton** Nthumb
186 B6 **Middleton** P & K
113 K1 **Middleton** Rochdl
83 K7 **Middleton** Shrops
79 J2 **Middleton** Suffk
50 E7 **Middleton** Swans
85 L4 **Middleton** Warwks
73 G6 **Middleton Cheney** Nhants
113 K1 **Middleton Crematorium** Rochdl
139 L3 **Middleton-in-Teesdale** Dur
79 J2 **Middleton Moor** Suffk
141 J5 **Middleton One Row** Darltn
18 C5 **Middleton-on-Sea** W Susx
69 K2 **Middleton on the Hill** Herefs
125 L2 **Middleton on the Wolds** E R Yk
132 E4 **Middleton Quernhow** N York
141 J5 **Middleton St George** Darltn
84 C6 **Middleton Scriven** Shrops
57 K4 **Middleton Stoney** Oxon
141 G6 **Middleton Tyas** N York
2 a2 **Middle Town** IoS
82 F2 **Middletown** Powys
72 D5 **Middle Tysoe** Warwks
28 F4 **Middle Wallop** Hants
113 G7 **Middlewich** Ches E
28 E5 **Middle Winterslow** Wilts
5 L2 **Middlewood** Cnwll
28 C4 **Middle Woodford** Wilts
78 D3 **Middlewood Green** Suffk
163 M3 **Middleyard** E Ayrs
26 B5 **Middlezoy** Somset
39 H7 **Midford** BaNES
41 K6 **Midgham** W Berk

122 F5 **Midgley** Calder
123 K7 **Midgley** Wakefd
114 E2 **Midhopestones** Sheff
30 E6 **Midhurst** W Susx
18 B4 **Mid Lavant** W Susx
167 H4 **Midlem** Border
212 C6 **Mid Mains** Highld
173 H6 **Midpark** Ag & B
26 F1 **Midsomer Norton** BaNES
229 J4 **Midtown** Highld
72 C3 **Mid Warwickshire Crematorium** Warwks
235 d3 **Mid Yell** Shet
205 K4 **Migvie** Abers
26 F7 **Milborne Port** Somset
14 F3 **Milborne St Andrew** Dorset
26 F7 **Milborne Wick** Somset
158 E6 **Milbourne** Nthumb
39 L3 **Milbourne** Wilts
138 F2 **Milburn** Cumb
38 F3 **Milbury Heath** S Glos
132 F6 **Milby** N York
72 E7 **Milcombe** Oxon
77 L5 **Milden** Suffk
91 G8 **Mildenhall** Suffk
40 E6 **Mildenhall** Wilts
105 L8 **Mileham** Norfk
19 H4 **Mile Oak** Br & H
176 E2 **Milesmark** Fife
113 J2 **Miles Platting** Manch
46 F5 **Mile Town** Kent
168 D3 **Milfield** Nthumb
101 G4 **Milford** Derbys
22 C6 **Milford** Devon
99 L7 **Milford** Staffs
30 F3 **Milford** Surrey
48 F6 **Milford Haven** Pembks
16 C4 **Milford on Sea** Hants
54 E6 **Milkwall** Gloucs
30 D5 **Milland** W Susx
122 F6 **Mill Bank** Calder
217 J5 **Millbreck** Abers
30 D3 **Millbridge** Surrey
74 E6 **Millbrook** C Beds
29 G8 **Millbrook** C Sotn
6 B5 **Millbrook** Cnwll
236 c7 **Millbrook** Jersey
113 L4 **Mill Brow** Stockp
206 F4 **Millbuie** Abers
212 E4 **Millbuie** Highld
163 K4 **Millburn** S Ayrs
21 G2 **Millcorner** E Susx
222 E7 **Millcraig** Highld
100 C2 **Milldale** Staffs
42 C4 **Mill End** Bucks
60 B2 **Mill End** Herts
177 J4 **Millerhill** Mdloth
114 C6 **Miller's Dale** Derbys
175 H5 **Millerston** C Glas
76 F5 **Mill Green** Cambs
61 G7 **Mill Green** Essex
103 L7 **Mill Green** Lincs
77 L6 **Mill Green** Suffk
78 B3 **Mill Green** Suffk
78 D3 **Mill Green** Suffk
68 F5 **Millhalf** Herefs
175 K7 **Millheugh** S Lans
44 E2 **Mill Hill** Gt Lon
173 G4 **Millhouse** Ag & B
155 K5 **Millhousebridge** D & G
114 E2 **Millhouse Green** Barns
115 G5 **Millhouses** Sheff
174 D6 **Milliken Park** Rens
125 J1 **Millington** E R Yk
99 J5 **Millmeece** Staffs
185 H4 **Mill of Drummond** P & K
174 D2 **Mill of Haldane** W Duns
128 E4 **Millom** Cumb

173 K7 **Millport** N Ayrs
78 C1 **Mill Street** Suffk
130 C2 **Millthrop** Cumb
207 G5 **Milltimber** C Aber
205 G4 **Milltown** Abers
205 K3 **Milltown** Abers
156 C6 **Milltown** D & G
23 J4 **Milltown** Devon
206 C5 **Milltown of Campfield** Abers
215 G6 **Milltown of Edinvillie** Moray
206 C5 **Milltown of Learney** Abers
186 B6 **Milnathort** P & K
175 G4 **Milngavie** E Duns
122 D7 **Milnrow** Rochdl
129 K3 **Milnthorpe** Cumb
208 B4 **Milovaig** Highld
84 B8 **Milson** Shrops
34 B3 **Milstead** Kent
28 D3 **Milston** Wilts
73 H5 **Milthorpe** Nhants
76 C2 **Milton** Cambs
148 F3 **Milton** Cumb
144 F4 **Milton** D & G
154 E7 **Milton** D & G
100 F7 **Milton** Derbys
209 L5 **Milton** Highld
212 D7 **Milton** Highld
212 E4 **Milton** Highld
223 G6 **Milton** Highld
231 L5 **Milton** Highld
174 C5 **Milton** Inver
46 A5 **Milton** Kent
204 E2 **Milton** Moray
215 L2 **Milton** Moray
37 M7 **Milton** N Som
116 B6 **Milton** Notts
41 J3 **Milton** Oxon
72 F7 **Milton** Oxon
195 G4 **Milton** P & K
195 H5 **Milton** P & K
49 H6 **Milton** Pembks
26 C6 **Milton** Somset
184 B6 **Milton** Stirlg
174 D4 **Milton** W Duns
14 F3 **Milton Abbas** Dorset
9 K8 **Milton Abbot** Devon
177 H5 **Milton Bridge** Mdloth
58 F3 **Milton Bryan** C Beds
26 F4 **Milton Clevedon** Somset
6 D3 **Milton Combe** Devon
9 K3 **Milton Damerel** Devon
74 E4 **Milton Ernest** Bed
98 C2 **Milton Green** Ches W
41 J3 **Milton Hill** Oxon
74 C6 **Milton Keynes** M Keyn
40 D7 **Milton Lilbourne** Wilts
73 K4 **Milton Malsor** Nhants
184 D1 **Milton Morenish** P & K
206 B5 **Milton of Auchinhove** Abers
186 E7 **Milton of Balgonie** Fife
174 E1 **Milton of Buchanan** Stirlg
175 H3 **Milton of Campsie** E Duns
213 G6 **Milton of Leys** Highld
205 J6 **Milton of Tullich** Abers
27 J5 **Milton on Stour** Dorset
46 E6 **Milton Regis** Kent
56 E4 **Milton-under-Wychwood** Oxon
25 H6 **Milverton** Somset
72 C2 **Milverton** Warwks
99 L6 **Milwich** Staffs
182 D7 **Minard** Ag & B

55 K7 **Minchinhampton** Gloucs
24 F3 **Minehead** Somset
97 L3 **Minera** Wrexhm
40 A3 **Minety** Wilts
95 K5 **Minffordd** Gwynd
190 D3 **Mingarrypark** Highld
118 D8 **Miningsby** Lincs
5 L2 **Minions** Cnwll
163 J6 **Minishant** S Ayrs
81 J2 **Minllyn** Gwynd
145 J2 **Minnigaff** D & G
216 E3 **Minnonie** Abers
132 F6 **Minskip** N York
16 C1 **Minstead** Hants
30 D7 **Minsted** W Susx
35 J2 **Minster** Kent
46 F5 **Minster** Kent
83 G3 **Minsterley** Shrops
56 F5 **Minster Lovell** Oxon
55 H5 **Minsterworth** Gloucs
14 C2 **Minterne Magna** Dorset
117 K6 **Minting** Lincs
217 J5 **Mintlaw** Abers
105 G8 **Mintlyn Crematorium** Norfk
167 H5 **Minto** Border
83 H5 **Minton** Shrops
136 D4 **Mirehouse** Cumb
231 K4 **Mireland** Highld
123 J6 **Mirfield** Kirk
55 L6 **Miserden** Gloucs
37 G4 **Miskin** Rhondd
116 B3 **Misson** Notts
87 G6 **Misterton** Leics
116 C3 **Misterton** Notts
13 L2 **Misterton** Somset
62 D2 **Mistley** Essex
44 F6 **Mitcham** Gt Lon
54 F4 **Mitcheldean** Gloucs
4 D5 **Mitchell** Cnwll
155 G3 **Mitchellslacks** D & G
54 C6 **Mitchel Troy** Mons
158 F5 **Mitford** Nthumb
3 J2 **Mithian** Cnwll
73 H7 **Mixbury** Oxon
113 H5 **Mobberley** Ches E
100 A4 **Mobberley** Staffs
82 B5 **Moccas** Powys
145 H5 **Mochrum** D & G
33 J4 **Mockbeggar** Kent
136 F3 **Mockerkin** Cumb
6 F5 **Modbury** Devon
99 L5 **Moddershall** Staffs
109 G4 **Moelfre** IoA
97 J6 **Moelfre** Powys
155 J2 **Moffat** D & G
75 G5 **Moggerhanger** C Beds
86 C1 **Moira** Leics
34 D4 **Molash** Kent
199 G3 **Mol-chlach** Highld
111 H8 **Mold** Flints
123 H7 **Moldgreen** Kirk
60 E3 **Molehill Green** Essex
126 C3 **Molescroft** E R Yk
88 F7 **Molesworth** Cambs
24 C5 **Molland** Devon
111 L7 **Mollington** Ches W
72 F5 **Mollington** Oxon
175 J4 **Mollinsburn** N Lans
197 J1 **Mondynes** Abers
78 F3 **Monewden** Suffk
185 M2 **Moneydie** P & K
154 D4 **Moniaive** D & G
187 H2 **Monifieth** Angus
196 E8 **Monikie** Angus
186 E5 **Monimail** Fife
44 E1 **Monken Hadley** Gt Lon
124 D5 **Monk Fryston** N York
70 B5 **Monkhide** Herefs
148 C3 **Monkhill** Cumb
84 B5 **Monkhopton** Shrops

69 J3 **Monkland** Herefs
23 G7 **Monkleigh** Devon
36 E6 **Monknash** V Glam
10 E4 **Monkokehampton** Devon
159 H7 **Monkseaton** N Tyne
77 L5 **Monks Eleigh** Suffk
31 K6 **Monk's Gate** W Susx
113 J6 **Monks Heath** Ches E
29 L1 **Monk Sherborne** Hants
34 F6 **Monks Horton** Kent
25 G4 **Monksilver** Somset
86 F6 **Monks Kirby** Warwks
78 E2 **Monk Soham** Suffk
58 D6 **Monks Risborough** Bucks
118 F7 **Monksthorpe** Lincs
60 F3 **Monk Street** Essex
53 M7 **Monkswood** Mons
12 F2 **Monkton** Devon
47 M6 **Monkton** Kent
163 J4 **Monkton** S Ayrs
151 H3 **Monkton** S Tyne
39 H7 **Monkton Combe** BaNES
27 J4 **Monkton Deverill** Wilts
39 J7 **Monkton Farleigh** Wilts
25 K6 **Monkton Heathfield** Somset
13 J3 **Monkton Wyld** Dorset
151 J4 **Monkwearmouth** Sundld
30 A5 **Monkwood** Hants
85 G4 **Monmore Green** Wolves
54 D5 **Monmouth** Mons
69 G5 **Monnington on Wye** Herefs
145 H6 **Monreith** D & G
26 D7 **Montacute** Somset
83 H1 **Montford** Shrops
83 H1 **Montford Bridge** Shrops
206 B2 **Montgarrie** Abers
82 E4 **Montgomery** Powys
197 H5 **Montrose** Angus
236 D3 **Mont Saint** Guern
28 F3 **Monxton** Hants
114 D7 **Monyash** Derbys
206 D3 **Monymusk** Abers
185 H3 **Monzie** P & K
175 J4 **Moodiesburn** N Lans
186 E4 **Moonzie** Fife
123 L3 **Moor Allerton** Leeds
118 D8 **Moorby** Lincs
15 J2 **Moor Crichel** Dorset
15 K4 **Moordown** Bmouth
112 E5 **Moore** Halton
122 F5 **Moor End** Calder
125 G7 **Moorends** Donc
101 J3 **Moorgreen** Notts
123 H3 **Moorhead** C Brad
148 B4 **Moorhouse** Cumb
116 C7 **Moorhouse** Notts
32 D3 **Moorhouse Bank** Surrey
26 B4 **Moorlinch** Somset
133 H7 **Moor Monkton** N York
142 E4 **Moorsholm** R & Cl
27 H7 **Moorside** Dorset
5 K3 **Moorswater** Cnwll
124 C7 **Moorthorpe** Wakefd
123 K3 **Moortown** Leeds
117 H2 **Moortown** Lincs
223 G5 **Morangie** Highld
199 L6 **Morar** Highld
215 J3 **Moray Crematorium** Moray
89 G5 **Morborne** Cambs
11 H4 **Morchard Bishop** Devon

13 K4 **Morcombelake** Dorset
88 D4 **Morcott** Rutlnd
97 L6 **Morda** Shrops
15 H4 **Morden** Dorset
44 E6 **Morden** Gt Lon
69 L6 **Mordiford** Herefs
141 H2 **Mordon** Dur
83 G5 **More** Shrops
24 E6 **Morebath** Devon
168 B4 **Morebattle** Border
129 J6 **Morecambe** Lancs
40 C3 **Moredon** Swindn
220 E3 **Morefield** Highld
35 G7 **Morehall** Kent
7 H5 **Moreleigh** Devon
184 D1 **Morenish** P & K
29 K4 **Morestead** Hants
14 F4 **Moreton** Dorset
60 E6 **Moreton** Essex
69 K2 **Moreton** Herefs
58 B6 **Moreton** Oxon
111 J4 **Moreton** Wirral
98 E7 **Moreton Corbet** Shrops
11 H7 **Moretonhampstead** Devon
56 D2 **Moreton-in-Marsh** Gloucs
69 L5 **Moreton Jeffries** Herefs
72 C4 **Moreton Morrell** Warwks
69 K5 **Moreton on Lugg** Herefs
73 H5 **Moreton Pinkney** Nhants
98 F5 **Moreton Say** Shrops
55 H6 **Moreton Valence** Gloucs
94 E4 **Morfa Nefyn** Gwynd
178 C4 **Morham** E Loth
138 E3 **Morland** Cumb
113 J5 **Morley** Ches E
101 H4 **Morley** Derbys
123 K5 **Morley** Leeds
113 J5 **Morley Green** Ches E
92 C4 **Morley St Botolph** Norfk
177 H4 **Morningside** C Edin
175 L7 **Morningside** N Lans
92 F5 **Morningthorpe** Norfk
158 F5 **Morpeth** Nthumb
197 H4 **Morphie** Abers
100 C8 **Morrey** Staffs
51 J6 **Morriston** Swans
106 B4 **Morston** Norfk
23 G3 **Mortehoe** Devon
115 J4 **Morthen** Rothm
41 M7 **Mortimer** W Berk
41 M7 **Mortimer West End** Hants
44 E5 **Mortlake** Gt Lon
44 D5 **Mortlake Crematorium** Gt Lon
148 C4 **Morton** Cumb
101 H1 **Morton** Derbys
103 H7 **Morton** Lincs
116 D3 **Morton** Lincs
102 B3 **Morton** Notts
97 L7 **Morton** Shrops
177 H5 **Mortonhall Crematorium** C Edin
132 E2 **Morton-on-Swale** N York
92 D1 **Morton on the Hill** Norfk
2 D4 **Morvah** Cnwll
200 E2 **Morvich** Highld
84 C5 **Morville** Shrops
6 C3 **Morwellham Quay** Devon
9 G2 **Morwenstow** Cnwll
115 H5 **Mosborough** Sheff
163 L2 **Moscow** E Ayrs
85 J6 **Moseley** Birm

85 G4 **Moseley** Wolves
70 E3 **Moseley** Worcs
188 B7 **Moss** Ag & B
124 F7 **Moss** Donc
205 K2 **Mossat** Abers
235 d4 **Mossbank** Shet
112 D3 **Moss Bank** St Hel
136 D2 **Mossbay** Cumb
163 K4 **Mossblown** S Ayrs
167 K6 **Mossburnford** Border
154 B7 **Mossdale** D & G
153 K2 **Mossdale** E Ayrs
120 F2 **Moss Edge** Lancs
175 K6 **Mossend** N Lans
113 L2 **Mossley** Tamesd
156 D3 **Mosspaul Hotel** Border
213 K4 **Moss-side** Highld
215 H3 **Mosstodloch** Moray
145 L5 **Mossyard** D & G
121 H7 **Mossy Lea** Lancs
13 L2 **Mosterton** Dorset
113 K2 **Moston** Manch
111 G5 **Mostyn** Flints
27 J6 **Motcombe** Dorset
6 F6 **Mothecombe** Devon
138 B2 **Motherby** Cumb
175 K6 **Motherwell** N Lans
44 E6 **Motspur Park** Gt Lon
45 H5 **Mottingham** Gt Lon
28 F6 **Mottisfont** Hants
16 E5 **Mottistone** IoW
113 M3 **Mottram in Longdendale** Tamesd
113 K3 **Mottram St Andrew** Ches E
112 D7 **Mouldsworth** Ches W
194 E4 **Moulin** P & K
19 J4 **Moulsecoomb** Br & H
41 L4 **Moulsford** Oxon
74 C6 **Moulsoe** M Keyn
222 E7 **Moultavie** Highld
112 F7 **Moulton** Ches W
104 A7 **Moulton** Lincs
141 G6 **Moulton** N York
73 L2 **Moulton** Nhants
77 G2 **Moulton** Suffk
37 G6 **Moulton** V Glam
103 M8 **Moulton Chapel** Lincs
93 H3 **Moulton St Mary** Norfk
104 A6 **Moulton Seas End** Lincs
5 J3 **Mount** Cnwll
123 G4 **Mountain** C Brad
53 G7 **Mountain Ash** Rhondd
176 F8 **Mountain Cross** Border
3 J3 **Mount Ambrose** Cnwll
61 L2 **Mount Bures** Essex
20 E2 **Mountfield** E Susx
212 E3 **Mountgerald House** Highld
3 J2 **Mount Hawke** Cnwll
4 D4 **Mountjoy** Cnwll
177 H6 **Mount Lothian** Mdloth
60 F8 **Mountnessing** Essex
38 D2 **Mounton** Mons
101 J2 **Mount Pleasant** Derbys
77 G5 **Mount Pleasant** Suffk
150 E4 **Mountsett Crematorium** Dur
87 H2 **Mountsorrel** Leics
122 F5 **Mount Tabor** Calder
30 F3 **Mousehill** Surrey
2 E6 **Mousehole** Cnwll
155 J7 **Mouswald** D & G
99 J2 **Mow Cop** Ches E
168 B5 **Mowhaugh** Border
87 J5 **Mowsley** Leics
202 C8 **Moy** Highld
213 J7 **Moy** Highld

200 D2 **Moyle** Highld
64 F5 **Moylegrove** Pembks
161 H2 **Muasdale** Ag & B
207 G6 **Muchalls** Abers
54 D3 **Much Birch** Herefs
70 B5 **Much Cowarne** Herefs
54 C2 **Much Dewchurch** Herefs
26 B6 **Muchelney** Somset
26 C6 **Muchelney Ham** Somset
60 C4 **Much Hadham** Herts
120 F6 **Much Hoole** Lancs
5 K5 **Muchlarnick** Cnwll
54 F2 **Much Marcle** Herefs
84 B4 **Much Wenlock** Shrops
189 K1 **Muck** Highld
106 D4 **Muckleburgh Collection** Norfk
99 G5 **Mucklestone** Staffs
118 E5 **Muckton** Lincs
23 J4 **Muddiford** Devon
20 B3 **Muddles Green** E Susx
16 A4 **Mudeford** Dorset
26 E7 **Mudford** Somset
26 E7 **Mudford Sock** Somset
175 G3 **Mugdock** Stirlg
209 G6 **Mugginby** Highld
100 F4 **Mugginton** Derbys
216 D4 **Muirden** Abers
196 F8 **Muirdrum** Angus
216 D5 **Muiresk** Abers
186 E1 **Muirhead** Angus
186 E6 **Muirhead** Fife
175 J4 **Muirhead** N Lans
164 D4 **Muirkirk** E Ayrs
175 J2 **Muirmill** Stirlg
206 B3 **Muir of Fowlis** Abers
214 E3 **Muir of Miltonduff** Moray
212 E4 **Muir of Ord** Highld
195 G8 **Muir of Thorn** P & K
192 B1 **Muirshearlich** Highld
217 J6 **Muirtack** Abers
185 J5 **Muirton** P & K
212 C4 **Muirton Mains** Highld
195 J7 **Muirton of Ardblair** P & K
139 K7 **Muker** N York
92 E4 **Mulbarton** Norfk
215 H4 **Mulben** Moray
181 J1 **Mull** Ag & B
3 H7 **Mullion** Cnwll
3 H7 **Mullion Cove** Cnwll
119 G6 **Mumby** Lincs
70 B4 **Munderfield Row** Herefs
70 B4 **Munderfield Stocks** Herefs
107 G5 **Mundesley** Norfk
91 H5 **Mundford** Norfk
93 G4 **Mundham** Norfk
61 K7 **Mundon Hill** Essex
137 K2 **Mungrisdale** Cumb
213 G4 **Munlochy** Highld
174 B8 **Munnoch** N Ayrs
70 B6 **Munsley** Herefs
83 K6 **Munslow** Shrops
11 G7 **Murchington** Devon
57 L5 **Murcott** Oxon
231 H2 **Murkle** Highld
200 F6 **Murlaggan** Highld
187 G1 **Murroes** Angus
89 L3 **Murrow** Cambs
58 D3 **Mursley** Bucks
196 D5 **Murthill** Angus
195 H8 **Murthly** P & K
133 K8 **Murton** C York
139 G3 **Murton** Cumb
151 J5 **Murton** Dur
179 K8 **Murton** Nthumb
13 H4 **Musbury** Devon
177 K4 **Musselburgh** E Loth

102 D5 **Muston** Leics
135 H4 **Muston** N York
44 F1 **Muswell Hill** Gt Lon
146 C5 **Mutehill** D & G
93 K6 **Mutford** Suffk
185 H4 **Muthill** P & K
231 H5 **Mybster** Highld
52 B3 **Myddfai** Carmth
98 C7 **Myddle** Shrops
66 B4 **Mydroilyn** Cerdgn
4 C8 **Mylor** Cnwll
4 C8 **Mylor Bridge** Cnwll
49 K2 **Mynachlog ddu** Pembks
83 H5 **Myndtown** Shrops
38 C2 **Mynydd-bach** Mons
51 J6 **Mynydd-Bach** Swans
111 J8 **Mynydd Isa** Flints
206 E5 **Myrebird** Abers
157 G3 **Myredykes** Border
30 E1 **Mytchett** Surrey
122 E5 **Mytholm** Calder
122 F5 **Mytholmroyd** Calder
132 F6 **Myton-on-Swale** N York

N

219 J5 **Naast** Highld
232 d4 **Na Buirgh** W Isls
124 F2 **Naburn** C York
123 H3 **Nab Wood Crematorium** C Brad
34 F4 **Nackington** Kent
78 F6 **Nacton** Suffk
135 G7 **Nafferton** E R Yk
25 K5 **Nailsbourne** Somset
38 C6 **Nailsea** N Som
86 E3 **Nailstone** Leics
55 J7 **Nailsworth** Gloucs
213 K3 **Nairn** Highld
111 G7 **Nannerch** Flints
87 G1 **Nanpantan** Leics
4 F5 **Nanpean** Cnwll
5 G3 **Nanstallon** Cnwll
65 L3 **Nanternis** Cerdgn
50 F2 **Nantgaredig** Carmth
96 F1 **Nantglyn** Denbgs
68 B2 **Nantmel** Powys
95 K4 **Nantmor** Gwynd
95 K2 **Nant Peris** Gwynd
98 F3 **Nantwich** Ches E
53 J6 **Nantyglo** Blae G
36 E2 **Nant-y-moel** Brdgnd
42 D2 **Naphill** Bucks
72 F3 **Napton on the Hill** Warwks
49 J4 **Narberth** Pembks
87 G4 **Narborough** Leics
91 H2 **Narborough** Norfk
95 H3 **Nasareth** Gwynd
87 K7 **Naseby** Nhants
73 L7 **Nash** Bucks
37 M4 **Nash** Newpt
69 L1 **Nash** Shrops
88 F4 **Nassington** Nhants
139 H6 **Nateby** Cumb
120 F2 **Nateby** Lancs
85 L1 **National Memorial Arboretum** Staffs
87 H3 **National Space Science Centre** C Leic
129 L2 **Natland** Cumb
78 B5 **Naughton** Suffk
56 C4 **Naunton** Gloucs
70 F6 **Naunton** Worcs
71 G4 **Naunton Beauchamp** Worcs
103 G2 **Navenby** Lincs
45 K1 **Navestock** Essex
60 E8 **Navestock Side** Essex
227 J5 **Navidale House Hotel** Highld
213 J2 **Navity** Highld
133 K3 **Nawton** N York

77 L7 **Nayland** Suffk
60 C6 **Nazeing** Essex
235 d5 **Neap** Shet
100 B4 **Near Cotton** Staffs
137 K7 **Near Sawrey** Cumb
44 E3 **Neasden** Gt Lon
141 H5 **Neasham** Darltn
51 L6 **Neath** Neath
30 C4 **Neatham** Hants
107 H7 **Neatishead** Norfk
66 D2 **Nebo** Cerdgn
96 C2 **Nebo** Conwy
95 H3 **Nebo** Gwynd
108 F4 **Nebo** IoA
91 K2 **Necton** Norfk
224 D3 **Nedd** Highld
78 B5 **Nedging** Suffk
78 B4 **Nedging Tye** Suffk
92 F6 **Needham** Norfk
78 C4 **Needham Market** Suffk
75 L1 **Needingworth** Cambs
84 C7 **Neen Savage** Shrops
84 B8 **Neen Sollars** Shrops
84 B6 **Neenton** Shrops
94 E4 **Nefyn** Gwynd
174 E6 **Neilston** E Rens
37 H2 **Nelson** Caerph
122 C3 **Nelson** Lancs
165 G1 **Nemphlar** S Lans
38 D7 **Nempnett Thrubwell** BaNES
149 K6 **Nenthead** Cumb
167 K2 **Nenthorn** Border
97 K1 **Nercwys** Flints
170 E7 **Nereabolls** Ag & B
175 H6 **Nerston** S Lans
168 E3 **Nesbit** Nthumb
123 G1 **Nesfield** N York
111 J6 **Ness Botanic Gardens** Ches W
98 B8 **Nesscliffe** Shrops
111 J6 **Neston** Ches W
39 K6 **Neston** Wilts
84 B5 **Netchwood** Shrops
113 J6 **Nether Alderley** Ches E
28 D2 **Netheravon** Wilts
167 H2 **Nether Blainslie** Border
216 F3 **Netherbrae** Abers
102 B7 **Nether Broughton** Leics
175 L8 **Netherburn** S Lans
13 L3 **Netherbury** Dorset
123 L2 **Netherby** N York
14 C3 **Nether Cerne** Dorset
155 K5 **Nethercleuch** D & G
26 E7 **Nether Compton** Dorset
206 F2 **Nether Crimond** Abers
215 H2 **Nether Dallachy** Moray
54 E7 **Netherend** Gloucs
11 L5 **Nether Exe** Devon
20 E2 **Netherfield** E Susx
20 E3 **Netherfield Road** E Susx
165 H7 **Nether Fingland** S Lans
28 C5 **Netherhampton** Wilts
196 B7 **Nether Handwick** Angus
115 H3 **Nether Haugh** Rothm
13 K2 **Netherhay** Dorset
116 C6 **Nether Headon** Notts
101 G3 **Nether Heage** Derbys
73 J3 **Nether Heyford** Nhants
165 K6 **Nether Howcleugh** S Lans
129 K6 **Nether Kellet** Lancs
217 K5 **Nether Kinmundy** Abers

115 K7 **Nether Langwith** Notts
146 C6 **Netherlaw** D & G
207 G6 **Netherley** Abers
155 H5 **Nethermill** D & G
217 G5 **Nethermuir** Abers
32 B3 **Netherne-on-the-Hill** Surrey
123 H6 **Netheroyd Hill** Kirk
114 E6 **Nether Padley** Derbys
174 F7 **Netherplace** E Rens
133 J8 **Nether Poppleton** C York
86 C2 **Netherseal** Derbys
133 G2 **Nether Silton** N York
25 J4 **Nether Stowey** Somset
123 H8 **Netherthong** Kirk
196 E5 **Netherton** Angus
7 K5 **Netherton** Devon
85 G6 **Netherton** Dudley
123 H7 **Netherton** Kirk
175 K7 **Netherton** N Lans
168 E7 **Netherton** Nthumb
195 J6 **Netherton** P & K
84 D6 **Netherton** Shrops
175 G3 **Netherton** Stirlg
123 K6 **Netherton** Wakefd
136 D5 **Nethertown** Cumb
231 L1 **Nethertown** Highld
100 C8 **Nethertown** Staffs
165 L1 **Netherurd** Border
28 F4 **Nether Wallop** Hants
136 F6 **Nether Wasdale** Cumb
56 E4 **Nether Westcote** Gloucs
86 B5 **Nether Whitacre** Warwks
165 G5 **Nether Whitecleuch** S Lans
58 B3 **Nether Winchendon** Bucks
158 D4 **Netherwitton** Nthumb
204 B2 **Nethy Bridge** Highld
16 F2 **Netley** Hants
29 G8 **Netley Marsh** Hants
42 B3 **Nettlebed** Oxon
26 F2 **Nettlebridge** Somset
13 M4 **Nettlecombe** Dorset
59 G6 **Nettleden** Herts
117 G6 **Nettleham** Lincs
33 H3 **Nettlestead** Kent
33 H3 **Nettlestead Green** Kent
17 H4 **Nettlestone** IoW
151 G5 **Nettlesworth** Dur
117 J2 **Nettleton** Lincs
39 J5 **Nettleton** Wilts
28 C4 **Netton** Wilts
64 F6 **Nevern** Pembks
88 B5 **Nevill Holt** Leics
147 G2 **New Abbey** D & G
217 G2 **New Aberdour** Abers
45 G7 **New Addington** Gt Lon
123 J2 **Newall** Leeds
29 L5 **New Alresford** Hants
195 K6 **New Alyth** P & K
234 e4 **Newark** Ork
102 D2 **Newark-on-Trent** Notts
175 K6 **Newarthill** N Lans
45 L6 **New Ash Green** Kent
102 D3 **New Balderton** Notts
45 L6 **New Barn** Kent
44 F2 **New Barnet** Gt Lon
177 J5 **Newbattle** Mdloth
169 G5 **New Bewick** Nthumb
147 L3 **Newbie** D & G
138 C2 **Newbiggin** Cumb
138 F2 **Newbiggin** Cumb
148 F5 **Newbiggin** Cumb
139 K2 **Newbiggin** Dur
131 J3 **Newbiggin** N York

159 H5 Newbiggin-by-the-
Sea Nthumb
187 H1 Newbigging Angus
195 L7 Newbigging Angus
196 C8 Newbigging Angus
165 K1 Newbigging S Lans
139 G6 Newbigging-on-Lune
Cumb
86 F7 New Bilton Warwks
115 G6 Newbold Derbys
86 F7 Newbold on Avon
Warwks
72 B5 Newbold on Stour
Warwks
72 C3 Newbold Pacey
Warwks
86 F3 Newbold Verdon
Leics
104 A2 New Bolingbroke
Lincs
89 H3 Newborough C Pete
108 E7 Newborough IoA
100 C7 Newborough Staffs
116 F7 New Boultham Lincs
78 F6 Newbourne Suffk
74 B6 New Bradwell M Keyn
115 G7 New Brampton
Derbys
151 G6 New Brancepeth Dur
176 F4 Newbridge C Edin
37 K2 Newbridge Caerph
2 D5 Newbridge Cnwll
155 G6 Newbridge D & G
28 F7 Newbridge Hants
16 E5 Newbridge IoW
70 E6 Newbridge Green
Worcs
67 L3 Newbridge on Wye
Powys
111 J3 New Brighton Wirral
149 L2 Newbrough Nthumb
92 C5 New Buckenham
Norfk
11 J4 Newbuildings Devon
207 J1 Newburgh Abers
217 H3 Newburgh Abers
186 D4 Newburgh Fife
121 G7 Newburgh Lancs
133 H4 Newburgh Priory
N York
150 F2 Newburn N u Ty
27 G2 Newbury Somset
41 J6 Newbury W Berk
45 J3 Newbury Park Gt Lon
138 E3 Newby Cumb
122 B2 Newby Lancs
130 D5 Newby N York
142 B5 Newby N York
129 H3 Newby Bridge Cumb
148 E4 Newby East Cumb
216 F4 New Byth Abers
148 C4 Newby West Cumb
54 C5 Newcastle Mons
82 E6 Newcastle Shrops
158 F7 Newcastle Airport
Nthumb
65 J6 Newcastle Emlyn
Carmth
156 E5 Newcastleton Border
99 J4 Newcastle-under-
Lyme Staffs
151 G3 Newcastle upon
Tyne N u Ty
65 H6 Newchapel Pembks
32 C5 Newchapel Surrey
17 G5 Newchurch IoW
34 E7 Newchurch Kent
38 C2 Newchurch Mons
68 E4 Newchurch Powys
100 D7 Newchurch Staffs
92 E2 New Costessey Norfk
177 J4 Newcraighall C Edin
124 B6 New Crofton Wakefd
45 G5 New Cross Gt Lon
26 B7 New Cross Somset
164 C6 New Cumnock E Ayrs

217 G5 New Deer Abers
43 H4 New Denham Bucks
31 K3 Newdigate Surrey
73 K3 New Duston Nhants
133 J7 New Earswick C York
115 K2 New Edlington Donc
214 F3 New Elgin Moray
126 E3 New Ellerby E R Yk
42 E6 Newell Green Br For
45 H5 New Eltham Gt Lon
71 J3 New End Worcs
33 L7 Newenden Kent
89 H4 New England C Pete
55 G3 Newent Gloucs
150 F7 Newfield Dur
223 H6 Newfield Highld
89 H4 New Fletton C Pete
16 C2 New Forest National
Park
48 E3 Newgale Pembks
154 B6 New Galloway D & G
59 M6 Newgate Street Herts
187 H3 New Gilston Fife
2 a1 New Grimsby IoS
98 E4 Newhall Ches E
159 H6 New Hartley Nthumb
177 H3 Newhaven C Edin
19 L5 Newhaven E Susx
43 H7 New Haw Surrey
49 J6 New Hedges Pembks
126 D5 New Holland N Linc
143 H5 Newholm N York
115 J7 New Houghton
Derbys
105 J6 New Houghton Norfk
175 L6 Newhouse N Lans
130 B2 New Hutton Cumb
19 L2 Newick E Susx
35 G7 Newington Kent
46 E6 Newington Kent
41 L2 Newington Oxon
66 B6 New Inn Carmth
53 L7 New Inn Torfn
82 F7 New Invention
Shrops
165 G2 New Lanark S Lans
126 F4 Newland C KuH
54 D6 Newland Gloucs
125 G5 Newland N York
24 C4 Newland Somset
70 E5 Newland Worcs
177 K6 Newlandrig Mdloth
156 E4 Newlands Border
150 D4 Newlands Nthumb
215 G4 Newlands of
Dundurcas Moray
156 C5 New Langholm D & G
104 C2 New Leake Lincs
217 J4 New Leeds Abers
123 L8 New Lodge Barns
121 G5 New Longton Lancs
144 E3 New Luce D & G
2 E5 Newlyn Cnwll
4 C5 Newlyn East Cnwll
207 G2 Newmachar Abers
175 L6 Newmains N Lans
44 E6 New Malden Gt Lon
77 K5 Newman's Green
Suffk
76 F2 Newmarket Suffk
232 F2 Newmarket W Isls
142 D3 New Marske R & Cl
57 K6 New Marston Oxon
206 E8 New Mill Abers
167 G7 Newmill Border
2 E4 New Mill Cnwll
123 H8 New Mill Kirk
215 K4 Newmill Moray
123 L7 Newmillerdam
Wakefd
196 C4 Newmill of Inshewan
Angus
177 G5 Newmills C Edin
113 M4 New Mills Derbys
176 D2 Newmills Fife
54 D6 Newmills Mons

82 C4 New Mills Powys
186 B2 Newmiln P & K
164 B2 Newmilns E Ayrs
16 B4 New Milton Hants
62 D2 New Mistley Essex
49 H3 New Moat Pembks
61 G6 Newney Green Essex
55 G5 Newnham Gloucs
30 B2 Newnham Hants
75 J6 Newnham Herts
34 C3 Newnham Kent
73 H3 Newnham Nhants
70 B2 Newnham Worcs
116 A7 New Ollerton Notts
217 G3 New Pitsligo Abers
9 J7 Newport Cnwll
125 K4 Newport E R Yk
76 D7 Newport Essex
39 G2 Newport Gloucs
227 K4 Newport Highld
16 F5 Newport IoW
37 L3 Newport Newpt
64 E6 Newport Pembks
99 H8 Newport Wrekin
187 G2 Newport-on-Tay Fife
74 C5 Newport Pagnell
M Keyn
74 C5 Newport Pagnell
Services M Keyn
163 J4 New Prestwick S Ayrs
65 L3 New Quay Cerdgn
4 C4 Newquay Cnwll
4 D3 Newquay Airport
Cnwll
93 G2 New Rackheath
Norfk
68 E3 New Radnor Powys
150 D3 New Ridley Nthumb
21 L2 New Romney Kent
115 L2 New Rossington
Donc
185 J7 New Sauchie Clacks
216 D7 Newseat Abers
121 G4 Newsham Lancs
132 E3 Newsham N York
140 E5 Newsham N York
159 H6 Newsham Nthumb
124 B6 New Sharlston
Wakefd
125 H5 Newsholme E R Yk
151 J4 New Silksworth
Sundld
123 H7 Newsome Kirk
102 F5 New Somerby Lincs
44 F2 New Southgate
Crematorium Gt Lon
167 H3 Newstead Border
101 K3 Newstead Notts
169 H4 Newstead Nthumb
175 K6 New Stevenston
N Lans
124 C2 Newthorpe N York
101 J4 Newthorpe Notts
182 F7 Newton Ag & B
167 J5 Newton Border
36 C5 Newton Brdgnd
75 J5 Newton C Beds
76 B5 Newton Cambs
90 B1 Newton Cambs
98 D1 Newton Ches W
112 B7 Newton Ches W
128 F5 Newton Cumb
101 H2 Newton Derbys
53 M2 Newton Herefs
69 K4 Newton Herefs
212 F4 Newton Highld
213 H5 Newton Highld
213 J2 Newton Highld
231 L5 Newton Highld
121 K1 Newton Lancs
103 H5 Newton Lincs
177 J4 Newton Mdloth
214 E2 Newton Moray
215 H2 Newton Moray
88 C6 Newton Nhants
91 J1 Newton Norfk

102 B4 Newton Notts
150 C3 Newton Nthumb
165 H3 Newton S Lans
175 H6 Newton S Lans
100 B7 Newton Staffs
77 K6 Newton Suffk
176 E3 Newton W Loth
87 G7 Newton Warwks
7 K2 Newton Abbot Devon
147 L4 Newton Arlosh Cumb
141 G3 Newton Aycliffe Dur
141 K2 Newton Bewley
Hartpl
74 D4 Newton Blossomville
M Keyn
74 E2 Newton Bromswold
Nhants
86 D2 Newton Burgoland
Leics
169 J4 Newton-by-the-Sea
Nthumb
117 H4 Newton by Toft Lincs
6 A3 Newton Ferrers Cnwll
6 E6 Newton Ferrers
Devon
232 C5 Newton Ferry W Isls
92 E4 Newton Flotman
Norfk
177 J5 Newtongrange
Mdloth
87 J4 Newton Harcourt
Leics
113 K2 Newton Heath Manch
207 G6 Newtonhill Abers
124 C2 Newton Kyme N York
132 C2 Newton-le-Willows
N York
112 E3 Newton-le-Willows
St Hel
177 J5 Newtonloan Mdloth
58 D2 Newton Longville
Bucks
174 F7 Newton Mearns
E Rens
196 F4 Newtonmill Angus
203 H5 Newtonmore Highld
141 G5 Newton Morrell
N York
186 B5 Newton of
Balcanquhal P & K
187 H6 Newton of Balcormo
Fife
133 H7 Newton on Ouse
N York
134 C2 Newton-on-
Rawcliffe N York
158 F2 Newton-on-the-
Moor Nthumb
116 D6 Newton on Trent
Lincs
12 E4 Newton Poppleford
Devon
57 L3 Newton Purcell Oxon
86 C3 Newton Regis
Warwks
138 C2 Newton Reigny
Cumb
11 K5 Newton St Cyres
Devon
92 F1 Newton St Faith
Norfk
39 G7 Newton St Loe BaNES
9 K3 Newton St Petrock
Devon
100 F7 Newton Solney
Derbys
29 H4 Newton Stacey Hants
145 J3 Newton Stewart
D & G
28 E4 Newton Tony Wilts
23 H6 Newton Tracey
Devon
142 C5 Newton under
Roseberry R & Cl
125 H2 Newton upon
Derwent E R Yk

30 B5 **Newton Valence** Hants
155 K3 **Newton Wamphray** D & G
120 F4 **Newton with Scales** Lancs
147 J5 **Newtown** Cumb
148 E3 **Newtown** Cumb
164 F7 **Newtown** D & G
12 D3 **Newtown** Devon
24 B6 **Newtown** Devon
27 L7 **New Town** Dorset
27 M7 **New Town** Dorset
19 M2 **New Town** E Susx
54 F7 **Newtown** Gloucs
29 L8 **Newtown** Hants
70 B5 **Newtown** Herefs
70 C6 **Newtown** Herefs
202 B4 **Newtown** Highld
16 E4 **Newtown** IoW
158 C3 **Newtown** Nthumb
168 F4 **Newtown** Nthumb
15 K4 **Newtown** Poole
82 C5 **Newtown** Powys
98 B7 **Newtown** Shrops
98 C6 **Newtown** Shrops
25 L8 **Newtown** Somset
99 K1 **Newtown** Staffs
112 E1 **Newtown** Wigan
70 F4 **Newtown** Worcs
87 G2 **Newtown Linford** Leics
174 D6 **Newtown of Beltrees** Rens
167 J3 **Newtown St Boswells** Border
53 H7 **New Tredegar** Caerph
164 F2 **New Trows** S Lans
195 L7 **Newtyle** Angus
90 C2 **New Walsoken** Cambs
118 C1 **New Waltham** NE Lin
177 L4 **New Winton** E Loth
182 D5 **Newyork** Ag & B
103 L2 **New York** Lincs
49 G6 **Neyland** Pembks
25 H7 **Nicholashayne** Devon
51 G7 **Nicholaston** Swans
132 D7 **Nidd** N York
207 H5 **Nigg** C Aber
223 H6 **Nigg** Highld
149 K4 **Ninebanks** Nthumb
40 C3 **Nine Elms** Swindn
70 B2 **Nineveh** Worcs
20 E3 **Ninfield** E Susx
16 E5 **Ningwood** IoW
167 K4 **Nisbet** Border
179 G7 **Nisbet Hill** Border
17 F6 **Niton** IoW
174 F6 **Nitshill** C Glas
117 H8 **Nocton** Lincs
57 K5 **Noke** Oxon
48 E4 **Nolton** Pembks
48 E4 **Nolton Haven** Pembks
98 D3 **No Man's Heath** Ches W
86 C2 **No Man's Heath** Warwks
11 J3 **Nomansland** Devon
28 E7 **Nomansland** Wilts
98 C6 **Noneley** Shrops
35 H4 **Nonington** Kent
129 L3 **Nook** Cumb
44 D6 **Norbiton** Gt Lon
98 E3 **Norbury** Ches E
100 C4 **Norbury** Derbys
44 F6 **Norbury** Gt Lon
83 G5 **Norbury** Shrops
99 H7 **Norbury** Staffs
70 F2 **Norchard** Worcs
90 D4 **Nordelph** Norfk
84 C4 **Nordley** Shrops
93 K2 **Norfolk Broads** Norfk
179 J8 **Norham** Nthumb
112 E6 **Norley** Ches W

16 D3 **Norleywood** Hants
117 G4 **Normanby** Lincs
125 K7 **Normanby** N Linc
134 B3 **Normanby** N York
142 C4 **Normanby** R & Cl
117 J3 **Normanby le Wold** Lincs
30 F2 **Normandy** Surrey
12 D2 **Norman's Green** Devon
101 G5 **Normanton** C Derb
102 D4 **Normanton** Leics
102 F4 **Normanton** Lincs
102 B2 **Normanton** Notts
124 B6 **Normanton** Wakefd
86 D2 **Normanton le Heath** Leics
101 K7 **Normanton on Soar** Notts
101 L6 **Normanton on the Wolds** Notts
116 C7 **Normanton on Trent** Notts
86 D1 **Norris Hill** Leics
58 F4 **Northall** Bucks
141 J7 **Northallerton** N York
29 H8 **Northam** C Sotn
23 G5 **Northam** Devon
73 L3 **Northampton** Nhants
70 E2 **Northampton** Worcs
115 K5 **North Anston** Rothm
42 E6 **North Ascot** Br For
57 J3 **North Aston** Oxon
59 L7 **Northaw** Herts
13 H1 **Northay** Somset
29 H7 **North Baddesley** Hants
191 L4 **North Ballachulish** Highld
26 E5 **North Barrow** Somset
105 L5 **North Barsham** Norfk
46 C3 **North Benfleet** Essex
18 C5 **North Bersted** W Susx
178 C2 **North Berwick** E Loth
17 H1 **North Boarhunt** Hants
89 H3 **Northborough** C Pete
35 J4 **Northbourne** Kent
11 H7 **North Bovey** Devon
27 J1 **North Bradley** Wilts
10 C8 **North Brentor** Devon
27 G4 **North Brewham** Somset
29 K4 **Northbrook** Hants
23 G4 **North Buckland** Devon
93 H2 **North Burlingham** Norfk
26 F6 **North Cadbury** Somset
116 F6 **North Carlton** Lincs
115 L4 **North Carlton** Notts
125 K4 **North Cave** E R Yk
56 A6 **North Cerney** Gloucs
19 K2 **North Chailey** E Susx
30 F5 **Northchapel** W Susx
28 D7 **North Charford** Hants
169 H5 **North Charlton** Nthumb
44 E6 **North Cheam** Gt Lon
27 G6 **North Cheriton** Somset
13 K4 **North Chideock** Dorset
58 F6 **Northchurch** Herts
125 K3 **North Cliffe** E R Yk
116 D6 **North Clifton** Notts
118 E4 **North Cockerington** Lincs
182 C1 **North Connel** Ag & B
36 C3 **North Cornelly** Brdgnd
118 E2 **North Cotes** Lincs
9 J6 **Northcott** Devon
57 J7 **Northcourt** Oxon
93 K5 **North Cove** Suffk

141 G6 **North Cowton** N York
74 D5 **North Crawley** M Keyn
105 K5 **North Creake** Norfk
25 L6 **North Curry** Somset
125 L1 **North Dalton** E R Yk
124 B1 **North Deighton** N York
23 H5 **North Devon Crematorium** Devon
35 K2 **Northdown** Kent
34 B4 **North Downs**
125 G3 **North Duffield** N York
218 C6 **North Duntulm** Highld
44 E6 **North East Surrey Crematorium** Gt Lon
35 G5 **North Elham** Kent
106 B7 **North Elmham** Norfk
124 D7 **North Elmsall** Wakefd
17 J3 **North End** C Port
61 G4 **North End** Essex
28 C7 **North End** Hants
74 D2 **North End** Nhants
18 D5 **North End** W Susx
72 E4 **Northend** Warwks
113 J4 **Northenden** Manch
219 H5 **North Erradale** Highld
87 J3 **North Evington** C Leic
61 K7 **North Fambridge** Essex
126 B5 **North Ferriby** E R Yk
85 H7 **Northfield** Birm
207 G4 **Northfield** C Aber
126 C5 **Northfield** E R Yk
88 E2 **Northfields** Lincs
45 M5 **Northfleet** Kent
135 H8 **North Frodingham** E R Yk
15 M1 **North Gorley** Hants
79 G3 **North Green** Suffk
117 G6 **North Greetwell** Lincs
134 C6 **North Grimston** N York
17 K2 **North Hayling** Hants
5 L1 **North Hill** Cnwll
43 H4 **North Hillingdon** Gt Lon
57 J6 **North Hinksey Village** Oxon
31 K3 **North Holmwood** Surrey
7 G5 **North Huish** Devon
116 F7 **North Hykeham** Lincs
21 G2 **Northiam** E Susx
75 G5 **Northill** C Beds
29 K4 **Northington** Hants
117 H2 **North Kelsey** Lincs
213 G5 **North Kessock** Highld
126 E6 **North Killingholme** N Linc
132 F3 **North Kilvington** N York
87 H6 **North Kilworth** Leics
103 J3 **North Kyme** Lincs
135 K5 **North Landing** E R Yk
104 B2 **Northlands** Lincs
56 C5 **Northleach** Gloucs
58 D6 **North Lee** Bucks
12 F3 **Northleigh** Devon
57 H5 **North Leigh** Oxon
116 C5 **North Leverton with Habblesthorpe** Notts
10 D5 **Northlew** Devon
71 J5 **North Littleton** Worcs
92 C6 **North Lopham** Norfk
88 D3 **North Luffenham** Rutlnd
30 D7 **North Marden** W Susx
58 C4 **North Marston** Bucks
177 K6 **North Middleton** Mdloth
216 F5 **North Millbrex** Abers
144 C4 **North Milmain** D & G
24 B5 **North Molton** Devon
57 H7 **Northmoor** Oxon

41 K3 **North Moreton** Oxon
196 C5 **Northmuir** Angus
18 B5 **North Mundham** W Susx
102 D2 **North Muskham** Notts
125 L3 **North Newbald** E R Yk
72 E6 **North Newington** Oxon
40 C8 **North Newnton** Wilts
25 L5 **North Newton** Somset
17 K2 **Northney** Hants
39 H2 **North Nibley** Gloucs
43 J4 **Northolt** Gt Lon
111 H7 **Northop** Flints
111 J7 **Northop Hall** Flints
142 B4 **North Ormesby** Middsb
118 C3 **North Ormsby** Lincs
103 K5 **Northorpe** Lincs
116 E3 **Northorpe** Lincs
132 E2 **North Otterington** N York
117 H3 **North Owersby** Lincs
123 G5 **Northowram** Calder
13 L1 **North Perrott** Somset
25 L5 **North Petherton** Somset
9 H6 **North Petherwin** Cnwll
91 J3 **North Pickenham** Norfk
71 G4 **North Piddle** Worcs
13 M3 **North Poorton** Dorset
15 H5 **Northport** Dorset
176 F3 **North Queensferry** Fife
103 G3 **North Rauceby** Lincs
106 F5 **Northrepps** Norfk
118 E5 **North Reston** Lincs
123 K1 **North Rigton** N York
113 K7 **North Rode** Ches E
234 e3 **North Ronaldsay** Ork
234 e3 *North Ronaldsay Airport* Ork
90 F1 **North Runcton** Norfk
116 D7 **North Scarle** Lincs
191 H7 **North Shian** Ag & B
151 J2 **North Shields** N Tyne
46 F3 **North Shoebury** Sthend
120 D3 **North Shore** Bpool
89 K4 **North Side** C Pete
118 F3 **North Somercotes** Lincs
132 D4 **North Stainley** N York
45 L4 **North Stifford** Thurr
39 G6 **North Stoke** BaNES
41 L3 **North Stoke** Oxon
18 D4 **North Stoke** W Susx
34 D3 **North Street** Kent
41 M6 **North Street** W Berk
169 J3 **North Sunderland** Nthumb
9 J5 **North Tamerton** Cnwll
10 F4 **North Tawton** Devon
175 K1 **North Third** Stirlg
118 D2 **North Thoresby** Lincs
232 d5 **Northton** W Isls
10 D3 **North Town** Devon
26 E3 **North Town** Somset
42 E4 **North Town** W & M
92 C2 **North Tuddenham** Norfk
233 b6 **North Uist** W Isls
157 L2 **Northumberland National Park** Nthumb
107 G6 **North Walsham** Norfk
29 K3 **North Waltham** Hants
30 B2 **North Warnborough** Hants

60 D7 **North Weald Bassett** Essex
116 C4 **North Wheatley** Notts
112 F6 **Northwich** Ches W
70 E3 **Northwick** Worcs
38 E8 **North Widcombe** BaNES
117 K4 **North Willingham** Lincs
115 H8 **North Wingfield** Derbys
102 F7 **North Witham** Lincs
91 H4 **Northwold** Norfk
43 H3 **Northwood** Gt Lon
16 F4 **Northwood** IoW
98 C6 **Northwood** Shrops
55 G5 **Northwood Green** Gloucs
26 F8 **North Wootton** Dorset
105 G7 **North Wootton** Norfk
26 E3 **North Wootton** Somset
39 J5 **North Wraxall** Wilts
142 F6 **North York Moors National Park**
124 E7 **Norton** Donc
19 M5 **Norton** E Susx
55 J3 **Norton** Gloucs
134 C5 **Norton** N York
73 H2 **Norton** Nhants
115 L6 **Norton** Notts
68 F2 **Norton** Powys
141 K3 **Norton** S on T
84 D4 **Norton** Shrops
77 L2 **Norton** Suffk
18 C4 **Norton** W Susx
39 K4 **Norton** Wilts
70 F4 **Norton** Worcs
71 J5 **Norton** Worcs
27 K3 **Norton Bavant** Wilts
99 K6 **Norton Bridge** Staffs
85 H2 **Norton Canes** Staffs
85 H3 *Norton Canes Services* Staffs
69 H5 **Norton Canon** Herefs
102 E2 **Norton Disney** Lincs
25 J6 **Norton Fitzwarren** Somset
16 D5 **Norton Green** IoW
38 E7 **Norton Hawkfield** BaNES
60 F6 **Norton Heath** Essex
99 G5 **Norton in Hales** Shrops
86 D3 **Norton-Juxta-Twycross** Leics
132 F5 **Norton-le-Clay** N York
72 B2 **Norton Lindsey** Warwks
77 L2 **Norton Little Green** Suffk
38 E7 **Norton Malreward** BaNES
27 H1 **Norton St Philip** Somset
93 J4 **Norton Subcourse** Norfk
26 C7 **Norton sub Hamdon** Somset
102 C1 **Norwell** Notts
116 B8 **Norwell Woodhouse** Notts
92 F2 **Norwich** Norfk
92 E2 *Norwich Airport* Norfk
92 F2 **Norwich Cathedral** Norfk
92 F1 **Norwich (St Faith) Crematorium** Norfk
235 e1 **Norwick** Shet
185 J8 **Norwood** Clacks
43 J5 **Norwood Green** Gt Lon
31 L3 **Norwood Hill** Surrey
87 K4 **Noseley** Leics

6 E6 **Noss Mayo** Devon
132 D4 **Nosterfield** N York
210 D8 **Nostie** Highld
56 C4 **Notgrove** Gloucs
36 C5 **Nottage** Brdgnd
101 L5 **Nottingham** C Nott
123 L7 **Notton** Wakefd
39 K6 **Notton** Wilts
70 E2 **Noutard's Green** Worcs
83 H2 **Nox** Shrops
42 A3 **Nuffield** Oxon
125 K2 **Nunburnholme** E R Yk
86 D5 **Nuneaton** Warwks
57 K7 **Nuneham Courtenay** Oxon
45 G5 **Nunhead** Gt Lon
126 E1 **Nunkeeling** E R Yk
133 H7 **Nun Monkton** N York
27 G3 **Nunney** Somset
133 K4 **Nunnington** N York
127 G8 **Nunsthorpe** NE Lin
124 F1 **Nunthorpe** C York
142 C4 **Nunthorpe** Middsb
142 C5 **Nunthorpe Village** Middsb
28 D6 **Nunton** Wilts
132 E5 **Nunwick** N York
29 G7 **Nursling** Hants
17 L2 **Nutbourne** W Susx
18 E3 **Nutbourne** W Susx
32 B3 **Nutfield** Surrey
101 K4 **Nuthall** Notts
76 B7 **Nuthampstead** Herts
31 K6 **Nuthurst** W Susx
32 D7 **Nutley** E Susx
231 L3 **Nybster** Highld
18 B6 **Nyetimber** W Susx
30 D6 **Nyewood** W Susx
11 G4 **Nymet Rowland** Devon
11 G5 **Nymet Tracey** Devon
55 J7 **Nympsfield** Gloucs
25 H6 **Nynehead** Somset
18 C5 **Nyton** W Susx

O

87 J4 **Oadby** Leics
34 B3 **Oad Street** Kent
100 B4 **Oakamoor** Staffs
176 E5 **Oakbank** W Loth
10 D5 **Oak Cross** Devon
37 J2 **Oakdale** Caerph
25 J6 **Oake** Somset
84 F3 **Oaken** Staffs
121 H2 **Oakenclough** Lancs
84 C2 **Oakengates** Wrekin
150 F7 **Oakenshaw** Dur
123 H5 **Oakenshaw** Kirk
66 B3 **Oakford** Cerdgn
24 E6 **Oakford** Devon
88 C2 **Oakham** Rutlnd
30 C4 **Oakhanger** Hants
26 F3 **Oakhill** Somset
76 B2 **Oakington** Cambs
55 H4 **Oakle Street** Gloucs
74 E4 **Oakley** Bed
57 M5 **Oakley** Bucks
176 D1 **Oakley** Fife
29 K2 **Oakley** Hants
92 E7 **Oakley** Suffk
55 K7 **Oakridge** Gloucs
39 M2 **Oaksey** Wilts
86 D2 **Oakthorpe** Leics
101 G5 **Oakwood** C Derb
122 F3 **Oakworth** C Brad
34 D3 **Oare** Kent
24 C3 **Oare** Somset
40 D7 **Oare** Wilts
103 G5 **Oasby** Lincs
26 B6 **Oath** Somset
196 D5 **Oathlaw** Angus
43 H7 **Oatlands Park** Surrey

182 B2 **Oban** Ag & B
83 G7 **Obley** Shrops
195 M8 **Obney** P & K
26 F7 **Oborne** Dorset
78 D1 **Occold** Suffk
231 J7 **Occumster** Highld
163 L5 **Ochiltree** E Ayrs
101 H5 **Ockbrook** Derbys
31 H1 **Ockham** Surrey
190 B3 **Ockle** Highld
31 J4 **Ockley** Surrey
69 L5 **Ocle Pychard** Herefs
26 D7 **Odcombe** Somset
39 H7 **Odd Down** BaNES
71 G3 **Oddingley** Worcs
56 E3 **Oddington** Gloucs
57 K5 **Oddington** Oxon
74 D3 **Odell** Bed
30 C2 **Odiham** Hants
123 H5 **Odsal** C Brad
75 K6 **Odsey** Cambs
28 D6 **Odstock** Wilts
86 E3 **Odstone** Leics
72 D2 **Offchurch** Warwks
71 J5 **Offenham** Worcs
113 K4 **Offerton** Stockp
19 L3 **Offham** E Susx
33 H2 **Offham** Kent
18 D4 **Offham** W Susx
75 J2 **Offord Cluny** Cambs
75 J2 **Offord D'Arcy** Cambs
78 C5 **Offton** Suffk
12 F3 **Offwell** Devon
40 D6 **Ogbourne Maizey** Wilts
40 D6 **Ogbourne St Andrew** Wilts
40 D5 **Ogbourne St George** Wilts
158 E6 **Ogle** Nthumb
112 C5 **Oglet** Lpool
36 D5 **Ogmore** V Glam
36 D5 **Ogmore-by-Sea** V Glam
36 E3 **Ogmore Vale** Brdgnd
14 F1 **Okeford Fitzpaine** Dorset
10 E5 **Okehampton** Devon
100 F1 **Oker Side** Derbys
31 J4 **Okewood Hill** Surrey
87 L8 **Old** Nhants
207 H4 **Old Aberdeen** C Aber
29 L5 **Old Alresford** Hants
224 D2 **Oldany** Highld
154 D3 **Old Auchenbrack** D & G
101 K4 **Old Basford** C Nott
30 A2 **Old Basing** Hants
106 A8 **Old Beetley** Norfk
71 K2 **Oldberrow** Warwks
169 G5 **Old Bewick** Nthumb
118 E8 **Old Bolingbroke** Lincs
123 J2 **Old Bramhope** Leeds
115 G6 **Old Brampton** Derbys
146 D2 **Old Bridge of Urr** D & G
92 C5 **Old Buckenham** Norfk
41 J8 **Old Burghclere** Hants
85 H5 **Oldbury** Sandw
84 C5 **Oldbury** Shrops
86 C5 **Oldbury** Warwks
38 E2 **Oldbury-on-Severn** S Glos
39 J3 **Oldbury on the Hill** Gloucs
133 H3 **Old Byland** N York
115 L2 **Old Cantley** Donc
53 L3 **Oldcastle** Mons
127 G8 **Old Clee** NE Lin
25 G3 **Old Cleeve** Somset
115 L8 **Old Clipstone** Notts
110 B6 **Old Colwyn** Conwy
115 L4 **Oldcotes** Notts
152 F3 **Old Dailly** S Ayrs
102 A7 **Old Dalby** Leics

217 J5 **Old Deer** Abers
115 K3 **Old Edlington** Donc
126 E3 **Old Ellerby** E R Yk
79 G7 **Old Felixstowe** Suffk
70 E2 **Oldfield** Worcs
89 H4 **Old Fletton** C Pete
27 H2 **Oldford** Somset
54 E4 **Old Forge** Herefs
2 a1 **Old Grimsby** IoS
60 B4 **Old Hall Green** Herts
113 L1 **Oldham** Oldham
178 F4 **Oldhamstocks** E Loth
60 D5 **Old Harlow** Essex
105 G4 **Old Hunstanton** Norfk
89 K7 **Old Hurst** Cambs
130 B2 **Old Hutton** Cumb
174 E4 **Old Kilpatrick** W Duns
59 L4 **Old Knebworth** Herts
38 F6 **Oldland** S Glos
121 K4 **Old Langho** Lancs
104 C3 **Old Leake** Lincs
134 C5 **Old Malton** N York
216 F8 **Oldmeldrum** Abers
124 C4 **Old Micklefield** Leeds
6 B2 **Oldmill** Cnwll
72 C2 **Old Milverton** Warwks
37 M8 **Oldmixon** N Som
78 C3 **Old Newton** Suffk
68 E3 **Old Radnor** Powys
216 D8 **Old Rayne** Abers
21 K2 **Old Romney** Kent
19 G4 **Old Shoreham** W Susx
228 C4 **Oldshoremore** Highld
39 H4 **Old Sodbury** S Glos
102 F5 **Old Somerby** Lincs
133 H4 **Oldstead** N York
73 L6 **Old Stratford** Nhants
194 C4 **Old Struan** P & K
84 F6 **Old Swinford** Dudley
132 F3 **Old Thirsk** N York
130 B3 **Old Town** Cumb
20 C5 **Old Town** E Susx
2 b2 **Old Town** IoS
113 J3 **Old Trafford** Traffd
148 E3 **Oldwall** Cumb
50 F6 **Oldwalls** Swans
75 G5 **Old Warden** C Beds
89 G7 **Old Weston** Cambs
231 L5 **Old Wick** Highld
43 G5 **Old Windsor** W & M
34 E4 **Old Wives Lees** Kent
43 G8 **Old Woking** Surrey
231 G5 **Olgrinmore** Highld
100 C8 **Olive Green** Staffs
165 L4 **Oliver** Border
29 J6 **Oliver's Battery** Hants
235 c3 **Ollaberry** Shet
209 H6 **Ollach** Highld
113 H6 **Ollerton** Ches E
116 A7 **Ollerton** Notts
98 F7 **Ollerton** Shrops
74 C4 **Olney** M Keyn
231 H3 **Olrig House** Highld
85 K6 **Olton** Solhll
38 E3 **Olveston** S Glos
70 C2 **Ombersley** Worcs
116 B7 **Ompton** Notts
237 d5 **Onchan** IoM
100 B2 **Onecote** Staffs
83 J7 **Onibury** Shrops
191 K4 **Onich** Highld
52 C6 **Onllwyn** Neath
99 H4 **Onneley** Staffs
31 G2 **Onslow Village** Surrey
112 E6 **Onston** Ches W
219 H6 **Opinan** Highld
215 G3 **Orbliston** Moray
208 D5 **Orbost** Highld
119 G7 **Orby** Lincs
25 K6 **Orchard Portman** Somset
28 B3 **Orcheston** Wilts
54 D3 **Orcop** Herefs
54 C3 **Orcop Hill** Herefs
216 C3 **Ord** Abers

206 C3 Ordhead Abers	12 E5 Otterton Devon
205 K5 Ordie Abers	12 E4 Ottery St Mary Devon
215 H3 Ordiequish Moray	34 F6 Ottinge Kent
150 B3 Ordley Nthumb	127 G5 Ottringham E R Yk
116 B5 Ordsall Notts	147 K6 Oughterside Cumb
21 G4 Ore E Susx	114 F3 Oughtibridge Sheff
79 J4 Orford Suffk	113 G4 Oughtrington Warrtn
112 E4 Orford Warrtn	133 H5 Oulston N York
15 H4 Organford Dorset	147 M5 Oulton Cumb
34 D7 Orlestone Kent	106 D6 Oulton Norfk
69 J2 Orleton Herefs	99 K5 Oulton Staffs
70 C2 Orleton Worcs	93 L5 Oulton Suffk
74 C1 Orlingbury Nhants	93 L5 Oulton Broad Suffk
142 C4 Ormesby R & Cl	106 D6 Oulton Street Norfk
93 K1 Ormesby St	88 F6 Oundle Nhants
Margaret Norfk	84 F5 Ounsdale Staffs
93 K1 Ormesby St Michael	149 G7 Ousby Cumb
Norfk	77 G3 Ousden Suffk
219 K4 Ormiscaig Highld	125 K6 Ousefleet E R Yk
177 L4 Ormiston E Loth	151 L4 Ouston Dur
189 L4 Ormsaigmore Highld	137 K7 Outgate Cumb
172 C4 Ormsary Ag & B	139 H6 Outhgill Cumb
120 F8 Ormskirk Lancs	71 K2 Outhill Warwks
171 G2 Oronsay Ag & B	123 G6 Outlane Kirk
234 b6 Orphir Ork	120 E3 Out Rawcliffe Lancs
45 J6 Orpington Gt Lon	90 D3 Outwell Norfk
111 K3 Orrell Sefton	32 B4 Outwood Surrey
112 D2 Orrell Wigan	99 H8 Outwoods Staffs
146 D5 Orroland D & G	123 L5 Ouzlewell Green
45 M4 Orsett Thurr	Leeds
84 E1 Orslow Staffs	75 L1 Over Cambs
102 C4 Orston Notts	71 G6 Overbury Worcs
138 F5 Orton Cumb	14 D6 Overcombe Dorset
88 B7 Orton Nhants	26 E7 Over Compton Dorset
84 F4 Orton Staffs	121 K8 Overdale
89 H4 Orton Longueville	Crematorium Bolton
C Pete	114 D7 Over Haddon Derbys
86 C3 Orton-on-the-Hill	129 L5 Over Kellet Lancs
Leics	57 H4 Over Kiddington
89 H4 Orton Waterville	Oxon
C Pete	26 C4 Overleigh Somset
75 L4 Orwell Cambs	56 F3 Over Norton Oxon
121 J4 Osbaldeston Lancs	113 H6 Over Peover Ches E
124 F1 Osbaldwick C York	111 L6 Overpool Ches W
86 E3 Osbaston Leics	225 J4 Overscaig Hotel
97 L7 Osbaston Shrops	Highld
17 G4 Osborne House IoW	86 C1 Overseal Derbys
103 H5 Osbournby Lincs	133 G2 Over Silton N York
112 D7 Oscroft Ches W	34 E3 Oversland Kent
208 E6 Ose Highld	74 B2 Overstone Nhants
101 H8 Osgathorpe Leics	25 J4 Over Stowey Somset
117 H3 Osgodby Lincs	106 F4 Overstrand Norfk
124 F4 Osgodby N York	26 B7 Over Stratton Somset
135 G3 Osgodby N York	72 F6 Overthorpe Nhants
209 H6 Oskaig Highld	207 G3 Overton C Aber
189 L7 Oskamull Ag & B	29 K2 Overton Hants
61 G4 Onslow Green Essex	129 J7 Overton Lancs
100 D4 Osmaston Derbys	133 H7 Overton N York
14 D5 Osmington Dorset	69 K1 Overton Shrops
14 E6 Osmington Mills	50 F7 Overton Swans
Dorset	123 K7 Overton Wakefd
123 L4 Osmondthorpe Leeds	98 A4 Overton Wrexhm
141 K7 Osmotherley N York	130 C4 Overtown Lancs
57 J6 Osney Oxon	175 L7 Overtown N Lans
34 D3 Ospringe Kent	28 F4 Over Wallop Hants
123 K6 Ossett Wakefd	86 B5 Over Whitacre
116 C8 Ossington Notts	Warwks
44 D5 Osterley Gt Lon	57 H3 Over Worton Oxon
133 K4 Oswaldkirk N York	58 C4 Oving Bucks
121 L5 Oswaldtwistle Lancs	18 B5 Oving W Susx
97 L6 Oswestry Shrops	19 K5 Ovingdean Br & H
32 F2 Otford Kent	150 D3 Ovingham Nthumb
33 K3 Otham Kent	140 E4 Ovington Dur
26 B5 Othery Somset	77 H6 Ovington Essex
123 J2 Otley Leeds	29 K5 Ovington Hants
78 E4 Otley Suffk	91 K3 Ovington Norfk
29 J6 Otterbourne Hants	150 D3 Ovington Nthumb
131 G7 Otterburn N York	28 F7 Ower Hants
157 M4 Otterburn Nthumb	14 E5 Owermoigne Dorset
172 F2 Otter Ferry Ag & B	115 G4 Owlerton Sheff
8 F6 Otterham Cnwll	42 D7 Owlsmoor Br For
25 K3 Otterhampton	58 C6 Owlswick Bucks
Somset	117 A4 Owmby Lincs
232 c5 Otternish W Isls	117 H1 Owmby Lincs
43 G7 Ottershaw Surrey	29 K6 Owslebury Hants
235 d3 Otterswick Shet	124 E7 Owston Donc
87 L3 Owston Leics	61 H3 Panfield Essex
116 D2 Owston Ferry N Linc	41 M5 Pangbourne W Berk
127 G4 Owstwick E R Yk	19 J4 Pangdean W Susx
127 H5 Owthorne E R Yk	123 L1 Pannal N York
102 A5 Owthorpe Notts	132 D8 Pannal Ash N York
141 L2 Owton Manor Hartpl	205 J6 Pannanich Wells
91 G3 Oxborough Norfk	Hotel Abers
118 D6 Oxcombe Lincs	97 L7 Pant Shrops
61 G3 Oxen End Essex	111 G6 Pantasaph Flints
129 L2 Oxenholme Cumb	36 E4 Pant-ffrwyth Brdgnd
122 F4 Oxenhope C Brad	95 H3 Pant Glas Gwynd
129 G3 Oxen Park Cumb	81 G4 Pantglas Powys
26 C3 Oxenpill Somset	117 K5 Panton Lincs
55 L2 Oxenton Gloucs	81 L8 Pant-y-dwr Powys
40 F8 Oxenwood Wilts	111 H8 Pant-y-mwyn Flints
57 K6 Oxford Oxon	93 H2 Panxworth Norfk
57 J5 Oxford Airport Oxon	234 c3 Papa Westray Airport
57 K6 Oxford Crematorium	Ork
Oxon	136 F2 Papcastle Cumb
57 L6 Oxford Services Oxon	231 L5 Papigoe Highld
43 J2 Oxhey Herts	178 D4 Papple E Loth
72 C5 Oxhill Warwks	101 K3 Papplewick Notts
84 F3 Oxley Wolves	75 K3 Papworth Everard
61 L5 Oxley Green Essex	Cambs
90 C6 Oxlode Cambs	75 J2 Papworth St Agnes
167 L5 Oxnam Border	Cambs
106 F7 Oxnead Norfk	5 G5 Par Cnwll
43 J7 Oxshott Surrey	121 G7 Parbold Lancs
114 F2 Oxspring Barns	26 E4 Parbrook Somset
32 C3 Oxted Surrey	96 D5 Parc Gwynd
178 B7 Oxton Border	49 K5 Parc Gwyn
124 D2 Oxton N York	Crematorium Pembks
101 M3 Oxton Notts	38 B3 Parc Seymour Newpt
51 G7 Oxwich Swans	136 F3 Pardshaw Cumb
50 F7 Oxwich Green Swans	79 G3 Parham Suffk
221 K2 Oykel Bridge Hotel	154 F4 Park D & G
Highld	149 H3 Park Nthumb
206 D1 Oyne Abers	42 B3 Park Corner Oxon
51 H7 Oystermouth Swans	120 E5 Park Crematorium
	Lancs
	54 E6 Parkend Gloucs
	33 G4 Parkers Green Kent
P	34 D6 Park Farm Kent
	111 J6 Parkgate Ches W
232 g2 Pabail W Isls	155 H4 Parkgate D & G
86 D1 Packington Leics	17 G2 Park Gate Hants
196 C6 Padanaram Angus	123 J3 Park Gate Leeds
58 B2 Padbury Bucks	31 K3 Parkgate Surrey
44 F4 Paddington Gt Lon	196 F6 Parkgrove
35 G6 Paddlesworth Kent	Crematorium Angus
46 B7 Paddlesworth Kent	174 E4 Parkhall W Duns
33 H4 Paddock Wood Kent	22 F6 Parkham Devon
122 B4 Padiham Lancs	207 G3 Parkhill House Abers
132 B7 Padside N York	51 G7 Parkmill Swans
4 E2 Padstow Cnwll	44 D4 Park Royal Gt Lon
41 L7 Padworth W Berk	151 K5 Parkside Dur
18 B6 Pagham W Susx	175 L6 Parkside N Lans
46 F2 Paglesham Essex	15 J4 Parkstone Poole
7 K4 Paignton Torbay	59 J6 Park Street Herts
86 F6 Pailton Warwks	123 G6 Park Wood
68 D5 Painscastle Powys	Crematorium Calder
150 D3 Painshawfield	60 C6 Parndon Essex
Nthumb	60 C6 Parndon Wood
134 C7 Painsthorpe E R Yk	Crematorium Essex
55 K6 Painswick Gloucs	23 L3 Parracombe Devon
34 D3 Painter's Forstal Kent	89 L2 Parson Drove Cambs
174 E5 Paisley Rens	62 B3 Parson's Heath Essex
93 L5 Pakefield Suffk	174 F5 Partick C Glas
77 L2 Pakenham Suffk	113 G3 Partington Traffd
42 E5 Paley Street W & M	118 F7 Partney Lincs
85 H4 Palfrey Wsall	136 D3 Parton Cumb
92 D7 Palgrave Suffk	19 G2 Partridge Green
14 E2 Pallington Dorset	W Susx
163 L5 Palmerston E Ayrs	100 D2 Parwich Derbys
146 E4 Palnackie D & G	73 L6 Passenham Nhants
145 J3 Palnure D & G	107 G5 Paston Norfk
115 J7 Palterton Derbys	19 J4 Patcham Br & H
41 L8 Pamber End Hants	18 E4 Patching W Susx
41 L8 Pamber Green Hants	38 E4 Patchway S Glos
41 L7 Pamber Heath Hants	132 B6 Pateley Bridge N York
55 L2 Pamington Gloucs	186 E8 Pathhead Fife
15 J3 Pamphill Dorset	177 K5 Pathhead Mdloth
76 C5 Pampisford Cambs	185 M5 Path of Condie P & K
187 J1 Panbride Angus	163 K7 Patna E Ayrs
9 H4 Pancrasweek Devon	40 B8 Patney Wilts
53 M4 Pandy Mons	237 b5 Patrick IoM
110 B8 Pandy Tudur Conwy	

132 C2 **Patrick Brompton** N York
113 H2 **Patricroft** Salfd
127 H6 **Patrington** E R Yk
127 H6 **Patrington Haven** E R Yk
35 G4 **Patrixbourne** Kent
137 L4 **Patterdale** Cumb
84 E4 **Pattingham** Staffs
73 J4 **Pattishall** Nhants
61 K3 **Pattiswick Green** Essex
2 E5 **Paul** Cnwll
73 K5 **Paulerspury** Nhants
126 E5 **Paull** E R Yk
28 C5 **Paul's Dene** Wilts
26 F1 **Paulton** BaNES
158 D3 **Pauperhaugh** Nthumb
74 E4 **Pavenham** Bed
25 L3 **Pawlett** Somset
71 L6 **Paxford** Gloucs
179 J7 **Paxton** Border
12 E3 **Payhembury** Devon
122 C1 **Paythorne** Lancs
19 L5 **Peacehaven** E Susx
114 D3 **Peak District National Park**
114 C5 **Peak Forest** Derbys
89 H3 **Peakirk** C Pete
39 G8 **Peasedown St John** BaNES
92 C1 **Peaseland Green** Norfk
41 J5 **Peasemore** W Berk
79 H2 **Peasenhall** Suffk
31 L5 **Pease Pottage** W Susx
31 L5 **Pease Pottage Services** W Susx
31 H3 **Peaslake** Surrey
112 D3 **Peasley Cross** St Hel
21 H2 **Peasmarsh** E Susx
217 H2 **Peathill** Abers
187 G5 **Peat Inn** Fife
87 H5 **Peatling Magna** Leics
87 H5 **Peatling Parva** Leics
77 J7 **Pebmarsh** Essex
71 K5 **Pebworth** Worcs
122 E5 **Pecket Well** Calder
98 D2 **Peckforton** Ches E
45 G5 **Peckham** Gt Lon
86 F4 **Peckleton** Leics
34 F7 **Pedlinge** Kent
85 G6 **Pedmore** Dudley
26 B4 **Pedwell** Somset
166 C2 **Peebles** Border
237 b4 **Peel** IoM
35 G6 **Peene** Kent
59 J2 **Pegsdon** C Beds
159 G5 **Pegswood** Nthumb
35 K2 **Pegwell** Kent
209 H7 **Peinchorran** Highld
208 F3 **Peinlich** Highld
62 B5 **Peldon** Essex
85 H3 **Pelsall** Wsall
151 G4 **Pelton** Dur
5 K5 **Pelynt** Cnwll
51 G5 **Pemberton** Carmth
112 D2 **Pemberton** Wigan
50 E5 **Pembrey** Carmth
69 H3 **Pembridge** Herefs
49 G7 **Pembroke** Pembks
49 G6 **Pembroke Dock** Pembks
48 E4 **Pembrokeshire Coast National Park** Pembks
33 G3 **Pembury** Kent
54 E3 **Pen-allt** Herefs
54 D6 **Penallt** Mons
49 J7 **Penally** Pembks
37 J6 **Penarth** V Glam
80 F6 **Pen-bont Rhydybeddau** Cerdgn

65 J4 **Penbryn** Cerdgn
66 B7 **Pencader** Carmth
177 L5 **Pencaitland** E Loth
108 D6 **Pencarnisiog** IoA
66 C5 **Pencarreg** Carmth
53 H3 **Pencelli** Powys
51 G6 **Penclawdd** Swans
36 E4 **Pencoed** Brdgnd
69 L4 **Pencombe** Herefs
54 E4 **Pencraig** Herefs
97 G6 **Pencraig** Powys
2 C4 **Pendeen** Cnwll
52 E6 **Penderyn** Rhondd
50 B4 **Pendine** Carmth
113 H2 **Pendlebury** Salfd
121 L3 **Pendleton** Lancs
55 H2 **Pendock** Worcs
8 D8 **Pendoggett** Cnwll
13 M1 **Pendomer** Somset
37 G5 **Pendoylan** V Glam
81 G4 **Penegoes** Powys
49 J3 **Pen-ffordd** Pembks
37 J2 **Pengam** Caerph
37 K5 **Pengam** Cardif
45 G6 **Penge** Gt Lon
8 E7 **Pengelly** Cnwll
3 K2 **Penhallow** Cnwll
3 J4 **Penhalvean** Cnwll
40 D3 **Penhill** Swindn
38 B3 **Penhow** Newpt
177 H6 **Penicuik** Mdloth
209 G6 **Penifiler** Highld
161 J4 **Peninver** Ag & B
114 E2 **Penistone** Barns
152 F3 **Penkill** S Ayrs
85 G2 **Penkridge** Staffs
98 B4 **Penley** Wrexhm
36 F5 **Penllyn** V Glam
96 C3 **Penmachno** Conwy
37 J2 **Penmaen** Caerph
51 G7 **Penmaen** Swans
109 K6 **Penmaenmawr** Conwy
95 M8 **Penmaenpool** Gwynd
37 G6 **Penmark** V Glam
4 C6 **Penmount Crematorium** Cnwll
109 G6 **Penmynydd** IoA
42 F2 **Penn** Bucks
80 F4 **Pennal** Gwynd
216 F2 **Pennan** Abers
81 J4 **Pennant** Powys
83 G4 **Pennerley** Shrops
122 E4 **Pennines**
128 F4 **Pennington** Cumb
53 H3 **Pennorth** Powys
42 F2 **Penn Street** Bucks
129 G3 **Penny Bridge** Cumb
181 G3 **Pennycross** Ag & B
181 H3 **Pennyghael** Ag & B
163 H7 **Pennyglen** S Ayrs
11 K3 **Pennymoor** Devon
65 H5 **Penparc** Cerdgn
53 L6 **Penperlleni** Mons
5 J5 **Penpoll** Cnwll
3 H4 **Penponds** Cnwll
154 E4 **Penpont** D & G
65 H6 **Pen-rhiw** Pembks
37 G2 **Penrhiwceiber** Rhondd
51 L4 **Pen Rhiwfawr** Neath
65 K6 **Penrhiw-llan** Cerdgn
65 K5 **Penrhiw-pal** Cerdgn
94 F5 **Penrhos** Gwynd
54 B5 **Penrhos** Mons
110 A5 **Penrhyn Bay** Conwy
109 H6 **Penrhyn Castle** Gwynd
95 K5 **Penrhyndeudraeth** Gwynd
50 F7 **Penrice** Swans
161 L1 **Penrioch** N Ayrs
138 D2 **Penrith** Cumb
4 D2 **Penrose** Cnwll
138 B2 **Penruddock** Cumb
3 K4 **Penryn** Cnwll

110 C5 **Pensarn** Conwy
70 C2 **Pensax** Worcs
27 H5 **Penselwood** Somset
38 F7 **Pensford** BaNES
71 G5 **Pensham** Worcs
151 H4 **Penshaw** Sundld
32 F4 **Penshurst** Kent
5 L2 **Pensilva** Cnwll
4 F6 **Pentewan** Cnwll
109 H7 **Pentir** Gwynd
4 C4 **Pentire** Cnwll
77 J5 **Pentlow** Essex
91 G2 **Pentney** Norfk
156 D6 **Pentonbridge** Cumb
29 G3 **Penton Mewsey** Hants
109 G5 **Pentraeth** IoA
54 B7 **Pentre** Mons
36 F2 **Pentre** Rhondd
98 A8 **Pentre** Shrops
53 G7 **Pentrebach** Myr Td
52 E2 **Pentre-bach** Powys
108 F6 **Pentre Berw** IoA
97 L3 **Pentrebychan Crematorium** Wrexhm
97 J2 **Pentre-celyn** Denbgs
81 J3 **Pentre-celyn** Powys
51 J6 **Pentre-chwyth** Swans
65 L6 **Pentre-cwrt** Carmth
97 J3 **Pentredwr** Denbgs
95 J5 **Pentrefelin** Gwynd
96 D3 **Pentrefoelas** Conwy
65 K4 **Pentregat** Cerdgn
51 H3 **Pentre-Gwenlais** Carmth
83 G7 **Pentre Hodrey** Shrops
110 F8 **Pentre Llanrhaeadr** Denbgs
36 E5 **Pentre Meyrick** V Glam
96 C1 **Pentre-tafarn-y-fedw** Conwy
101 G3 **Pentrich** Derbys
28 B7 **Pentridge** Dorset
54 D6 **Pen-twyn** Mons
37 J2 **Pentwynmaur** Caerph
37 H4 **Pentyrch** Cardif
5 G5 **Penwithick** Cnwll
51 H2 **Penybanc** Carmth
68 C2 **Penybont** Powys
97 K7 **Pen-y-bont** Powys
97 G7 **Pen-y-bont-fawr** Powys
65 G6 **Pen-y-bryn** Pembks
97 L4 **Pencycae** Wrexhm
54 C6 **Pen-y-clawdd** Mons
37 G3 **Pen-y-coedcae** Rhondd
48 E3 **Pen-y-cwn** Pembks
111 G7 **Pen-y-felin** Flints
97 L1 **Penyffordd** Flints
97 H7 **Pen-y-Garnedd** Powys
94 D5 **Pen-y-graig** Gwynd
36 F3 **Penygraig** Rhondd
51 H3 **Penygroes** Carmth
95 H2 **Penygroes** Gwynd
50 F5 **Pen-y-Mynydd** Carmth
97 L1 **Penymynydd** Flints
108 F4 **Penysarn** IoA
97 J3 **Pen-y-stryt** Denbgs
52 F6 **Penywaun** Rhondd
2 E5 **Penzance** Cnwll
2 E5 **Penzance Heliport** Cnwll
71 G4 **Peopleton** Worcs
98 F7 **Peplow** Shrops
163 J2 **Perceton** N Ayrs
217 H2 **Percyhorner** Abers
28 E2 **Perham Down** Wilts
24 E3 **Periton** Somset

44 D4 **Perivale** Gt Lon
12 D4 **Perkins Village** Devon
115 M7 **Perlethorpe** Notts
3 K4 **Perranarworthal** Cnwll
3 K1 **Perranporth** Cnwll
2 F5 **Perranuthnoe** Cnwll
3 K4 **Perranwell** Cnwll
3 K2 **Perranzabuloe** Cnwll
85 J5 **Perry Barr** Birm
85 J5 **Perry Barr Crematorium** Birm
39 L3 **Perry Green** Wilts
99 J6 **Pershall** Staffs
71 G5 **Pershore** Worcs
74 F2 **Pertenhall** Bed
186 B3 **Perth** P & K
186 A3 **Perth Crematorium** P & K
98 A5 **Perthy** Shrops
69 L6 **Perton** Herefs
84 F4 **Perton** Staffs
89 H4 **Peterborough** C Pete
89 H3 **Peterborough Crematorium** C Pete
89 G5 **Peterborough Services** Cambs
69 G6 **Peterchurch** Herefs
206 F5 **Peterculter** C Aber
217 L5 **Peterhead** Abers
151 K6 **Peterlee** Dur
30 C6 **Petersfield** Hants
59 J4 **Peter's Green** Herts
44 D5 **Petersham** Gt Lon
10 C3 **Peters Marland** Devon
37 K4 **Peterstone Wentlooge** Newpt
37 G5 **Peterston-super-Ely** V Glam
54 E3 **Peterstow** Herefs
6 D1 **Peter Tavy** Devon
34 F4 **Petham** Kent
9 H6 **Petherwin Gate** Cnwll
10 D3 **Petrockstow** Devon
21 H3 **Pett** E Susx
78 E3 **Pettaugh** Suffk
196 C7 **Petterden** Angus
165 J2 **Pettinain** S Lans
79 G4 **Pettistree** Suffk
24 F6 **Petton** Devon
45 J6 **Petts Wood** Gt Lon
177 H2 **Pettycur** Fife
207 G1 **Pettymuk** Abers
31 G6 **Petworth** W Susx
20 D5 **Pevensey** E Susx
20 D5 **Pevensey Bay** E Susx
40 D7 **Pewsey** Wilts
71 G3 **Phepson** Worcs
22 D6 **Philham** Devon
166 F4 **Philiphaugh** Border
2 F4 **Phillack** Cnwll
4 D7 **Philleigh** Cnwll
176 E3 **Philpstoun** W Loth
30 C1 **Phoenix Green** Hants
203 G6 **Phoines** Highld
26 C6 **Pibsbury** Somset
136 E3 **Pica** Cumb
115 K1 **Pickburn** Donc
134 C3 **Pickering** N York
86 C6 **Pickford** Covtry
132 E3 **Pickhill** N York
83 J4 **Picklescott** Shrops
113 G6 **Pickmere** Ches E
25 J5 **Pickney** Somset
121 K6 **Pickup Bank** Bl w D
87 L2 **Pickwell** Leics
103 H5 **Pickworth** Lincs
88 E2 **Pickworth** Rutlnd
112 B7 **Picton** Ches W
141 K5 **Picton** N York
19 L5 **Piddinghoe** E Susx
74 B4 **Piddington** Nhants
57 M5 **Piddington** Oxon
14 D3 **Piddlehinton** Dorset

14 D3 **Piddletrenthide** Dorset
89 K7 **Pidley** Cambs
140 F4 **Piercebridge** Darltn
234 c3 **Pierowall** Ork
45 L2 **Pilgrims Hatch** Essex
116 E3 **Pilham** Lincs
6 A3 **Pillaton** Cnwll
72 C5 **Pillerton Hersey** Warwks
72 C5 **Pillerton Priors** Warwks
115 G2 **Pilley** Barns
16 D3 **Pilley** Hants
120 E2 **Pilling** Lancs
38 D4 **Pilning** S Glos
114 C8 **Pilsbury** Derbys
13 K3 **Pilsdon** Dorset
101 H1 **Pilsley** Derbys
114 E7 **Pilsley** Derbys
93 H2 **Pilson Green** Norfk
19 L2 **Piltdown** E Susx
23 J5 **Pilton** Devon
88 E6 **Pilton** Nhants
88 D3 **Pilton** Rutlnd
26 E3 **Pilton** Somset
15 G1 **Pimperne** Dorset
103 L7 **Pinchbeck** Lincs
59 L3 **Pin Green** Herts
12 C4 **Pinhoe** Devon
72 B2 **Pinley Green** Warwks
152 E4 **Pinminnoch** S Ayrs
152 E4 **Pinmore** S Ayrs
12 E5 **Pinn** Devon
43 J3 **Pinner** Gt Lon
43 J3 **Pinner Green** Gt Lon
71 G5 **Pinvin** Worcs
152 E5 **Pinwherry** S Ayrs
101 J2 **Pinxton** Derbys
69 K5 **Pipe and Lyde** Herefs
69 J1 **Pipe Aston** Herefs
99 G4 **Pipe Gate** Shrops
213 K4 **Piperhill** Highld
88 B6 **Pipewell** Nhants
30 F1 **Pirbright** Surrey
167 K4 **Pirnie** Border
161 L1 **Pirnmill** N Ayrs
59 J2 **Pirton** Herts
70 F5 **Pirton** Worcs
42 B3 **Pishill** Oxon
94 F4 **Pistyll** Gwynd
194 C3 **Pitagowan** P & K
217 J2 **Pitblae** Abers
185 M3 **Pitcairngreen** P & K
223 H6 **Pitcalnie** Highld
206 D1 **Pitcaple** Abers
196 B4 **Pitcarity** Angus
55 J6 **Pitchcombe** Gloucs
58 C4 **Pitchcott** Bucks
83 K3 **Pitchford** Shrops
58 C7 **Pitch Green** Bucks
214 E6 **Pitchroy** Moray
26 F5 **Pitcombe** Somset
178 E4 **Pitcox** E Loth
206 D3 **Pitfichie** Abers
216 D5 **Pitglassie** Abers
223 H3 **Pitgrudy** Highld
196 E5 **Pitkennedy** Angus
186 E5 **Pitlessie** Fife
194 E5 **Pitlochry** P & K
216 C8 **Pitmachie** Abers
203 H5 **Pitmain** Highld
217 G8 **Pitmedden** Abers
217 G8 **Pitmedden Garden** Abers
25 K7 **Pitminster** Somset
196 F6 **Pitmuies** Angus
206 C3 **Pitmunie** Abers
26 C5 **Pitney** Somset
186 C3 **Pitroddie** P & K
187 G5 **Pitscottie** Fife
46 C3 **Pitsea** Essex
73 L2 **Pitsford** Nhants
58 F5 **Pitstone** Bucks
197 H2 **Pittarrow** Abers
27 J6 **Pittenweem** Fife

186 D7 **Pitteuchar** Fife
151 H6 **Pittington** Dur
206 D1 **Pittodrie House Hotel** Abers
28 E5 **Pitton** Wilts
217 H2 **Pittulie** Abers
151 G5 **Pity Me** Dur
31 K2 **Pixham** Surrey
175 L5 **Plains** N Lans
83 K4 **Plaish** Shrops
45 H4 **Plaistow** Gt Lon
31 G5 **Plaistow** W Susx
28 F7 **Plaitford** Hants
108 C6 **Plas Cymyran** IoA
33 G2 **Platt** Kent
151 G5 **Plawsworth** Dur
33 G3 **Plaxtol** Kent
21 H2 **Playden** E Susx
78 F5 **Playford** Suffk
42 C5 **Play Hatch** Oxon
4 C7 **Playing Place** Cnwll
55 H2 **Playley Green** Gloucs
83 H3 **Plealey** Shrops
175 L2 **Plean** Stirlg
186 D5 **Pleasance** Fife
121 J5 **Pleasington** Bl w D
121 J5 **Pleasington Crematorium** Bl w D
115 J8 **Pleasley** Derbys
112 C7 **Plemstall** Ches W
61 G5 **Pleshey** Essex
210 C7 **Plockton** Highld
83 H6 **Plowden** Shrops
83 G3 **Plox Green** Shrops
34 B5 **Pluckley** Kent
34 B5 **Pluckley Thorne** Kent
147 K6 **Plumbland** Cumb
113 G6 **Plumley** Ches E
148 E7 **Plumpton** Cumb
19 K3 **Plumpton** E Susx
73 H5 **Plumpton** Nhants
19 K3 **Plumpton Green** E Susx
45 J4 **Plumstead** Gt Lon
106 D5 **Plumstead** Norfk
101 L6 **Plumtree** Notts
102 C5 **Plungar** Leics
34 C7 **Plurenden** Kent
14 D3 **Plush** Dorset
65 K4 **Plwmp** Cerdgn
6 C5 **Plymouth** C Plym
6 D4 *Plymouth Airport C Plym*
6 D5 **Plympton** C Plym
6 D5 **Plymstock** C Plym
12 D2 **Plymtree** Devon
133 K3 **Pockley** N York
125 J2 **Pocklington** E R Yk
26 D6 **Podimore** Somset
74 D3 **Podington** Bed
99 H5 **Podmore** Staffs
103 J6 **Pointon** Lincs
15 L4 **Pokesdown** Bmouth
6 A4 **Polbain** Highld
6 A4 **Polbathic** Cnwll
176 D5 **Polbeth** W Loth
3 H5 **Poldark Mine** Cnwll
88 F6 **Polebrook** Nhants
20 C5 **Polegate** E Susx
86 C3 **Polesworth** Warwks
224 C6 **Polglass** Highld
4 F5 **Polgooth** Cnwll
154 C2 **Polgown** D & G
18 E5 **Poling** W Susx
18 E5 **Poling Corner** W Susx
5 H5 **Polkerris** Cnwll
124 F6 **Pollington** E R Yk
190 F3 **Polloch** Highld
175 G6 **Pollokshaws** C Glas
175 G5 **Pollokshields** C Glas
4 F6 **Polmassick** Cnwll
176 C3 **Polmont** Falk
200 B8 **Polnish** Highld
5 K5 **Polperro** Cnwll
5 H5 **Polruan** Cnwll
78 B6 **Polstead** Suffk

182 B7 **Poltalloch** Ag & B
12 C3 **Poltimore** Devon
177 J5 **Polton** Mdloth
178 F7 **Polwarth** Border
9 H7 **Polyphant** Cnwll
4 E1 **Polzeath** Cnwll
177 H6 **Pomathorn** Mdloth
89 J5 **Pondersbridge** Cambs
45 G2 **Ponders End** Gt Lon
3 K4 **Ponsanooth** Cnwll
7 G2 **Ponsworthy** Devon
51 H4 *Pont Abraham Services* Carmth
50 F3 **Pontantwn** Carmth
51 K5 **Pontardawe** Neath
51 H5 **Pontarddulais** Swans
51 G2 **Pont-ar-gothi** Carmth
66 B8 **Pontarsais** Carmth
97 L1 **Pontblyddyn** Flints
124 C6 **Pontefract** Wakefd
124 C6 **Pontefract Crematorium** Wakefd
158 F7 **Ponteland** Nthumb
81 G7 **Ponterwyd** Cerdgn
83 H3 **Pontesbury** Shrops
83 H3 **Pontesford** Shrops
97 K5 **Pontfadog** Wrexhm
64 E7 **Pontfaen** Pembks
67 L7 **Pont-faen** Powys
65 K4 **Pontgarreg** Cerdgn
50 F4 **Ponthenry** Carmth
37 M2 **Ponthir** Torfn
65 J5 **Ponthirwaun** Cerdgn
37 J2 **Pontllanfraith** Caerph
51 H5 **Pontlliw** Swans
53 H6 **Pontlottyn** Caerph
95 G3 **Pontlyfni** Gwynd
52 D6 **Pontneddfechan** Neath
37 L2 **Pontnewydd** Torfn
150 E4 **Pontop** Dur
67 G2 **Pontrhydfendigaid** Cerdgn
36 C2 **Pont-rhyd-y-fen** Neath
81 G8 **Pontrhydygroes** Cerdgn
54 B3 **Pontrilas** Herefs
82 C2 **Pont Robert** Powys
20 D3 **Ponts Green** E Susx
66 B5 **Pontshaen** Cerdgn
54 F4 **Pontshill** Herefs
53 G5 **Pontsticill** Myr Td
65 L6 **Pontwelly** Carmth
50 F4 **Pontyates** Carmth
51 G4 **Pontyberem** Carmth
97 L2 **Pontybodkin** Flints
37 G4 **Pontyclun** Rhondd
36 D3 **Pontycymer** Brdgnd
96 B2 **Pont-y-pant** Conwy
53 L7 **Pontypool** Torfn
37 G3 **Pontypridd** Rhondd
37 K2 **Pontywaun** Caerph
3 H3 **Pool** Cnwll
123 J2 **Pool** Leeds
15 J4 **Poole** Poole
15 J3 **Poole Crematorium** Poole
39 M2 **Poole Keynes** Gloucs
219 K5 **Poolewe** Highld
138 C3 **Pooley Bridge** Cumb
99 K1 **Poolfold** Staffs
55 G3 **Poolhill** Gloucs
185 L7 **Pool of Muckhart** Clacks
77 H6 **Pool Street** Essex
45 G4 **Poplar** Gt Lon
16 F4 **Porchfield** IoW
92 F3 **Poringland** Norfk
3 J5 **Porkellis** Cnwll
24 D3 **Porlock** Somset
24 D2 **Porlock Weir** Somset
172 C6 **Portachoillan** Ag & B
210 B7 **Port-an-Eorna** Highld
191 H7 **Port Appin** Ag & B

171 H5 **Port Askaig** Ag & B
172 H4 **Portavadie** Ag & B
173 J5 **Port Bannatyne** Ag & B
38 D5 **Portbury** N Som
147 M3 **Port Carlisle** Cumb
170 E6 **Port Charlotte** Ag & B
17 H2 **Portchester** Hants
17 H2 **Portchester Crematorium** Hants
173 G4 **Port Driseach** Ag & B
50 F7 **Port Einon** Swans
160 C1 **Port Ellen** Ag & B
206 E2 **Port Elphinstone** Abers
152 B7 **Portencalzie** D & G
173 K8 **Portencross** N Ayrs
237 a6 **Port Erin** IoM
14 B5 **Portesham** Dorset
215 K2 **Portessie** Moray
48 F4 **Portfield Gate** Pembks
10 B7 **Portgate** Devon
8 D8 **Port Gaverne** Cnwll
174 C4 **Port Glasgow** Inver
215 J2 **Portgordon** Moray
227 H5 **Portgower** Highld
4 C4 **Porth** Cnwll
36 F3 **Porth** Rhondd
3 K6 **Porthallow** Cnwll
5 K5 **Porthallow** Cnwll
36 C5 **Porthcawl** Brdgnd
4 D2 **Porthcothan** Cnwll
2 C6 **Porthcurno** Cnwll
219 H6 **Port Henderson** Highld
64 A7 **Porthgain** Pembks
2 C6 **Porthgwarra** Cnwll
37 G6 **Porthkerry** V Glam
3 H6 **Porthleven** Cnwll
95 K5 **Porthmadog** Gwynd
3 K5 **Porth Navas** Cnwll
3 K6 **Porthoustock** Cnwll
5 G5 **Porthpean** Cnwll
3 J2 **Porthtowan** Cnwll
51 G3 **Porthyrhyd** Carmth
183 J8 **Portincaple** Ag & B
125 J4 **Portington** E R Yk
182 D5 **Portinnisherrich** Ag & B
137 H3 **Portinscale** Cumb
8 D8 **Port Isaac** Cnwll
38 C5 **Portishead** N Som
215 K2 **Portknockie** Moray
14 D7 **Portland** Dorset
207 H6 **Portlethen** Abers
146 F4 **Portling** D & G
4 E7 **Portloe** Cnwll
144 D6 **Port Logan** D & G
223 K5 **Portmahomack** Highld
95 K5 **Portmeirion** Gwynd
4 F6 **Portmellon** Cnwll
189 K1 **Port Mor** Highld
191 H6 **Portnacroish** Ag & B
232 g2 **Portnaguran** W Isls
170 D7 **Portnahaven** Ag & B
208 E7 **Portnalong** Highld
232 g2 **Port nan Giuran** W Isls
232 c5 **Port nan Long** W Isls
232 g1 **Port Nis** W Isls
177 J4 **Portobello** C Edin
85 G4 **Portobello** Wolves
184 D6 **Port of Menteith** Stirlg
232 g1 **Port of Ness** W Isls
28 D4 **Porton** Wilts
144 B4 **Portpatrick** D & G
8 C8 **Port Quin** Cnwll
191 H7 **Port Ramsay** Ag & B
3 H3 **Portreath** Cnwll
209 G5 **Portree** Highld
237 b7 **Port St Mary** IoM
4 D8 **Portscatho** Cnwll
17 J3 **Portsea** C Port

230 C3 **Portskerra** Highld
38 D3 **Portskewett** Mons
19 H4 **Portslade** Br & H
19 H5 **Portslade-by-Sea** Br & H
144 B3 **Portslogan** D & G
17 J3 **Portsmouth** C Port
122 D5 **Portsmouth** Calder
237 C6 **Port Soderick** IoM
182 F3 **Portsonachan Hotel** Ag & B
216 B2 **Portsoy** Abers
111 K5 **Port Sunlight** Wirral
29 H8 **Portswood** C Sotn
36 B3 **Port Talbot** Neath
189 K3 **Portuairk** Highld
85 J8 **Portway** Worcs
170 D7 **Port Wemyss** Ag & B
145 H6 **Port William** D & G
6 A5 **Portwrinkle** Cnwll
145 K7 **Portyerrock** D & G
77 H5 **Poslingford** Suffk
166 B3 **Posso** Border
10 F8 **Postbridge** Devon
58 B7 **Postcombe** Oxon
34 F6 **Postling** Kent
93 G2 **Postwick** Norfk
206 B6 **Potarch** Abers
58 F3 **Potsgrove** C Beds
59 G6 **Potten End** Herts
134 F4 **Potter Brompton** N York
117 H7 **Potterhanworth** Lincs
117 H7 **Potterhanworth Booths** Lincs
107 J8 **Potter Heigham** Norfk
39 M8 **Potterne** Wilts
39 M8 **Potterne Wick** Wilts
59 L7 **Potters Bar** Herts
59 J6 **Potters Crouch** Herts
86 D6 **Potters Green** Covtry
87 G4 **Potters Marston** Leics
73 L6 **Potterspury** Nhants
207 H3 **Potterton** Abers
141 L6 **Potto** N York
75 J5 **Potton** C Beds
113 L5 **Pott Shrigley** Ches E
9 G4 **Poughill** Cnwll
11 K3 **Poughill** Devon
15 M2 **Poulner** Hants
39 L7 **Poulshot** Wilts
56 C7 **Poulton** Gloucs
120 D3 **Poulton-le-Fylde** Lancs
51 H6 **Poundffald** Swans
20 B2 **Pound Green** E Susx
77 G4 **Pound Green** Suffk
32 B5 **Pound Hill** W Susx
57 M3 **Poundon** Bucks
7 G2 **Poundsgate** Devon
9 G5 **Poundstock** Cnwll
145 K5 **Pouton** D & G
31 L3 **Povey Cross** Surrey
168 F6 **Powburn** Nthumb
12 C5 **Powderham** Devon
13 M3 **Powerstock** Dorset
147 K2 **Powfoot** D & G
147 M4 **Powhill** Cumb
70 E4 **Powick** Worcs
185 L7 **Powmill** P & K
14 E5 **Poxwell** Dorset
43 G5 **Poyle** Slough
19 H4 **Poynings** W Susx
26 F7 **Poyntington** Dorset
113 L5 **Poynton** Ches E
98 E8 **Poynton Green** Wrekin
3 G5 **Praa Sands** Cnwll
45 J7 **Pratt's Bottom** Gt Lon
3 H4 **Praze-an-Beeble** Cnwll
98 D5 **Prees** Shrops
120 E2 **Preesall** Lancs
98 E6 **Prees Green** Shrops

98 E5 **Prees Heath** Shrops
98 E5 **Prees Higher Heath** Shrops
168 E6 **Prendwick** Nthumb
65 L5 **Pren-gwyn** Cerdgn
95 K4 **Prenteg** Gwynd
112 C3 **Prescot** Knows
25 H8 **Prescott** Devon
195 J3 **Presnerb** Angus
110 E5 **Prestatyn** Denbgs
113 K6 **Prestbury** Ches E
55 L4 **Prestbury** Gloucs
69 G2 **Presteigne** Powys
26 F4 **Prestleigh** Somset
179 G6 **Preston** Border
19 J4 **Preston** Br & H
7 K2 **Preston** Devon
14 D5 **Preston** Dorset
126 F4 **Preston** E R Yk
56 B7 **Preston** Gloucs
59 K3 **Preston** Herts
34 D3 **Preston** Kent
35 H3 **Preston** Kent
121 H4 **Preston** Lancs
169 H4 **Preston** Nthumb
88 C3 **Preston** Rutlnd
25 H4 **Preston** Somset
77 L4 **Preston** Suffk
7 K4 **Preston** Torbay
40 B5 **Preston** Wilts
71 L2 **Preston Bagot** Warwks
58 A3 **Preston Bissett** Bucks
25 H6 **Preston Bowyer** Somset
98 D7 **Preston Brockhurst** Shrops
112 E5 **Preston Brook** Halton
29 L3 **Preston Candover** Hants
73 H4 **Preston Capes** Nhants
121 H4 **Preston Crematorium** Lancs
71 L2 **Preston Green** Warwks
98 C8 **Preston Gubbals** Shrops
72 B4 **Preston on Stour** Warwks
112 E5 **Preston on the Hill** Halton
69 H6 **Preston on Wye** Herefs
177 K4 **Prestonpans** E Loth
129 L3 **Preston Patrick** Cumb
26 D7 **Preston Plucknett** Somset
131 K2 **Preston-under-Scar** N York
84 C1 **Preston upon the Weald Moors** Wrekin
69 L5 **Preston Wynne** Herefs
113 J1 **Prestwich** Bury
163 J4 **Prestwick** S Ayrs
163 J4 Prestwick Airport S Ayrs
58 F7 **Prestwood** Bucks
90 E6 **Prickwillow** Cambs
26 D2 **Priddy** Somset
129 L5 **Priest Hutton** Lancs
164 B2 **Priestland** E Ayrs
82 F4 **Priest Weston** Shrops
179 G6 **Primrosehill** Border
168 B4 **Primsidemill** Border
58 D7 **Princes Risborough** Bucks
72 F4 **Princethorpe** Warwks
6 E2 **Princetown** Devon
72 F4 **Priors Hardwick** Warwks
84 C2 **Priorslee** Wrekin
72 F3 **Priors Marston** Warwks

55 K3 **Priors Norton** Gloucs
40 C3 **Priory Vale** Swindn
39 G7 **Priston** BaNES
46 E3 **Prittlewell** Sthend
30 B6 **Privett** Hants
23 J4 **Prixford** Devon
4 E6 **Probus** Cnwll
178 C3 **Prora** E Loth
147 K6 **Prospect** Cumb
3 H5 **Prospidnick** Cnwll
216 F2 **Protstonhill** Abers
150 D3 **Prudhoe** Nthumb
38 F7 **Publow** BaNES
60 C4 **Puckeridge** Herts
26 B7 **Puckington** Somset
39 G5 **Pucklechurch** S Glos
111 K6 **Puddington** Ches W
11 J3 **Puddington** Devon
14 E4 **Puddletown** Dorset
123 J4 **Pudsey** Leeds
18 E3 **Pulborough** W Susx
98 A2 **Pulford** Ches W
14 D2 **Pulham** Dorset
92 E6 **Pulham Market** Norfk
92 E6 **Pulham St Mary** Norfk
74 F7 **Pulloxhill** C Beds
176 E4 **Pumpherston** W Loth
66 E6 **Pumsaint** Carmth
49 G2 **Puncheston** Pembks
14 A5 **Puncknowle** Dorset
20 C2 **Punnett's Town** E Susx
17 J2 **Purbrook** Hants
45 K4 **Purfleet** Thurr
25 L3 **Puriton** Somset
61 K7 **Purleigh** Essex
44 F7 **Purley** Gt Lon
42 A5 **Purley** W Berk
27 G7 **Purse Caundle** Dorset
13 K2 **Purtington** Somset
54 F6 **Purton** Gloucs
55 G7 **Purton** Gloucs
40 C3 **Purton** Wilts
40 C3 **Purton Stoke** Wilts
73 K5 **Pury End** Nhants
41 G2 **Pusey** Oxon
70 B6 **Putley** Herefs
70 B6 **Putley Green** Herefs
44 E5 **Putney** Gt Lon
44 E5 **Putney Vale Crematorium** Gt Lon
30 F7 **Puttenham** Surrey
73 L6 **Puxley** Nhants
38 B7 **Puxton** N Som
50 F5 **Pwll** Carmth
97 H2 **Pwll-glas** Denbgs
68 B7 **Pwllgloyw** Powys
94 F5 **Pwllheli** Gwynd
38 D2 **Pwllmeyric** Mons
50 C3 **Pwll Trap** Carmth
36 C2 **Pwll-y-glaw** Neath
101 H3 **Pye Bridge** Derbys
19 J3 **Pyecombe** W Susx
36 C4 **Pyle** Brdgnd
25 H5 **Pyleigh** Somset
26 E4 **Pylle** Somset
90 C6 **Pymoor** Cambs
13 L4 **Pymore** Dorset
43 H8 **Pyrford** Surrey
42 B2 **Pyrton** Oxon
88 C8 **Pytchley** Nhants
9 J4 **Pyworthy** Devon

Q

103 L6 **Quadring** Lincs
103 L5 **Quadring Eaudike** Lincs
58 C4 **Quainton** Bucks
25 J4 **Quantock Hills** Somset
235 C6 **Quarff** Shet
28 F3 **Quarley** Hants
101 G4 **Quarndon** Derbys

174 C5 **Quarrier's Village** Inver
103 H4 **Quarrington** Lincs
151 H7 **Quarrington Hill** Dur
85 G6 **Quarry Bank** Dudley
214 E2 **Quarrywood** Moray
173 L6 **Quarter** N Ayrs
175 J7 **Quarter** S Lans
84 D5 **Quatford** Shrops
84 D6 **Quatt** Shrops
150 F6 **Quebec** Dur
55 J5 **Quedgeley** Gloucs
90 E7 **Queen Adelaide** Cambs
46 E5 **Queenborough** Kent
26 E6 **Queen Camel** Somset
38 F6 **Queen Charlton** BaNES
184 B6 **Queen Elizabeth Forest Park** Stirlg
70 F6 **Queenhill** Worcs
27 H5 **Queen Oak** Dorset
17 H5 **Queen's Bower** IoW
123 G4 **Queensbury** C Brad
111 K7 **Queensferry** Flints
175 H5 **Queenslie** C Glas
33 H4 **Queen Street** Kent
175 J3 **Queenzieburn** N Lans
60 E3 **Quendon** Essex
87 J2 **Queniborough** Leics
56 C7 **Quenington** Gloucs
85 J4 **Queslett** Birm
5 L3 **Quethiock** Cnwll
92 B6 **Quidenham** Norfk
28 C5 **Quidhampton** Wilts
73 L4 **Quinton** Nhants
4 D4 **Quintrell Downs** Cnwll
179 G5 **Quixwood** Border
9 K5 **Quoditch** Devon
185 H3 **Quoig** P & K
87 H1 **Quorn** Leics
165 J2 **Quothquan** S Lans
234 C6 **Quoyburray** Ork
234 b5 **Quoyloo** Ork

R

209 J5 **Raasay** Highld
165 L3 **Rachan Mill** Border
109 J7 **Rachub** Gwynd
24 D7 **Rackenford** Devon
18 E3 **Rackham** W Susx
93 G1 **Rackheath** Norfk
155 H7 **Racks** D & G
234 a7 **Rackwick** Ork
100 F5 **Radbourne** Derbys
113 H4 **Radcliffe** Bury
159 G2 **Radcliffe** Nthumb
101 M5 **Radcliffe on Trent** Notts
73 J7 **Radclive** Bucks
213 H3 **Raddery** Highld
187 G5 **Radernie** Fife
86 D7 **Radford** Covtry
72 D2 **Radford Semele** Warwks
59 K7 **Radlett** Herts
57 K7 **Radley** Oxon
60 F6 **Radley Green** Essex
42 C2 **Radnage** Bucks
27 G1 **Radstock** BaNES
73 H6 **Radstone** Nhants
72 D5 **Radway** Warwks
74 E3 **Radwell** Bed
75 J7 **Radwell** Herts
76 E6 **Radwinter** Essex
37 H4 **Radyr** Cardif
214 C3 **Rafford** Moray
102 A8 **Ragdale** Leics
54 B6 **Raglan** Mons
116 D6 **Ragnall** Notts
213 J8 **Raigbeg** Highld
70 F4 **Rainbow Hill** Worcs
112 C2 **Rainford** St Hel

45 K4 **Rainham** Gt Lon	35 H4 **Ratling** Kent	234 b5 **Redland** Ork	223 H2 **Rhives** Highld
46 D6 **Rainham** Medway	83 H4 **Ratlinghope** Shrops	78 E1 **Redlingfield** Suffk	37 J4 **Rhiwbina** Cardif
112 C4 **Rainhill** St Hel	231 J2 **Rattar** Highld	78 E1 **Redlingfield Green** Suffk	37 K3 **Rhiwderyn** Newpt
112 B4 **Rainhill Stoops** St Hel	7 H4 **Rattery** Devon		109 H7 **Rhiwlas** Gwynd
113 L6 **Rainow** Ches E	77 L3 **Rattlesden** Suffk	77 G1 **Red Lodge** Suffk	33 H4 **Rhoden Green** Kent
132 E4 **Rainton** N York	20 C5 **Ratton Village** E Susx	27 C5 **Redlynch** Somset	34 F6 **Rhodes Minnis** Kent
101 L2 **Rainworth** Notts	195 J7 **Rattray** P & K	28 D7 **Redlynch** Wilts	48 C3 **Rhodiad-y-brenin** Pembks
186 D3 **Rait** P & K	88 E8 **Raunds** Nhants	70 D2 **Redmarley** Worcs	146 C3 **Rhonehouse** D & G
118 D5 **Raithby** Lincs	115 J3 **Ravenfield** Rothm	55 H2 **Redmarley D'Abitot** Gloucs	37 G6 **Rhoose** V Glam
118 E7 **Raithby** Lincs	136 F7 **Ravenglass** Cumb	141 J3 **Redmarshall** S on T	65 L7 **Rhos** Carmth
30 D5 **Rake** Hants	93 H4 **Raveningham** Norfk	102 D5 **Redmile** Leics	51 L5 **Rhos** Neath
203 H5 **Ralia** Highld	143 K6 **Ravenscar** N York	131 K2 **Redmire** N York	108 E3 **Rhosbeirio** IoA
208 B5 **Ramasaig** Highld	74 F4 **Ravensden** Bed	197 J2 **Redmyre** Abers	108 C6 **Rhoscolyn** IoA
3 J4 **Rame** Cnwll	101 K2 **Ravenshead** Notts	98 A6 **Rednal** Shrops	48 F6 **Rhoscrowther** Pembks
6 B6 **Rame** Cnwll	123 J6 **Ravensthorpe** Kirk	167 J3 **Redpath** Border	111 H7 **Rhosesmor** Flints
14 B3 **Rampisham** Dorset	73 J1 **Ravensthorpe** Nhants	219 H7 **Redpoint** Highld	68 D5 **Rhosgoch** Powys
128 F6 **Rampside** Cumb	86 E2 **Ravenstone** Leics	49 L5 **Red Roses** Carmth	65 H6 **Rhoshill** Pembks
76 B2 **Rampton** Cambs	74 B4 **Ravenstone** M Keyn	159 G3 **Red Row** Nthumb	94 D6 **Rhoshirwaun** Gwynd
116 D5 **Rampton** Notts	139 G6 **Ravenstonedale** Cumb	3 J3 **Redruth** Cnwll	80 D3 **Rhoslefain** Gwynd
122 B6 **Ramsbottom** Bury	165 H1 **Ravenstruther** S Lans	186 C1 **Redstone** P & K	97 L3 **Rhosllanerchrugog** Wrexhm
40 F6 **Ramsbury** Wilts	140 E5 **Ravensworth** N York	109 G5 **Red Wharf Bay** IoA	
227 K3 **Ramscraigs** Highld	133 J8 **Rawcliffe** C York	38 B4 **Redwick** Newpt	108 F6 **Rhosmeirch** IoA
30 B6 **Ramsdean** Hants	125 G6 **Rawcliffe** E R Yk	38 D3 **Redwick** S Glos	108 D6 **Rhosneigr** IoA
41 L8 **Ramsdell** Hants	123 J5 **Rawdon** Leeds	141 G3 **Redworth** Darltn	97 M3 **Rhosnesni** Wrexhm
57 G5 **Ramsden** Oxon	123 J3 **Rawdon Crematorium** Leeds	75 L7 **Reed** Herts	110 B5 **Rhôs-on-Sea** Conwy
46 B2 **Ramsden Bellhouse** Essex	34 B3 **Rawling Street** Kent	93 J3 **Reedham** Norfk	50 E7 **Rhossili** Swans
89 K6 **Ramsey** Cambs	115 H3 **Rawmarsh** Rothm	125 J6 **Reedness** E R Yk	95 H2 **Rhostryfan** Gwynd
62 E2 **Ramsey** Essex	46 C2 **Rawreth** Essex	117 H6 **Reepham** Lincs	97 L3 **Rhostyllen** Wrexhm
237 e3 **Ramsey** IoM	12 F2 **Rawridge** Devon	106 D7 **Reepham** Norfk	108 F4 **Rhosybol** IoA
89 K6 **Ramsey Forty Foot** Cambs	122 B6 **Rawtenstall** Lancs	140 C7 **Reeth** N York	96 E5 **Rhos-y-gwaliau** Gwynd
89 J6 **Ramsey Heights** Cambs	78 C6 **Raydon** Suffk	86 C7 **Reeves Green** Solhll	97 L4 **Rhosymedre** Wrexhm
61 M6 **Ramsey Island** Essex	46 D2 **Rayleigh** Essex	224 B5 **Reiff** Highld	174 B2 **Rhu** Ag & B
48 B3 **Ramsey Island** Pembks	61 H4 **Rayne** Essex	31 L2 **Reigate** Surrey	110 F6 **Rhualt** Denbgs
89 K5 **Ramsey Mereside** Cambs	44 E6 **Raynes Park** Gt Lon	135 H4 **Reighton** N York	173 H4 **Rhubodach** Ag & B
89 J6 **Ramsey St Mary's** Cambs	76 E2 **Reach** Cambs	207 G2 **Reisque** Abers	110 E6 **Rhuddlan** Denbgs
35 K2 **Ramsgate** Kent	122 B4 **Read** Lancs	231 L5 **Reiss** Highld	172 C8 **Rhunahaorine** Ag & B
131 L5 **Ramsgill** N York	42 B5 **Reading** Readg	2 F5 **Relubbus** Cnwll	95 L4 **Rhyd** Gwynd
157 J2 **Ramshope** Nthumb	42 B5 **Reading Crematorium** Readg	214 B5 **Relugas** Moray	50 F1 **Rhydargaeau** Carmth
100 B4 **Ramshorn** Staffs	42 A6 **Reading Services** W Berk	42 C4 **Remenham** Wokham	66 D6 **Rhydcymerau** Carmth
30 F5 **Ramsnest Common** Surrey	34 B8 **Reading Street** Kent	42 C4 **Remenham Hill** Wokham	95 K3 **Rhyd-Ddu** Gwynd
118 B5 **Ranby** Lincs	35 K2 **Reading Street** Kent	101 L7 **Rempstone** Notts	65 K5 **Rhydlewis** Cerdgn
116 A5 **Ranby** Notts	138 E4 **Reagill** Cumb	56 A6 **Rendcomb** Gloucs	66 B5 **Rhydowen** Cerdgn
117 J5 **Rand** Lincs	3 G4 **Realwa** Cnwll	79 H2 **Rendham** Suffk	96 D5 **Rhyd-uchaf** Gwynd
44 D8 **Randalls Park Crematorium** Surrey	223 G3 **Rearquhar** Highld	79 H4 **Rendlesham** Suffk	94 F5 **Rhyd-y-clafdy** Gwynd
55 J6 **Randwick** Gloucs	87 J2 **Rearsby** Leics	174 F5 **Renfrew** Rens	110 C6 **Rhyd-y-foel** Conwy
174 D5 **Ranfurly** Rens	230 D3 **Reay** Highld	74 F4 **Renhold** Bed	51 K4 **Rhydyfro** Neath
100 D7 **Rangemore** Staffs	47 L6 **Reculver** Kent	115 J6 **Renishaw** Derbys	109 H7 **Rhyd-y-groes** Gwynd
39 G3 **Rangeworthy** S Glos	25 H7 **Red Ball** Devon	169 J5 **Rennington** Nthumb	80 E6 **Rhyd-y pennau** Cerdgn
163 L6 **Rankinston** E Ayrs	49 J6 **Redberth** Pembks	174 D3 **Renton** W Duns	
121 K5 **Rann** B L	59 J5 **Redbourn** Herts	149 G6 **Renwick** Cumb	110 D5 **Rhyl** Denbgs
193 G5 **Rannoch Station** P & K	116 F2 **Redbourne** N Linc	93 J1 **Repps** Norfk	53 H6 **Rhymney** Caerph
	54 D6 **Redbrook** Gloucs	100 F6 **Repton** Derbys	186 B4 **Rhynd** P & K
24 E3 **Ranscombe** Somset	98 D4 **Redbrook** Wrexhm	213 H5 **Resaurie** Highld	215 L8 **Rhynie** Abers
116 A4 **Ranskill** Notts	34 C7 **Redbrook Street** Kent	4 F7 **Rescassa** Cnwll	223 J5 **Rhynie** Highld
99 J7 **Ranton** Staffs	213 L5 **Redburn** Highld	190 E4 **Resipole** Highld	84 D8 **Ribbesford** Worcs
99 J7 **Ranton Green** Staffs	142 D3 **Redcar** R & Cl	3 H3 **Reskadinnick** Cnwll	121 H4 **Ribbleton** Lancs
93 H1 **Ranworth** Norfk	146 E2 **Redcastle** D & G	213 G2 **Resolis** Highld	121 J4 **Ribchester** Lancs
185 G7 **Raploch** Stirlg	212 E4 **Redcastle** Highld	52 C7 **Resolven** Neath	126 F8 **Riby** Lincs
234 C4 **Rapness** Ork	176 C3 **Redding** Falk	183 J6 **Rest and be thankful** Ag & B	124 F3 **Riccall** N York
146 D5 **Rascarrel** D & G	176 C3 **Reddingmuirhead** Falk	179 H6 **Reston** Border	156 F3 **Riccarton** Border
173 K2 **Rashfield** Ag & B	71 J2 **Redditch** Worcs	196 E6 **Reswallie** Angus	163 K3 **Riccarton** E Ayrs
71 G2 **Rashwood** Worcs	71 J2 **Redditch Crematorium** Worcs	116 B5 **Retford** Notts	69 J1 **Richards Castle** Herefs
133 G5 **Raskelf** N York	77 J4 **Rede** Suffk	61 J7 **Rettendon** Essex	44 D5 **Richmond** Gt Lon
123 H6 **Rastrick** Calder	92 F6 **Redenhall** Norfk	103 M1 **Revesby** Lincs	140 F6 **Richmond** N York
200 E2 **Ratagan** Highld	157 L5 **Redesmouth** Nthumb	12 B3 **Rewe** Devon	115 H4 **Richmond** Sheff
87 G3 **Ratby** Leics	197 J3 **Redford** Abers	16 F4 **Rew Street** IoW	99 L7 **Rickerscote** Staffs
86 D4 **Ratcliffe Culey** Leics	196 F7 **Redford** Angus	93 K7 **Reydon** Suffk	38 C8 **Rickford** N Som
101 J6 **Ratcliffe on Soar** Notts	30 E6 **Redford** W Susx	92 B3 **Reymerston** Norfk	7 H7 **Rickham** Devon
87 J1 **Ratcliffe on the Wreake** Leics	166 E6 **Redfordgreen** Border	49 J5 **Reynalton** Pembks	92 C7 **Rickinghall** Suffk
217 J3 **Rathen** Abers	186 A2 **Redgorton** P & K	50 F7 **Reynoldston** Swans	60 E3 **Rickling Green** Essex
186 F3 **Rathillet** Fife	92 C7 **Redgrave** Suffk	6 A1 **Rezare** Cnwll	43 H2 **Rickmansworth** Herts
130 F7 **Rathmell** N York	206 E4 **Redhill** Abers	67 H5 **Rhandirmwyn** Carmth	167 H4 **Riddell** Border
176 F4 **Ratho** C Edin	15 K4 **Red Hill** Bmouth	67 L2 **Rhayader** Powys	10 F3 **Riddlecombe** Devon
176 F4 **Ratho Station** C Edin	59 M2 **Redhill** Herts	212 D5 **Rheindown** Highld	123 G3 **Riddlesden** C Brad
215 K2 **Rathven** Moray	38 D7 **Redhill** N Som	111 H7 **Rhes-y-cae** Flints	15 H5 **Ridge** Dorset
72 E5 **Ratley** Warwks	32 B3 **Redhill** Surrey	97 H1 **Rhewl** Denbgs	59 K7 **Ridge** Herts
	71 K4 **Red Hill** Warwks	97 J4 **Rhewl** Denbgs	27 L5 **Ridge** Wilts
	93 J6 **Redisham** Suffk	224 D4 **Rhicarn** Highld	38 D7 **Ridgehill** N Som
	38 E5 **Redland** Bristl	228 C5 **Rhiconich** Highld	86 C4 **Ridge Lane** Warwks
		222 F6 **Rhicullen** Highld	115 H5 **Ridgeway** Derbys
		52 E6 **Rhigos** Rhondd	
		220 D3 **Rhireavach** Highld	

77 G6 **Ridgewell** Essex
19 M2 **Ridgewood** E Susx
74 E7 **Ridgmont** C Beds
150 C3 **Riding Mill** Nthumb
107 H6 **Ridlington** Norfk
88 B3 **Ridlington** Rutlnd
158 A5 **Ridsdale** Nthumb
133 J3 **Rievaulx** N York
133 J3 **Rievaulx Abbey** N York
148 B2 **Rigg** D & G
175 K4 **Riggend** N Lans
213 K4 **Righoul** Highld
118 F6 **Rigsby** Lincs
165 G3 **Rigside** S Lans
121 J5 **Riley Green** Lancs
5 L2 **Rilla Mill** Cnwll
134 D5 **Rillington** N York
122 B2 **Rimington** Lancs
26 E6 **Rimpton** Somset
127 H5 **Rimswell** E R Yk
49 G3 **Rinaston** Pembks
84 D4 **Rindleford** Shrops
146 C4 **Ringford** D & G
92 D2 **Ringland** Norfk
19 L3 **Ringmer** E Susx
6 F6 **Ringmore** Devon
7 L2 **Ringmore** Devon
215 G5 **Ringorm** Moray
93 J5 **Ringsfield** Suffk
93 J6 **Ringsfield Corner** Suffk
59 G5 **Ringshall** Herts
78 C4 **Ringshall** Suffk
78 C4 **Ringshall Stocks** Suffk
88 E7 **Ringstead** Nhants
105 H4 **Ringstead** Norfk
15 L2 **Ringwood** Hants
35 K5 **Ringwould** Kent
20 B4 **Ripe** E Susx
101 H3 **Ripley** Derbys
15 M3 **Ripley** Hants
132 D7 **Ripley** N York
31 H1 **Ripley** Surrey
30 A6 **Riplington** Hants
132 D5 **Ripon** N York
103 H6 **Rippingale** Lincs
35 J5 **Ripple** Kent
70 F6 **Ripple** Worcs
122 F6 **Ripponden** Calder
160 B2 **Risabus** Ag & B
69 K4 **Risbury** Herefs
77 H2 **Risby** Suffk
37 K3 **Risca** Caerph
126 E3 **Rise** E R Yk
103 K6 **Risegate** Lincs
74 F3 **Riseley** Bed
42 B7 **Riseley** Wokham
78 E2 **Rishangles** Suffk
121 L4 **Rishton** Lancs
122 F6 **Rishworth** Calder
101 J5 **Risley** Derbys
112 F3 **Risley** Warrtn
132 C5 **Risplith** N York
35 J6 **River** Kent
30 F6 **River** W Susx
212 E4 **Riverford** Highld
32 F3 **Riverhead** Kent
121 J7 **Rivington** Lancs
73 L4 **Roade** Nhants
176 B7 **Roadmeetings** S Lans
164 B5 **Roadside** E Ayrs
231 H4 **Roadside** Highld
25 G4 **Roadwater** Somset
208 D5 **Roag** Highld
153 G2 **Roan of Craigoch** S Ayrs
37 J5 **Roath** Cardif
166 F6 **Roberton** Border
165 H4 **Roberton** S Lans
20 E2 **Robertsbridge** E Susx
123 J6 **Roberttown** Kirk
49 J4 **Robeston Wathen** Pembks
155 M7 **Robgill Tower** D & G

85 K7 **Robin Hood Crematorium** Solhll
116 A2 *Robin Hood Doncaster Sheffield Airport* Donc
143 K6 **Robin Hood's Bay** N York
6 D4 **Roborough** Devon
10 E2 **Roborough** Devon
112 B4 **Roby** Knows
100 C5 **Rocester** Staffs
48 E3 **Roch** Pembks
122 D7 **Rochdale** Rochdl
122 C7 **Rochdale Crematorium** Rochdl
4 F4 **Roche** Cnwll
46 C6 **Rochester** Medway
157 L3 **Rochester** Nthumb
46 E3 **Rochford** Essex
70 B2 **Rochford** Worcs
4 E2 **Rock** Cnwll
169 J5 **Rock** Nthumb
70 D1 **Rock** Worcs
12 C4 **Rockbeare** Devon
28 C7 **Rockbourne** Hants
148 C3 **Rockcliffe** Cumb
146 E4 **Rockcliffe** D & G
7 L4 **Rockend** Torbay
111 K4 **Rock Ferry** Wirral
223 K5 **Rockfield** Highld
54 C5 **Rockfield** Mons
24 B2 **Rockford** Devon
38 F2 **Rockhampton** S Glos
82 F7 **Rockhill** Shrops
88 C5 **Rockingham** Nhants
92 B4 **Rockland All Saints** Norfk
93 G3 **Rockland St Mary** Norfk
92 B4 **Rockland St Peter** Norfk
116 B6 **Rockley** Notts
40 D6 **Rockley** Wilts
173 L1 **Rockville** Ag & B
42 D3 **Rockwell End** Bucks
55 J6 **Rodborough** Gloucs
40 C4 **Rodbourne** Swindn
39 L4 **Rodbourne** Wilts
14 B5 **Rodden** Dorset
27 J2 **Rode** Somset
99 J2 **Rode Heath** Ches E
232 d5 **Rodel** W Isls
83 L1 **Roden** Wrekin
24 F4 **Rodhuish** Somset
83 L1 **Rodington** Wrekin
83 L1 **Rodington Heath** Wrekin
55 H5 **Rodley** Gloucs
39 L2 **Rodmarton** Gloucs
19 L4 **Rodmell** E Susx
34 B3 **Rodmersham** Kent
34 B3 **Rodmersham Green** Kent
26 C2 **Rodney Stoke** Somset
100 D4 **Rodsley** Derbys
132 E6 **Roecliffe** N York
59 K6 **Roe Green** Herts
75 K7 **Roe Green** Herts
44 E5 **Roehampton** Gt Lon
31 K5 **Roffey** W Susx
226 C7 **Rogart** Highld
30 D6 **Rogate** W Susx
37 L3 **Rogerstone** Newpt
232 d5 **Roghadal** W Isls
38 C3 **Rogiet** Mons
41 L2 **Roke** Oxon
151 J3 **Roker** Sundld
93 J1 **Rollesby** Norfk
87 K4 **Rolleston** Leics
102 C3 **Rolleston** Notts
100 E6 **Rolleston on Dove** Staffs
126 F2 **Rolston** E R Yk
33 L6 **Rolvenden** Kent

33 L7 **Rolvenden Layne** Kent
140 C3 **Romaldkirk** Dur
39 H7 **Roman Baths & Pump Room** BaNES
132 E2 **Romanby** N York
177 G8 **Romanno Bridge** Border
24 B7 **Romansleigh** Devon
208 F4 **Romesdal** Highld
15 K1 **Romford** Dorset
45 K3 **Romford** Gt Lon
113 L4 **Romiley** Stockp
29 G6 **Romsey** Hants
84 D6 **Romsley** Shrops
85 G7 **Romsley** Worcs
209 K3 **Rona** Highld
172 C7 **Ronachan** Ag & B
150 B6 **Rookhope** Dur
17 G5 **Rookley** IoW
26 A2 **Rooks Bridge** Somset
25 H5 **Rooks Nest** Somset
132 C3 **Rookwith** N York
127 G4 **Roos** E R Yk
75 G3 **Roothams Green** Bed
29 M5 **Ropley** Hants
29 L5 **Ropley Dean** Hants
103 G5 **Ropsley** Lincs
217 K4 **Rora** Abers
82 F4 **Rorrington** Shrops
215 J4 **Rosarie** Moray
3 K1 **Rose** Cnwll
24 C6 **Rose Ash** Devon
175 L7 **Rosebank** S Lans
49 J2 **Rosebush** Pembks
142 F7 **Rosedale Abbey** N York
61 L3 **Rose Green** Essex
77 L5 **Rose Green** Suffk
77 L6 **Rose Green** Suffk
18 B5 **Rose Green** W Susx
225 K7 **Rosehall** Highld
217 H2 **Rosehearty** Abers
122 C4 **Rose Hill** Lancs
214 E2 **Roseisle** Moray
20 C5 **Roselands** E Susx
49 G5 **Rosemarket** Pembks
213 H3 **Rosemarkie** Highld
25 J7 **Rosemary Lane** Devon
195 J7 **Rosemount** P & K
4 E3 **Rosenannon** Cnwll
177 J6 **Rosewell** Mdloth
141 K3 **Roseworth** S on T
138 D4 **Rosgill** Cumb
208 D5 **Roskhill** Highld
148 B6 **Rosley** Cumb
177 H5 **Roslin** Mdloth
86 B1 **Rosliston** Derbys
174 B2 **Rosneath** Ag & B
146 B6 **Ross** D & G
98 A2 **Rossett** Wrexhm
132 D8 **Rossett Green** N York
115 L2 **Rossington** Donc
174 E4 **Rossland** Rens
54 E4 **Ross-on-Wye** Herefs
231 J7 **Roster** Highld
113 H5 **Rostherne** Ches E
137 H4 **Rosthwaite** Cumb
100 C4 **Roston** Derbys
176 F2 **Rosyth** Fife
158 D2 **Rothbury** Nthumb
87 J1 **Rotherby** Leics
32 F7 **Rotherfield** E Susx
42 B4 **Rotherfield Greys** Oxon
42 B4 **Rotherfield Peppard** Oxon
115 H3 **Rotherham** Rothm
115 J3 **Rotherham Crematorium** Rothm
73 K3 **Rothersthorpe** Nhants
73 K3 *Rothersthorpe Services* Nhants
30 B1 **Rotherwick** Hants

215 G4 **Rothes** Moray
173 J5 **Rothesay** Ag & B
216 E6 **Rothiebrisbane** Abers
215 M5 **Rothiemay** Moray
204 B4 **Rothiemurchus Lodge** Highld
216 D7 **Rothienorman** Abers
87 H2 **Rothley** Leics
216 D7 **Rothmaise** Abers
123 L5 **Rothwell** Leeds
117 J2 **Rothwell** Lincs
88 B7 **Rothwell** Nhants
196 B3 **Rottal Lodge** Angus
19 K5 **Rottingdean** Br & H
136 D5 **Rottington** Cumb
155 H6 **Roucan** D & G
155 H6 **Roucan Loch Crematorium** D & G
105 K7 **Rougham** Norfk
77 L3 **Rougham Green** Suffk
34 F3 **Rough Common** Kent
205 H3 **Roughpark** Abers
118 C8 **Roughton** Lincs
106 F5 **Roughton** Norfk
84 D5 **Roughton** Shrops
60 F5 **Roundbush Green** Essex
59 J4 **Round Green** Luton
13 K1 **Roundham** Somset
123 L3 **Roundhay** Leeds
40 A7 **Roundway** Wilts
196 C6 **Roundyhill** Angus
234 c4 **Rousay** Ork
13 H4 **Rousdon** Devon
57 J3 **Rousham** Oxon
71 H4 **Rous Lench** Worcs
173 L6 **Routenburn** N Ayrs
126 D3 **Routh** E R Yk
129 K2 **Row** Cumb
156 D6 **Rowanburn** D & G
183 J7 **Rowardennan** Stirlg
114 A4 **Rowarth** Derbys
38 C8 **Rowberrow** Somset
39 L7 **Rowde** Wilts
109 L6 **Rowen** Conwy
149 H3 **Rowfoot** Nthumb
62 B4 **Rowhedge** Essex
72 B2 **Rowington** Warwks
114 E6 **Rowland** Derbys
17 K1 **Rowland's Castle** Hants
150 E4 **Rowland's Gill** Gatesd
30 D4 **Rowledge** Surrey
150 D5 **Rowley** Dur
76 E2 **Rowley Mile Services** Suffk
85 H6 **Rowley Regis** Sandw
85 H6 **Rowley Regis Crematorium** Sandw
54 A3 **Rowlstone** Herefs
31 H4 **Rowly** Surrey
17 H3 **Rowner** Hants
71 J1 **Rowney Green** Worcs
29 G7 **Rownhams** Hants
29 H7 *Rownhams Services* Hants
136 E4 **Rowrah** Cumb
58 D4 **Rowsham** Bucks
114 E7 **Rowsley** Derbys
103 H2 **Rowston** Lincs
112 C8 **Rowton** Ches W
98 E8 **Rowton** Wrekin
167 L4 **Roxburgh** Border
125 L6 **Roxby** N Linc
75 G4 **Roxton** Bed
61 G6 **Roxwell** Essex
192 D1 **Roy Bridge** Highld
60 E5 **Roydon** Essex
92 D7 **Roydon** Norfk
105 H7 **Roydon** Norfk
60 C6 **Roydon Hamlet** Essex
124 B7 **Royston** Barns
75 L6 **Royston** Herts
122 D8 **Royton** Oldham
236 e6 **Rozel** Jersey

97 L4 **Ruabon** Wrexhm
188 D6 **Ruaig** Ag & B
4 D7 **Ruan Lanihorne** Cnwll
3 J7 **Ruan Major** Cnwll
3 J7 **Ruan Minor** Cnwll
54 F4 **Ruardean** Gloucs
54 F5 **Ruardean Hill** Gloucs
54 F5 **Ruardean Woodside** Gloucs
85 H7 **Rubery** Birm
233 c9 **Rubha Ban** W Isls
69 J6 **Ruckhall** Herefs
34 D7 **Ruckinge** Kent
83 K4 **Ruckley** Shrops
141 L6 **Rudby** N York
150 E2 **Rudchester** Nthumb
101 L6 **Ruddington** Notts
27 J2 **Rudge** Somset
38 F3 **Rudgeway** S Glos
31 H5 **Rudgwick** W Susx
112 F6 **Rudheath** Ches W
61 K7 **Rudley Green** Essex
39 J6 **Rudloe** Wilts
37 J3 **Rudry** Caerph
135 H6 **Rudston** E R Yk
99 L2 **Rudyard** Staffs
167 J5 **Ruecastle** Border
120 F7 **Rufford** Lancs
124 D1 **Rufforth** C York
87 G7 **Rugby** Warwks
100 B8 **Rugeley** Staffs
25 K6 **Ruishton** Somset
43 H3 **Ruislip** Gt Lon
198 F6 **Rùm** Highld
215 J4 **Rumbach** Moray
185 L7 **Rumbling Bridge** P & K
93 H7 **Rumburgh** Suffk
4 D2 **Rumford** Cnwll
176 C3 **Rumford** Falk
37 K5 **Rumney** Cardif
112 D5 **Runcorn** Halton
18 B5 **Runcton** W Susx
90 E2 **Runcton Holme** Norfk
30 E3 **Runfold** Surrey
92 C3 **Runhall** Norfk
93 K2 **Runham** Norfk
25 H6 **Runnington** Somset
143 G4 **Runswick** N York
195 L3 **Runtaleave** Angus
46 C2 **Runwell** Essex
42 D5 **Ruscombe** Wokham
70 B7 **Rushall** Herefs
92 E6 **Rushall** Norfk
28 C1 **Rushall** Wilts
77 K3 **Rushbrooke** Suffk
83 K5 **Rushbury** Shrops
60 A2 **Rushden** Herts
74 D2 **Rushden** Nhants
46 E5 **Rushenden** Kent
91 K7 **Rushford** Norfk
62 E5 **Rush Green** Essex
45 K3 **Rush Green** Gt Lon
20 D3 **Rushlake Green** E Susx
93 K6 **Rushmere** Suffk
30 E4 **Rushmoor** Surrey
70 F1 **Rushock** Worcs
113 J3 **Rusholme** Manch
88 B6 **Rushton** Nhants
113 L8 **Rushton Spencer** Staffs
70 E4 **Rushwick** Worcs
141 G2 **Rushyford** Dur
184 D7 **Ruskie** Stirlg
103 H3 **Ruskington** Lincs
129 H2 **Rusland** Cumb
31 K4 **Rusper** W Susx
54 F5 **Ruspidge** Gloucs
42 B3 **Russell's Water** Oxon
31 L4 **Russ Hill** Surrey
32 F5 **Rusthall** Kent
18 E5 **Rustington** W Susx
134 E3 **Ruston** N York
135 G6 **Ruston Parva** E R Yk

143 H5 **Ruswarp** N York
167 K4 **Rutherford** Border
175 H6 **Rutherglen** S Lans
4 F3 **Ruthernbridge** Cnwll
97 H2 **Ruthin** Denbgs
207 H4 **Ruthrieston** C Aber
215 L5 **Ruthven** Abers
195 L6 **Ruthven** Angus
203 H5 **Ruthven** Highld
4 E4 **Ruthvoes** Cnwll
147 J2 **Ruthwell** D & G
98 B7 **Ruyton-XI-Towns** Shrops
158 C7 **Ryal** Nthumb
13 K4 **Ryall** Dorset
70 F6 **Ryall** Worcs
33 H7 **Ryarsh** Kent
137 K6 **Rydal** Cumb
17 H4 **Ryde** IoW
21 H2 **Rye** E Susx
21 H2 **Rye Foreign** E Susx
70 D7 **Rye Street** Worcs
88 F2 **Ryhall** Rutlnd
124 B7 **Ryhill** Wakefd
151 K4 **Ryhope** Sundld
117 G5 **Ryland** Lincs
101 K5 **Rylands** Notts
131 H7 **Rylstone** N York
14 B1 **Ryme Intrinseca** Dorset
124 E3 **Ryther** N York
150 E3 **Ryton** Gatesd
84 D3 **Ryton** Shrops
86 E8 **Ryton-on-Dunsmore** Warwks

S

122 B3 **Sabden** Lancs
60 B4 **Sacombe** Herts
151 G5 **Sacriston** Dur
141 H4 **Sadberge** Darltn
161 K3 **Saddell** Ag & B
87 J5 **Saddington** Leics
90 E1 **Saddle Bow** Norfk
19 H4 **Saddlescombe** W Susx
76 D6 **Saffron Walden** Essex
49 H6 **Sageston** Pembks
91 K3 **Saham Hills** Norfk
91 K3 **Saham Toney** Norfk
98 C1 **Saighton** Ches W
179 J5 **St Abbs** Border
178 E5 **St Agnes** Border
3 J2 **St Agnes** Cnwll
2 a2 **St Agnes** IoS
59 J6 **St Albans** Herts
4 C5 **St Allen** Cnwll
236 c3 **St Andrew** Guern
187 H4 **St Andrews** Fife
187 H4 **St Andrews Botanic Garden** Fife
37 H6 **St Andrew's Major** V Glam
13 L4 **St Andrews Well** Dorset
120 D5 **St Anne's** Lancs
155 J4 **St Ann's** D & G
6 B2 **St Ann's Chapel** Cnwll
6 F6 **St Ann's Chapel** Devon
3 K6 **St Anthony** Cnwll
20 D5 **St Anthony's Hill** E Susx
38 D2 **St Arvans** Mons
110 E6 **St Asaph** Denbgs
36 F6 **St Athan** V Glam
236 b7 **St Aubin** Jersey
4 F5 **St Austell** Cnwll
136 D5 **St Bees** Cumb
5 G5 **St Blazey** Cnwll
167 J3 **St Boswells** Border
236 b7 **St Brelade** Jersey
236 b7 **St Brelade's Bay** Jersey

4 F2 **St Breock** Cnwll
5 H1 **St Breward** Cnwll
54 E6 **St Briavels** Gloucs
36 D5 **St Bride's Major** V Glam
37 H5 **St Brides super-Ely** V Glam
37 L4 **St Brides Wentlooge** Newpt
6 C4 **St Budeaux** C Plym
71 K6 **Saintbury** Gloucs
2 D6 **St Buryan** Cnwll
183 G6 **St Catherines** Ag & B
55 J7 **St Chloe** Gloucs
50 C3 **St Clears** Carmth
5 K3 **St Cleer** Cnwll
4 D6 **St Clement** Cnwll
236 e8 **St Clement** Jersey
9 G7 **St Clether** Cnwll
173 H5 **St Colmac** Ag & B
4 E3 **St Columb Major** Cnwll
4 D4 **St Columb Minor** Cnwll
4 E4 **St Columb Road** Cnwll
217 K2 **St Combs** Abers
93 G6 **St Cross South Elmham** Suffk
197 J4 **St Cyrus** Abers
185 K4 **St David's** P & K
48 C3 **St David's** Pembks
3 J3 **St Day** Cnwll
4 E4 **St Dennis** Cnwll
65 G5 **St Dogmaels** Pembks
6 B3 **St Dominick** Cnwll
36 E6 **St Donats** V Glam
4 F1 **St Endellion** Cnwll
4 D4 **St Enoder** Cnwll
4 D6 **St Erme** Cnwll
6 B4 **St Erney** Cnwll
2 F4 **St Erth** Cnwll
3 G4 **St Erth Praze** Cnwll
4 D2 **St Ervan** Cnwll
4 D3 **St Eval** Cnwll
4 F6 **St Ewe** Cnwll
37 H5 **St Fagans** Cardif
37 H5 **St Fagans Welsh Life Museum** Cardif
217 K4 **St Fergus** Abers
184 F3 **St Fillans** P & K
49 J7 **St Florence** Pembks
8 F5 **St Gennys** Cnwll
110 D6 **St George** Conwy
38 B7 **St Georges** N Som
37 H5 **St George's** V Glam
6 A4 **St Germans** Cnwll
23 H7 **St Giles in the Wood** Devon
9 K6 **St Giles-on-the-Heath** Devon
81 L8 **St Harmon** Powys
140 F2 **St Helen Auckland** Dur
17 J5 **St Helens** IoW
112 D3 **St Helens** St Hel
112 C3 **St Helens Crematorium** St Hel
44 E6 **St Helier** Gt Lon
236 d7 **St Helier** Jersey
2 F5 **St Hilary** Cnwll
36 F5 **St Hilary** V Glam
59 K3 **St Ippollitts** Herts
48 E6 **St Ishmael's** Pembks
4 E2 **St Issey** Cnwll
5 L3 **St Ive** Cnwll
75 K1 **St Ives** Cambs
2 F3 **St Ives** Cnwll
73 L3 **St James's End** Nhants
93 G7 **St James South Elmham** Suffk
4 E3 **St Jidgey** Cnwll
6 B5 **St John** Cnwll
236 c5 **St John** Jersey
237 b5 **St John's** IoM

32 F3 **St Johns** Kent
43 G8 **St Johns** Surrey
70 E4 **St Johns** Worcs
23 H5 **St John's Chapel** Devon
149 M7 **St John's Chapel** Dur
90 D2 **St John's Fen End** Norfk
165 J3 **St John's Kirk** S Lans
154 B6 **St John's Town of Dalry** D & G
44 F4 **St John's Wood** Gt Lon
237 d3 **St Jude's** IoM
2 C5 **St Just** Cnwll
4 D8 **St Just-in-Roseland** Cnwll
216 E7 **St Katherines** Abers
3 K6 **St Keverne** Cnwll
5 G1 **St Kew** Cnwll
5 G2 **St Kew Highway** Cnwll
5 K4 **St Keyne** Cnwll
62 A6 **St Lawrence** Essex
17 G6 **St Lawrence** IoW
236 c6 **St Lawrence** Jersey
35 K2 **St Lawrence** Kent
58 E6 **St Leonards** Bucks
15 L2 **St Leonards** Dorset
20 F4 **St Leonards** E Susx
2 C6 **St Levan** Cnwll
37 H6 **St Lythans** V Glam
5 G2 **St Mabyn** Cnwll
186 C3 **St Madoes** P & K
69 G7 **St Margarets** Herefs
60 B5 **St Margarets** Herts
35 K5 **St Margaret's at Cliffe** Kent
234 c7 **St Margaret's Hope** Ork
93 G6 **St Margaret South Elmham** Suffk
237 c6 **St Marks** IoM
3 J6 **St Martin** Cnwll
5 K5 **St Martin** Cnwll
236 d3 **St Martin** Guern
236 e6 **St Martin** Jersey
2 b1 **St Martin's** IoS
186 B2 **St Martin's** P & K
97 L5 **St Martins** Shrops
236 b6 **St Mary** Jersey
29 H2 **St Mary Bourne** Hants
7 L3 **St Marychurch** Torbay
36 F6 **St Mary Church** V Glam
45 J6 **St Mary Cray** Gt Lon
21 L1 **St Mary in the Marsh** Kent
44 E3 **St Marylebone Crematorium** Gt Lon
2 b1 **St Mary's** IoS
234 c6 **St Mary's** Ork
21 L1 **St Mary's Bay** Kent
46 D5 **St Mary's Hoo** Medway
54 C5 **St Maughans Green** Mons
3 L5 **St Mawes** Cnwll
4 D3 **St Mawgan** Cnwll
6 B3 **St Mellion** Cnwll
37 K4 **St Mellons** Cardif
4 D2 **St Merryn** Cnwll
4 F7 **St Michael Caerhays** Cnwll
25 L5 **St Michael Church** Somset
4 D7 **St Michael Penkevil** Cnwll
34 B7 **St Michaels** Kent
69 L2 **St Michaels** Worcs
120 F3 **St Michael's on Wyre** Lancs
4 F1 **St Minver** Cnwll
187 H6 **St Monans** Fife
5 J3 **St Neot** Cnwll
75 H3 **St Neots** Cambs

64 C7 **St Nicholas** Pembks
37 H5 **St Nicholas** V Glam
47 L6 **St Nicholas at Wade** Kent
185 G8 **St Ninians** Stirlg
93 J4 **St Olaves** Norfk
62 D5 **St Osyth** Essex
236 b6 **St Ouen** Jersey
54 D3 **St Owens Cross** Herefs
45 J6 **St Pauls Cray** Gt Lon
59 K4 **St Paul's Walden** Herts
236 b6 **St Peter** Jersey
236 d3 **St Peter Port** Guern
236 b3 **St Peter's** Guern
35 K2 **St Peter's** Kent
5 J3 **St Pinnock** Cnwll
163 J5 **St Quivox** S Ayrs
236 d2 **St Sampson** Guern
236 c3 **St Saviour** Guern
236 d7 **St Saviour** Jersey
4 E5 **St Stephen** Cnwll
6 B4 **St Stephens** Cnwll
9 J7 **St Stephens** Cnwll
8 E8 **St Teath** Cnwll
5 G1 **St Tudy** Cnwll
48 F7 **St Twynnells** Pembks
5 J5 **St Veep** Cnwll
197 G7 **St Vigeans** Angus
4 F3 **St Wenn** Cnwll
54 D3 **St Weonards** Herefs
7 H7 **Salcombe** Devon
12 F5 **Salcombe Regis** Devon
61 M5 **Salcott-cum-Virley** Essex
113 H3 **Sale** Traffd
118 F5 **Saleby** Lincs
71 G3 **Sale Green** Worcs
20 F2 **Salehurst** E Susx
80 F6 **Salem** Cerdgn
190 C7 **Salen** Ag & B
190 D4 **Salen** Highld
74 D6 **Salford** C Beds
56 F3 **Salford** Oxon
113 J2 **Salford** Salfd
71 J4 **Salford Priors** Warwks
32 B4 **Salfords** Surrey
93 G1 **Salhouse** Norfk
185 L8 **Saline** Fife
28 C5 **Salisbury** Wilts
28 C5 **Salisbury Cathedral** Wilts
28 D5 **Salisbury Crematorium** Wilts
28 B3 **Salisbury Plain** Wilts
148 F7 **Salkeld Dykes** Cumb
106 D7 **Salle** Norfk
118 D6 **Salmonby** Lincs
56 B4 **Salperton** Gloucs
175 L5 **Salsburgh** N Lans
99 L6 **Salt** Staffs
123 H3 **Saltaire** C Brad
6 B4 **Saltash** Cnwll
223 G7 **Saltburn** Highld
142 E3 **Saltburn-by-the-Sea** R & Cl
102 D7 **Saltby** Leics
163 G2 **Saltcoats** N Ayrs
19 K5 **Saltdean** Br & H
136 D3 **Salterbeck** Cumb
122 D2 **Salterforth** Lancs
28 C4 **Salterton** Wilts
118 F3 **Saltfleet** Lincs
118 F4 **Saltfleetby All Saints** Lincs
118 F3 **Saltfleetby St Clement** Lincs
118 F4 **Saltfleetby St Peter** Lincs
39 G6 **Saltford** BaNES
106 C4 **Salthouse** Norfk
125 J5 **Saltmarshe** E R Yk
111 L8 **Saltney** Flints
133 L4 **Salton** N York

23 G6 **Saltrens** Devon
151 G3 **Saltwell Crematorium** Gatesd
34 F7 **Saltwood** Kent
18 F5 **Salvington** W Susx
70 F3 **Salwarpe** Worcs
13 L3 **Salway Ash** Dorset
71 J3 **Sambourne** Warwks
99 G7 **Sambrook** Wrekin
121 H4 **Samlesbury** Lancs
25 H7 **Sampford Arundel** Somset
25 G3 **Sampford Brett** Somset
10 F5 **Sampford Courtenay** Devon
25 H7 **Sampford Moor** Somset
25 G8 **Sampford Peverell** Devon
6 D2 **Sampford Spiney** Devon
234 d5 **Samsonlane** Ork
178 B4 **Samuelston** E Loth
170 E4 **Sanaigmore** Ag & B
2 D5 **Sancreed** Cnwll
125 L3 **Sancton** E R Yk
199 L5 **Sandaig** Highld
123 L6 **Sandal Magna** Wakefd
199 G7 **Sandavore** Highld
234 d4 **Sanday** Ork
234 d4 *Sanday Airport* Ork
99 H1 **Sandbach** Ches E
99 H1 *Sandbach Services* Ches E
173 K3 **Sandbank** Ag & B
15 K5 **Sandbanks** Poole
216 B2 **Sandend** Abers
45 G7 **Sanderstead** Gt Lon
139 G4 **Sandford** Cumb
11 J4 **Sandford** Devon
15 H5 **Sandford** Dorset
15 M3 **Sandford** Hants
17 G6 **Sandford** IoW
38 B8 **Sandford** N Som
164 E2 **Sandford** S Lans
57 K7 **Sandford-on-Thames** Oxon
26 F7 **Sandford Orcas** Dorset
57 H3 **Sandford St Martin** Oxon
35 G7 **Sandgate** Kent
217 H2 **Sandhaven** Abers
144 D5 **Sandhead** D & G
124 B3 **Sand Hills** Leeds
57 K6 **Sandhills** Oxon
30 F4 **Sandhills** Surrey
150 B2 **Sandhoe** Nthumb
182 E7 **Sandhole** Ag & B
125 J3 **Sand Hole** E R Yk
125 J4 **Sandholme** E R Yk
42 D7 **Sandhurst** Br For
55 J4 **Sandhurst** Gloucs
33 K7 **Sandhurst** Kent
132 F3 **Sandhutton** N York
133 L7 **Sand Hutton** N York
101 J5 **Sandiacre** Derbys
119 G5 **Sandilands** Lincs
28 C7 **Sandleheath** Hants
57 J7 **Sandleigh** Oxon
27 H6 **Sandley** Dorset
235 b5 **Sandness** Shet
61 H6 **Sandon** Essex
75 K7 **Sandon** Herts
99 L6 **Sandon** Staffs
99 L6 **Sandon Bank** Staffs
17 H5 **Sandown** IoW
5 K4 **Sandplace** Cnwll
59 K6 **Sandridge** Herts
105 H6 **Sandringham** Norfk
143 H5 **Sandsend** N York
125 H8 **Sandtoft** N Linc
34 B5 **Sandway** Kent
35 J3 **Sandwich** Kent

235 C7 **Sandwick** Shet
232 g2 **Sandwick** W Isls
136 D4 **Sandwith** Cumb
75 H5 **Sandy** C Beds
155 L4 **Sandyford** D & G
7 K2 **Sandygate** Devon
237 d3 **Sandygate** IoM
146 F4 **Sandyhills** D & G
129 J6 **Sandylands** Lancs
39 L6 **Sandy Lane** Wilts
11 G6 **Sandy Park** Devon
228 F3 **Sangobeg** Highld
228 F3 **Sangomore** Highld
70 E2 **Sankyn's Green** Worcs
189 K3 **Sanna Bay** Highld
232 g2 **Sanndabhaig** W Isls
162 C1 **Sannox** N Ayrs
164 F7 **Sanquhar** D & G
136 F6 **Santon Bridge** Cumb
91 J6 **Santon Downham** Suff
86 F5 **Sapcote** Leics
70 C2 **Sapey Common** Herefs
91 K7 **Sapiston** Suffk
55 L7 **Sapperton** Gloucs
103 G5 **Sapperton** Lincs
104 B6 **Saracen's Head** Lincs
231 L6 **Sarclet** Highld
17 G2 **Sarisbury** Hants
94 D6 **Sarn** Gwynd
81 K4 **Sarn** Powys
82 E5 **Sarn** Powys
65 K4 **Sarnau** Cerdgn
82 E1 **Sarnau** Powys
36 D4 **Sarn Park Services** Brdgnd
51 H3 **Saron** Carmth
109 G7 **Saron** Gwynd
59 H7 **Sarratt** Herts
47 L6 **Sarre** Kent
56 F4 **Sarsden** Oxon
150 E6 **Satley** Dur
23 L6 **Satterleigh** Devon
129 H2 **Satterthwaite** Cumb
206 D3 **Sauchen** Abers
186 C2 **Saucher** P & K
197 G3 **Sauchieburn** Abers
55 H6 **Saul** Gloucs
116 C4 **Saundby** Notts
49 K6 **Saundersfoot** Pembks
58 C7 **Saunderton** Bucks
23 G4 **Saunton** Devon
118 E7 **Sausthorpe** Lincs
123 K6 **Savile Town** Kirk
73 G2 **Sawbridge** Warwks
60 D5 **Sawbridgeworth** Herts
134 E3 **Sawdon** N York
122 B2 **Sawley** Lancs
132 C6 **Sawley** N York
76 C5 **Sawston** Cambs
89 H6 **Sawtry** Cambs
102 D8 **Saxby** Leics
117 G4 **Saxby** Lincs
126 B7 **Saxby All Saints** N Linc
102 B7 **Saxelbye** Leics
78 C3 **Saxham Street** Suffk
116 E6 **Saxilby** Lincs
106 B5 **Saxlingham** Norfk
92 F4 **Saxlingham Green** Norfk
92 F4 **Saxlingham Nethergate** Norfk
92 F4 **Saxlingham Thorpe** Norfk
79 H2 **Saxmundham** Suff
102 B4 **Saxondale** Notts
76 F3 **Saxon Street** Cambs
78 F2 **Saxtead** Suffk
78 F2 **Saxtead Green** Suffk
78 F2 **Saxtead Little Green** Suffk

106 D6 **Saxthorpe** Norfk
124 D3 **Saxton** N York
19 H3 **Sayers Common** W Susx
133 K5 **Scackleton** N York
137 H5 **Scafell Pike** Cumb
116 A3 **Scaftworth** Notts
134 C5 **Scagglethorpe** N York
180 E8 **Scalasaig** Ag & B
125 K5 **Scalby** E R Yk
134 F2 **Scalby** N York
73 L1 **Scaldwell** Nhants
148 D3 **Scaleby** Cumb
148 D3 **Scalebyhill** Cumb
129 G5 **Scales** Cumb
137 K2 **Scales** Cumb
102 C7 **Scalford** Leics
142 F4 **Scaling** N York
235 c6 **Scalloway** Shet
209 J7 **Scalpay** Highld
118 C5 **Scamblesby** Lincs
191 L2 **Scamodale** Highld
134 D4 **Scampston** N York
116 F5 **Scampton** Lincs
212 F6 **Scaniport** Highld
123 G7 **Scapegoat Hill** Kirk
181 K6 **Scarba** Ag & B
135 G2 **Scarborough** N York
4 E5 **Scarcewater** Cnwll
115 J7 **Scarcliffe** Derbys
124 B3 **Scarcroft** Leeds
231 J2 **Scarfskerry** Highld
140 D5 **Scargill** Dur
188 D7 **Scarinish** Ag & B
120 E7 **Scarisbrick** Lancs
91 L2 **Scarning** Norfk
102 B4 **Scarrington** Notts
118 C1 **Scartho** NE Lin
235 c4 *Scatsta Airport* Shet
116 F1 **Scawby** N Linc
115 K1 **Scawby** Donc
115 K1 **Scawthorpe** Donc
133 H3 **Scawton** N York
19 K2 **Scayne's Hill** W Susx
53 H3 **Scethrog** Powys
99 J2 **Scholar Green** Ches E
123 H4 **Scholemoor Crematorium** C Brad
123 H8 **Scholes** Kirk
124 B3 **Scholes** Leeds
115 H3 **Scholes** Rothm
112 E1 **Scholes** Wigan
123 K7 **Scissett** Kirk
64 C7 **Scleddau** Pembks
115 L5 **Scofton** Notts
92 D7 **Scole** Norfk
186 B3 **Scone** P & K
209 H7 **Sconser** Highld
186 F6 **Scoonie** Fife
103 H2 **Scopwick** Lincs
220 C3 **Scoraig** Highld
126 C2 **Scorborough** E R Yk
3 J3 **Scorrier** Cnwll
121 G2 **Scorton** Lancs
141 G7 **Scorton** N York
148 D2 **Scotby** Cumb
140 F6 **Scotch Corner** N York
140 F6 **Scotch Corner Services** N York
125 K7 **Scotforth** Lancs
117 G6 **Scothern** Lincs
186 C6 **Scotlandwell** P & K
231 G4 **Scotscalder Station** Highld
158 C5 **Scot's Gap** Nthumb
206 B3 **Scotsmill** Abers
174 F5 **Scotstoun** C Glas
150 F3 **Scotswood** N u Ty
116 E2 **Scotter** Lincs
116 E2 **Scotterthorpe** Lincs
116 E2 **Scotton** Lincs
132 E7 **Scotton** N York
140 F7 **Scotton** N York
92 B4 **Scoulton** Norfk
228 B6 **Scourie** Highld
228 B6 **Scourie More** Highld

235 C7 **Scousburgh** Shet
231 G2 **Scrabster** Highld
167 K5 **Scraesburgh** Border
104 C4 **Scrane End** Lincs
87 J3 **Scraptoft** Leics
93 K1 **Scratby** Norfk
133 L7 **Scrayingham** N York
103 H4 **Scredington** Lincs
118 F7 **Scremby** Lincs
179 L8 **Scremerston** Nthumb
102 B4 **Screveton** Notts
132 E7 **Scriven** N York
115 M4 **Scrooby** Notts
100 D6 **Scropton** Derbys
103 L2 **Scrub Hill** Lincs
195 K5 **Scruschloch** Angus
132 D2 **Scruton** N York
229 J4 **Scullomie** Highld
105 L6 **Sculthorpe** Norfk
125 K7 **Scunthorpe** N Linc
13 K2 **Seaborough** Dorset
35 G7 **Seabrook** Kent
151 J3 **Seaburn** Sundld
124 B4 **Seacroft** Leeds
209 G5 **Seafield** Highld
176 D5 **Seafield** W Loth
177 J4 **Seafield**
  Crematorium C Edin
20 A6 **Seaford** E Susx
111 K3 **Seaforth** Sefton
101 L8 **Seagrave** Leics
151 K5 **Seaham** Dur
169 J3 **Seahouses** Nthumb
32 F2 **Seal** Kent
30 E2 **Seale** Surrey
134 F3 **Seamer** N York
142 B5 **Seamer** N York
173 L8 **Seamill** N Ayrs
107 J6 **Sea Palling** Norfk
117 H1 **Searby** Lincs
47 H6 **Seasalter** Kent
136 E6 **Seascale** Cumb
137 H7 **Seathwaite** Cumb
137 H4 **Seatoller** Cumb
5 L5 **Seaton** Cnwll
136 E2 **Seaton** Cumb
13 G4 **Seaton** Devon
126 E2 **Seaton** E R Yk
35 G3 **Seaton** Kent
159 H6 **Seaton** Nthumb
88 C4 **Seaton** Rutlnd
142 B2 **Seaton Carew** Hartpl
159 H6 **Seaton Delaval**
  Nthumb
125 J3 **Seaton Ross** E R Yk
159 H6 **Seaton Sluice**
  Nthumb
13 K4 **Seatown** Dorset
142 C7 **Seave Green** N York
17 J4 **Seaview** IoW
147 K4 **Seaville** Cumb
26 B7 **Seavington St Mary**
  Somset
26 B7 **Seavington St**
  Michael Somset
148 C6 **Sebergham** Cumb
86 C3 **Seckington** Warwks
130 C2 **Sedbergh** Cumb
38 D2 **Sedbury** Gloucs
131 G2 **Sedbusk** N York
71 H6 **Sedgeberrow** Worcs
102 D5 **Sedgebrook** Lincs
141 J2 **Sedgefield** Dur
105 H5 **Sedgeford** Norfk
27 K5 **Sedgehill** Wilts
26 A2 **Sedgemoor Services**
  Somset
85 G5 **Sedgley** Dudley
129 L3 **Sedgwick** Cumb
20 F3 **Sedlescombe** E Susx
58 D5 **Sedrup** Bucks
39 L7 **Seend** Wilts
39 L7 **Seend Cleeve** Wilts
42 F3 **Seer Green** Bucks
93 G4 **Seething** Norfk
111 K2 **Sefton** Sefton

99 K7 **Seighford** Staffs
109 H7 **Seion** Gwynd
84 E4 **Seisdon** Staffs
97 K5 **Selattyn** Shrops
30 C5 **Selborne** Hants
124 F4 **Selby** N York
30 F7 **Selham** W Susx
45 G6 **Selhurst** Gt Lon
167 G4 **Selkirk** Border
54 E3 **Sellack** Herefs
235 d2 **Sellafirth** Shet
34 E6 **Sellindge** Kent
34 D4 **Selling** Kent
39 L7 **Sells Green** Wilts
85 J6 **Selly Oak** Birm
20 B4 **Selmeston** E Susx
45 G7 **Selsdon** Gt Lon
55 J7 **Selsey** Gloucs
18 B6 **Selsey** W Susx
130 E4 **Selside** N York
55 G5 **Selsted** Kent
101 J2 **Selston** Notts
24 E3 **Selworthy** Somset
78 B5 **Semer** Suffk
39 K7 **Semington** Wilts
27 K6 **Semley** Wilts
31 G1 **Send** Surrey
37 H3 **Senghenydd** Caerph
2 C6 **Sennen** Cnwll
2 C6 **Sennen Cove** Cnwll
52 E3 **Sennybridge** Powys
133 G4 **Sessay** N York
90 F2 **Setchey** Norfk
177 L4 **Seton Mains** E Loth
130 F6 **Settle** N York
134 C5 **Settrington** N York
56 B4 **Sevenhampton**
  Gloucs
40 E3 **Sevenhampton**
  Swindn
45 J3 **Seven Kings** Gt Lon
32 F3 **Sevenoaks** Kent
32 F3 **Sevenoaks Weald**
  Kent
52 C6 **Seven Sisters** Neath
61 M3 **Seven Star Green**
  Essex
38 D4 **Severn Beach** S Glos
70 F5 **Severn Stoke** Worcs
38 E3 **Severn View Services**
  S Glos
34 D6 **Sevington** Kent
76 E6 **Sewards End** Essex
59 G4 **Sewell** C Beds
135 J5 **Sewerby** E R Yk
3 J5 **Sewerby** Cnwll
102 E7 **Sewstern** Leics
232 g1 **Sgiogarstaigh** W Isls
58 A6 **Shabbington** Bucks
86 D3 **Shackerstone** Leics
30 F3 **Shackleford** Surrey
232 f1 **Shader** W Isls
151 H6 **Shadforth** Dur
93 J6 **Shadingfield** Suffk
34 C7 **Shadoxhurst** Kent
91 L6 **Shadwell** Norfk
76 B6 **Shaftenhoe End**
  Herts
27 K6 **Shaftesbury** Dorset
124 B7 **Shafton** Barns
113 G2 **Shakerley** Wigan
40 F7 **Shalbourne** Wilts
30 B3 **Shalden** Hants
7 L2 **Shaldon** Devon
16 E5 **Shalfleet** IoW
61 H3 **Shalford** Essex
31 G3 **Shalford** Surrey
61 H3 **Shalford Green** Essex
34 E4 **Shalmsford Street**
  Kent
73 J7 **Shalstone** Bucks
31 G3 **Shamley Green**
  Surrey
196 E6 **Shandford** Angus
174 B2 **Shandon** Ag & B
223 J6 **Shandwick** Highld

87 K4 **Shangton** Leics
17 H6 **Shanklin** IoW
138 E4 **Shap** Cumb
234 C5 **Shapinsay** Ork
15 H3 **Shapwick** Dorset
26 B4 **Shapwick** Somset
101 H6 **Shardlow** Derbys
85 G3 **Shareshill** Staffs
124 B6 **Sharlston** Wakefd
74 E3 **Sharnbrook** Bed
86 F5 **Sharnford** Leics
121 G4 **Sharoe Green** Lancs
132 E5 **Sharow** N York
59 H2 **Sharpenhoe** C Beds
158 B2 **Sharperton** Nthumb
54 F7 **Sharpness** Gloucs
106 C5 **Sharrington** Norfk
84 E7 **Shatterford** Worcs
6 D3 **Shaugh Prior** Devon
99 G3 **Shavington** Ches E
122 D8 **Shaw** Oldham
41 J6 **Shaw** W Berk
39 K7 **Shaw** Wilts
84 B2 **Shawbirch** Wrekin
232 e2 **Shawbost** W Isls
98 E7 **Shawbury** Shrops
87 G7 **Shawell** Leics
29 J6 **Shawford** Hants
154 F6 **Shawhead** D & G
132 C6 **Shaw Mills** N York
175 K7 **Shawsburn** S Lans
147 H2 **Shearington** D & G
87 J5 **Shearsby** Leics
25 L5 **Shearston** Somset
10 C3 **Shebbear** Devon
99 H7 **Shebdon** Staffs
230 E3 **Shebster** Highld
175 G6 **Sheddens** E Rens
29 K8 **Shedfield** Hants
100 C1 **Sheen** Staffs
123 H6 **Sheepridge** Kirk
123 L4 **Sheepscar** Leeds
55 K6 **Sheepscombe** Gloucs
6 E3 **Sheepstor** Devon
10 C4 **Sheepwash** Devon
86 D3 **Sheepy Magna** Leics
86 D3 **Sheepy Parva** Leics
60 E5 **Sheering** Essex
46 F5 **Sheerness** Kent
43 H7 **Sheerwater** Surrey
30 C6 **Sheet** Hants
115 G4 **Sheffield** Sheff
115 G4 **Sheffield City Road**
  Crematorium Sheff
75 G6 **Shefford** C Beds
228 B4 **Sheigra** Highld
83 L3 **Sheinton** Shrops
83 H7 **Shelderton** Shrops
85 L6 **Sheldon** Birm
114 D7 **Sheldon** Derbys
12 E2 **Sheldon** Devon
34 D4 **Sheldwich** Kent
92 D6 **Shelfanger** Norfk
102 A4 **Shelford** Notts
123 J7 **Shelley** Kirk
78 B6 **Shelley** Suffk
40 F2 **Shellingford** Oxon
60 F6 **Shellow Bowells**
  Essex
70 D2 **Shelsley Beauchamp**
  Worcs
70 C2 **Shelsley Walsh** Worcs
74 F7 **Shelton** Bed
92 F5 **Shelton** Norfk
102 C4 **Shelton** Notts
99 J5 **Shelton Under**
  Harley Staffs
83 G4 **Shelve** Shrops
69 K6 **Shelwick** Herefs
45 L2 **Shenfield** Essex
72 D6 **Shenington** Oxon
59 K7 **Shenley** Herts
74 B7 **Shenley Brook End**
  M Keyn
74 B7 **Shenley Church End**
  M Keyn

69 H6 **Shenmore** Herefs
145 H3 **Shennanton** D & G
85 K3 **Shenstone** Staffs
84 F8 **Shenstone** Worcs
86 E4 **Shenton** Leics
59 L4 **Shenval** Herts
44 E4 **Shepherd's Bush**
  Gt Lon
35 H5 **Shepherdswell** Kent
123 J8 **Shepley** Kirk
43 H6 **Shepperton** Surrey
76 B5 **Shepreth** Cambs
101 J8 **Shepshed** Leics
26 B7 **Shepton Beauchamp**
  Somset
26 F3 **Shepton Mallet**
  Somset
27 G5 **Shepton Montague**
  Somset
33 K3 **Shepway** Kent
151 K7 **Sheraton** Dur
26 F7 **Sherborne** Dorset
56 D5 **Sherborne** Gloucs
26 E1 **Sherborne** Somset
29 L1 **Sherborne St John**
  Hants
72 C3 **Sherbourne** Warwks
151 H6 **Sherburn** Dur
134 E4 **Sherburn** N York
151 H6 **Sherburn Hill** Dur
124 D4 **Sherburn in Elmet**
  N York
31 H2 **Shere** Surrey
105 L6 **Shereford** Norfk
28 F6 **Sherfield English**
  Hants
42 B8 **Sherfield on Loddon**
  Hants
7 H6 **Sherford** Devon
84 D2 **Sheriffhales** Shrops
133 K6 **Sheriff Hutton** N York
106 E4 **Sheringham** Norfk
74 C5 **Sherington** M Keyn
105 H6 **Shernborne** Norfk
27 L4 **Sherrington** Wilts
39 J3 **Sherston** Wilts
101 K4 **Sherwood** C Nott
101 L2 **Sherwood Forest**
  Notts
116 A7 **Sherwood Forest**
  Crematorium Notts
175 H5 **Shettleston** C Glas
121 H8 **Shevington** Wigan
6 B5 **Sheviock** Cnwll
123 G5 **Shibden Head** C Brad
16 F5 **Shide** IoW
168 B2 **Shidlaw** Nthumb
200 E2 **Shiel Bridge** Highld
210 C4 **Shieldaig** Highld
155 H5 **Shieldhill** D & G
176 B3 **Shieldhill** Falk
165 J2 **Shieldhill House**
  Hotel S Lans
175 K7 **Shields** N Lans
190 D3 **Shielfoot** Highld
196 C5 **Shielhill** Angus
173 L4 **Shielhill** Inver
84 D2 **Shifnal** Shrops
169 J7 **Shilbottle** Nthumb
141 G3 **Shildon** Dur
174 E6 **Shillford** E Rens
24 F6 **Shillingford** Devon
41 L2 **Shillingford** Oxon
11 K6 **Shillingford Abbot**
  Devon
11 K7 **Shillingford St**
  George Devon
14 F1 **Shillingstone** Dorset
75 G7 **Shillington** C Beds
56 E6 **Shilton** Oxon
86 E6 **Shilton** Warwks
92 D6 **Shimpling** Norfk
77 J4 **Shimpling** Suffk
77 K4 **Shimpling Street**
  Suffk
151 H6 **Shincliffe** Dur

151 H4 **Shiney Row** Sundld
42 B6 **Shinfield** Wokham
225 L5 **Shinness** Highld
33 G3 **Shipbourne** Kent
91 L3 **Shipdham** Norfk
38 C8 **Shipham** Somset
7 K3 **Shiphay** Torbay
42 C5 **Shiplake** Oxon
123 H3 **Shipley** C Brad
31 J6 **Shipley** W Susx
32 B5 **Shipley Bridge** Surrey
93 H5 **Shipmeadow** Suffk
41 J2 **Shippon** Oxon
72 B6 **Shipston on Stour** Warwks
56 B4 **Shipton** Gloucs
133 H7 **Shipton** N York
83 L5 **Shipton** Shrops
28 E3 **Shipton Bellinger** Hants
13 L4 **Shipton Gorge** Dorset
17 L3 **Shipton Green** W Susx
39 K3 **Shipton Moyne** Gloucs
57 J5 **Shipton-on-Cherwell** Oxon
125 K2 **Shiptonthorpe** E R Yk
56 F4 **Shipton-under-Wychwood** Oxon
42 B2 **Shirburn** Oxon
120 E7 **Shirdley Hill** Lancs
115 K4 **Shirebrook** Derbys
115 G3 **Shiregreen** Sheff
38 D5 **Shirehampton** Bristl
159 H7 **Shiremoor** N Tyne
38 C2 **Shirenewton** Mons
115 K5 **Shireoaks** Notts
101 H2 **Shirland** Derbys
29 H8 **Shirley** C Sotn
100 E4 **Shirley** Derbys
45 G6 **Shirley** Gt Lon
85 K7 **Shirley** Solhll
29 L8 **Shirrell Heath** Hants
172 E2 **Shirvan** Ag & B
23 J4 **Shirwell** Devon
162 B4 **Shiskine** N Ayrs
69 H3 **Shobdon** Herefs
11 K5 **Shobrooke** Devon
102 B7 **Shoby** Leics
98 C3 **Shocklach** Ches W
46 F3 **Shoeburyness** Sthend
35 K4 **Sholden** Kent
16 F1 **Sholing** C Sotn
9 G2 **Shop** Cnwll
45 G4 **Shoreditch** Gt Lon
25 K6 **Shoreditch** Somset
45 K7 **Shoreham** Kent
19 G5 *Shoreham Airport W Susx*
19 H5 **Shoreham-by-Sea** W Susx
29 L6 **Shorley** Hants
46 B5 **Shorne** Kent
20 A3 **Shortgate** E Susx
4 C6 **Shortlanesend** Cnwll
163 K3 **Shortlees** E Ayrs
74 F5 **Shortstown** Bed
16 F5 **Shorwell** IoW
27 G1 **Shoscombe** BaNES
92 F4 **Shotesham** Norfk
46 C2 **Shotgate** Essex
78 F7 **Shotley** Suffk
150 D4 **Shotley Bridge** Dur
78 F7 **Shotley Gate** Suffk
78 F7 **Shotley Street** Suffk
34 D4 **Shottenden** Kent
71 L4 **Shottery** Warwks
72 E5 **Shotteswell** Warwks
79 G5 **Shottisham** Suffk
100 F3 **Shottle** Derbys
100 F3 **Shottlegate** Derbys
151 K6 **Shotton** Dur
111 J7 **Shotton** Flints
151 J6 **Shotton Colliery** Dur
176 B6 **Shotts** N Lans
111 K6 **Shotwick** Ches W

214 F4 **Shougle** Moray
90 F2 **Shouldham** Norfk
90 F2 **Shouldham Thorpe** Norfk
70 E3 **Shoulton** Worcs
83 H1 **Shrawardine** Shrops
70 E2 **Shrawley** Worcs
72 B2 **Shrewley** Warwks
83 J2 **Shrewsbury** Shrops
28 B3 **Shrewton** Wilts
18 C5 **Shripney** W Susx
40 E3 **Shrivenham** Oxon
92 B5 **Shropham** Norfk
69 L6 **Shucknall** Herefs
76 E5 **Shudy Camps** Cambs
181 M5 **Shuna** Ag & B
55 L4 **Shurdington** Gloucs
42 D5 **Shurlock Row** W & M
230 F4 **Shurrery** Highld
230 F4 **Shurrery Lodge** Highld
25 J3 **Shurton** Somset
86 B5 **Shustoke** Warwks
11 K5 **Shute** Devon
13 G3 **Shute** Devon
72 E6 **Shutford** Oxon
99 K7 **Shut Heath** Staffs
70 F7 **Shuthonger** Gloucs
73 K4 **Shutlanger** Nhants
86 B3 **Shuttington** Warwks
115 J6 **Shuttlewood** Derbys
122 B6 **Shuttleworth** Bury
232 e2 **Siabost** W Isls
232 f1 **Siadar** W Isls
87 K6 **Sibbertoft** Nhants
72 D6 **Sibford Ferris** Oxon
72 D6 **Sibford Gower** Oxon
77 H7 **Sible Hedingham** Essex
60 F3 **Sibley's Green** Essex
104 B3 **Sibsey** Lincs
89 G4 **Sibson** Cambs
86 D4 **Sibson** Leics
231 K5 **Sibster** Highld
102 C4 **Sibthorpe** Notts
116 B6 **Sibthorpe** Notts
79 H1 **Sibton** Suffk
77 K3 **Sicklesmere** Suffk
124 B2 **Sicklinghall** N York
12 E4 **Sidbury** Devon
84 C6 **Sidbury** Shrops
38 B8 **Sidcot** N Som
45 J5 **Sidcup** Gt Lon
113 J7 **Siddington** Ches E
56 B7 **Siddington** Gloucs
106 F4 **Sidestrand** Norfk
12 E4 **Sidford** Devon
18 B6 **Sidlesham** W Susx
20 E4 **Sidley** E Susx
12 E5 **Sidmouth** Devon
126 E2 **Sigglesthorne** E R Yk
36 F6 **Sigingstone** V Glam
41 L7 **Silchester** Hants
87 H1 **Sileby** Leics
128 D3 **Silecroft** Cumb
92 D4 **Silfield** Norfk
114 F1 **Silkstone** Barns
114 F1 **Silkstone Common** Barns
151 J4 **Silksworth** Sundld
103 H4 **Silk Willoughby** Lincs
147 K4 **Silloth** Cumb
134 E2 **Silpho** N York
122 F2 **Silsden** C Brad
74 F7 **Silsoe** C Beds
27 H5 **Silton** Dorset
177 G6 **Silverburn** Mdloth
129 K4 **Silverdale** Lancs
99 J3 **Silverdale** Staffs
61 K4 **Silver End** Essex
216 E2 **Silverford** Abers
73 J5 **Silverstone** Nhants
12 B2 **Silverton** Devon
84 B7 **Silvington** Shrops
157 L7 **Simonburn** Nthumb
24 B4 **Simonsbath** Somset

122 B4 **Simonstone** Lancs
168 C1 **Simprim** Border
74 C7 **Simpson** M Keyn
48 F4 **Simpson Cross** Pembks
179 G7 **Sinclair's Hill** Border
163 L6 **Sinclairston** E Ayrs
132 E3 **Sinderby** N York
113 G4 **Sinderland Green** Traffd
42 C6 **Sindlesham** Wokham
101 G6 **Sinfin** C Derb
34 D6 **Singleton** Kent
120 E3 **Singleton** Lancs
18 B3 **Singleton** W Susx
46 A6 **Singlewell** Kent
205 K3 **Sinnarhard** Abers
134 B3 **Sinnington** N York
70 E3 **Sinton** Worcs
70 E3 **Sinton Green** Worcs
33 K5 **Sissinghurst** Kent
39 G5 **Siston** S Glos
3 H5 **Sithney** Cnwll
34 B3 **Sittingbourne** Kent
84 E5 **Six Ashes** Shrops
117 K4 **Sixhills** Lincs
76 E3 **Six Mile Bottom** Cambs
34 F5 **Sixmile Cottages** Kent
27 M7 **Sixpenny Handley** Dorset
129 K3 **Sizergh Castle** Cumb
234 d6 **Skaill** Ork
164 B6 **Skares** E Ayrs
207 G6 **Skateraw** Abers
178 F4 **Skateraw** E Loth
208 F5 **Skeabost** Highld
140 F6 **Skeeby** N York
87 L3 **Skeffington** Leics
127 J6 **Skeffling** E R Yk
101 J1 **Skegby** Notts
116 C7 **Skegby** Notts
119 H8 **Skegness** Lincs
223 H3 **Skelbo** Highld
223 H3 **Skelbo Street** Highld
124 D7 **Skelbrooke** Donc
104 B5 **Skeldyke** Lincs
116 F6 **Skellingthorpe** Lincs
124 E7 **Skellow** Donc
123 J7 **Skelmanthorpe** Kirk
112 C1 **Skelmersdale** Lancs
173 L5 **Skelmorlie** N Ayrs
229 L4 **Skelpick** Highld
154 E5 **Skelston** D & G
133 J7 **Skelton** C York
148 D7 **Skelton** Cumb
125 H5 **Skelton** E R Yk
132 E5 **Skelton** N York
142 E4 **Skelton** R & Cl
137 K6 **Skelwith Bridge** Cumb
118 F7 **Skendleby** Lincs
206 E4 **Skene House** Abers
54 C4 **Skenfrith** Mons
135 G7 **Skerne** E R Yk
229 K3 **Skerray** Highld
228 C5 **Skerricha** Highld
129 K6 **Skerton** Lancs
86 E5 **Sketchley** Leics
51 J6 **Sketty** Swans
51 K6 **Skewen** Neath
133 K5 **Skewsby** N York
230 E3 **Skiall** Highld
126 C4 **Skidby** E R Yk
232 g1 **Skigersta** W Isls
24 F6 **Skilgate** Somset
102 E7 **Skillington** Lincs
147 K4 **Skinburness** Cumb
176 B2 **Skinflats** Falk
208 C5 **Skinidin** Highld
172 F6 **Skipness** Ag & B
156 C5 **Skipper's Bridge** D & G
135 J8 **Skipsea** E R Yk
122 E1 **Skipton** N York

132 E4 **Skipton-on-Swale** N York
125 G3 **Skipwith** N York
126 E3 **Skirlaugh** E R Yk
165 L2 **Skirling** Border
42 C5 **Skirmett** Bucks
134 B7 **Skirpenbeck** E R Yk
149 G7 **Skirwith** Cumb
231 L2 **Skirza** Highld
48 C6 **Skokholm Island** Pembks
48 C5 **Skomer Island** Pembks
199 K2 **Skulamus** Highld
61 L4 **Skye Green** Essex
204 B1 **Skye of Curr** Highld
122 E5 **Slack** Calder
216 F5 **Slacks of Cairnbanno** Abers
55 K6 **Slad** Gloucs
23 H3 **Slade** Devon
45 K5 **Slade Green** Gt Lon
115 K4 **Slade Hooton** Rothm
149 H4 **Slaggyford** Nthumb
130 D8 **Slaidburn** Lancs
123 G7 **Slaithwaite** Kirk
150 B4 **Slaley** Nthumb
176 B4 **Slamannan** Falk
58 F4 **Slapton** Bucks
7 J6 **Slapton** Devon
73 J5 **Slapton** Nhants
31 L5 **Slaugham** W Susx
39 J5 **Slaughterford** Wilts
87 L5 **Slawston** Leics
30 D4 **Sleaford** Hants
103 H4 **Sleaford** Lincs
138 E4 **Sleagill** Cumb
84 B1 **Sleapford** Wrekin
222 E8 **Sleasdairidh** Highld
134 E6 **Sledmere** E R Yk
156 E6 **Sleetbeck** Cumb
140 B5 **Sleightholme** Dur
143 H5 **Sleights** N York
231 K3 **Slickly** Highld
162 B5 **Sliddery** N Ayrs
209 G7 **Sligachan** Highld
173 K1 **Sligrachan** Ag & B
55 H7 **Slimbridge** Gloucs
99 J6 **Slindon** Staffs
18 C4 **Slindon** W Susx
31 J5 **Slinfold** W Susx
133 L4 **Slingsby** N York
59 H4 **Slip End** C Beds
75 K6 **Slip End** Herts
88 D7 **Slipton** Nhants
100 B8 **Slitting Mill** Staffs
182 B7 **Slockavullin** Ag & B
146 B2 **Slogarie** D & G
11 H7 **Sloncombe** Devon
119 G7 **Sloothby** Lincs
43 G4 **Slough** Slough
43 G4 **Slough Crematorium** Bucks
25 L7 **Slough Green** Somset
210 D6 **Slumbay** Highld
129 K6 **Slyne** Lancs
167 K3 **Smailholm** Border
107 G7 **Smallburgh** Norfk
19 G3 **Small Dole** W Susx
101 H4 **Smalley** Derbys
32 B5 **Smallfield** Surrey
85 K6 **Small Heath** Birm
34 B8 **Small Hythe** Kent
13 H3 **Smallridge** Devon
92 B7 **Smallworth** Norfk
29 G2 **Smannell** Hants
34 B6 **Smarden** Kent
34 B6 **Smarden Bell** Kent
32 F5 **Smart's Hill** Kent
190 D2 **Smearisary** Highld
12 F1 **Smeatharpe** Devon
34 E6 **Smeeth** Kent
87 K5 **Smeeton Westerby** Leics
227 L2 **Smerral** Highld
84 F5 **Smestow** Staffs

85 H6 **Smethwick** Sandw
101 G8 **Smisby** Derbys
148 D2 **Smithfield** Cumb
76 F6 **Smith's Green** Essex
219 J6 **Smithstown** Highld
213 H5 **Smithton** Highld
228 F3 **Smoo** Highld
61 L4 **Smythe's Green** Essex
154 E5 **Snade** D & G
83 G3 **Snailbeach** Shrops
76 F2 **Snailwell** Cambs
134 E3 **Snainton** N York
124 F6 **Snaith** E R Yk
132 D3 **Snape** N York
79 H3 **Snape** Suffk
79 H3 **Snape Street** Suffk
45 H3 **Snaresbrook** Gt Lon
86 D2 **Snarestone** Leics
117 H5 **Snarford** Lincs
34 D8 **Snargate** Kent
34 D8 **Snave** Kent
143 J5 **Sneaton** N York
117 H5 **Snelland** Lincs
100 D4 **Snelston** Derbys
92 B5 **Snetterton** Norfk
105 G5 **Snettisham** Norfk
158 C2 **Snitter** Nthumb
117 G3 **Snitterby** Lincs
72 B3 **Snitterfield** Warwks
83 L7 **Snitton** Shrops
46 B7 **Snodland** Kent
95 K2 **Snowdon** Gwynd
96 C6 **Snowdonia National Park**
60 C2 **Snow End** Herts
71 K7 **Snowshill** Gloucs
17 J1 **Soake** Hants
199 G3 **Soay** Highld
29 L7 **Soberton** Hants
29 L8 **Soberton Heath** Hants
141 J5 **Sockburn** Darltn
90 E8 **Soham** Cambs
232 C5 **Solas** W Isls
29 M4 **Soldridge** Hants
34 E5 **Sole Street** Kent
46 A6 **Sole Street** Kent
85 L7 **Solihull** Solhll
69 H4 **Sollers Dilwyn** Herefs
54 E2 **Sollers Hope** Herefs
48 D3 **Solva** Pembks
156 B6 **Solwaybank** D & G
87 L2 **Somerby** Leics
117 H1 **Somerby** Lincs
101 H2 **Somercotes** Derbys
15 M4 **Somerford** Dorset
40 A2 **Somerford Keynes** Gloucs
17 M3 **Somerley** W Susx
93 K4 **Somerleyton** Suffk
100 C5 **Somersal Herbert** Derbys
118 D6 **Somersby** Lincs
89 L7 **Somersham** Cambs
78 C5 **Somersham** Suffk
57 J3 **Somerton** Oxon
26 C5 **Somerton** Somset
77 J4 **Somerton** Somset
19 G5 **Sompting** W Susx
42 C5 **Sonning** Wokham
42 B4 **Sonning Common** Oxon
15 M3 **Sopley** Hants
39 J3 **Sopworth** Wilts
145 J5 **Sorbie** D & G
231 G3 **Sordale** Highld
189 H4 **Sorisdale** Ag & B
164 B4 **Sorn** E Ayrs
231 K3 **Sortat** Highld
117 K5 **Sotby** Lincs
117 J8 **Sots Hole** Lincs
93 J6 **Sotterley** Suffk
111 H7 **Soughton** Flints
58 E3 **Soulbury** Bucks
139 H5 **Soulby** Cumb
57 K2 **Souldern** Oxon

74 E3 **Souldrop** Bed
98 F3 **Sound** Ches E
215 H4 **Sound Muir** Moray
38 F5 **Soundwell** S Glos
10 D6 **Sourton** Devon
128 F3 **Soutergate** Cumb
91 J2 **South Acre** Norfk
35 H6 **South Alkham** Kent
43 J4 **Southall** Gt Lon
7 J7 **South Allington** Devon
185 J8 **South Alloa** Falk
55 L3 **Southam** Gloucs
72 E3 **Southam** Warwks
30 E7 **South Ambersham** W Susx
29 H8 **Southampton** C Sotn
29 J7 *Southampton Airport* Hants
29 H7 **Southampton Crematorium** Hants
115 K5 **South Anston** Rothm
34 D6 **South Ashford** Kent
16 D3 **South Baddesley** Hants
191 L5 **South Ballachulish** Highld
124 F1 **South Bank** C York
26 E5 **South Barrow** Somset
44 F7 **South Beddington** Gt Lon
46 C3 **South Benfleet** Essex
18 C5 **South Bersted** W Susx
45 H6 **Southborough** Gt Lon
33 G5 **Southborough** Kent
15 L4 **Southbourne** Bmouth
17 L2 **Southbourne** W Susx
124 F7 **South Bramwith** Donc
7 G4 **South Brent** Devon
27 G4 **South Brewham** Somset
38 E6 **South Bristol Crematorium** Bristl
159 G3 **South Broomhill** Nthumb
92 B3 **Southburgh** Norfk
93 H3 **South Burlingham** Norfk
134 F8 **Southburn** E R Yk
26 F6 **South Cadbury** Somset
116 F6 **South Carlton** Lincs
115 L5 **South Carlton** Notts
125 L4 **South Cave** E R Yk
40 B2 **South Cerney** Gloucs
19 K3 **South Chailey** E Susx
169 H5 **South Charlton** Nthumb
27 G6 **South Cheriton** Somset
140 F2 **South Church** Dur
46 E3 **Southchurch** Sthend
125 K4 **South Cliffe** E R Yk
116 D7 **South Clifton** Notts
118 E4 **South Cockerington** Lincs
36 C4 **South Cornelly** Brdgnd
9 G5 **Southcott** Cnwll
11 H8 **Southcott** Devon
58 D5 **Southcourt** Bucks
93 K7 **South Cove** Suffk
105 K5 **South Creake** Norfk
87 K2 **South Croxton** Leics
126 B2 **South Dalton** E R Yk
45 K6 **South Darenth** Kent
19 K4 **South Downs**
125 G4 **South Duffield** N York
19 L5 **Southease** E Susx
118 D4 **South Elkington** Lincs
124 D7 **South Elmsall** Wakefd
161 H7 **Southend** Ag & B

46 E3 *Southend Airport* Essex
46 E3 **Southend Crematorium** Sthend
46 E3 **Southend-on-Sea** Sthend
36 D5 **Southerndown** V Glam
147 G4 **Southerness** D & G
219 H7 **South Erradale** Highld
12 D4 **Southerton** Devon
90 E5 **Southery** Norfk
45 L3 **South Essex Crematorium** Gt Lon
46 E2 **South Fambridge** Essex
126 B6 **South Ferriby** N Linc
126 C5 **South Field** E R Yk
175 L4 **Southfield** Falk
45 L5 **Southfleet** Kent
44 F2 **Southgate** Gt Lon
51 G7 **Southgate** Swans
15 M1 **South Gorley** Hants
151 G2 **South Gosforth** N u Ty
46 B2 **South Green** Essex
33 L2 **South Green** Kent
92 C2 **South Green** Norfk
177 G4 **South Gyle** C Edin
61 H8 **South Hanningfield** Essex
30 C7 **South Harting** W Susx
17 K3 **South Hayling** Hants
58 E7 **South Heath** Bucks
19 L5 **South Heighton** E Susx
151 J6 **South Hetton** Dur
124 B7 **South Hiendley** Wakefd
5 M2 **South Hill** Cnwll
57 K7 **South Hinksey** Oxon
31 K3 **South Holmwood** Surrey
45 K4 **South Hornchurch** Gt Lon
7 G7 **South Huish** Devon
116 F8 **South Hykeham** Lincs
151 J4 **South Hylton** Sundld
75 H6 **Southill** C Beds
29 J2 **Southington** Hants
117 H2 **South Kelsey** Lincs
213 G5 **South Kessock** Highld
126 E7 **South Killingholme** N Linc
132 F3 **South Kilvington** N York
87 H6 **South Kilworth** Leics
124 C7 **South Kirkby** Wakefd
103 K3 **South Kyme** Lincs
175 J7 **South Lanarkshire Crematorium** S Lans
12 F4 **Southleigh** Devon
57 H6 **South Leigh** Oxon
116 C5 **South Leverton** Notts
71 J5 **South Littleton** Worcs
44 F6 **South London Crematorium** Gt Lon
92 C7 **South Lopham** Norfk
88 D3 **South Luffenham** Rutlnd
19 L4 **South Malling** E Susx
40 D3 **South Marston** Swindn
32 B3 **South Merstham** Surrey
124 D4 **South Milford** N York
7 G7 **South Milton** Devon
59 L7 **South Mimms** Herts
59 L7 *South Mimms Services* Herts
62 A7 **Southminster** Essex
23 L6 **South Molton** Devon
150 F5 **South Moor** Dur
41 H2 **Southmoor** Oxon
41 K3 **South Moreton** Oxon

196 C5 **Southmuir** Angus
18 B5 **South Mundham** W Susx
125 L4 **South Newbald** E R Yk
57 H2 **South Newington** Oxon
28 C4 **South Newton** Wilts
101 H2 **South Normanton** Derbys
45 G6 **South Norwood** Gt Lon
45 L4 **South Ockendon** Thurr
75 H2 **Southoe** Cambs
78 E2 **Southolt** Suffk
118 E6 **South Ormsby** Lincs
88 F3 **Southorpe** C Pete
132 E3 **South Otterington** N York
14 C4 **Southover** Dorset
117 H3 **South Owersby** Lincs
123 G5 **Southowram** Calder
31 L2 **South Park** Surrey
13 L2 **South Perrott** Dorset
26 B7 **South Petherton** Somset
9 J8 **South Petherwin** Cnwll
91 J3 **South Pickenham** Norfk
6 B4 **South Pill** Cnwll
7 H7 **South Pool** Devon
13 M3 **South Poorton** Dorset
120 D6 **Southport** Sefton
120 E7 **Southport Crematorium** Lancs
176 F3 **South Queensferry** C Edin
103 G4 **South Rauceby** Lincs
105 L7 **South Raynham** Norfk
106 F5 **Southrepps** Norfk
118 E5 **South Reston** Lincs
117 J7 **Southrey** Lincs
234 c7 **South Ronaldsay** Ork
56 D7 **Southrop** Gloucs
30 A3 **Southrope** Hants
90 F2 **South Runcton** Norfk
116 D8 **South Scarle** Notts
17 J3 **Southsea** C Port
191 H7 **South Shian** Ag & B
151 J2 **South Shields** S Tyne
151 J3 **South Shields Crematorium** S Tyne
120 D4 **South Shore** Bpool
140 E2 **Southside** Dur
132 D6 **South Stainley** N York
39 H7 **South Stoke** BaNES
41 L4 **South Stoke** Oxon
18 D4 **South Stoke** W Susx
34 E3 **South Street** Kent
47 J6 **South Street** Kent
176 D7 **South Tarbrax** S Lans
10 F6 **South Tawton** Devon
3 H3 **South Tehidy** Cnwll
118 E6 **South Thoresby** Lincs
93 L3 **Southtown** Norfk
233 c8 **South Uist** W Isls
148 D6 **Southwaite** Cumb
148 D6 *Southwaite Services* Cumb
93 H2 **South Walsham** Norfk
44 F4 **Southwark** Gt Lon
30 B3 **South Warnborough** Hants
31 J6 **Southwater** W Susx
45 L2 **South Weald** Essex
102 B2 **Southwell** Notts
43 J5 **South West Middlesex Crematorium** Gt Lon
42 B2 **South Weston** Oxon
17 J2 **Southwick** Hants

88 E5 **Southwick** Nhants
151 J4 **Southwick** Sundld
19 H5 **Southwick** W Susx
27 J1 **Southwick** Wilts
38 E8 **South Widcombe** BaNES
87 H4 **South Wigston** Leics
34 D6 **South Willesborough** Kent
117 K5 **South Willingham** Lincs
151 K7 **South Wingate** Dur
101 G2 **South Wingfield** Derbys
102 F8 **South Witham** Lincs
93 K7 **Southwold** Suffk
61 J7 **South Woodham Ferrers** Essex
105 G7 **South Wootton** Norfk
39 J7 **South Wraxall** Wilts
10 F6 **South Zeal** Devon
122 F6 **Sowerby** Calder
132 F4 **Sowerby** N York
122 F5 **Sowerby Bridge** Calder
123 G6 **Sowood** Calder
6 D3 **Sowton** Devon
12 C4 **Sowton** Devon
122 F6 **Soyland Town** Calder
76 F6 **Spain's End** Essex
103 L7 **Spalding** Lincs
125 H4 **Spaldington** E R Yk
89 G8 **Spaldwick** Cambs
116 D7 **Spalford** Notts
103 H5 **Spanby** Lincs
106 C8 **Sparham** Norfk
129 G3 **Spark Bridge** Cumb
26 E6 **Sparkford** Somset
85 K6 **Sparkhill** Birm
6 E4 **Sparkwell** Devon
114 C5 **Sparrowpit** Derbys
33 H6 **Sparrows Green** E Susx
29 H5 **Sparsholt** Hants
41 G3 **Sparsholt** Oxon
133 L2 **Spaunton** N York
25 K4 **Spaxton** Somset
201 K8 **Spean Bridge** Highld
28 F6 **Spearywell** Hants
58 D7 **Speen** Bucks
41 J6 **Speen** W Berk
135 J5 **Speeton** N York
112 C5 **Speke** Lpool
32 F5 **Speldhurst** Kent
60 D4 **Spellbrook** Herts
42 B6 **Spencers Wood** Wokham
99 J1 **Spen Green** Ches E
131 L2 **Spennithorne** N York
151 G7 **Spennymoor** Dur
70 F4 **Spetchley** Worcs
15 G3 **Spetisbury** Dorset
93 H7 **Spexhall** Suffk
215 H2 **Spey Bay** Moray
204 C1 **Speybridge** Highld
215 G6 **Speyview** Moray
118 E7 **Spilsby** Lincs
115 J5 **Spinkhill** Derbys
222 F4 **Spinningdale** Highld
115 L3 **Spital Hill** Donc
178 B3 **Spittal** E Loth
231 H5 **Spittal** Highld
179 L7 **Spittal** Nthumb
49 G3 **Spittal** Pembks
195 H7 **Spittalfield** P & K
205 G7 **Spittal of Glenmuick** Abers
195 H3 **Spittal of Glenshee** P & K
167 J5 **Spittal-on-Rule** Border
92 F1 **Spixworth** Norfk
10 E4 **Splatt** Devon
19 L2 **Splayne's Green** E Susx
37 K5 **Splottlands** Cardif

124 B1 **Spofforth** N York
101 H5 **Spondon** C Derb
92 D4 **Spooner Row** Norfk
91 J2 **Sporle** Norfk
178 E4 **Spott** E Loth
178 D7 **Spottiswoode** Border
73 K1 **Spratton** Nhants
30 D3 **Spreakley** Surrey
11 G5 **Spreyton** Devon
6 D5 **Spriddlestone** Devon
117 G5 **Spridlington** Lincs
175 G5 **Springburn** C Glas
148 B2 **Springfield** D & G
61 H6 **Springfield** Essex
186 E5 **Springfield** Fife
154 E7 **Springholm** D & G
163 J2 **Springside** N Ayrs
116 E4 **Springthorpe** Lincs
151 H4 **Springwell** Sundld
112 B4 **Springwood Crematorium** Lpool
126 F4 **Sproatley** E R Yk
113 G7 **Sproston Green** Ches W
115 K2 **Sprotbrough** Donc
78 D5 **Sproughton** Suffk
168 A3 **Sprouston** Border
92 F2 **Sprowston** Norfk
102 D7 **Sproxton** Leics
133 J3 **Sproxton** N York
98 D2 **Spurstow** Ches E
14 A4 **Spyway** Dorset
84 D4 **Stableford** Shrops
114 F4 **Stacey Bank** Sheff
130 F6 **Stackhouse** N York
49 G7 **Stackpole** Pembks
6 D5 **Staddiscombe** C Plym
57 L7 **Stadhampton** Oxon
233 b7 **Stadhlaigearraidh** W Isls
148 F6 **Staffield** Cumb
218 D7 **Staffin** Highld
99 L7 **Stafford** Staffs
99 L7 **Stafford Crematorium** Staffs
99 K6 **Stafford Services (northbound)** Staffs
99 K6 **Stafford Services (southbound)** Staffs
74 E5 **Stagsden** Bed
136 E2 **Stainburn** Cumb
123 K2 **Stainburn** N York
102 E7 **Stainby** Lincs
123 L7 **Staincross** Barns
140 E3 **Staindrop** Dur
43 G6 **Staines** Surrey
124 F7 **Stainforth** Donc
130 F6 **Stainforth** N York
120 D4 **Staining** Lancs
123 G6 **Stainland** Calder
143 J5 **Stainsacre** N York
129 L3 **Stainton** Cumb
138 C2 **Stainton** Cumb
115 K3 **Stainton** Donc
140 D4 **Stainton** Dur
141 L4 **Stainton** Middsb
117 H6 **Stainton by Langworth** Lincs
143 K7 **Staintondale** N York
117 K3 **Stainton le Vale** Lincs
128 F5 **Stainton with Adgarley** Cumb
163 K5 **Stair** E Ayrs
144 E4 **Stairhaven** D & G
143 G4 **Staithes** N York
159 G5 **Stakeford** Nthumb
17 K2 **Stakes** Hants
27 G7 **Stalbridge** Dorset
27 G7 **Stalbridge Weston** Dorset
107 H7 **Stalham** Norfk
34 C4 **Stalisfield Green** Kent
26 E7 **Stallen** Dorset
126 F7 **Stallingborough** NE Lin
120 E2 **Stalmine** Lancs

113 L2 **Stalybridge** Tamesd
77 G6 **Stambourne** Essex
77 G6 **Stambourne Green** Essex
88 E3 **Stamford** Lincs
169 J5 **Stamford** Nthumb
112 C7 **Stamford Bridge** Ches W
133 L7 **Stamford Bridge** E R Yk
158 D7 **Stamfordham** Nthumb
45 G3 **Stamford Hill** Gt Lon
58 F3 **Stanbridge** C Beds
122 F3 **Stanbury** C Brad
175 K5 **Stand** N Lans
176 C4 **Standburn** Falk
85 G3 **Standeford** Staffs
33 L5 **Standen** Kent
27 J2 **Standerwick** Somset
30 D4 **Standford** Hants
147 J7 **Standingstone** Cumb
121 H7 **Standish** Wigan
57 H7 **Standlake** Oxon
29 H6 **Standon** Hants
60 C4 **Standon** Herts
99 J5 **Standon** Staffs
176 B6 **Stane** N Lans
105 M7 **Stanfield** Norfk
75 H6 **Stanford** C Beds
34 F6 **Stanford** Kent
70 C4 **Stanford Bishop** Herefs
70 C2 **Stanford Bridge** Worcs
41 L6 **Stanford Dingley** W Berk
41 G2 **Stanford in the Vale** Oxon
46 B4 **Stanford le Hope** Thurr
87 H7 **Stanford on Avon** Nhants
101 K7 **Stanford on Soar** Notts
70 C2 **Stanford on Teme** Worcs
115 J6 **Stanfree** Derbys
142 E4 **Stanghow** R & Cl
89 H4 **Stanground** C Pete
105 J5 **Stanhoe** Norfk
165 L4 **Stanhope** Border
150 C6 **Stanhope** Dur
34 D6 **Stanhope** Kent
88 D6 **Stanion** Nhants
101 H4 **Stanley** Derbys
150 F4 **Stanley** Dur
186 B2 **Stanley** P & K
99 L3 **Stanley** Staffs
150 E7 **Stanley Crook** Dur
55 M3 **Stanley Pontlarge** Gloucs
19 K4 **Stanmer** Br & H
44 D2 **Stanmore** Gt Lon
29 J5 **Stanmore** Hants
157 J5 **Stannersburn** Nthumb
77 K3 **Stanningfield** Suffk
158 F6 **Stannington** Nthumb
114 F4 **Stannington** Sheff
158 F5 **Stannington Station** Nthumb
69 G3 **Stansbatch** Herefs
77 H4 **Stansfield** Suffk
77 J5 **Stanstead** Suffk
60 C5 **Stanstead Abbotts** Herts
77 J5 **Stanstead Street** Suffk
45 L7 **Stansted** Kent
60 E4 **Stansted Airport** Essex
60 E3 **Stansted Mountfitchet** Essex
71 J7 **Stanton** Gloucs
158 E4 **Stanton** Nthumb

100 C4 **Stanton** Staffs
91 L8 **Stanton** Suffk
101 G6 **Stanton by Bridge** Derbys
101 J5 **Stanton by Dale** Derbys
38 E7 **Stanton Drew** BaNES
40 D3 **Stanton Fitzwarren** Swindn
57 H6 **Stanton Harcourt** Oxon
114 E8 **Stanton in Peak** Derbys
83 K7 **Stanton Lacy** Shrops
114 E8 **Stanton Lees** Derbys
83 L5 **Stanton Long** Shrops
101 M6 **Stanton on the Wolds** Notts
39 G7 **Stanton Prior** BaNES
40 C7 **Stanton St Bernard** Wilts
57 L6 **Stanton St John** Oxon
39 K4 **Stanton St Quintin** Wilts
77 L2 **Stanton Street** Suffk
86 F2 **Stanton under Bardon** Leics
98 E7 **Stanton upon Hine Heath** Shrops
38 E7 **Stanton Wick** BaNES
61 M3 **Stanway** Essex
56 B2 **Stanway** Gloucs
43 H5 **Stanwell** Surrey
74 E1 **Stanwick** Nhants
148 D4 **Stanwix** Cumb
233 b8 **Staoinebrig** W Isls
143 G7 **Stape** N York
99 G3 **Stapeley** Ches E
100 E7 **Stapenhill** Staffs
35 H4 **Staple** Kent
25 C7 **Staple Cross** Devon
20 F2 **Staple Cross** E Susx
32 B7 **Staplefield** W Susx
25 K7 **Staple Fitzpaine** Somset
76 C4 **Stapleford** Cambs
60 A5 **Stapleford** Herts
102 D8 **Stapleford** Leics
102 E2 **Stapleford** Lincs
101 J5 **Stapleford** Notts
28 B4 **Stapleford** Wilts
45 K2 **Stapleford Abbotts** Essex
25 K6 **Staplegrove** Somset
25 K6 **Staplehay** Somset
33 K5 **Staplehurst** Kent
34 E3 **Staplestreet** Kent
69 G2 **Stapleton** Herefs
86 E4 **Stapleton** Leics
141 G5 **Stapleton** N York
83 J3 **Stapleton** Shrops
26 C7 **Stapleton** Somset
25 J8 **Stapley** Somset
75 G3 **Staploe** Bed
70 C6 **Staplow** Herefs
186 E6 **Star** Fife
65 H7 **Star** Pembks
38 C8 **Star** Somset
132 E7 **Starbeck** N York
131 H5 **Starbotton** N York
12 C6 **Starcross** Devon
72 D1 **Stareton** Warwks
60 D2 **Starlings Green** Essex
92 F6 **Starston** Norfk
140 D4 **Startforth** Dur
39 L4 **Startley** Wilts
35 J4 **Statenborough** Kent
26 A5 **Stathe** Somset
102 C6 **Stathern** Leics
75 G2 **Staughton Green** Cambs
54 D5 **Staunton** Gloucs
55 H3 **Staunton** Gloucs
69 G3 **Staunton on Arrow** Herefs

69 G5 **Staunton on Wye** Herefs
129 H3 **Staveley** Cumb
138 C7 **Staveley** Cumb
115 H6 **Staveley** Derbys
132 E6 **Staveley** N York
7 J3 **Staverton** Devon
55 K4 **Staverton** Gloucs
73 G3 **Staverton** Nhants
39 J7 **Staverton** Wilts
26 A4 **Stawell** Somset
25 G6 **Stawley** Somset
231 L5 **Staxigoe** Highld
134 F4 **Staxton** N York
120 E2 **Staynall** Lancs
131 K5 **Stean** N York
133 J5 **Stearsby** N York
25 L3 **Steart** Somset
61 G3 **Stebbing** Essex
61 H4 **Stebbing Green** Essex
30 E6 **Stedham** W Susx
185 L8 **Steelend** Fife
156 F4 **Steele Road** Border
69 K3 **Steen's Bridge** Herefs
30 C6 **Steep** Hants
122 F5 **Steep Lane** Calder
61 M7 **Steeple** Essex
27 K1 **Steeple Ashton** Wilts
57 J3 **Steeple Aston** Oxon
76 F6 **Steeple Bumpstead** Essex
58 B3 **Steeple Claydon** Bucks
89 G7 **Steeple Gidding** Cambs
28 B4 **Steeple Langford** Wilts
75 K6 **Steeple Morden** Cambs
122 F2 **Steeton** C Brad
208 D3 **Stein** Highld
34 F5 **Stelling Minnis** Kent
26 B7 **Stembridge** Somset
4 F4 **Stenalees** Cnwll
154 D4 **Stenhouse** D & G
176 B2 **Stenhousemuir** Falk
218 D7 **Stenscholl** Highld
101 G6 **Stenson Fields** Derbys
178 D4 **Stenton** E Loth
232 f2 **Steornabhagh** W Isls
49 K6 **Stepaside** Pembks
45 G4 **Stepney** Gt Lon
74 E7 **Steppingley** C Beds
175 H5 **Stepps** N Lans
79 H3 **Sternfield** Suffk
40 B8 **Stert** Wilts
76 F3 **Stetchworth** Cambs
59 L3 **Stevenage** Herts
163 H2 **Stevenston** N Ayrs
29 K2 **Steventon** Hants
41 J3 **Steventon** Oxon
76 E6 **Steventon End** Essex
74 E4 **Stevington** Bed
74 E6 **Stewartby** Bed
175 H7 **Stewartfield** S Lans
163 K1 **Stewarton** E Ayrs
58 D3 **Stewkley** Bucks
25 L7 **Stewley** Somset
19 G4 **Steyning** W Susx
48 F6 **Steynton** Pembks
9 G3 **Stibb** Cnwll
106 B6 **Stibbard** Norfk
10 C2 **Stibb Cross** Devon
40 E7 **Stibb Green** Wilts
88 F4 **Stibbington** Cambs
167 L2 **Stichill** Border
4 F5 **Sticker** Cnwll
104 B1 **Stickford** Lincs
10 F6 **Sticklepath** Devon
104 B2 **Stickney** Lincs
106 A4 **Stiffkey** Norfk
233 b7 **Stilligarry** W Isls
124 F3 **Stillingfleet** N York
133 J6 **Stillington** N York
141 J3 **Stillington** S on T

89 H5 **Stilton** Cambs
55 G7 **Stinchcombe** Gloucs
14 D4 **Stinsford** Dorset
83 G4 **Stiperstones** Shrops
84 C3 **Stirchley** Wrekin
217 L6 **Stirling** Abers
185 G8 **Stirling** Stirlg
175 L2 **Stirling Services** Stirlg
75 H2 **Stirtloe** Cambs
131 H8 **Stirton** N York
61 J3 **Stisted** Essex
3 J4 **Stithians** Cnwll
86 D7 **Stivichall** Covtry
117 K7 **Stixwould** Lincs
112 B6 **Stoak** Ches W
166 B2 **Stobo** Border
15 H5 **Stoborough** Dorset
167 G7 **Stobs Castle** Border
158 F3 **Stobswood** Nthumb
61 H7 **Stock** Essex
38 C7 **Stock** N Som
29 G4 **Stockbridge** Hants
164 F3 **Stockbriggs** S Lans
46 D7 **Stockbury** Kent
41 H6 **Stockcross** W Berk
88 B4 **Stockerston** Leics
71 H3 **Stock Green** Worcs
54 F2 **Stocking** Herefs
86 D5 **Stockingford** Warwks
60 D3 **Stocking Pelham** Herts
13 G2 **Stockland** Devon
25 K3 **Stockland Bristol** Somset
11 K4 **Stockleigh English** Devon
11 K4 **Stockleigh Pomeroy** Devon
39 M6 **Stockley** Wilts
26 B7 **Stocklinch** Somset
113 K4 **Stockport** Stockp
113 K4 **Stockport Crematorium** Stockp
114 E2 **Stocksbridge** Sheff
150 D3 **Stocksfield** Nthumb
69 K3 **Stockton** Herefs
93 H5 **Stockton** Norfk
84 C4 **Stockton** Shrops
72 E2 **Stockton** Warwks
27 M4 **Stockton** Wilts
84 D1 **Stockton** Wrekin
112 E4 **Stockton Heath** Warrtn
141 K4 **Stockton-on-Tees** S on T
70 C2 **Stockton on Teme** Worcs
133 K7 **Stockton on the Forest** C York
38 F6 **Stockwood** Bristl
14 B2 **Stockwood** Dorset
71 H3 **Stock Wood** Worcs
35 G3 **Stodmarsh** Kent
106 C5 **Stody** Norfk
224 C3 **Stoer** Highld
26 E8 **Stoford** Somset
28 B4 **Stoford** Wilts
25 H4 **Stogumber** Somset
25 J3 **Stogursey** Somset
86 D7 **Stoke** Covtry
22 C6 **Stoke** Devon
17 K3 **Stoke** Hants
29 H2 **Stoke** Hants
46 D5 **Stoke** Medway
13 L3 **Stoke Abbott** Dorset
88 B5 **Stoke Albany** Nhants
78 D1 **Stoke Ash** Suffk
101 M4 **Stoke Bardolph** Notts
70 B2 **Stoke Bliss** Worcs
73 L4 **Stoke Bruerne** Nhants
77 G5 **Stoke by Clare** Suffk
78 B7 **Stoke-by-Nayland** Suffk
12 B3 **Stoke Canon** Devon
29 J4 **Stoke Charity** Hants

6 A2 **Stoke Climsland** Cnwll
70 B4 **Stoke Cross** Herefs
43 J8 **Stoke D'Abernon** Surrey
88 E6 **Stoke Doyle** Nhants
88 C4 **Stoke Dry** Rutlnd
69 L6 **Stoke Edith** Herefs
28 B6 **Stoke Farthing** Wilts
91 G4 **Stoke Ferry** Norfk
7 K6 **Stoke Fleming** Devon
15 G5 **Stokeford** Dorset
7 J4 **Stoke Gabriel** Devon
38 F4 **Stoke Gifford** S Glos
86 E4 **Stoke Golding** Leics
74 B5 **Stoke Goldington** M Keyn
116 C6 **Stokeham** Notts
58 E3 **Stoke Hammond** Bucks
92 F3 **Stoke Holy Cross** Norfk
7 L2 **Stokeinteignhead** Devon
70 B5 **Stoke Lacy** Herefs
57 K3 **Stoke Lyne** Oxon
58 D6 **Stoke Mandeville** Bucks
42 C2 **Stokenchurch** Bucks
45 G3 **Stoke Newington** Gt Lon
7 J7 **Stokenham** Devon
99 K3 **Stoke-on-Trent** C Stke
55 K3 **Stoke Orchard** Gloucs
42 F4 **Stoke Poges** Bucks
69 K3 **Stoke Prior** Herefs
71 G2 **Stoke Prior** Worcs
23 K4 **Stoke Rivers** Devon
102 F6 **Stoke Rochford** Lincs
42 B4 **Stoke Row** Oxon
25 M6 **Stoke St Gregory** Somset
25 K6 **Stoke St Mary** Somset
26 F3 **Stoke St Michael** Somset
83 L6 **Stoke St Milborough** Shrops
83 H6 **Stokesay Castle** Shrops
93 J2 **Stokesby** Norfk
142 B5 **Stokesley** N York
26 C7 **Stoke sub Hamdon** Somset
58 B7 **Stoke Talmage** Oxon
27 H5 **Stoke Trister** Somset
98 F6 **Stoke upon Tern** Shrops
99 K4 **Stoke-upon-Trent** C Stke
14 E2 **Stoke Wake** Dorset
25 K3 **Stolford** Somset
60 F7 **Stondon Massey** Essex
58 C5 **Stone** Bucks
39 G2 **Stone** Gloucs
21 J1 **Stone** Kent
115 K4 **Stone** Rothm
99 K5 **Stone** Staffs
84 F7 **Stone** Worcs
26 B2 **Stone Allerton** Somset
26 F2 **Ston Easton** Somset
38 B7 **Stonebridge** N Som
86 B6 **Stonebridge** Warwks
101 H2 **Stonebroom** Derbys
35 J4 **Stone Cross** Kent
33 J6 **Stonecrouch** Kent
126 D4 **Stoneferry** C KuH
172 E4 **Stonefield Castle Hotel** Ag & B
33 H7 **Stonegate** E Susx
133 K4 **Stonegrave** N York
207 G7 **Stonehaven** Abers
28 C3 **Stonehenge** Wilts
6 C5 **Stonehouse** C Plym

55 J6 **Stonehouse** Gloucs
175 K8 **Stonehouse** S Lans
86 D8 **Stoneleigh** Warwks
102 D7 **Stonesby** Leics
57 H4 **Stonesfield** Oxon
62 E3 **Stones Green** Essex
33 G3 **Stone Street** Kent
93 H6 **Stone Street** Suffk
215 G2 **Stonewells** Moray
233 b8 **Stoneybridge** W Isls
176 D5 **Stoneyburn** W Loth
87 H3 **Stoneygate** C Leic
144 C4 **Stoneykirk** D & G
114 E6 **Stoney Middleton** Derbys
86 F4 **Stoney Stanton** Leics
27 G5 **Stoney Stoke** Somset
26 F4 **Stoney Stratton** Somset
83 H2 **Stoney Stretton** Shrops
207 G3 **Stoneywood** C Aber
175 L2 **Stoneywood** Falk
78 D3 **Stonham Aspal** Suffk
85 J3 **Stonnall** Staffs
42 B3 **Stonor** Oxon
87 K4 **Stonton Wyville** Leics
115 J7 **Stony Houghton** Derbys
73 L6 **Stony Stratford** M Keyn
23 K5 **Stoodleigh** Devon
24 E7 **Stoodleigh** Devon
34 F7 **Stop 24 Services** Kent
18 D2 **Stopham** W Susx
59 J3 **Stopsley** Luton
232 f2 **Stornoway** W Isls
232 g2 **Stornoway Airport** W Isls
18 E3 **Storrington** W Susx
125 H2 **Storwood** E R Yk
214 F1 **Stotfield** Moray
75 J7 **Stotfold** C Beds
84 C6 **Stottesdon** Shrops
87 J3 **Stoughton** Leics
31 G2 **Stoughton** Surrey
17 L1 **Stoughton** W Susx
70 F4 **Stoulton** Worcs
84 F6 **Stourbridge** Dudley
84 F6 **Stourbridge Crematorium** Dudley
15 G1 **Stourpaine** Dorset
70 E1 **Stourport-on-Severn** Worcs
27 H6 **Stour Provost** Dorset
27 J7 **Stour Row** Dorset
84 F6 **Stourton** Staffs
72 C6 **Stourton** Warwks
27 H5 **Stourton** Wilts
27 G7 **Stourton Caundle** Dorset
235 c7 **Stove** Shet
93 J6 **Stoven** Suffk
167 G1 **Stow** Border
116 E5 **Stow** Lincs
90 F3 **Stow Bardolph** Norfk
91 L4 **Stow Bedon** Norfk
90 E3 **Stowbridge** Norfk
76 D3 **Stow-cum-Quy** Cambs
82 F8 **Stowe** Shrops
100 A6 **Stowe by Chartley** Staffs
27 G6 **Stowell** Somset
38 E7 **Stowey** BaNES
10 C5 **Stowford** Devon
10 C7 **Stowford** Devon
77 L2 **Stowlangtoft** Suffk
75 G1 **Stow Longa** Cambs
61 K7 **Stow Maries** Essex
78 C3 **Stowmarket** Suffk
56 D3 **Stow-on-the-Wold** Gloucs
34 F6 **Stowting** Kent
34 F6 **Stowting Common** Kent

78 C3 **Stowupland** Suffk
204 B3 **Straanruie** Highld
197 G4 **Stracathro Hospital** Angus
206 D6 **Strachan** Abers
182 F6 **Strachur** Ag & B
92 F8 **Stradbroke** Suffk
77 H4 **Stradishall** Suffk
90 F3 **Stradsett** Norfk
102 E3 **Stragglethorpe** Lincs
177 H5 **Straiton** Mdloth
153 H2 **Straiton** S Ayrs
207 G2 **Straloch** Abers
195 G4 **Straloch** P & K
100 B5 **Stramshall** Staffs
237 C5 **Strang** IoM
113 J2 **Strangeways** Salfd
54 E3 **Strangford** Herefs
144 C3 **Stranraer** D & G
42 A7 **Stratfield Mortimer** W Berk
42 B7 **Stratfield Saye** Hants
42 B7 **Stratfield Turgis** Hants
45 H3 **Stratford** Gt Lon
79 H3 **Stratford St Andrew** Suffk
78 C7 **Stratford St Mary** Suffk
28 C6 **Stratford Tony** Wilts
72 B4 **Stratford-upon-Avon** Warwks
219 J5 **Strath** Highld
224 D4 **Strathan** Highld
229 J3 **Strathan** Highld
164 D1 **Strathaven** S Lans
175 G3 **Strathblane** Stirlg
220 F2 **Strathcanaird** Highld
210 E6 **Strathcarron** Highld
181 K2 **Strathcoil** Ag & B
205 H3 **Strathdon** Abers
187 G4 **Strathkinness** Fife
176 C4 **Strathloanhead** W Loth
202 F6 **Strathmashie House** Highld
186 C5 **Strathmiglo** Fife
212 D3 **Strathpeffer** Highld
194 E5 **Strathtay** P & K
162 D3 **Strathwhillan** N Ayrs
230 B3 **Strathy** Highld
230 B3 **Strathy Inn** Highld
184 C4 **Strathyre** Stirlg
9 G4 **Stratton** Cnwll
14 C4 **Stratton** Dorset
56 A7 **Stratton** Gloucs
57 L3 **Stratton Audley** Oxon
26 F2 **Stratton-on-the-Fosse** Somset
40 D3 **Stratton St Margaret** Swindn
92 E5 **Stratton St Michael** Norfk
106 F7 **Stratton Strawless** Norfk
187 J5 **Stravithie** Fife
19 K3 **Streat** E Susx
44 F5 **Streatham** Gt Lon
59 H3 **Streatley** C Beds
41 L4 **Streatley** W Berk
12 F5 **Street** Devon
26 C4 **Street** Somset
86 F6 **Street Ashton** Warwks
97 M5 **Street Dinas** Shrops
34 F4 **Street End** Kent
18 A5 **Street End** W Susx
85 K2 **Streethay** Staffs
141 H7 **Streetlam** N York
85 J4 **Streetly Crematorium** Wsall
76 E5 **Streetly End** Cambs
26 F4 **Street on the Fosse** Somset
186 C1 **Strelitz** P & K
101 K4 **Strelley** Notts

133 K7 **Strensall** C York
70 F6 **Strensham Services (northbound)** Worcs
70 F6 **Strensham Services (southbound)** Worcs
25 L3 **Stretcholt** Somset
7 J6 **Strete** Devon
113 H3 **Stretford** Traffd
76 C6 **Strethall** Essex
90 D8 **Stretham** Cambs
18 B4 **Strettington** W Susx
101 H1 **Stretton** Derbys
88 D1 **Stretton** Rutlnd
84 F2 **Stretton** Staffs
100 E7 **Stretton** Staffs
112 F5 **Stretton** Warrtn
70 B5 **Stretton Grandison** Herefs
86 E8 **Stretton-on-Dunsmore** Warwks
72 B6 **Stretton on Fosse** Warwks
69 J6 **Stretton Sugwas** Herefs
86 F7 **Stretton under Fosse** Warwks
83 L4 **Stretton Westwood** Shrops
217 H4 **Strichen** Abers
25 J3 **Stringston** Somset
74 C3 **Strixton** Nhants
38 E2 **Stroat** Gloucs
231 L1 **Stroma** Highld
210 D7 **Stromeferry** Highld
234 D6 **Stromness** Ork
183 L5 **Stronachlachar** Stirlg
173 H3 **Stronafian** Ag & B
224 F5 **Stronchrubie** Highld
173 L3 **Strone** Ag & B
192 B1 **Strone** Highld
201 J8 **Stronenaba** Highld
183 G2 **Stronmilchan** Ag & B
234 d5 **Stronsay** Ork
234 d5 *Stronsay Airport* Ork
191 G4 **Strontian** Highld
46 B6 **Strood** Medway
55 J6 **Stroud** Gloucs
30 B6 **Stroud** Hants
55 J6 **Stroud Green** Gloucs
102 E6 **Stroxton** Lincs
208 E6 **Struan** Highld
194 C4 **Struan** P & K
93 H3 **Strumpshaw** Norfk
175 K7 **Strutherhill** S Lans
186 F5 **Struthers** Fife
212 B6 **Struy** Highld
217 H5 **Stuartfield** Abers
17 G2 **Stubbington** Hants
122 B6 **Stubbins** Lancs
102 E3 **Stubton** Lincs
28 D8 **Stuckton** Hants
59 G5 **Studham** C Beds
148 A4 **Studholme** Cumb
15 J6 **Studland** Dorset
71 J2 **Studley** Warwks
39 L6 **Studley** Wilts
132 D5 **Studley Roger** N York
132 D5 **Studley Royal** N York
90 D7 **Stuntney** Cambs
77 G5 **Sturmer** Essex
27 H8 **Sturminster Common** Dorset
15 H3 **Sturminster Marshall** Dorset
27 H8 **Sturminster Newton** Dorset
35 G3 **Sturry** Kent
116 F2 **Sturton** N Linc
116 E5 **Sturton by Stow** Lincs
116 C5 **Sturton le Steeple** Notts
92 D7 **Stuston** Suffk
124 D3 **Stutton** N York
78 D7 **Stutton** Suffk
113 J5 **Styal** Ches E

215 H3 **Stynie** Moray
115 L4 **Styrrup** Notts
183 K6 **Succoth** Ag & B
70 C4 **Suckley** Worcs
88 D6 **Sudborough** Nhants
79 J4 **Sudbourne** Suffk
102 F4 **Sudbrook** Lincs
38 D3 **Sudbrook** Mons
117 G6 **Sudbrooke** Lincs
100 D6 **Sudbury** Derbys
44 D3 **Sudbury** Gt Lon
77 K6 **Sudbury** Suffk
70 F2 **Suddington** Worcs
134 F2 **Suffield** N York
106 F6 **Suffield** Norfk
99 H6 **Sugnall** Staffs
69 J6 **Sugwas Pool** Herefs
199 J3 **Suisnish** Highld
237 d3 **Sulby** IoM
73 G5 **Sulgrave** Nhants
73 H5 **Sulgrave Manor** Nhants
41 M5 **Sulham** W Berk
41 M6 **Sulhamstead** W Berk
235 C4 **Sullom** Shet
235 C4 **Sullom Voe** Shet
37 J6 **Sully** V Glam
235 c8 *Sumburgh Airport* Shet
132 C6 **Summerbridge** N York
4 D5 **Summercourt** Cnwll
105 J5 **Summerfield** Norfk
49 K6 **Summerhill** Pembks
140 F4 **Summerhouse** Darltn
18 B4 **Summersdale** W Susx
122 B7 **Summerseat** Bury
57 K6 **Summertown** Oxon
43 J6 **Sunbury** Surrey
154 E5 **Sundaywell** D & G
170 E5 **Sunderland** Ag & B
147 L1 **Sunderland** Cumb
129 J7 **Sunderland** Lancs
151 J4 **Sunderland** Sundld
151 G7 **Sunderland Bridge** Dur
151 J4 **Sunderland Crematorium** Sundld
166 E4 **Sundhope** Border
59 H3 **Sundon Park** Luton
32 E3 **Sundridge** Kent
42 F4 **Sunningdale** W & M
42 F6 **Sunninghill** W & M
57 J7 **Sunningwell** Oxon
150 E7 **Sunniside** Dur
150 F3 **Sunniside** Gatesd
101 K4 **Sunnyhill** C Derb
121 K6 **Sunnyhurst** Bl w D
185 G7 **Sunnylaw** Stirlg
57 J6 **Sunnymead** Oxon
44 D6 **Surbiton** Gt Lon
103 L6 **Surfleet** Lincs
93 G3 **Surlingham** Norfk
61 L4 **Surrex** Essex
32 B5 **Surrey & Sussex Crematorium** W Susx
106 E5 **Sustead** Norfk
116 D2 **Susworth** Lincs
9 J3 **Sutcombe** Devon
9 J3 **Sutcombemill** Devon
118 E6 **Sutterby** Lincs
103 M5 **Sutterton** Lincs
75 J5 **Sutton** C Beds
89 G4 **Sutton** C Pete
90 C7 **Sutton** Cambs
7 G7 **Sutton** Devon
20 A5 **Sutton** E Susx
44 E7 **Sutton** Gt Lon
35 J5 **Sutton** Kent
124 D5 **Sutton** N York
107 H7 **Sutton** Norfk
102 C5 **Sutton** Notts
84 D6 **Sutton** Shrops
99 H7 **Sutton** Staffs
79 G5 **Sutton** Suffk
18 D3 **Sutton** W Susx

45 K6 **Sutton at Hone** Kent
87 L5 **Sutton Bassett** Nhants
39 L5 **Sutton Benger** Wilts
101 K7 **Sutton Bonington** Notts
104 D7 **Sutton Bridge** Lincs
86 E4 **Sutton Cheney** Leics
85 K4 **Sutton Coldfield** Birm
85 K4 **Sutton Coldfield Crematorium** Birm
41 J2 **Sutton Courtenay** Oxon
116 B5 **Sutton cum Lound** Notts
31 G1 **Sutton Green** Surrey
132 D4 **Sutton Howgrave** N York
101 J2 **Sutton in Ashfield** Notts
122 F2 **Sutton-in-Craven** N York
84 C3 **Sutton Maddock** Shrops
26 A4 **Sutton Mallet** Somset
27 M5 **Sutton Mandeville** Wilts
26 F6 **Sutton Montis** Somset
126 E4 **Sutton-on-Hull** C KuH
119 G5 **Sutton on Sea** Lincs
133 J6 **Sutton-on-the-Forest** N York
100 E5 **Sutton on the Hill** Derbys
116 D7 **Sutton on Trent** Notts
89 L2 **Sutton St Edmund** Lincs
104 C8 **Sutton St James** Lincs
69 K5 **Sutton St Nicholas** Herefs
29 J4 **Sutton Scotney** Hants
29 J4 **Sutton Scotney Services** Hants
72 C6 **Sutton-under-Brailes** Warwks
133 G3 **Sutton-under-Whitestonecliffe** N York
125 G2 **Sutton upon Derwent** E R Yk
33 L4 **Sutton Valence** Kent
27 K3 **Sutton Veny** Wilts
27 K7 **Sutton Waldron** Dorset
112 D5 **Sutton Weaver** Ches W
38 E8 **Sutton Wick** BaNES
41 J2 **Sutton Wick** Oxon
118 E6 **Swaby** Lincs
100 F8 **Swadlincote** Derbys
91 J2 **Swaffham** Norfk
76 D3 **Swaffham Bulbeck** Cambs
76 E2 **Swaffham Prior** Cambs
107 G6 **Swafield** Norfk
141 L6 **Swainby** N York
92 F4 **Swainsthorpe** Norfk
39 H6 **Swainswick** BaNES
72 E6 **Swalcliffe** Oxon
47 J6 **Swalecliffe** Kent
117 K2 **Swallow** Lincs
116 F7 **Swallow Beck** Lincs
27 L6 **Swallowcliffe** Wilts
42 B7 **Swallowfield** Wokham
15 J6 **Swanage** Dorset
58 D3 **Swanbourne** Bucks
113 G6 **Swan Green** Ches W
126 B5 **Swanland** E R Yk
45 K6 **Swanley** Kent
45 K6 **Swanley Village** Kent
29 L7 **Swanmore** Hants
86 E1 **Swannington** Leics

106 D8 **Swannington** Norfk
116 F7 **Swanpool Garden Suburb** Lincs
45 L5 **Swanscombe** Kent
51 J6 **Swansea** Swans
51 H7 *Swansea Airport* Swans
51 J5 **Swansea Crematorium** Swans
51 J5 *Swansea West Services* Swans
106 F7 **Swanton Abbot** Norfk
92 B1 **Swanton Morley** Norfk
106 B6 **Swanton Novers** Norfk
101 H2 **Swanwick** Derbys
17 G1 **Swanwick** Hants
103 H4 **Swarby** Lincs
92 E3 **Swardeston** Norfk
101 G6 **Swarkestone** Derbys
158 E2 **Swarland** Nthumb
29 K4 **Swarraton** Hants
129 G4 **Swarthmoor** Cumb
103 J5 **Swaton** Lincs
75 L2 **Swavesey** Cambs
16 C3 **Sway** Hants
103 G7 **Swayfield** Lincs
29 H7 **Swaythling** C Sotn
11 K5 **Sweetham** Devon
32 E7 **Sweethaws** E Susx
8 F5 **Sweets** Cnwll
5 H4 **Sweetshouse** Cnwll
79 H2 **Swefling** Suffk
86 D2 **Swepstone** Leics
57 G2 **Swerford** Oxon
113 J7 **Swettenham** Ches E
78 E4 **Swilland** Suffk
124 B4 **Swillington** Leeds
23 K5 **Swimbridge** Devon
23 J5 **Swimbridge Newland** Devon
56 F5 **Swinbrook** Oxon
132 C7 **Swincliffe** N York
116 E8 **Swinderby** Lincs
55 L3 **Swindon** Gloucs
84 F5 **Swindon** Staffs
40 D4 **Swindon** Swindn
126 E4 **Swine** E R Yk
125 H6 **Swinefleet** E R Yk
74 F2 **Swineshead** Bed
103 L4 **Swineshead** Lincs
227 M2 **Swiney** Highld
87 H7 **Swinford** Leics
35 G6 **Swingfield Minnis** Kent
35 H6 **Swingfield Street** Kent
77 L5 **Swingleton Green** Suffk
169 J4 **Swinhoe** Nthumb
131 K2 **Swinithwaite** N York
100 C3 **Swinscoe** Staffs
137 H3 **Swinside** Cumb
103 G7 **Swinstead** Lincs
179 H8 **Swinton** Border
132 C4 **Swinton** N York
134 B5 **Swinton** N York
115 J2 **Swinton** Rothm
113 H2 **Swinton** Salfd
87 G2 **Swithland** Leics
212 E2 **Swordale** Highld
200 B6 **Swordland** Highld
229 M3 **Swordly** Highld
99 J5 **Swynnerton** Staffs
13 M5 **Swyre** Dorset
81 L3 **Sychtyn** Powys
55 L5 **Syde** Gloucs
45 G5 **Sydenham** Gt Lon
58 B7 **Sydenham** Oxon
6 B2 **Sydenham Damerel** Devon
105 K6 **Syderstone** Norfk
14 C3 **Sydling St Nicholas** Dorset

41 J8 **Sydmonton** Hants
102 C3 **Syerston** Notts
95 K3 **Sygun Copper Mine** Gwynd
124 F6 **Sykehouse** Donc
235 d4 **Symbister** Shet
163 J3 **Symington** S Ayrs
165 J3 **Symington** S Lans
13 K4 **Symondsbury** Dorset
54 E5 **Symonds Yat** Herefs
229 L6 **Syre** Highld
56 B4 **Syreford** Gloucs
73 J6 **Syresham** Nhants
87 J2 **Syston** Leics
102 F4 **Syston** Lincs
70 E2 **Sytchampton** Worcs
74 B2 **Sywell** Nhants

T

57 J4 **Tackley** Oxon
92 D4 **Tacolneston** Norfk
124 D2 **Tadcaster** N York
114 C7 **Taddington** Derbys
56 C2 **Taddington** Gloucs
41 L7 **Tadley** Hants
75 K5 **Tadlow** Cambs
72 E6 **Tadmarton** Oxon
44 E8 **Tadworth** Surrey
37 H4 **Taff's Well** Rhondd
36 B3 **Taibach** Neath
223 G5 **Tain** Highld
231 J3 **Tain** Highld
232 e4 **Tairbeart** W Isls
60 F4 **Takeley** Essex
60 E4 **Takeley Street** Essex
12 D3 **Talaton** Devon
48 E5 **Talbenny** Pembks
12 E3 **Taleford** Devon
81 K4 **Talerddig** Powys
65 L4 **Talgarreg** Cerdgn
68 D7 **Talgarth** Powys
208 E7 **Talisker** Highld
99 J2 **Talke** Staffs
148 F4 **Talkin** Cumb
219 L7 **Talladale** Highld
165 M5 **Talla Linnfoots** Border
153 J3 **Tallaminnock** S Ayrs
98 C4 **Tallarn Green** Wrexhm
147 K2 **Tallentire** Cumb
66 E7 **Talley** Carmth
88 F2 **Tallington** Lincs
229 J3 **Talmine** Highld
50 D1 **Talog** Carmth
66 D4 **Talsarn** Cerdgn
95 K5 **Talsarnau** Gwynd
4 E3 **Talskiddy** Cnwll
109 G6 **Talwrn** IoA
80 E5 **Tal-y-bont** Cerdgn
109 L7 **Tal-y-Bont** Conwy
95 K7 **Tal-y-bont** Gwynd
109 J7 **Tal-y-bont** Gwynd
53 H4 **Talybont-on-Usk** Powys
109 M7 **Tal-y-Cafn** Conwy
54 B5 **Tal-y-coed** Mons
95 H2 **Talysarn** Gwynd
6 C4 **Tamerton Foliot** C Plym
86 B3 **Tamworth** Staffs
86 B4 *Tamworth Services* Warwks
32 C3 **Tandridge** Surrey
150 F4 **Tanfield** Dur
150 F4 **Tanfield Lea** Dur
28 F2 **Tangley** Hants
18 B4 **Tangmere** W Susx
233 b9 **Tangusdale** W Isls
234 c6 **Tankerness** Ork
115 G2 **Tankersley** Barns
47 J6 **Tankerton** Kent
231 K6 **Tannach** Highld
206 E8 **Tannachie** Abers

196 D5 **Tannadice** Angus
85 J8 **Tanner's Green** Worcs
78 F2 **Tannington** Suffk
175 J6 **Tannochside** N Lans
100 F1 **Tansley** Derbys
88 F5 **Tansor** Nhants
150 F4 **Tantobie** Dur
142 B5 **Tanton** N York
71 K1 **Tanworth in Arden** Warwks
65 J5 **Tan-y-groes** Cerdgn
232 d5 **Taobh Tuath** W Isls
42 E4 **Taplow** Bucks
172 B7 **Tarbert** Ag & B
172 E5 **Tarbert** Ag & B
232 e4 **Tarbert** W Isls
183 K6 **Tarbet** Ag & B
200 B6 **Tarbet** Highld
228 B5 **Tarbet** Highld
163 K4 **Tarbolton** S Ayrs
176 D7 **Tarbrax** S Lans
71 H2 **Tardebigge** Worcs
196 D1 **Tarfside** Angus
205 K4 **Tarland** Abers
120 F6 **Tarleton** Lancs
55 L7 **Tarlton** Gloucs
26 B2 **Tarnock** Somset
112 D8 **Tarporley** Ches W
15 H2 **Tarrant Crawford** Dorset
27 L8 **Tarrant Gunville** Dorset
15 H1 **Tarrant Hinton** Dorset
15 H2 **Tarrant Keyneston** Dorset
15 H1 **Tarrant Launceston** Dorset
15 H2 **Tarrant Monkton** Dorset
15 H2 **Tarrant Rawston** Dorset
15 H2 **Tarrant Rushton** Dorset
19 L5 **Tarring Neville** E Susx
70 B6 **Tarrington** Herefs
199 J4 **Tarskavaig** Highld
217 G7 **Tarves** Abers
112 C7 **Tarvin** Ches W
92 E4 **Tasburgh** Norfk
100 D7 **Tatenhill** Staffs
118 D5 **Tathwell** Lincs
32 D2 **Tatsfield** Surrey
98 C2 **Tattenhall** Ches W
105 K6 **Tatterford** Norfk
105 K6 **Tattersett** Norfk
103 K2 **Tattershall** Lincs
103 L1 **Tattershall Thorpe** Lincs
78 D6 **Tattingstone** Suffk
78 D6 **Tattingstone White Horse** Suffk
13 J2 **Tatworth** Somset
215 J4 **Tauchers** Moray
25 K6 **Taunton** Somset
25 J6 **Taunton Deane Crematorium** Somset
25 J7 *Taunton Deane Services* Somset
92 E2 **Taverham** Norfk
49 K5 **Tavernspite** Pembks
6 C2 **Tavistock** Devon
10 F5 **Taw Green** Devon
23 J5 **Tawstock** Devon
114 A5 **Taxal** Derbys
182 F3 **Taychreggan Hotel** Ag & B
194 C4 **Tay Forest Park** P & K
161 H1 **Tayinloan** Ag & B
55 G4 **Taynton** Gloucs
56 E5 **Taynton** Oxon
182 E2 **Taynuilt** Ag & B
187 G2 **Tayport** Fife
172 C2 **Tayvallich** Ag & B
117 J4 **Tealby** Lincs
151 G3 **Team Valley** Gatesd

199 K4 **Teangue** Highld
212 F2 **Teanord** Highld
138 E6 **Tebay** Cumb
138 E6 *Tebay Services* Cumb
59 G3 **Tebworth** C Beds
11 J6 **Tedburn St Mary** Devon
55 L2 **Teddington** Gloucs
44 D6 **Teddington** Gt Lon
70 C3 **Tedstone Delamere** Herefs
70 C3 **Tedstone Wafer** Herefs
141 L4 **Teesside Crematorium** Middsb
73 K1 **Teeton** Nhants
27 M5 **Teffont Evias** Wilts
27 M5 **Teffont Magna** Wilts
65 H7 **Tegryn** Pembks
88 C1 **Teigh** Rutlnd
7 K2 **Teigngrace** Devon
12 B7 **Teignmouth** Devon
166 F7 **Teindside** Border
84 C2 **Telford** Wrekin
84 D2 **Telford Crematorium** Wrekin
84 D2 *Telford Services* Shrops
27 J1 **Tellisford** Somset
19 L5 **Telscombe** E Susx
193 L5 **Tempar** P & K
155 J5 **Templand** D & G
5 J2 **Temple** Cnwll
177 J6 **Temple** Mdloth
66 C4 **Temple Bar** Cerdgn
38 F8 **Temple Cloud** BaNES
27 G6 **Templecombe** Somset
35 H5 **Temple Ewell** Kent
71 K4 **Temple Grafton** Warwks
56 C3 **Temple Guiting** Gloucs
124 F5 **Temple Hirst** N York
115 H7 **Temple Normanton** Derbys
197 K1 **Temple of Fiddes** Abers
212 E7 **Temple Pier** Highld
138 E2 **Temple Sowerby** Cumb
11 K3 **Templeton** Devon
49 J5 **Templeton** Pembks
150 E5 **Templetown** Dur
75 H4 **Tempsford** C Beds
69 L2 **Tenbury Wells** Worcs
49 J7 **Tenby** Pembks
62 D3 **Tendring** Essex
62 D3 **Tendring Green** Essex
62 D3 **Tendring Heath** Essex
90 E4 **Ten Mile Bank** Norfk
34 B7 **Tenterden** Kent
61 J5 **Terling** Essex
98 F6 **Ternhill** Shrops
155 G6 **Terregles** D & G
133 K5 **Terrington** N York
104 E7 **Terrington St Clement** Norfk
90 D2 **Terrington St John** Norfk
33 J3 **Teston** Kent
29 G8 **Testwood** Hants
39 K2 **Tetbury** Gloucs
98 B6 **Tetchill** Shrops
9 J5 **Tetcott** Devon
118 D6 **Tetford** Lincs
118 D2 **Tetney** Lincs
58 B7 **Tetsworth** Oxon
84 F4 **Tettenhall** Wolves
101 J1 **Teversal** Notts
76 C3 **Teversham** Cambs
156 D2 **Teviothead** Border
59 L5 **Tewin** Herts
55 K2 **Tewkesbury** Gloucs
34 C3 **Teynham** Kent
123 H3 **Thackley** C Brad

18 F3	Thakeham W Susx	120 E3	Thistleton Lancs	86 F3	Thornton Leics
58 B6	Thame Oxon	102 E8	Thistleton Rutlnd	118 C7	Thornton Lincs
44 D6	Thames Ditton Surrey	90 F7	Thistley Green Suffk	141 L4	Thornton Middsb
45 J4	Thamesmead Gt Lon	134 C7	Thixendale N York	179 K8	Thornton Nthumb
35 K2	Thanet Crematorium Kent	158 B6	Thockrington Nthumb	126 D6	Thornton Curtis N Linc
34 F4	Thanington Kent	90 B3	Tholomas Drove Cambs	111 K2	Thornton Garden of Rest Crematorium Sefton
165 J2	Thankerton S Lans	133 G6	Tholthorpe N York		
92 E5	Tharston Norfk	216 B6	Thomastown Abers	175 G7	Thorntonhall S Lans
41 K6	Thatcham W Berk	91 K4	Thompson Norfk	44 F6	Thornton Heath Gt Lon
60 F2	Thaxted Essex	46 B6	Thong Kent		
132 D3	Theakston N York	131 J3	Thoralby N York	111 J5	Thornton Hough Wirral
125 K6	Thealby N Linc	117 K3	Thoresway Lincs		
26 C3	Theale Somset	117 K3	Thorganby Lincs	122 D2	Thornton-in-Craven N York
41 M6	Theale W Berk	125 G3	Thorganby N York		
126 D3	Thearne E R Yk	142 E7	Thorgill N York	130 D5	Thornton in Lonsdale N York
56 B7	The Beeches Gloucs	93 J8	Thorington Suffk		
79 J2	Theberton Suffk	78 B7	Thorington Street Suffk	132 F2	Thornton-le-Beans N York
209 H7	The Braes Highld				
178 E4	The Brunt E Loth	131 H8	Thorlby N York	133 L6	Thornton-le-Clay N York
237 d4	The Bungalow IoM	60 D4	Thorley Herts		
70 E2	The Burf Worcs	16 D5	Thorley Street IoW	134 C3	Thornton le Dale N York
55 K5	The Butts Gloucs	133 G5	Thormanby N York		
42 C2	The City Bucks	141 K4	Thornaby-on-Tees S on T	117 H3	Thornton le Moor Lincs
28 E5	The Common Wilts				
83 J6	The Corner Shrops	106 C5	Thornage Norfk	132 F2	Thornton-le-Moor N York
73 K3	The Counties Crematorium Nhants	73 L7	Thornborough Bucks		
		132 D4	Thornborough N York	112 C6	Thornton-le-Moors Ches W
87 J6	Theddingworth Leics	123 J4	Thornbury C Brad		
118 F4	Theddlethorpe All Saints Lincs	9 K3	Thornbury Devon	132 F3	Thornton-le-Street N York
		70 B3	Thornbury Herefs		
119 G4	Theddlethorpe St Helen Lincs	38 F3	Thornbury S Glos	178 F4	Thorntonloch E Loth
		87 J7	Thornby Nhants	131 H2	Thornton Rust N York
174 C7	The Den N Ayrs	100 A2	Thorncliff Staffs	132 B3	Thornton Steward N York
54 F5	The Forest of Dean Crematorium Gloucs	128 E5	Thorncliffe Crematorium Cumb		
				132 C3	Thornton Watlass N York
34 B5	The Forstal Kent	13 J2	Thorncombe Dorset		
34 D6	The Forstal Kent	78 D1	Thorndon Suffk	178 D8	Thornydykes Border
46 E6	The Garden of England Crematorium Kent	10 D6	Thorndon Cross Devon	137 L3	Thornythwaite Cumb
				102 C4	Thoroton Notts
128 E3	The Green Cumb	125 G7	Thorne Donc	124 C2	Thorp Arch Leeds
61 J4	The Green Essex	26 D7	Thorne Somset	100 D3	Thorpe Derbys
143 G6	The Green N York	124 B3	Thorner Leeds	126 B2	Thorpe E R Yk
27 K5	The Green Wilts	25 H7	Thorne St Margaret Somset	131 J6	Thorpe N York
151 M7	The Headland Hartpl			102 C3	Thorpe Notts
128 E3	The Hill Cumb	89 K3	Thorney C Pete	43 G6	Thorpe Surrey
58 E6	The Lee Bucks	116 E6	Thorney Notts	92 E7	Thorpe Abbotts Norfk
237 d2	The Lhen IoM	26 B6	Thorney Somset		
175 G6	The Linn Crematorium E Rens	16 A3	Thorney Hill Hants	102 C7	Thorpe Arnold Leics
		17 L2	Thorney Island W Susx	124 D7	Thorpe Audlin Wakefd
92 B7	Thelnetham Suffk				
215 G2	The Lochs Moray	25 L6	Thornfalcon Somset	134 D5	Thorpe Bassett N York
92 E7	Thelveton Norfk	26 E8	Thornford Dorset		
112 F4	Thelwall Warrtn	149 K2	Thorngrafton Nthumb	46 E3	Thorpe Bay Sthend
113 J3	The Manchester Crematorium Manch			88 C4	Thorpe by Water Rutlnd
		126 F5	Thorngumbald E R Yk		
106 C7	Themelthorpe Norfk	105 H4	Thornham Norfk	86 C2	Thorpe Constantine Staffs
33 K7	The Moor Kent	78 D1	Thornham Magna Suffk		
51 J7	The Mumbles Swans			93 G2	Thorpe End Norfk
175 H7	The Murray S Lans	92 D8	Thornham Parva Suffk	62 E4	Thorpe Green Essex
206 D5	The Neuk Abers			77 L4	Thorpe Green Suffk
73 G6	Thenford Nhants	88 F4	Thornhaugh C Pete	115 G3	Thorpe Hesley Rothm
30 E2	The Park Crematorium Hants	29 J8	Thornhill C Sotn	124 F7	Thorpe in Balne Donc
		154 F3	Thornhill D & G		
55 K4	The Reddings Gloucs	114 D5	Thornhill Derbys	87 L5	Thorpe Langton Leics
75 L6	Therfield Herts	123 K6	Thornhill Kirk	43 G6	Thorpe Lea Surrey
115 L2	The Rose Hill Crematorium Donc	184 E7	Thornhill Stirlg	62 E4	Thorpe-le-Soken Essex
		37 J4	Thornhill Crematorium Cardif		
185 G3	The Ross P & K			125 K2	Thorpe le Street E R Yk
21 H1	The Stocks Kent	135 H6	Thornholme E R Yk		
39 L8	The Strand Wilts	15 G2	Thornicombe Dorset	88 B7	Thorpe Malsor Nhants
91 K6	Thetford Norfk	168 D3	Thornington Nthumb		
91 J5	Thetford Forest Park Suffk	150 E7	Thornley Dur	73 G5	Thorpe Mandeville Nhants
59 J3	The Vale Crematorium Luton	151 J6	Thornley Dur		
		174 F6	Thornliebank E Rens	106 F5	Thorpe Market Norfk
60 D7	Theydon Bois Essex	77 G4	Thorns Suffk	92 E1	Thorpe Marriot Norfk
39 J5	Thickwood Wilts	114 A4	Thornsett Derbys	77 L4	Thorpe Morieux Suffk
118 C7	Thimbleby Lincs	137 H3	Thornthwaite Cumb	79 K3	Thorpeness Suffk
141 K7	Thimbleby N York	132 B7	Thornthwaite N York	116 E7	Thorpe on the Hill Lincs
111 J5	Thingwall Wirral	196 C6	Thornton Angus		
133 G4	Thirkleby N York	73 L7	Thornton Bucks	43 G6	Thorpe Park Surrey
133 G3	Thirlby N York	123 G4	Thornton C Brad	92 F2	Thorpe St Andrew Norfk
178 C8	Thirlestane Border	125 H2	Thornton E R Yk		
132 C3	Thirn N York	186 E7	Thornton Fife	104 D1	Thorpe St Peter Lincs
132 F3	Thirsk N York	120 D3	Thornton Lancs	115 K5	Thorpe Salvin Rothm

87 K2	Thorpe Satchville Leics			
141 J3	Thorpe Thewles S on T			
103 J2	Thorpe Tilney Lincs			
133 G7	Thorpe Underwood N York			
88 E7	Thorpe Waterville Nhants			
124 E4	Thorpe Willoughby N York			
62 C4	Thorrington Essex			
11 L4	Thorverton Devon			
92 D7	Thrandeston Suffk			
88 E7	Thrapston Nhants			
98 C4	Threapwood Ches W			
100 B4	Threapwood Staffs			
163 J7	Threave S Ayrs			
146 C3	Threave Castle D & G			
32 B5	Three Bridges W Susx			
33 L5	Three Chimneys Kent			
68 D6	Three Cocks Powys			
51 H6	Three Crosses Swans			
20 D2	Three Cups Corner E Susx			
103 H5	Threekingham Lincs			
33 H6	Three Leg Cross E Susx			
15 K2	Three Legged Cross Dorset			
42 B6	Three Mile Cross Wokham			
3 K3	Threemilestone Cnwll			
176 E3	Three Miletown W Loth			
21 G3	Three Oaks E Susx			
167 H2	Threepwood Border			
137 J3	Threlkeld Cumb			
60 D6	Threshers Bush Essex			
131 J6	Threshfield N York			
93 K2	Thrigby Norfk			
86 E1	Thringstone Leics			
132 D2	Thrintoft N York			
76 B5	Thriplow Cambs			
60 B3	Throcking Herts			
150 E2	Throckley N u Ty			
71 H4	Throckmorton Worcs			
15 L4	Throop Bmouth			
158 C2	Thropton Nthumb			
176 B1	Throsk Stirlg			
154 F5	Throughgate D & G			
11 G6	Throwleigh Devon			
34 C4	Throwley Forstal Kent			
101 J6	Thrumpton Notts			
231 L6	Thrumster Highld			
127 H8	Thrunscoe NE Lin			
55 K7	Thrupp Gloucs			
87 J1	Thrussington Leics			
28 F3	Thruxton Hants			
69 J7	Thruxton Herefs			
115 J3	Thrybergh Rothm			
101 H6	Thulston Derbys			
46 C3	Thundersley Essex			
87 H2	Thurcaston Leics			
115 J4	Thurcroft Rothm			
106 E5	Thurgarton Norfk			
102 B3	Thurgarton Notts			
114 F2	Thurgoland Barns			
87 G4	Thurlaston Leics			
72 F1	Thurlaston Warwks			
25 K7	Thurlbear Somset			
89 G1	Thurlby Lincs			
102 E1	Thurlby Lincs			
119 G6	Thurlby Lincs			
74 F3	Thurleigh Bed			
7 G7	Thurlestone Devon			
76 F4	Thurlow Suffk			
25 L5	Thurloxton Somset			
114 E2	Thurlstone Barns			
93 J4	Thurlton Norfk			
87 H2	Thurmaston Leics			
87 J3	Thurnby Leics			
93 J1	Thurne Norfk			
33 K2	Thurnham Kent			
88 F6	Thurning Nhants			

106 C6 **Thurning** Norfk
115 J1 **Thurnscoe** Barns
45 L4 **Thurrock Services** Thurr
148 B5 **Thursby** Cumb
106 B5 **Thursford** Norfk
30 E4 **Thursley** Surrey
231 G2 **Thurso** Highld
111 H5 **Thurstaston** Wirral
77 L2 **Thurston** Suffk
148 B4 **Thurstonfield** Cumb
123 H7 **Thurstonland** Kirk
93 G4 **Thurton** Norfk
100 E5 **Thurvaston** Derbys
92 B3 **Thuxton** Norfk
139 K7 **Thwaite** N York
78 D2 **Thwaite** Suffk
129 H2 **Thwaite Head** Cumb
93 G4 **Thwaite St Mary** Norfk
135 G5 **Thwing** E R Yk
185 L3 **Tibbermore** P & K
154 E3 **Tibbers** D & G
55 H4 **Tibberton** Gloucs
70 F3 **Tibberton** Worcs
99 G7 **Tibberton** Wrekin
166 C5 **Tibbie Shiels Inn** Border
92 D5 **Tibenham** Norfk
101 H1 **Tibshelf** Derbys
134 E7 **Tibthorpe** E R Yk
33 H7 **Ticehurst** E Susx
29 L5 **Tichborne** Hants
88 E2 **Tickencote** Rutlnd
38 C6 **Tickenham** N Som
115 L3 **Tickhill** Donc
83 J5 **Ticklerton** Shrops
101 G7 **Ticknall** Derbys
126 D3 **Tickton** E R Yk
40 F8 **Tidcombe** Wilts
57 M6 **Tiddington** Oxon
72 B4 **Tiddington** Warwks
33 G7 **Tidebrook** E Susx
6 A4 **Tideford** Cnwll
38 E2 **Tidenham** Gloucs
114 D6 **Tideswell** Derbys
41 M5 **Tidmarsh** W Berk
72 C6 **Tidmington** Warwks
28 E2 **Tidworth** Wilts
48 F5 **Tiers Cross** Pembks
73 K4 **Tiffield** Nhants
196 E4 **Tigerton** Angus
233 b6 **Tigh a Ghearraidh** W Isls
233 b6 **Tigharry** W Isls
173 G4 **Tighnabruaich** Ag & B
7 H4 **Tigley** Devon
74 F2 **Tilbrook** Cambs
45 M5 **Tilbury** Thurr
86 C7 **Tile Hill** Covtry
42 A5 **Tilehurst** Readg
30 E3 **Tilford** Surrey
31 L4 **Tilgate** W Susx
26 E4 **Tilham Street** Somset
185 J7 **Tillicoultry** Clacks
164 F1 **Tillietudlem** S Lans
62 B7 **Tillingham** Essex
69 J5 **Tillington** Herefs
30 F6 **Tillington** W Susx
69 J5 **Tillington Common** Herefs
206 D4 **Tillybirloch** Abers
206 C3 **Tillyfourie** Abers
207 G2 **Tillygreig** Abers
186 B6 **Tillyrie** P & K
35 J4 **Tilmanstone** Kent
104 F8 **Tilney All Saints** Norfk
104 E8 **Tilney High End** Norfk
90 D2 **Tilney St Lawrence** Norfk
28 B2 **Tilshead** Wilts
98 D5 **Tilstock** Shrops
98 C3 **Tilston** Ches W
98 E1 **Tilstone Fearnall** Ches W
59 G3 **Tilsworth** C Beds

87 L3 **Tilton on the Hill** Leics
39 J2 **Tiltups End** Gloucs
103 J2 **Timberland** Lincs
113 K8 **Timbersbrook** Ches E
24 E3 **Timberscombe** Somset
132 B3 **Timble** N York
156 B7 **Timpanheck** D & G
113 H4 **Timperley** Traffd
38 F8 **Timsbury** BaNES
29 G6 **Timsbury** Hants
232 d2 **Timsgarry** W Isls
232 d2 **Timsgearraidh** W Isls
77 J2 **Timworth** Suffk
77 J2 **Timworth Green** Suffk
14 E4 **Tincleton** Dorset
149 G3 **Tindale** Cumb
140 F2 **Tindale Crescent** Dur
58 A2 **Tingewick** Bucks
123 K5 **Tingley** Leeds
59 G2 **Tingrith** C Beds
235 c6 **Tingwall Airport** Shet
9 K7 **Tinhay** Devon
115 H4 **Tinsley** Sheff
32 B5 **Tinsley Green** W Susx
8 E7 **Tintagel** Cnwll
8 D6 **Tintagel Castle** Cnwll
54 D7 **Tintern Abbey** Mons
54 D7 **Tintern Parva** Mons
26 D7 **Tintinhull** Somset
114 A3 **Tintwistle** Derbys
155 H5 **Tinwald** D & G
88 E3 **Tinwell** Rutlnd
85 G5 **Tipton** Sandw
12 E4 **Tipton St John** Devon
61 L5 **Tiptree** Essex
61 L5 **Tiptree Heath** Essex
67 J6 **Tirabad** Powys
188 D7 **Tiree** Ag & B
188 C7 **Tiree Airport** Ag & B
172 C6 **Tiretigan** Ag & B
55 J3 **Tirley** Gloucs
53 H7 **Tirphil** Caerph
138 D2 **Tirril** Cumb
27 L5 **Tisbury** Wilts
100 D3 **Tissington** Derbys
22 C6 **Titchberry** Devon
17 G2 **Titchfield** Hants
88 E7 **Titchmarsh** Nhants
105 J4 **Titchwell** Norfk
102 B5 **Tithby** Notts
69 G3 **Titley** Herefs
32 D3 **Titsey** Surrey
9 H5 **Titson** Cnwll
99 K5 **Tittensor** Staffs
105 L7 **Tittleshall** Norfk
70 E1 **Titton** Worcs
98 D1 **Tiverton** Ches W
24 E8 **Tiverton** Devon
92 E6 **Tivetshall St Margaret** Norfk
92 E6 **Tivetshall St Mary** Norfk
24 E3 **Tivington** Somset
99 L7 **Tixall** Staffs
88 E4 **Tixover** Rutlnd
235 c8 **Toab** Shet
189 L5 **Tobermory** Ag & B
181 L5 **Toberonochy** Ag & B
233 b7 **Tobha Mor** W Isls
216 D7 **Tocher** Abers
215 L2 **Tochieneal** Moray
40 B4 **Tockenham** Wilts
121 K6 **Tockholes** Bl w D
38 E3 **Tockington** S Glos
133 G8 **Tockwith** N York
27 J7 **Todber** Dorset
158 E3 **Todburn** Nthumb
59 G3 **Toddington** C Beds
56 B2 **Toddington** Gloucs
59 G3 **Toddington Services** C Beds
72 B7 **Todenham** Gloucs
196 C8 **Todhills** Angus

148 C3 **Todhills Services** Cumb
122 D5 **Todmorden** Calder
115 J5 **Todwick** Rothm
75 L4 **Toft** Cambs
88 F1 **Toft** Lincs
235 C3 **Toft** Shet
140 E2 **Toft Hill** Dur
93 J4 **Toft Monks** Norfk
117 H4 **Toft next Newton** Lincs
105 L6 **Toftrees** Norfk
159 G2 **Togston** Nthumb
199 J3 **Tokavaig** Highld
42 B5 **Tokers Green** Oxon
232 g2 **Tolastadh** W Isls
25 H5 **Tolland** Somset
27 L7 **Tollard Royal** Wilts
124 E8 **Toll Bar** Donc
14 B3 **Toller Fratrum** Dorset
14 B3 **Toller Porcorum** Dorset
133 H6 **Tollerton** N York
101 L5 **Tollerton** Notts
13 M3 **Toller Whelme** Dorset
62 A6 **Tollesbury** Essex
61 L5 **Tolleshunt D'Arcy** Essex
61 L5 **Tolleshunt Knights** Essex
61 L5 **Tolleshunt Major** Essex
14 E4 **Tolpuddle** Dorset
232 g2 **Tolsta** W Isls
44 D6 **Tolworth** Gt Lon
213 J8 **Tomatin** Highld
201 K3 **Tomchrasky** Highld
201 H5 **Tomdoun** Highld
211 L8 **Tomich** Highld
212 E5 **Tomich** Highld
222 F7 **Tomich** Highld
226 A7 **Tomich** Highld
204 E2 **Tomintoul** Moray
212 D6 **Tomnacross** Highld
204 F1 **Tomnavoulin** Moray
33 G4 **Tonbridge** Kent
36 D4 **Tondu** Brdgnd
25 H6 **Tonedale** Somset
123 J4 **Tong** C Brad
34 C4 **Tong** Kent
84 E3 **Tong** Shrops
101 H7 **Tonge** Leics
30 E2 **Tongham** Surrey
146 C4 **Tongland** D & G
84 E2 **Tong Norton** Shrops
123 J4 **Tong Street** C Brad
229 J4 **Tongue** Highld
37 H4 **Tongwynlais** Cardif
36 C2 **Tonmawr** Neath
52 B7 **Tonna** Neath
60 B5 **Tonwell** Herts
36 F3 **Tonypandy** Rhondd
36 F3 **Tonyrefail** Rhondd
57 K7 **Toot Baldon** Oxon
60 E7 **Toot Hill** Essex
40 C4 **Toothill** Swindn
44 F5 **Tooting** Gt Lon
44 F5 **Tooting Bec** Gt Lon
132 F4 **Topcliffe** N York
92 F5 **Topcroft** Norfk
92 F5 **Topcroft Street** Norfk
77 G6 **Toppesfield** Essex
92 E4 **Toprow** Norfk
12 C5 **Topsham** Devon
162 A4 **Torbeg** N Ayrs
223 G2 **Torboll** Highld
213 G6 **Torbreck** Highld
7 J3 **Torbryan** Devon
192 B2 **Torcastle** Highld
7 J7 **Torcross** Devon
212 F4 **Tore** Highld
172 D5 **Torinturk** Ag & B
116 D5 **Torksey** Lincs
39 H5 **Tormarton** S Glos
161 M3 **Tormore** N Ayrs
213 J4 **Tornagrain** Highld

206 C4 **Tornaveen** Abers
212 E8 **Torness** Highld
140 F2 **Toronto** Dur
181 L1 **Torosay Castle** Ag & B
147 L6 **Torpenhow** Cumb
176 C4 **Torphichen** W Loth
206 C5 **Torphins** Abers
6 C5 **Torpoint** Cnwll
7 L3 **Torquay** Torbay
7 K3 **Torquay Crematorium** Torbay
177 L8 **Torquhan** Border
209 J5 **Torran** Highld
175 H4 **Torrance** E Duns
163 J1 **Torranyard** N Ayrs
210 D3 **Torridon** Highld
210 D3 **Torridon House** Highld
199 J2 **Torrin** Highld
161 K3 **Torrisdale** Ag & B
229 K3 **Torrisdale** Highld
227 G5 **Torrish** Highld
129 K6 **Torrisholme** Lancs
226 A7 **Torrobull** Highld
207 H4 **Torry** C Aber
176 D2 **Torryburn** Fife
236 b4 **Torteval** Guern
155 H6 **Torthorwald** D & G
18 D5 **Tortington** W Susx
84 E8 **Torton** Worcs
39 G2 **Tortworth** S Glos
209 H5 **Torvaig** Highld
137 J7 **Torver** Cumb
175 L2 **Torwood** Falk
167 G2 **Torwoodlee** Border
116 A4 **Torworth** Notts
209 L6 **Toscaig** Highld
75 J3 **Toseland** Cambs
130 E7 **Tosside** Lancs
77 L2 **Tostock** Suffk
208 C4 **Totaig** Highld
208 F5 **Tote** Highld
209 H3 **Tote** Highld
16 D5 **Totland** IoW
114 F5 **Totley** Sheff
7 J4 **Totnes** Devon
101 J5 **Toton** Notts
188 F5 **Totronald** Ag & B
208 F2 **Totscore** Highld
45 G3 **Tottenham** Gt Lon
90 F2 **Tottenhill** Norfk
44 E2 **Totteridge** Gt Lon
59 G4 **Totternhoe** C Beds
122 B7 **Tottington** Bury
29 G8 **Totton** Hants
25 J5 **Toulston** Somset
223 J5 **Toulvaddie** Highld
33 K3 **Tovil** Kent
173 K5 **Toward** Ag & B
173 J5 **Toward Quay** Ag & B
73 K5 **Towcester** Nhants
2 E4 **Towednack** Cnwll
58 B6 **Towersey** Oxon
205 K3 **Towie** Abers
150 E6 **Tow Law** Dur
90 B4 **Town End** Cambs
128 F2 **Town End** Cumb
174 D3 **Townend** W Duns
114 D2 **Townhead** Barns
155 H4 **Townhead** D & G
146 C3 **Townhead of Greenlaw** D & G
176 F1 **Townhill** Fife
19 L3 **Town Littleworth** E Susx
41 K8 **Towns End** Hants
3 G5 **Townshend** Cnwll
91 H6 **Town Street** Suffk
168 B4 **Town Yetholm** Border
133 K7 **Towthorpe** C York
124 D3 **Towton** N York
110 D5 **Towyn** Conwy
111 K4 **Toxteth** Lpool
118 E8 **Toynton All Saints** Lincs

32 E3	**Toy's Hill** Kent
163 K5	**Trabboch** E Ayrs
163 L5	**Trabbochburn** E Ayrs
213 K3	**Tradespark** Highld
52 E3	**Trallong** Powys
101 G2	**Tramway Museum** Derbys
177 L4	**Tranent** E Loth
111 J4	**Tranmere** Wirral
230 C5	**Trantelbeg** Highld
230 C5	**Trantlemore** Highld
51 J2	**Trapp** Carmth
178 D4	**Traprain** E Loth
166 E3	**Traquair** Border
122 D3	**Trawden** Lancs
96 A5	**Trawsfynydd** Gwynd
36 F3	**Trealaw** Rhondd
120 F4	**Treales** Lancs
108 C5	**Trearddur Bay** IoA
208 F4	**Treaslane** Highld
4 E1	**Trebetherick** Cnwll
24 F4	**Treborough** Somset
5 M1	**Trebullett** Cnwll
6 A1	**Treburley** Cnwll
52 D3	**Trecastle** Powys
64 D7	**Trecwn** Pembks
52 F7	**Trecynon** Rhondd
53 H6	**Tredegar** Blae G
55 K3	**Tredington** Gloucs
72 C5	**Tredington** Warwks
38 B2	**Tredunnock** Mons
2 D6	**Treen** Cnwll
115 H4	**Treeton** Rothm
64 C6	**Trefasser** Pembks
53 H2	**Trefecca** Powys
81 L5	**Trefeglwys** Powys
49 G3	**Treffgarne** Pembks
48 E3	**Treffgarne Owen** Pembks
37 G3	**Trefforest** Rhondd
66 D3	**Trefilan** Cerdgn
64 B7	**Trefin** Pembks
110 E7	**Trefnant** Denbgs
97 K6	**Trefonen** Shrops
94 F4	**Trefor** Gwynd
109 L8	**Trefriw** Conwy
9 H7	**Tregadillett** Cnwll
54 B6	**Tregare** Mons
66 F3	**Tregaron** Cerdgn
109 H7	**Tregarth** Gwynd
9 H7	**Tregeare** Cnwll
97 J5	**Tregeiriog** Wrexhm
108 D3	**Tregele** IoA
48 D2	**Treglemais** Pembks
4 E3	**Tregonetha** Cnwll
4 E6	**Tregony** Cnwll
68 E6	**Tregoyd** Powys
65 L5	**Tre-groes** Cerdgn
82 C4	**Tregynon** Powys
50 E2	**Tre-gynwr** Carmth
37 G3	**Trehafod** Rhondd
6 B4	**Trehan** Cnwll
37 H2	**Treharris** Myr Td
52 E7	**Treherbert** Rhondd
6 A1	**Trekenner** Cnwll
8 D7	**Treknow** Cnwll
110 F5	**Trelawnyd** Flints
65 J7	**Trelech** Carmth
48 C2	**Treleddyd-fawr** Pembks
37 H2	**Trelewis** Myr Td
8 C8	**Trelights** Cnwll
5 G1	**Trelill** Cnwll
4 C7	**Trelissick Garden** Cnwll
54 D6	**Trelleck** Mons
110 F5	**Trelogan** Flints
95 K4	**Tremadog** Gwynd
8 F7	**Tremail** Cnwll
65 H5	**Tremain** Cerdgn
9 G6	**Tremaine** Cnwll
5 K3	**Tremar** Cnwll
6 B4	**Trematon** Cnwll
110 F6	**Tremeirchion** Denbgs
4 D3	**Trenance** Cnwll
4 E2	**Trenance** Cnwll
84 C2	**Trench** Wrekin
3 H5	**Trenear** Cnwll
9 G7	**Treneglos** Cnwll
26 E7	**Trent** Dorset
99 K4	**Trentham** C Stke
23 K2	**Trentishoe** Devon
36 E5	**Treoes** V Glam
36 E2	**Treorchy** Rhondd
5 G1	**Trequite** Cnwll
36 F5	**Trerhyngyll** V Glam
5 M4	**Trerulefoot** Cnwll
65 J4	**Tresaith** Cerdgn
2 a1	**Tresco** IoS
2 a1	*Tresco Heliport* IoS
3 G5	**Trescowe** Cnwll
4 C4	**Tresean** Cnwll
39 H3	**Tresham** Gloucs
189 G7	**Treshnish Isles** Ag & B
4 D6	**Tresillian** Cnwll
9 G5	**Treskinnick Cross** Cnwll
9 G7	**Tresmeer** Cnwll
8 F6	**Tresparrett** Cnwll
194 C4	**Tressait** P & K
235 C5	**Tresta** Shet
235 e3	**Tresta** Shet
116 C5	**Treswell** Notts
80 E5	**Tre Taliesin** Cerdgn
8 E6	**Trethevey** Cnwll
2 C6	**Trethewey** Cnwll
5 G5	**Trethurgy** Cnwll
54 D4	**Tretire** Herefs
53 J4	**Tretower** Powys
97 K2	**Treuddyn** Flints
8 E6	**Trevalga** Cnwll
98 B2	**Trevalyn** Wrexhm
4 D3	**Trevarrian** Cnwll
4 C4	**Treveal** Cnwll
8 E8	**Treveighan** Cnwll
3 J2	**Trevellas Downs** Cnwll
5 K3	**Trevelmond** Cnwll
3 K5	**Treverva** Cnwll
2 C6	**Trevescan** Cnwll
4 E5	**Treviscoe** Cnwll
4 D2	**Trevone** Cnwll
97 L4	**Trevor** Wrexhm
8 E7	**Trewalder** Cnwll
8 E7	**Trewarmett** Cnwll
9 H7	**Trewen** Cnwll
9 G8	**Trewint** Cnwll
4 D7	**Trewithian** Cnwll
4 F5	**Trewoon** Cnwll
30 D7	**Treyford** W Susx
151 J7	**Trimdon** Dur
151 J7	**Trimdon Colliery** Dur
151 J7	**Trimdon Grange** Dur
107 G5	**Trimingham** Norfk
78 F6	**Trimley St Martin** Suffk
79 G7	**Trimley St Mary** Suffk
50 F5	**Trimsaran** Carmth
23 H3	**Trimstone** Devon
194 B4	**Trinafour** P & K
58 F5	**Tring** Herts
196 F4	**Trinity** Angus
236 d6	**Trinity** Jersey
185 K4	**Trinity Gask** P & K
25 J4	**Triscombe** Somset
191 L2	**Trislaig** Highld
4 D5	**Trispen** Cnwll
158 F4	**Tritlington** Nthumb
194 F7	**Trochry** P & K
65 K5	**Troedyraur** Cerdgn
53 G7	**Troedyrhiw** Myr Td
3 H4	**Troon** Cnwll
163 H3	**Troon** S Ayrs
123 L3	**Tropical World Roundhay Park** Leeds
184 B5	**Trossachs** Stirlg
184 B6	**Trossachs Pier** Stirlg
91 K8	**Troston** Suffk
70 F4	**Trotshill** Worcs
33 H2	**Trottiscliffe** Kent
30 D6	**Trotton** W Susx
157 L4	**Troughend** Nthumb
137 L6	**Troutbeck** Cumb
137 L7	**Troutbeck Bridge** Cumb
115 H5	**Troway** Derbys
39 J4	**Trowbridge** Wilts
101 J4	**Trowell** Notts
101 J4	**Trowell Services** Notts
92 F3	**Trowse Newton** Norfk
27 H3	**Trudoxhill** Somset
25 K6	**Trull** Somset
208 D3	**Trumpan** Highld
70 B6	**Trumpet** Herefs
76 C4	**Trumpington** Cambs
107 G5	**Trunch** Norfk
4 C6	**Truro** Cnwll
4 C6	**Truro Cathedral** Cnwll
11 K7	**Trusham** Devon
100 E5	**Trusley** Derbys
119 G5	**Trusthorpe** Lincs
84 F5	**Trysull** Staffs
57 H7	**Tubney** Oxon
7 J5	**Tuckenhay** Devon
84 E6	**Tuckhill** Shrops
3 H3	**Tuckingmill** Cnwll
27 L5	**Tuckingmill** Wilts
15 L4	**Tuckton** Bmouth
77 G1	**Tuddenham** Suffk
78 E5	**Tuddenham** Suffk
33 G4	**Tudeley** Kent
151 G2	**Tudhoe** Dur
94 D5	**Tudweiliog** Gwynd
55 J5	**Tuffley** Gloucs
29 J3	**Tufton** Hants
49 H2	**Tufton** Pembks
87 L4	**Tugby** Leics
83 L6	**Tugford** Shrops
169 J4	**Tughall** Nthumb
185 H7	**Tullibody** Clacks
212 F8	**Tullich** Highld
223 J6	**Tullich** Highld
194 F5	**Tulliemet** P & K
216 F7	**Tulloch** Abers
182 D7	**Tullochgorm** Ag & B
192 F1	**Tulloch Station** Highld
185 L1	**Tullybeagles Lodge** P & K
195 J5	**Tullymurdoch** P & K
206 B2	**Tullynessle** Abers
44 F5	**Tulse Hill** Gt Lon
51 G3	**Tumble** Carmth
103 L1	**Tumby** Lincs
103 L2	**Tumby Woodside** Lincs
194 B5	**Tummel Bridge** P & K
33 G5	**Tunbridge Wells** Kent
155 L6	**Tundergarth** D & G
39 G8	**Tunley** BaNES
99 K3	**Tunstall** C Stke
127 H4	**Tunstall** E R Yk
34 B3	**Tunstall** Kent
130 B5	**Tunstall** Lancs
140 F7	**Tunstall** N York
93 J2	**Tunstall** Norfk
99 H6	**Tunstall** Staffs
79 H4	**Tunstall** Suffk
151 J4	**Tunstall** Sundld
114 C6	**Tunstead** Derbys
107 G7	**Tunstead** Norfk
114 B5	**Tunstead Milton** Derbys
42 B8	**Turgis Green** Hants
56 C4	**Turkdean** Gloucs
87 K5	**Tur Langton** Leics
39 J7	**Turleigh** Wilts
69 G7	**Turnastone** Herefs
152 E2	**Turnberry** S Ayrs
100 F3	**Turnditch** Derbys
32 C6	**Turner's Hill** W Susx
177 G4	**Turnhouse** C Edin
14 F7	**Turnworth** Dorset
216 D4	**Turriff** Abers
121 L7	**Turton Bottoms** Bl w D
89 L4	**Turves** Cambs
74 D4	**Turvey** Bed
42 C3	**Turville** Bucks
73 H6	**Turweston** Bucks
166 D5	**Tushielaw Inn** Border
100 E6	**Tutbury** Staffs
38 D2	**Tutshill** Gloucs
106 F6	**Tuttington** Norfk
116 C7	**Tuxford** Notts
234 b5	**Twatt** Ork
235 c5	**Twatt** Shet
175 J3	**Twechar** E Duns
167 H3	**Tweedbank** Border
179 K7	**Tweedmouth** Nthumb
165 L4	**Tweedsmuir** Border
3 K3	**Twelveheads** Cnwll
113 H7	**Twemlow Green** Ches E
103 J7	**Twenty** Lincs
39 G7	**Twerton** BaNES
44 D5	**Twickenham** Gt Lon
55 J4	**Twigworth** Gloucs
19 H2	**Twineham** W Susx
77 J6	**Twinstead** Essex
24 C5	**Twitchen** Devon
114 F8	**Two Dales** Derbys
86 B4	**Two Gates** Staffs
86 D3	**Twycross** Leics
86 C3	**Twycross Zoo** Leics
58 A3	**Twyford** Bucks
29 J6	**Twyford** Hants
87 K2	**Twyford** Leics
106 B7	**Twyford** Norfk
42 C5	**Twyford** Wokham
146 B4	**Twynholm** D & G
70 F7	**Twyning** Gloucs
70 F6	**Twyning Green** Gloucs
51 L2	**Twynllanan** Carmth
88 D7	**Twywell** Nhants
69 H6	**Tyberton** Herefs
51 H4	**Tycroes** Carmth
97 H8	**Tycrwyn** Powys
104 D8	**Tydd Gote** Lincs
90 B1	**Tydd St Giles** Cambs
104 C8	**Tydd St Mary** Lincs
76 E7	**Tye Green** Essex
113 G2	**Tyldesley** Wigan
34 F3	**Tyler Hill** Kent
36 F2	**Tylorstown** Rhondd
96 F4	**Ty-nant** Conwy
183 K2	**Tyndrum** Stirlg
97 K4	**Ty'n-dwr** Denbgs
151 J2	**Tynemouth** N Tyne
151 J2	**Tynemouth Crematorium** N Tyne
178 D3	**Tyninghame** E Loth
154 E4	**Tynron** D & G
38 D6	**Tyntesfield** N Som
66 F1	**Tynygraig** Cerdgn
109 L7	**Ty'n-y-Groes** Conwy
37 G4	**Tyn-y-nant** Rhondd
74 C5	**Tyringham** M Keyn
36 D5	**Tythegston** Brdgnd
113 K6	**Tytherington** Ches E
38 F3	**Tytherington** S Glos
27 K3	**Tytherington** Wilts
13 H2	**Tytherleigh** Devon
39 L5	**Tytherton Lucas** Wilts
5 H5	**Tywardreath** Cnwll
80 D4	**Tywyn** Gwynd

U

79 G1	**Ubbeston Green** Suffk
38 D8	**Ubley** BaNES
141 G6	**Uckerby** N York
19 M2	**Uckfield** E Susx
70 F6	**Uckinghall** Worcs
55 K3	**Uckington** Gloucs
83 L2	**Uckington** Shrops
175 J6	**Uddingston** S Lans
165 G3	**Uddington** S Lans

21 H2 **Udimore** E Susx
207 G1 **Udny Green** Abers
207 G1 **Udny Station** Abers
25 G8 **Uffculme** Devon
88 F3 **Uffington** Lincs
40 F3 **Uffington** Oxon
83 K2 **Uffington** Shrops
89 G3 **Ufford** C Pete
79 G4 **Ufford** Suffk
72 E3 **Ufton** Warwks
41 M6 **Ufton Nervet** W Berk
161 K4 **Ugadale** Ag & B
7 G5 **Ugborough** Devon
93 J7 **Uggeshall** Suffk
143 H5 **Ugglebarnby** N York
114 E4 **Ughill** Sheff
60 E3 **Ugley** Essex
60 E3 **Ugley Green** Essex
143 G5 **Ugthorpe** N York
233 C8 **Uibhist A Deas** W Isls
233 b6 **Uibhist A Tuath** W Isls
188 F5 **Uig** Ag & B
208 C4 **Uig** Highld
208 F2 **Uig** Highld
232 d2 **Uig** W Isls
209 G5 **Uigshader** Highld
180 E4 **Uisken** Ag & B
231 K7 **Ulbster** Highld
137 L3 **Ulcat Row** Cumb
118 F6 **Ulceby** Lincs
126 D7 **Ulceby** N Linc
126 E7 **Ulceby Skitter** N Linc
33 L4 **Ulcombe** Kent
147 M7 **Uldale** Cumb
55 H7 **Uley** Gloucs
159 G4 **Ulgham** Nthumb
220 E3 **Ullapool** Highld
71 K2 **Ullenhall** Warwks
124 D3 **Ulleskelf** N York
87 G6 **Ullesthorpe** Leics
115 J4 **Ulley** Rothm
69 L4 **Ullingswick** Herefs
208 E6 **Ullinish Lodge Hotel** Highld
136 E3 **Ullock** Cumb
138 B3 **Ullswater** Cumb
128 E2 **Ulpha** Cumb
135 J7 **Ulrome** E R Yk
235 d3 **Ulsta** Shet
189 K7 **Ulva** Ag & B
129 G4 **Ulverston** Cumb
15 J6 **Ulwell** Dorset
164 F7 **Ulzieside** D & G
23 J6 **Umberleigh** Devon
224 F2 **Unapool** Highld
129 K2 **Underbarrow** Cumb
156 E5 **Under Burnmouth** Border
123 J4 **Undercliffe** C Brad
83 K2 **Underdale** Shrops
32 F3 **Under River** Kent
101 J3 **Underwood** Notts
38 C3 **Undy** Mons
237 c5 **Union Mills** IoM
235 d1 **Unst** Shet
115 G6 **Unstone** Derbys
28 C1 **Upavon** Wilts
14 C2 **Up Cerne** Dorset
46 D6 **Upchurch** Kent
24 B5 **Upcott** Devon
12 B2 **Up Exe** Devon
106 D8 **Upgate** Norfk
14 B2 **Uphall** Dorset
176 E4 **Uphall** W Loth
11 K3 **Upham** Devon
29 K7 **Upham** Hants
69 H2 **Uphampton** Herefs
70 E2 **Uphampton** Worcs
37 L8 **Uphill** N Som
112 D1 **Up Holland** Lancs
174 E7 **Uplawmoor** E Rens
55 H3 **Upleadon** Gloucs
142 D4 **Upleatham** R & Cl
13 L4 **Uploders** Dorset
24 F7 **Uplowman** Devon
13 H4 **Uplyme** Devon

30 D8 **Up Marden** W Susx
45 K3 **Upminster** Gt Lon
26 E7 **Up Mudford** Somset
30 B2 **Up Nately** Hants
12 F2 **Upottery** Devon
83 J6 **Upper Affcot** Shrops
222 E4 **Upper Ardchronie** Highld
84 D7 **Upper Arley** Worcs
41 L5 **Upper Basildon** W Berk
19 G4 **Upper Beeding** W Susx
88 E5 **Upper Benefield** Nhants
71 H2 **Upper Bentley** Worcs
230 C4 **Upper Bighouse** Highld
72 F4 **Upper Boddington** Nhants
72 C6 **Upper Brailes** Warwks
199 L2 **Upper Breakish** Highld
70 E4 **Upper Broadheath** Worcs
102 B7 **Upper Broughton** Notts
41 K6 **Upper Bucklebury** W Berk
28 D7 **Upper Burgate** Hants
148 D4 **Upperby** Cumb
75 H5 **Upper Caldecote** C Beds
67 L6 **Upper Chapel** Powys
27 L5 **Upper Chicksgrove** Wilts
28 F2 **Upper Chute** Wilts
45 G3 **Upper Clapton** Gt Lon
29 G3 **Upper Clatford** Hants
55 M5 **Upper Coberley** Gloucs
83 K3 **Upper Cound** Shrops
123 J8 **Upper Cumberworth** Kirk
215 H2 **Upper Dallachy** Moray
35 K4 **Upper Deal** Kent
74 F2 **Upper Dean** Bed
114 E1 **Upper Denby** Kirk
20 B4 **Upper Dicker** E Susx
230 E3 **Upper Dounreay** Highld
62 F2 **Upper Dovercourt** Essex
184 E6 **Upper Drumbane** Stirlg
133 G6 **Upper Dunsforth** N York
30 F3 **Upper Eashing** Surrey
213 J2 **Upper Eathie** Highld
70 B5 **Upper Egleton** Herefs
100 B2 **Upper Elkstone** Staffs
100 C4 **Upper Ellastone** Staffs
30 B4 **Upper Farringdon** Hants
55 H6 **Upper Framilode** Gloucs
30 C3 **Upper Froyle** Hants
208 E4 **Upperglen** Highld
26 C3 **Upper Godney** Somset
75 G7 **Upper Gravenhurst** C Beds
76 E7 **Upper Green** Essex
41 E7 **Upper Green** W Berk
54 E3 **Upper Grove Common** Herefs
30 D2 **Upper Hale** Surrey
43 H6 **Upper Halliford** Surrey
88 C3 **Upper Hambleton** Rutlnd
34 F3 **Upper Harbledown** Kent

32 E6 **Upper Hartfield** E Susx
55 L4 **Upper Hatherley** Gloucs
123 H6 **Upper Heaton** Kirk
133 L7 **Upper Helmsley** N York
68 F4 **Upper Hergest** Herefs
73 J3 **Upper Heyford** Nhants
57 J3 **Upper Heyford** Oxon
69 J4 **Upper Hill** Herefs
123 J6 **Upper Hopton** Kirk
100 A1 **Upper Hulme** Staffs
40 D2 **Upper Inglesham** Swindn
51 H6 **Upper Killay** Swans
183 G2 **Upper Kinchrackine** Ag & B
40 F4 **Upper Lambourn** W Berk
85 H3 **Upper Landywood** Staffs
38 C7 **Upper Langford** N Som
115 K7 **Upper Langwith** Derbys
187 G6 **Upper Largo** Fife
100 A5 **Upper Leigh** Staffs
206 D6 **Upper Lochton** Abers
85 J2 **Upper Longdon** Staffs
75 H7 **Upper & Lower Stondon** C Beds
231 J7 **Upper Lybster** Highld
54 E5 **Upper Lydbrook** Gloucs
69 H2 **Upper Lye** Herefs
113 M1 **Uppermill** Oldham
84 E8 **Upper Milton** Worcs
40 A3 **Upper Minety** Wilts
215 H4 **Upper Mulben** Moray
83 L5 **Upper Netchwood** Shrops
100 B5 **Upper Nobut** Staffs
18 C3 **Upper Norwood** W Susx
133 H8 **Upper Poppleton** C York
71 L5 **Upper Quinton** Warwks
28 F6 **Upper Ratley** Hants
56 D4 **Upper Rissington** Gloucs
70 B2 **Upper Rochford** Worcs
145 L3 **Upper Ruscoe** D & G
70 C2 **Upper Sapey** Herefs
39 L4 **Upper Seagry** Wilts
74 E5 **Upper Shelton** C Beds
106 D4 **Upper Sheringham** Norfk
173 L5 **Upper Skelmorlie** N Ayrs
56 D4 **Upper Slaughter** Gloucs
54 F6 **Upper Soudley** Gloucs
35 H6 **Upper Standen** Kent
154 E5 **Upper Stepford** D & G
92 F3 **Upper Stoke** Norfk
73 J3 **Upper Stowe** Nhants
28 D7 **Upper Street** Hants
93 H1 **Upper Street** Norfk
107 G8 **Upper Street** Norfk
77 H4 **Upper Street** Suffk
78 D4 **Upper Street** Suffk
59 H3 **Upper Sundon** C Beds
56 D3 **Upper Swell** Gloucs
92 E4 **Upper Tasburgh** Norfk
100 A5 **Upper Tean** Staffs
123 H8 **Upperthong** Kirk
30 F6 **Upperton** W Susx
69 L5 **Uppertown** Herefs
231 L1 **Uppertown** Highld
38 D7 **Upper Town** N Som
77 K2 **Upper Town** Suffk

51 G3 **Upper Tumble** Carmth
72 D5 **Upper Tysoe** Warwks
187 J1 **Upper Victoria** Angus
72 F5 **Upper Wardington** Oxon
19 L3 **Upper Wellingham** E Susx
92 F7 **Upper Weybread** Suffk
29 L4 **Upper Wield** Hants
58 C5 **Upper Winchendon** Bucks
28 C4 **Upper Woodford** Wilts
39 J5 **Upper Wraxall** Wilts
88 C4 **Uppingham** Rutlnd
83 L2 **Uppington** Shrops
133 G3 **Upsall** N York
168 C1 **Upsettlington** Border
60 C7 **Upshire** Essex
29 H5 **Up Somborne** Hants
35 G3 **Upstreet** Kent
14 C3 **Up Sydling** Dorset
58 C5 **Upton** Bucks
89 G4 **Upton** C Pete
89 H7 **Upton** Cambs
112 B7 **Upton** Ches W
5 L2 **Upton** Cnwll
7 G7 **Upton** Devon
12 E2 **Upton** Devon
14 E5 **Upton** Dorset
15 J4 **Upton** Dorset
29 G1 **Upton** Hants
29 G7 **Upton** Hants
86 D4 **Upton** Leics
116 E4 **Upton** Lincs
93 H2 **Upton** Norfk
102 B2 **Upton** Notts
116 C6 **Upton** Notts
41 K3 **Upton** Oxon
43 G5 **Upton** Slough
24 F5 **Upton** Somset
26 C6 **Upton** Somset
124 D7 **Upton** Wakefd
111 J4 **Upton** Wirral
54 F3 **Upton Bishop** Herefs
39 G6 **Upton Cheyney** S Glos
84 B5 **Upton Cressett** Shrops
30 B2 **Upton Grey** Hants
11 J4 **Upton Hellions** Devon
27 L4 **Upton Lovell** Wilts
83 K2 **Upton Magna** Shrops
27 G4 **Upton Noble** Somset
11 L5 **Upton Pyne** Devon
55 K5 **Upton St Leonards** Gloucs
27 K2 **Upton Scudamore** Wilts
71 G4 **Upton Snodsbury** Worcs
70 F6 **Upton upon Severn** Worcs
71 G2 **Upton Warren** Worcs
18 C3 **Upwaltham** W Susx
90 C3 **Upwell** Norfk
89 J6 **Upwood** Cambs
40 B8 **Urchfont** Wilts
113 H3 **Urmston** Traffd
215 G2 **Urquhart** Moray
142 C6 **Urra** N York
212 D4 **Urray** Highld
197 H5 **Usan** Angus
151 G6 **Ushaw Moor** Dur
54 B7 **Usk** Mons
117 H3 **Usselby** Lincs
151 H4 **Usworth** Sundld
112 D7 **Utkinton** Ches W
122 F3 **Utley** C Brad
11 J5 **Uton** Devon
118 D3 **Utterby** Lincs
100 C5 **Uttoxeter** Staffs
43 H4 **Uxbridge** Gt Lon
235 d2 **Uyeasound** Shet

49 G5 **Uzmaston** Pembks

V

236 d2 **Vale** Guern
80 F7 **Vale of Rheidol Railway** Cerdgn
108 C5 **Valley** IoA
209 H2 **Valtos** Highld
232 d2 **Valtos** W Isls
46 B3 **Vange** Essex
235 d3 **Vatsetter** Shet
208 D5 **Vatten** Highld
53 G6 **Vaynor** Myr Td
235 c6 **Veensgarth** Shet
68 D7 **Velindre** Powys
9 K3 **Venngreen** Devon
12 D4 **Venn Ottery** Devon
17 G6 **Ventnor** IoW
6 E4 **Venton** Devon
29 G1 **Vernham Dean** Hants
41 G8 **Vernham Street** Hants
15 K2 **Verwood** Dorset
4 E7 **Veryan** Cnwll
128 E5 **Vickerstown** Cumb
4 F4 **Victoria** Cnwll
235 d4 **Vidlin** Shet
215 G2 **Viewfield** Moray
175 J6 **Viewpark** N Lans
45 M7 **Vigo** Kent
236 d3 **Village de Putron** Guern
20 C3 **Vines Cross** E Susx
33 K2 **Vinters Park Crematorium** Kent
43 G6 **Virginia Water** Surrey
9 K6 **Virginstow** Devon
27 G2 **Vobster** Somset
235 c4 **Voe** Shet
69 G7 **Vowchurch** Herefs

W

140 E3 **Wackerfield** Dur
92 E5 **Wacton** Norfk
70 F5 **Wadborough** Worcs
58 C5 **Waddesdon** Bucks
7 K4 **Waddeton** Devon
117 G3 **Waddingham** Lincs
121 L2 **Waddington** Lancs
116 F8 **Waddington** Lincs
4 F2 **Wadebridge** Cnwll
13 H1 **Wadeford** Somset
88 E6 **Wadenhoe** Nhants
60 B4 **Wadesmill** Herts
33 H6 **Wadhurst** E Susx
114 F7 **Wadshelf** Derbys
115 K3 **Wadworth** Donc
104 D2 **Wainfleet All Saints** Lincs
104 D2 **Wainfleet St Mary** Lincs
9 G5 **Wainhouse Corner** Cnwll
46 C6 **Wainscott** Medway
122 F5 **Wainstalls** Calder
139 H5 **Waitby** Cumb
118 C2 **Waithe** Lincs
123 L6 **Wakefield** Wakefd
123 L7 **Wakefield Crematorium** Wakefd
88 D4 **Wakerley** Nhants
61 L3 **Wakes Colne** Essex
93 K8 **Walberswick** Suffk
18 C4 **Walberton** W Susx
146 D2 **Walbutt** D & G
26 D3 **Walcombe** Somset
103 H5 **Walcot** Lincs
83 L2 **Walcot** Shrops
40 D4 **Walcot** Swindn
87 H6 **Walcote** Leics
92 D7 **Walcot Green** Norfk
103 J2 **Walcott** Lincs

107 H6 **Walcott** Norfk
124 E6 **Walden Stubbs** N York
46 C7 **Walderslade** Medway
17 L1 **Walderton** W Susx
13 L4 **Walditch** Dorset
151 L5 **Waldridge** Dur
79 G5 **Waldringfield** Suffk
20 B2 **Waldron** E Susx
115 J5 **Wales** Rothm
26 E6 **Wales** Somset
117 J3 **Walesby** Lincs
116 B7 **Walesby** Notts
54 E4 **Walford** Herefs
83 H8 **Walford** Herefs
98 C8 **Walford Heath** Shrops
99 G3 **Walgherton** Ches E
74 B1 **Walgrave** Nhants
113 G2 **Walkden** Salfd
151 H3 **Walker** N u Ty
166 E3 **Walkerburn** Border
116 C3 **Walkeringham** Notts
116 C3 **Walkerith** Lincs
59 M3 **Walkern** Herts
186 D6 **Walkerton** Fife
16 B4 **Walkford** Dorset
6 D2 **Walkhampton** Devon
126 B3 **Walkington** E R Yk
115 G4 **Walkley** Sheff
122 C5 **Walk Mill** Lancs
71 J2 **Walkwood** Worcs
150 A2 **Wall** Nthumb
85 K3 **Wall** Staffs
153 C2 **Wallacetown** S Ayrs
163 J5 **Wallacetown** S Ayrs
19 L4 **Wallands Park** E Susx
111 J3 **Wallasey** Wirral
41 L3 **Wallingford** Oxon
44 F6 **Wallington** Gt Lon
17 H2 **Wallington** Hants
75 K7 **Wallington** Herts
15 K4 **Wallisdown** Poole
235 b5 **Walls** Shet
151 H2 **Wallsend** N Tyne
177 K4 **Wallyford** E Loth
35 K5 **Walmer** Kent
121 G5 **Walmer Bridge** Lancs
85 K5 **Walmley** Birm
93 H8 **Walpole** Suffk
104 E8 **Walpole Cross Keys** Norfk
90 D2 **Walpole Highway** Norfk
104 D8 **Walpole St Andrew** Norfk
90 C1 **Walpole St Peter** Norfk
85 H4 **Walsall** Wsall
122 D6 **Walsden** Calder
86 E7 **Walsgrave on Sowe** Covtry
78 B1 **Walsham le Willows** Suffk
132 F8 **Walshford** N York
90 C2 **Walsoken** Norfk
165 K1 **Walston** S Lans
59 K3 **Walsworth** Herts
42 D2 **Walter's Ash** Bucks
34 E5 **Waltham** Kent
118 C2 **Waltham** NE Lin
60 C7 **Waltham Abbey** Essex
29 K7 **Waltham Chase** Hants
60 B7 **Waltham Cross** Herts
102 D7 **Waltham on the Wolds** Leics
42 D5 **Waltham St Lawrence** W & M
45 G3 **Walthamstow** Gt Lon
148 D2 **Walton** Cumb
115 G7 **Walton** Derbys
124 C2 **Walton** Leeds
87 H6 **Walton** Leics
74 C7 **Walton** M Keyn
68 F3 **Walton** Powys

26 C4 **Walton** Somset
79 G7 **Walton** Suffk
17 M2 **Walton** W Susx
123 L6 **Walton** Wakefd
98 E8 **Walton** Wrekin
55 K2 **Walton Cardiff** Gloucs
49 H3 **Walton East** Pembks
38 B5 **Walton-in-Gordano** N Som
112 E4 **Walton Lea Crematorium** Warrtn
121 H5 **Walton-le-Dale** Lancs
43 J6 **Walton-on-Thames** Surrey
99 L7 **Walton-on-the-Hill** Staffs
31 L1 **Walton on the Hill** Surrey
62 F4 **Walton on the Naze** Essex
101 L8 **Walton on the Wolds** Leics
100 E8 **Walton-on-Trent** Derbys
38 B6 **Walton Park** N Som
48 E5 **Walton West** Pembks
122 E1 **Waltonwrays Crematorium** N York
141 G4 **Walworth** Darltn
45 G4 **Walworth** Gt Lon
48 E5 **Walwyn's Castle** Pembks
13 H2 **Wambrook** Somset
30 F2 **Wanborough** Surrey
40 E4 **Wanborough** Swindn
44 E5 **Wandsworth** Gt Lon
93 K7 **Wangford** Suffk
87 H2 **Wanlip** Leics
165 G6 **Wanlockhead** D & G
20 C5 **Wannock** E Susx
88 F4 **Wansford** C Pete
135 G7 **Wansford** E R Yk
33 K4 **Wanshurst Green** Kent
45 H3 **Wanstead** Gt Lon
27 G3 **Wanstrow** Somset
55 G7 **Wanswell** Gloucs
41 H3 **Wantage** Oxon
72 E2 **Wappenbury** Warwks
73 J5 **Wappenham** Nhants
20 C3 **Warbleton** E Susx
41 L2 **Warborough** Oxon
89 K7 **Warboys** Cambs
120 D3 **Warbreck** Bpool
9 G6 **Warbstow** Cnwll
113 G4 **Warburton** Traffd
139 H4 **Warcop** Cumb
150 A2 **Warden** Nthumb
72 F5 **Wardington** Oxon
98 E2 **Wardle** Ches E
122 D6 **Wardle** Rochdl
151 H3 **Wardley** Gatesd
88 B4 **Wardley** Rutlnd
114 D6 **Wardlow** Derbys
90 C6 **Wardy Hill** Cambs
60 B5 **Ware** Herts
15 H5 **Wareham** Dorset
34 D7 **Warehorne** Kent
169 H4 **Warenford** Nthumb
60 C5 **Wareside** Herts
75 J4 **Waresley** Cambs
42 E6 **Warfield** Br For
7 K6 **Warfleet** Devon
42 C5 **Wargrave** Wokham
105 M4 **Warham All Saints** Norfk
105 M4 **Warham St Mary** Norfk
157 L6 **Wark** Nthumb
168 C2 **Wark** Nthumb
23 K6 **Warkleigh** Devon
88 C7 **Warkton** Nhants
72 F6 **Warkworth** Nhants
159 G2 **Warkworth** Nthumb
132 E2 **Warlaby** N York
5 J3 **Warleggan** Cnwll

122 F5 **Warley Town** Calder
32 C2 **Warlingham** Surrey
147 L2 **Warmanbie** D & G
124 B6 **Warmfield** Wakefd
99 G1 **Warmingham** Ches E
88 F5 **Warmington** Nhants
72 E5 **Warmington** Warwks
27 K3 **Warminster** Wilts
38 F5 **Warmley** S Glos
115 K2 **Warmsworth** Donc
14 E5 **Warmwell** Dorset
29 L6 **Warnford** Hants
31 J5 **Warnham** W Susx
18 D4 **Warningcamp** W Susx
31 L6 **Warninglid** W Susx
113 K7 **Warren** Ches E
48 F7 **Warren** Pembks
165 J2 **Warrenhill** S Lans
42 D4 **Warren Row** W & M
34 C4 **Warren Street** Kent
74 C4 **Warrington** M Keyn
112 E4 **Warrington** Warrtn
177 H4 **Warriston** C Edin
177 H3 **Warriston Crematorium** C Edin
16 F2 **Warsash** Hants
100 C2 **Warslow** Staffs
125 K1 **Warter** E R Yk
132 C4 **Warthermaske** N York
133 K7 **Warthill** N York
20 D4 **Wartling** E Susx
102 B7 **Wartnaby** Leics
120 E5 **Warton** Lancs
129 K5 **Warton** Lancs
86 C3 **Warton** Warwks
72 C2 **Warwick** Warwks
148 E4 **Warwick Bridge** Cumb
72 C2 **Warwick Castle** Warwks
72 D3 **Warwick Services** Warwks
234 c4 **Wasbister** Ork
137 G5 **Wasdale Head** Cumb
5 G2 **Washaway** Cnwll
7 J5 **Washbourne** Devon
78 D6 **Washbrook** Suffk
11 L2 **Washfield** Devon
140 D6 **Washfold** N York
25 G3 **Washford** Somset
11 J3 **Washford Pyne** Devon
117 G7 **Washingborough** Lincs
151 H4 **Washington** Sundld
18 F3 **Washington** W Susx
151 G4 **Washington Services** Gatesd
72 C3 **Wasperton** Warwks
133 H4 **Wass** N York
25 G3 **Watchet** Somset
40 E3 **Watchfield** Oxon
138 D7 **Watchgate** Cumb
11 H8 **Water** Devon
76 C2 **Waterbeach** Cambs
18 B4 **Waterbeach** W Susx
155 M6 **Waterbeck** D & G
125 J3 **Water End** E R Yk
100 B3 **Waterfall** Staffs
175 G7 **Waterfoot** E Rens
60 A5 **Waterford** Herts
177 H7 **Waterheads** Border
100 B3 **Waterhouses** Staffs
33 H3 **Wateringbury** Kent
199 K2 **Waterloo** Highld
175 L7 **Waterloo** N Lans
195 G8 **Waterloo** P & K
49 G6 **Waterloo** Pembks
111 K2 **Waterloo** Sefton
17 J1 **Waterlooville** Hants
138 C3 **Watermillock** Cumb
89 G4 **Water Newton** Cambs
85 L5 **Water Orton** Warwks
57 L6 **Waterperry** Oxon

25 G6	**Waterrow** Somset	
18 D3	**Watersfield** W Susx	
121 K5	**Waterside** Bl w D	
163 K7	**Waterside** E Ayrs	
163 L2	**Waterside** E Ayrs	
175 J4	**Waterside** E Duns	
208 B5	**Waterstein** Highld	
57 M6	**Waterstock** Oxon	
48 F6	**Waterston** Pembks	
73 J7	**Water Stratford** Bucks	
98 F8	**Waters Upton** Wrekin	
43 J2	**Watford** Herts	
73 H2	**Watford** Nhants	
73 H2	**Watford Gap Services** Nhants	
132 B6	**Wath** N York	
132 E4	**Wath** N York	
115 H2	**Wath upon Dearne** Rothm	
90 E2	**Watlington** Norfk	
42 B2	**Watlington** Oxon	
231 J5	**Watten** Highld	
92 B8	**Wattisfield** Suffk	
78 B4	**Wattisham** Suffk	
13 L4	**Watton** Dorset	
126 C1	**Watton** E R Yk	
91 K4	**Watton** Norfk	
60 A4	**Watton-at-Stone** Herts	
175 K4	**Wattston** N Lans	
37 J3	**Wattsville** Caerph	
206 C6	**Waulkmill** Abers	
51 H6	**Waunarlwydd** Swans	
80 E6	**Waunfawr** Cerdgn	
95 J2	**Waunfawr** Gwynd	
74 C6	**Wavendon** M Keyn	
147 L5	**Waverbridge** Cumb	
112 C8	**Waverton** Ches W	
147 L5	**Waverton** Cumb	
126 D3	**Wawne** E R Yk	
107 J7	**Waxham** Norfk	
13 K2	**Wayford** Somset	
13 L3	**Waytown** Dorset	
11 K3	**Way Village** Devon	
25 H4	**Weacombe** Somset	
56 F7	**Weald** Oxon	
44 D3	**Wealdstone** Gt Lon	
123 K2	**Weardley** Leeds	
26 B2	**Weare** Somset	
23 G6	**Weare Giffard** Devon	
149 L6	**Wearhead** Dur	
26 B5	**Wearne** Somset	
105 K7	**Weasenham All Saints** Norfk	
105 K7	**Weasenham St Peter** Norfk	
113 J2	**Weaste** Salfd	
112 E6	**Weaverham** Ches W	
134 E5	**Weaverthorpe** N York	
71 H2	**Webheath** Worcs	
216 F7	**Wedderlairs** Abers	
86 D5	**Weddington** Warwks	
40 B8	**Wedhampton** Wilts	
26 C2	**Wedmore** Somset	
85 H4	**Wednesbury** Sandw	
85 G4	**Wednesfield** Wolves	
58 D4	**Weedon** Bucks	
73 J3	**Weedon** Nhants	
73 H5	**Weedon Lois** Nhants	
85 K3	**Weeford** Staffs	
29 J5	**Weeke** Hants	
88 C7	**Weekley** Nhants	
9 H5	**Week St Mary** Cnwll	
126 D3	**Weel** E R Yk	
62 D4	**Weeley** Essex	
62 D4	**Weeley Crematorium** Essex	
62 D4	**Weeley Heath** Essex	
194 D6	**Weem** P & K	
71 J4	**Weethley** Warwks	
91 H5	**Weeting** Norfk	
127 H6	**Weeton** E R Yk	
120 E4	**Weeton** Lancs	
123 K2	**Weeton** N York	
123 K3	**Weetwood** Leeds	
122 C5	**Weir** Lancs	
6 C3	**Weir Quay** Devon	
235 c5	**Weisdale** Shet	
92 C2	**Welborne** Norfk	
102 F2	**Welbourn** Lincs	
133 L6	**Welburn** N York	
141 J6	**Welbury** N York	
102 F5	**Welby** Lincs	
22 C7	**Welcombe** Devon	
87 J7	**Welford** Nhants	
41 H5	**Welford** W Berk	
71 K4	**Welford-on-Avon** Warwks	
87 L5	**Welham** Leics	
116 B5	**Welham** Notts	
59 L6	**Welham Green** Herts	
30 C3	**Well** Hants	
118 F6	**Well** Lincs	
132 D3	**Well** N York	
70 E6	**Welland** Worcs	
196 D8	**Wellbank** Angus	
72 C4	**Wellesbourne** Warwks	
59 K3	**Well Head** Herts	
45 J5	**Welling** Gt Lon	
74 C2	**Wellingborough** Nhants	
105 L7	**Wellingham** Norfk	
103 G2	**Wellingore** Lincs	
136 F6	**Wellington** Cumb	
69 K5	**Wellington** Herefs	
25 H7	**Wellington** Somset	
84 B2	**Wellington** Wrekin	
70 C6	**Wellington Heath** Herefs	
39 H8	**Wellow** BaNES	
16 E5	**Wellow** IoW	
116 A7	**Wellow** Notts	
26 D3	**Wells** Somset	
105 L4	**Wells-next-the-sea** Norfk	
61 G4	**Wellstye Green** Essex	
185 K3	**Welltree** P & K	
176 E2	**Wellwood** Fife	
90 D5	**Welney** Norfk	
98 C5	**Welshampton** Shrops	
98 A6	**Welsh Frankton** Shrops	
54 D4	**Welsh Newton** Herefs	
82 E3	**Welshpool** Powys	
36 F5	**Welsh St Donats** V Glam	
148 C6	**Welton** Cumb	
126 B5	**Welton** E R Yk	
117 G5	**Welton** Lincs	
73 H2	**Welton** Nhants	
119 G7	**Welton le Marsh** Lincs	
118 C4	**Welton le Wold** Lincs	
127 H6	**Welwick** E R Yk	
59 L5	**Welwyn** Herts	
59 L5	**Welwyn Garden City** Herts	
98 D6	**Wem** Shrops	
25 L4	**Wembdon** Somset	
44 D3	**Wembley** Gt Lon	
6 D6	**Wembury** Devon	
10 F3	**Wemworthy** Devon	
173 L4	**Wemyss Bay** Inver	
76 D7	**Wendens Ambo** Essex	
57 K4	**Wendlebury** Oxon	
91 L2	**Wendling** Norfk	
58 E6	**Wendover** Bucks	
3 H5	**Wendron** Cnwll	
75 K5	**Wendy** Cambs	
93 J7	**Wenhaston** Suffk	
89 J7	**Wennington** Cambs	
45 K4	**Wennington** Gt Lon	
130 C5	**Wennington** Lancs	
100 E1	**Wensley** Derbys	
131 K2	**Wensley** N York	
124 D6	**Wentbridge** Wakefd	
83 H5	**Wentnor** Shrops	
90 C7	**Wentworth** Cambs	
115 G2	**Wentworth** Rothm	
37 H6	**Wenvoe** V Glam	
69 H4	**Weobley** Herefs	
69 H4	**Weobley Marsh** Herefs	
18 E4	**Wepham** W Susx	
90 F3	**Wereham** Norfk	
89 H3	**Werrington** C Pete	
9 J7	**Werrington** Cnwll	
112 B6	**Wervin** Ches W	
120 F4	**Wesham** Lancs	
101 G2	**Wessington** Derbys	
91 H1	**West Acre** Norfk	
7 G6	**West Alvington** Devon	
24 D6	**West Anstey** Devon	
118 C6	**West Ashby** Lincs	
17 M2	**West Ashling** W Susx	
27 K1	**West Ashton** Wilts	
140 F3	**West Auckland** Dur	
134 F3	**West Ayton** N York	
25 J5	**West Bagborough** Somset	
112 D5	**West Bank** Halton	
117 K5	**West Barkwith** Lincs	
143 G5	**West Barnby** N York	
178 E3	**West Barns** E Loth	
105 L5	**West Barsham** Norfk	
13 L4	**West Bay** Dorset	
106 D5	**West Beckham** Norfk	
43 H5	**West Bedfont** Surrey	
35 G3	**Westbere** Kent	
62 A3	**West Bergholt** Essex	
41 K6	**West Berkshire Crematorium** W Berk	
14 A5	**West Bexington** Dorset	
91 G1	**West Bilney** Norfk	
19 J4	**West Blatchington** Br & H	
91 G1	**West Boldon** S Tyne	
102 D4	**Westborough** Lincs	
15 K4	**Westbourne** Bmouth	
17 L2	**Westbourne** W Susx	
123 H4	**West Bowling** C Brad	
34 E6	**West Brabourne** Kent	
91 K2	**West Bradenham** Norfk	
121 L2	**West Bradford** Lancs	
26 E4	**West Bradley** Somset	
123 K7	**West Bretton** Wakefd	
101 L5	**West Bridgford** Notts	
85 H5	**West Bromwich** Sandw	
85 H5	**West Bromwich Crematorium** Sandw	
35 J2	**Westbrook** Kent	
41 H6	**Westbrook** W Berk	
23 K5	**West Buckland** Devon	
25 J7	**West Buckland** Somset	
131 J3	**West Burton** N York	
73 J7	**Westbury** Bucks	
83 G2	**Westbury** Shrops	
27 K2	**Westbury** Wilts	
27 K2	**Westbury Leigh** Wilts	
55 G5	**Westbury on Severn** Gloucs	
38 E5	**Westbury-on-Trym** Bristl	
26 D2	**Westbury-sub-Mendip** Somset	
116 D1	**West Butterwick** N Linc	
120 E4	**Westby** Lancs	
43 H7	**West Byfleet** Surrey	
144 D8	**West Cairngaan** D & G	
93 K2	**West Caister** Norfk	
176 D5	**West Calder** W Loth	
26 E6	**West Camel** Somset	
14 E5	**West Chaldon** Dorset	
41 G3	**West Challow** Oxon	
7 H7	**West Charleton** Devon	
159 G3	**West Chevington** Nthumb	
18 E3	**West Chiltington** W Susx	
26 C8	**West Chinnock** Somset	
31 H2	**West Clandon** Surrey	
35 J5	**West Cliffe** Kent	
46 E3	**Westcliff-on-Sea** Sthend	
26 D8	**West Coker** Somset	
27 G4	**Westcombe** Somset	
26 E3	**West Compton** Somset	
14 B4	**West Compton Abbas** Dorset	
56 E4	**Westcote** Gloucs	
57 H3	**Westcote Barton** Oxon	
58 B5	**Westcott** Bucks	
12 C2	**Westcott** Devon	
31 J2	**Westcott** Surrey	
125 G3	**West Cottingwith** N York	
40 E7	**Westcourt** Wilts	
124 F6	**West Cowick** E R Yk	
51 H7	**West Cross** Swans	
148 B5	**West Curthwaite** Cumb	
20 B5	**Westdean** E Susx	
18 B3	**West Dean** W Susx	
28 E6	**West Dean** Wilts	
89 G2	**West Deeping** Lincs	
111 L3	**West Derby** Lpool	
90 F4	**West Dereham** Norfk	
23 H3	**West Down** Devon	
8 E7	**Westdowns** Cnwll	
43 H4	**West Drayton** Gt Lon	
116 B6	**West Drayton** Notts	
231 J2	**West Dunnet** Highld	
126 C5	**West Ella** E R Yk	
74 E4	**West End** Bed	
29 J8	**West End** Hants	
38 C6	**West End** N Som	
93 K2	**West End** Norfk	
42 F7	**West End** Surrey	
27 M6	**West End** Wilts	
42 A7	**West End Green** Hants	
231 G5	**Westerdale** Highld	
142 E6	**Westerdale** N York	
212 F7	**Wester Drumashie** Highld	
78 E5	**Westerfield** Suffk	
18 C5	**Westergate** W Susx	
32 D3	**Westerham** Kent	
150 F2	**Westerhope** N u Ty	
7 K4	**Westerland** Devon	
39 G4	**Westerleigh** S Glos	
39 G5	**Westerleigh Crematorium** S Glos	
176 D4	**Wester Ochiltree** W Loth	
187 J6	**Wester Pitkierie** Fife	
220 C5	**Wester Ross** Highld	
197 G5	**Westerton** Angus	
235 c6	**Westerwick** Shet	
33 J3	**West Farleigh** Kent	
73 G4	**West Farndon** Nhants	
97 M7	**West Felton** Shrops	
26 F2	**Westfield** BaNES	
136 D2	**Westfield** Cumb	
21 G3	**Westfield** E Susx	
230 F3	**Westfield** Highld	
175 J4	**Westfield** N Lans	
92 B2	**Westfield** Norfk	
176 C4	**Westfield** W Loth	
195 J6	**Westfields of Rattray** P & K	
150 A3	**Westgate** Dur	
125 J8	**Westgate** N Linc	
35 J2	**Westgate on Sea** Kent	
40 E7	**West Grafton** Wilts	
30 C1	**West Green** Hants	
28 E6	**West Grimstead** Wilts	
31 K6	**West Grinstead** W Susx	
14 E5	**West Haddlesey** N York	

Ref	Place
73 J1	West Haddon Nhants
41 K3	West Hagbourne Oxon
84 F7	West Hagley Worcs
93 J7	Westhall Suffk
101 H4	West Hallam Derbys
125 L6	West Halton N Linc
14 C6	Westham Dorset
20 D5	Westham E Susx
45 H4	West Ham Gt Lon
26 B3	Westham Somset
18 B4	Westhampnett W Susx
115 H6	West Handley Derbys
41 H2	West Hanney Oxon
61 H7	West Hanningfield Essex
28 C5	West Harnham Wilts
38 E8	West Harptree BaNES
30 C7	West Harting W Susx
25 L7	West Hatch Somset
27 L5	West Hatch Wilts
187 J1	West Haven Angus
26 C3	Westhay Somset
85 J7	West Heath Birm
227 H5	West Helmsdale Highld
41 H3	West Hendred Oxon
59 J7	West Hertfordshire Crematorium Herts
134 E4	West Heslerton N York
38 B7	West Hewish N Som
69 L5	Westhide Herefs
206 F4	Westhill Abers
12 D4	West Hill Devon
32 C6	West Hoathly W Susx
15 G5	West Holme Dorset
69 J4	Westhope Herefs
83 J6	Westhope Shrops
45 M3	West Horndon Essex
103 L6	Westhorpe Lincs
78 C2	Westhorpe Suffk
26 E3	West Horrington Somset
31 H2	West Horsley Surrey
35 H6	West Hougham Kent
112 F1	Westhoughton Bolton
130 D5	Westhouse N York
101 H2	Westhouses Derbys
15 K4	West Howe Bmouth
31 K2	Westhumble Surrey
185 M3	West Huntingtower P & K
25 L3	West Huntspill Somset
34 F7	West Hythe Kent
41 J4	West Ilsley W Berk
17 L3	West Itchenor W Susx
40 C6	West Kennett Wilts
173 L8	West Kilbride N Ayrs
45 L7	West Kingsdown Kent
39 J5	West Kington Wilts
111 H4	West Kirby Wirral
134 D4	West Knapton N York
14 D5	West Knighton Dorset
27 K5	West Knoyle Wilts
6 F5	Westlake Devon
26 B7	West Lambrook Somset
35 J5	West Langdon Kent
191 L5	West Laroch Highld
30 E7	West Lavington W Susx
28 A2	West Lavington Wilts
140 E5	West Layton N York
101 K7	West Leake Notts
11 G4	West Leigh Devon
23 G5	Westleigh Devon
25 G7	Westleigh Devon
25 H5	West Leigh Somset
79 J2	Westleton Suffk
91 J1	West Lexham Norfk
77 J2	Westley Suffk
76 E3	Westley Waterless Cambs
133 K6	West Lilling N York
58 C6	Westlington Bucks
176 F7	West Linton Border
148 D3	Westlinton Cumb
39 H5	West Littleton S Glos
41 H3	West Lockinge Oxon
44 E4	West London Crematorium Gt Lon
14 F6	West Lulworth Dorset
134 E5	West Lutton N York
26 E5	West Lydford Somset
25 L5	West Lyng Somset
104 F7	West Lynn Norfk
33 H2	West Malling Kent
70 D5	West Malvern Worcs
30 C8	West Marden W Susx
116 B6	West Markham Notts
35 H3	Westmarsh Kent
127 G8	West Marsh NE Lin
122 D1	West Marton N York
27 K7	West Melbury Dorset
29 M6	West Meon Hants
62 B5	West Mersea Essex
19 K3	Westmeston E Susx
84 E7	West Midland Safari Park Worcs
60 B3	Westmill Herts
13 L3	West Milton Dorset
44 F4	Westminster Gt Lon
46 E5	West Minster Kent
43 J6	West Molesey Surrey
25 K5	West Monkton Somset
15 K2	West Moors Dorset
15 G4	West Morden Dorset
167 J2	West Morriston Border
26 E7	West Mudford Somset
196 B5	Westmuir Angus
133 L4	West Ness N York
147 K6	Westnewton Cumb
126 F3	West Newton E R Yk
105 H6	West Newton Norfk
25 L5	West Newton Somset
44 F5	West Norwood Gt Lon
44 F5	West Norwood Crematorium Gt Lon
151 J2	Weston S Tyne
7 J2	West Ogwell Devon
39 G6	Weston BaNES
99 G3	Weston Ches E
12 E3	Weston Devon
12 F5	Weston Devon
30 B6	Weston Hants
59 L3	Weston Herts
103 M7	Weston Lincs
123 H2	Weston N York
73 H5	Weston Nhants
116 C7	Weston Notts
83 L5	Weston Shrops
97 L6	Weston Shrops
99 L6	Weston Staffs
41 H5	Weston W Berk
69 L6	Weston Beggard Herefs
39 J3	Westonbirt Gloucs
87 L5	Weston by Welland Nhants
76 E4	Weston Colville Cambs
30 B3	Weston Corbett Hants
99 L4	Weston Coyney C Stke
73 L3	Weston Favell Nhants
76 F4	Weston Green Cambs
84 D2	Weston Heath Shrops
59 G2	Westoning C Beds
38 C5	Weston-in-Gordano N Som
99 H7	Weston Jones Staffs
92 D1	Weston Longville Norfk
98 B7	Weston Lullingfields Shrops
6 C4	Weston Mill Crematorium C Plym
57 K4	Weston-on-the-Green Oxon
30 B3	Weston Patrick Hants
97 L5	Weston Rhyn Shrops
71 K6	Weston Subedge Gloucs
37 L7	Weston-Super-Mare N Som
38 A7	Weston-super-Mare Crematorium N Som
58 D6	Weston Turville Bucks
84 E2	Weston-under-Lizard Staffs
54 F4	Weston under Penyard Herefs
98 E6	Weston-under-Redcastle Shrops
72 D1	Weston under Wetherley Warwks
100 F4	Weston Underwood Derbys
74 C4	Weston Underwood M Keyn
101 H6	Weston-upon-Trent Derbys
25 M4	Westonzoyland Somset
27 J7	West Orchard Dorset
40 C6	West Overton Wilts
134 B6	Westow N York
206 E5	West Park Abers
15 K3	West Parley Dorset
33 H3	West Peckham Kent
151 G4	West Pelton Dur
26 D4	West Pennard Somset
4 B4	West Pentire Cnwll
75 G2	West Perry Cambs
24 D3	West Porlock Somset
26 B7	Westport Somset
14 D2	West Pulham Dorset
9 K2	West Putford Devon
25 H3	West Quantoxhead Somset
176 B3	Westquarter Falk
151 H5	West Rainton Dur
117 H4	West Rasen Lincs
234 c3	Westray Ork
234 c3	*Westray Airport* Ork
105 L7	West Raynham Norfk
41 K4	Westridge Green W Berk
176 B5	Westrigg W Loth
150 F2	West Road Crematorium N u Ty
40 C7	Westrop Swindn
141 K6	West Rounton N York
90 F7	West Row Suffk
105 K6	West Rudham Norfk
106 E4	West Runton Norfk
178 D7	Westruther Border
90 B4	Westry Cambs
178 B5	West Saltoun E Loth
11 J4	West Sandford Devon
235 d3	West Sandwick Shet
131 K3	West Scrafton N York
14 D4	West Stafford Dorset
116 C3	West Stockwith Notts
17 M2	West Stoke W Susx
27 H6	West Stour Dorset
35 H3	West Stourmouth Kent
77 J1	West Stow Suffk
40 C7	West Stowell Wilts
78 B1	West Street Suffk
77 J2	West Suffolk Crematorium Suffk
132 D4	West Tanfield N York
5 J3	West Taphouse Cnwll
172 E5	West Tarbert Ag & B
18 F5	West Tarring W Susx
158 F3	West Thirston Nthumb
17 L3	West Thorney W Susx
101 L7	West Thorpe Notts
45 L4	West Thurrock Thurr
46 A4	West Tilbury Thurr
29 M5	West Tisted Hants
117 J5	West Torrington Lincs
17 K3	West Town Hants
38 C6	West Town N Som
28 F5	West Tytherley Hants
90 C2	West Walton Norfk
90 C2	West Walton Highway Norfk
148 B6	Westward Cumb
23 G5	Westward Ho! Devon
34 D5	Westwell Kent
56 E6	Westwell Oxon
34 C5	Westwell Leacon Kent
28 F7	West Wellow Hants
6 D6	West Wembury Devon
186 E7	West Wemyss Fife
76 B2	Westwick Cambs
76 E5	West Wickham Cambs
45 G6	West Wickham Gt Lon
49 H6	West Williamston Pembks
39 K7	West Wiltshire Crematorium Wilts
90 F1	West Winch Norfk
28 E5	West Winterslow Wilts
17 L3	West Wittering W Susx
131 K2	West Witton N York
12 C3	Westwood Devon
35 K2	Westwood Kent
39 J8	Westwood Wilts
157 M5	West Woodburn Nthumb
41 H7	West Woodhay W Berk
116 C2	Westwoodside N Linc
30 C4	West Worldham Hants
18 F5	West Worthing W Susx
76 E4	West Wratting Cambs
148 E4	Wetheral Cumb
124 B2	Wetherby Leeds
78 B3	Wetherden Suffk
78 D2	Wetheringsett Suffk
61 H2	Wethersfield Essex
78 D2	Wetherup Street Suffk
99 L3	Wetley Rocks Staffs
98 F1	Wettenhall Ches E
100 C2	Wetton Staffs
134 E7	Wetwang E R Yk
99 H5	Wetwood Staffs
40 F8	Wexcombe Wilts
106 D4	Weybourne Norfk
30 D2	Weybourne Surrey
92 F7	Weybread Suffk
92 F7	Weybread Street Suffk
43 H7	Weybridge Surrey
13 H3	Weycroft Devon
231 H3	Weydale Highld
28 F3	Weyhill Hants
14 D6	Weymouth Dorset
14 C6	Weymouth Crematorium Dorset
74 B7	Whaddon Bucks
75 L5	Whaddon Cambs
55 J5	Whaddon Gloucs
28 D6	Whaddon Wilts
39 K7	Whaddon Wilts
115 K7	Whaley Derbys
114 A5	Whaley Bridge Derbys

115 K7 **Whaley Thorns** Derbys
231 K7 **Whaligoe** Highld
121 L4 **Whalley** Lancs
235 d4 **Whalsay** Shet
158 E6 **Whalton** Nthumb
104 A7 **Whaplode** Lincs
89 K2 **Whaplode Drove** Lincs
72 E4 **Wharf** Warwks
130 E5 **Wharfe** N York
120 F4 **Wharles** Lancs
74 D5 **Wharley End** C Beds
114 F3 **Wharncliffe Side** Sheff
134 D6 **Wharram-le-Street** N York
69 K4 **Wharton** Herefs
140 E6 **Whashton** N York
129 L4 **Whasset** Cumb
72 C5 **Whatcote** Warwks
86 B4 **Whateley** Warwks
78 B5 **Whatfield** Suffk
13 J2 **Whatley** Somset
27 G3 **Whatley** Somset
20 F3 **Whatlington** E Susx
34 F5 **Whatsole Street** Kent
101 G2 **Whatstandwell** Derbys
102 C5 **Whatton** Notts
145 J5 **Whauphill** D & G
93 K5 **Wheatacre** Norfk
59 K5 **Wheathampstead** Herts
84 B6 **Wheathill** Shrops
30 C4 **Wheatley** Hants
57 L6 **Wheatley** Oxon
151 J6 **Wheatley Hill** Dur
115 L1 **Wheatley Hills** Donc
84 F2 **Wheaton Aston** Staffs
24 E4 **Wheddon Cross** Somset
99 H2 **Wheelock** Ches E
121 J6 **Wheelton** Lancs
125 G2 **Wheldrake** C York
56 D7 **Whelford** Gloucs
59 G6 **Whelpley Hill** Bucks
60 A4 **Whempstead** Herts
133 K5 **Whenby** N York
77 J3 **Whepstead** Suffk
78 E6 **Wherstead** Suffk
29 H3 **Wherwell** Hants
114 C6 **Wheston** Derbys
33 H4 **Whetsted** Kent
87 G4 **Whetstone** Leics
128 D3 **Whicham** Cumb
72 C7 **Whichford** Warwks
150 F3 **Whickham** Gatesd
11 G6 **Whiddon Down** Devon
196 D7 **Whigstreet** Angus
73 J2 **Whilton** Nhants
12 D3 **Whimple** Devon
107 H6 **Whimpwell Green** Norfk
92 B2 **Whinburgh** Norfk
146 C4 **Whinnie Liggate** D & G
217 K7 **Whinnyfold** Abers
17 G4 **Whippingham** IoW
59 G4 **Whipsnade** C Beds
59 G4 **Whipsnade Wild Animal Park** C Beds
12 B4 **Whipton** Devon
116 E7 **Whisby** Lincs
88 B2 **Whissendine** Rutlnd
105 L7 **Whissonsett** Norfk
183 J8 **Whistlefield** Ag & B
183 G8 **Whistlefield Inn** Ag & B
42 C5 **Whistley Green** Wokham
112 C3 **Whiston** Knows
74 B3 **Whiston** Nhants
115 H4 **Whiston** Rothm
84 F2 **Whiston** Staffs

100 B3 **Whiston** Staffs
128 D3 **Whitbeck** Cumb
70 D3 **Whitbourne** Herefs
151 J3 **Whitburn** S Tyne
176 C5 **Whitburn** W Loth
143 J5 **Whitby** N York
178 F6 **Whitchester** Border
38 F6 **Whitchurch** BaNES
58 D4 **Whitchurch** Bucks
37 J4 **Whitchurch** Cardif
6 D2 **Whitchurch** Devon
29 J2 **Whitchurch** Hants
54 D4 **Whitchurch** Herefs
41 M5 **Whitchurch** Oxon
48 D3 **Whitchurch** Pembks
98 D4 **Whitchurch** Shrops
13 K4 **Whitchurch Canonicorum** Dorset
41 M5 **Whitchurch Hill** Oxon
14 D5 **Whitcombe** Dorset
83 H5 **Whitcot** Shrops
82 F6 **Whitcott Keysett** Shrops
86 B5 **Whiteacre Heath** Warwks
25 H7 **White Ball** Somset
202 D3 **Whitebridge** Highld
54 D6 **Whitebrook** Mons
207 H2 **Whitecairns** Abers
45 G4 **Whitechapel** Gt Lon
121 H3 **White Chapel** Lancs
54 E6 **Whitecliffe** Gloucs
61 L3 **White Colne** Essex
177 K4 **Whitecraig** E Loth
144 E4 **Whitecrook** D & G
3 H6 **White Cross** Cnwll
176 C3 **Whitecross** Falk
70 E7 **White End** Worcs
222 F4 **Whiteface** Highld
161 L2 **Whitefarland** N Ayrs
163 H7 **Whitefaulds** S Ayrs
113 J1 **Whitefield** Bury
25 G5 **Whitefield** Somset
206 D1 **Whiteford** Abers
112 F7 **Whitegate** Ches W
234 d5 **Whitehall** Ork
136 D4 **Whitehaven** Cumb
30 C5 **Whitehill and Bordon** Hants
216 C2 **Whitehills** Abers
206 C3 **Whitehouse** Abers
172 N6 **Whitehouse** Ag & B
178 D3 **Whitekirk** E Loth
14 D3 **White Lackington** Dorset
26 B7 **Whitelackington** Somset
71 G4 **White Ladies Aston** Worcs
58 D6 **Whiteleaf** Bucks
17 G6 **Whiteley Bank** IoW
214 B4 **Whitemire** Moray
101 K4 **Whitemoor** C Nott
4 F4 **Whitemoor** Cnwll
235 c6 **Whiteness** Shet
61 J4 **White Notley** Essex
28 E6 **Whiteparish** Wilts
118 E6 **White Pit** Lincs
206 F2 **Whiterashes** Abers
60 E5 **White Roding** Essex
231 L5 **Whiterow** Highld
214 C3 **Whiterow** Moray
55 J6 **Whiteshill** Gloucs
20 B3 **Whitesmith** E Susx
13 H1 **Whitestaunton** Somset
11 K6 **Whitestone Cross** Devon
42 D5 **White Waltham** W & M
121 K2 **Whitewell** Lancs
35 J5 **Whitfield** Kent
73 H6 **Whitfield** Nhants
149 K4 **Whitfield** Nthumb
38 F3 **Whitfield** S Glos
13 G4 **Whitford** Devon

111 G5 **Whitford** Flints
125 J6 **Whitgift** E R Yk
99 K6 **Whitgreave** Staffs
145 J6 **Whithorn** D & G
162 D4 **Whiting Bay** N Ayrs
124 B4 **Whitkirk** Leeds
49 L4 **Whitland** Carmth
167 G6 **Whitlaw** Border
163 J5 **Whitletts** S Ayrs
124 E6 **Whitley** N York
42 B6 **Whitley** Readg
115 G3 **Whitley** Sheff
39 K6 **Whitley** Wilts
159 J7 **Whitley Bay** N Tyne
159 H7 **Whitley Bay Crematorium** N Tyne
150 B4 **Whitley Chapel** Nthumb
123 J6 **Whitley Lower** Kirk
55 H6 **Whitminster** Gloucs
99 J4 **Whitmore** Staffs
25 G7 **Whitnage** Devon
72 D2 **Whitnash** Warwks
68 F5 **Whitney-on-Wye** Herefs
147 M4 **Whitrigglees** Cumb
28 C7 **Whitsbury** Hants
179 H7 **Whitsome** Border
38 B4 **Whitson** Newpt
47 J6 **Whitstable** Kent
9 H5 **Whitstone** Cnwll
168 F6 **Whittingham** Nthumb
83 H5 **Whittingslow** Shrops
115 G6 **Whittington** Derbys
56 A4 **Whittington** Gloucs
130 B4 **Whittington** Lancs
91 G4 **Whittington** Norfk
97 L6 **Whittington** Shrops
84 F6 **Whittington** Staffs
85 L2 **Whittington** Staffs
86 C4 **Whittington** Warwks
70 F4 **Whittington** Worcs
73 K5 **Whittlebury** Nhants
121 H6 **Whittle-le-Woods** Lancs
89 J4 **Whittlesey** Cambs
76 C5 **Whittlesford** Cambs
125 L5 **Whitton** N Linc
158 D3 **Whitton** Nthumb
68 F2 **Whitton** Powys
141 J3 **Whitton** S on T
83 L8 **Whitton** Shrops
150 D4 **Whittonstall** Nthumb
41 J8 **Whitway** Hants
115 K6 **Whitwell** Derbys
59 K4 **Whitwell** Herts
17 G6 **Whitwell** IoW
141 G7 **Whitwell** N York
88 D2 **Whitwell** Rutlnd
133 L6 **Whitwell-on-the-Hill** N York
106 D7 **Whitwell Street** Norfk
86 E1 **Whitwick** Leics
122 D6 **Whitworth** Lancs
98 D5 **Whixall** Shrops
133 G7 **Whixley** N York
140 E4 **Whorlton** Dur
141 L6 **Whorlton** N York
69 L3 **Whyle** Herefs
32 C2 **Whyteleafe** Surrey
123 H4 **Wibsey** C Brad
86 F6 **Wibtoft** Warwks
70 D3 **Wichenford** Worcs
34 B4 **Wichling** Kent
15 L4 **Wick** Bmouth
231 L5 **Wick** Highld
39 G5 **Wick** S Glos
36 E6 **Wick** V Glam
18 D5 **Wick** W Susx
71 G5 **Wick** Worcs
231 L5 *Wick Airport* Highld
76 E1 **Wicken** Cambs
73 L6 **Wicken** Nhants

60 D2 **Wicken Bonhunt** Essex
117 H5 **Wickenby** Lincs
115 J3 **Wickersley** Rothm
77 L6 **Wicker Street Green** Suffk
46 C2 **Wickford** Essex
17 H1 **Wickham** Hants
41 H6 **Wickham** W Berk
61 K5 **Wickham Bishops** Essex
35 G3 **Wickhambreaux** Kent
77 H4 **Wickhambrook** Suffk
71 J6 **Wickhamford** Worcs
78 D2 **Wickham Green** Suffk
79 G4 **Wickham Market** Suffk
93 J3 **Wickhampton** Norfk
77 J7 **Wickham St Paul** Essex
78 C2 **Wickham Skeith** Suffk
78 C1 **Wickham Street** Suffk
92 C3 **Wicklewood** Norfk
106 E5 **Wickmere** Norfk
38 A7 **Wick St Lawrence** N Som
39 G3 **Wickwar** S Glos
60 E2 **Widdington** Essex
159 G3 **Widdrington** Nthumb
159 G4 **Widdrington Station** Nthumb
7 G1 **Widecombe in the Moor** Devon
5 L4 **Widegates** Cnwll
9 G4 **Widemouth Bay** Cnwll
159 G7 **Wide Open** N Tyne
61 H6 **Widford** Essex
60 C5 **Widford** Herts
42 E2 **Widmer End** Bucks
101 M6 **Widmerpool** Notts
45 H6 **Widmore** Gt Lon
112 D5 **Widnes** Halton
112 D4 **Widnes Crematorium** Halton
13 G3 **Widworthy** Devon
112 E1 **Wigan** Wigan
112 E2 **Wigan Crematorium** Wigan
26 C7 **Wigborough** Somset
12 E4 **Wiggaton** Devon
90 E2 **Wiggenhall St Germans** Norfk
90 E2 **Wiggenhall St Mary Magdalen** Norfk
90 E2 **Wiggenhall St Mary the Virgin** Norfk
133 J7 **Wigginton** C York
58 F6 **Wigginton** Herts
57 H2 **Wigginton** Oxon
86 B3 **Wigginton** Staffs
130 F7 **Wigglesworth** N York
148 B4 **Wiggonby** Cumb
124 D2 **Wighill** N York
105 M4 **Wighton** Norfk
84 F4 **Wightwick** Wolves
29 G7 **Wigley** Hants
69 H2 **Wigmore** Herefs
46 D6 **Wigmore** Medway
116 E7 **Wigsley** Notts
88 F6 **Wigsthorpe** Nhants
87 H4 **Wigston** Leics
86 F5 **Wigston Parva** Leics
115 L5 **Wigthorpe** Notts
103 L5 **Wigtoft** Lincs
148 A5 **Wigton** Cumb
145 J4 **Wigtown** D & G
123 L3 **Wike** Leeds
88 B5 **Wilbarston** Nhants
125 H1 **Wilberfoss** E R Yk
90 C7 **Wilburton** Cambs
74 C2 **Wilby** Nhants
92 B5 **Wilby** Norfk
78 F1 **Wilby** Suffk
40 C7 **Wilcot** Wilts

98 B8 **Wilcott** Shrops
113 M7 **Wildboarclough** Ches E
75 G4 **Wilden** Bed
84 E8 **Wilden** Worcs
175 L7 **Wildmanbridge** S Lans
85 G7 **Wildmoor** Worcs
116 D3 **Wildsworth** Lincs
101 L5 **Wilford Hill Crematorium** Notts
98 F4 **Wilkesley** Ches E
223 K4 **Wilkhaven** Highld
176 F5 **Wilkieston** W Loth
12 D1 **Willand** Devon
99 G3 **Willaston** Ches E
111 K6 **Willaston** Ches W
74 C6 **Willen** M Keyn
86 D7 **Willenhall** Covtry
85 H4 **Willenhall** Wsall
126 C4 **Willerby** E R Yk
134 F4 **Willerby** N York
71 K6 **Willersey** Gloucs
68 F5 **Willersley** Herefs
34 D6 **Willesborough** Kent
34 D6 **Willesborough Lees** Kent
44 E3 **Willesden** Gt Lon
39 J3 **Willesley** Wilts
25 H5 **Willett** Somset
84 C4 **Willey** Shrops
86 F6 **Willey** Warwks
30 F2 **Willey Green** Surrey
72 F5 **Williamscot** Oxon
59 L2 **Willian** Herts
60 F6 **Willingale** Essex
20 C5 **Willingdon** E Susx
76 B1 **Willingham** Cambs
116 E5 **Willingham by Stow** Lincs
76 F4 **Willingham Green** Cambs
75 G4 **Willington** Bed
100 F6 **Willington** Derbys
150 F7 **Willington** Dur
33 K3 **Willington** Kent
72 C6 **Willington** Warwks
151 H2 **Willington Quay** N Tyne
125 H4 **Willitoft** E R Yk
25 H4 **Williton** Somset
119 G6 **Willoughby** Lincs
73 G2 **Willoughby** Warwks
101 M7 **Willoughby-on-the-Wolds** Notts
87 H5 **Willoughby Waterleys** Leics
116 F3 **Willoughton** Lincs
61 H4 **Willows Green** Essex
26 B6 **Willtown** Somset
71 L3 **Wilmcote** Warwks
13 G3 **Wilmington** Devon
20 B5 **Wilmington** E Susx
45 K5 **Wilmington** Kent
113 J5 **Wilmslow** Ches E
121 K4 **Wilpshire** Lancs
123 G3 **Wilsden** C Brad
103 G4 **Wilsford** Lincs
28 C4 **Wilsford** Wilts
40 C8 **Wilsford** Wilts
123 G8 **Wilshaw** Kirk
132 B6 **Wilsill** N York
101 H7 **Wilson** Leics
176 C7 **Wilsontown** S Lans
74 F5 **Wilstead** Bed
88 F2 **Wilsthorpe** Lincs
58 E5 **Wilstone** Herts
54 E3 **Wilton** Herefs
134 D3 **Wilton** N York
142 C4 **Wilton** R & Cl
28 C5 **Wilton** Wilts
40 E7 **Wilton** Wilts
167 G6 **Wilton Dean** Border
76 E6 **Wimbish** Essex
76 E7 **Wimbish Green** Essex
44 E6 **Wimbledon** Gt Lon

90 B5 **Wimblington** Cambs
113 G8 **Wimboldsley** Ches W
15 J3 **Wimborne Minster** Dorset
28 B8 **Wimborne St Giles** Dorset
90 E3 **Wimbotsham** Norfk
75 L4 **Wimpole** Cambs
72 B5 **Wimpstone** Warwks
27 G5 **Wincanton** Somset
176 E4 **Winchburgh** W Loth
56 A3 **Winchcombe** Gloucs
21 H3 **Winchelsea** E Susx
29 J5 **Winchester** Hants
29 K4 *Winchester Services Hants*
33 J5 **Winchet Hill** Kent
30 C1 **Winchfield** Hants
42 F7 **Winchmore Hill** Bucks
44 F7 **Winchmore Hill** Gt Lon
113 L7 **Wincle** Ches E
115 G3 **Wincobank** Sheff
137 L7 **Windermere** Cumb
72 D6 **Winderton** Warwks
212 E5 **Windhill** Highld
42 F7 **Windlesham** Surrey
56 D5 **Windrush** Gloucs
216 B4 **Windsole** Abers
42 F5 **Windsor** W & M
42 F5 **Windsor Castle** W & M
55 J7 **Windsoredge** Gloucs
77 K4 **Windsor Green** Suffk
72 C1 **Windy Arbour** Warwks
186 E7 **Windygates** Fife
31 L7 **Wineham** W Susx
127 G5 **Winestead** E R Yk
92 D6 **Winfarthing** Norfk
17 G5 **Winford** IoW
38 D7 **Winford** N Som
68 F5 **Winforton** Herefs
14 F5 **Winfrith Newburgh** Dorset
58 E4 **Wing** Bucks
88 C3 **Wing** Rutlnd
151 J7 **Wingate** Dur
115 G7 **Wingerworth** Derbys
59 G3 **Wingfield** C Beds
92 F7 **Wingfield** Suffk
27 J1 **Wingfield** Wilts
35 H3 **Wingham** Kent
35 G5 **Wingmore** Kent
58 E4 **Wingrave** Bucks
102 B2 **Winkburn** Notts
42 E6 **Winkfield** Br For
42 E6 **Winkfield Row** Br For
100 B3 **Winkhill** Staffs
10 F4 **Winkleigh** Devon
132 C5 **Winksley** N York
150 F3 **Winlaton** Gatesd
231 K5 **Winless** Highld
120 F7 **Winmarleigh** Lancs
29 J5 **Winnall** Hants
42 C4 **Winnersh** Wokham
112 F6 **Winnington** Ches W
38 B8 **Winscombe** N Som
112 F7 **Winsford** Ches W
24 E4 **Winsford** Somset
13 J2 **Winsham** Somset
100 F7 **Winshill** Staffs
51 K6 **Winshwen** Swans
149 G7 **Winskill** Cumb
39 J7 **Winsley** Wilts
58 C3 **Winslow** Bucks
56 C6 **Winson** Gloucs
28 F8 **Winsor** Hants
129 J2 **Winster** Cumb
100 E1 **Winster** Derbys
140 E4 **Winston** Dur
78 E3 **Winston** Suffk
55 L6 **Winstone** Gloucs

10 D3 **Winswell** Devon
14 D5 **Winterborne Came** Dorset
14 F2 **Winterborne Clenston** Dorset
14 F2 **Winterborne Houghton** Dorset
15 G3 **Winterborne Kingston** Dorset
14 D5 **Winterborne Monkton** Dorset
14 F2 **Winterborne Stickland** Dorset
14 F3 **Winterborne Whitechurch** Dorset
15 G3 **Winterborne Zelston** Dorset
38 F4 **Winterbourne** S Glos
41 J6 **Winterbourne** W Berk
14 C4 **Winterbourne Abbas** Dorset
40 C5 **Winterbourne Bassett** Wilts
28 D4 **Winterbourne Dauntsey** Wilts
28 D5 **Winterbourne Earls** Wilts
28 D4 **Winterbourne Gunner** Wilts
40 C6 **Winterbourne Monkton** Wilts
14 C4 **Winterbourne Steepleton** Dorset
28 B3 **Winterbourne Stoke** Wilts
131 H7 **Winterburn** N York
125 L6 **Winteringham** N Linc
99 H2 **Winterley** Ches E
28 E5 **Winterslow** Wilts
125 L6 **Winterton** N Linc
107 K8 **Winterton-on-Sea** Norfk
102 D2 **Winthorpe** Notts
15 K4 **Winton** Bmouth
139 H5 **Winton** Cumb
134 D5 **Wintringham** N York
89 G7 **Winwick** Cambs
87 J8 **Winwick** Nhants
112 E3 **Winwick** Warrtn
100 F2 **Wirksworth** Derbys
111 J4 **Wirral** Wirral
98 D4 **Wirswall** Ches E
90 C2 **Wisbech** Cambs
90 B2 **Wisbech St Mary** Cambs
31 H6 **Wisborough Green** W Susx
49 K6 **Wiseman's Bridge** Pembks
116 B4 **Wiseton** Notts
175 L7 **Wishaw** N Lans
85 L5 **Wishaw** Warwks
43 H8 **Wisley Gardens** Surrey
117 K6 **Wispington** Lincs
93 H7 **Wissett** Suffk
62 A2 **Wissington** Suffk
83 H6 **Wistanstow** Shrops
98 F6 **Wistanswick** Shrops
99 G2 **Wistaston** Ches E
49 H4 **Wiston** Pembks
165 J3 **Wiston** S Lans
18 F3 **Wiston** W Susx
89 K7 **Wistow** Cambs
124 F4 **Wistow** N York
121 L3 **Wiswell** Lancs
90 C7 **Witcham** Cambs
15 J2 **Witchampton** Dorset
90 C7 **Witchford** Cambs
26 C6 **Witcombe** Somset
61 K5 **Witham** Essex
27 H3 **Witham Friary** Somset
88 F1 **Witham on the Hill** Lincs
118 C5 **Withcall** Lincs

19 J4 **Withdean** Br & H
33 H7 **Witherenden Hill** E Susx
11 J3 **Witheridge** Devon
86 D4 **Witherley** Leics
118 F5 **Withern** Lincs
127 H5 **Withernsea** E R Yk
126 F3 **Withernwick** E R Yk
92 F7 **Withersdale Street** Suffk
76 F5 **Withersfield** Suffk
129 J3 **Witherslack** Cumb
4 F3 **Withiel** Cnwll
24 F5 **Withiel Florey** Somset
56 B5 **Withington** Gloucs
69 L5 **Withington** Herefs
113 J3 **Withington** Manch
83 L2 **Withington** Shrops
100 B5 **Withington** Staffs
11 K3 **Withleigh** Devon
85 H8 **Withybed Green** Worcs
86 E6 **Withybrook** Warwks
24 F3 **Withycombe** Somset
32 E6 **Withyham** E Susx
24 D4 **Withypool** Somset
38 E6 **Withywood** Bristl
30 F4 **Witley** Surrey
78 E4 **Witnesham** Suffk
57 G6 **Witney** Oxon
88 F3 **Wittering** C Pete
21 H1 **Wittersham** Kent
85 J5 **Witton** Birm
93 G2 **Witton** Norfk
107 H6 **Witton** Norfk
151 G5 **Witton Gilbert** Dur
140 E2 **Witton le Wear** Dur
140 F2 **Witton Park** Dur
25 G5 **Wiveliscombe** Somset
30 A4 **Wivelrod** Hants
19 K2 **Wivelsfield** E Susx
19 K2 **Wivelsfield Green** E Susx
62 C4 **Wivenhoe** Essex
106 C4 **Wiveton** Norfk
62 E3 **Wix** Essex
71 K4 **Wixford** Warwks
77 G6 **Wixoe** Suffk
58 F2 **Woburn** C Beds
58 F2 **Woburn Abbey** C Beds
74 D7 **Woburn Sands** M Keyn
43 G8 **Woking** Surrey
42 F8 **Woking Crematorium** Surrey
42 D6 **Wokingham** Wokham
32 C3 **Woldingham** Surrey
135 G5 **Wold Newton** E R Yk
118 C3 **Wold Newton** NE Lin
165 K3 **Wolfclyde** S Lans
105 G6 **Wolferton** Norfk
186 B2 **Wolfhill** P & K
49 G3 **Wolf's Castle** Pembks
48 F3 **Wolfsdale** Pembks
84 F6 **Wollaston** Dudley
74 C2 **Wollaston** Nhants
83 G2 **Wollaston** Shrops
101 K4 **Wollaton** C Nott
98 F6 **Wollerton** Shrops
85 G6 **Wollescote** Dudley
100 A7 **Wolseley Bridge** Staffs
150 D7 **Wolsingham** Dur
99 J3 **Wolstanton** Staffs
86 E7 **Wolston** Warwks
57 J6 **Wolvercote** Oxon
85 G4 **Wolverhampton** Wolves
84 E5 *Wolverhampton Business Airport Staffs*
84 E7 **Wolverley** Worcs
41 K8 **Wolverton** Hants

74 B6 **Wolverton** M Keyn
72 B3 **Wolverton** Warwks
27 H5 **Wolverton** Wilts
54 C7 **Wolvesnewton** Mons
86 E6 **Wolvey** Warwks
86 E5 **Wolvey Heath** Warwks
141 K3 **Wolviston** S on T
133 K3 **Wombleton** N York
84 F5 **Wombourne** Staffs
115 H2 **Wombwell** Barns
35 G5 **Womenswold** Kent
124 E6 **Womersley** N York
31 G3 **Wonersh** Surrey
12 B4 **Wonford** Devon
29 J4 **Wonston** Hants
42 E3 **Wooburn** Bucks
42 E3 **Wooburn Green** Bucks
9 K4 **Woodacott** Devon
115 J5 **Woodall** Rothm
115 J5 **Woodall Services** Rothm
93 G1 **Woodbastwick** Norfk
71 J4 **Wood Bevington** Warwks
101 M3 **Woodborough** Notts
40 C7 **Woodborough** Wilts
78 F5 **Woodbridge** Suffk
12 C5 **Woodbury** Devon
12 C5 **Woodbury Salterton** Devon
55 J7 **Woodchester** Gloucs
34 C7 **Woodchurch** Kent
24 E3 **Woodcombe** Somset
44 F7 **Woodcote** Gt Lon
41 M4 **Woodcote** Oxon
84 D1 **Woodcote** Wrekin
38 D2 **Woodcroft** Gloucs
106 C6 **Wood Dalling** Norfk
76 F3 **Woodditton** Cambs
57 K5 **Woodeaton** Oxon
43 J4 **Wood End** Gt Lon
60 B3 **Wood End** Herts
190 F4 **Woodend** Highld
73 H5 **Woodend** Nhants
176 C4 **Woodend** W Loth
17 M2 **Woodend** W Susx
71 K1 **Wood End** Warwks
118 C8 **Wood Enderby** Lincs
28 D7 **Woodfalls** Wilts
9 G3 **Woodford** Cnwll
39 G2 **Woodford** Gloucs
45 H2 **Woodford** Gt Lon
88 D7 **Woodford** Nhants
113 K5 **Woodford** Stockp
45 H2 **Woodford Bridge** Gt Lon
73 G4 **Woodford Halse** Nhants
45 H2 **Woodford Wells** Gt Lon
85 H6 **Woodgate** Birm
25 H7 **Woodgate** Devon
18 C5 **Woodgate** W Susx
71 H2 **Woodgate** Worcs
44 F2 **Wood Green** Gt Lon
28 D7 **Woodgreen** Hants
131 J2 **Woodhall** N York
117 K8 **Woodhall Spa** Lincs
58 B4 **Woodham** Bucks
43 H7 **Woodham** Surrey
61 J7 **Woodham Ferrers** Essex
61 K6 **Woodham Mortimer** Essex
61 K6 **Woodham Walter** Essex
85 G3 **Wood Hayes** Wolves
216 E6 **Woodhead** Abers
26 A6 **Woodhill** Somset
159 H4 **Woodhorn** Nthumb
123 K4 **Woodhouse** Leeds
87 G1 **Woodhouse** Leics
115 H4 **Woodhouse** Sheff
124 B6 **Woodhouse** Wakefd

87 G2 **Woodhouse Eaves** Leics
177 H5 **Woodhouselee** Mdloth
156 D6 **Woodhouselees** D & G
100 D8 **Woodhouses** Staffs
89 K7 **Woodhurst** Cambs
19 K5 **Woodingdean** Br & H
123 K5 **Woodkirk** Leeds
207 G2 **Woodland** Abers
6 F5 **Woodland** Devon
7 J3 **Woodland** Devon
140 D2 **Woodland** Dur
34 F6 **Woodland** Kent
152 E3 **Woodland** S Ayrs
206 E6 **Woodlands** Abers
124 E8 **Woodlands** Donc
15 K2 **Woodlands** Dorset
16 C1 **Woodlands** Hants
132 E8 **Woodlands** N York
85 L5 **Woodlands (Coleshill) Crematorium** Warwks
42 E5 **Woodlands Park** W & M
134 F3 **Woodlands (Scarborough) Crematorium** N York
125 K7 **Woodlands (Scunthorpe) Crematorium** N Linc
7 H6 **Woodleigh** Devon
42 C5 **Woodley** Wokham
39 H7 **Woodmancote** Gloucs
55 L3 **Woodmancote** Gloucs
56 A6 **Woodmancote** Gloucs
17 L2 **Woodmancote** W Susx
19 H3 **Woodmancote** W Susx
29 K3 **Woodmancott** Hants
126 C3 **Woodmansey** E R Yk
30 E6 **Woodmansgreen** W Susx
32 B2 **Woodmansterne** Surrey
12 C5 **Woodmanton** Devon
35 J4 **Woodnesborough** Kent
88 F5 **Woodnewton** Nhants
106 B6 **Wood Norton** Norfk
121 G4 **Woodplumpton** Lancs
92 B3 **Woodrising** Norfk
20 D2 **Wood's Corner** E Susx
99 H7 **Woodseaves** Staffs
115 K5 **Woodsetts** Rothm
14 E4 **Woodsford** Dorset
33 H6 **Wood's Green** E Susx
42 F6 **Woodside** Br For
187 G5 **Woodside** Fife
45 G6 **Woodside** Gt Lon
195 K8 **Woodside** P & K
57 H5 **Woodstock** Oxon
89 H4 **Woodston** C Pete
107 H7 **Wood Street** Norfk
30 F2 **Wood Street Village** Surrey
93 G5 **Woodton** Norfk
22 F6 **Woodtown** Devon
19 J4 **Woodvale Crematorium** Br & H
89 J7 **Wood Walton** Cambs
69 K2 **Woofferton** Shrops
26 D3 **Wookey** Somset
26 D2 **Wookey Hole** Somset
14 F5 **Wool** Dorset
23 G3 **Woolacombe** Devon
35 H5 **Woolage Green** Kent
54 E7 **Woolaston** Gloucs
54 E7 **Woolaston Common** Gloucs

25 M3 **Woolavington** Somset
30 E6 **Woolbeding** W Susx
12 E5 **Woolbrook** Devon
168 E4 **Wooler** Nthumb
11 J3 **Woolfardisworthy** Devon
22 E7 **Woolfardisworthy** Devon
176 D6 **Woolfords** S Lans
41 L6 **Woolhampton** W Berk
69 L7 **Woolhope** Herefs
14 E2 **Woolland** Dorset
39 H6 **Woolley** BaNES
89 G8 **Woolley** Cambs
123 L7 **Woolley** Wakefd
123 K7 **Woolley Edge Services** Wakefd
71 G2 **Woolmere Green** Worcs
59 L4 **Woolmer Green** Herts
13 K2 **Woolminstone** Somset
77 L3 **Woolpit** Suffk
83 J4 **Woolstaston** Shrops
102 D5 **Woolsthorpe** Lincs
102 F7 **Woolsthorpe-by-Colsterworth** Lincs
16 E1 **Woolston** C Sotn
83 H6 **Woolston** Shrops
97 L7 **Woolston** Shrops
25 H4 **Woolston** Somset
26 F5 **Woolston** Somset
112 F4 **Woolston** Warrtn
55 L3 **Woolstone** Gloucs
74 C6 **Woolstone** M Keyn
40 F3 **Woolstone** Oxon
7 H3 **Woolston Green** Devon
112 B4 **Woolton** Lpool
41 H7 **Woolton Hill** Hants
78 E6 **Woolverstone** Suffk
27 H2 **Woolverton** Somset
45 H4 **Woolwich** Gt Lon
69 G4 **Woonton** Herefs
99 G4 **Woore** Shrops
92 F8 **Wootten Green** Suffk
74 E5 **Wootton** Bed
35 G5 **Wootton** Kent
126 D7 **Wootton** N Linc
73 L3 **Wootton** Nhants
57 H4 **Wootton** Oxon
57 J7 **Wootton** Oxon
100 C4 **Wootton** Staffs
40 B4 **Wootton Bassett** Wilts
17 G4 **Wootton Bridge** IoW
24 E3 **Wootton Courtenay** Somset
13 J4 **Wootton Fitzpaine** Dorset
40 D7 **Wootton Rivers** Wilts
29 L2 **Wootton St Lawrence** Hants
71 L2 **Wootton Wawen** Warwks
70 F4 **Worcester** Worcs
44 E6 **Worcester Park** Gt Lon
84 F6 **Wordsley** Dudley
84 D4 **Worfield** Shrops
136 D2 **Workington** Cumb
115 L5 **Worksop** Notts
126 C7 **Worlaby** N Linc
29 M8 **Worlds End** Hants
41 J5 **World's End** W Berk
19 J2 **Worlds End** W Susx
38 A7 **Worle** N Som
98 F2 **Worleston** Ches E
93 J5 **Worlingham** Suffk
11 H3 **Worlington** Devon
91 G8 **Worlington** Suffk
78 F2 **Worlingworth** Suffk
132 D6 **Wormald Green** N York

54 B2 **Wormbridge** Herefs
90 F2 **Wormegay** Norfk
54 C3 **Wormelow Tump** Herefs
114 C6 **Wormhill** Derbys
61 M2 **Wormingford** Essex
57 M6 **Worminghall** Bucks
71 J7 **Wormington** Gloucs
186 F3 **Wormit** Fife
72 F4 **Wormleighton** Warwks
60 B6 **Wormley** Herts
30 F4 **Wormley** Surrey
34 B3 **Wormshill** Kent
69 H5 **Wormsley** Herefs
30 F2 **Worplesdon** Surrey
114 F3 **Worrall** Sheff
115 G2 **Worsbrough** Barns
115 G2 **Worsbrough Bridge** Barns
115 G2 **Worsbrough Dale** Barns
113 H2 **Worsley** Salfd
107 G7 **Worstead** Norfk
122 C4 **Worsthorne** Lancs
6 E5 **Worston** Devon
122 B3 **Worston** Lancs
35 J4 **Worth** Kent
92 C7 **Wortham** Suffk
83 G3 **Worthen** Shrops
98 B4 **Worthenbury** Wrexhm
106 B8 **Worthing** Norfk
18 F5 **Worthing** W Susx
18 F4 **Worthing Crematorium** W Susx
101 H7 **Worthington** Leics
15 H6 **Worth Matravers** Dorset
114 F2 **Wortley** Barns
123 K4 **Wortley** Leeds
131 H2 **Worton** N York
39 L8 **Worton** Wilts
92 F6 **Wortwell** Norfk
39 H7 **Wotton-under-Edge** Gloucs
58 B5 **Wotton Underwood** Bucks
74 C6 **Woughton on the Green** M Keyn
46 B7 **Wouldham** Kent
84 D5 **Woundale** Shrops
62 E2 **Wrabness** Essex
23 H4 **Wrafton** Devon
117 J6 **Wragby** Lincs
124 C6 **Wragby** Wakefd
7 G4 **Wrangaton** Devon
104 C3 **Wrangle** Lincs
25 H7 **Wrangway** Somset
25 L6 **Wrantage** Somset
126 C3 **Wrawby** N Linc
38 C6 **Wraxall** N Som
26 E4 **Wraxall** Somset
130 B6 **Wray** Lancs
43 G5 **Wraysbury** W & M
130 C5 **Wrayton** Lancs
120 E4 **Wrea Green** Lancs
148 D5 **Wreay** Cumb
30 D3 **Wrecclesham** Surrey
151 G3 **Wrekenton** Gatesd
134 B3 **Wrelton** N York
98 E3 **Wrenbury** Ches E
92 E4 **Wreningham** Norfk
93 K6 **Wrentham** Suffk
83 H3 **Wrentnall** Shrops
125 G4 **Wressle** E R Yk
126 B8 **Wressle** N Linc
75 J5 **Wrestlingworth** C Beds
91 G4 **Wrexham** Wrexhm
97 M3 **Wrexham** Wrexhm
84 E7 **Wribbenhall** Worcs
99 H3 **Wrinehill** Staffs
38 C7 **Wrington** N Som
27 G1 **Writhlington** BaNES
61 G6 **Writtle** Essex

84 B2 **Wrockwardine** Wrekin
116 B2 **Wroot** N Linc
123 H3 **Wrose** C Brad
33 G2 **Wrotham** Kent
40 C4 **Wroughton** Swindn
17 G6 **Wroxall** IoW
72 B1 **Wroxall** Warwks
83 L2 **Wroxeter** Shrops
107 G8 **Wroxham** Norfk
72 E6 **Wroxton** Oxon
100 D4 **Wyaston** Derbys
104 B4 **Wyberton East** Lincs
75 H3 **Wyboston** Bed
99 G3 **Wybunbury** Ches E
71 G2 **Wychbold** Worcs
85 L1 **Wychnor** Staffs
56 D4 **Wyck Rissington** Gloucs
140 E4 **Wycliffe** Dur
122 D3 **Wycoller** Lancs
102 C7 **Wycomb** Leics
42 E3 **Wycombe Marsh** Bucks
60 B2 **Wyddial** Herts
34 E5 **Wye** Kent
123 H5 **Wyke** C Brad
27 H6 **Wyke** Dorset
26 F4 **Wyke Champflower** Somset
134 E3 **Wykeham** N York
86 D7 **Wyken** Covtry
84 D4 **Wyken** Shrops
14 C6 **Wyke Regis** Dorset
98 B7 **Wykey** Shrops
150 E3 **Wylam** Nthumb
85 K5 **Wylde Green** Birm
28 A4 **Wylye** Wilts
101 L7 **Wymeswold** Leics
74 D2 **Wymington** Bed
102 D8 **Wymondham** Leics
92 D3 **Wymondham** Norfk
14 B3 **Wynford Eagle** Dorset
71 G5 **Wyre Piddle** Worcs
101 L6 **Wysall** Notts
85 J7 **Wythall** Worcs
57 J6 **Wytham** Oxon
113 J4 **Wythenshawe** Manch
89 K8 **Wyton** Cambs
126 E4 **Wyton** E R Yk
78 C2 **Wyverstone** Suffk
78 B2 **Wyverstone Street** Suffk

116 E1 **Yaddlethorpe** N Linc
141 H7 **Yafforth** N York
7 K4 **Yalberton** Torbay
33 J3 **Yalding** Kent
138 D2 **Yanwath** Cumb
56 B5 **Yanworth** Gloucs
125 J1 **Yapham** E R Yk
18 D5 **Yapton** W Susx

38 B8 **Yarborough** N Som
118 E3 **Yarburgh** Lincs
13 G2 **Yarcombe** Devon
24 B6 **Yard** Devon
85 K6 **Yardley** Birm
85 K6 **Yardley Crematorium** Birm
73 L5 **Yardley Gobion** Nhants
74 C3 **Yardley Hastings** Nhants
85 K7 **Yardley Wood** Birm
69 L6 **Yarkhill** Herefs
26 D3 **Yarley** Somset
26 F5 **Yarlington** Somset
141 K5 **Yarm** S on T
16 D4 **Yarmouth** IoW
27 K1 **Yarnbrook** Wilts
99 K6 **Yarnfield** Staffs
23 J6 **Yarnscombe** Devon
57 J5 **Yarnton** Oxon
69 J2 **Yarpole** Herefs
166 E4 **Yarrow** Border
166 E4 **Yarrow Feus** Border
166 F4 **Yarrowford** Border
88 F4 **Yarwell** Nhants
39 G4 **Yate** S Glos
42 D7 **Yateley** Hants
40 B6 **Yatesbury** Wilts
41 K5 **Yattendon** W Berk
69 H2 **Yatton** Herefs
38 B7 **Yatton** N Som
39 K5 **Yatton Keynell** Wilts
17 H5 **Yaverland** IoW
92 B2 **Yaxham** Norfk
89 H5 **Yaxley** Cambs
92 D8 **Yaxley** Suffk
69 H5 **Yazor** Herefs
43 J4 **Yeading** Gt Lon
123 J3 **Yeadon** Leeds
129 K5 **Yealand Conyers** Lancs
129 K4 **Yealand Redmayne** Lancs
6 E5 **Yealmpton** Devon
133 J5 **Yearsley** N York
98 B8 **Yeaton** Shrops
100 D4 **Yeaveley** Derbys
168 D4 **Yeavering** Nthumb
134 D4 **Yedingham** N York
57 G6 **Yelford** Oxon
235 d3 **Yell** Shet
75 J3 **Yelling** Cambs
87 H7 **Yelvertoft** Nhants
6 D3 **Yelverton** Devon
93 G3 **Yelverton** Norfk
27 G7 **Yenston** Somset
11 H5 **Yeoford** Devon
9 J7 **Yeolmbridge** Cnwll
26 D7 **Yeovil** Somset
26 D7 **Yeovil Crematorium** Somset
26 D7 **Yeovil Marsh** Somset
26 D6 **Yeovilton** Somset
26 D6 **Yeovilton Fleet Air Arm Museum** Somset
234 b5 **Yesnaby** Ork

14 B1 **Yetminster** Dorset
12 D5 **Yettington** Devon
185 L6 **Yetts o'Muckhart** Clacks
85 H4 **Yew Tree** Sandw
109 G7 **Y Felinheli** Gwynd
65 G5 **Y Ferwig** Cerdgn
95 G5 **Y Ffor** Gwynd
97 G2 **Y Gyffylliog** Denbgs
74 E2 **Yielden** Bed
176 B7 **Yieldshields** S Lans
43 H4 **Yiewsley** Gt Lon
96 F4 **Y Maerdy** Conwy
37 G2 **Ynysboeth** Rhondd
37 J2 **Ynysddu** Caerph
36 F3 **Ynyshir** Rhondd
51 K5 **Ynystawe** Swans
37 G2 **Ynysybwl** Rhondd
83 H2 **Yockleton** Shrops
125 J5 **Yokefleet** E R Yk
174 F5 **Yoker** C Glas
124 F1 **York** C York
124 F2 **York City Crematorium** C York
34 E3 **Yorkletts** Kent
54 F6 **Yorkley** Gloucs
124 F1 **York Minster** C York
131 G4 **Yorkshire Dales National Park**
42 E7 **York Town** Surrey
114 E8 **Youlgreave** Derbys
134 B7 **Youlthorpe** E R Yk
133 G6 **Youlton** N York
61 H4 **Young's End** Essex
100 C8 **Yoxall** Staffs
79 H2 **Yoxford** Suffk
94 D6 **Y Rhiw** Gwynd
96 C3 **Ysbyty Ifan** Conwy
67 G1 **Ysbyty Ystwyth** Cerdgn
111 G7 **Ysceifiog** Flints
52 B6 **Ystalyfera** Neath
36 F2 **Ystrad** Rhondd
66 C4 **Ystrad Aeron** Cerdgn
52 E5 **Ystradfellte** Powys
52 C6 **Ystradgynlais** Powys
66 F2 **Ystrad Meurig** Cerdgn
37 H2 **Ystrad Mynach** Caerph
36 F5 **Ystradowen** V Glam
217 G7 **Ythanbank** Abers
216 C6 **Ythanwells** Abers
217 G7 **Ythsie** Abers

11 G4 **Zeal Monachorum** Devon
27 H5 **Zeals** Wilts
4 C5 **Zelah** Cnwll
2 E4 **Zennor** Cnwll
101 J7 **Zouch** Notts

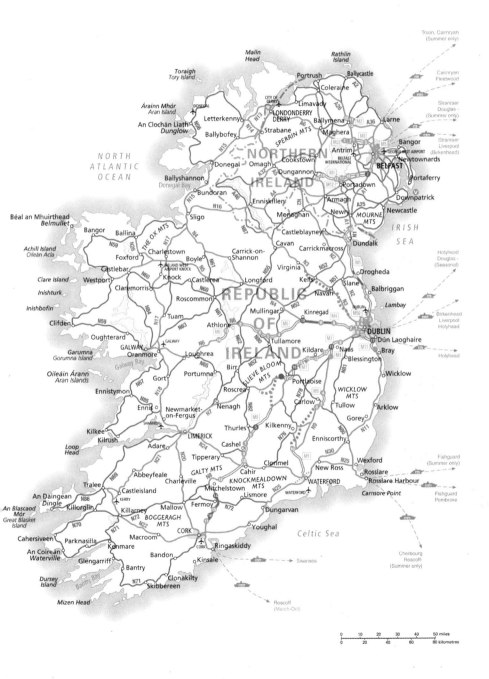

Map pages north

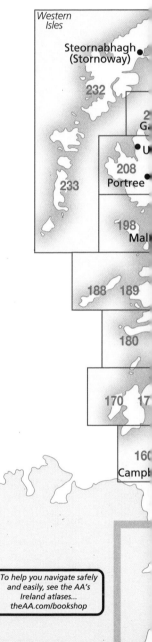

Western
Isles

Steornabhagh
(Stornoway)

232

2
G.

U

208
Portree

233

198
Mal

188   189

180

170   17

16
Camp

**Europe's clearest road
mapping by miles...**

theAA.com/bookshop

To help you navigate safely
and easily, see the AA's
Ireland atlases...
theAA.com/bookshop